Excursions in
LITERATURE
THIRD EDITION

DONNALYNN HESS

bju press®
Greenville, South Carolina

NOTE: The fact that materials produced by other publishers may be referred to in this volume does not constitute an endorsement of the content or theological position of materials produced by such publishers. Any references and ancillary materials are listed as an aid to the student or the teacher and in an attempt to maintain the accepted academic standards of the publishing industry.

EXCURSIONS IN LITERATURE
Third Edition
Donnalynn Hess, MA

Coordinating Writers
June W. Cates
Judith W. Lanier, MA
Elizabeth Rose, MEd, MA
Stephen Rowley, MA
Kimberly Y. Stegall, MEd

Consultant
Steven N. Skaggs, MEd
Director of Content Development, BJU Press

Designers
Christy B. Matias
Drew Fields

Compositor
Carol Ingalls

Editor
Rebecca Moore

Photo Acquisition
Joyce Landis
Rita Mitchell
Sarah C. Strawhorn

Project Manager
Lesley Morris

Bible Integration
Adam Mayo
Bryan Smith, PhD

Acknowledgments begin on page v, which is an extension of this copyright page.

Illustrators and Photograph Credits appear on pages 607–9.

Some Scripture quoted in the novel *In Search of Honor* is from the New King James Version. Copyright © 1982 by Thomas Nelson, Inc. Used by permission. All rights reserved.

© 2008, 2015 BJU Press
Greenville, South Carolina 29609
First Edition © 1985 BJU Press
Second Edition © 1997 BJU Press

Printed in the United States of America
All rights reserved

ISBN 978-1-60682-696-1

15 14 13 12 11 10 9 8 7 6 5

ACKNOWLEDGMENTS

A careful effort has been made to trace the ownership of selections included in this textbook in order to secure permission to reprint copyrighted material and to make full acknowledgment of their use. If any error or omission has occurred, it is purely inadvertent and will be corrected in subsequent editions, provided written notification is made to the publisher.

The Aaron M. Priest Literary Agency: "Elusive Rest Area—July 11, 1976" by Erma Bombeck from FOREVER ERMA. Reprinted with permission from The Aaron M. Priest Literary Agency.

The American-Scandinavian Foundation: "The Brothers" by Björnstjerne Björnson. First published by The American-Scandinavian Foundation, 1927, in *Told in Norway*, edited by Hanna Astrup Larsen. Printed with permission.

BJU Press: *In Search of Honor* by Donnalynn Hess. Copyright © 1991 BJU Press. All rights reserved.

Christian Literature Crusade: "Make Me Thy Fuel" by Amy Carmichael. *Mountain Breezes: The Collected Poems of Amy Carmichael* (Fort Washington, PA: CLC Publications, 1999), p. 223.

Curtis Brown Ltd: "Mama and the Graduation Present" from MAMA'S BANK ACCOUNT, copyright © 1943 by Kathryn Forbes. Reprinted by permission of Curtis Brown, Ltd.

Curtis Brown Group Ltd: "You Need to Go Upstairs" by Rumer Godden. Reproduced with permission of Curtis Brown Group Ltd, London on behalf of The Rumer Godden Literary Trust. Copyright © Rumer Godden 1953.

Don Congdon Associates, Inc.: "Fry, Fry Again" by Russell Baker. Reprinted by permission of Don Congdon Associates, Inc. Copyright © 1982 by Russell Baker

Faber and Faber Ltd.: "Some Like Poetry" from POEMS, NEW AND COLLECTED 1957–1997 by Wislawa Szymborksa, translated from the Polish by Stanislaw Baranczak and Clare Cavanagh. Reprinted by permission of Faber and Faber Ltd (UK & Commonwealth).

"The Sloth," copyright © 1950 by Theodore Roethke from THE COLLECTED POEMS OF THEODORE ROETHKE by Theodore Roethke. Used by permission of Faber and Faber Ltd (UK & Commonwealth).

Farrar, Straus and Giroux, LLC: "Thank You, M'am" from Short Stories by Langston Hughes. Copyright © 1996 by Ramona Bass and Arnold Rampersad. Reprinted by permission of Hill and Wang, a division of Farrar, Straus and Giroux, LLC for use in the United States, Canada and open market throughout the world excluding the UK and British Commonwealth.

Harold Matson Co., Inc.: "Weep No More, My Lady" by James Street. © 1941 by James Street. © renewed 1969 by Lucy Nash Street. Reprinted by permission of the Harold Matson Co., Inc.

"The Torn Invitation" by Norman Katkov. Copyright © 1952 by Norman Katkov. Reprinted by permission of the Harold Matson Co., Inc.

Harold Ober Associates Incorporated: "Thank You, Ma'm" from *Short Stories* by Langston Hughes. Copyright © 1996 by Ramona Bass and Arnold Rampersad. Reprinted by permission of Harold Ober Associates Incorporated for use in the UK and Commonwealth.

"You've Got to Learn" by Robert Murphy. Reprinted by permission of Harold Ober Associates Incorporated. Copyright © 1945 by Robert Murphy.

HarperCollins Publishers: Excerpt from pp. 147–50 from EVIDENCE NOT SEEN A WOMAN'S MIRACULOUS FAITH IN THE JUNGLES OF WORLD WAR II by DARLENE DEIBLER ROSE. Copyright © 1988 by Darlene Rose. Reprinted by permission of HarperCollins Publishers. Published in the UK

CONTENTS

CHOICES
UNIT TWO

HEROES
UNIT THREE

DISCOVERIES
UNIT FOUR

ADVENTURERS
UNIT FIVE

VIEWPOINTS
UNIT SIX

TO THE STUDENT

"Why do I need to study literature?" Perhaps you have been asking that question even as you thumbed through the opening pages of this book. It's a good question with an equally good answer—one that can be given in just two words. *Deep reading*. "But I already know how to read," you may say. Deep reading, however, is more than skill in letter-sound correspondence, word recognition, and phonics. Deep reading requires you to read closely and think critically about a text, to question it for additional meaning, to connect similar ideas, and to evaluate concepts from your worldview. Deep reading, while sometimes demanding, is always rewarding.

But such a skill does not develop automatically. Like an athletic skill, it requires great effort and years of practice. One reason is that texts vary greatly in how they convey their ideas. A poem, for instance, communicates by different rules than does a story, and a story communicates differently than an essay. To read these kinds of texts deeply, you have to learn how

each conveys meaning and then practice deriving meaning again and again. Another reason is that evaluating texts from your worldview is complicated. The Christian knows that the Bible is God's Word and everything that is good and right aligns with its teachings. But how do we know what the Bible teaches, and how do we demonstrate that something agrees with the Bible? We learn what the Bible teaches by reading it deeply. And we evaluate texts by comparing their meanings to the teachings of Scripture.

The task before you is big—or should I say deep! But don't worry. You have time, all this year—and several years after that. And you have help, the book you hold in your hands.

EXCURSIONS IN LITERATURE, Third Edition, is divided into six units that contain selections in a variety of genres and from diverse periods and cultures. Each unit focuses on a different theme: friends, choices, heroes, discoveries, adventurers, and viewpoints. A piece of artwork or a photograph opens the unit, and questions about the piece give you practice in visual analysis. Following the visual analysis is an essay about the unit theme. Each selection

within a unit begins with a short introduction to prepare you for the literary piece. A brief biographical sketch of the author follows most selections.

Following each work or group of pieces will be a *Thinking Zone* page. You will be asked to answer questions based on what you have read and what you think in reference to the selection. The questions are categorized as *literal*, requiring you to recall what you have read; *interpretive*, asking you to interpret what you have read; *critical*, stimulating analysis of what you have read; or *appreciative*, encouraging evaluation of what you have read. Now, let's get busy with some deep reading.

CHOICES

THERE IS A SIMPLE RULE IN FICTION: INTRIGUING CHARACTERS IN
INTRIGUING STORIES NEVER STAND STILL. WHEN A CHARACTER MAKES
ANY DECISION, HE MOVES EITHER FORWARD OR BACKWARD. HE MAY
TAKE ONLY ONE STEP, BUT HE IS ONE STEP CLOSER TO EVENTUAL
SUCCESS OR FAILURE. THE SAME IS TRUE OF PEOPLE IN REAL LIFE.

Consider yourself. You face choices
every day. Of course, some of your choices
are more important than others. But the
ones that determine whether you will eventually become "fit'n" or "unfit," as Uncle
Jesse says in "Weep No More, My Lady,"
are choices between right and wrong. How
are you to determine right fro[m]
You must first establish a fixed
You cannot, however, rely on n[…]
and values for a standard, for n[…]
of right and wrong are colored [by…]
ness and pride. As Solomon said[…]
"All the ways of a man are clean [in his]
eyes; but the Lord weigheth th[e…]
(Prov. 16:2). The only unfailing
authority you have for determin[ing]
is right is the Bible, and it is ess[…]
you know God's Word so that you[…]
right choices.

Making one choice is only [begin]-
ning. There is in the decisio[n…]
process a "domino theory." W[…]
domino theory? Well, take a se[t of domi]-
nos and set them up one behin[…]
Then push the first one into the s[…]
What happens? Not just two, but[…]
set topples. Like the dominos[…]
whether they are good ones or[…]

are followed by a whole series of additional
choices and consequences.

As you read the following stories and
poems, carefully consider that we are not the
only ones who make choices. God chooses
too. In fact, His choices matter much more
than ours. Our choices shape our lives, but
[…]

72   CHOICES

Literature selections are grouped by six different topics so that you learn to appreciate and assess an author's theme.

The introductory essays reveal the relevance of Scripture to the unit theme.

Each unit concludes with a Bible passage that supports the unit's theme.

THE CONVERSION OF SAUL

In Acts 8 we are told that Saul had persecuted believers and assisted in
the stoning of Stephen. In this selection, a remarkable change occurs. This
change is the result of more than one person's choice. What choices were
made and by whom? Which choice do you think is most important? Why?

And Saul, yet breathing out threatenings
and slaughter against the disciples of
the Lord, went unto the high priest,

2 And desired of him letters to Damascus to
the synagogues, that if he found any of this
way, whether they were men or women, he
might bring them bound unto Jerusalem.

3 And as he journeyed, he came near
Damascus: and suddenly there shined round
about him a light from heaven:

4 And he fell to the earth, and heard a voice
saying unto him, Saul, Saul, why persecutest
thou me?

5 And he said, Who art thou, Lord? And
the Lord said, I am Jesus whom thou persecutest: it is hard for thee to kick against the
pricks.

6 And he trembling and astonished said,
Lord, what wilt thou have me to do? And
the Lord said unto him, Arise, and go into
the city, and it shall be told thee what thou
must do.

7 And the men which journeyed with him
stood speechless, hearing a voice, but seeing
no man.

8 And Saul arose from the earth; and when
his eyes were opened, he saw no man: but
they led him by the hand, and brought him
into Damascus.

9 And he was three days without sight, and
neither did eat nor drink.

10 And there was a certain disciple at
Damascus, named Ananias; and to him said
the Lord in a vision, Ananias. And he said,
Behold, I am here, Lord.

11 And the Lord said unto him, Arise, and
go into the street which is called Straight, and
inquire in the house of Judas for one called
Saul of Tarsus: for, behold, he prayeth.

12 And hath seen in a vision a man named
Ananias coming in, and putting his hand on
him, that he might receive his sight.

13 Then Ananias answered, Lord, I have
heard by many of this man, how much evil
he hath done to thy saints at Jerusalem:

14 And here he hath authority from the chief
priests to bind all that call on thy name.

15 But the Lord said unto him, Go thy way:
for he is a chosen vessel unto me, to bear my
name before the Gentiles, and kings, and
the children of Israel:

16 For I will shew him how great things he
must suffer for my name's sake.

17 And Ananias went his way, and entered
into the house; and putting his hands on
him said, Brother Saul, the Lord, even Jesus,
that appeared unto thee in the way as thou
camest, hath sent me, that thou mightest receive thy sight, and be filled with the Holy
Ghost,

18 And immediately there fell from his eyes
as it had been scales: and he received sight
forthwith, and arose, and was baptized.

19 And when he had received meat, he was
strengthened. Then was Saul certain days
with the disciples which were at Damascus.

20 And straightway he preached Christ in
the synagogues, that he is the Son of God.

21 But all that heard him were amazed,
and said; Is not this he that destroyed them
which called on this name in Jerusalem, and

158   CHOICES

THE UGLY DUCKLING

A.A. MILNE

Have you ever planned with a friend to "pull off" something on another person? Did your plan succeed? Milne's play, which is quite different from the Hans Christian Andersen fairy tale, focuses on the attempt to "pull off" a wedding between the Princess and a suitor.

The scene is the Throne Room of the Palace; a room of many doors, or, if preferred, curtain-openings: simply furnished with three thrones for Their Majesties and Her Royal Highness the PRINCESS CAMILLA—in other words, with three handsome chairs. At each side is a long seat: reserved, as it might be, for His Majesty's Council (if any), but useful, as to-day, for other purposes. The KING is asleep on his throne with a handkerchief over his face. He is a king of any country from any story-book, in whatever costume you please. But he should be wearing his crown.

A VOICE: *(announcing).* His Excellency the Chancellor! *(The CHANCELLOR, an elderly man in horn-rimmed spectacles,* enters, bowing. The KING wakes up with a start and removes the handkerchief from his face.)*

horn-rimmed spectacles: eyeglasses with frames made of material like tortoiseshell

KING: *(with simple dignity).* I was thinking.

CHANCELLOR: *(bowing).* Never, Your Majesty, was greater need for thought than now.

KING: That's what I was thinking. *(He struggles into a more dignified position).* Well, what is it? More trouble?

CHANCELLOR: What we might call the old trouble, Your Majesty.

KING: It's what I was saying last night to the Queen. "Uneasy lies the head that wears a crown," was how I put it.

CHANCELLOR: A profound and original thought, which may well go down to posterity.

KING: You mean it may go down well with posterity. I hope so. Remind me to tell you some time of another

ETRY

me another. Szymborska poetry.

have been given to this question.
But I don't know and don't know and hold on to it
like to a sustaining railing.

— ABOUT THE AUTHOR —

Wislawa Szymborska (b. 1923) was born in Kornik, Poland. She studied Polish literature and sociology at Jagiellonian University and then from 1953 to 1981 was a columnist and poetry editor at a literary magazine in Krakow. She published her first poem, "Szukam slowa" ("I Am Looking for a Word"), in March 1945. Since then sixteen collections of her poetry have been published, and many of her poems have been translated into more than twelve languages. In addition, her poems have been published in for-

eign anthologies of Polish poetry. Szymborska is both a Goethe and Herder Prize winner. She has received many additional honors, including an honorary doctorate from Poznan University in 1995 and the 1996 Polish PEN Club prize. She was awarded the Nobel Prize for literature in 1996. A 2002 work, *Nonrequired Reading: Prose Pieces*, was a break from her usual genre. An intensely private person, Szymborska avoids the public eye of literary society and continues to write from her home in Krakow.

SOME LIKE POETRY 501

Callout boxes:

The book includes interesting selections from a variety of literary genres.

Each selection begins with the title, author, and brief headnote about the selection.

Glosses identify difficult or unfamiliar words and provide meaningful explanations.

Four-color illustrations and photographs throughout not only add visual interest but also reinforce theme and tone.

Both contemporary and classic authors are included.

When information is available, a brief biographical sketch of the author accompanies the selection.

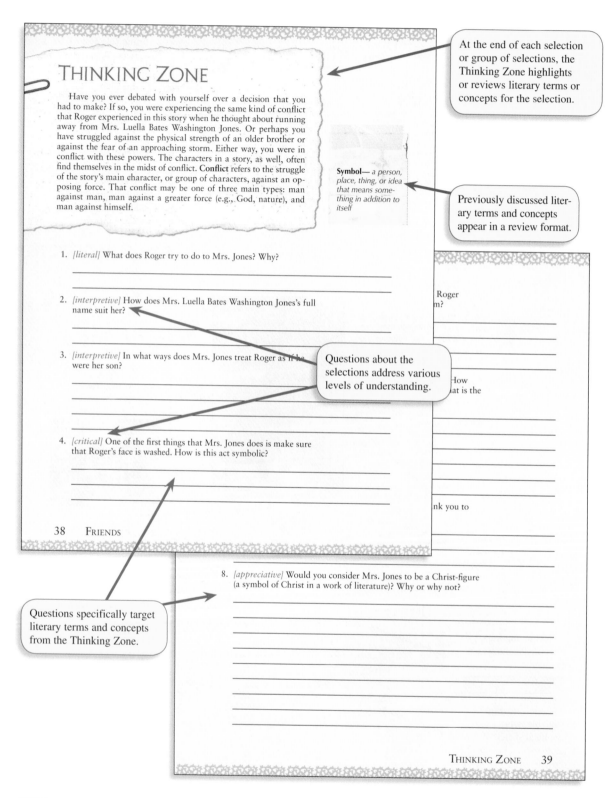

THINKING ZONE

Have you ever debated with yourself over a decision that you had to make? If so, you were experiencing the same kind of conflict that Roger experienced in this story when he thought about running away from Mrs. Luella Bates Washington Jones. Or perhaps you have struggled against the physical strength of an older brother or against the fear of an approaching storm. Either way, you were in conflict with these powers. The characters in a story, as well, often find themselves in the midst of conflict. **Conflict** refers to the struggle of the story's main character, or group of characters, against an opposing force. That conflict may be one of three main types: man against man, man against a greater force (e.g., God, nature), and man against himself.

Symbol— *a person, place, thing, or idea that means something in addition to itself*

At the end of each selection or group of selections, the Thinking Zone highlights or reviews literary terms or concepts for the selection.

Previously discussed literary terms and concepts appear in a review format.

1. *[literal]* What does Roger try to do to Mrs. Jones? Why?

2. *[interpretive]* How does Mrs. Luella Bates Washington Jones's full name suit her?

3. *[interpretive]* In what ways does Mrs. Jones treat Roger as if he were her son?

Questions about the selections address various levels of understanding.

4. *[critical]* One of the first things that Mrs. Jones does is make sure that Roger's face is washed. How is this act symbolic?

Roger
m?

How
at is the

nk you to

38   FRIENDS

Questions specifically target literary terms and concepts from the Thinking Zone.

8. *[appreciative]* Would you consider Mrs. Jones to be a Christ-figure (a symbol of Christ in a work of literature)? Why or why not?

UNIT 1 REVIEW

SHORT ANSWER

Write the word, phrase, or sentence that best answers the question.

1. In "A Most Important Person," Chester compares his rescue by Miss Lucy with what previous experience?

2. "A Most Important Person" is an example of what genre?

3. In the excerpt "Being Neighborly" from *Little Women*, which of the gifts that Jo brings helps Laurie overcome his bashfulness?

4. What does Laurie mean when he says, "A fellow can't live on books"?

5. In "The Doll's House," wh[...]
   the doll's house?

6. In what ways does the lam[...]

7. What symbolic action does [...]
   You, M'am"? What does it [...]

8. At the end of the story "Ha[...]
   ing his mother? Why did h[...]
   the comb?

9. What do we know about th[...]

10. In "Seeing Off a Friend," w[...]

MATCHING

Match the following literary terms with their correct definitions.

_____ 16. language used to convey meaning other than what is stated

_____ 17. struggle of the story's characters against an opposing force

_____ 18. development that violates the reader's expectations

_____ 19. hinting at events that will occur later in the story

_____ 20. departure from the literal way of saying something

A. foreshadowing

B. conflict

C. figurative language

D. irony

E. plot twist

SHORT ANSWER

Give examples of the following literary devices used in the stories indicated.

21. foreshadowing in "After Twenty Years"

22. types of conflict in "Thank You, M'am"

23. irony in Isaiah 52:13–53:12

The Unit Reviews help you prepare for unit tests through multiple choice, matching, short answer, true/false, and essay questions.

1

FRIENDS

Colin Bootman (contemporary artist) moved to the United States from Trinidad when he was seven years old. He cites the vibrancy of life in the islands as having an influence on his artistic expression.

What mood has the artist conveyed in his painting entitled *Friends*?

What do you think the relationships are among the girls in the painting?

Where might these girls be headed? Where might they be coming from?

What do you think is the emphasis of this painting? How does the artist accomplish that emphasis?

Can you tell anything about the time period of the painting?

FRIENDS

FRIENDSHIP IS A GOD-GIVEN GIFT. WHEN ADAM WAS ONLY HOURS OLD, GOD SAID, "IT IS NOT GOOD THAT THE MAN SHOULD BE ALONE" (GEN. 2:18). THUS, TOWARD THE END OF OUR RACE'S FIRST DAY, THE FIRST HUMAN FRIENDSHIP BEGAN.

But it did not take long for our first parents to damage God's gift of friendship. Adam and Eve disobeyed God, and this first sin brought selfishness, pride, and betrayal (Gen. 3:12).

On the same day that sin entered our race, God promised to intervene and to remedy mankind's fallen condition (Gen. 3:15) by making the ultimate sacrifice for sin. Through that sacrifice, Christ has given His people an example of true friendship. He is the loyal, patient, gracious, generous, honest, sacrificial, and forgiving Friend, the perfect embodiment of the qualities found in 1 Corinthians 13.

As you read this unit's selections, ask yourself how certain characters' attitudes and actions differ from those of other characters. Then evaluate the quality of their friendships by Christ's standard. A person who is a good friend will exhibit behavior that mirrors the example of Christ. You will discover that His example has had a great impact on literature. The account of Christ's love, sacrifice, and victory over evil is part of the greatest story ever told. For this reason many authors purposefully construct their stories so that one or more of the characters remind the reader of Jesus Christ. In stud-

ies of literature, such a character is called a Christ-figure. See whether you recognize any Christ-figures in these selections.

Your study of friendship in literature is not complete until you have thought about your own friendships. What kind of friends do you have? If they do not exemplify to some degree the positive qualities you find in literature and in the Bible, your friendships may be nothing more than destructive influences. As Solomon warned, the wrong friend can ruin a person's life: "Make no friendship with an angry man; . . . Lest thou learn his ways, and get a snare to thy soul" (Prov. 22:24–25). Of course, the most important question for you to consider concerns you as a friend. What kind of friend are you? Do you befriend people for what you can get from them? Christ's example teaches us that we should view friendship as an opportunity to give to others and help them become what God wants them to be. It is not easy to sacrifice so that others can flourish spiritually. But Christ has promised His joy to those who will follow His example: "These things have I spoken unto you, that my joy might remain in you, and that your joy might be full. This is my commandment, That ye love one another, as I have loved you" (John 15:11–12).

GREATER LOVE HATH NO MAN THAN THIS,
THAT A MAN LAY DOWN HIS LIFE FOR HIS FRIENDS.
YE ARE MY FRIENDS.

—JOHN 15:13–14

A Most Important Person

Margaret Weymouth Jackson

Miss Lucy Quinn has been "brought up on the fixed idea that there was only a small group of people in the city with whom [she] might associate." As the years pass, however, Miss Lucy discovers that refinement and wealth are lonely companions and that "the aloof manner imposed on her in her youth imprison[s] her now like a suit of armor." But Chester, an energetic, mischievous young boy, finds a way to pierce the armor and becomes the most important person Miss Lucy will ever meet.

The old-fashioned high-bodied automobile drew up at the curbing at Fourth Street and the Boulevard, and the liveried* chauffeur descended and opened the car door as grandly as though it were some new imported model carrying a queen. Miss Lucy Quinn hesitated with one gloved hand on the open car door and one small foot on the pavement. She looked as though she did not want to get out of the car, and the elderly chauffeur said quickly, kindly:

"Maybe you'd better not walk today, Miss Quinn. The wind is cold and it might snow again."

---

liveried: uniformed

"Yes, Arthur, I must walk, thank you," Miss Quinn said firmly and stepped down onto the pavement.

It was her custom always to stop at this corner and walk the six blocks down the Boulevard and around the corner to her house on Maple Drive. She walked off now, her narrow back erect, the little hat bobbing on her smooth gray hair, and the chauffeur looked after her.

"It's the Christmas trimmings," he told himself. "She's that lonely."

It was true. It was Christmas and Miss Lucy Quinn was lonely. There was no one for whom she could make a Christmas. The rest of the year she endured her loneliness with composure, but at Christmas it came upon her like an illness.

"It's the way we were brought up," Miss Quinn told herself; and then, hastily: "Yet we had a happy childhood. Our parents were always good and kind to us."

But Miss Lucy and her sister Agatha had been brought up on the fixed idea that there was only a small group of people in the city with whom they might associate. The idea once planted, the years had done the rest. Miss Lucy's parents, loving though they were, had had to die. Miss Lucy's sister Agatha and her husband had died. All the friends of Miss Lucy's youth had either died or moved away or lost touch with her, until now there was no one left—no one at all near Miss Lucy. The society of the town moved briskly on without her, bristling with strange names.

There had been three delightful years when Miss Lucy's grandnephew, Agatha's only grandson, George, had lived in her house and studied at the university. He had been a quiet, studious young man, a true Quinn and a scholar, not much given to gaiety, but Miss Lucy had enjoyed him tremendously. Now he was studying in England; and in the casual manner of young males, he occasionally wrote to her.

There must be many interesting things one could do in a great city, Miss Lucy knew, but she did not know how to do them. The aloof* manner imposed on her in her youth imprisoned her now like a suit of armor.

aloof: withdrawn; keeping to oneself

She was reflecting rather vaguely on these and wishing—almost—for a catastrophe that might hurl her out of her rut, when suddenly, it seemed right out of the pavement beneath her feet, a violent fight sprang up. Miss Lucy stopped and trembled. She did not like fighting at all, and this was nothing more than a brawl. Three small boys, two larger than the other, were fighting in deadly earnest, with the sounds like a dog-fight which arise from small boys in battle. Miss Lucy looked at them horrified. The two big boys were beating and pounding the small one, and though he fought like a young wildcat, he was being overcome.

Miss Lucy looked all around. No one was near. No policeman was in sight. The horrible idea occurred to her that the little boy might be killed, right before her eyes. Briskly she raised her umbrella and brought it down smartly* on first one pair of young shoulders and then the other. The bigger boys howled and departed as abruptly and inexplicably* as they had come, and the small boy stood, still braced for battle, still snorting through his nose, and looked at Miss Lucy.

smartly: forcibly, sharply
inexplicably: incapable of being explained

Miss Lucy was very upset. She had never struck another human being in her life. She was completely demoralized* and astonished, and she also felt a strange glow. She pulled herself together and resumed her walk. The small boy reached up and put his hand inside of hers and walked beside her. His hand was shaking a little and he was still breathing very hard. Miss Lucy looked down at him but went on walking, and the small boy measured his step to hers and walked with her. They proceeded so to the very corner and the small boy drew a deep quivering breath and said:

"You saved me!"

Miss Lucy did not know what to say. She walked on across the street, holding the little hand firmly now, because of the traffic. In the next block her young friend, who had quite recovered, said to her again:

"You saved me! I have never been saved before."

Miss Lucy felt required to make some answer. "I'm glad," she told him, "glad I was there." And she found that she was very glad. He was such a dear little boy!

"I know how you feel," he answered eagerly. "I know just how you feel. I saved a cat once. I was awf'ly fond of it afterwards. It wasn't much of a cat," he explained. "Its ears were chewed and it had fleas, but then—it liked me."

"Yes, indeed," said Miss Lucy. The little hand was now warm and safe and friendly in her own.

"I think you are a very good fighter for your size," Miss Lucy said, a little shyly.

"Yes," he agreed complacently,* "I'm a good fighter. And I like to fight. But not two at once, and both so big."

"Little boys should not fight on the street," said Miss Lucy, but she did not say it severely, and he answered at once:

"I know. It is better to get in an alley, or somewheres where the cops or teachers won't stop you."

They had come unaccountably to her very door. Miss Lucy was amazed. The walk had never seemed so short. She stopped and explained, "I live here. This is my house."

The little boy looked at the house.

"I think that I'll come in and visit you awhile," he offered then. "I don't have to be home until dark, and I like to go visiting. I like to visit my friends."

"I always have tea when I come in from my walk," said Miss Lucy, who was ashamed that he had needed to invite himself. "Wouldn't you like to come in and have tea with me?"

"I don't care," he said, and they went up the steps and Mitzie, the grizzled* parlor-maid, opened the door for Miss Lucy.

Miss Lucy walked in proudly with her guest. "There will be two of us for tea, Mitzie," she said, and Mitzie said, "Yes, Ma'am," and helped Miss Lucy out of her coat and took the small boy's jacket and cap. Miss Lucy led him into the little parlor where she always sat. A coal fire was burning on the hearth. The brass coal scuttle* and the brass fender* were shining. He stood and looked all around. Miss Lucy felt suddenly proud of her parlor. It seemed to her it had never looked so nice. But the small boy said:

"Where is your Christmas tree?"

"Why," said Miss Lucy, "I haven't got it up yet."

"Oh," he said, and his face broke into a vivid smile, "I know! You are keeping it back for a surprise for someone. Will you have it up tomorrow? May I come to see it?"

"Yes," said Miss Lucy, "I will have the tree up tomorrow. I'll be glad if you will come to see it."

"I'll come early," he assured her. "I love Christmas trees. I'll bet I've seen every tree on our whole street and I'll bet that you will have the biggest tree and the best tree of all!"

Mitzie appeared with the tea tray and placed it on the low table before Miss Lucy. Cook had put a chocolate pot beside the silver teapot, and there was a plate with three great sugary buns on the usually Spartan* tray. But they had made a mistake. A large kitchen cup and saucer stood on the tray. Miss Lucy picked them up and handed them to Mitzie with a stern glance.

Spartan: simple; avoiding luxury

"Bring me the delft-blue* cup," she said. "The big one that my father used."

delft-blue: a style of glazed earthenware pottery, usually blue and white, originally made in Delft, Netherlands

Mitzie turned red and took the cup without a word and brought back Miss Lucy's great treasure, her father's cup which held almost a pint. Miss Lucy filled it with chocolate and gave it to her guest, who placed it carefully on the edge of a small table. She gave him a fringed napkin and passed the buns. He began at once to eat in a businesslike manner and with much pleasure.

"My mother says the lankest* part of the day is between school's out and supper," he remarked.

lankest: longest

Miss Lucy felt a vague disappointment. She didn't know why. "Oh, you have a mother?" she said.

The small boy looked astonished. *Whoever heard of anyone without a mother?* his look said. "Sure," he told her. "I have a mother and father and two brothers and two sisters, besides the baby."

"And the baby?" Miss Lucy asked.

"The baby is a girl," he said. "Her name is Marie. She's got blue eyes and she's bowlegged."

"Oh, I'm sorry," said Miss Lucy.

"It's on account of her temper'ment," the boy explained. "She has such a for'd* temper'ment."

for'd: forward

Miss Lucy put her cup down and looked at him. "I don't understand," she said.

"She does everything before she should," he answered. "She's that way. She wanted to sit up too soon, and now she is walking before she should and that makes her bow-legged. My mother says she doesn't know how she is going to cope with her, her being always so for'd."

"Oh," said Miss Lucy.

"Our baby is quite a care," he admitted.

"Now she is causing a lot of trouble because she is determined to eat things off the Christmas tree; and when she is determined, she is determined, and there's nothing anyone can do about it. She's a nice baby. You

mustn't think we don't like her. I'm just telling you about her."

"I understand," Miss Lucy assured him. "She sounds like an interesting baby. But I shouldn't think Christmas-tree ornaments would be very good for her."

"They're not! But what does she care? They are pretty and she wants to eat them— that's the way she is."

"Wouldn't you like another bun?" said Miss Lucy.

He would. He said, eating it, "If you would like to see our baby—since you're so interested in her and everything—I could bring her over to see you. Not in the morning when I come to see the tree, but after lunch, I could bring her. I take her out every day. That's what the fight was about," he added, "because those guys think it is sissy to take the baby out. But my mother says family responsibility is not sissy."

Miss Lucy almost said she always took a nap after lunch, but she caught herself back in time. Her young guest was offering her a great favor, in showing her the baby. "I will be looking for you," she said. She rang the bell and Mitzie came and took the tray away and Miss Lucy said: "It is getting almost dark. You mustn't worry your mother. You haven't told me yet what your name is, or where you live."

"My name is Chester," he said, embarrassed, "Chester Chilton. My mother is smart but she admits herself that my name was a mistake, and my father thinks so too. However, what can they do about it now? But everyone calls me Chuck, so it isn't important, I guess. I live on Basalt-1028. On the third floor. It isn't far from here."

Miss Lucy went to the door with him. She knew where Basalt Street was. A crowded street, three blocks long, a half mile or so to the west of the Boulevard. "I have enjoyed your visit," she said, "and you must come again."

"I'm coming in the morning," he reminded her, "to see your Christmas tree. School's out so I can come early."

Miss Lucy closed the door gently after him and looked out through the glass and saw him hop down the stairs and light out for Basalt Street on the run. She returned to her fire. She rang the bell again.

"Please send Arthur to me," she said and in a moment the chauffeur stood in the door. "I want to go out again," Miss Lucy told him. "Are the shops still open? I want to buy a Christmas tree."

"I can get it for you, Miss Quinn," said Arthur.

But Miss Lucy thought to herself that one thing that made her so lonely was that she never did anything for herself, or for anyone else. She simply said, "Mitzie, do this," or "Cook, I want so and so—" She smiled, thinking what the child had said about family responsibilities. He would expect something pretty wonderful of her, in the way of a tree. She wanted to choose it herself!

It was very crowded and busy at the market. After some searching they found a tree that suited Miss Lucy. It filled up the back of the car and stuck out of the window and Miss Lucy had to ride with Arthur.

"We will have to go downtown for ornaments," she said. "There is a box of things in the attic, but I am sure there are not enough."

So they went to the dime store and Arthur went in with Miss Lucy. She was almost crushed to death. White people and black ones jammed the aisles, and babies in their mothers' arms wailed or slept or gazed around at the great world. They bought boxes and boxes of ornaments.

"I need a gift for him too," Miss Lucy shouted at Arthur. Her hat was on one side of her head and she said in a firm, annoyed tone, "Please take your elbow out of my ribs," to a tall, thin man who tried to oblige her. "What do you buy," she shouted again, "for a seven-year-old who lives on Basalt and likes to fight, and for a girl baby who eats Christmas-tree ornaments?"

Arthur blinked a little. "I'd buy him boxing gloves," said Arthur, solemn as an owl. "And I'd buy her some of these candy canes."

So they left the car where it was and found a sporting goods store, and a candy store. When they got back to the car, they found that the tires were marked with chalk, and they had been given a ticket! Arthur took it out from under the windshield wiper. He was quite disconcerted.*

---

disconcerted: unpleasantly surprised

"I've not had a ticket for years, Miss Quinn," he said.

"Never mind," said Miss Lucy, "we'll just pay the fine."

"They're getting very strict about traffic violations," explained Arthur, stowing packages away under the tree. "But if you'll call Mr. Henderson, Ma'am."

"No," said Miss Lucy firmly, "I will pay the fine."

When they got home again, Mitzie ran out to help Arthur with all the packages, and Cook came to see what they had bought.

Miss Lucy was very excited. "We'll have dinner," she announced, "and then you will all have to help me with the tree. There are some boxes in the attic. But I am very hungry now."

"If you will tell me what you want, Miss Quinn," Mitzie said, when she served Miss Lucy, "I will get it from the attic."

"No," said Miss Lucy, "I want to get it. I know where the things are. The last time we had a tree in this house was when George

was twelve years old, the year before my father died. I put the things away then."

When Miss Lucy went up to the attic, Arthur and Cook and Mitzie all followed her. The attic was in perfect order. Miss Lucy found the box just where she had expected to find it and Mitzie helped Arthur carry it down.

Cook looked around. "My, wouldn't a lively young one have a time up here," said Cook, "dressing up in these old clothes and parading around?"

"Yes," said Miss Lucy. "I'm sure I don't know why I have saved all this junk. It is no good to anyone."

Cook followed Miss Lucy down, talking a blue streak. They discussed the position of the tree, and had some trouble making it stand up straight. Arthur had to take his coat off and go down to the basement and hammer and pound until he contrived a sturdy base. At last the tree was in place and Cook brought the ladder they used for window washing, and they began to trim the tree.

Miss Lucy wanted the same old angel on the top of the tree they had had when she was a child.

"It is faded," she said, "but it is like Chester's cat—it is mine," and she told them about the cat. "You mustn't put anything near the bottom that the baby might eat," said Miss Lucy and she told them about the baby who was determined to eat Christmas-tree things, and when she was determined, she was determined!

Cook knew a child that had done the same thing and Arthur said, "I had a cat when I was a lad that simply went wild over a Christmas tree—simply wild. Once he got so excited he sprang right into the middle of the tree—just lost all reason!"

Mitzie got the giggles at this, and Miss Lucy laughed aloud. They worked very hard and by nine o'clock there the tree stood, covered with gorgeous bright balls and silver icicles, and strung with lights, with candy canes on the lower branches for the baby.

Miss Lucy had to sit down and admire it, and she could not hear enough praise from the others. She was so tired she was no sooner in bed than asleep and she slept so soundly that Mitzie had to waken her.

"The young gentleman is here," Mitzie explained. "I thought you would want to see him."

Miss Lucy got downstairs in a hurry. Chester was standing in the middle of the parlor staring at the tree with round excited eyes.

"I knew it!" he said, when he saw her. "I told my mother you would have the best tree of anyone. I told her, 'That's the way she is!'"

Miss Lucy glowed with pride. "I haven't had my breakfast," she said. "Wouldn't you like to eat with me?" That was one thing she remembered—George could always eat, when he was little.

Chester said politely, "I will be glad to keep you company," and Mitzie put a plate on the dining-room table for him.

But before they had finished with breakfast Mitzie summoned her mistress to the door, and Chester followed her. There was a policeman with a summons. Miss Lucy had to appear in the police court at ten o'clock.

"Have you been arrested?" Chester asked with eager interest.

"Yes," said Miss Lucy, bragging about it, and she explained: "We got a ticket, Arthur and I, for parking too long on Front Street."

The last fine touch of glamour had been added to Miss Lucy. Her young friend looked at her with shining eyes. "Will you have to go to jail?" he said hopefully. "I will come and visit you if you do."

"No," said Miss Lucy, "I am afraid they will not imprison me. I will be home before you get here with the baby."

Chester offered to ride down to the courthouse with them, but Miss Lucy dropped him off at his own door. The police court was crowded. Arthur stood very stiff and severe beside Miss Lucy. They had to wait their turn. The judge was cross. He was scolding and fining everyone. A young man at a table near the judge's bench nudged another young man and they watched Miss Lucy when she came forward to answer the complaint.

"Miss Lucy Quinn," said the judge. "Parking on Front Street for forty-five minutes, between five and six." He looked over his glasses. "You are certainly the last person I expected to see in this court, Miss Lucy."

"Yes, Your Honor—yes, Judge Hennesy."

The judge turned to Arthur. "You are Miss Quinn's chauffeur?" he demanded.

"Yes sir."

"Don't you know the traffic rules?"

"Yes sir."

"It was my fault," said Miss Quinn. "I was buying a Christmas tree and boxing gloves and candy—you see, the child thinks things on the tree are to eat. The dime store was crowded, and it took us a long time. I will pay my fine."

"Seven dollars and costs," said the judge. "And I want to speak to you in my chambers."

Miss Lucy paid her fine to the clerk, and went into the judge's little room. When the door closed he shook hands with her, his blue eyes twinkling.

"So you have a Christmas tree, Miss Lucy?" he said. "My wife and I were speaking about you the other day. We haven't seen you for years."

"Why don't you come to call on me, and see my tree?" said Miss Lucy Quinn. "I will leave it up until the New Year."

"We'll do it. We will come to see you some time next week, Miss Lucy."

When they reached home Miss Lucy got out of the car and looked at their front door. "We ought to have a wreath on our door, Arthur—a big one, with a great red bow of ribbon on it. Everyone has a wreath on the front door." So she got back into the car and they went and bought a wreath for the door.

Inside, Miss Lucy was surprised to see that there were packages tucked under the tree, and she went up to her room and got the gifts she had purchased for Mitzie and Cook and Arthur and put them under the tree. She was a little late for luncheon, but it seemed the servants did not mind anything today.

Chester arrived with the baby tied securely into a small cart, and he untied her and carried her up the stairs, staggering a little. Mitzie ran to help him and Miss Lucy stood in the door. When Mitzie had unwrapped the baby from her blankets and taken off her bonnet and coat, there she stood, no bigger than a minute, with bright red cheeks and bright blue eyes and silky-soft fair hair.

The baby put her arms up to Miss Lucy. "Up!" she said, and Miss Lucy lifted her uncertainly. They went into the parlor and Miss Lucy sat down with the baby in her lap. But the baby gave a great lunge at sight of the tree and almost leaped out of Miss Lucy's arms. Miss Lucy gave a cry and clutched the infant firmly.

"She wants down," explained Chester, and Miss Lucy put the baby on the floor. She went on her active small legs, which were undeniably a little bowed, straight for the tree and grabbed one of the candy canes and stuffed it in her mouth and looked around with a defiant "come-and-get-it" air. Cook and Arthur hovered in the doorway, smiling and murmuring.

Chester's visit was a great success. Marie was an altogether delightful small person, noisy and gay and not afraid of anyone or anything in the world. She got into the desk and into the bookcase, and the magazine stand and the bric-a-brac.* She was quick as a flash and curious as a monkey. It took both Cook and Mitzie to regulate her. But a delicate sense of loyalty prevented Miss Lucy from becoming too enamored of the baby. She made Chester her special guest and responsibility. She told him about the police court, and about Judge Hennesy, who had been the policeman on this very beat* when they were both young. He had married their upstairs girl, as pretty a girl as ever came from the country to work in town. Then he had studied law and he had become a lawyer and a politician and now he was a judge!

bric-a-brac: small ornamental object
beat: area regularly covered by a police officer

"And a very fine judge too," Miss Lucy said, who knew nothing at all of what kind of judge he was.

"I am going to be a pilot," Chester told her and they talked about that.

Finally the baby began to rub her eyes and cry, and Arthur took Marie and Chester home in the car with the little cart strapped onto the trunk! Miss Lucy toiled upstairs to her nap. She was as sleepy as Marie. When she came downstairs again, the evening paper was lying on the table near her chair by the fireplace and the tree was blazing with lights. Miss Lucy felt very happy.

She opened the paper and there on the first page was a candid-camera picture of Miss Lucy and Judge Hennesy! "Society Leader in Traffic Court" the legend ran. Miss Lucy blushed bright red, and then looked at the picture critically. It was re-

ally quite good. She was looking very pert, and Judge Hennesy was leaning down with his mouth open, and Arthur looked like an undertaker!

Miss Lucy read the story through twice. It was most absurd. It told a great deal about her family, about her position as "titular* head of local Society," and went on about how simple everything would be when people stepped up and paid their fines instead of using their influence to get stickers "fixed." While Miss Lucy was reading the story the third time the telephone rang for her. It was old Mr. Henderson, for many years the family lawyer. He said, quite excited, that Miss Lucy should have called him and he would have taken care of the ticket for her, or at least taken care of the fine without her appearing in court. She must always let him know—

titular: in name only

"It was no trouble at all," said Miss Lucy.

She asked after Mr. Henderson's health, and his wife's health.

"We are quite well," said Mr. Henderson.

Before she knew it she had agreed to go to Hendersons' to dinner the following Tuesday.

Before she had finished her dinner, she was called again. It was her sister Agatha's husband's niece, Mrs. Morrison.

"We wondered, Miss Lucy, if you would not like to go to the community Christmas tree, at the Settlement House. We will call for you and take you home again, if you would go, as a favor to the committee."

Miss Lucy almost refused, and then she remembered that Chester had seen every tree on his block, and that Agatha's husband's family had given a great deal of money to the Settlement House. Miss Lucy was far too excited to eat any more dinner. But she was ready when Mrs. Morrison came for her.

There was an enormous tree at the Settlement House, and there were swarms of children from the ghetto. Miss Lucy was quite confused; but after she had recovered herself sufficiently to watch the games being played on the floor, she decided it was the lights in the great dark room which confused her.

"Something should be done about these lights," she told Mrs. Morrison. "And the room shouldn't be brown—it is such a dreary, sad color. Couldn't the room be painted cream—or even pink? And couldn't the lights be softer?"

Mrs. Morrison explained that this was the gymnasium and it got very dirty, and there was never enough money for decorating and lighting the place—there were so many needs.

"If you could come to a committee meeting," she suggested, "if you feel strong enough—you would see what our problems are."

"I am perfectly well," Miss Lucy told her tartly*. "There isn't a thing the matter with me. And I will come to your committee meeting. There," she said, pointing down at a shy child, smitten with stage fright, trying to hide behind an older brother, "there is your real problem—people shouldn't be allowed to grow up to be shy."

---

tartly: sharp or bitter in tone or meaning

Mrs. Morrison agreed, but Miss Lucy did not listen to what they were saying about child psychology. It had come to Miss Lucy that the problems were always the same; people had the same things to overcome, wherever they lived! And she grew suddenly warmly interested in what they were trying to do for all these children. If she worked on this committee, they would have to listen to her.

When she reached home, Arthur and Cook and Mitzie were all waiting up to see that their mistress got home safely and safely to bed. Miss Lucy was quite touched.

"I am going to be going out a good deal," she scolded them, "and you must not begin waiting up for me."

In the morning they gathered around the tree, Arthur and Cook and Mitzie and Miss Lucy, and opened their gifts. Miss Lucy was exceedingly gratified at the little things her old servants had given her. And she was even more gratified at the things she had given them, and their pleasure in them! And there, under the tree, was a grimy little package, labeled, "To Miss Quinn from her friend Chuck." Miss Lucy opened it with brimming eyes. It was a string of glass beads with a huge brass clasp.

When she went out for her drive that afternoon, Arthur took her to Basalt Street, and delivered the boxing gloves for Chester, and a bright ball for Marie. Chester came down to the car to see Miss Lucy and they took him for a short ride. He chattered all the way, and Miss Lucy was very much surprised to find that she had invited him and his brothers and sisters and a few friends, if he liked, to come to her house to an attic party the next week.

Chester was vivid with excitement, and he asked her, in a whisper, to park in the street for a minute, so that all the "kids" could see her.

Miss Lucy sat parked while Chester went and got some of his friends. They were clean, rosy children. The street, though crowded, was not a slum, and the other children, like Chester, looked healthy and well cared for. And Miss Lucy did not know that the ancient high bodied car was a great curiosity to the children.

But she felt dissatisfied to go home and eat the small turkey Cook had prepared for

Christmas dinner, all by herself. For two years George had had a young friend of his in for Christmas dinner, a young professor who had no family.

"But he wouldn't want to eat with an old woman like me," Miss Lucy thought. And then she remembered how Chester had invited himself visiting, remembered the baby who could not wait until time to taste of life, and she was ashamed. She spoke to Arthur. "Do you know where Professor Tilden lives?" she asked him. "The young man George had for dinner last Christmas."

"Yes, Miss Quinn," said Arthur. "He lives near the university."

So they drove there, and Arthur went into Professor Tilden's boarding house and found him sitting alone over his book. He came down to the car. He would be delighted to have dinner with Miss Quinn.

"How kind you are to remember me," he said.

He was a very shy young man. And all through the formal dinner he and Miss Quinn talked about poetry. And later by the fire he said to her:

"I wonder if you would be kind enough to come to visit the Shelley Club? We have some gifted young people, trying to write verse. You are so gracious and kind—you might be a great help to them, and I think you would enjoy it."

Miss Lucy said she had got out of touch with the university since her father died.

"But he was a regent* for years," Professor Tilden objected. "You ought to know what we are doing out there."

regent: board member

When Professor Tilden had gone home, Miss Lucy sat by the fire looking at the Christmas tree and thinking about Chester.

"What a dear little boy he is," she thought, and then she stared, amazed at all that had happened to her in the last two days. Since she had lifted her umbrella to Chester's adversaries all her life had changed. She decided soberly, "I am seventy years old, and he is the most important person I ever knew—and Christmas the most important time."

ABOUT THE AUTHOR

Margaret Weymouth Jackson (1895–1974), who was born in Eureka Springs, Arkansas, began her writing career at the age of twenty as a contributor of short stories to *Farm Life*. Even as a wife and mother of three, Jackson found time to further her writing career, publishing more than three hundred short stories in such magazines as *McCall's* and *Saturday Evening Post*. Jackson, who served as an editor, educator, and author, was recognized for her achievements with several literary awards. Perhaps the greatest tribute to her success is the continued popularity of her stories, which continue to delight readers of all ages.

THINKING ZONE

As you read the selections in this book, you will encounter many different **genres** or types of literature. The genre of "A Most Important Person" by Margaret Weymouth Jackson is **short story**, a brief work of prose fiction that tells a tale that resonates with realistic human emotions. Short stories like "A Most Important Person" usually chronicle people and happenings invented by the author—even though they can at times seem very real. The term *fiction* refers to literature that contains events made up by the author.

1. *[interpretive]* Look closely at the details given about Miss Lucy in the first five paragraphs of the **short story**. What does this description tell you about her?

   _____

   _____

   _____

2. *[literal]* How does Miss Lucy meet Chester?

   _____

   _____

   _____

3. *[interpretive]* How does Chester feel about Miss Lucy?

   _____

   _____

4. *[interpretive]* What does Miss Lucy's response to the traffic ticket say about her character?

   _____

   _____

   _____

5. *[interpretive]* Why does Miss Lucy call Chester "the most important person" she has ever known?

_____

_____

_____

_____

_____

6. *[critical]* At the end of the story, how has Miss Lucy changed? How is the ending similar to or different from the beginning of the story?

_____

_____

_____

_____

_____

_____

_____

_____

7. *[appreciative]* Although "A Most Important Person" is a work of **fiction**, you may have had a real-life experience in which you met a person or participated in an event that changed your life. If so, briefly describe that experience.

_____

_____

_____

_____

_____

_____

BEING NEIGHBORLY
FROM *LITTLE WOMEN*

LOUISA MAY ALCOTT

Sometimes making a new friend—even one who lives right next door—can be a challenge. In this story young Jo March meets a couple of neighbors whom she has only seen peering at her through curtained windows. They are rich, that much she knows, but will they make good friends?

"What in the world are you going to do now, Jo?" asked Meg one snowy afternoon as her sister came tramping through the hall in rubber boots, old sack* and hood, with a broom in one hand and a shovel in the other.

---
sack: loose coat

"Going out for exercise," answered Jo.

"I should think two long walks this morning would have been enough! It's cold and dull out, and I advise you to stay warm and dry by the fire, as I do," said Meg with a shiver.

"Never take advice! Can't keep still all day, and not being a pussycat, I don't like to doze by the fire. I like adventures, and I'm going to find some."

Meg went back to toast her feet and read *Ivanhoe*, and Jo began to dig paths with great energy. The snow was light, and with her broom she soon swept a path all round the garden. Now the garden separated the Marches' house from that of Mr. Laurence. Both stood in a suburb of the city, which was still countrylike, with groves and lawns, large gardens, and quiet streets. A low hedge parted the two estates. On one side was an old brown house, looking rather bare and shabby robbed of the vines that in summer covered its walls and the flowers which then surrounded it. On the other side was a

stately stone mansion, plainly betokening* every sort of comfort and luxury, from the big coach house and well-kept grounds to the conservatory.* Yet it seemed a lonely, lifeless sort of house; for no children frolicked on the lawn, no motherly face ever smiled at the windows, and few people went in and out except the old gentleman and his grandson.

---
betokening: indicating
conservatory: greenhouse

To Jo's lively fancy*, this fine house seemed a kind of enchanted palace full of splendors and delights which no one enjoyed. She had long wanted to behold these hidden glories, and to know the "Laurence boy," who looked as if he would like to be known if he only knew how to begin. Since the party, she had been more eager than ever and had planned many ways of making friends with him; but he had not been seen lately, and Jo began to think he had gone away when she one day spied a brown face at the upper window, looking wishfully down into their garden, where Beth and Amy were snowballing one another.

---
fancy: imagination

"That boy is suffering for society and fun," she said to herself. "His grandpa does not know what's good for him and keeps him shut up all alone. He needs a party of jolly boys to play with, or somebody young and lively. I've a great mind to go over and tell the old gentleman so!"

The idea amused Jo, who liked to do daring things and was always scandalizing* Meg by her odd performances. The plan of "going over" was not forgotten, and when the snowy afternoon came, Jo resolved to try what could be done. She saw Mr. Laurence drive off, and then sallied out* to dig her way down to the hedge, where she paused and took a survey. All quiet—curtains down at the lower windows, servants out of sight, and nothing human visible but a curly black head leaning on a thin hand at the upper window.

scandalizing: shocking
sallied out: rushed out

"There he is," thought Jo, "poor boy! All alone and sick this dismal day. It's a shame! I'll toss up a snowball and make him look out, and then say a kind word to him."

Up went a handful of soft snow, and the head turned at once, showing a face which lost its listless look in a minute. Jo nodded and laughed, and flourished her broom as she called out: "How do you do? Are you sick?" Laurie* opened the window, and croaked out as hoarsely as a raven:

Laurie: nickname for Theodore Laurence

"Better, thank you. I've had a bad cold and been shut up a week."

"I'm sorry. What do you amuse yourself with?"

"Nothing. It's as dull as tombs up here."

"Don't you read?"

"Not much. They won't let me."

"Can't somebody read to you?"

"Grandpa does, sometimes; but my books don't interest him, and I hate to ask Brooke* all the time."

Brooke: Laurie's private teacher

"Have someone come and see you, then."

"There isn't anyone I'd like to see. Boys make such a row, and my head is weak."

"Isn't there some nice girl who'd read and amuse you? Girls are quiet, and like to play nurse."

"Don't know any."

"You know us," began Jo, then laughed, and stopped.

"So I do! Will you come, please?" cried Laurie.

"I'm not quiet and nice, but I'll come if Mother will let me. I'll go ask her. Shut that window, like a good boy, and wait till I come."

With that, Jo shouldered her broom and marched into the house, wondering what

they would all say to her. Laurie was in a flutter of excitement at the idea of having company and flew about to get ready. Presently there came a loud ring, then a decided voice asking for "Mr. Laurie," and a surprised-looking servant came running up to announce a young lady.

"All right, show her up. It's Miss Jo," said Laurie, going to the door of his little parlor to meet Jo, who appeared with a covered dish in one hand and Beth's three kittens in the other.

"Here I am, bag and baggage," she said briskly. "Mother sent her love, and was glad if I could do anything for you. Meg wanted me to bring some of her blancmange*—she makes it very nicely—and Beth thought her cats would be comforting. I knew you'd laugh at them, but I couldn't refuse, she was so anxious to do something."

blancmange: a cornstarch pudding

It so happened that Beth's funny loan was just the thing, for in laughing over the kits Laurie forgot his bashfulness, and grew sociable at once.

"That looks too pretty to eat," he said, smiling with pleasure as Jo uncovered the dish and showed the blancmange, surrounded by a garland of green leaves and the scarlet flowers of Amy's pet geranium.

"It isn't anything, only they all felt kindly, and wanted to show it. Tell the girl to put it away for your tea. It's so simple you can eat it, and it will slip down without hurting your sore throat. What a cozy room this is!"

"It might be if it was kept nice."

"I'll right it up in two minutes; for it only needs to have the hearth brushed, so—and the things made straight on the mantelpiece, so— and the books put here, and the bottles there, and your sofa turned from the light, and the pillows plumped up a bit. Now then, you're fixed."

And so he was, for as she laughed and talked Jo had whisked things into place and given quite a different air to the room. Laurie watched her in respectful silence and when she beckoned him to his sofa, he sat down with a sigh of satisfaction, saying gratefully: "How kind you are! Yes, that's what it wanted. Now please take the big chair, and let me do something to amuse my company."

"No—I came to amuse you. Shall I read aloud?" And Jo looked affectionately toward some inviting books near by.

"Thank you, I've read all those, and if you don't mind, I'd rather talk," answered Laurie.

"Not a bit. I'll talk all day if you'll only set me going. Beth says I never know when to stop."

"Is Beth the rosy one who stays at home a good deal, and sometimes goes out with a little basket?" asked Laurie.

"Yes, that's Beth. She's my girl, and a regular good one she is, too."

"The pretty one is Meg, and the curly-haired one is Amy, I believe?"

"How did you find that out?"

Laurie colored up, but answered frankly: "Why, you see I often hear you calling to one another, and when I'm alone up here, I can't help looking over at your house, you always seem to be having such good times. I beg your pardon for being so rude, but sometimes you forget to put down the curtain at the window where the flowers are; and when the lamps are lighted, it's like looking at a picture to see the fire, and you all round the table with your mother. I can't help watching it. I haven't got any mother, you know."

The solitary, hungry look in his eyes went straight to Jo's warm heart. She had been so simply taught that there was no nonsense in her head, and at fifteen she was as innocent and frank as any child. Laurie was sick and lonely, and feeling how rich she was in home, love and happiness, she gladly tried to share it with him. Her face was very friendly and her sharp voice unusually gentle as she said:

"We'll never draw that curtain any more, and I give you leave to look as much as you like. I just wish, though, instead of peeping, you'd come over and see us. Mother is so splendid she'd do you heaps of good, and Beth would sing to you if *I* begged her to, and Amy would dance, Meg and I would make you laugh over our funny stage properties, and we'd have jolly times. Wouldn't your grandpa let you?"

"I think he would, if your mother asked him. He's very kind, though he does not look so; and he lets me do what I like, pretty much, only he's afraid I might be a bother to strangers," began Laurie, brightening more and more.

"We are not strangers, we are neighbors, and you needn't think you'd be a bother. We want to know you, and I've been trying to do this ever so long. We haven't been here a great while, you know, but we have got acquainted with all our neighbors but you."

"You see Grandpa lives among his books, and doesn't mind much what happens outside. Mr. Brooke, my tutor, doesn't stay here, you know, and I have no one to go about with me, so I just stop at home and get on as I can."

"That's bad. You ought to make an effort, and go visiting everywhere you are asked. Then you'll have plenty of friends and pleasant places to go to. Never mind being bashful; it won't last long if you keep going."

Laurie turned red again, but wasn't offended at being accused of bashfulness, for there was so much goodwill in Jo it was impossible not to take her blunt speeches as kindly as they were meant.

"Do you like your school?" asked the boy, changing the subject.

"Don't go to school. I'm a businessman—girl, I mean. I go to wait on my great-aunt, and a dear, cross old soul she is, too," answered Jo.

Laurie opened his mouth to ask another question, but remembering just in time that it wasn't good manners to make too many inquiries into people's affairs, he shut it again, and looked uncomfortable. Jo liked his good breeding, and didn't mind having a laugh at Aunt March, so she gave him a lively description of the fidgety old lady, her fat poodle, the parrot, and the library where she reveled.* Laurie enjoyed that immensely.

---

reveled: took great delight

"Oh, that does me no end of good! Tell on, please."

Much elated with her success, Jo did "tell on," all about their plays and plans, their hopes and fears for father, and the most interesting events of the little world in which the sisters lived. Then they got to talking about books, and to Jo's delight, she found that Laurie loved them as well as she did, and had read even more than herself.

"If you like them so much, come down and see ours. Grandpa is out, so you needn't be afraid," said Laurie.

"I'm not afraid," returned Jo, with a toss of the head.

"I don't believe you are!" exclaimed the boy, looking at her with much admiration, though he privately thought she would have good reason to be a trifle afraid of the old gentleman if she met him in some of his moods.

The atmosphere of the whole house being summerlike, Laurie led the way from room to room, letting Jo stop to examine whatever struck her fancy; and so at last they came to the library, where she clapped her hands and pranced, as she always did when especially delighted. It was lined with books, and there were pictures and statues, and distracting little cabinets full of coins and curiosities, and sleepy-hollow chairs, and odd tables, and bronzes; and best of all a great open fireplace, with quaint tiles all round it.

"What richness!" sighed Jo, sinking into the depth of a velvet chair and gazing about her with an air of intense satisfaction. "Theodore Laurence, you ought to be the happiest boy in the world," she added impressively.

"A fellow can't live on books," said Laurie, shaking his head.

Before he could say more, a bell rang, and Jo flew up, exclaiming with alarm: "Mercy me! It's your grandpa!"

"Well, what if it is? You aren't afraid of anything, you know," returned the boy, looking wicked.

"I think I am a little bit afraid of him, but I don't know why I should be. Marmee said I might come, and I don't think you're any the worse for it," said Jo, composing herself.

"I'm a great deal better for it, and ever so much obliged. I'm only afraid you are very tired talking to me. It was so pleasant I couldn't bear to stop," said Laurie gratefully.

"The doctor to see you, sir," and the maid beckoned as she spoke.

"Would you mind if I left you for a minute? I suppose I must see him," said Laurie.

"Don't mind me. I'm as happy as a cricket here."

Laurie went away, and his guest amused herself in her own way. She was standing before a fine portrait of the old gentleman when the door opened again, and, without turning, she said decidedly: "I'm sure now that I shouldn't be afraid of him, for he's got kind eyes, though his mouth is grim and he looks as if he had a tremendous will of his own. He isn't as handsome as my grandfather, but I like him."

"Thank you, ma'am," said a gruff voice behind her, and there, to her great dismay, stood old Mr. Laurence.

Poor Jo blushed till she couldn't blush any redder, and her heart began to beat uncomfortably fast as she thought what she had said. For a minute a wild desire to run away possessed her; but that was cowardly, and the girls would laugh at her, so she resolved to stay and get out of the scrape as she could. A second look showed her that the living eyes under the bushy gray eyebrows were kinder even than the painted ones, and there was a sly twinkle in them which lessened her fear a good deal. The gruff voice was gruffer than ever as the old gentleman said abruptly, "So you're not afraid of me, hey?"

"Not much, sir."

"And you don't think me as handsome as your grandfather?"

"Not quite, sir."

"And I've got a tremendous will, have I?"

"I only said I thought so."

"But you like me, in spite of it?"

"Yes, I do, sir."

That answer pleased the old gentleman. He gave a short laugh, shook hands with her, and putting his finger under her chin, turned up her face, examined it gravely, and let it go, saying with a nod:

"You've got your grandfather's spirit, if you haven't his face. He was a fine man, my dear, but what is better, he was a brave and an honest one, and I was proud to be his friend."

"Thank you, sir."

"What have you been doing to this boy of mine, hey?" was the next question, sharply put.

"Only trying to be neighborly, sir." And Jo told how her visit came about.

"You think he needs cheering up a bit, do you?"

"Yes, sir. He seems a little lonely, and young folks would do him good perhaps. We are only girls, but we should be glad to help if we could, for we don't forget the splendid Christmas present you sent us," said Jo eagerly.

"I shall come and see your mother some fine day. Tell her so. There's the tea bell; we have it early, on the boy's account. Come down, and go on being neighborly."

"If you'd like to have me, sir."

"Shouldn't ask you if I didn't." And Mr. Laurence offered her his arm with old-fashioned courtesy.

"What would Meg say to this?" thought Jo as she was marched away.

"Hey! Why, what the dickens has come to the fellow?" said the old gentleman as Laurie came running downstairs and brought up with a start of surprise at the astonishing sight of Jo arm-in-arm with his redoubtable* grandfather.

redoubtable: frightening; intimidating

"I didn't know you'd come, sir."

"That's evident by the way you racket* downstairs. Come to your tea, sir, and behave like a gentleman." And having pulled the boy's hair by way of a caress, Mr. Laurence walked on, while Laurie went through a series of comic evolutions* behind their backs which nearly produced an explosion of laughter from Jo.

racket: move with a loud distressing noise
evolutions: changes

The old gentleman did not say much as he drank his four cups of tea, but he watched the young people, who soon chatted away like old friends, and the change in his grandson did not escape him. There was color, light, and life in the boy's face now, vivacity* in his manner, and genuine merriment in his laugh.

vivacity: liveliness

"She's right, the lad is lonely. I'll see what these little girls can do for him," thought Mr. Laurence. He liked Jo, for her odd, blunt ways suited him, and she seemed to understand the boy almost as well as if she had been one herself.

If the Laurences had been what Jo called "prim and poky," she would not have got on at all, for such people always made her shy and awkward; but finding them free and easy, she was so herself, and made a good impression. When they rose she proposed to go, but Laurie said he had something more to show her and took her away to the conservatory. It seemed quite fairylike to Jo as she went up and down the walks enjoying the blooming walls on either side, the soft light, the damp sweet air, and the won-

derful vines and trees that hung above her. Her new friend cut the finest flowers till his hands were full; then he tied them up, saying, with the happy look Jo liked to see: "Please give these to your mother, and tell her I like the medicine she sent me very much."

ABOUT THE AUTHOR

Little Women is a literary picture of an ideal American home, and, for the most part, it was Louisa May Alcott's home. Growing up in the Alcott home was an exciting experience. Louisa May Alcott (1832–88) was tutored by her father and by some of his friends, including Ralph Waldo Emerson and Henry David Thoreau. Although her early ambition was to be an actress, she also spent time writing, and by age sixteen she had published her first book. After working as a nurse in a Union hospital during the Civil War, she turned her letters home about her nursing experiences into the book *Hospital Sketches*.

Although she became known as the "Children's Friend," Alcott wrote in almost every genre, including the thriller, before she began focusing on her famed series of domestic novels. She was remarkable in her ability to use her own life as the source for her work and yet adapt it to the format of the juvenile novel: she and her sisters became the March girls. Alcott followed the maxim "never use a long word when a short one will do as well" and turned all her words, both short and long, into some of America's best-loved children's fiction.

THINKING ZONE

Louisa May Alcott's famous little women—Jo, Amy, Beth, and Meg—are some of the best-known characters in American literature. For an author, the **characters**, the persons or beings who perform the action of the story, are some of the most important tools of the trade. Each character is endowed by the author with certain **character traits**, features or attributes that distinguish one character from another. These traits affect what a character thinks and how that character behaves. Perhaps most important, character traits emerge through an author's use of **dialogue**, or conversation between characters. Note how the dialogue in "Being Neighborly" tells you something about each of the characters.

1. *[interpretive]* What does the opening **dialogue** between Meg and Jo tell you about them as **characters**?

   _____

   _____

   _____

2. *[interpretive]* What **character traits** does Jo display in her response to Laurie?

   _____

   _____

   _____

   _____

3. *[literal]* What was Laurie's response to Jo's friendliness?

   _____

   _____

4. *[literal]* How do Jo's and Laurie's character traits differ?

   _____

   _____

   _____

5. *[interpretive]* What character traits does Mr. Laurence exhibit? How do they contrast with what everyone seems to think of him?

_____

_____

_____

6. *[critical]* Read the following words spoken by old Mr. Laurence. Was his assessment of Jo correct?

> "You've got your grandfather's spirit. . . . He was a fine man . . . a brave and an honest one, and I was proud to be his friend."

_____

_____

_____

_____

_____

7. *[appreciative]* Do you think Jo would make a good friend?

_____

_____

8. *[interpretive]* What does the following dialogue between Jo and Laurie reveal about Laurie's character traits?

> "Shall I read aloud?" And Jo looked affectionately toward some inviting books near by.

> "Thank you, I've read all those, and if you don't mind, I'd rather talk," answered Laurie.

_____

_____

_____

9. *[interpretive]* What two things might Laurie mean when he hands Jo the flowers and says, "Please give these to your mother, and tell her I like the medicine she sent me very much"? What is the significance of the message?

_____

_____

_____

THE DOLL'S HOUSE

KATHERINE MANSFIELD

What happens when one little girl determines to show herself friendly despite pressure to be snobbish? Mansfield's highly symbolic story of a magnificent new doll's house and its admirers is a sad reminder of the damage that misplaced pride and the resulting unfriendliness can do.

When dear old Mrs. Hay went back to town after staying with the Burnells she sent the children a doll's house. It was so big that the carter and Pat carried it into the courtyard, and there it stayed, propped up on two wooden boxes beside the feed-room door. No harm could come of it: it was summer. And perhaps the smell of paint would have gone off by the time it had to be taken in. For, really, the smell of paint coming from that doll's house ("Sweet of old Mrs. Hay, of course; most sweet and generous!")—but the smell of paint was quite enough to make anyone seriously ill, in Aunt Beryl's opinion. Even before the sacking* was taken off. And when it was . . .

sacking: wrapper made from brown paper

There stood the doll's house, a dark, oily, spinach green, picked out with bright yellow. Its two solid little chimneys, glued on to the roof, were painted red and white, and the door, gleaming with yellow varnish, was like a little slab of toffee. Four windows, real windows, were divided into panes by a broad streak of green. There was actually a tiny porch, too, painted yellow, with big lumps of congealed paint hanging along the edge.

But perfect, perfect little house! Who could possibly mind the smell? It was part of the joy, part of the newness.

"Open it quickly, someone!"

The hook at the side was stuck fast. Pat pried it open with his penknife, and the whole house-front swung back, and—there you were, gazing at one and the same moment into the drawing-room* and dining-room, the kitchen and two bedrooms. That is the way for a house to open! Why don't all houses open like that? How much more exciting than peering through the slit of a door into a mean little hall with a hatstand and two umbrellas! That is—isn't it?—what you long to know about a house when you put your hand on the knocker. Perhaps it is the way God opens houses at dead of night when He is taking a quiet turn with an angel. . . .

drawing-room: a large room for greeting guests

"O-oh!" The Burnell children sounded as though they were in despair. It was too marvelous; it was too much for them. They had never seen anything like it in their lives. All the rooms were papered. There were pictures on the walls, painted on the paper, with gold frames complete. Red carpet covered all the floors except the kitchen; red plush chairs in the drawing-room, green in the dining-room; tables, beds with real bedclothes, a cradle, a stove, a dresser with tiny plates and one big jug. But what Kezia liked more than anything, what she liked frightfully, was the lamp. It stood in the middle of the dining-room table, an exquisite little amber lamp with a white globe. It was even filled, all ready for lighting, though, of course, you couldn't light it. But there was something inside that looked like oil, and that moved when you shook it.

The father and mother dolls, who sprawled very stiff as though they had fainted in the drawing-room, and their two little children asleep upstairs, were really too big for the doll's house. They didn't look as though they belonged. But the lamp was perfect. It seemed to smile at Kezia, to say, "I live here." The lamp was real.

The Burnell children could hardly walk to school fast enough the next morning. They burned to tell everybody, to describe, to—well—to boast about their doll's house before the school-bell rang.

"I'm to tell," said Isabel, "because I'm the eldest. And you two can join in after. But I'm to tell first."

There was nothing to answer. Isabel was bossy, but she was always right, and Lottie and Kezia knew too well the powers that went with being eldest. They brushed through the thick buttercups at the road edge and said nothing.

"And I'm to choose who's to come and see it first. Mother said I might."

For it had been arranged that while the doll's house stood in the courtyard they might ask the girls at school, two at a time, to come and look. Not to stay to tea, of course, or to come traipsing* through the house. But just to stand quietly in the courtyard while Isabel pointed out the beauties, and Lottie and Kezia looked pleased. . . .

traipsing: walking or tramping about

But hurry as they might, by the time they had reached the tarred palings* of the boys' playground the bell had begun to jangle. They only just had time to whip off their hats and fall into line before the roll was called. Never mind. Isabel tried to make up

for it by looking very important and mysterious and by whispering behind her hand to the girls near her, "Got something to tell you at playtime."

palings: fence posts

Playtime came and Isabel was surrounded. The girls of her class nearly fought to put their arms around her, to walk away with her, to beam flatteringly, to be her special friend. She held quite a court under the huge pine trees at the side of the playground. Nudging, giggling together, the little girls pressed up close. And the only two who stayed outside the ring were the two who were always outside, the little Kelveys. They knew better than to come anywhere near the Burnells.

For the fact was, the school the Burnell children went to was not at all the kind of place their parents would have chosen if there had been any choice. But there was none. It was the only school for miles. And the consequence was all the children in the neighborhood, the Judge's little girls, the doctor's daughters, the storekeeper's children, the milkman's, were forced to mix together. Not to speak of there being an equal number of rude, rough little boys as well. But the line had to be drawn somewhere. It was drawn at the Kelveys. Many of the children, including the Burnells, were not allowed even to speak to them. They walked past the Kelveys with their heads in the air, and as they set the fashion in all matters of behavior, the Kelveys were shunned by everybody. Even the teacher had a special voice for them, and a special smile for the other children when Lil Kelvey came up to her desk with a bunch of dreadfully common-looking flowers.

They were the daughters of a spry, hard-working little washerwoman who went about from house to house by the day. This was awful enough. But where was Mr. Kelvey? Nobody knew for certain. But everybody said he was in prison. So they were the daughters of a washerwoman and a jailbird. Very nice company for other people's children! And they looked it. Why Mrs. Kelvey made them so conspicuous was hard to understand. The truth was they were dressed in "bits" given to her by the people for whom she worked. Lil, for instance, who was a stout, plain child with big freckles, came to school in a dress made from a green art-serge table-cloth of the Burnells', with red plush sleeves from the Logans' curtains. Her hat, perched on top of her high forehead, was a grown-up woman's hat, once the property of Miss Lecky, the postmistress. It was turned up at the back and trimmed with a large scarlet quill. What a little guy* she looked! It was impossible not to laugh. And her little sister, our Else, wore a long white dress, rather like a nightgown, and a pair of little boy's boots. But whatever our Else wore she would have looked strange. She was a tiny wishbone of a child, with cropped hair and enormous solemn eyes—a little white owl. Nobody had ever seen her smile: she scarcely ever spoke. She went through life holding on to Lil, with a piece of Lil's skirt screwed up in her hand. Where Lil went our Else followed. In the playground, on the road going to and from school, there was Lil marching in front and our Else holding on behind. Only when she wanted anything, or when she was out of breath, our Else gave Lil a tug, a twitch, and Lil stopped and turned round. The Kelveys never failed to understand each other.

little guy: one who resembled the rag dolls representing the British traitor Guy Fawkes

Now they hovered at the edge; you couldn't stop them listening. When the little girls turned round and sneered, Lil, as

usual, gave her silly, shamefaced smile, but our Else only looked.

And Isabel's voice, so very proud, went on telling. The carpet made a great sensation, but so did the bed with real bedclothes, and the stove with an oven door.

When she finished Kezia broke in. "You've forgotten the lamp, Isabel."

"Oh, yes," said Isabel, "and there's a teeny little lamp, all made of yellow glass, with a white globe that stands on the dining-room table. You couldn't tell it from a real one."

"The lamps's best of all," cried Kezia. She thought Isabel wasn't making half enough of the little lamp. But nobody paid any attention. Isabel was choosing the two who were to come back with them that afternoon and see it. She chose Emmie Cole and Lena Logan. But when the others knew they were all to have a chance, they couldn't be nice enough to Isabel. One by one they put their arms round Isabel's waist and walked her off. They had something to whisper to her, a secret. "Isabel's *my* friend."

Only the little Kelveys moved away forgotten; there was nothing more for them to hear.

Days passed, and as more children saw the doll's house, the fame of it spread. It became the one subject, the rage. The one question was, "Have you seen Burnells' doll's house? Oh, ain't it lovely?" "Haven't you seen it? Oh, I say!"

Even the dinner hour was given up to talking about it. The little girls sat under the pines eating their thick mutton* sandwiches and big slabs of johnny cake* spread with butter. While always, as near as they could get, sat the Kelveys, our Else holding on to Lil, listening too, while they chewed their jam sandwiches out of a newspaper soaked with large red blobs. . . .

mutton: meat from a sheep

johnny cake: cornmeal bread shaped into a flat cake

"Mother," said Kezia, "can't I ask the Kelveys just once?"

"Certainly not, Kezia."

"But why not?"

"Run away, Kezia; you know quite well why not."

At last everybody had seen it except them. On that day the subject rather flagged.* It was the dinner hour. The children stood together under the pine trees, and suddenly, as they looked at the Kelveys eating out of their paper, always by themselves, always listening, they wanted to be horrid to them. Emmie Cole started the whisper.

flagged: declined in strength

"Lil Kelvey's going to be a servant when she grows up."

"O-oh, how awful!" said Isabel Burnell, and she made eyes at Emmie.

Emmie swallowed in a very meaning way and nodded to Isabel as she'd seen her mother do on those occasions.

"It's true—it's true—it's true," she said.

Then Lena Logan's little eyes snapped. "Shall I ask her?" she whispered.

"Bet you don't," said Jessie May.

"Pooh, I'm not frightened," said Lena. Suddenly she gave a little squeal and danced in front of the other girls. "Watch! Watch me! Watch me now!" said Lena. And sliding, gliding, dragging one foot, giggling behind her hand, Lena went over to the Kelveys.

Lil looked up from her dinner. She wrapped the rest quickly away. Our Else stopped chewing. What was coming now?

"Is it true you're going to be a servant when you grow up, Lil Kelvey?" shrilled Lena.

Dead silence. But instead of answering Lil only gave her silly, shamefaced smile. She didn't seem to mind the question at all.

What a sell* for Lena! The girls began to titter.

sell: disappointment

Lena couldn't stand that. She put her hands on her hips: she shot forward. "Yah, yer father's in prison!" she hissed, spitefully.

This was such a marvelous thing to have said that the little girls rushed away in a body, deeply, deeply excited, wild with joy. Someone found a long rope, and they began skipping. And never did they skip so high, run in and out so fast, or do such daring things as on that morning.

In the afternoon Pat called for the Burnell children with the buggy and they drove home. There were visitors. Isabel and Lottie, who liked visitors, went upstairs to change their pinafores.* But Kezia thieved out at the back. Nobody was about; she began to swing on the big white gates of the courtyard. Presently, looking along the road, she saw two little dots. They grew bigger, they were coming towards her. Now she could see that one was in front and one close behind. Now she could see that they were the Kelveys. Kezia stopped swinging. She slipped off the gate as if she was going to run away. Then she hesitated. The Kelveys came nearer, and beside them walked their shadows, very long, stretching right across the road with their heads in the buttercups. Kezia clambered back on the gate; she had made up her mind; she swung out.

pinafore: sleeveless garment like an apron over a dress

"Hullo," she said to the passing Kelveys.

They were so astounded that they stopped. Lil gave her silly smile. Our Else stared.

"You can come and see our doll's house if you want to," said Kezia, and she dragged one toe on the ground. But at that Lil turned red and shook her head quickly.

"Why not?" asked Kezia.

Lil gasped, then she said, "Your ma told our ma you wasn't to speak to us."

"Oh, well," said Kezia. She didn't know what to reply. "It doesn't matter. You can come and see our doll's house all the same. Come on. Nobody's looking."

But Lil shook her head still harder.

"Don't you want to?" asked Kezia.

Suddenly there was a twitch, a tug at Lil's skirt. She turned around. Our Else was looking at her with big, imploring eyes; she was frowning; she wanted to go. For a moment Lil looked at our Else very doubtfully. But then our Else twitched her skirt again. She started forward. Kezia led the way. Like two little stray cats they followed across the courtyard to where the doll's house stood.

"There it is," said Kezia.

There was a pause. Lil breathed loudly, almost snorted; our Else was still as a stone.

"I'll open it for you," said Kezia kindly. She undid the hook and they looked inside.

"There's the drawing-room and the dining-room, and that's the—"

"Kezia!"

Oh, what a start they gave!

"Kezia!"

It was Aunt Beryl's voice. They turned round. At the back door stood Aunt Beryl, staring as if she couldn't believe what she saw.

"How dare you ask the little Kelveys into the courtyard?" said her cold, furious voice. "You know as well as I do, you're not allowed to talk to them. Run away, children, run away at once. And don't come back again," said Aunt Beryl. And she stepped into the yard and shooed them out as if they were chickens.

"Off you go immediately!" she called, cold and proud.

They did not need telling twice. Burning with shame, shrinking together, Lil huddling along like her mother, our Else dazed, somehow they crossed the big courtyard and squeezed through the white gate.

"Wicked, disobedient little girl!" said Aunt Beryl bitterly to Kezia, and she slammed the doll's house to.

The afternoon had been awful. A letter had come from Willie Brent, a terrifying, threatening letter, saying if she did not meet him that evening in Pulman's Bush, he'd come to the front door and ask the reason why! But now that she had frightened those little rats of Kelveys and given Kezia a good scolding, her heart felt lighter. That ghastly pressure was gone. She went back to the house humming.

When the Kelveys were well out of sight of Burnells', they sat down to rest on a big red drain-pipe by the side of the road. Lil's cheeks were still burning; she took off the hat with the quill and held it on her knee. Dreamily they looked over the hay paddocks,* past the creek, to the group of wattles* where Logan's cows stood waiting to be milked. What were their thoughts?

paddocks: fields

wattles: crude shelters constructed of woven twigs and branches

Presently our Else nudged up close to her sister. But now she had forgotten the cross lady. She put out a finger and stroked her sister's quill; she smiled her rare smile.

"I seen the little lamp," she said, softly.

Then both were silent once more.

ABOUT THE AUTHOR

Born into a middle-class family, Katherine Mansfield (1888–1923) spent her early years in Wellington, New Zealand. As a very young child, she was interested in writing, and she published her first text at the age of nine. As a teenager she developed an interest in music and became an accomplished musician. Her interest in music did not please her father; in fact, he forbade her to pursue music as a career. Mansfield's young adult years were times of rebellion, discontent, and unhappiness. Eventually she returned to her writing. *Bliss* and *The Garden Party* are collections of short stories that established her as a major writer and as one of the masters of the short story. In fact, it was through Mansfield's influence that the short story became recognized as a form of literature. Her stories rely on symbols and atmosphere to communicate the emotions of her characters. In Mansfield's *The Garden Party*, the character Laura says, "'Isn't life . . .' But what life was she couldn't explain." Like Laura, others of Mansfield's characters experience great sadness in their lives just as Mansfield did in her life.

Mansfield did not limit her writing to short stories, however. A collection of her critical essays appears in *Novels and Novelists*. During her adult years Mansfield lived in southern France, where she received treatment for tuberculosis. In spite of her illness, she continued to write, producing some of her best works during this time. After her death, her husband, John Murry, organized some of her writings. Using her journal writings and letters, he edited *Journal of Katherine Mansfield* and *The Letters of Katherine Mansfield*.

THINKING ZONE

When you see the Stars and Stripes flying from a flagpole or see a photograph of the Statue of Liberty, you are seeing symbols that probably remind you of America and freedom. What comes to your mind when you see a scepter? You most likely think of a king on his royal throne. In "The Doll's House" Mansfield makes use of **symbol**—a person, place, thing, or idea that means something in addition to itself—to get across some important ideas. We call the use of symbols **symbolism**. One of her main symbols is the doll's house itself. It represents the Burnell household, in which values are based only on appearance.

Besides the symbolism in this story, you may also recognize some examples of **irony**, which is language used to convey meaning other than what is stated. One type of irony occurs when there is a contrast between what characters see and understand and what the reader sees and understands. Situations that fit this description are said to be **ironic**. Notice the description of what the characters in "The Doll's House" believe to be their "perfect, perfect little house." The reader realizes from the sloppy paint and garish trimmings that the doll's house is anything but perfect. The effect of irony sometimes is that the reader feels an emotion for the characters—pity or anger or humor, for example—because it seems that the characters in the story are in the dark about some aspect of what is happening around them.

Another type of irony is a contradiction between what is expected and what in reality happens. One such scriptural irony is the truth that Christians must die to self in order to live in Christ. The idea that we live by dying is ironic. Miss Lucy's situation in "A Most Important Person" is ironic when her getting a ticket and appearing in court make her seem more glamorous to her new friend Chester—just the opposite of what you expect.

> **Character**—*the person or being who performs the action of the story*

1. *[interpretive]* What is the response of the Burnell children to the doll's house? What is **ironic** about the children's sounding "as though they were in despair"?

   _____

   _____

   _____

2. *[literal]* What does Kezia like most about the doll's house? Why?

   _____

   _____

3. *[literal]* According to the Burnells and the townspeople, what was "awful" about the Kelvey girls?

_____

_____

_____

4. *[interpretive]* How do the children learn to behave the way they do toward the Kelveys?

_____

_____

_____

5. *[critical]* The Burnell children love the doll's house despite its appearance and smell, yet the whole family (except for Kezia) despises the Kelveys because of their poverty and social status. How does this demonstrate **irony**?

_____

_____

_____

6. *[interpretive/critical]* One **symbol** in the story is the little lamp in the doll's house. Often in a literary work, light is symbolic of enlightenment or revelation. The two who are most impressed by the lamp are Kezia and Else. What do Kezia and Else both seem to realize that the others in the story do not?

_____

_____

_____

_____

7. *[critical]* What is the significance of Else's final statement: "I seen the little lamp"?

_____

_____

_____

THANK YOU, M'AM

LANGSTON HUGHES

Mrs. Luella Bates Washington Jones is no ordinary person, as Roger quickly discovers. She is a "large woman with a large purse"—and a heart as big as both. As you read this story, ask yourself how her behavior mirrors that of a true friend. Does she desire comradeship with the boy? Or is her friendship something deeper?

She was a large woman with a large purse that had everything in it but a hammer and nails. It had a long strap, and she carried it slung across her shoulder. It was about eleven o'clock at night, dark, and she was walking alone, when a boy ran up behind her and tried to snatch her purse. The strap broke with the sudden single tug the boy gave it from behind. But the boy's weight and the weight of the purse combined caused him to lose his balance. Instead of taking off full blast as he had hoped, the boy fell on his back on the sidewalk and his legs flew up. The large woman simply turned around and kicked him right square in his blue-jeaned sitter. Then she reached down, picked the boy up by his shirt front, and shook him until his teeth rattled.

After that the woman said, "Pick up my pocketbook, boy, and give it here."

She still held him tightly. But she bent down enough to permit him to stoop and pick up her purse. Then she said, "Now ain't you ashamed of yourself?"

Firmly gripped by his shirt front, the boy said, "Yes'm."

The woman said, "What did you want to do it for?"

The boy said, "I didn't aim to."

She said, "You a lie!"

By that time two or three people passed, stopped, turned to look, and some stood watching.

"If I turn you loose, will you run?" asked the woman.

"Yes'm," said the boy.

"Then I won't turn you loose," said the woman. She did not release him.

"Lady, I'm sorry," whispered the boy.

"Um-hum. Your face is dirty. I got a great mind to wash your face for you. Ain't you got nobody home to tell you to wash your face?"

"No'm," said the boy.

"Then it will get washed this evening," said the large woman, starting up the street, dragging the frightened boy behind her.

He looked as if he were fourteen or fifteen, frail and willow-wild; in tennis shoes and blue jeans.

The woman said, "You ought to be my son. I would teach you right from wrong. Least I can do right now is to wash your face. Are you hungry?"

"No'm," said the being-dragged boy. "I just want you to turn me loose."

"Was I bothering *you* when I turned that corner?" asked the woman.

"No'm."

"But you put yourself in contact with *me*," said the woman. "If you think that that contact is not going to last awhile, you got another thought coming. When I get through with you, sir, you are going to remember Mrs. Luella Bates Washington Jones."

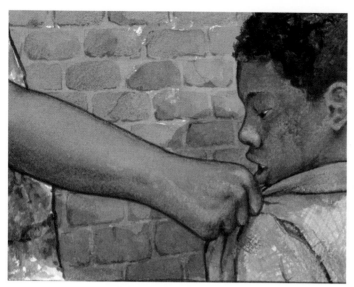

Sweat popped out on the boy's face, and he began to struggle. Mrs. Jones stopped, jerked him around in front of her, put a half nelson* about his neck, and continued to drag him up the street. When she got to her door, she dragged the boy inside, down a hall, and into a large kitchenette-furnished room at the rear of the house. She switched on the light and left the door open. The boy could hear other roomers laughing and talking in the large house. Some of their doors were open, too, so he knew that he and the woman were not alone. The woman still had him by the neck in the middle of her room.

half nelson: a wrestling hold

She said, "What is your name?"

"Roger," answered the boy.

"Then, Roger, you go to that sink and wash your face," said the woman, whereupon she turned him loose—at last. Roger looked at the door—looked at the woman—looked at the door—*and went to the sink.*

"Let the water run until it gets warm," she said. "Here's a clean towel."

"You gonna take me to jail?" asked the boy, bending over the sink.

"Not with that face; I would not take you nowhere," said the woman. "Here I am trying to get home to cook me a bite to eat, and you snatch my pocketbook! Maybe you ain't been to your supper either, late as it be. Have you?"

"There's nobody home at my house," said the boy.

"Then we'll eat," said the woman. "I believe you're hungry—or been hungry—to try to snatch my pocketbook!"

"I want a pair of blue suede shoes," said the boy.

"Well, you didn't have to snatch *my* pocketbook to get some suede shoes," said Mrs. Luella Bates Washington Jones. "You could of asked me."

"M'am?"

The water dripping from his face, the boy looked at her. There was a long pause. A very long pause. After he had dried his face and not knowing what else to do, dried it again, the boy turned around, wondering what next. The door was open. He could make a dash for it down the hall. He could run, run, run, *run!*

The woman was sitting on the day bed. After a while she said, "I were young once and I wanted things I could not get."

There was another long pause. The boy's mouth opened. Then he frowned, not knowing he frowned.

The woman said, "Um-hum! You thought I was going to say *but,* didn't you? You thought I was going to say, *but I didn't snatch people's pocketbooks.* Well I wasn't going to say that." Pause. Silence. "I have done things, too, which I would not tell you, son—neither tell God, if He didn't already know. Everybody's got something in common. So you set down while I fix us something to eat. You might run that comb through your hair so you will look presentable."

In another corner of the room behind a screen was a gas plate and an icebox. Mrs. Jones got up and went behind the screen. The woman did not watch the boy to see if he was going to run now, nor did she watch her purse, which she left behind her on the day bed. But the boy took care to sit on the far side of the room, away from the purse, where he thought she could easily see him out of the corner of her eye if she wanted to. He did not trust the woman *not* to trust him. And he did not want to be mistrusted now.

"Do you need somebody to go to the store," asked the boy, "maybe to get some milk or something?"

"Don't believe I do," said the woman, "unless you just want sweet milk yourself. I was going to make cocoa out of this canned milk I got here."

"That will be fine," said the boy.

She heated some lima beans and ham she had in the icebox, made the cocoa, and set the table. The woman did not ask the boy anything about where he lived, or his folks, or anything else that would embarrass him. Instead, as they ate, she told him about her job in a hotel beauty shop that stayed open late, what the work was like, and how all kinds of women came in and out, blondes, redheads, and Spanish. Then she cut him a half of her ten-cent cake.

"Eat some more, son," she said.

When they were finished eating, she got up and said, "Now here, take this ten dollars and buy yourself some blue suede shoes. And next time, do not make the mistake of latching onto *my* pocketbook *nor nobody else's*—because shoes got by devilish ways will burn your feet. I got to get my rest now. But from here on in, son, I hope you will behave yourself."

She led him down the hall to the front door and opened it. "Good night! Behave yourself, boy!" she said, looking out into the street as he went down the steps.

The boy wanted to say something other than, "Thank you, m'am," to Mrs. Luella Bates Washington Jones; but although his lips moved, he couldn't even say that as he turned at the foot of the barren stoop and looked up at the large woman in the door. Then she shut the door.

ABOUT THE AUTHOR

Langston Hughes (1902–67) succeeded in making a name for himself as one of America's greatest African American writers. During much of his childhood, Hughes lived with his grandmother. They were very poor, but early in his life, he discovered books. Books and language became very important to him.

Although he loved to read, Hughes's interest in writing did not develop until he was elected class poet when he was thirteen years old. He had had no thought of writing anything himself until then. Not only did Hughes become a writer of poetry that has been translated into numerous other languages, but he also wrote short stories, plays, and song lyrics. The distinctive characters in his stories exude a zest for life that makes his stories both flavorful and memorable.

THINKING ZONE

Have you ever debated with yourself over a decision that you had to make? If so, you were experiencing the same kind of conflict that Roger experienced in this story when he thought about running away from Mrs. Luella Bates Washington Jones. Or perhaps you have struggled against the physical strength of an older brother or against the fear of an approaching storm. Either way, you were in conflict with these powers. The characters in a story, as well, often find themselves in the midst of conflict. **Conflict** refers to the struggle of the story's main character, or group of characters, against an opposing force. That conflict may be one of three main types: man against man, man against a greater force (e.g., God, nature), and man against himself.

Symbol— *a person, place, thing, or idea that means something in addition to itself*

1. *[literal]* What does Roger try to do to Mrs. Jones? Why?

   _____

   _____

2. *[interpretive]* How does Mrs. Luella Bates Washington Jones's full name suit her?

   _____

   _____

3. *[interpretive]* In what ways does Mrs. Jones treat Roger as if he were her son?

   _____

   _____

   _____

   _____

4. *[critical]* One of the first things that Mrs. Jones does is make sure that Roger's face is washed. How is this act symbolic?

   _____

   _____

   _____

5. *[critical]* What does Mrs. Jones suggest when she tells Roger about her own past? What is her purpose in telling him?

_____

_____

_____

_____

6. *[literal/critical]* What is the **conflict** that begins the story? How does the conflict change? How is the conflict resolved? What is the irony in this?

_____

_____

_____

_____

_____

_____

7. *[critical]* Why do you think Roger is unable to say thank you to Mrs. Jones?

_____

_____

_____

8. *[appreciative]* Would you consider Mrs. Jones to be a Christ-figure (a symbol of Christ in a work of literature)? Why or why not?

_____

_____

_____

_____

_____

_____

_____

After Twenty Years

O. Henry

Sometimes those we have loved as friends may choose the way of vice despite our admonitions and example. In such cases, we would do well to remember Abraham Lincoln's words: "I desire so to conduct [my affairs] that if at the end . . . I have lost every other friend on earth, I shall at least have one friend left, and that friend shall be down inside of me."

The policeman on the beat moved up the avenue impressively. The impressiveness was habitual and not for show, for spectators were few. The time was barely ten o'clock at night, but chilly gusts of wind with a taste of rain in them had well nigh depeopled the streets.

Trying doors as he went, twirling his club with many intricate and artful movements, turning now and then to cast his watchful eye adown the pacific thoroughfare, the officer, with his stalwart* form and slight swagger, made a fine picture of a guardian of the peace. The vicinity was one that kept early hours. Now and then you might see the lights of a cigar store or of an all-night lunch counter; but the majority of the doors belonged to business places that had long since been closed.

---

stalwart: sturdy

When about midway of a certain block the policeman suddenly slowed his walk. In the doorway of a darkened hardware store a man leaned, with an unlighted cigar in his mouth. As the policeman walked up to him, the man spoke up quickly.

"It's all right, officer," he said, reassuringly. "I'm just waiting for a friend. It's an appointment made twenty years ago. Sounds a little funny to you, doesn't it? Well, I'll explain if you'd like to make certain it's all straight. About that long ago there used to

be a restaurant where this store stands—'Big Joe' Brady's restaurant."

"Until five years ago," said the policeman. "It was torn down then."

The man in the doorway struck a match and lit his cigar. The light showed a pale, square-jawed face with keen eyes, and a little white scar near his right eyebrow. His scarfpin was a large diamond, oddly set.

"Twenty years ago tonight," said the man, "I dined here at 'Big Joe' Brady's with Jimmy Wells, my best chum, and the finest chap in the world. He and I were raised here in New York, just like two brothers, together. I was eighteen and Jimmy was twenty. The next morning I was to start for the West to make my fortune. You couldn't have dragged Jimmy out of New York; he thought it was the only place on earth. Well, we agreed that night that we would meet here again in exactly twenty years from that date and time, no matter what our conditions might be or from what distance we might have to come. We figured that in twenty years each of us ought to have our destiny worked out and our fortunes made, whatever they were going to be."

"It sounds pretty interesting," said the policeman. "Rather a long time between meets, though, it seems to me. Haven't you heard from your friend since you left?"

"Well, yes, for a time we corresponded," said the other. "But after a year or two we

with some of the sharpest wits going to get my pile. A man gets in a groove in New York. It takes the West to put a razor-edge on him."

The policeman twirled his club and took a step or two. "I'll be on my way. Hope your friend comes around all right. Going to call time on him sharp?"

"I should say not!" said the other. "I'll give him half an hour at least. If Jimmy is alive on earth, he'll be here by that time. So long, officer."

"Good night, sir," said the policeman, passing on along his beat, trying doors as he went.

There was now a fine, cold drizzle falling, and the wind had risen from its uncertain puffs into a steady blow. The few foot passengers astir in that quarter hurried dismally and silently along with coat collars turned high and pocketed hands. And in the door of the hardware store the man who had come a thousand miles to fill an appointment, uncertain almost to absurdity, with the friend of his youth, smoked his cigar and waited.

About twenty minutes he waited, and then a tall man in a long overcoat, with collar turned up to his ears, hurried across from the opposite side of the street. He went directly to the waiting man.

"Is that you, Bob?" he asked, doubtfully.

"Is that you, Jimmy Wells?" cried the man in the door.

"Bless my heart!" exclaimed the new arrival, grasping both the other's hands with his own. "It's Bob, sure as fate. I was certain I'd find you here if you were still in existence. Well, well, well! Twenty years is a long time. The old restaurant's gone, Bob; I wish it had lasted, so we could have had another

lost track of each other. You see, the West is a pretty big proposition*, and I kept hustling around over it pretty lively. But I know Jimmy will meet me here if he's alive, for he always was the truest, staunchest old chap in the world. He'll never forget. I came a thousand miles to stand in this door tonight, and it's worth it if my old partner turns up."

The waiting man pulled out a handsome watch, the lids of it set with small diamonds.

"Three minutes to ten," he announced. "It was exactly ten o'clock when we parted here at the restaurant door."

"Did pretty well out West, didn't you?" asked the policeman.

"You bet! I hope Jimmy has done half as well. He was a kind of plodder*, though, good fellow as he was. I've had to compete

dinner there. How has the West treated you, old man?"

"Bully;* it has given me everything I asked it for. You've changed lots, Jimmy. I never thought you were so tall by two or three inches."

---

bully: excellently

"Oh, I grew a bit after I was twenty."

"Doing well in New York, Jimmy?"

"Moderately. I have a position in one of the city departments. Come on, Bob; we'll go around to a place I know of, and have a good long talk about old times."

The two men started up the street, arm in arm. The man from the West, his egotism enlarged by success, was beginning to outline the history of his career. The other, submerged in his overcoat, listened with interest.

At the corner stood a drugstore, brilliant with electric lights. When they came into this glare, each of them turned simultaneously to gaze upon the other's face.

The man from the West stopped suddenly and released his arm.

"You're not Jimmy Wells," he snapped. "Twenty years is a long time, but not long enough to change a man's nose from a Roman to a pug."

"It sometimes changes a good man into a bad one," said the tall man. "You've been under arrest for ten minutes, 'silky' Bob. Chicago thinks you may have dropped over our way and wires us she wants to have a chat with you. Going quietly, are you? That's sensible. Now, before we go to the station, here's a note I was asked to hand to you. You may read it here at the window. It's from Patrolman Wells."

The man from the West unfolded the little piece of paper handed him. His hand was steady when he began to read, but it trembled a little by the time he had finished. The note was rather short.

Bob: I was at the appointed place on time. When you struck the match to light your cigar, I saw it was the face of the man wanted in Chicago. Somehow I couldn't do it myself, so I went around and got a plainclothesman to do the job.

JIMMY

About the Author

Born on Polecat Creek in Guilford County, North Carolina, William Sydney Porter (1862–1910) is considered the most popular short story writer of his time. Better known as O. Henry, a name he adopted after a brief jail stay, Porter began writing his short stories to support his young daughter. O. Henry's focus on ordinary people and ordinary events endeared him to the reading public but brought little praise from critics. At the age of forty, O. Henry moved to New York City, where he wrote a story a week for the *New York World* and published in magazines as well. During his lifetime he published over six hundred short stories that include well-known stories such as "The Gift of the Magi," "The Furnished Room," "The Last Leaf," and "The Ransom of Red Chief." A typical O. Henry story concludes with a series of coincidences and a surprise ending.

THINKING ZONE

You have already learned about important details that contribute to the short story, such as character and conflict. An author must consider these (and many other) details when determining how best to arrange the **plot,** the series of events that tell the story.

Would you rather read a story with a predictable ending or a story that ends in a way different from what you expected? The author whose story you just read, O. Henry, capitalizes on the **plot twist,** a plot development that violates the reader's expectations. When a plot twist occurs at the end of the story, it may also be referred to as a **surprise ending.** The author may give clues that a plot twist or surprise ending is coming by including details of foreshadowing. **Foreshadowing** is hinting at events that will occur later in the story. As you read this story, did any details clue you in to what would happen at the end?

Short story—a brief work of prose fiction

1. *[literal]* Why is the man waiting in the doorway of the hardware store?

   _____

   _____

2. *[interpretive]* When all is revealed, the men are standing in front of a drugstore "brilliant with electric lights." How might it be said that this is symbolic?

   _____

   _____

   _____

3. *[interpretive]* What is the **plot twist?** Is it also a **surprise ending?** What element (or elements) did the author include to try to trick you?

   _____

   _____

   _____

   _____

4. [interpretive/critical] What might be symbolic about the fact that the first meeting place, "Big Joe" Brady's restaurant, was torn down?

_____

_____

_____

5. [interpretive/critical] Look at the story again, paying close attention to the descriptive details. What elements or clues **foreshadow** the ending?

_____

_____

_____

_____

_____

_____

_____

6. [critical] What does the following character revelation suggest about Bob? "The light showed a pale, square-jawed face with keen eyes, and a little white scar near his right eyebrow. His scarfpin was a large diamond, oddly set."

_____

_____

_____

7. [critical] Was Jimmy right to have his friend arrested? Why or why not?

_____

_____

_____

HALF A GIFT

ROBERT ZACKS

Nick and Joe understood that "it is more blessed to give than to receive" (Acts 20:35), and each one thoroughly enjoyed secretly planning the purchase of a special Mother's Day gift. But their secret plans resulted in their learning another important principle.

I was ten years old then, and my brother, Nick, was fourteen. For both of us, this purchase of a gift for our mother on Mother's Day was an occasion of excitement and great importance.

It was our first gift to her. We were very poor. It was just after the first World War and we lived in a time of trouble. Our father worked now and then as a waiter. Birthday and Christmas gifts were taken care of by him as well as he could, but such a thing as a Mother's Day gift was an out-of-the-ordinary luxury. But we had been fortunate, Nick and myself. A secondhand furniture store had opened on the block, and deliveries were made by means of loading the

furniture on a wobbly pushcart which we carefully pushed through traffic to the customer's home. We had a nickel each and, perhaps, a tip.

I remember how Nick's thin, dark face blazed with the joy of the present. He had been given the thought in school; and the anticipation of surprise and giving grew in him, and myself, until we were almost frantic.

When we secretly told our father, he was very pleased. He stroked our heads proudly.

"It's a fine idea," he said. "It will make your mother very happy."

From his wistful tone, we knew what he was thinking. He had given our mother little enough in their life together. She worked all day, cooking and buying and tending to us in illness and stoking the stove in the kitchen with wood and coal to keep us warm in winter. She did her own washing of the family clothes in the bathtub. And she did all these things silently. She did not laugh much, but when she smiled at us it was a beautiful thing—well worth waiting for.

"What are you going to give her?" asked Father, thoughtfully. "How much money have you?"

"We're going to give separate presents," I announced importantly.

"Pick carefully," my father counseled.

"You tell Mother," said Nick, looking at me for approval, "so she can enjoy thinking about it."

I nodded. My father said, "That is a big thought to come from so small a head. And wise."

Nick flushed with joy. Then he put a hand on my shoulder and said quickly, "Joe thought of it, too."

"No," I said, "I didn't." I wanted no credit for what was not mine. "But my present will make up for it."

"The thought belongs to everybody," said Father smiling. "Everybody. Nick, too, got the thought elsewhere."

For the next few days we enjoyed the game of secrecy with my mother. A shining look came into her face as she worked near

us, pretending not to know, and she smiled often. The air was full of love.

Nick and I discussed what to buy. We became involved in competition of taste.

"Let's not tell each other what we're getting," said Nick, exasperated with me, for my mind was not as settled as his and scooted around like a fly in summertime.

"We might get the same thing," I wailed.

"No, we won't," said Nick. "I have more money than you."

I did not like this remark, though it was fair enough, since I had spent some of my earnings for candy, while Nick had determined to spend every thing on the gift.

After careful deliberation I bought for my mother a comb decorated with little shiny stones that could even be mistaken for diamonds. Nick came back from the store with a pleased look. He liked my gift very much and wouldn't tell about his.

"We will give the gifts at a certain moment I have picked," he said.

"What moment?" I asked mystified.

"I can't tell, because it has something to do with my gift. And don't ask me again what it is."

The next morning Nick kept me close and when my mother got ready to wash the floor he nodded to me and we ran to get our gifts. When I came back, Mother was, as usual, on her knees, wearily scrubbing the floor with scouring powder and scrubbing brush, and mopping up the dirty water with old rags made of discarded underwear. It was the job she hated most in the world.

Then Nick returned with his present, and Mother sat back on her heels staring unbelievingly at the gift. Her face went pale with disappointment as she looked at the new scrubbing pail with the wringer and the fresh mop in it.

"A scrubbing pail?" she said. Her voice almost broke.

Tears sprang to Nick's eyes. Without a word he picked up the scrubbing pail and mop. "I will take it back," he sobbed.

"No," said Father, taking the pail. He soaked the puddle of dirty water up with the mop and using the foot wringer on the bucket, neatly squeezed it dry.

"You did not let Nick finish," he said to Mother. "Part of his gift is that he is going to wash the floor from now on." He looked at Nick. "Isn't that so, Nick?"

With a flush of shame Nick understood the lesson. "Yes, oh, yes," he said in a low, eager tone.

Quickly, repentantly, Mother said, "It is too heavy work for a fourteen-year-old boy."

It was then I realized how smart Father was. "Ah," he said cunningly, "not with this wonderful wringer and scrub pail. It's much easier. Your hands stay clean, and your knees don't hurt." Again Father demonstrated quickly.

Mother said, looking sadly at Nick, "Ah, a woman can become so stupid." She kissed Nick and he felt better. Then they turned to me.

"What is your gift?" asked Father. Nick looked at me and paled. I felt the comb in my pocket. It would make the scrubbing pail, again, just a scrubbing pail. After all, a comb with shining stones just like diamonds.

"Half the scrubbing pail," I said mournfully, and Nick looked at me with love in his eyes.

THINKING ZONE

Think about a time when you were talking with your friends about something that had happened. Perhaps it was a discussion of a soccer tournament or a basketball game or perhaps a trip that you took with your friends. Were you surprised that there were different versions of the story? Your **point of view**, the perspective or angle from which a story is told, may have been different from that of someone else. If you were a participant, your point of view would most likely be different from the point of view of the person who only observed what happened.

When a character tells his own story and refers to himself as "I" throughout, he is the **narrator** and is speaking from the **first-person point of view**. The reader of a first-person narrative will find out the details from only the narrator's perspective. In the stories you have read up to this point, the narrator has been an outside observer of the story. Think about how the first-person point of view affects a story. How is it beneficial to the reader? How might it be limiting?

1. *[interpretive]* Who is the **narrator** of the story? From what **point of view** is the story told?

   _____

   _____

   _____

2. *[literal]* Why is the purchase of a Mother's Day gift so special for Nick and Joe?

   _____

   _____

   _____

   _____

3. *[literal]* What does each son buy?

   _____

   _____

   _____

4. *[literal]* What makes Joe realize how "smart" his father is?

_____

_____

_____

_____

5. *[critical]* How does Joe remedy a potentially awkward situation? What does this act say about Joe?

_____

_____

_____

_____

_____

6. *[critical]* Do you think that the title of the story is appropriate? Explain.

_____

_____

_____

_____

_____

_____

7. *[critical]* In 1 Corinthians 13 Paul lists several characteristics of true love. One of these characteristics is that "Charity . . . seeketh not her own." How does Paul's statement apply to Nick? How does Paul's statement apply to Joe?

_____

_____

_____

_____

_____

CHRISTIAN BEHOLDS THE CROSS
FROM *THE PILGRIM'S PROGRESS*

JOHN BUNYAN

"Jesus, what a Friend for sinners!" penned hymnwriter John Wilbur Chapman. As Bunyan's pilgrim gazes at the cross, he realizes that Christ is indeed the Friend who saves, helps, keeps, and loves—the One Who will stay with him to the end.

> Thus far did I come loaden with my sin,
> Nor could aught ease the grief that I was in,
> Till I came hither. What a place is this!
> Must here be the beginning of my bliss?
> Must here the burden fall from off my back? 5
> Must here the strings that bound it to me, crack?
> Blessed Cross! Blessed Sepulchre! Blessed rather be
> The man that there was put to shame for me.

John Bunyan's *The Pilgrim's Progress* is no tall tale. Often confused with the legendary American figure Paul Bunyan, John Bunyan (1628–88) was, nonetheless, a giant among men. He has proved to be the most popular religious writer in the English language, and his work has been translated more and put into more editions than any other English book except the Bible.

What accounts for a poor Bedford tinker's popularity? One factor is the character of the author himself. As a young hooligan, Bunyan led a miserable, wayward life. His vivid imagination and his knowledge of the Bible combined to keep him convicted of his sins even while he continued in them. During his time in the army, he experienced God's protection when his replacement on sentry duty was shot. Afterwards, Bunyan married a poor girl whose only dowry was two devotional books, and these books served as the catalyst for Bunyan's conversion. By age twenty-seven he was preaching, although such unlicensed activity was illegal. He was soon arrested, and his three-month sentence was extended to twelve years, for he refused to promise not to preach.

Bunyan paid a terrible price for his convictions as he watched his family undergo great hardship without his provision for them. However, he used his time in prison to write. His autobiography, *Grace Abounding to the Chief of Sinners*, was a product of the prison years, as was *The Pilgrim's Progress*, which was probably begun during his first jail term and finished during or shortly after his second imprisonment. Bunyan's fictionalized autobiography owes its popularity to its content and style. The book is characterized by its universalized experiences and "every Christian" character, as well as its use of the common people's speech and the beautiful language of the King James Version of the Bible, one of two books Bunyan had in prison (the other was *Foxe's Book of Martyrs*). *The Pilgrim's Progress* communicates Bunyan's, and indeed every Christian's, best tale, for its happy ending is guaranteed for all who enter at the Wicket Gate and lose their burden at the cross.

THINKING ZONE

Another literary genre that you may learn to enjoy is **poetry**. Poetry can be described as artfully compressed thought or as elevated expression. Poetry shows what experiences and insights are precious to a writer. So what an author says in a poem reveals an important aspect of the author's values. Because the poet seeks to present a subject from a unique perspective using as few words as possible, he relies more on imaginative comparisons and vivid imagery to get the reader's attention, to illuminate his subject, and to evoke an emotional response than does the writer of prose. The more a poet compresses or reduces the thought, the more he must rely on the artful use of language.

However, this shortened form does not always mean that a poem is easier to understand than a short story or essay. Because a poet relies heavily on symbols and other literary devices in order to communicate, the resulting poem may be more difficult for a reader to grasp in one sitting.

You probably remember reciting poems when you were younger. What made them easy to remember? Probably the simple arrangement of the lines and the rhyming words helped you memorize the poem. The excerpt from Bunyan's *The Pilgrim's Progress* is a poem with **rhyme**, the repetition of the last stressed vowel and all of the sounds following that vowel in two or more words. Perhaps the most familiar type of rhyme is **end rhyme**, rhyme that occurs at the ends of corresponding lines of poetry. As you examine most rhyming poems, you will notice a pattern developing in the rhymed lines. This pattern is known as the poem's **rhyme scheme**. Letters of the alphabet are used to mark a poem's rhyme scheme, with the first line marked as *a* and the second as *b* and so on. If the third line rhymes with the first, that line is marked as *a* again.

Genre—*a type or category of literature*

1. *[interpretive]* From whose point of view is this work of **poetry** written?

_____

_____

_____

_____

Point of view— *perspective or angle from which a story is told*

2. *[interpretive]* Look at the first two lines of the poem. What is Christian's attitude? Why does he feel this way?

_____

_____

3. *[critical]* What is Christian's first response to the cross? How does Bunyan communicate this reaction to the reader?

_____

_____

4. *[interpretive]* What do the symbols of the cross and sepulcher represent in Bunyan's poem?

_____

_____

5. *[critical]* Why do you think Bunyan chose the order he did for the list of the final two lines?

_____

_____

_____

6. *[interpretive]* What does the burden falling from Christian's back symbolize?

_____

_____

7. *[literal/interpretive]* The first four lines of "Christian Beholds the Cross" exhibit **end rhyme** with a **rhyme scheme** of *aabb*. "Sin" (line 1) **rhymes** with "in" (line 2), and "this" (line 3) rhymes with "bliss" (line 4). What would the rhyme scheme of the remaining lines be?

_____

_____

8. *[critical]* Why do you think Bunyan chose to include a poem at this point in his prose story?

_____

_____

_____

Seeing Off a Friend

Li Bai

Translated from the Chinese by Greg Whincup

Saying goodbye to a dear friend is often very difficult. Li Bai uses elements of nature to create the feeling of saying goodbye.

Green mountains
Lie across the northern outskirts
Of the city.
White water
Winds around the eastern   5
City wall.

Once we make our parting
Here in this place,
Like a solitary tumbleweed
You will go   10
Ten thousand miles.

Floating clouds
Are the thoughts of the wanderer.
Setting sun
Is the mood of his old friend.   15

With a wave of the hand
Now you go from here.
Your horse gives a whinny
As it departs.

About the Author

Li Bai (701–62), one of the best-known Chinese poets, led an unconventional life. Leaving home at age nineteen, he spent the next twenty years roaming the Chinese countryside. Occasionally he sought official employment but refused to take the state exam that typically marked one's entry into public life. In 742 Li Bai joined the entourage of court poets with the hope of gaining political favor with the emperor. Although he earned acclaim as a poet, he achieved nothing politically, and, disillusioned, resumed his wandering lifestyle until his death in 762.

THINKING ZONE

You may notice that this poem is divided into groupings of verse lines. These groupings are known as **stanzas**. Depending on what type of poem you read, the stanza divisions may serve different purposes. Some stanza forms in rhymed poetry are precisely measured and lend order to the poem. For instance, each stanza might have its own grouping of rhymed words. Stanza forms in unrhymed poetry many times serve to separate completed thoughts from each other. As you reread this poem by Li Bai, try to think about the purpose of each individual stanza.

Li Bai also fills each stanza of his poem with vivid descriptions and phrases used to create impressions. Poets often rely on details or images that are **concrete** or that specifically appeal to one or more of the five senses. The term often used throughout literature for these descriptions is **imagery**. Imagery helps to make descriptive passages more real and imaginable to the reader. They help us to perceive what the writer is trying to convey.

1. *[interpretive]* What **concrete imagery** does the poet use in the first **stanza**? What sense does the poet appeal to?

_____

_____

_____

2. *[literal/interpretive]* Look at the second stanza. To what does the poet compare his friend? What can we deduce about his friend from this comparison?

_____

_____

_____

_____

3. *[literal/interpretive]* Look at the third stanza. What image is used to describe the "thoughts of the wanderer"? What does this comparison suggest about his thoughts?

_____

_____

_____

_____

_____

4. *[interpretive]* What image in the third stanza describes the mood of the wanderer's friend? What does this image suggest?

_____

_____

_____

_____

_____

5. *[critical]* What is the prevalent emotion that the **imagery** helps to convey?

_____

_____

_____

_____

_____

6. *[appreciative]* If you were to write a poem about parting, what images would you choose to use?

_____

_____

_____

_____

_____

_____

_____

FROM

VERSOS SENCILLOS

José Martí

Translated from the Spanish by Elinor Randall

Do you befriend someone who wrongs you? Or do you respond in the same way you were treated? Martí challenges us to show kindness to both friends and foes.

XXXIX

I cultivate white roses
In January as in July
For the honest friend who freely
Offers me his hand.

And for the brute who tears from me
The heart with which I live,
I nurture neither grubs nor thistles,
But cultivate white roses.

ABOUT THE AUTHOR

José Martí (1853–95), the apostle of Cuban independence, influenced his native Cuba both literarily and politically. He firmly believed in the need for Cuba's independence from Spain and did all he could to aid in the struggle, including using the power of the written word and wielding a sword himself. A poet by age fifteen, he found himself sentenced to hard labor and then deportation by age seventeen because of his political writings. Though he lived in Spain, France, Venezuela, Guatemala, and the United States, he devoted all his energies to the liberation of Cuba. He was killed in 1895 while leading Cuban troops against the Spanish.

Martí's literary contributions extended past his death. His poetry was a forerunner of modern Latin American style, and the personal style of his essays prompted changes in later Latin American prose. Themes of friendship, love, justice, and freedom flavor not only his writing but his life as well.

THINKING ZONE

The **literal meaning** is the standard definition of a word or expression. If, for instance, a friend comes in shivering and tells you, "It's cold outside," he is using the word *cold* in the literal sense to mean that the temperature is low. The literal meaning of a word can almost always be found in its dictionary definition.

On the other hand, **figurative language** is a departure or artful deviation from the literal way of saying something.

Many of the day-to-day expressions that we use are examples of figurative language. For example, if you remark that someone's manner is cold, you do not mean that he is behaving in a low-temperature way. Rather, you mean that the person lacks emotion or feeling. Figurative language encompasses the many creative comparisons that writers use to convey appearances and feelings.

1. *[literal]* What do lines 1 and 8 each describe the speaker doing?

   _____

   _____

   _____

   _____

2. *[critical]* What do you think is the effect of the author's repetition?

   _____

   _____

   _____

   _____

3. *[literal/interpretive]* In stanza 1, for whom is the speaker cultivating roses? For whom is he working in stanza 2? How are the two different?

   _____

   _____

   _____

   _____

4. *[critical]* Throughout the poem, do you think that the poet uses mostly **literal** or **figurative language**? Explain.

_____

_____

_____

_____

5. *[interpretive]* What is represented by what the friend offers in line 4? What is represented by what the brute takes in line 6?

_____

_____

_____

_____

6. *[critical]* Why do you think the poet chose the color white for the roses?

_____

_____

_____

_____

7. *[critical]* What is the main idea of Martí's poem?

_____

_____

_____

_____

8. *[critical]* How do Matthew 5:44 and 46 compare to the main idea of the poem?

_____

_____

_____

_____

GOD'S VICTORIOUS SERVANT

Isaiah's prophecy is a marvelous book of opposites. This prophet presents Israel as rebellious and wicked. But he also states that they are beloved of God and certain to receive His richest blessings. Isaiah presents God as a righteous judge Who will punish all wrongdoing. But God is also merciful and forgiving. How can these opposites be harmonized? The poem found in Isaiah 52:13–53:12 answers this question with remarkable beauty and power.

The Christ of Derision. Andrea Solario.
From the Bob Jones University Collection

Behold, my servant shall deal prudently,
He shall be exalted and extolled, and be very high.
As many were astonied* at thee;   astonied: bewildered, shocked
His visage was so marred more than any man,
And his form more than the sons of men: 5
So shall he sprinkle many nations;
The kings shall shut their mouths at him:
For that which had not been told them shall they see;
And that which they had not heard shall they consider.

Who hath believed our report?   10
And to whom is the arm of the Lord revealed?
For he shall grow up before him as a tender plant,
And as a root out of a dry ground:
He hath no form nor comeliness;*   comeliness: attractiveness
And when we shall see him, there is no beauty that we
    should desire him.   15
He is despised and rejected of men;
A man of sorrows, and acquainted with grief:
And we hid as it were our faces from him;
He was despised, and we esteemed* him not.   esteemed: regarded with respect

Surely he hath borne our griefs,   20
And carried our sorrows:
Yet we did esteem him stricken,
Smitten of God, and afflicted.
But he was wounded for our transgressions,
He was bruised for our iniquities: 25
The chastisement* of our peace was upon him;   chastisement: punishment
And with his stripes we are healed.
All we like sheep have gone astray;
We have turned every one to his own way;
And the Lord hath laid on him   30
The iniquity of us all.

He was oppressed, and he was afflicted,
Yet he opened not his mouth:
He is brought as a lamb to the slaughter,
And as a sheep before her shearers is dumb,   35
So he openeth not his mouth.
He was taken from prison and from judgment:
And who shall declare his generation?
For he was cut off out of the land of the living:
For the transgression of my people was he stricken.   40
And he made his grave with the wicked,
And with the rich in his death;
Because he had done no violence,
Neither was any deceit in his mouth.

Yet it pleased the Lord to bruise him;   45
He hath put him to grief:
When thou shalt make his soul an offering for sin,
He shall see his seed, he shall prolong his days,
And the pleasure of the Lord shall prosper in his hand.
He shall see of the travail* of his soul,   50   travail: agony
And shall be satisfied:
By his knowledge shall my righteous servant justify many;
For he shall bear their iniquities.
Therefore will I divide him a portion with the great,
And he shall divide the spoil with the strong;   55
Because he hath poured out his soul unto death:
And he was numbered with the transgressors;
And he bare the sin of many,
And made intercession for the transgressors.

THINKING ZONE

You have probably read this prophetic passage many times. But have you ever realized it is not just a biblical prophecy? It is also an example of Hebrew poetry. One of the key features of Hebrew poetry is **parallelism**, similarity in the structure of two or more phrases, sentences, or stanzas. Parallelism can be found throughout many types of poetry, but it is especially noticeable in Old Testament Hebrew poetry. Often, phrases and sentences are repeated in order to emphasize a truth. Sometimes, the first sentence or phrase will contain a general statement, and the second will be more specific. For instance, consider the parallelism of Psalm 140:1: "Deliver me, O Lord, *from the evil man*: preserve me *from the violent man*." You will also encounter a reverse style of parallelism, in which the second phrase or sentence reverses the structure of the first. For example, Psalm 142:1 states: "I cried unto the Lord *with my voice; with my voice* unto the Lord did I make my supplication." An important result of this reverse parallelism is that it focuses the reader's attention on the central member. By placing "with my voice" at the center, the writer emphasizes the eagerness with which he has been seeking the Lord's help. This kind of parallelism can be seen in the stanzas of a poem as well. The five stanzas of Isaiah 52:13–53:12 are a fine example.

Similes, comparisons of unlike objects using *like* or *as*, are also prevalent throughout Hebrew poetry, as well as the rest of literature. Similes are a type of figurative language that help the reader better understand the qualities of a thing. One often-heard simile is the phrase "[something] is as hard as a rock." Note the similes that are used to describe both the reader and God's Servant in this Bible passage.

1. *[interpretive]* Who is the speaker of the prophecy, and whom is the prophecy about? What does the prophecy say about this person?

_____

_____

_____

_____

2. *[interpretive]* How are stanzas 1 and 5 parallel?

_____

_____

_____

3. *[interpretive]* What are the **similes** in lines 12–13? What do they communicate about God's Servant?

_____

_____

_____

_____

_____

_____

4. *[critical]* What part of stanza 3 exhibits reverse parallelism?

_____

_____

5. *[critical]* What is the irony found in stanza 3?

_____

_____

_____

> **irony**—*language used to convey meaning other than what is stated or a contradiction between what is expected and what in reality happens*

6. *[interpretive]* What simile is used in stanza 3 to describe our attitudes toward God? What aspect of our attitudes does the verse emphasize?

_____

_____

_____

7. *[critical]* What aspect of Christ do the similes in stanza 4 emphasize?

_____

_____

8. *[literal]* Stanza 5 focuses on the Servant's victory and exaltation. What four reasons does God give in this stanza for honoring His triumphant Servant?

_____

_____

_____

_____

WHAT A FRIEND WE HAVE IN JESUS

JOSEPH SCRIVEN

What a Friend we have in Jesus,
All our sins and griefs to bear!
What a privilege to carry
Everything to God in prayer!
O what peace we often forfeit,
O what needless pain we bear,
All because we do not carry
Everything to God in prayer!

Have we trials and temptations?
Is there trouble anywhere?
We should never be discouraged,
Take it to the Lord in prayer.
Can we find a friend so faithful
Who will all our sorrows share?
Jesus knows our every weakness,
Take it to the Lord in prayer.

Are we weak and heavy laden,
Cumbered* with a load of care? cumbered: weighed down
Precious Savior, still our refuge
Take it to the Lord in prayer.
Do thy friends despise, forsake thee?
Take it to the Lord in prayer;
In His arms He'll take and shield thee,
Thou wilt find a solace* there. solace: comfort

ABOUT THE AUTHOR

October 10, 1886, was a sad day for the community of Lake Rice, Canada, where Joseph Scriven (1820–86) had lived with various families for forty years. On that day, the community lost a beloved citizen. Scriven, who was born in Dublin, Ireland, was a man who had suffered a great personal loss. In 1846, one day before his wedding, Scriven's wife-to-be drowned. In an effort to forget his grief, Scriven moved to Canada. There he took it upon himself to help the unfortunate: widows, orphans, the poor—anyone incapable of paying him for his services. In Port Hope, Ontario, Joseph Scriven became known as a man who, without pay, would chop wood for widows and aged people. Scriven demonstrated Christian love to others in a way that few men do. In fact, even though he accomplished no great acts of heroism by men's standards, his neighbors were so touched by his love for them in giving to meet their needs that they erected a monument in his honor.

The hymn "What a Friend We Have in Jesus" was published in one of Ira D. Sankey's early hymnals. Scriven had written the poem as a comfort to his mother during an illness and had not intended to publish it. A friend found the poem and asked him who wrote it. Scriven replied, "The Lord and I did it together." As a man who had been acquainted with heartache, he had to learn the simple message of his hymn: "Take it to the Lord in prayer."

MERCY FOR MEPHIBOSHETH

Why is David's response to Mephibosheth mentioned in the Bible? First, it is the last part of the story of the friendship of Jonathan and David. Perhaps more important, the king's response is evidence of a Christlike love. In David's day, a new king would often kill any descendents of the previous king in order to prevent relatives from trying to reclaim the throne. When David called for Mephibosheth, the boy probably thought that he was going to be killed. But David did not execute the young man; instead, the king showed mercy. Why did David show mercy to Mephibosheth?

And David said, Is there yet any that is left of the house of Saul, that I may shew him kindness for Jonathan's sake?

2 And there was of the house of Saul a servant whose name was Ziba. And when they had called him unto David, the king said unto him, Art thou Ziba? And he said, Thy servant is he.

3 And the king said, Is there not yet any of the house of Saul, that I may shew the kindness of God unto him? And Ziba said unto the king, Jonathan hath yet a son, which is lame on his feet.

4 And the king said unto him, Where is he? And Ziba said unto the king, Behold, he is in the house of Machir, the son of Ammiel, in Lodebar.

5 Then king David sent, and fetched him out of the house of Machir, the son of Ammiel, from Lodebar.

6 Now when Mephibosheth, the son of Jonathan, the son of Saul, was come unto David, he fell on his face, and did reverence. And David said, Mephibosheth. And he answered, Behold thy servant!

7 And David said unto him, Fear not: for I will surely shew thee kindness for Jonathan thy father's sake, and will restore thee all the land of Saul thy father; and thou shalt eat bread at my table continually.

8 And he bowed himself, and said, What is thy servant, that thou shouldest look upon such a dead dog as I am?

9 Then the king called to Ziba, Saul's servant, and said unto him, I have given unto thy master's son all that pertained to Saul and to all his house.

10 Thou therefore, and thy sons, and thy servants, shall till the land for him, and thou shalt bring in the fruits, that thy master's son may have food to eat: but Mephibosheth thy master's son shall eat bread alway at my table. Now Ziba had fifteen sons and twenty servants.

11 Then said Ziba unto the king, According to all that my lord the king hath commanded his servant, so shall thy servant do. As for Mephibosheth, said the king, he shall eat at my table, as one of the king's sons.

12 And Mephibosheth had a young son, whose name was Micha. And all that dwelt in the house of Ziba were servants unto Mephibosheth.

13 So Mephibosheth dwelt in Jerusalem: for he did eat continually at the king's table; and was lame on both his feet.

—2 Samuel 9

UNIT 1 REVIEW

SHORT ANSWER

Write the word, phrase, or sentence that best answers the question.

1. In "A Most Important Person," Chester compares his rescue by Miss Lucy with what previous experience?

   _____

2. "A Most Important Person" is an example of what genre?

   _____

3. In the excerpt "Being Neighborly" from *Little Women*, which of the gifts that Jo brings helps Laurie overcome his bashfulness?

   _____

4. What does Laurie mean when he says, "A fellow can't live on books"?

   _____

5. In "The Doll's House," what is wrong with the family of dolls in the doll's house?

   _____

6. In what ways does the lamp represent Kezia?

   _____

   _____

7. What symbolic action does Mrs. Jones do to Roger in "Thank You, M'am"? What does it symbolize?

   _____

8. At the end of the story "Half a Gift," what does Joe say he is giving his mother? Why did he decide to do that instead of giving her the comb?

   _____

   _____

9. What do we know about the friend talked about in "Seeing Off a Friend"?

   _____

10. In "Seeing Off a Friend," what emotion does the imagery suggest?

    _____

MULTIPLE CHOICE

Choose the best answer from the choices given.

_____ 11. Which of the following is true about Chester's statement "You saved me"?
  A. Chester was teasing when he said this.
  B. Miss Lucy did nothing to rescue Chester.
  C. Miss Lucy is the one who said "You saved me."
  D. The statement is ironic because in reality it is Chester who "saves" Miss Lucy from her pride and selfishness.

_____ 12. In "The Doll's House," the doll's house symbolizes the childish values of the
  A. Kelvey household.
  B. Burnell household.
  C. townspeople.
  D. religious establishment.

_____ 13. In "After Twenty Years," the most likely reason Jimmy Wells cannot arrest the man from the West himself is that he
  A. is afraid of the man.
  B. is not sure he has correctly identified the man.
  C. does not believe that his friend could have committed any crime.
  D. still feels a sense of loyalty because of their previous friendship.

_____ 14. In Li Bai's poem "Seeing Off a Friend," to what does he compare his friend?
  A. the city and the mountains
  B. floating clouds
  C. a high mountain
  D. a tumbleweed

_____ 15. The primary image in Martí's poem from _Versos Sencillos_ is the
  A. cultivating of white roses.
  B. passing of floating clouds.
  C. weeding out of grubs and thistles.
  D. mending of a broken heart.

MATCHING

Match the following literary terms with their correct definitions.

_____ 16. language used to convey meaning other than what is stated

_____ 17. struggle of the story's characters against an opposing force

_____ 18. development that violates the reader's expectations

_____ 19. hinting at events that will occur later in the story

_____ 20. departure from the literal way of saying something

A. foreshadowing

B. conflict

C. figurative language

D. irony

E. plot twist

SHORT ANSWER

Give examples of the following literary devices used in the stories indicated.

21. foreshadowing in "After Twenty Years"

_____

_____

_____

_____

22. types of conflict in "Thank You, M'am"

_____

_____

_____

_____

23. irony in Isaiah 52:13–53:12

_____

_____

_____

_____

TRUE OR FALSE

If the statement is completely true, write *true*. If any part of the statement is false, write *false*.

_____ 24. In "A Most Important Person," Miss Lucy is not lonely because she has a large group of friends in town.

_____ 25. Dialogue is a means by which an author reveals certain character traits.

_____ 26. One irony of the story "The Doll's House" is the unattractive doll's house being admired but the unattractive children being shunned.

_____ 27. The plot development of "After Twenty Years" meets the reader's expectations.

_____ 28. In the selection from *Versos Sencillos*, the author contrasts two types of people.

ESSAY

Write a complete answer in one paragraph for the question below, using specific examples from the unit.

29. Which of the characters in this unit would you most likely choose as a friend? Explain why you made your choice(s). Cite specific details from the story in your answer.

_____

_____

_____

_____

_____

_____

_____

_____

_____

_____

_____

CHOICES

This study for a stained glass window of Prodigal Son *by Einar Forseth (1892–1988) is in the cubist style. Cubist painters viewed their subjects as groups of intersecting abstract geometric shapes that could be moved around and reassembled in order to show various angles simultaneously. What in this painting would we be unable to see were the piece done in another style?*

How does this painting relate to the unit theme of choices?

How is the style of this painting different from *Friends* in Unit 1?

What mood is created by the colors and style of this painting?

The central figures in this painting are the father and his son. Who do you think the other figures in the painting are?

Only the father is wearing glasses. Why do you think the artist chose to represent the father in this way?

CHOICES

THERE IS A SIMPLE RULE IN FICTION: INTRIGUING CHARACTERS IN INTRIGUING STORIES NEVER STAND STILL. WHEN A CHARACTER MAKES ANY DECISION, HE MOVES EITHER FORWARD OR BACKWARD. HE MAY TAKE ONLY ONE STEP, BUT HE IS ONE STEP CLOSER TO EVENTUAL SUCCESS OR FAILURE. THE SAME IS TRUE OF PEOPLE IN REAL LIFE.

Consider yourself. You face choices every day. Of course, some of your choices are more important than others. But the ones that determine whether you will eventually become "fit'n" or "unfit," as Uncle Jesse says in "Weep No More, My Lady," are choices between right and wrong. How are you to determine right from wrong? You must first establish a fixed standard. You cannot, however, rely on men's laws and values for a standard, for men's ideas of right and wrong are colored by selfishness and pride. As Solomon said long ago, "All the ways of a man are clean in his own eyes; but the Lord weigheth the spirits" (Prov. 16:2). The only unfailing, absolute authority you have for determining what is right is the Bible, and it is essential that you know God's Word so that you can make right choices.

Making one choice is only the beginning. There is in the decision-making process a "domino theory." What is the domino theory? Well, take a set of dominos and set them up one behind another. Then push the first one into the second one. What happens? Not just two, but the whole set topples. Like the dominos, choices, whether they are good ones or bad ones,

are followed by a whole series of additional choices and consequences.

As you read the following stories and poems, carefully consider that we are not the only ones who make choices. God chooses too. In fact, His choices matter much more than ours. Our choices shape our lives, but His choices determine what will be. The power of God's choices should challenge and encourage us all. Those who consistently choose what is right must remember that God's choices have made their choices possible. How could a person choose right unless God had first shown him what is right and given him a desire to choose it? Those who have made many wrong choices should not despair that God cannot use them. God has decreed that a person will reap what he sows (Gal. 6:7), but God has also revealed that He is merciful and gracious. He delights in changing people and in rewarding them for changing. All of us are indebted to God's good and wise choices. The humble Christian chooses to praise God for these choices: "God hath chosen the foolish things of this world to confound the wise . . . that no flesh should glory in his presence. . . . According as it is written, He that glorieth, let him glory in the Lord" (1 Cor. 1:27–31). ✠

CERTAIN THINGS ARE RIGHT AND CERTAIN THINGS ARE
WRONG. AND NOTHING AIN'T GONNA EVER CHANGE THAT.
WHEN YOU LEARN THAT, THEN YOU'RE FIT'N TO BE A MAN.

—UNCLE JESSE
"WEEP NO MORE, MY LADY"

WEEP NO MORE, MY LADY

JAMES STREET

From the moment Skeeter and Uncle Jesse discover the strange dog in the swamp, Skeeter and My Lady become inseparable. But another discovery soon threatens their bond and creates a tug of war for Skeeter, forcing him to choose between his conscience and his desires.

The moonlight symphony of swamp creatures hushed abruptly, and the dismal bog* was as peaceful as unborn time and seemed to brood in its silence. The gaunt man glanced back at the boy and motioned for him to be quiet, but it was too late. Their presence was discovered. A jumbo frog rumbled a warning, and the swamp squirmed into life as its denizens* scuttled to safety.

---
bog: an area of wet, spongy ground; a swamp

denizens: inhabitants

Foxfire* was glowing to the west and the bayou was slapping the cypress trees when suddenly a haunting laugh echoed through the wilderness, a strange chuckling yodel ending in a weird "gro-o-o."

---
foxfire: emission of light, sometimes caused by fungi on decaying wood
---

The boy's eyes were wide and staring. "That's it, Uncle Jesse. Come on! Let's catch it!"

"Uh, oh." The man gripped his shotgun. "That ain't no animal. That's a thing."

They hurried noiselessly in the direction of the sound that Skeeter had been hearing for several nights. Swamp born and reared, they feared nothing they could shoot or outwit, so they slipped out of the morass* and to the side of a ridge. Suddenly, Jesse put out his hand and stopped the child; then he pointed up the slope. The animal, clearly visible in the moonlight, was sitting on its haunches, its head cocked sideways as it chuckled. It was a merry and rather melodious little chuckle.

---
morass: a swamp

Skeeter grinned in spite of his surprise, then said, "Sh-h-h. It'll smell us."

Jesse said, "Can't nothing smell that far. Wonder what the thing is?" He peered up the ridge, studying the creature. He had no intention of shooting unless attacked, for Jesse Tolliver and his nephew never killed wantonly.*

---
wantonly: senselessly; maliciously; without provocation

The animal, however, did smell them and whipped her nose into the wind, crouched and braced. She was about sixteen inches high and weighed about twenty-two pounds. Her coat was red and silky, and there was a blaze of white down her throat. Her face was wrinkled and sad, like a wise old man's.

Jesse shook his head. "Looks som'n like a mixture of bloodhound and terrier from here," he whispered. "It beats me—"

"It's a dog, all right," Skeeter said.

"Can't no dog laugh."

"That dog can." The boy began walking toward the animal, his right hand outstretched. "Heah, heah. I ain't gonna hurt you."

The dog, for she was a dog, cocked her head from one side to the other and watched Skeeter. She was trembling, but she didn't run. And when Skeeter knelt by her, she stopped trembling, for the ways of a boy with a dog are mysterious. He stroked her, and the trim little creature looked up at him and blinked her big hazel eyes. Then she turned over, and Skeeter scratched her. She closed her eyes, stretched, and chuckled, a happy mixture of chortle* and yodel. Jesse ambled* up, and the dog leaped to her feet and sprang between the boy and the man.

chortle: chuckling or snorting sound
ambled: walked leisurely

Skeeter calmed her. "That's just Uncle Jesse."

Jesse, still bewildered, shook his head again. "I still say that ain't no dog. She don't smell and she don't bark. Ain't natural. And look at her! Licking herself like a cat."

"Well, I'll be catty wampus*," Skeeter said. "Never saw a dog do that before." However, he was quick to defend any mannerism of his friend and said, "She likes to keep herself clean. She's a lady, and I'm gonna name her that, and she's mine 'cause I found her."

"Lady, huh?"

catty wampus: askew, off balance

"No, sir. My Lady. If I name her Lady, how folks gonna know she's mine?" He began stroking his dog again. "Uncle Jesse, I ain't never had nothing like this before."

"It still don't make sense to me," Jesse said. But he didn't care, for he was happy because the child was happy.

Like most mysteries, there was no mystery at all about My Lady. She was a lady, all right, an aristocratic basenji,* one of those strange barkless dogs of Africa. Her ancestors were pets of the Pharaohs, and her line was well established. A bundle of nerves and muscles, she would fight anything and could scent game up to eighty yards. She had the gait of an antelope and was odorless, washing herself before and after meals. However,

the only noises she could make were a piercing cry that sounded almost human and that chuckling little chortle. She could chuckle only when happy, and she had been happy in the woods. Now she was happy again.

---

basenji (bə-sĕn´jē)

As most men judge values, she was worth more than all the possessions of Jesse and his nephew. Several of the dogs had been shipped to New Orleans to avoid the dangerous upper route, thence by motor to a northern kennel. While crossing Mississippi, My Lady had escaped from a station wagon. Her keeper had advertised in several papers, but Jesse and Skeeter never saw papers.

Skeeter said, "Come on, M'Lady. Let's go home."

The dog didn't hesitate, but walked proudly at the boy's side to a cabin on the bank of the bayou. Skeeter crumbled corn bread, wet it with potlikker* and put it before her. She sniffed the food disdainfully* at first, eating it only when she saw the boy fix a bowl for his uncle. She licked herself clean and explored the cabin, sniffing the brush brooms, the piles of wild pecans and hickory nuts, and then the cots. Satisfied at last, she jumped on Skeeter's bed, tucked her nose under her paws, and went to sleep.

---

potlikker: a juice produced by cooking greens and meat together
disdainfully: scornfully

"Acts like she owns the place," Jesse said.

"Where you reckon she came from?" The boy slipped his overall straps from his shoulders, flexed his stringy muscles, and yawned.

"Circus maybe." He looked at M'Lady quickly. "Say, maybe she's freak and run off from some show. Bet they'd give us two dollars for her."

Skeeter's face got long. "You don't aim to get rid of her?"

The old man put his shotgun over the mantel and lit his pipe. "Skeets, if you want that thing, I wouldn't get shed of her for a piece of bottom land a mile long. Already plowed and planted."

"I reckoned you wouldn't, 'cause you like me so much. And I know how you like dogs, 'cause I saw you cry when yours got killed. But you can have part of mine."

Jesse sat down and leaned back, blowing smoke into the air to drive away mosquitos. The boy got a brick and hammer and began cracking nuts, pounding the meat to pulp so his uncle could chew it. Skeeter's yellow hair hadn't been cut for months and was tangled. He had freckles, too. And his real name was Jonathan. His mother was Jesse's only sister and died when the child was born. No one thereabouts ever knew what happened to his father. Jesse, a leathery, toothless old man with faded blue eyes, took him to bring up and called him Skeeter because he was so little.

In the village, where Jesse seldom visited, folks wondered if he were fit'n to rear a little boy. They considered him shiftless and no-count. Jesse had lived all his sixty years in the swamp. He earned a few dollars selling jumbo frogs and pelts,* but mostly he just paddled around the swamp, watching things and teaching Skeeter about life.

---

pelts: animal skins

The villagers might have tried to send Skeeter to an orphanage, but for Joe (Cash) Watson, the storekeeper. Cash was a hard man, but fair. He often hunted with Jesse, and the old man trained Cash's bird dogs. When there was talk of sending Skeeter away, Cash said, "You ain't gonna do it. You just don't take young'uns away from their folks." And that's all there was to it.

Jesse yearned for only two things—a twenty-gauge shotgun for Skeeter and a set of Roebuckers for himself, as he called store-bought teeth. Cash had promised him the gun and the best false teeth in the catalog for forty-six dollars. Jesse had saved nine dollars and thirty-seven cents.

"Someday I'm gonna get them Roebuckers," he often told Skeeter. "Then I'm gonna eat me enough roastin' ears to kill a goat. Maybe I can get a set with a couple of gold teeth in 'em. I seen a man once with six gold teeth."

The boy cracked as many nuts as his uncle wanted, then put the hammer away. He was undressing when he glanced over at his dog. "Uncle Jesse, I'm scared somebody'll come get her."

"I ain't heard of nobody losing no things around here. If'n they had, they'd been to me fo' now, beings I know all about dogs and the swamp."

"That's so," Skeeter said. "But you don't reckon she belonged to another fellow like me, do you? I know how I'd feel if I had a dog like her and she got lost."

Jesse said, "She don't belong to another fellow like you. If'n she had, she wouldn't be so happy here."

Skeeter fed M'Lady biscuits and molasses for breakfast, and although the basenji ate it, she still was hungry when she went into the swamp with the boy. He was hoping he could find a bee tree or signs of wild hogs. They were at the edge of a clearing when M'Lady's chokebore* nose suddenly tilted and she froze to a flash point, pausing only long enough to get set. Then she darted to the bayou, at least sixty yards away, dived into a clump of reeds, and snatched a water rat. She was eating it when Skeeter ran up.

chokebore: tapered

"Don't do that," he scolded. "Ain't you got no more sense than to run into the water after things? A snake or a 'gator might snatch you."

The basenji dropped the rat and tucked her head. She knew the boy was displeased, and when she looked up at him, her eyes were filled, and a woebegone expression was on her face.

Skeeter tried to explain. "I didn't mean to hurt your feelings. Don't cry." He stepped back quickly and stared at her, at the tears in her eyes. "She is crying!" Skeeter called her and ran toward the cabin, where Uncle Jesse was cutting splinters.

"Uncle Jesse! Guess what else my dog can do!"

"Whistle," the old man laughed.

"She can cry! I declare! Not out loud, but she can cry just the same."

Jesse knew that most dogs will get watery-eyed on occasion, but, not wanting to ridicule M'Lady's accomplishments, asked, "What made her cry?"

"Well, sir, we were walking along an all of a sudden she got scent and flash pointed and then . . ." Skeeter remembered something.

"Then what?"

Skeeter sat on the steps. "Uncle Jesse," he said slowly, "we must have been fifty or sixty yards from that rat when she smelled it."

"What rat? What's eating you?"

The child told him the story, and Jesse couldn't believe it. For a dog to pick up the scent of a water rat at sixty yards simply isn't credible.* Jesse reckoned Skeeter's love for M'Lady had led him to exaggerate.

credible: believable

Skeeter knew Jesse didn't believe the story, so he said, "Come on. I'll show you." He whistled for M'Lady.

The dog came up. "Hey," Jesse said. "That thing knows what a whistle means.

Shows she's been around folks." He caught the dog's eye and commanded, "Heel!"

But M'Lady cocked her head quizzically. Then she turned to the boy and chuckled softly. She'd never heard the order before. That was obvious. Her nose came up into the breeze and she wheeled.

Her curved tail suddenly was still and her head was poised.

"Flash pointing," Jesse said. "Well, I'll be a monkey's uncle!"

M'Lady held the strange point only for a second, though, then dashed toward a corn patch about eighty yards from the cabin.

Halfway to the patch, she broke her gait and began creeping. A whir of feathered lightning sounded in the corn, and a covey* of quail exploded almost under her nose. She sprang and snatched a bird.

covey: small group

"Partridges!" Jesse's jaw dropped.

The child was motionless as stone, his face white and his eyes wide in amazement. Finally he found his voice, "She was right here when she smelled them birds. A good eighty yards."

"I know she ain't no dog now," Jesse said. "Can't no dog do that."

"She's fast as greased lightning and ain't scared of nothing." Skeeter still was under the spell of the adventure. "She's a hunting dog from way back."

"She ain't no dog a-tall, I'm telling you. It ain't human." Jesse walked toward M'Lady and told her to fetch the bird, but the dog didn't understand. Instead, she pawed it. "Well," Jesse said. "One thing's certain. She ain't no bird hunter."

"She can do anything," Skeeter said. "Even hunt birds. Maybe I can make a bird dog out'n her. Wouldn't that be som'n?"

"You're batty. Maybe a coon dog, but not a bird dog. I know 'bout dogs."

"Me too," said Skeeter. And he did. He'd seen Jesse train many dogs, even pointers, and had helped him train Big Boy, Cash Watson's prize gun dog.

Jesse eyed Skeeter and read his mind.

"It can't be done, Skeets."

"Maybe not, but I aim to try. Ain't no sin in trying, is it?"

"Naw," Jesse said slowly. "But she'll flush* birds."

flush: frighten from cover

"I'll learn her not to."

"She won't hold no point. Any dog'll flash point. And she'll hunt rats."

"I'm gonna learn her just to hunt birds," Skeeter said.

"Wanta bet?" Jesse issued the challenge in an effort to keep Skeeter's enthusiasm and determination at the high-water mark.

"Yes, sir. If I don't train my dog, then I'll cut all the splinters for a year. If I do, you cut 'em."

"It's a go," Jesse said.

Skeeter ran to the bayou and recovered the rat M'Lady had killed. He tied it round his dog's neck. The basenji was indignant* and tried to claw off the hateful burden. Failing, she ran into the house and under the bed, but Skeeter made her come out. M'Lady filled up then, and her face assumed that don't-nobody-love-me look. The boy steeled himself, tapped M'Lady's nose with the rat, and left it around her neck.

indignant: angry

"You done whittled out a job for yourself," Jesse said. "If'n you get her trained, you'll lose her in the brush. She's too fast and too little to keep up with."

"I'll bell her," Skeeter said. "I'm gonna learn her ever'thing. I got us a gun dog, Uncle Jesse."

The old man sat on the porch and propped against the wall. "Bud, I don't know what that thing is. But you're a thoroughbred. John dog my hide!"

If Skeeter had loved M'Lady one bit less, his patience would have exploded during the ordeal of training the basenji. It takes judgment and infinite patience to train a bird dog properly, but to train a basenji, that'll hunt anything, to concentrate only on quail took something more than discipline and patience. It never could have been done except for that strange affinity* between a boy and a dog, and the blind faith of a child.

affinity: natural attraction

M'Lady's devotion to Skeeter was so complete that she was anxious to do anything to earn a pat. It wasn't difficult to teach her to heel and follow at Skeeter's feet regardless of the urge to dash away and chase rabbits. The boy used a clothesline as a guide rope and made M'Lady follow him. The first time the dog tried to chase an animal, Skeeter pinched the rope around her neck just a bit and commanded "Heel!" And when she obeyed, Skeeter released the noose. It took M'Lady only a few hours to associate disobedience with disfavor.

The dog learned that when she chased and killed a rat or rabbit, the thing would be tied around her neck. The only things she could hunt without being disciplined were quail. Of course, she often mistook the scent of game chickens for quail and hunted them, but Skeeter punished her by scolding. He never switched his dog, but to M'Lady a harsh word from the boy hurt more than a hickory limb.

Jesse watched the dog's progress and pretended not to be impressed. He never volunteered suggestions. M'Lady learned quickly, but the task of teaching her to point birds seemed hopeless. Skeeter knew she'd never point as pointers do, so he worked out his own system. He taught her to stand motionless when he shouted "Hup!" One day she got a scent of birds, paused and pointed for a moment as most animals will, and was ready to spring away when Skeeter said "Hup!"

M'Lady was confused. Every instinct urged her to chase the birds, but her master had said stand still. She broke, however, and Skeeter scolded her. She pouted at first, then filled up, but the boy ignored her until she obeyed the next command, then he patted her and she chuckled.

The lessons continued for days and weeks, and slowly and surely M'Lady learned her chores. She learned that the second she smelled birds she must stop and stand still until Skeeter flushed them; that she must not quiver when he shot.

Teaching her to fetch was easy, but teaching her to retrieve dead birds without damaging them was another matter. M'Lady had a hard mouth—that is, she sank her teeth into the birds. Skeeter used one of the oldest hunting tricks of the backwoods to break her.

He got a stick and wrapped it with wire and taught his dog to fetch it. Only once did M'Lady bite hard on the stick, and then the wire hurt her sensitive mouth. Soon she developed a habit of carrying the stick on her tongue and supporting it lightly with her teeth. Skeeter tied quail feathers on the stick, and soon M'Lady's education was complete.

Skeeter led Jesse into a field one day and turned his dog loose. She flashed to a point almost immediately. It was a funny point, and Jesse almost laughed. The dog's curved tail poked up over her back, she straddled her front legs and sort of squatted, her nose pointing the birds, more than forty yards away. She remained rigid until the boy flushed and shot, then she leaped away, seeking and fetching dead birds.

Jesse was mighty proud. "Well, Skeets, looks like you got yourself a bird hunter."

"Yes, sir," Skeeter said. "And you got yourself a job." He pointed toward the kindling pile.

The swamp was dressing for winter when Cash Watson drove down that day to give his Big Boy a workout in the wild brush.

He locked his fine pointer in the corncrib for the night and was warming himself in the cabin when he noticed M'Lady for the first time. She was sleeping in front of the fire.

"What's that?" he asked.

"My dog," said Skeeter. "Ain't she a beaut?"

"She sure is," Cash grinned at Jesse. Skeeter went out to the well, and Cash asked his old friend, "What kind of mutt is that?"

"Search me," said Jesse. "Skeets found her in the swamp. I reckon she's got a trace of bloodhound in her and some terrier and a heap of just plain dog."

M'Lady cocked one ear and got up and stretched; then, apparently not liking the company, she turned her tail toward Cash and strutted out, looking for Skeeter.

The men laughed. "Som'n wrong with her throat," Jesse said. "She can't bark. When she tries, she makes a funny sound, sort of a cackling, chuckling yodel. Sounds like she's laughing."

"Well," Cash said, "trust a young'un to love the orner'st dog he can find."

"Wait a minute," Jesse said. "She ain't no-count. She's a bird-hunting fool."

Just then Skeeter entered and Cash jestingly said, "Hear you got yourself a bird dog, son."

The boy clasped his hands behind him and rocked on the balls of his feet as he had seen men do. "Well, now, I'll tell you, Mr. Cash. M'Lady does ever'thing except tote the gun."

"She must be fair to middling. Why not take her out with Big Boy tomorrow? Do my dog good to hunt in a brace."*

---

brace: a pair

"Me and my dog don't want to show Big Boy up. He's a pretty good ol' dog."

"Whoa!" Cash was every inch a bird-dog man and nobody could challenge him without a showdown. Besides, Skeeter was shooting up and should be learning a few things about life. "Any old boiler can pop off steam." Cash winked at Jesse.

"Well, sir, if you're itching for a run, I'll run your dog against mine."

Cash admired the boy's confidence. "All right, son. What are the stakes?"

Skeeter started to mention the twenty-gauge gun he wanted, but changed his mind quickly. He reached down and patted M'Lady, then looked up. "If my dog beats yours, then you get them Roebuckers for Uncle Jesse."

Jesse's chest suddenly was tight. Cash glanced from the boy to the man, and he, too, was proud of Skeeter. "I wasn't aiming to go that high. But all right. What do I get if I win?"

"I'll cut ten cords of stove wood."

"And a stack of splinters?"

"Yes, sir."

Cash offered his hand, and Skeeter took it. "It's a race," Cash said. "Jesse will be the judge."

The wind was rustling the sage and there was a nip in the early-morning air when they took the dogs to a clearing and set them down. Skeeter snapped a belt around M'Lady's neck, and, at a word from Jesse, the dogs were released.

Big Boy bounded away and began circling, ranging into the brush. M'Lady tilted her nose into the wind and ripped away toward the sage, her bell tinkling. Cash said, "She sure covers ground." Skeeter made no effort to keep up with her, but waited until he couldn't hear the bell, then ran for a clearing where he had last heard it. And there was M'Lady on a point.

Cash laughed out loud. "That ain't no point, son. That's a squat."

"She's got birds."

"Where?"

Jesse leaned against a tree and watched the fun.

Skeeter pointed toward a clump of sage. "She's pointing birds in that sage."

Cash couldn't restrain his mirth. "Boy, now that's what I call some pointing. Why, Skeeter, it's sixty or seventy yards to that sage."

Just then Big Boy flashed by M'Lady, his head high. He raced to the edge of the sage, caught the wind, then whipped around,
freezing to a point. Cash called Jesse's attention to the point.

"That's M'Lady's point," Skeeter said. "She's got the same birds Big Boy has."

Jesse sauntered up. "The boy's right, Cash. I aimed to keep my mouth out'n this race, but M'Lady's pointing them birds. She can catch scents up to eighty yards."

Cash said, "Aw, go on. You're crazy." He walked over and flushed the birds.

Skeeter picked one off and ordered M'Lady to fetch it. When she returned with the bird, the boy patted her, and she began chuckling.

Cash really studied her then for the first time. "Hey!" he said suddenly. "A basenji! That's a basenji!"

"A what?" Jesse asked.

"I should have known." Cash was very excited. "That's the dog that was lost by them rich Yankees. I saw about it in the paper." He happened to look at Skeeter then and wished he had cut out his tongue.

The boy's lips were compressed and his face drawn and white. Jesse had closed his eyes and was rubbing his forehead.

Cash, trying to dismiss the subject, said, "Just 'cause it was in the paper don't make it so. I don't believe that's the same dog, come to think of it."

"I know she's the same dog," Skeeter said. "On account of I just know it. But she's mine now." His voice rose and trembled. "And ain't nobody gonna take her away from me." He ran into the swamp. M'Lady was at his heels.

Cash said, "I'm sorry, Jesse. If I'd kept my mouth shut he'd never known the difference."

"It can't be helped, now," Jesse said.

"'Course she beat Big Boy. Them's the best hunting dogs in the world. And she's worth a mint of money."

They didn't feel like hunting and returned to the cabin and sat on the porch. Neither had much to say, but kept glancing toward the swamp where Skeeter and M'Lady were walking along the bayou.

"Don't you worry," Skeeter said tenderly, "ain't nobody gonna bother you." He sat on a stump and M'Lady put her head on his knee. She wasn't worrying. Nothing could have been more contented than she was.

"I don't care if the sheriff comes down." Skeeter pulled her onto his lap and held her. "I don't give a whoop if the governor comes down. Even the President of the United States! The whole shebang can come, but ain't nobody gonna mess with you."

His words gave him courage, and he felt better, but only for a minute. Then the tug-of-war between him and his conscience started.

"Once I found a Barlow knife and kept it, and it was all right," he mumbled.

"*But this is different.*"

"Finders, keepers; losers, weepers."

"*No, Skeeter.*"

"Well, I don't care. She's mine."

"*Remember what your Uncle Jesse said.*"

"He said a heap of things."

"*Yes, but you remember one thing more than the rest. He said, 'Certain things are right and certain things are wrong. And nothing ain't gonna ever change that. When you learn that, then you're fit'n to be a man.' Remember, Skeeter?*"

A feeling of despair and loneliness almost overwhelmed him. He fought off the tears as long as he could, but finally he gave in, and his sobs caused M'Lady to peer into his face and wonder why he was acting that way when she was so happy. He put his arms around her neck and pulled her to him. "My li'l old puppy dog. Poor li'l old puppy dog. But I got to do it."

He sniffed back his tears and got up and walked to the cabin. M'Lady curled up by the fire, and the boy sat down, watching the logs splutter for several minutes. Then he said, almost in a whisper, "Uncle Jesse, if you keep som'n that ain't yours, it's the same as stealing, ain't it?"

Jesse puffed his pipe slowly. "Son, that's som'n you got to settle with yourself."

Skeeter stood and turned his back to the flames warming his hands. "Mr. Cash," he said slowly, "when you get back to your store, please let them folks know their dog is here."

"If that's how it is—"

"That's how it is," Skeeter said.

The firelight dancing on Jesse's face revealed the old man's dejection, and Skeeter, seeing it, said quickly, "It's best for M'Lady. She's too good for the swamp. They'll give her a good home."

Jesse flinched, and Cash, catching the hurt in his friend's eyes, said, "Your dog outhunted mine, Skeets. You win them Roebuckers for your uncle."

"I don't want 'em," Jesse said, rather childishly. "I don't care if'n I never eat no roastin' ears." He got up quickly and hurried outside. Cash reckoned he'd better be going and left Skeeter by the fire, rubbing his dog.

Jesse came back in directly and pulled up a chair. Skeeter started to speak, but Jesse spoke first. "I been doing a heap of thinking lately. You're sprouting up. The swamp ain't no place for you."

Skeeter forgot about his dog and faced his uncle, bewildered.

"I reckon you're too good for the swamp too," Jesse said. "I'm aiming to send you into town for a spell. I can make enough to keep you in fit'n clothes and all." He dared not look at the boy.

"Uncle Jesse!" Skeeter said reproachfully.* "You don't mean that. You're just saying that on account of what I said about M'Lady. I said it just to keep you from feeling so bad about our dog going away. I ain't ever gonna leave you." He buried his face in his uncle's shoulder. M'Lady put her head on Jesse's knee, and he patted the boy and rubbed the dog.

reproachfully: disapprovingly

"Reckon I'll take them Roebuckers," he said at last. "I been wanting some for a long, long time."

Several days later Cash drove down and told them the man from the kennels was at his store. Skeeter didn't say a word, but called M'Lady and they got in Cash's car. All the way to town, the boy was silent. He held his dog's head in his lap.

The keeper took just one look at M'Lady and said, "That's she, all right. Miss Congo III." He turned to speak to Skeeter, but the boy was walking away. He got a glance at Skeeter's face, however. "I wish you fellows hadn't told me," he muttered. "I hate to take a dog away from a kid."

"Mister"—Jesse closed his left eye and struck his swapping pose—"I'd like to swap you out'n that hound. Now, course she ain't much 'count . . ."

The keeper smiled in spite of himself. "If she was mine, I'd give her to the kid. But she's not for sale. The owner wants to breed her

and establish her line in this country. And if she was for sale, she'd cost more money than any of us will ever see." He called Skeeter and offered his hand. Skeeter shook it.

"You're a good kid. There's a reward for this dog."

"I don't want no reward." The boy's words tumbled out. "I don't want nothing, except to be left alone. You've got your dog, mister. Take her and go on. Please." He walked away again, fearing he would cry.

Cash said, "I'll take the reward and keep it for him. Some day he'll want it."

Jesse went out to the store porch to be with Skeeter. The keeper handed Cash the money. "It's tough, but the kid'll get over it. The dog never will."

"Is that a fact?"

"Yep. I know the breed. They never forget. That dog'll never laugh again. They never laugh unless they're happy."

He walked to the post where Skeeter had tied M'Lady. He untied the leash and started toward his station wagon. M'Lady braced her front feet and looked around for the boy. Seeing him on the porch, she jerked away from the keeper and ran to her master.

She rubbed against his legs. Skeeter tried to ignore her. The keeper reached for the leash again, and M'Lady crouched, baring her fangs. The keeper shrugged, a helpless gesture.

"Wild elephants couldn't pull that dog away from that boy," he said.

"That's all right, mister." Skeeter unsnapped the leash and tossed it to the keeper. Then he walked to the station wagon, opened the door of a cage, and called, "Heah, M'Lady!" She bounded to him. "Up!" he commanded. She didn't hesitate, but leaped into the cage. The keeper locked the door.

M'Lady, having obeyed a command, poked her nose between the bars, expecting a pat. The boy rubbed her head. She tried to move closer to him, but the bars held her. She looked quizzically at the bars, then tried to nudge them aside. Then she clawed them. A look of fear suddenly came to her eyes, and she fastened them on Skeeter, wistfully* at first, then pleadingly. She couldn't make a sound, for her unhappiness had sealed her throat. Slowly her eyes filled up.

---

wistfully: longingly

"Don't cry no more, M'Lady. Ever'thing's gonna be all right." He reached out to pat her, but the station wagon moved off, leaving him standing there in the dust.

Back on the porch, Jesse lit his pipe and said to his friend, "Cash, the boy has lost his dog, and I've lost a boy."

"Aw, Jesse, Skeeter wouldn't leave you."

"That ain't what I mean. He growed up that day in the swamp."

Skeeter walked into the store and Cash followed him. "I've got that reward money for you, Jonathan."

It was the first time anyone ever had called him that, and it sounded like man talk.

"And that twenty-gauge is waiting for you," Cash said. "I'm gonna give it to you."

"Thank you, Mr. Cash." The boy bit his lower lip. "But I don't aim to do no more hunting. I don't never want no more dogs."

"Know how you feel. But if you change you mind, the gun's here for you."

Skeeter looked back toward the porch where Jesse was waiting, and said, "Tell you what, though. When you get them Roebuckers, get some with a couple of gold teeth in 'em. Take it out of the reward money."

"Sure, Jonathan."

Jesse joined them and Skeeter said, "We better be getting back toward the house."

"I'll drive you down," Cash said. "But first I aim to treat you to some lemon pop and sardines."

"That's mighty nice of you," Jesse said, "but we better be gettin' on."

"What's your hurry?" Cash opened the pop.

"It's my time to cut splinters," Jesse said. "That's what I get for betting with a good man."

THINKING ZONE

As you know, a story's point of view refers to the perspective from which the story is told. "Weep No More, My Lady" is told from the **third-person point of view**, which uses third-person pronouns such as *it*, *he*, and *she* to tell a story. Usually, the narrator is not a character in a story that is told in the third person.

Throughout this story, you may also have noticed several expressions, such as "I'll be catty wampus," that Uncle Jesse, Skeeter, and Cash use to communicate with one another. These unique expressions, known as **idioms**, cannot be defined by the meanings of the individual words. In "The Doll's House," Mansfield writes about Isabel's "holding court" and the Burnells' needing to "draw the line" on whom the girls could associate with. Both of these terms are idioms because Isabel does not literally have anything in her arms, and no one in the family uses a writing implement to make a mark on anyone. We know what the author means because those words in combination have a meaning other than their individual literal definitions.

First-person point of view—*perspective in literature in which the narrator refers to himself as "I"*

1. *[appreciative]* Do you think that **third-person point of view** was the best choice for this story? How would the story have been different if told from another point of view?

_____

_____

_____

2. *[literal/critical]* List some characteristics that make M'Lady unusual. Do you think Skeeter was attracted to the dog only because of these uncommon traits?

_____

_____

_____

_____

3. *[interpretive]* What is the main conflict in "Weep No More, My Lady"? Cite the specific portion of the story that shows the beginning of the conflict.

_____

_____

_____

4. *[interpretive]* What events serve to further the conflict?

_____

_____

5. *[interpretive]* What is the main idea of the story? Where is this idea stated?

_____

_____

_____

6. *[critical]* Why does Cash call Skeeter "Jonathan" at the end of the story?

_____

_____

_____

_____

_____

7. *[appreciative]* Do you think that the author was wise to use so many **idioms** when writing the dialogue? Why or why not?

_____

_____

_____

8. *[critical]* How is Uncle Jesse and Skeeter's relationship like the injunction in Philippians 2:3–4?

_____

_____

_____

MAMA AND THE GRADUATION PRESENT

KATHRYN FORBES

The past months had proved very difficult financially. But now that Papa was home from the hospital and the new boarders were happily settled, finances were bound to improve, Katrin told herself. In this story Katrin has a decision to make. Have you ever had to make a difficult choice—one that affected other people's happiness as well as your own?

During the last week that Papa was in the hospital, we rented the big downstairs bedroom to two brothers, Mr. Sam and Mr. George Stanton.

The Stantons worked in the office of the Gas and Electric Company, and they paid a whole month's rent in advance, which was a very good thing for us. They were nice young men, and after dinner every night they would come out to the kitchen to tell Mama how much they enjoyed her cooking.

After they got better acquainted with Miss Durant, they teased her about her "rabbit food" and made bets with each other as to which of them would be the first to coax her to eat a big, thick steak—medium rare.

Mama was very proud of her three boarders; she listened to their chattering and laughter and said it was going to be fine when we had the hospital bills paid up and the money back to the Aunts. Then we would get more furniture and more boarders. Enough to fill all the chairs in the dining room. The Stanton brothers said they knew two more men from their place who would like to board with us.

On the day that Papa came home from the hospital, it was like a big party. We all stayed home from school, and Mama let Dagmar decorate the table real fancy.

Everything seemed all right again when Papa walked carefully into the kitchen and sat down in the rocking chair. His face was white, and he looked thinner, but his smile was just the same.

He had a bandage on his head, and he made little jokes about how they shaved off his hair when he wasn't looking.

It was strange, having Papa about the house during the day, but it was nice, too. He would be there in the kitchen when I came home from school, and I would tell him all that had happened.

Winford School had become the most important thing in life to me. I was friendly with the girls, and Carmelita and I were invited to all their parties. Every other Wednesday they came to my house, and we would sit up in my attic, drink chocolate, eat cookies, and make plans about our graduation.

We discussed "High"* and vowed that we would stay together all through the next four years. We were the only ones in our class going on to Lowell. Lowell, we told each other loftily, was "academic."

High: high school

We were enthralled* with our superiority. We were going to be the first class at Winford to have evening graduation exercises; we were having a graduation play; and we were

making our own graduation dresses in sewing class.

And when I was given the second lead in the play—the part of the Grecian boy—I found my own great importance hard to bear. I alone, of all the girls, had to go downtown to the costumer's to rent a wig. A coarse black wig that smelled of disinfectant, but made me feel like Geraldine Farrar.* At every opportunity, I would put it on and have Papa listen to my part of the play.

Geraldine Farrar: an American opera singer (1882–1967)

Then the girls started talking about their graduation presents.

Madeline said she was getting an onyx ring with a small diamond. Hester was getting a real honest-to-goodness wrist watch, and Thyra's family was going to add seven pearls to the necklace they had started for her when she was a baby. Even Carmelita was getting something special; her sister

Rose was putting a dollar every payday into an ivory manicure set.

I was intrigued, and wondered what great surprise my family had in store for me. I talked about it endlessly, hoping for some clue. It would be terrible if my present weren't as nice as the rest.

"It is the custom, then," Mama asked, "the giving of gifts when one graduates?"

"My goodness, Mama," I said, "it's practically the most important time there is in a girl's life—when she graduates."

I had seen a beautiful pink celluloid* dresser set at Mr. Schiller's drugstore, and I set my heart upon it. I dropped hint after hint, until Nels took me aside and reminded me that we did not have money for that sort of thing. Had I forgotten that the Aunts and the hospital must be paid up? That just as soon as Papa was well enough, he must do the Beauchamp job for no pay?

celluloid: similar to plastic

"I don't care," I cried recklessly, "I must have a graduation present. Why, Nels, think how I will feel if I don't get any. When the girls ask me—"

Nels got impatient and said he thought I was turning into a spoiled brat. And I retorted that since he was a boy, he naturally couldn't be expected to understand.

When Mama and I were alone one day, she asked me how I would like her silver brooch for a graduation present. Mama thought a lot of that brooch—it had been her mother's.

"Mama," I said reasonably, "what in the world would I want an old brooch for?"

"It would be like an—an heirloom, Katrin. It was your grandmother's."

"No, thank you, Mama."

"I could polish it up, Katrin."

I shook my head. "Look, Mama, a graduation present is something like—well, it's like that beautiful dresser set in Mr. Schiller's window."

There, now, I had told. Surely, with such a hint—

Mama looked worried, but she didn't say anything. Just pinned the silver brooch back on her dress.

I was so sure that Mama would find some way to get me the dresser set, I bragged to the girls as if it were a sure thing. I even took them by Schiller's window to admire it. They agreed with me that it was wonderful. There was a comb, a clothesbrush, and even something called a "hair receiver*."

---

hair receiver: ceramic, bronze, or crystal container in which hair from a hair brush was placed

---

Graduation night was a flurry of excitement.

I didn't forget a single word of my part in the play. Flushed and triumphant, I heard Miss Scanlon say that I was every bit as good as Hester, who had taken elocution* lessons for years. And when I went up to the platform for my diploma, the applause for me was long and loud. Of course, the Aunts and Uncles were all there, and Uncle Ole and Uncle Peter could clap very loud, but I pretended that it was because I was so popular.

---

elocution: art of speaking that emphasizes gesture, manner, and delivery

---

And when I got home—there was the pink celluloid dresser set!

Mama and Papa beamed at my delight, but Nels and Christine, I noticed, didn't say anything. I decided that they were jealous, and felt sorry that they would not join me in my joy.

I carried the box up to my attic and placed the comb and brush carefully on my dresser. It took me a long while to arrange everything

to my satisfaction. The mirror, so. The pincushion, here. The hair receiver, there.

Mama let me sleep late the next morning. When I got down for breakfast, she had already gone downtown to do her shopping. Nels was reading the want-ad section of the paper. Since it was vacation, he was going to try to get a job. He read the jobs aloud to Papa, and they discussed each one.

After my breakfast, Christine and I went upstairs to make the beds. I made her wait while I ran up to my attic to look again at my wonderful present. Dagmar came with me, and when she touched the mirror, I scolded her so hard she started to cry.

Christine came up then and wiped Dagmar's tears and sent her down to Papa. She looked at me for a long time.

"Why do you look at me like that, Christine?"

"What do you care? You got what you wanted, didn't you?" And she pointed to the dresser set. "Trash," she said, "cheap trash."

"Don't you dare talk about my lovely present like that! You're jealous, that's what. I'll tell Mama on you."

"And while you're telling her," Christine said, "ask her what she did with her silver brooch. The one her very own dear mother gave her. Ask her that."

I looked at Christine with horror. "What? You mean—did Mama—?"

Christine walked away.

I grabbed up the dresser set and ran down the stairs to the kitchen. Papa was drinking his second cup of coffee, and Dagmar was playing with her doll in front of the stove. Nels had left. "Papa, oh, Papa!" I cried. "Did Mama— Christine says—" I started to cry then, and Papa had me sit on his lap.

"There now," he said, and patted my shoulder. "There now."

And he dipped a cube of sugar into his coffee and fed it to me. We were not allowed to drink coffee—even with lots of milk in it—until we were considered grown-up, but all of us children loved that occasional lump of sugar dipped in a cup of coffee.

After my hiccuping and sobbing had stopped, Papa talked to me very seriously. It was like this, he said. I had wanted the graduation present. Mama had wanted my happiness more than she had wanted the silver brooch. So she had traded it to Mr. Schiller for the dresser set.

"But I never wanted her to do that, Papa. If I had known—I would never have let her—"

"It was what Mama wanted to do, Katrin."

"But she loved it so. It was all she had of Grandmother's."

"She always meant it to be for you, Katrin."

I stood up slowly; I knew what I must do.

And all the way up to Mr. Schiller's drugstore, the graduation present in my arms, I thought of how hard it must have been for Mama to ask Mr. Schiller to take the brooch as payment. It was never easy for Mama to talk to strangers.

Mr. Schiller examined the dresser set with care. He didn't know, he said, about taking it back. After all, a bargain was a bargain, and he had been thinking of giving the brooch to his wife for her birthday next month.

Recklessly, I mortgaged my vacation.

If he would take back the dresser set, if he would give me back my brooch, I would come in and work for him every single day, even Saturdays. "I'll shine the showcases," I begged. "I'll sweep the floor for you."

Mr. Schiller said that would not be necessary. Since I wanted the brooch back so

badly, he would call the deal off. But if I was serious about working during vacation, he might be able to use me.

So I walked out of Mr. Schiller's drugstore not only with Mama's brooch, but with a job that started the next morning. I felt very proud. The dresser set suddenly seemed a childish and silly thing.

I put the brooch on the table in front of Papa.

He looked at me proudly. "Was it so hard to do, Daughter?"

"Not so hard as I thought." I pinned the brooch to my dress. "I'll wear it always," I said. "I'll keep it forever."

"Mama will be glad, Katrin."

Papa dipped a lump of sugar and held it out to me. I shook my head. "Somehow," I said, "I just don't feel like it, Papa."

"So?" Papa said. "So?"

And he stood up and poured out a cup of coffee and handed it to me.

"For me?" I asked wonderingly.

Papa smiled and nodded. "For my grown-up daughter," he said.

I sat up straight in my chair. And felt very proud as I drank my first cup of coffee.

ABOUT THE AUTHOR

Kathryn Forbes (1909–66) was born Kathryn Anderson to her American father and Norwegian-immigrant mother. After graduating from high school, the San Francisco native married Robert McLean. Under the pen name "Forbes" (from her paternal grandmother), she began writing magazine articles and radio scripts in addition to short stories. Her book *Mama's Bank Account*, a collection of semiautobiographical stories such as "Mama and the Graduation Present," is about a Norwegian-American family early in the 1900s. The book began as a single story published in the *Toronto Star Weekly* and was then republished in *Reader's Digest*. Mama and her unique ability to stretch every penny as far as it could go was an instant success with American readers, for whom the Great Depression was scarcely a thing of the past. Thousands wrote, clamoring for more stories about Mama. The book was so popular that the U.S. War Department ordered 50,000 copies sent to the soldiers overseas. It was made into a talking book for the blind, became a popular television series that ran for eight years (1949–57), and was dramatized under the title *I Remember Mama*.

THINKING ZONE

When you hear someone talk about the **theme** of a piece of literature, that person is referring to the recurring or emerging idea that exists within the work. When an author states the theme outright through the words of the characters or through the narration, the theme is said to be an **explicit theme**. In "Weep No More, My Lady," the theme is explicitly stated by Uncle Jesse when he tells Skeeter that "Certain things are right and certain things are wrong. . . . When you learn that, then you're fit'n to be a man." Sometimes an author chooses instead to suggest a theme through the details of the story. This type of theme is an **implicit theme**. A story or novel may have more than one theme. Look again at this portion from *Mama's Bank Account* and consider the theme of the story and the way (or ways) in which the author reveals the theme.

Third-person point of view—*perspective in literature that uses third-person pronouns such as it, he, and she to tell a story*

1. *[interpretive]* From what point of view—first- or third-person—is the story told? How can you tell? How does this affect the story?

   _____

   _____

   _____

2. *[literal]* Why did Katrin initially choose the dresser set over her mother's brooch?

   _____

   _____

   _____

3. *[critical]* What is ironic about Katrin's wanting the dresser set more than the brooch?

   _____

   _____

   _____

4. *[literal]* At what specific point in the story does Katrin undergo a change in attitude?

_____

_____

_____

_____

_____

5. *[interpretive/critical]* What is the **theme** of this selection? Is the theme **explicit** or **implicit**?

_____

_____

_____

_____

_____

6. *[critical]* In what ways might one say that the themes of "Weep No More, My Lady" and "Mama and the Graduation Present" are alike? List specific actions by the characters that point to the themes.

_____

_____

_____

_____

_____

7. *[critical]* What is the meaning of the title "Mama and the Graduation Present"?

_____

_____

_____

_____

_____

THE BROTHERS

BJÖRNSTJERNE BJÖRNSON

Solomon, the wisest of men, wrote, "A brother offended is harder to be won than a strong city: and their contentions are like the bars of a castle" (Prov. 18:19). The following story vividly illustrates this proverb. More importantly, this narrative shows how personal choices rooted in pride and selfishness can turn minor misunderstandings into bitter rivalries.

The schoolmaster's name was Baard, and he had a brother named Anders. They thought a great deal of each other, enlisted together, lived together in town, went through the war together, served in the same company, and both rose to the rank of corporal. When they came home from the war, people said they were two fine stalwart fellows.

Then their father died. He left much personal property, which it was difficult to divide, and therefore they said to each other that they would not let this come between them, but would put the property up at auction, that each might buy what he wanted, and both share the proceeds. And it was so done.

But the father had owned a large gold watch, which had come to be known far and wide, for it was the only gold watch people in those parts had ever seen. When this watch was put up, there were many wealthy men who wanted it, but when both brothers began to bid, all the others desisted. Now Baard expected that Anders would let him have it, and Anders expected the same of Baard. They bid in turn, each trying the other out, and as they bid they looked hard at each other. When the watch had gone up to twenty dollars, Baard began to feel that this was not kind of his brother, and bid over him until he almost reached thirty. When Anders did not withdraw even then, Baard felt that Anders no longer remembered how good he had often been to him, and that he was furthermore the elder of the two; and the watch went over thirty. Anders still kept on. Baard then raised the price to forty dollars with one bound, and no longer looked at his brother. It grew very still in the auction room; only the bailiff* repeated the figures quietly. Anders thought, as he stood there, that if Baard could afford to go to forty dollars, so could he, and if Baard begrudged him the watch, he might as well take it, and bid over him.

This to Baard seemed the greatest disgrace that had ever befallen him; he bid fifty dollars in a low voice. There were many people there, and Anders said to himself that he would not let his brother mock him before them all, and again raised the bid. Baard burst out laughing.

bailiff: a court officer

"One hundred dollars and my brotherhood into the bargain," he said, as he turned on his heel, and left the room.

A little later, as he stood saddling the horse he had just bought at the auction, a man came out to him.

"The watch is yours; Anders gave in."

The instant he heard the news, there welled up in him a sense of remorse; he thought of his brother and not of the watch. The saddle was already in place, but he paused, his hand on his horse, uncertain whether to mount. Many people came out, Anders among them, and when he saw his brother, with horse saddled, ready to leave, he little knew what Baard was turning over in his mind.

"Thanks for the watch, Baard!" he shouted over to him. "You shall never see the day when your brother shall tread on your heels!"

"Nor the day I shall darken your doors again!" Baard answered, his face pale, as he swung himself on his horse.

After that day neither of them ever set foot in the home where they had both lived with their father.

Anders married into a crofter's* family, not long afterwards, but he did not invite Baard to the wedding. Nor did Baard go to the church. The first year he was married, Anders lost his only cow. It was found dead one morning on the north side of the house, where it had been tethered, and no one could explain what it had died of. Other misfortunes befell him, and he fared from bad to worse. But the heaviest blow came when his hayloft and all it contained burned down one night in the dead of winter. No one knew how the fire had started.

crofter: a tenant farmer

"This has been done by someone who wishes me ill," Anders said, and all that night he wept. He became a poor man, and he lost all inclination to work.

The evening after the fire, Baard appeared at his brother's house. Anders lay on his bed, but sprang up as Baard entered.

"What do you want here?" he asked, then stopped short, and stood staring fixedly at his brother.

Baard waited a little before he answered.

"I want to help you, Anders; you're in a bad way."

"I'm faring no worse than you wished me to fare! Go—else I'm not sure I can master myself."

"You're mistaken, Anders; I regret—"

"Go, Baard, or God have mercy on us both!"

Baard drew back a step.

"If you want the watch," he said in a trembling voice, "you can have it."

"Go, Baard!" shrieked his brother, and Baard, unwilling to stay any longer, left.

In the meanwhile* Baard had fared thus. As soon as he heard of his brother's misfortunes, he had suffered a change of heart, but pride held him back. He felt urged to go to church, and there he vowed many a good resolve, but he lacked strength to carry them out. He frequently went so far that he could see the house, but either someone was just coming out, or there were strangers there, or Anders stood chopping wood outside—there was always something in the way.

---

*in the meanwhile: The translators intend to indicate the beginning of an extended recounting of events leading up to the fire.

But one Sunday, late in the winter, he again went to church, and that Sunday Anders too was there. Baard saw him. He had grown pale and thin, and he wore the same clothes he had worn when the brothers were together, although now they were old and patched. All through the service Anders looked steadily at the minister. To Baard it seemed that he was kind and gentle, and he recalled their childhood days and what a good boy Anders had been. That day Baard even went to communion, and he made a solemn vow to God that he would make up with his brother, come what might. This resolution swept through his soul as he drank the wine, and when he arose he felt an impulse to go over and take a seat beside him, but there was someone in the way, and Anders did not look up. After the service there was still something in the way; there were too many people about; Anders's wife was with him, and her he did not know. He decided it would be better to seek Anders in his home and have a quiet talk with him.

When evening came, he set out. He went right up to the door. Then he paused, and as he stood there listening, he heard his name mentioned; it was the wife speaking.

"He went to communion this morning," she was saying. "I am sure he was thinking of you."

"No, it wasn't of me he was thinking," Anders replied. "I know him; he thinks only of himself."

For a long time nothing was said, and Baard sweat, as he stood there, although it was a cold night. The wife inside was busy with a kettle; the fire on the hearth crackled and hissed; a child cried now and then, and Anders rocked it. At length the wife spoke again.

"I believe you are both thinking of each other though you won't admit it."

"Let us talk of something else," Anders answered.

After a little he got up to go out. Baard had to hide in the woodshed; but then Anders, too, came to the shed to get an armful of wood. From where he stood in the corner Baard could see him clearly. He had taken off his threadbare Sunday clothes and put on his uniform, just like Baard's own. These they had promised each other never to wear, but to pass on as heirlooms* to their children. Anders's was now patched and worn out, so that his strong, well-built frame seemed bundled in rags, while at the same time Baard could hear the gold watch ticking in his own pocket. Anders went over to the brushwood, but instead of bending down immediately to gather up his load, he leaned back against a pile of wood and looked up at the sky glimmering brightly with stars. Then he sighed heavily and muttered to himself, "Well—well—well—oh, Lord, oh, Lord!"

---

heirlooms: treasured objects passed down from generation to generation

---

As long as he lived, Baard never forgot those words. He wanted to step forward then, but the brother coughed, and it seemed so difficult. No more was needed to hold him back. Anders took his armful of fagots,* and as he went out, brushed past Baard so close that the twigs struck him in the face.

---

fagots: bundles of sticks or twigs

For fully ten minutes more he stood rooted to the spot, and it is doubtful how much longer he might have stayed, had not a chill, on top of the emotional stress, seized him, and set him shivering through and through. Then he went out. He frankly confessed to himself that he was too cowardly to enter now; wherefore he conceived another plan. From an ash barrel, which stood in the corner he had just left, he selected some bits of charcoal, found a pitchpine splinter, went up into the hayloft, closed the door, and struck a light. When he had lit the torch he searched about for the peg on which Anders hung his lantern when he came out early in the morning to thresh. Baard then took his gold watch and hung it on the peg, put out his light, and left. He felt so relieved in his mind that he raced over the snow like a youngster.

The day following he heard that the hayloft had burned down during the night. Presumably sparks had flown from the torch he had used while hanging up the watch.

This so overwhelmed Baard that all day he kept to himself as though he were ill, brought out his hymnbook, and sang until the people in the house thought something was wrong with him. But in the evening he went out. It was bright moonlight. He went over to his brother's place, dug around in the charred ruins of the fire, and found, sure enough, a little lump of melted gold—all that remained of the watch.*

---

all that remained of the watch: This is the end of the sequence of events leading up to the fire.

It was with this in his hand that he had gone in to his brother, anxious to explain everything, and to sue* for peace. But how he fared that evening has already been told.

---

sue: to petition or to appeal

A little girl had seen him digging in the ashes; some boys, on their way to a dance, had observed him go down toward his brother's the Sunday evening in question; and the people where he lived explained how strangely he had acted on the Monday following. And inasmuch as everyone knew that he and his brother were bitter enemies, these details were reported to the authorities, and an inquiry instituted. No one could prove anything against him, yet suspicion hovered around him. He could now less than ever approach his brother.

Anders had thought of Baard when the hayloft burned, but had said nothing. When he had seen him enter his house, the following evening, pale and strange, he had forthwith thought: he is smitten with remorse, but for such a terrible outrage against his brother there can be no forgiveness. Since then he heard how people had seen Baard go down toward his home the evening of the fire, and although nothing was brought to light in the inquiry, he felt convinced that his brother was the guilty one.

They met at the hearing, Baard in his good clothes, Anders in his worn-out rags. Baard looked at his brother as he entered, and Anders was conscious, in his inmost heart, of an anxious pleading in his eyes. He doesn't want me to say anything, thought Anders; and when he was asked whether he suspected his brother of the deed, he answered loudly and decisively, "No!"

Anders took to drinking heavily after that day, and it was not long before he was in a bad way. Even worse, however, fared Baard, although he did not drink; he was so changed that people hardly knew him.

Then late one evening a poor woman entered the little room Baard rented and asked him to come with her. He recognized her; it was his brother's wife. Baard understood at once what her errand was, turned deathly pale, dressed himself, and followed her without a word. A pale glimmer shone from Anders's window, now flickering, now vanishing, and this light they followed, for there was no path across the snow. When Baard again stood in the doorway, he was met with a strange odor which almost made him ill. They went in. A little child sat eating charcoal over by the hearth, its face all black, but it looked up and laughed and showed its white teeth. It was his brother's child.

Over on the bed, with all sorts of clothes over him, lay Anders, pale, emaciated,* his forehead high and smooth, and he stared at his brother with hollow eyes. Baard's knees trembled. He sat down at the foot of the bed and burst into uncontrollable weeping. The sick man looked at him intently and said nothing. At length he asked his wife to go out, but Baard motioned for her to remain. And then the two brothers began to talk to each other. They explained everything, from the day they bid for the watch down through the years to this day when they finally met again. Baard ended by taking out the lump of gold, which he always carried about him, and it came to light in the course of their talk that never for one single day in all these years had they been really happy.

---

emaciated: extremely thin

Anders did not say much, for he had little strength, but Baard watched by the bedside as long as Anders was ill.

"Now I am perfectly well," Anders said one morning, on awakening. "Now, brother, we shall live together always, just as in the old days, and never leave each other."

But that day he died.

The widow and the child Baard took home with him, and they were henceforth well taken care of. But what the brothers had talked of at the bedside came out through the walls and the night, and became generally known to all the people in the valley. Baard grew to be the most highly respected man among them. They all honored him as one who had had a great sorrow and had found peace again, or as one who had returned after a long absence. And Baard grew in strength of mind by reason of all their friendliness. He became a godly man, and wishing to be of some use, as he said, the old corporal turned schoolmaster. What he impressed upon the children, first and last, was love, and he himself practiced it till the children came to love him as a playmate and a father.

ABOUT THE AUTHOR

Björnstjerne Björnson (1832–1910) began writing while still a child. Although he was not an exceptional student, he edited a handwritten newspaper and enjoyed writing poetry. As a young adult, he combined his considerable journalistic skills with his love of the theater by reviewing plays for a local newspaper. In addition to serving as the stage director for the national theater in Bergen, he founded the Society for Norwegian Culture. His multitude of stories, poems, and plays all greatly enriched Norwegian literary heritage, an achievement for which he received the Nobel Prize in literature in 1903. Undoubtedly, Björnson's single greatest contribution to Norwegian culture is the poem "Ja Vi Elsker Dette Landet," which became Norway's national anthem.

Today Björnson is recognized primarily for his folktales and poetry. These tales, like "The Brothers," portray the struggles of the peasant class with nature and sometimes with each other. They also reflect Norwegian history in their resemblance to Old Norse tales in both style and characterization. In spite of the love of country that Björnson expresses in his stories, his radical political views caused him to be suspected of treason, and he spent most of the last thirty years of his life abroad.

THINKING ZONE

    Character flaws are weaknesses or moral faults that are revealed about characters in a story. Near the beginning of the previous story, Katrin's attitude toward her mother's brooch demonstrated some major character flaws in Katrin—selfishness, thoughtlessness, and arrogance. As the story progressed, Katrin underwent a change of heart and corrected her attitude. Of course, this is not true of every character in every story. In "The Brothers" you read about two men who, although aware of their faults, seem unwilling to change.

    Character flaws often lead to conflict between sets of characters. All conflict falls under one of two types: **external conflict**, or conflict between a character and an outside force such as society or nature (or your own brother), and **internal conflict**, or conflict within a character's mind between opposing thoughts and emotions. Look again at some of the stories you have read so far in this book. Which stories have external conflict and which have internal conflict?

1. *[critical]* What initial **character flaw** or flaws do both brothers demonstrate after their father dies and during the auction?

   _____

   _____

   _____

   _____

2. *[critical]* What **conflicts** are present within the story? Name at least one **external conflict** and one **internal conflict.**

   _____

   _____

   _____

   _____

3. *[interpretive]* Baard vows to God that he will make peace with his brother but cannot force himself to do so after church because "there was still something in the way." What kept Baard from speaking to Anders?

_____

_____

_____

_____

_____

_____

4. *[literal/critical]* What finally happens to the watch? How is this ironic?

_____

_____

_____

_____

5. *[interpretive]* A *tragedy* may be defined as a narrative in which the consequences of the action are disastrous for the protagonist(s). In what way is "The Brothers" a tragedy? Is the ending completely tragic?

_____

_____

_____

_____

6. *[appreciative]* Name a biblical story that is similar to "The Brothers."

_____

_____

_____

_____

PLEASING ALL THE WORLD

YIDDISH FOLKTALE

Sometimes a choice must be made about whom to please since no task is so daunting or so futile as attempting to satisfy everyone. This classic tale of a parent, a child, and a beast of burden appears in the folktales of many cultures. Sometimes the story includes a mother and daughter, sometimes a donkey or a horse—but always the same moral.

An old man and his ten-year-old son were leading a camel through the desert. Their way was long, the sun was hot, and they were tired. They met a man who looked at them amazed. "How foolish that you both go on foot," he said, "when the camel was created to carry people."

Heeding the stranger's words, the old man mounted the camel and his son followed on foot. A while later they met a second traveler, who said, "Have you no pity on your son? He's still a child with tender feet; look at them, cut to ribbons. How can a father allow his own child to suffer like that?"

The father, ashamed, dismounted and set his son upon the camel. But a while later they met a third traveler, who cried, "For shame—and in the heat of the day, too! A child has no right to ride while his old father walks."

So the old man hit on another idea. He and his son both mounted the camel, making themselves comfortable while the camel went on. But then they met a fourth traveler who threw up his hands in horror. "Abusing a dumb creature! Making him carry a double load! Have you no pity in your hearts?"

The father and son quickly dismounted. The father said, "Well, there's no help for it, we'll just have to carry the camel ourselves. Though someone will probably come along and say that it's stupid. No matter what we do, we can't please all the world."

THE MAGIC BROCADE

CHINESE FOLKTALE

Folktales often make use of conventions, which are devices, techniques, or plot points that appear throughout literature. Examples of conventional devices in folklore include the oft-quoted opening "Once upon a time" and stock characters (e.g., a wicked stepmother or stepfather, a prince or princess who appears in a different form, such as a frog or beast). As you read "The Magic Brocade," look for examples of literary conventions. Are there any elements that seem to part with what you consider conventional?

Once upon a time, long, long ago, there lived in a small village in the southern part of China a mother and her three sons. Since the poor woman was a widow, she had to support her growing family as best she could. Fortunately she was very skilled at weaving fine brocade.* This material was a specialty of the Chuang area where they lived and it was made of rich fabric with designs of silver, gold, and silk woven upon it. The widow was quite famous in the surrounding countryside for her brocades, as she had a special talent for making the birds and other animals and the flowers that she wove into her cloth appear lifelike. Some people even said that her flowers and animals and birds were even more beautiful than real ones.

brocade: fabric with intricate raised design

One day the widow had to go into the market place to sell some cloth she had just finished. It took her no time at all to get rid of it, for everyone was anxious to buy her work. When she had completed her business she strolled among the stalls, looking at all the interesting objects for sale. Suddenly her glance was caught by a beautiful picture and she paused. In the painting was a marvellous white house surrounded by vast fields and grand walks which led to glorious gardens bursting with fruit and flowers. Between the stately trees in the background could be glimpsed some smaller buildings, and among the fluttering leaves flew rare brightly plumed birds of all kinds.

Instantly the widow fell in love with the picture and bought it. When she got home she showed it to her three sons, who also thought it was very beautiful.

"Oh," sighed the widow, "wouldn't it be wonderful if we lived in such a place!"

The two elder sons shook their heads and laughed.

"My dear mother, that's only an idle dream," said the eldest.

"Perhaps it might happen in the next world," agreed the second son, "but not in this one."

Only the youngest son comforted her.

"Why don't you weave a copy of the picture into a brocade?" he suggested. With a gentle smile on his face, he added, "That will be nearly as good as living in it."

This thought made the mother very happy. Right away she went out and bought all the coloured silk yarns she needed. Then she set up her loom and began to weave the design of the painting into the brocade.

Day and night, month after month, the mother sat at her loom weaving her silks. Though her back ached and her eyes grew strained from the exacting work, still she would not stop. She worked as if possessed. Gradually the two elder sons became annoyed.

One day the eldest one said with irritation, "Mother, you weave all day but you never sell anything."

"Yes!" grumbled the second. "And we have to earn money for the rice you eat by chopping wood. We're tired of all this hard work."

The youngest son didn't want his mother to be worried. He told his brothers not to complain and promised that he would look after everything. From then on, every morning he went up the mountain by himself and chopped enough wood to take care of the whole family.

Day after day the mother continued her weaving. At night she burned pine branches to make enough light. The branches smoked so much that her eyes became sore and bloodshot. But still she would not stop.

A year passed.

Tears from the mother's eyes began to drop upon the picture. She wove the crystal liquid into a bright clear river and also into a charming little fish pond.

Another year went by.

Now the tears from the mother's eyes turned into blood and dropped like red jewels upon the cloth. Quickly she wove them into a flaming sun and into brilliant red flowers.

Hour after hour, without a moment's stop, the widow went on weaving.

Finally, at the end of the third year, her brocade was done. The mother stepped away from her work and smiled with pride and with great happiness. There it all was: the beautiful house, the breathtaking gardens filled with exotic flowers and fruit, the

brilliant birds, and beyond in the vast fields sheep and cattle grazing contentedly upon the grass.

Suddenly a great wind from the west howled through the house. Catching up the rare brocade it sped through the door and disappeared over the hill. Frantically the mother chased after her beautiful treasure, only to see it blown high into the sky, far beyond her reach. It flew straight towards the east and in a twinkling it had completely vanished.

The heartbroken mother, unable to bear such a calamity,* fell into a deep faint. Carefully her three sons carried her into the house and laid her upon the bed. Hours later, after sipping some ginger broth, the widow slowly came to herself.

---

calamity: disaster or loss

"My son," she implored her eldest, "go to the east and find my brocade for me. It means more to me than life."

The boy nodded and quickly set out on his journey. After travelling eastward for more than a month, he came to a mountain pass where an old white-haired woman sat in front of a stone house. Beside her stood a handsome stone horse which looked as though it longed to eat the red fruit off the pretty tree that grew next to it. As the eldest boy passed by, the old lady stopped him.

"Where are you going, young man?" she asked.

"East," he said, and told her the story of the brocade.

"Ah!" she said, "the brocade your mother wove has been carried away by the fairies of the Sun Mountain because it was so beautifully made. They are going to copy it."

"But, tell me, how can I recover it?" begged the boy.

"That will be very difficult," said the old woman. "First, you have to knock out two

of your front teeth and put them into the mouth of my stone horse. Then he will be able to move and to eat the red fruit hanging from this tree. When he has eaten ten pieces, then you can mount him. He will take you directly to the Sun Mountain. But first you will have to pass through the Flame Mountain which burns with a continuous fierceness."

Here the old lady offered a warning. "You must not utter a word of complaint, for if you do you will instantly be burned to ashes. When you have arrived at the other side, you must then cross an icy sea." With a grave nod she whispered, "And if you give the slightest shudder, you will immediately sink to the bottom."

After hearing all this, the eldest son felt his jaw and thought anxiously of the burning fire and lashing sea waves. He went white as a ghost.

The old woman looked at him and laughed.

"You won't be able to stand it, I can see," she said. "Don't go. I'll give you a small iron box full of gold. Take it and live comfortably."

She fetched the box of gold from the stone house and gave it to the boy. He took it happily and went away. On his way home he began thinking about all the money he now had. "This gold will enable me to live very well. If I take it home, I will have to share it. Spending it all on myself will be much more fun than spending it on four people."

He decided right then and there not to go home and turned instead to the path which led to a big city.

At home the poor mother waited two months for her eldest son to return, but he did not come back. Gradually her illness got worse. At length she sent her second son to bring the brocade back.

When the boy reached the mountain pass he came upon the old woman at the stone house, who told him the same things she had told his older brother. As he learned all that he must do in order to obtain the brocade, he became frightened and his face paled. Laughing, the woman offered him a box of gold, just as she had his brother. Greatly relieved, the boy took it and went on his way, deciding also to head for the city instead of returning home.

After waiting and waiting for the second son to return home, the widow became desperately ill. At last she turned blind from weeping. Still neither of her sons ever came back.

The youngest son, beside himself with worry, begged his mother to let him go in search of the brocade.

"I'll bring it back to you, mother, I promise."

Faint with exhaustion and despair, the widow nodded weakly.

Travelling swiftly, the youngest son took only half a month to arrive at the mountain pass. There he met the old woman in front of the stone house. She told him exactly the same things that she had told his two brothers, but added, "My son, your brothers each went away with a box of gold. You may have one, too."

With steady firmness the boy refused. "I shall not let these difficulties stop me," he declared. "I am going to bring back the brocade that took my mother three years to weave."

Instantly he knocked two teeth out of his mouth and put them into the mouth of the handsome stone horse. The stone horse came alive and went to the tall green tree and ate ten pieces of red fruit hanging from its branches. As soon as it had done this, the horse lifted its elegant head, tossed its silver mane, and neighed. Quickly the boy mounted its back, and together they galloped off towards the east.

After three days and nights the young son came to Flame Mountain. On every side fires spat forth wildly. The boy stared for a moment at the terrifying sight, then spurring his horse he dashed courageously up the flaming mountain, enduring the ferocious heat without once uttering a sound.

Once on the other side of the mountain, he came to a vast sea. Great waves frosted with chunks of ice crashed upon him as he made his way painfully across the freezing water. Though cold and aching, he held the horse's mane tightly, persisting in his journey without allowing himself to shudder.

Emerging on the opposite shore, he saw at once the Sun Mountain. Warm light flooded the air and flowers blossomed everywhere. On top of the mountain stood a marvellous palace and from it he could hear sounds of girlish laughter and singing.

Quickly the boy tapped his horse. It reared up and flew with great speed to the door of the palace. The boy got down and entered the front hall. There he found one hundred beautiful fairies, each sitting at a loom and weaving a copy of his mother's brocade.

The fairies were all very surprised to see him. One came forth at last and spoke.

"We shall finish our weaving tonight and you may have your mother's brocade tomorrow. Will it please you to wait here for the night?"

"Yes," said the son. He sat down, prepared to wait forever if necessary for his mother's treasure. Several fairies graciously attended him, bringing delicious fruit to refresh him. Instantly all his fatigue* disappeared.

fatigue: weariness

When dusk fell, the fairies hung from the centre of the ceiling an enormous pearl which shone so brilliantly it lit the entire room. Then, while they went on weaving, the youngest son went to sleep.

One fairy finally finished her brocade, but it was not nearly as well done as the one the widow had made. The sad fairy felt she could not part with the widow's brocade and longed to live in that beautiful human world, so she embroidered a picture of herself on the original work.

When the young son woke up just before daylight, the fairies had all gone, leaving his mother's cloth under the shining pearl. Not waiting for daybreak the boy quickly clasped it to his chest and, mounting his horse, galloped off in the waning* moonlight. Bending low upon the stallion's flowing mane and clamping his mouth tightly shut, he passed again through the icy sea and up and down the flaming mountain. Soon he reached the mountain pass where the old woman stood waiting for him in front of her stone house. Smiling warmly, she greeted him.

waning: fading, declining

"Young man, I see you have come back."

"Yes, old woman." After he dismounted, the woman took his teeth from the horse and put them back into his mouth. Instantly the horse turned back to stone. Then she went inside the house and returned with a pair of deerskin shoes.

"Take these," she said, "they will help you get home."

When the boy put them on he found he could move as though he had wings. In a moment he was back in his own house. He entered his mother's room and unrolled the brocade. It gleamed so brightly that the widow gasped and opened her eyes, finding her sight entirely restored.

Instantly cured of all illness, she rose from her bed. Together she and her son took the precious work outside to see it in the bright light. As they unrolled it, a strange, fragrant breeze sprang up and blew upon the

brocade, drawing it out longer and longer and wider and wider until at last it covered all the land in sight. Suddenly the silken threads trembled and the picture burst into life. Scarlet flowers waved in the soft wind. Animals stirred and grazed upon the tender grasses of the vast fields. Golden birds darted in and out of the handsome trees and about the grand white house that commanded the landscape.

It was all exactly as the mother had woven it, except that now there was a beautiful girl in red standing by the fish pond. It was the fairy who had embroidered herself into the brocade.

The kind widow, thrilled with her good fortune, went out among her poor neighbours and asked them to come to live with her on her new land, and share the abundance of her fields and gardens.

It will not surprise you to learn that the youngest son married the beautiful fairy girl and that they lived together very happily for many, many years.

One day two beggars walked slowly down the road. They were the two elder sons of the widow, and it was clear from their appearance that they had long ago squandered all the gold they had. Astonished to see such a beautiful place, they decided to stop and beg something from the owner. But when they looked across the fields, they suddenly recognized that the people happily picnicking by the pretty stream were none other than their very own mother and brother—and a beautiful lady who must be their brother's wife. Blushing with shame, they quickly picked up their begging sticks and crept silently away.

THINKING ZONE

If as a child you heard the story of the Three Bears or Aesop's fable about the Crow and the Pitcher, you have heard an example of **folklore**. *Folklore* is the term applied to the songs, fairy tales, tall tales, and legends transmitted primarily by word of mouth—something called **oral tradition**. In most instances, speaking was the primary means of passing along these stories in cultures where there was either no written language or few people who could read or write. Usually the author is unknown. A **folktale** is the general term given to a popular myth, legend, tall tale, or fairy tale that has been passed on from person to person through diverse cultures. Many folktales are adopted by several different cultures and are easily recognizable as the same basic story with the same theme and similar characters. The story of Cinderella is an example of such a tale. It is estimated that there are over five hundred versions of this folktale just in Europe!

Folktales were often used to teach **morals** (truths about life) and to illustrate **proverbs** (brief but wise sayings). As you review the folktales in this unit, notice the proverbs and consider what truth or moral is being taught.

1. *[interpretive/appreciative]* What is the **moral** expressed in "Pleasing All the World"? Do you agree? Is there a solution to this problem?

   _____

   _____

   _____

   _____

   _____

2. *[appreciative]* The story of "Pleasing All the World" has been passed down in the **oral tradition** all over the world, making it a staple in the **folklore** of many different countries. Relate a variation of this tale that you have heard or that you can think of.

   _____

   _____

3. *[critical]* Where do you find an example of foreshadowing in the **folktale** "The Magic Brocade"?

_____

_____

_____

_____

_____

Foreshadowing— *hinting at events that will occur later in the story.*

4. *[critical]* To which of the sons in "The Magic Brocade" would you apply the Kurdish **proverb** "One can never repay one's debt to one's mother"? Explain.

_____

_____

_____

_____

5. *[literal/interpretive]* What do the first two sons choose over the dangers involved in retrieving their mother's magic brocade? What does this tell you about them?

_____

_____

_____

6. *[interpretive]* What do you think the moral of "The Magic Brocade" is? Can you find similar admonitions in the Bible?

_____

_____

_____

_____

_____

_____

THE BLACKSMITH'S DILEMMA

AFRICAN FOLKTALE

Perhaps you are familiar with the saying "Old friends are the best friends." Have you ever thought about why this saying is true? In this folktale, the blacksmith realizes this very thing. Not only does he profit from his old friend, but his old friend, in turn, profits from him.

There was once a blacksmith* called Walukaga, who was very skilled at all kinds of metal-work. Every day a small crowd of people would gather at his smithy and watch him at work making hoes for the farmers, knives and spears for the hunters, or armlets and bracelets to decorate the young men and maidens.

blacksmith: one who forms and shapes iron with an anvil and hammer

Early one morning, as Walukaga was beginning work, pumping his sheepskin bellows* to make a glowing charcoal fire; a messenger from the king's court arrived.

bellows: a device for making a strong current of air

"His Majesty says you are to go and see him immediately. He has a job for you to do," said the messenger.

Walukaga was delighted and hastily putting on his best white robes he hurried off to the palace, wondering what the king wanted him to do. He passed many of his friends about their early-morning tasks in the dusty roads, and to all of them he shouted happily:

"The king has sent for me! He has some work for me to do. Wish me luck!"

Walukaga reached the palace and was shown into a little room by the gate, where he waited some time until the king was ready to receive him. Then he was taken into the inner courtyard where the king sat on a stool carved from a single piece of tree-trunk.

The blacksmith bowed to the ground, and when he rose the king said:

"I have sent for you, the most skilful blacksmith in the district, because I have a very special task to give you." He clapped his hands and several servants appeared with their arms full of odd-shaped pieces of iron which they placed at the king's feet.

"You are to take this metal and change it into a man," said the king. "Not just a statue, but a living man of iron who can walk and talk and think, and who has blood in his veins."

Walukaga was flabbergasted.* He searched the king's face to see whether perhaps this was a joke, but the king's dark, serious eyes

showed that he was in earnest, so Walukaga decided to go home and think it over.

flabbergasted: overcome with great surprise

"Yes, Your Majesty," he replied, bowing low once more, and the interview was over.

The king's servants helped the blacksmith carry the iron to his smithy,* and Walukaga followed them slowly, scarcely returning the greetings of his friends in the town, who wondered what was wrong. Later in the day they came to see him and when he told them what the king had commanded, they too fell silent.

smithy: forge

Everyone in that country knew that the king had the power of life and death over his subjects and that if anyone failed to carry out an order, he would be put to death, so poor Walukaga began to think his days were numbered. All day and all night he sat with his head in his hands, wondering how to find a solution to his problem. Of course, a number of people made suggestions. Could he not make an iron shell of a man and persuade somebody to get inside it and speak and walk? Should he run away to a far country and begin life afresh where he

was not known? Someone even suggested he bribe the palace cook to put poison in the king's food, since Walukaga himself would surely die within a few days unless the king died first.

Poor Walukaga! He became ill and thin, since he could not sleep or eat, and began roaming the bush* alone, speaking his thoughts aloud as he tried to think of a plan to save himself from death.

bush: land remote from settlement

One evening, as he walked through a deserted stretch of bush, he heard weird singing, and going closer to investigate, he discovered a boyhood friend of his who had now, alas, become mad and lived alone in the wild country outside the town.

"Greetings, Walukaga," called the madman, who had no difficulty in remembering the blacksmith, even though his mind was so often muddled about other things. "How kind of you to visit me. Come, sit down and share my supper."

The madman was harmless enough and Walukaga had nothing else to do, so he sat on a rock beside him and together they ate ripe berries and some honey which the madman had collected from the wild bees.

Walukaga suddenly realized that this was the first food he had eaten for several days, and felt better for it, so he decided to humour his old friend and told him the story of the king's demand. To his surprise, the madman sat quite still and listened to the end without interrupting.

"Well," concluded Walukaga, "that is my story; and if you can tell me what I am to do, you will be a better friend than any other, for they cannot help me."

Almost immediately the madman had the answer.

"I know what you must do," he said. "Go to the king and tell him that you can only make the kind of man he requires if you have special kinds of charcoal and water. Ask him to make all his subjects shave their heads and bring the hair to be burnt into charcoal and when you have a thousand loads of such charcoal, that will be enough. Then say you must have a hundred pots of water made up from the tears of the king's people, since only such water may be used to keep your fire from burning too fiercely."

When the madman had said this, he laughed uproariously for some minutes, while the blacksmith tried in vain to thank him for such good advice and then hurried off to the king's palace, in spite of the lateness of the hour.

He bowed low before the king and explained what he must have before he could begin work on the iron man. The king was quite agreeable and sent messages to all his subjects the next morning, commanding them to shave their heads for charcoal and to weep into their water-pots.

The people did their best, wondering at this strange request, and not daring to disobey the powerful king, but try as they would, it was impossible to collect more than two pots of tears or even one load of charcoal.

When the results of this proclamation were brought to the king, he sighed.

"Alas! I can see that we shall never be able to collect all the charcoal and water that Walukaga needs. Send for him to come here at once."

With shaking legs Walukaga approached the king, and as he looked up was relieved to see a smile on his face.

"Walukaga," he said. "You have asked something impossible. I see now that my people can never grow enough hair to produce a thousand loads of charcoal, nor weep enough tears to fill a hundred water-pots. I therefore exempt you from your task."

"Your Majesty," replied Walukaga. "I am indeed grateful to you, for you too, asked something impossible of me. I could never have made a living man from iron, try as I would."

Then all the people laughed when they realized how cleverly Walukaga had got out of his fix*, and the king allowed him to go home and continue his work at the smithy. But the blacksmith never forgot that it was his friend's advice which had saved him, and saw that the madman never went hungry or thirsty to the end of his life.

fix: difficult or embarrassing situation

THE NAIL

JAKOB AND WILHELM GRIMM

It is quite possible that the well-educated Grimm Brothers knew of a famous quotation of Ben Franklin's when they wrote this fable. Wrong thinking leads to wrong choices like those made by the careless and self-justifying merchant.

A merchant had done good business at the fair. All his wares had been sold, and his money bag was lined with gold and silver. Now he wanted to begin the journey homeward so that he could reach his house before nightfall. After he had packed his saddlebags with the money and set them on his horse, he rode away. At noon he rested in a city, and when he wanted to continue on his way, the stableboy brought his horse to him but said, "Sir, there's a nail missing in the shoe of the left hind foot."

"Let it stay missing," responded the merchant. "The shoe will certainly hold during the six hours I have yet to go. I'm in a hurry."

In the afternoon, when he dismounted again and had the horse fed, a stableboy came to him and said, "Sir, there's a shoe missing from the left hind foot of your horse. Should I take the horse to a blacksmith?"

"Let it stay missing," replied the man. "The horse will certainly be able to hold out during the couple of hours that are left. I'm in a hurry."

He rode on, but not for long. The horse began to limp. It did not limp for very long before it began to stumble, and it did not stumble for very long before it fell to the ground and broke a leg. The merchant had to leave the horse lying there, while he took the saddlebags, swung them over his shoulder, and made his way home on foot. It was not until late in the night that he reached his house. "It was the cursed nail," he said to himself, "that caused all my misfortune."

Haste makes waste.

About the Author

Wilhelm Carl Grimm (1786–1859) and Jacob Ludwig Carl Grimm (1785–1863) were born in Hanau, Germany. After the death of their father, the brothers sought admission to the University of Marburg, where they planned to study law. Wilhelm received his law degree, but his brother Jacob moved to Paris to study. In 1808 the Grimm brothers' mother died, and Jacob returned to Germany. The brothers began collecting fairy tales from neighbors and relatives who lived in the surrounding area. The brothers worked well together, and in 1812 they published their first volume of eighty-six stories and folktales. The entire collection numbered eight editions, with two hundred stories and folktales and ten legends.

The brothers worked at both the University of Göttingen and the University of Berlin as professors and librarians. In 1838 the Brothers Grimm began work on a thirty-two-volume German dictionary that attempted to trace the origin of every word in the language. The first volume, through the word *Biermolke*, was published in 1854 with 1,824 pages. Both brothers died long before the completion of the final publication of the German dictionary in 1960, but during their lifetimes they made lasting contributions to the field of linguistics.

THINKING ZONE

If you were to examine the folktales of different parts of the world, it is likely that you would notice both similarities and differences. For example, the characters, themes, and techniques used to tell the stories are very similar. The differences lie in the conventions of a particular group's culture. The previous Thinking Zone mentioned the story of Cinderella as being a folktale that appears in many forms and cultures. In some versions the little ash girl is mistreated by a stepmother, and in others it is a stepfather who is so cruel. In some a beautiful fairy godmother helps her escape her misery, and in others it is a kindly tutor. Disney made famous a version in which several comic mice help Cinderella outfit herself for the prince's ball.

Regardless of country or culture, it is typical for many stories to feature a decision that must be made by the **protagonist**, or main character. In many instances, the protagonist's fate is determined by whether he makes the right choice or is able to think quickly and say or do the right thing. The protagonist may also be referred to as a **hero** or **heroine**.

1. *[critical]* Who is the **protagonist** or **hero** in "The Blacksmith's Dilemma"?

_____

_____

2. *[critical]* A popular type of African folktale is the trickster tale, in which a weak character uses his wits to survive against a greater or stronger character. Do you think that "The Blacksmith's Dilemma" is a trickster tale? Why or why not?

_____

_____

_____

_____

_____

_____

3. *[critical]* Name a biblical story in which a character used creative means to solve a dilemma.

_____

_____

_____

_____

_____

4. *[interpretive]* In what way does the saying "Haste makes waste" sum up the story of "The Nail"?

_____

_____

_____

_____

_____

5. *[critical]* Are there any other morals that "The Nail" teaches?

_____

_____

_____

_____

_____

6. *[appreciative]* Which of the folktales that you have read so far has been the most memorable or effective? What has made it so?

_____

_____

_____

_____

_____

THE GOLDEN TOUCH

NATHANIEL HAWTHORNE

Too often people desire things that really do not matter. Perhaps the desire is the prestige of friends or the glamour of a position or the salary of a particular job. But when the desire is achieved, does it really satisfy? This fable, like others you have read, appears in the literature of many cultures. The common thread is the early realization that the king has made a disastrous choice.

Once upon a time, there lived a very rich man, and a king besides, whose name was Midas; and he had a little daughter, whom nobody but myself had ever heard of, and whose name I either never knew, or have entirely forgotten. So, because I love odd names for little girls, I choose to call her Marygold.

This King Midas was fonder of gold than of anything else in the world. He valued his royal crown chiefly because it was composed of that precious metal. If he loved anything better, or half so well, it was the one little maiden who played so merrily around her father's footstool. But the more Midas loved his daughter, the more did he desire and seek for wealth. He thought, foolish man! that the best thing he could possibly do for this dear child would be to bequeath her the immensest pile of yellow, glistening coin, that had ever been heaped together since the world was made.

At length (as people always grow more and more foolish, unless they take care to grow wiser and wiser), Midas had got to be so exceedingly unreasonable, that he could scarcely bear to see or touch any object that was not gold. He made it his custom, therefore, to pass a large portion of every day in a dark and dreary apartment, under ground, at the basement of his palace. It was here that he kept his wealth. To this dismal hole—for it was little better than a dungeon—Midas took himself, whenever he wanted to be particularly happy. Here, after carefully locking the door, he would take a bag of gold coin, or a gold cup as big as a wash-bowl, or a heavy golden bar, or a peck-measure of gold-dust, and bring them from the obscure corners of the room into the one bright and narrow sunbeam that fell from the dungeon-like window. He valued the sunbeam for no other reason but that his treasure would not shine without its help.

Midas was enjoying himself in his treasure-room, one day, as usual, when he perceived a shadow fall over the heaps of gold; and, looking suddenly up, what should he behold but the figure of a stranger, standing in the bright and narrow sunbeam! It was a young man, with a cheerful and ruddy face. The stranger's aspect, indeed, was so good-humoured and kindly, if not beneficent,* that it would have been unreasonable to suspect him of intending any mischief. It was far more probable that he came to do Midas a favour. And what could that favour be, unless to multiply his heaps of treasure?

beneficent: characterized by performing acts of kindness

The stranger gazed about the room; and when his lustrous smile had glistened upon all the golden objects that were there, he turned again to Midas.

"You are a wealthy man, friend Midas!" he observed. "I doubt whether any other four walls on earth contain so much gold as you have contrived to pile up in this room."

"I have done pretty well—pretty well," answered Midas, in a discontented tone. "But, after all, it is but a trifle,* when you consider that it has taken me my whole life to get it together. If one could live a thousand years, he might have time to grow rich!"

trifle: small amount

"What!" exclaimed the stranger. "Then you are not satisfied?"

Midas shook his head.

"And pray what would satisfy you?" asked the stranger. "Merely for the curiosity of the thing, I should be glad to know."

Midas paused and meditated. He felt a presentiment* that this stranger, with such a golden lustre in his good-humoured smile, had come hither with both the power and the purpose of gratifying his utmost wishes. Now, therefore, was the fortunate moment, when he had but to speak, and obtain whatever possible, or seemingly impossible thing, it might come into his head to ask. So he thought, and thought, and thought, and heaped up one golden mountain upon another, in his imagination, without being able to imagine them big enough. At last, a bright idea occurred to King Midas.

presentiment: a sense that something is about to occur

Raising his head he looked the lustrous stranger in the face.

"Well, Midas," observed the visitor, "I see that you have at length hit upon something that will satisfy you. Tell me your wish.'

"It is only this," replied Midas. "I am weary of collecting my treasures with so much trouble, and beholding the heap so diminutive* after I have done my best. I wish everything that I touch to be changed to gold."

"The Golden Touch!" exclaimed he. "You certainly deserve credit, friend Midas, for striking out so brilliant a conception. But are you quite sure that this will satisfy you?"

"How could it fail?" said Midas.

"And will you never regret the possession of it?"

"What could induce me?" asked Midas. "I ask nothing else to render me perfectly happy."

"Be it as you wish, then," replied the stranger, waving his hand in token of farewell. "To-morrow, at sunrise, you will find yourself gifted with the Golden Touch."

Whether Midas slept as usual that night the story does not say. At any rate, day had hardly peeped over the hills, when King Midas was broad awake, and, stretching his arms out of bed, began to touch the objects that were within reach. He was anxious to prove whether the Golden Touch had really come, according to the stranger's promise. So he laid his finger on a chair by the bedside, and on various other things, but was grievously disappointed to perceive that they remained of exactly the same substance as before.

He lay in a very disconsolate mood, regretting the downfall of his hopes, and kept growing sadder and sadder, until the earliest sunbeam shone through the window, and gilded the ceiling over his head. It seemed to Midas that this bright yellow sunbeam was reflected in rather a singular way on the white covering of the bed. Looking more closely, what was his astonishment and delight, when he found that this linen fabric had been transmuted* to what seemed a woven texture of the purest and brightest gold! The Golden Touch had come to him, with the first sunbeam!

Midas started up, in a kind of joyful frenzy, and ran about the room grasping at everything that happened to be in his way. He seized one of the bed-posts, and it became immediately a fluted* golden pillar. He pulled aside a window curtain, in order to admit a clear spectacle of the wonders which he was performing; and the tassel grew heavy in his hand—a mass of gold. He took up a book from the table. At his first touch, it assumed the appearance of such a splendidly bound and gilt-edged volume as one often meets with nowadays; but, on running his fingers through the leaves, behold! it was a bundle of thin golden plates, in which all the wisdom of the book had grown illegible. He hurriedly put on his clothes, and was enraptured to see himself in a magnificent suit of gold cloth, which retained its flexibility and softness, although it burdened him a little with its weight. He drew out his handkerchief, which little Marygold had hemmed for him. That was likewise gold, with the dear child's neat and pretty stitches running all along the border, in gold thread!

Somehow or other, this last transformation did not quite please King Midas. He would rather that his little daughter's handiwork should have remained just the same as when she climbed his knee, and put it into his hand.

But it was not worth while to vex* himself about a trifle. Midas now took his spectacles from his pocket, and put them on his nose, in order that he might see more distinctly what he was about. In those days, spectacles for common people had not been invented, but were already worn by kings;

ordinary purposes, and little Marygold will soon be old enough to read to me."

Wise King Midas was so exalted by his good fortune that the palace seemed not sufficiently spacious to contain him. He therefore went downstairs, and smiled, on observing that the balustrade* of the staircase became a bar of burnished gold, as his hand passed over it in his descent. He lifted the door latch (it was brass only a moment ago, but golden when his fingers quitted* it), and emerged into the garden. Here, as it happened, he found a great number of beautiful roses in full bloom, and others in all the stages of lovely bud and blossom. Very delicious was their fragrance in the morning breeze. Their delicate blush was one of the fairest sights in the world; so gentle, so modest, and so full of sweet tranquillity did these roses seem to be.

balustrade: a rail and row of posts
quitted: released

But Midas knew a way to make them far more precious, according to his way of thinking, than roses had ever been before. So he took great pains in going from bush to bush, and exercised his magic touch most indefatigably;* until every individual flower and bud, and even the worms at the heart of some of them, were changed to gold. By the time this good work was completed, King Midas was summoned to breakfast; and, as the morning air had given him an excellent appetite, he made haste back to the palace.

indefatigably: tireless

else, how could Midas have had any? To his great perplexity, however, excellent as the glasses were, he discovered that he could not possibly see through them. But this was the most natural thing in the world; for, on taking them off, the transparent crystals turned out to be plates of yellow metal, and, of course, were worthless as spectacles, though valuable as gold. It struck Midas as rather inconvenient, that with all his wealth, he could never again be rich enough to own a pair of serviceable spectacles.

vex: to annoy

"It is no great matter, nevertheless," said he to himself, very philosophically. "We cannot expect any great good, without its being accompanied by some small inconvenience. The Golden Touch is worth the sacrifice of a pair of spectacles, at least, if not of one's very eyesight. My own eyes will serve for

Little Marygold had not yet made her appearance. Her father ordered her to be called, and, seating himself at table, awaited the child's coming, in order to begin his own breakfast. To do Midas justice, he really loved his daughter, and loved her so much the more this morning, on account of the good fortune which had befallen him. It was not a great while before he heard her coming along the passage crying bitterly. This circumstance surprised him, because Marygold was one of the cheerfullest little people whom you would see in a summer's day, and hardly shed a thimbleful of tears in a twelvemonth. Marygold slowly and disconsolately* opened the door, and showed herself with her apron at her eyes, still sobbing as if her heart would break.

disconsolately: dejectedly

"How now, my little lady?" cried Midas. "Pray what is the matter with you, this bright morning?"

Marygold, without taking the apron from her eyes, held out her hand, in which

was one of the roses which Midas had so recently transmuted.

"Beautiful!" exclaimed her father. "And what is there in this magnificent golden rose to make you cry?"

"Ah, dear father!" answered the child, as well as her sobs would let her; "it is not beautiful, but the ugliest flower that ever grew! As soon as I was dressed, I ran into the garden to gather some roses for you; because I know you like them, and like them better when gathered by your little daughter. But, oh dear, dear me! What do you think has happened? Such a misfortune! All the beautiful roses, that smelled so sweetly and had so many lovely blushes, are blighted and spoilt! They are grown quite yellow, as you see this one, and have no longer any fragrance! What can have been the matter with them?"

"Poh, my dear little girl—pray don't cry about it!" said Midas, who was ashamed to confess that he himself had wrought the change which so greatly afflicted her. "Sit down and eat your bread and milk! You will find it easy enough to exchange a golden rose like that (which will last hundreds of years) for an ordinary one, which would wither in a day."

"I don't care for such roses as this!" cried Marygold, tossing it contemptuously* away. "It has no smell, and the hard petals prick my nose!"

contemptuously: scornfully

Midas, meanwhile, had poured out a cup of coffee; and as he lifted a spoonful of coffee to his lips, and, sipping it, was astonished to perceive that, the instant his lips touched the liquid, it became molten gold, and, the next moment, hardened into a lump.

"Ha!" exclaimed Midas, rather aghast.

"What is the matter, father?" asked little Marygold, gazing at him, with the tears still standing in her eyes.

"Nothing, child, nothing," said Midas. "Eat your milk, before it gets quite cold."

He took one of the nice little trouts on his plate, and, by way of experiment, touched its tail with his finger. To his horror, it was immediately transmuted from an admirably fried brook trout into a gold fish, though not one of those goldfishes which people often keep in glass globes, as ornaments for the parlour. No; but it was really a metallic fish, and looked as if it had been very cunningly made by the nicest goldsmith in the world. Its little bones were now golden wires; its fins and tail were thin plates of gold; and there were marks of the fork in it, and all the delicate, frothy appearance of a nicely fried fish, exactly imitated in metal. A very pretty piece of work, as you may suppose; only King Midas, just at that moment, would much rather have had a real trout in his dish than this elaborate and valuable imitation of one.

"I don't quite see," thought he to himself, "how I am to get any breakfast!"

"Well, this is a quandary!"* thought he, leaning back in his chair, and looking quite enviously at little Marygold, who was now eating her bread and milk with great satisfaction. Such a costly breakfast before me, and nothing that can be eaten!"

quandary: a state of uncertainty

Hoping that, by dint* of great dispatch, he might avoid what he now felt to be a considerable inconvenience, King Midas next snatched a hot potato, and attempted to cram it into his mouth, and swallow it in a hurry. But the Golden Touch was too nimble for him. He found his mouth full, not of mealy potato, but of solid metal, which so burnt his tongue that he roared aloud, and, jumping up from the table, began to dance and stamp about the room, both with pain and affright.

dint: effort

"Father, dear father!" cried little Marygold, who was a very affectionate child, "pray what is the matter? Have you burnt your mouth?"

"Ah, dear child," groaned Midas dolefully, I don't know what is to become of your poor father!"

And, truly, did you ever hear of such a pitiable* case in all your lives? Here was literally the richest breakfast that could be set before a king, and its very richness made it absolutely good for nothing! The poorest labourer, sitting down to his crust of bread and cup of water, was far better off than King Midas, whose delicate food was really worth its weight in gold. And what was to be done? Already, at breakfast, Midas was excessively hungry. Would he be less so by dinner-time? And how ravenous would be his appetite for supper, which must undoubtedly consist of the same sort of indigestible dishes as those now before him! How many days, think you, would he survive a continuance of this rich fare?

pitiable: deserving of pity

These reflections so troubled wise King Midas, that he began to doubt whether, after all, riches are the one desirable thing in the world, or even the most desirable. But this was only a passing thought. So fascinated was Midas with the glitter of the yellow metal, that he would still have refused to give up the Golden Touch for so paltry* a consideration as a breakfast.

paltry: trivial

Nevertheless, so great was his hunger, and the perplexity of his situation, that he again groaned aloud, and very grievously too. Our pretty Marygold could endure it no longer. She sat a moment gazing at her father, and trying, with all the might of her little wits, to find out what was the matter with him. Then, with a sweet and sorrow-

ful impulse to comfort him, she darted from her chair, and running to Midas, threw her arms affectionately about his knees. He bent down and kissed her. He felt that his little daughter's love was worth a thousand times more than he had gained by the Golden Touch.

"My precious, precious Marygold!" cried he.

But Marygold made no answer.

Alas, what had he done? How fatal was the gift which the stranger bestowed! The moment the lips of Midas touched Marygold's forehead, a change had taken place. Her sweet, rosy face, so full of affection as it had been, assumed a glittering yellow colour, with yellow tear-drops congealing on her cheeks. Her beautiful brown ringlets took the same tint. Her soft and tender little form grew hard and inflexible within her father's encircling arms. Oh, terrible misfortune! The victim of his insatiable* desire for wealth, little Marygold was a human child no longer, but a golden statue!

insatiable: impossible to satisfy

It had been a favourite phrase of Midas, whenever he felt particularly fond of the child, to say that she was worth her weight in gold. And now the phrase had become literally true. And now, at last, when it was too late, he felt how infinitely a warm and tender heart, that loved him, exceeded in value all the wealth that could be piled up betwixt the earth and sky!

It would be too sad a story if I were to tell you how Midas, in the fullness of all his gratified desires, began to wring his hands and bemoan himself; and how he could neither bear to look at Marygold, nor yet to look away from her. Midas had only to wring his hands, and to wish that he was the poorest man in the wide world, if the loss of all his wealth might bring back the faintest rose-colour to his dear child's face.

While he was in this tumult of despair, he suddenly beheld a stranger standing near the door. Midas bent down his head, without speaking; for he recognized the same figure which had appeared to him the day before in the treasure-room, and had bestowed on him this disastrous faculty of the Golden Touch. The stranger's countenance still wore a smile, which seemed to shed a yellow lustre all about the room, and gleamed on little Marygold's image, and on the other objects that had been transmuted by the touch of Midas.

"Well, friend Midas," said the stranger, "pray how do you succeed with the Golden Touch?"

Midas shook his head.

"I am very miserable," said he.

"Very miserable, indeed!" exclaimed the stranger. "And how, happens that? Have I not faithfully kept my promise with you? Have you not everything that your heart desired?"

"Gold is not everything," answered Midas. "And I have lost all that my heart really cared for."

"Ah! So you have made a discovery since yesterday?" observed the stranger. "Let us see, then. Which of these two things do you think is really worth the most—the gift of the Golden Touch, or one cup of clear cold water?"

"Oh, blessed water!" exclaimed Midas. "It will never moisten my parched throat again!"

"The Golden Touch," continued the stranger, "or a crust of bread?'

"A piece of bread," answered Midas, "is worth all the gold on earth!"

"The Golden Touch," asked the stranger, "or your own little Marygold, warm, soft, and loving as she was an hour ago?"

"Oh, my child, my dear child!" cried poor Midas, wringing his hands. "I would not have given that one small dimple in her chin for the power of changing this whole big earth into a solid lump of gold!"

"You are wiser than you were, King Midas!" said the stranger, looking seriously at him. "Your own heart, I perceive, has not been entirely changed from flesh to gold. Were it so, your case would indeed be desperate. But you appear to be still capable of understanding that the commonest things, such as lie within everybody's grasp, are more valuable than the riches which so many mortals sigh and struggle after. Tell me, now, do you sincerely desire to rid yourself of this Golden Touch?"

"It is hateful to me," replied Midas.

A fly settled on his nose, but immediately fell to the floor; for it, too, had become gold. Midas shuddered.

"Go, then," said the stranger, "and plunge into the river that glides past the bottom of your garden. Take likewise a vase of the same water, and sprinkle it over any object that you may desire to change back again from gold into its former substance. If you do this in earnestness and sincerity, it may possibly repair the mischief which your avarice* has occasioned."

---

avarice: great desire for wealth

You will easily believe that Midas lost no time in snatching up a great earthen pitcher (but, alas! it was no longer earthen after he touched it), and hastening to the river-side. As he scampered along, and forced his way through the shrubbery, it was positively marvellous to see how the foliage turned yellow behind him, as if the autumn had been there, and nowhere else. On reaching the river's brink, he plunged headlong in, without waiting so much as to pull off his shoes.

"Poof! poof poof!" snorted King Midas, as his head emerged out of the water. "Well, this is really a refreshing bath, and I think it must have quite washed away the Golden Touch. And now for filling my pitcher!"

As he dipped the pitcher into the water, it gladdened his very heart to see it change from gold into the same good, honest earthen vessel which it had been before he touched it. He was conscious, also, of a change within himself. A cold, hard, and heavy weight seemed to have gone out of his bosom. No doubt his heart had been gradually losing its human substance, and transmuting itself into insensible metal, but had now softened back again into flesh. Perceiving a violet, that grew on the bank of the river, Midas touched it with his finger, and was overjoyed to find that the delicate flower retained its purple hue, instead of undergoing a yellow blight. The curse of the Golden Touch had, therefore, really been removed from him.

King Midas hastened back to the palace: and I suppose the servants knew not what to make of it when they saw their royal master so carefully bringing home an earthen pitcher of water. But that water, which was to undo all the mischief that his folly had wrought, was more precious to Midas than an ocean of molten gold could have been. The first thing he did, as you need hardly be told, was to sprinkle it by handfuls over, the golden figure of little Marygold.

No sooner did it fall on her than you would have laughed to see how the rosy colour came back to the dear child's cheek!—and how she began to sneeze and splutter!— and how astonished she was to find herself dripping wet, and her father still throwing more water over her!

"Pray do not, dear father!" cried she. "See how you have wet my nice frock, which I put on only this morning!"

For Marygold did not know that she had been a little golden statue; nor could she remember anything that had happened since the moment when she ran, with outstretched arms, to comfort poor King Midas.

Her father did not think it necessary to tell his beloved child how very foolish he had been, but contented himself with showing how much wiser he had grown. For this purpose he led little Marygold into the garden, where he sprinkled all the remainder of the water over the rose-bushes, and

with such good effect that above five thousand roses recovered their beautiful bloom. There were two circumstances, however, which, as long as he lived, used to put King Midas in mind of the Golden Touch. One was, that the sands of the river sparkled like gold; the other, that little Marygold's hair had now a golden tinge, which he had never observed in it before she had been transmuted by the effect of his kiss.

When King Midas had grown quite an old man, and used to trot* Marygold's children on his knee, he was fond of telling them this marvellous story, pretty much as I have now told it to you. And then would he stroke their glossy ringlets, and tell them that their hair, likewise, had a rich shade of gold, which they had inherited from their mother. "And, to tell you the truth," quoth King Midas, "ever since that morning, I have hated the very sight of all other gold, save this!"

---

trot: move playfully, imitating gait of a horse

About the Author

Nathaniel Hawthorne (1804–64) was born in Salem, Massachusetts. At Bowdoin College Hawthorne was a classmate of Henry Wadsworth Longfellow and future president of the United States Franklin Pierce, for whom Hawthorne later wrote a campaign biography. Hawthorne is well known for his many short stories and four major novels. However, Hawthorne seems to have had a special desire to write for children. *A Wonder-Book for Girls and Boys* contains rewritings of several famous ancient Greek myths. Hawthorne believed that there was much to be learned from these myths. The original manuscript of *A Wonder-Book* is the only one of Hawthorne's completed manuscripts owned by a member of his family. Originally written on both sides of large blue pieces of paper, the manuscript contains few erasures or corrections, a sign, no doubt, that he gave careful consideration to his work.

THINKING ZONE

Myths are individual stories that exist within a greater **mythology**, a large group of stories that were at one time held by a cultural group to be true and that seek to teach or explain why things happen the way that they do. The ancient Greeks invented a complex mythology that sought to explain such everyday occurrences as the changing of the seasons, good harvests and famines, and why certain rulers conquered others.

Greek mythology contains stories about many gods and goddesses, as well as fantastic stories about real-life rulers and warriors. The Midas of the story you read in this book was a real king who ruled Phrygia in the late eighth century BC. Some of the earliest versions of the Midas story include a follower of the god Dionysus as the one who grants Midas the golden touch. Hawthorne has chosen to take the mythological references out of the story and has instead framed a folktale wherein no gods or goddesses are mentioned. Much of the great literature that you will read in future years contains references to mythological characters and stories. Many times, a writer will use the meaning of a myth in order to make a comparison or tell the story in an artful way. In certain cases, an entire story, poem, or play may be inspired by a mythological tale.

Within the story of Midas, you will notice a type of irony known as **situational irony**, in which the story's events violate normal expectations. Situational irony occurs, for instance, when something seemingly good happens to a character, but it later turns out to be bad. An example of this type of irony occurs in "Mama and the Graduation Present" when Katrin receives the dresser set but later finds out that her mother has sold her heirloom brooch to buy it for her.

1. *[interpretive]* Who is the protagonist of "The Golden Touch"?

_____

_____

Protagonist—*The main character of a story*

2. *[literal]* What else did Midas treasure besides gold?

_____

_____

3. *[literal/interpretive]* Where did Midas keep his wealth? How might this place be considered symbolic?

_____

_____

_____

4. *[interpretive]* Prior to Midas's sitting down to breakfast, what events in the story foreshadow that the "golden touch" is not as beneficial as he believes?

_____

_____

_____

_____

_____

_____

5. *[critical]* What do you think is the theme of this **myth**-like story? Is the theme implicit or explicit?

_____

_____

_____

_____

_____

_____

_____

_____

Explicit theme—*a theme that is stated outright through the words of the characters or through the narration*

Implicit theme—*a theme that is suggested through the details of the story*

6. *[critical]* Explain the **situational irony** that takes place in "The Golden Touch."

_____

_____

_____

_____

_____

THIS IS JUST TO SAY

WILLIAM CARLOS WILLIAMS

Explaining our choices can sometimes be difficult, especially if the choice made was contrary to what we knew would be best. Williams's brief poetic thought discusses one such struggle.

I have eaten
the plums
that were in
the icebox*   icebox: refrigerator

and which
you were probably
saving
for breakfast

Forgive me
they were delicious
so sweet
and so cold

ABOUT THE AUTHOR

A writer and medical doctor, William Carlos Williams (1883–1963) had a wide variety of experiences from which to write. While studying medicine at the University of Pennsylvania, Williams became friends with poet Ezra Pound, whose works greatly influenced the aspiring poet. After he established his medical practice in Rutherford, New Jersey, Williams began to publish his work in small magazines. Williams experimented with style, meter, and line length in his poems and was considered a member of the imagist movement along with fellow Americans Pound and T.S. Eliot. Williams did not limit himself to poetry but was a novelist, essayist, and playwright who focused on everyday circumstances of the common people. Williams's *Pictures from Brueghel and other Poems* was awarded a Pulitzer Prize after his death in 1963.

MAKE ME THY FUEL

AMY CARMICHAEL

Carmichael's poem deals with a choice: that of a Christian's willingness to give up his own will and desires out of gratitude for Christ's sacrifice. Are you willing to forfeit everything for Him Who sacrificed all for you?

From prayer that asks that I may be
Sheltered from winds that beat on Thee,
From fearing when I should aspire,
From faltering when I should climb higher,
From silken self, O Captain, free   5
Thy soldier who would follow Thee.

From subtle love of softening things,
From easy choices, weakenings,
Not thus are spirits fortified,
Not this way went the Crucified,   10
From all that dims Thy Calvary,
O Lamb of God, deliver me.

Give me the love that leads the way,
The faith that nothing can dismay,
The hope no disappointments tire,   15
The passion that will burn like fire,
Let me not sink to be a clod:
Make me Thy fuel, Flame of God.

ABOUT THE AUTHOR

Many young children have heard the story about a little girl who prayed that her brown eyes be turned to blue. As that three-year-old child, Amy Carmichael (1867–1951) first learned that "no" is an answer to prayer. God knew that she needed brown eyes for her missionary work in India, and Carmichael grew to know that her God never makes mistakes. In her midtwenties, she heard the unmistakable call of God to go tell those who had never heard about salvation. Obediently she went, denying herself the comforts of home and family. She learned to trust in God's care for the loved ones she had to leave in obedience to her Master.

Carmichael first went to China, then to Japan and Ceylon, settling finally in India, where her life-consuming work would unfold. She initially was involved in an itinerant ministry teaching the Bible to village women all over southern India. Then she became aware of the children who were in physical and moral danger. As she rescued child after child, she learned the truth of the Indian proverb, "Children tie the mother's feet." She found herself denied the traveling ministry she loved but was given in exchange the Dohnavur Fellowship, a ministry based on the truth that Jesus loves little children. Amy Carmichael spent fifty-three years in India without a furlough, rescuing hundreds of children and introducing them to Christ. She spent the last twenty years of her life bedridden as a result of her work. She had learned to deny herself and to accept God's denial of her desires that did not further His plan.

THINKING ZONE

You have already learned that a key element of poetry is the use of concrete imagery. Often, concrete language is used by poets to create **metaphors**, or expressions of one thing in terms of another. When a poet uses a concrete image to create a metaphor, the reader is better able to understand the idea that the poet is trying to convey. For instance, when we say that a person is a "lamb," we instantly think of qualities commonly associated with a lamb (such as gentleness and meekness) and associate those qualities with the person. Since symbolism and figurative language play such a large part in poetic expression, metaphors are commonly found throughout good poetry.

You have learned that another key feature of poetry is parallelism. One type of parallelism that is easily recognized is anaphora. In "Christian Beholds the Cross," Bunyan uses anaphora when he repeats the words "Must here" three times at the beginnings of lines 4–6. **Anaphora** is this repetition of words and phrases at the beginnings of lines of poetry. Notice how each of the poets uses these literary devices in the poems you just read.

Concrete imagery— *descriptive words or phrases that create an impression and that appeal to one or more of the five senses*

Parallelism— *similarity in the structure of two or more phrases, clauses, or sentences*

1. *[interpretive]* What examples of concrete imagery can you find in "This Is Just to Say"? To what senses do these images appeal?

_____

_____

_____

_____

2. *[interpretive/critical]* The speaker in "This Is Just to Say" asks the person to whom he is writing to forgive him for eating the plums. Do the last lines of the poem back up his claim that he is sorry, or do they seem ironic?

_____

_____

_____

_____

3. *[critical]* Which poem contains examples of **anaphora**?

_____

_____

_____

_____

4. *[interpretive]* What **metaphors** does Carmichael use to describe herself—both as she does and does not wish to be known—in "Make Me Thy Fuel"?

_____

_____

_____

_____

_____

5. *[interpretive]* What idea is Carmichael trying to convey through the line "From silken self, O Captain, free"?

_____

_____

_____

_____

_____

6. *[interpretive]* Read the final six lines of "Make Me Thy Fuel." How is it possible for Carmichael to be the "fuel" for the "Flame of God"?

_____

_____

_____

_____

_____

THE UGLY DUCKLING

A.A. MILNE

Have you ever planned with a friend to "pull off" something on another person? Did your plan succeed? Milne's play, which is quite different from the Hans Christian Andersen fairy tale, focuses on the attempt to "pull off" a wedding between the Princess and a suitor.

The scene is the Throne Room of the Palace; a room of many doors, or, if preferred, curtain-openings: simply furnished with three thrones for Their Majesties and Her Royal Highness the PRINCESS CAMILLA—in other words, with three handsome chairs. At each side is a long seat: reserved, as it might be, for His Majesty's Council (if any), but useful, as to-day, for other purposes. The KING is asleep on his throne with a handkerchief over his face. He is a king of any country from any story-book, in whatever costume you please. But he should be wearing his crown.

A VOICE:	(*announcing*). His Excellency the Chancellor! (*The* CHANCELLOR, *an elderly man in horn-rimmed spectacles,* enters, bowing. The* KING *wakes up with a start and removes the handkerchief from his face.*)

---

horn-rimmed spectacles: eyeglasses with frames made of material like tortoiseshell

KING:	(*with simple dignity*). I was thinking.
CHANCELLOR:	(*bowing*). Never, Your Majesty, was greater need for thought than now.
KING:	That's what I was thinking. (*He struggles into a more dignified position*). Well, what is it? More trouble?
CHANCELLOR:	What we might call the old trouble, Your Majesty.
KING:	It's what I was saying last night to the Queen. "Uneasy lies the head that wears a crown," was how I put it.
CHANCELLOR:	A profound and original thought, which may well go down to posterity.
KING:	You mean it may go down well with posterity. I hope so. Remind me to tell you some time of another

little thing I said to Her Majesty: something about a fierce light beating on a throne. Posterity would like that, too. Well, what is it?

CHANCELLOR: It is in the matter of Her Royal Highness' wedding.

KING: Oh . . . yes.

CHANCELLOR: As Your Majesty is aware, the young Prince Simon arrives to-day to seek Her Royal Highness' hand in marriage. He has been travelling in distant lands and, as I understand, has not—er—has not—

KING: You mean he hasn't heard anything.

CHANCELLOR: It is a little difficult to put this tactfully, Your Majesty.

KING: Do your best, and I will tell you afterwards how you got on.

CHANCELLOR: Let me put it this way. The Prince Simon will naturally assume that Her Royal Highness has the customary—so customary as to be, in my own poor opinion, slightly monotonous*—has what one might call the inevitable—so inevitable as to be, in my opinion again, almost in, assume, that she has the, as *I* think of it, faultily faultless, icily regular, splendidly—

---

monotonous: repetitious, lacking in variety

KING: What you are trying to say in the fewest words possible is that my daughter is not beautiful.

CHANCELLOR: Her beauty is certainly elusive, Your Majesty.

---

elusive: difficult to define or describe

KING: It is. It has eluded you, it has eluded me, it has eluded everybody who has seen her. It even eluded the Court Painter. His last words were, "Well, I did my best." His successor is now paint-ing the view across the water-meadows from the West Turret. He says that his doctor has advised him to keep to landscape.

CHANCELLOR: It is unfortunate, Your Majesty, but there it is. One just cannot understand how it can have occurred.

KING: You don't think she takes after me, at all? You don't detect a likeness?

CHANCELLOR: Most certainly not, Your Majesty.

KING: Good. . . . Your predecessor did.

CHANCELLOR: I have often wondered what happened to my predecessor.

KING: Well, now you know. (*There is a short silence.*)

CHANCELLOR: Looking at the bright side, although Her Royal Highness is not, strictly speaking, beautiful.

KING: Not, truthfully speaking, beautiful.

CHANCELLOR: Yet she has great beauty of character.

KING: My dear Chancellor, we are not considering Her Royal Highness' character, but her chances of getting married. You observe that there is a distinction.

CHANCELLOR: Yes, Your Majesty.

KING: Look at it from the suitor's point of view. If a girl is beautiful, it is easy to assume that she has, tucked away inside her, an equally beautiful character. But it is impossible to assume that an unattractive girl, however elevated in character, has, tucked away inside her, an equally beautiful face. That is, so to speak, not where you want it—tucked away.

CHANCELLOR: Quite so, Your Majesty.

KING: This doesn't, of course, alter the fact that the Princess Camilla is quite the nicest person in the Kingdom.

CHANCELLOR: (*enthusiastically*). She is indeed, Your Majesty. (*Hurriedly*). With the exception, I need hardly say, of Your Majesty—and Her Majesty.

KING: Your exceptions are tolerated for their loyalty and condemned for their extreme fatuity.*

---

fatuity: foolishness

CHANCELLOR: Thank you, Your Majesty.

KING: As an adjective for your King, the word "nice" is ill-chosen. As an adjective for Her Majesty, it is ill-chosen. (*At which moment* HER MAJESTY *comes in. The* KING *rises. The* CHANCELLOR *puts himself at right angles.*)

QUEEN: (*briskly*). Ah. Talking about Camilla? (*She sits down.*)

KING: (*returning to his throne*). As always, my dear, you are right.

QUEEN: (*to* CHANCELLOR). This fellow, Simon—What's he like?

CHANCELLOR: Nobody has seen him, Your Majesty.

QUEEN: How old is he?

CHANCELLOR: Five-and-twenty, I understand.

QUEEN: In twenty-five years he must have been seen by somebody.

KING: (*to the* CHANCELLOR). Just a fleeting glimpse.

CHANCELLOR: I meant, Your Majesty, that no detailed report of him has reached this country, save that he has the usual personal advantages and qualities expected of a Prince, and has been travelling in distant and dangerous lands.

QUEEN: Ah! Nothing gone wrong with his eyes? Sunstroke or anything?

CHANCELLOR: Not that I am aware of, Your Majesty. At the same time, as I was venturing to say to His Majesty. Her Royal Highness' character and disposition are so outstandingly—

QUEEN:	Stuff and nonsense. You remember what happened when we had the Tournament of Love last year.
CHANCELLOR:	I was not myself present, Your Majesty. I had not then the honour of—I was abroad, and never heard the full story.
QUEEN:	No; it was the other fool. They all rode up to Camilla to pay their homage*—it was the first time they had seen her. The heralds* blew their trumpets, and announced that she would marry

whichever Prince was left master of the field when all but one had been unhorsed. The trumpets were blown again, they charged enthusiastically into the fight, and— (*The* KING *looks nonchalantly at the ceiling and whistles a few bars.*)—don't do that.

---

homage: special honor; respect
heralds: messengers

KING:	I'm sorry, my dear.
QUEEN:	(*to* CHANCELLOR). And what happened? They all simultaneously fell off their horses and assumed a posture of defeat.
KING:	One of them was not quite so quick as the others. I was very quick. I proclaimed him the victor.
QUEEN:	At the Feast of Betrothal held that night—
KING:	We were all very quick.
QUEEN:	The Chancellor announced that by the laws of the country the successful suitor had to pass a further test. He had to give the correct answer to a riddle.
CHANCELLOR:	Such undoubtedly is the fact, Your Majesty.
KING:	There are times for announcing facts, and times for looking at things in a broadminded way. Please remember that, Chancellor.
CHANCELLOR:	Yes, Your Majesty.

QUEEN:	I invented the riddle myself. Quite an easy one. What is it which has four legs and barks like a dog? The answer is, "A dog."
KING:	(*to* CHANCELLOR). You see that?
CHANCELLOR:	Yes, Your Majesty.
KING:	It isn't difficult.
QUEEN:	He, however, seemed to find it so. He said an eagle. Then he said a serpent; a very high mountain with slippery sides; two peacocks; a moonlight night; the day after to-morrow—
KING:	Nobody could accuse him of not trying.
QUEEN:	*I* did.
KING:	I *should* have said that nobody could fail to recognize in his attitude an appearance of doggedness.*

---
doggedness: stubbornly persevering

QUEEN:	Finally he said "Death." I nudged the King—
KING:	Accepting the word "nudge" for the moment, I rubbed my ankle with one hand, clapped him on the shoulder with the other, and congratulated him on the correct answer. He disappeared under the table, and, personally, I never saw him again.
QUEEN:	His body was found in the moat next morning.
CHANCELLOR:	But what was he doing in the moat, Your Majesty?
KING:	Bobbing about. Try not to ask needless questions.
CHANCELLOR:	It all seems so strange.
QUEEN:	What does?
CHANCELLOR:	That Her Royal Highness, alone of all the Princesses one has ever heard of, should lack that invariable* attribute of Royalty, supreme beauty.

---
invariable: not changing

QUEEN:	(*to the* KING). That was your Great-Aunt Malkin. She came to the christening. You know what she said.
KING:	It was cryptic. Great-Aunt Malkin's besetting weakness. She came to *my* christening—she was one hundred and one then, and that was fifty-one years ago. (*To the* CHANCELLOR). How old would that make her?
CHANCELLOR:	One hundred and fifty-two, Your Majesty.
KING:	(*after thought*). About that, yes. She promised me that when I grew up I should have all the happiness which my wife deserved. It struck me at the time—well, when I say "at the time," I was only a week old—but it did strike me as soon as anything could strike me—I mean of that nature—well, work it out for yourself, Chancellor. It opens up a most interesting field

of speculation. Though naturally I have not liked to go into it at all deeply with Her Majesty.

QUEEN: I never heard anything less cryptic.* She was wishing you extreme happiness.

---

cryptic: having hidden meaning

KING: I don't think she was *wishing* me anything. However.

CHANCELLOR: (*to the* QUEEN). But what, Your Majesty, did she wish Her Royal Highness?

QUEEN: Her other godmother—on my side—had promised her the dazzling beauty for which all the women in my family are famous (*She pauses, and the* KING *snaps his fingers surreptitiously* in the direction of the* CHANCELLOR.)

---

surreptitiously: obtained or done to avoid notice

CHANCELLOR: (*hurriedly*). Indeed, yes, Your Majesty. (*The* KING *relaxes.*)

QUEEN: And Great-Aunt Malkin said—(*to the* KING)—what were the words?

KING: I give you with this kiss
A wedding-day surprise.
Where ignorance is bliss
'Tis folly to be wise.
I thought the last two lines rather neat. But what it *meant*—

QUEEN: We can all see what it meant. She was given beauty—and where is it? Great-Aunt Malkin took it away from her. The wedding-day surprise is that there will never be a wedding day.

KING: Young men being what they are, my dear, it would be much more surprising if there *were* a wedding day. So how— (*The* PRINCESS *comes in. She is young, happy, healthy, but not beautiful. Or let us say that by some trick of make-up or arrangement of hair she seems plain to us: unlike the* PRINCESS *of the story-books.*)

PRINCESS: (*to the* KING). Hallo, darling! (*Seeing the others*). Oh, I say! Affairs Of state? Sorry.

KING: (*holding out his hand*). Don't go, Camilla. (*She takes his hand.*)

CHANCELLOR: Shall I withdraw, Your Majesty?

QUEEN: You are aware, Camilla, that Prince Simon arrives to-day?

PRINCESS: He has arrived. They're just letting down the drawbridge.

KING: (*jumping up*). Arrived! I must—

PRINCESS:	Darling, you know what the drawbridge is like. It takes at least half an hour to let it down.
KING:	(*sitting down*). It wants oil. (*to the* CHANCELLOR). Have *you* been grudging it oil?
PRINCESS:	It wants a new drawbridge, darling.
CHANCELLOR:	Have I Your Majesty's permission—
KING:	Yes, yes. (*The* CHANCELLOR *bows and goes out.*)
QUEEN:	You've told him, of course? It's the only chance.
KING:	Er—no. I was just going to, when—
QUEEN:	Then I'd better. (*She goes to the door*). You can explain to the girl; I'll have her sent to you. You've told Camilla?
KING:	Er—no. I was just going to, when—
QUEEN:	Then you'd better tell her now.
KING:	My dear, are you sure—
QUEEN:	It's the only chance left. (*Dramatically to heaven*). My daughter! (*She goes out. There is a little silence when she is gone.*)
KING:	Camilla, I want to talk seriously to you about marriage.
PRINCESS:	Yes, father.
KING:	It is time that you learnt some of the facts of life.
PRINCESS:	Yes, father.
KING:	Now the great fact about marriage is that once you're married you live happy ever after. All our history books affirm this.
PRINCESS:	And your own experience too, darling.
KING:	(*with dignity*). Let us confine ourselves to history for the moment.
PRINCESS:	Yes, father.
KING:	Of course, there may be an exception here and there, which, as it were, proves the rule; just as oh, well, never mind.
PRINCESS:	(*smiling*). Go on, darling. You were going to say that an exception here and there proves the rule that all princesses are beautiful.
KING:	Well—leave that for the moment. The point is that it doesn't matter *how* you marry, or *who* you marry, as long as you *get* married. Because you'll be happy ever after in any case. Do you follow me so far?
PRINCESS:	Yes, father.
KING:	Well, your mother and I have a little plan—
PRINCESS:	Was that it, going out of the door just now?
KING:	Er—yes. It concerns your waiting-maid.
PRINCESS:	Darling, I have several.

KING: Only one that leaps to the eye, so to speak. The one with the— well, with everything.

PRINCESS: Dulcibella?

KING: That's the one. It is our little plan that at the first meeting she should pass herself off as the Princess—a harmless ruse,* of which you will find frequent record in the history books—and allure Prince Simon to his—that is to say, bring him up to the— In other words, the wedding will take place immediately afterwards, and as quietly as possible—well, naturally in view of the fact that your Aunt Malkin is one hundred and fifty-two; and since you will be wearing the family bridal veil—which is no doubt how the custom arose—the surprise after the ceremony will be his. Are you following me at all? Your attention seems to be wandering.

---

ruse: a crafty strategy

PRINCESS: I was wondering why you needed to tell me.

KING: Just a precautionary measure, in case you happened to meet the Prince or his attendant before the ceremony; in which case, of course, you would pass yourself off as the maid.

PRINCESS: A harmless ruse, of which, also, you will find frequent record in the history books.

KING: Exactly. But the occasion need not arise.

A VOICE: (*announcing*). The woman Dulcibella!

KING: Ah! (*to the* PRINCESS). Now, Camilla, if you will just retire to your own apartments, I will come to you there when we are ready for the actual ceremony. (*He leads her out as he is talking; and as he turns calls out*). Come in, my dear! (*She comes in. She is beautiful, but dumb*). Now don't be frightened, there is nothing to be frightened about. Has Her Majesty told you what you have to do?

DULCIBELLA: Y-yes, Your Majesty.

KING: Well now, let's see how well you can do it. You are sitting here, we will say. (*He leads her to a seat*). Now imagine that I am Prince Simon. (*He curls his moustache and puts his stomach in. She giggles*). You are the beautiful Princess Camilla whom he has never seen. (*She giggles again*). This is a serious moment in your life, and you will find that a giggle will not be helpful. (*He goes to the door*). I am announced: "His Royal Highness Prince Simon!" That's me being announced. Remember what I said about giggling. You should have a far-away look upon the face. (*She does her best*). Farther away than that. (*She tries again*). No, that's too far. You are sitting there, thinking

	beautiful thoughts. . . . You extend your hand graciously—*graciously*; you're not laying to push him in the face— that's better, and I raise it to my lips—so—and I kiss it . . . and I say, "Your Royal Highness, this is the most—er — Your Royal Highness, I shall ever be—no—Your Royal Highness, it is the proudest— Well, the point is that *he* will say it, and it will be something complimentary. . . . And then—what do *you* say?
DULCIBELLA:	Coo!
KING:	No, *not* Coo.
DULCIBELLA:	Never had anyone do that to me before.
KING:	That also strikes the wrong note. What you want to say is, "Oh, Prince Simon!" . . . Say it.
DULCIBELLA:	(*loudly*). Oh, Prince Simon!
KING:	No, no, You don't need to shout until he has said "What?" two or three times. Always consider the possibility that he *isn't* deaf. Softly, and giving the words a dying fall, letting them play around his head like a flight of doves.
DULCIBELLA:	(*still a little overloud*). O-o-o-o-h, Prinsimon!
KING:	Keep the idea in your mind of a flight of *doves* rather than a flight of panic-stricken elephants, and you will be all right. Now I'm going to get up, and you must, as it were, *waft** me into a seat by your side. (*She starts wafting*). *Not* rescuing a drowning man, that's another idea altogether, useful at times, but at the moment inappropriate. Wafting. Prince Simon will put the necessary muscles into play—all you require to do is to indicate by a gracious movement of the hand the seat you require him to take. Now! (*He gets up, a little stiffly, and sits next to her*). That was better. Well, here we are. Now, I think you give me a look: something . . . with an undertone of regal dignity, touched, as it were, with good comradeship. Now try that (*She gives him a vacant look of bewilderment*). Frankly, that didn't quite get it. There was just a little something missing. An absence, as it were, of all the qualities I asked for, and in their place an odd resemblance to an unsatisfied fish. Let us try to get at it another way. Dulcibella, have you a young man of your own?

waft: cause to go gently and smoothly through the air

DULCIBELLA:	(*eagerly, seizing his hand*). Oo, yes, he's ever so smart, he's an archer, well not as you might say a real archer, he works in the armoury, but old Bottlenose, *you* know who I mean, the Captain of the Guard, says the very next man they ever has to shoot, my Eg shall take his place, knowing Father and how it is with Eg and me, and me being maid to Her Royal Highness

	and can't marry me till he's a real soldier, but ever so loving, and funny like, the things he says, I said to him once, "Eg" I said—
KING:	(*getting up*). I rather fancy, Dulcibella, that if you think of Eg all the time, *say* as little as possible, and, when thinking of Eg, see that the mouth is not more than partially open, you will do very well, I will show you where you are to sit and wait for His Royal Highness. (*He leads her out, On the way he is saying*). Now remember —*waft*—*waft*—not *hoick*.* (PRINCE SIMON *wanders in from the back unannounced. He is a very ordinary-looking young man in rather dusty clothes. He gives a deep sigh of relief as he sinks into the* KING'S *throne . . . .* CAMILLA, *a new and strangely beautiful* CAMILLA, *comes in.*)

---

*hoick: variation of *yoick*; used as a hunting cry to urge hounds after a fox*

PRINCESS:	(*surprised*). Well!
PRINCE:	Oh, hallo!
PRINCESS:	Ought you?
PRINCE:	(*getting up*). Do sit down, won't you?
PRINCESS:	Who are you, and how did you get here?
PRINCE:	Well, that's rather a long story. Couldn't we sit down? You could sit here if you liked, but it isn't very comfortable.
PRINCESS:	That is the King's Throne.
PRINCE:	Oh, is that what it is?
PRINCESS:	Thrones are not meant to be comfortable.
PRINCE:	Well, I don't know if they're meant to be, but they certainly aren't.
PRINCESS:	Why were you sitting on the King's Throne, and who are you?
PRINCE:	My name is Carlo.
PRINCESS:	Mine is Dulcibella.
PRINCE:	Good. And now couldn't we sit down?
PRINCESS:	(*sitting down on the long seat to the left of the throne, and, as it were, wafting him to a place next to her*). You may sit here, if you like. Why are you so tired? (*He sits down.*)
PRINCE:	I've been taking very strenuous exercise.
PRINCESS:	Is that part of the long story?

PRINCE:	It is.
PRINCESS:	(*settling herself*). I love stories.
PRINCE:	This isn't a story really. You see, I'm attendant on Prince Simon, who is visiting here.
PRINCESS:	Oh? I'm attendant on Her Royal Highness.
PRINCE:	Then you know what he's here for.
PRINCESS:	Yes.
PRINCE:	She's very beautiful, I hear.
PRINCESS:	Did you hear that? Where have you been lately?
PRINCE:	Travelling in distant lands—with Prince Simon.
PRINCESS:	All the same, I don't understand. Is Prince Simon in the Palace now? The drawbridge *can't* be down yet!
PRINCE:	I don't suppose it is. *And* what a noise it makes coming down!
PRINCESS:	Isn't it terrible?
PRINCE:	I couldn't stand it any more. I just had to get away. That's why I'm here.
PRINCESS:	But how?
PRINCE:	Well, there's only one way, isn't there? That beech tree, and then a swing and a grab for the battlements, and don't ask me to remember it all— (*He shudders.*)

PRINCESS:	You mean you came across the moat by that beech tree?
PRINCE:	Yes. I got so tired of hanging about.
PRINCESS:	But it's terribly dangerous!
PRINCE:	That's why I'm so exhausted. Nervous shock. (*He lies back and breathes loudly.*)
PRINCESS:	Of course, it's different for *me*.
PRINCE:	(*sitting up*). Say that again. I must have got it wrong.
PRINCESS:	It's different for me, because I'm used to it. Besides, I'm so much lighter.
PRINCE:	You don't mean that *you*—
PRINCESS:	Oh yes, often.

PRINCE: And I thought I was a brave man! At least, I didn't until five minutes ago, and now I don't again.

PRINCESS: Oh, but you are! And I think it's wonderful to do it straight off the first time.

PRINCE: Well, *you* did.

PRINCESS: Oh no, not the first time. When I was a child.

PRINCE: You mean that you crashed?

PRINCESS: Well, you only fall into the moat.

PRINCE: Only! Can you *swim*?

PRINCESS: Of course.

PRINCE: So you swam to the castle walls, and yelled for help, and they fished you out and walloped you. And next day you tried again. Well, if *that* isn't pluck—

PRINCESS: Of course I didn't. I swam back, and did it at once; I mean I tried again at once. It wasn't until the third time that I actually did it. You see, I was afraid I might lose my nerve.

PRINCE: Afraid she might lose her nerve!

PRINCESS: There's a way of getting over from this side, too; a tree grows out from the wall and you jump into another tree—I don't think it's quite so easy.

PRINCE: Not quite so easy. Good. You must show me.

PRINCESS: Oh, I will.

PRINCE: Perhaps it might be as well if you taught me how to swim first. I've often heard about swimming, but never—

PRINCESS: You can't swim?

PRINCE: No. Don't look so surprised. There are a lot of other things which I can't do. I'll tell you about them as soon as you have a couple of years to spare.

PRINCESS: You can't swim and yet you crossed by the beech-tree! And you're *ever* so much heavier than I am! Now who's brave?

PRINCE: (*getting up*). You keep talking about how light you are. I must see if there's anything in it. Stand up! (*She stands obediently and he picks her up*). You're right, Dulcibella. I could hold you here for ever. (*Looking at her*). You're very lovely. Do you know how lovely you are?

PRINCESS: Yes. (*She laughs suddenly and happily.*)

PRINCE: Why do you laugh?

PRINCESS: Aren't you tired of holding me?

PRINCE: Frankly, yes. I exaggerated when I said I could hold you for ever. When you've been hanging by the arms for ten minutes over a very deep moat, wondering if it's too late to learn how to swim—(*he puts her down*)—what I meant was that I should *like* to hold you for ever. Why did you laugh?

PRINCESS: Oh, well, it was a little private joke of mine.

PRINCE: If it comes to that, I've got a private joke too. Let's exchange them.

PRINCESS: Mine's very private. One other woman in the whole world knows, and that's all.

PRINCE: Mine's just as private. One other man knows, and that's all.

PRINCESS: What fun. I love secrets . . . . Well, here's mine. When I was born, one of my godmothers promised that I should be very beautiful.

PRINCE: How right she was.

PRINCESS: But the other one said this:

I give you with this kiss
A wedding-day surprise.
Where ignorance is bliss
'Tis folly to be wise.

And nobody knew what it meant. And I grew up very plain. And then, when I was about ten, I met my godmother in the forest one day. It was my tenth birthday. Nobody knows this—except you.

PRINCE: Except us.

PRINCESS: Except us. And she told me what her gift meant. It meant that I *was* beautiful—but everybody else was to go on being ignorant, and thinking me plain, until my wedding-day. Because, she said, she didn't want me to grow up spoilt and wilful and vain, as I should have done if everybody had always been saying how beautiful I was; and the best thing in the world, she said, was to be quite sure of yourself, but not to expect admiration from other people. So ever since then my mirror has told me I'm beautiful, and everybody else thinks me ugly, and I get a lot of fun out of it.

PRINCE: Well, seeing that Dulcibella is the result, I can only say that your godmother was very, very wise.

PRINCESS: And now tell me *your* secret.

PRINCE: It isn't such a pretty one. You see, Prince Simon was going to woo Princess Camilla, and he'd heard that she was beautiful and haughty and imperious—all *you* would have been if your godmother hadn't been so wise. And being a very ordinary-looking fellow himself, he was afraid she wouldn't think much of him, so he suggested to one of his attendants, a man called Carlo, of extremely attractive appearance, that *he* should

	pretend to be the Prince, and win the Princess' hand; and then at the last moment they would change places—,
PRINCESS:	How would they do that?
PRINCE:	The Prince was going to have been married in full armour—with his visor down.
PRINCESS:	(*laughing happily*). Oh, what fun!
PRINCE:	Neat, isn't it?
PRINCESS:	(*laughing*). Oh, very . . . very . . . very.
PRINCE:	Neat, but not so terribly *funny*. Why do you keep laughing?
PRINCESS:	Well, that's another secret.
PRINCE:	If it comes to that, *I've* got another one up my sleeve. Shall we exchange again?
PRINCESS:	All right. You go first this time.
PRINCE:	Very well. I am not Carlo. (*Standing up and speaking dramatically*). I am Simon!—ow! (*He sits down and rubs his leg violently.*)
PRINCESS:	(*alarmed*). What is it?
PRINCE:	Cramp. (*In a mild voice, still rubbing*). I was saying that I was Prince Simon.
PRINCESS:	Shall I rub it for you? (*She rubs.*)
PRINCE:	(*still hopefully*). I am Simon.
PRINCESS:	Is that better?
PRINCE:	(*despairingly*). I am Simon.
PRINCESS:	I know.
PRINCE:	How did you know?
PRINCESS:	Well, you told me.
PRINCE:	But oughtn't you to swoon or something?
PRINCESS:	Why? History records many similar ruses.
PRINCE:	(*amazed*). Is that so? I've never read history. I thought I was being profoundly original.
PRINCESS:	Oh, no! Now I'll tell you *my* secret. For reasons very much like your own the Princess Camilla, who is held to be extremely plain, feared to meet Prince Simon. Is the drawbridge down yet?
PRINCE:	Do your people give a faint, surprised cheer every time it gets down?
PRINCESS:	Naturally.
PRINCE:	Then it came down about three minutes ago.
PRINCESS:	Ah! Then at this very moment your man Carlo is declaring his passionate love for my maid, Dulcibella. That, I think, is

funny. (*So does the* PRINCE. *He laughs heartily*). Dulcibella, by the way, is in love with a man she calls Eg, so I hope Carlo isn't getting carried away.

PRINCE: Carlo is married to a girl he calls "the little woman," so Eg has nothing to fear.

PRINCESS: By the way, I don't know if you heard, but I said, or as good as said, that I am the Princess Camilla.

PRINCE: I wasn't surprised. History, of which I read a great deal, records many similar ruses.

PRINCESS: (*laughing*). Simon!

PRINCE: (*laughing*). Camilla! (*He stands up*). May I try holding you again? (*She nods. He takes her in his arms and kisses her*). Sweetheart!

PRINCESS: You see, when you lifted me up before, you said, "You're very lovely," and my godmother said that the first person to whom I would seem lovely was the man I should marry; so I knew then that you were Simon and I should marry you.

PRINCE: I knew directly I saw you that I should marry you, even if you were Dulcibella. By the way, which of you *am* I marrying?

PRINCESS: When she lifts her veil, it will be Camilla. (*Voices are heard outside*). Until then it will be Dulcibella.

PRINCE: (*in a whisper*). Then goodbye, Camilla, until you lift your veil.

PRINCESS: Good-bye, Simon, until you raise your visor. (*The* KING *and* QUEEN *come in arm-in-arm, followed by* CARLO *and* DULCIBELLA, *also arm-in-arm. The* CHANCELLOR *precedes them, walking backwards, at a loyal angle*).

PRINCE: (*supporting the* CHANCELLOR *as an accident seems inevitable*). Careful! (*The* CHANCELLOR *turns indignantly round.*)

KING: Who and what is this? More accurately who and what are all these?

CARLO: My attendant, Carlo, Your Majesty. He will, with Your Majesty's permission, prepare me for the ceremony. (*The* PRINCE *bows.*)

KING: Of course, of course!

QUEEN: (*to* DULCIBELLA). Your maid, Dulcibella, is it not, my love? (DULCIBELLA *nods violently*). I thought so. (*To* CARLO). She will prepare Her Royal Highness. (*The* PRINCESS *curtsies.*)

KING: Ah, yes. Yes. *Most* important.

PRINCESS: (*curtsying*). I beg pardon, Your Majesty, if I've done wrong, but I found the gentleman wandering—

KING: (*crossing to her*). Quite right, my dear, quite right. (*He pinches her cheek, and takes advantage of this kingly gesture to say in a loud whisper*). We've pulled it off! (*They sit down; the* KING *and* QUEEN *on their thrones,* DULCIBELLA *on the* PRINCESS' *throne.* CARLO *stands behind* DULCIBELLA, *the* CHANCELLOR *on the* R. *of the* QUEEN, *and the* PRINCE *and* PRINCESS *behind the long seat on the left.*)

CHANCELLOR: (*consulting documents*). H'r'm! Have I Your Majesty's authority to put the final test to His Royal Highness?

QUEEN: (*whispering to* KING). Is this safe?

KING: (*whispering*). Perfectly, my dear. I told him the answer a minute ago. (*Over his shoulder to* CARLO). Don't forget. *Dog.*
(*Aloud*). Proceed, Your Excellency. It is my desire that the affairs of my country should ever be conducted in a strictly constitutional manner.

CHANCELLOR: (*oratorically*). By the constitution of the country, a suitor to Her Royal Highness' hand cannot be deemed successful until he has given the correct answer to a riddle. (*Conversationally*). The last suitor answered incorrectly, and thus failed to win his bride.

KING: By a coincidence he fell into the moat.

CHANCELLOR: (*to* CARLO). I have now to ask Your Royal Highness if you are prepared for the ordeal?

CARLO: (*cheerfully*). Absolutely.

CHANCELLOR: I may mention, as a matter, possibly, of some slight historical interest to our visitor, that by the constitution of the country the same riddle is not allowed to be asked on two successive occasions.

KING: (*startled*). What's that?

CHANCELLOR: This one, it is interesting to recall, was propounded exactly a century ago, and we must take it as a fortunate omen that it was well and truly solved.

KING: (*to* QUEEN). I may want my sword directly.

CHANCELLOR: The riddle is this. What is it which has four legs and mews like a cat?

CARLO: (*promptly*). A dog.

KING: (*still more promptly*). Bravo, bravo! (*He claps loudly and nudges the* QUEEN, *who claps too.*)

CHANCELLOR: (*peering at his documents*). According to the records of the occasion to which I referred, the correct answer would seem to be—

PRINCESS: (*to* PRINCE). Say some thing, quick!

CHANCELLOR: —not dog, but—

PRINCE: Your Majesty, have I permission to speak? Naturally His Royal Highness could not think of justifying himself on such an occasion, but I think that with Your Majesty's gracious permission, I could—

KING: Certainly, certainly.

PRINCE: In our country, we have an animal to which we have given the name "dog," or, in the local dialect of the more mountainous districts, "doggie." It sits by the fireside and purrs.

CARLO: That's right. It purrs like anything.

PRINCE: When it needs milk, which is its staple food, it mews.

CARLO: (*enthusiastically*). Mews like nobody's business.

PRINCE: It also has four legs.

CARLO: One at each corner.

PRINCE: In some countries, I understand, this animal is called a "cat." In one distant country to which His Royal Highness and I penetrated it was called by the very curious name of "hippopotamus."

CARLO: That's right. (*To the* PRINCE). Do you remember that ginger-coloured hippopotamus which used to climb onto my shoulder and lick my ear?

PRINCE: I shall never forget it, sir. (*To the* KING). So you see, Your Majesty—

KING: Thank you. I think that makes it perfectly clear. (*Firmly to the* CHANCELLOR). You are about to agree?

CHANCELLOR: Undoubtedly, Your Majesty. May I be the first to congratulate His Royal Highness on solving the riddle so accurately?

KING: You may be the first to see that all is in order for an immediate wedding.

CHANCELLOR: Thank you, Your Majesty, (*He bows and withdraws. The* KING *rises, as do the* QUEEN *and* DULCIBELLA.)

KING: (*to* CARLO). Doubtless, Prince Simon, you will wish to retire and prepare yourself for the ceremony.

CARLO: Thank you, sir.

PRINCE: Have I Your Majesty's permission to attend His Royal Highness? It is the custom of his country for Princes of the royal blood to be married in full armour, a matter which requires a certain adjustment—

KING: Of course, of course. (CARLO *bows to the* KING *and* QUEEN *and goes out. As the* PRINCE *is about to follow, the* KING *stops him*). Young man, you have a quality of quickness which I admire. It is my pleasure to reward it in any way which commends itself to you.

PRINCE: Your Majesty is ever gracious. May I ask for my reward *after* the ceremony? (*He catches the eye* of *the* PRINCESS, *and they give each other a secret smile.*)

KING: Certainly. (*The* PRINCE *bows and goes out. To* DULCIBELLA). Now, young woman, make yourself scarce. You've done your work excellently, and we will see that you and your—what was his name?

DULCIBELLA: Eg, Your Majesty.

KING: —that you and your Eg are not forgotten.

DULCIBELLA: Coo! (*She curtsies and goes out.*)

PRINCESS: (*calling*). Wait for me, Dulcibella!

KING: (*to* QUEEN). Well, my dear, we may congratulate ourselves. As I remember saying to somebody once, "You have not lost a daughter, you have gained a son." How does he strike you?

QUEEN: Stupid.

KING: They made a very handsome pair, I thought, he and Dulcibella.

QUEEN: Both stupid.

KING: I said nothing about stupidity. What I said was that they were both extremely handsome. That is the important thing. (*Struck by a sudden idea*). Or isn't it?

QUEEN: What do you think of Prince Simon, Camilla?

PRINCESS: I adore him. We shall be so happy together.
KING: Well, of course you will. I told you so. Happy ever after.
QUEEN: Run along now and get ready.
PRINCESS: Yes, mother. (*She throws a kiss to them and goes out.*)
KING: (*anxiously*). My dear, have we been wrong about Camilla all this time? It seemed to me that she wasn't looking *quite* so plain as usual just now. Did *you* notice anything?
QUEEN: (*carelessly*). Just the excitement of the marriage.
KING: (*relieved*). Ah, yes, that would account for it.

CURTAIN

ABOUT THE AUTHOR

Alan Alexander (A. A.) Milne (1882–1956) was born in Scotland but reared in England. Although Milne had attended college on a mathematics scholarship, he became a writer for a student magazine. In addition to this writing, he partnered with his brother to write articles for a British publication.

Milne is most noted for his Winnie the Pooh books. Christopher Robin, the main character, was named after Milne's son Christopher, while other characters were based on his son's stuffed animals. Although he was famous on both sides of the Atlantic, his children's works have been more widely accepted in the United States than in his homeland. In addition to his Pooh writings, Milne wrote a number of novels, numerous articles for magazines and newspapers, and a number of poems that were later compiled and published as the books *When We Were Very Young* and *Now We Are Six*. In addition, he wrote numerous plays dealing with a variety of subjects. Sometime after Milne's death in 1952, his wife sold the rights to Pooh to the Walt Disney Company.

THINKING ZONE

Another important and interesting literary genre is the drama or play. **Drama** is literature written to be acted. Perhaps you have attended a play or, better yet, been a part of one. Most plays are divided into **acts,** or major divisions in the action of a play. Shakespeare's *Hamlet* or Rostand's *Cyrano de Bergerac* are examples of multi-act plays. Each act may have multiple **scenes,** subdivisions of the act that do not contain a change of time or place. *The Ugly Duckling* is an example of a one-act play.

The director, the actors, and those backstage often rely upon **stage directions,** which are instructions for lighting, movement, and action included in the script. These instructions are written by the **playwright,** the name given to someone who writes plays. Imagine yourself playing a role in *The Ugly Duckling.* Which role would suit you best?

1. *[critical]* At what point did you realize that this is a humorous **drama?**

   _____

   _____

   _____

2. *[literal]* According to the play, on what basis would a suitor desire to marry the Princess?

   _____

   _____

   _____

3. *[appreciative]* As you read the King's dialogue with Dulcibella, how do the **stage directions** add to their conversation?

   _____

   _____

   _____

   Dialogue—*conversation between characters*

4. *[literal]* How did "Prince Simon's attendant" (in reality the Prince himself) get into the palace?

   _____

   _____

   _____

5. *[critical]* What is a plot twist in the play?

   _____

   _____

   _____

   _____

   Plot Twist— *a plot development that violates reader expectations*

6. *[literal]* Near the end of the **act** is a **scene** in which the Prince and Carlo discuss Carlo's inadvertently incorrect answer to the riddle. What name for a cat do they say is given in a distant country?

   _____

   _____

   _____

7. *[critical]* How does this response add to the humor of the play?

   _____

   _____

   _____

8. *[critical]* What do you think was the **playwright's** purpose in writing *The Ugly Duckling*? Do you think he accomplished that purpose?

   _____

   _____

   _____

9. *[critical]* How might the message of Isaiah 53:2 relate to the purpose mentioned in question 8: "He hath no form nor comeliness; and when we shall see him, there is no beauty that we should desire him"?

   _____

   _____

BENEATH THE CROSS OF JESUS

ELIZABETH C. CLEPHANE

Beneath the cross of Jesus
I fain* would take my stand,   fain: gladly
The shadow of a mighty rock
Within a weary land;
A home within the wilderness,
A rest upon the way,
From the burning of the noontide heat,
And the burden of the day.

Upon that cross of Jesus,
Mine eye at times can see
The very dying form of One
Who suffered there for me;
And from my smitten heart with tears
Two wonders I confess,—
The wonders of His glorious love
And my unworthiness.

I take, O Cross, thy shadow
For my abiding place;
I ask no other sunshine than
The sunshine of His face;
Content to let the world go by,
To know no gain nor loss,
My sinful self my only shame,
My glory all the cross.

Christ on the Cross. Unknown Flemish or Dutch.
From the Museum & Gallery at Bob Jones University
Collection

ABOUT THE AUTHOR

Elizabeth Cecilia Douglas Clephane (1830–69) was a Scottish poet who wrote several excellent hymns. She was an accomplished poet even as a child, and her father delighted in his daughter's poem-letters. The family moved to Melrose, Scotland, Sir Walter Scott's territory, and the bridge that appears in some of Scott's novels served as the inspiration for "Beneath the Cross of Jesus." Clephane was invited by the *Children's Hour* magazine to submit a poem. As she thought about what to write, she looked out the window at the nearby bridge and imagined a procession of monks from Melrose Abbey going across it. She was then impressed by the assurance that there is no other way to heaven but by the cross of Christ; no good works or life of piety will suffice. Clephane died a few months after writing her famous hymn. Singer-composer Ira Sankey saw her poem in a newspaper and set the words to music.

THE CONVERSION OF SAUL

In Acts 8 we are told that Saul had persecuted believers and assisted in the stoning of Stephen. In this selection, a remarkable change occurs. This change is the result of more than one person's choice. What choices were made and by whom? Which choice do you think is most important? Why?

And Saul, yet breathing out threatenings and slaughter against the disciples of the Lord, went unto the high priest,

2 And desired of him letters to Damascus to the synagogues, that if he found any of this way, whether they were men or women, he might bring them bound unto Jerusalem.

3 And as he journeyed, he came near Damascus: and suddenly there shined round about him a light from heaven:

4 And he fell to the earth, and heard a voice saying unto him, Saul, Saul, why persecutest thou me?

5 And he said, Who art thou, Lord? And the Lord said, I am Jesus whom thou persecutest: it is hard for thee to kick against the pricks.

6 And he trembling and astonished said, Lord, what wilt thou have me to do? And the Lord said unto him, Arise, and go into the city, and it shall be told thee what thou must do.

7 And the men which journeyed with him stood speechless, hearing a voice, but seeing no man.

8 And Saul arose from the earth; and when his eyes were opened, he saw no man: but they led him by the hand, and brought him into Damascus.

9 And he was three days without sight, and neither did eat nor drink.

10 And there was a certain disciple at Damascus, named Ananias; and to him said the Lord in a vision, Ananias. And he said, Behold, I am here, Lord.

11 And the Lord said unto him, Arise, and go into the street which is called Straight, and inquire in the house of Judas for one called Saul of Tarsus: for, behold, he prayeth.

12 And hath seen in a vision a man named Ananias coming in, and putting his hand on him, that he might receive his sight.

13 Then Ananias answered, Lord, I have heard by many of this man, how much evil he hath done to thy saints at Jerusalem:

14 And here he hath authority from the chief priests to bind all that call on thy name.

15 But the Lord said unto him, Go thy way: for he is a chosen vessel unto me, to bear my name before the Gentiles, and kings, and the children of Israel:

16 For I will shew him how great things he must suffer for my name's sake.

17 And Ananias went his way, and entered into the house; and putting his hands on him said, Brother Saul, the Lord, even Jesus, that appeared unto thee in the way as thou camest, hath sent me, that thou mightest receive thy sight, and be filled with the Holy Ghost,

18 And immediately there fell from his eyes as it had been scales: and he received sight forthwith, and arose, and was baptized.

19 And when he had received meat, he was strengthened. Then was Saul certain days with the disciples which were at Damascus.

20 And straightway he preached Christ in the synagogues, that he is the Son of God.

21 But all that heard him were amazed, and said; Is not this he that destroyed them which called on this name in Jerusalem, and

came hither for that intent, that he might bring them bound unto the chief priests?

22 But Saul increased the more in strength, and confounded the Jews which dwelt at Damascus, proving that this is very Christ.

23 And after that many days were fulfilled, the Jews took counsel to kill him:

24 But their laying await was known of Saul. And they watched the gates day and night to kill him.

25 Then the disciples took him by night, and let him down by the wall in a basket.

26 And when Saul was come to Jerusalem, he assayed to join himself to the disciples: but they were all afraid of him, and believed not that he was a disciple.

27 But Barnabas took him, and brought him to the apostles, and declared unto them how he had seen the Lord in the way, and that he had spoken to him, and how he had preached boldly at Damascus in the name of Jesus.

28 And he was with them coming in and going out at Jerusalem.

29 And he spake boldly in the name of the Lord Jesus, and disputed against the Grecians: but they went about to slay him.

30 Which when the brethren knew, they brought him down to Caesarea, and sent him forth to Tarsus.

31 Then had the churches rest throughout all Judea and Galilee and Samaria, and were edified; and walking in the fear of the Lord, and in the comfort of the Holy Ghost, were multiplied.

—Acts 9:1–31

UNIT 2 REVIEW

SHORT ANSWER

Write the word, phrase, or sentence that best answers the question.

1. From what point of view is "Weep No More, My Lady" told?

   _____

2. What are some characteristics that M'Lady shows that are not typical of dogs?

   _____

   _____

   _____

3. In "Mama and the Graduation Present," why does Katrin want something other than Mama's brooch for a graduation present?

   _____

   _____

   _____

4. How does Papa show that he believes Katrin has grown up?

   _____

5. In "The Brothers" what is the character trait that controls the action of the story?

   _____

6. What is the moral of "Pleasing All the World"?

   _____

7. In "The Magic Brocade" what do the actions of the sons reveal about them?

   _____

   _____

8. Who is the protagonist of "The Golden Touch"?

   _____

9. Name two things in "Make Me Thy Fuel" that Carmichael asks God to give her.

   _____

10. In the play *The Ugly Duckling*, what is the sole reason that a suitor would want to marry the Princess?

_____

MULTIPLE CHOICE

Choose the best answer from the choices given.

_____ 11. Why does Cash call Skeeter "Jonathan" at the end of the story?
   A. He thinks "Skeeter" is a silly name.
   B. He wants to treat Skeeter like a man.
   C. He does not know Skeeter very well.
   D. He forgets Skeeter's real name.

_____ 12. Throughout most of "Mama and the Graduation Present," Katrin is proud of all of the following *except*
   A. her graduation gift.
   B. her part in the school play.
   C. the fact that she is going to Lowell for high school.
   D. the sacrifice Mama makes to purchase her gift.

_____ 13. In "The Brothers," which of the following is true of the watch?
   A. Anders's wife hides the watch from both of them.
   B. The brothers eventually agree to share the watch.
   C. The watch becomes worthless.
   D. The watch increases in value when it is melted down for gold.

_____ 14. Which of the following is *not* a lesson to be learned from "The Nail"?
   A. Haste makes waste.
   B. Ignoring a problem won't solve it.
   C. Finding someone else to blame for problems makes one feel better.
   D. Take care of even the smallest problems before they turn into large ones.

_____ 15. Based on "Make Me Thy Fuel," which of the following things does the poet *not* ask God to grant her?
   A. a desire for joy
   B. a desire for love
   C. a desire for faith
   D. a desire for hope

_____ 16. What irony is revealed in "The Golden Touch"?

    A. that riches and roses are the most important things in life

    B. that success requires little effort

    C. that common things sometimes have the most value

    D. that extreme wealth brings extreme happiness

MATCHING

Match the following literary terms with their correct definitions.

_____ 17. weakness or moral flaw

_____ 18. expression of one thing in terms of another

_____ 19. truth about life

_____ 20. popular myth, legend, tall tale, or fairy tale

_____ 21. repetition at the beginning of lines of poetry

A. metaphor

B. folktale

C. anaphora

D. character flaw

E. moral

TRUE/FALSE

If the statement is completely true, write _true_. If any part of the statement is false, write _false_.

_____ 22. In "Weep No More, My Lady," M'Lady's winning the competition with Cash's dog does not further the conflict of the story.

_____ 23. The implicit theme of "Mama and the Graduation Present" is that a mature person is selfless and considerate of others.

_____ 24. In "The Brothers" only Baard demonstrates the character flaw of pride.

_____ 25. The protagonist in "The Blacksmith's Dilemma" is Walukaga.

_____ 26. In "The Golden Touch" Midas experiences events that foreshadowed that the "golden touch" would not be as beneficial as he thinks.

ESSAY

Write a complete answer in one paragraph for the question below, using specific examples from the unit.

27. Choose one of these characters: Skeeter, Anders, Baard, or King Midas. Write a paragraph that clearly answers the following questions about that character: What was the major choice he made? Was this a good choice or a poor choice? What were the results of this choice?

_____

_____

_____

_____

_____

_____

_____

_____

_____

_____

_____

_____

_____

_____

_____

_____

_____

_____

_____

_____

_____

_____

3

HEROES

Since the 1930s, photojournalists have played an important role in documenting not only the facts but also the emotions of war. Photographs are often seen as objective documents; however, photographers can also be subjective in the way they interpret the slices of life they depict.

What message do you think the unknown photographer wished to convey in this photograph of two men saluting in a World War II cemetery in the Ryukyu Islands?

What do you know about the men in the photograph? Do you think they are heroes?

What is the mood depicted by the rows of crosses? Are they all identical?

This photograph was shot in black and white. How would the mood of the photograph change if it were a color photograph?

HEROES

WHAT MAKES A HERO? A HERO MIGHT BE THE FIREFIGHTER WHO RUSHES INTO A BURNING APARTMENT TO SAVE A BABY, BUT A HERO MAY JUST AS WELL BE THE PARENT WHO GIVES UP HIS OWN AMBITION TO SUPPORT A FAMILY.

The daycare worker who herds her class to safety during a tornado is a hero, but so too is the friend who stands with you in trouble and in prosperity. A hero could be the stranger who chooses not to look the other way but who instead intervenes and offers encouragement and hope. Part of being heroic is doing the right thing despite the cost to one's self, one's reputation, or one's wallet.

The Bible is filled with people who could be considered heroes: Noah, Rahab, Paul, and Eunice, Timothy's mother, to name a few. These people believed God and His promises, and their faith was worked out in their everyday actions—to build an ark, to sequester the spies, to teach the young people in their care. They were not afraid to disregard personal pride or advancement for the glory of God.

By anyone's definition of heroism, the greatest hero in all history and literature is Jesus Christ. He lived meekly among His enemies. He refused to allow His followers to defend Him with weapons of war. And in the end, He chose death over denying what He knew was true—that He was indeed the Christ, the Son of God. But there is something grand and epic about His meek heroism. He died in shame, but three days later He rose again. By rising from the dead, He conquered death, proved that the sins of His people were forgiven, and took His triumphant place at His Father's right hand. Today He rules over the kings of the earth with glory and majesty. Christ's heroism is something He desires to share with His people. Because He has conquered death and sin, we too have the ability to live lives of courageous sacrifice.

The primary purpose for the literature selections in this unit is not to revere any human being or his actions; rather, it is to reinforce the belief that heroes are not shaped by the circumstances they face but by how they react to those circumstances. In this unit, you will meet some unlikely heroes. Be alert to the heroes' struggles and realize that it is heart, not environment, that determines a hero. The way that you act and react can glorify your Creator God and thereby be a testimony to someone who is watching. You, too, can be a hero. ✠

WORTHY IS THE LAMB THAT WAS SLAIN TO RECEIVE POWER,
AND RICHES, AND WISDOM, AND STRENGTH, AND HONOUR,
AND GLORY, AND BLESSING.

—REVELATION 5:12

In Search of Honor

Donnalynn Hess

The fear of the Lord is the instruction of wisdom;
and before honor is humility.—Proverbs 15:33

The triumphs and tragedies of the French Revolution (1789–93) were many, and like all revolutions, this one had both its heroes and its villains. For Jacques, the central character in this story, the process of searching for honor is a long and complicated one. The book begins with Jacques's own introduction to the story of his search for honor.

PROLOGUE
AUTUMN, 1793

Keep your heart with all diligence, for out of it spring the issues of life. —Proverbs 4:23

I have never been inclined to talk much about myself or my affairs. There are two reasons to account for this, I suppose. The first is simply that talk of others has always seemed more interesting to me than talk of myself. The second is that I was given by my Creator (whether as a thorn or a gift, I'm yet unsure) a reticent* nature. It may seem odd, therefore, that someone of my temperament should be suddenly struck with what might be called an "autobiographical impulse." But to be honest, I confess that even now as I begin to write, my inclination is the same as it has always been—to say nothing. My conscience, however, will not allow it.

---
reticent: reserved; shy

As may be guessed, much of what I must write is not flattering. I can only hope that those who read this narrative will believe me when I say that by the grace of God I am not as I once was. Such hope will seem less presumptuous if, from the outset, I make clear my determination to return to France and do what I can to set things right. I am re-

solved to do so even if it costs me my life, as well it might, for I've been warned that the Revolution has not ended—that the sharp blade of the guillotine is yet wet with the blood of the innocent.

Though I have little way of knowing exactly *what* I shall find when I return to Paris, I know *whom* I must find. His name is Phillipe Grammônd. Though he is several years younger than I, Phillipe was once my most loyal friend. He admired me at a time when I was unworthy of admiration and loved me with a faithfulness I did not deserve. It is for him especially that I've decided to write down these thoughts and take them with me. I hope that they will help him, and others like him, to understand the mercy of the God I've come to know and love.

I write for one other friend as well, a much older and wiser friend named Pierre-Joseph Aumônt. It was he who first shared with me the Scripture, that Word which has since given me the will to live and the courage to die. It was also he who made possible my safe flight from France to England.

My escape took place about a year ago in the autumn of 1792. Louis XVI had but recently been overthrown, and with the monarchy's demise, radicals in France increased their power until the tenuous* rule of law and order gave way to a reign of terror. Up to that time, I had imagined myself incapable of cowardice or cruelty. I was wrong.

---

tenuous: weak; flimsy

In my months away from home, I've come to understand many things, not the least of which is a truth that Pierre-Joseph tried with astonishing patience to pound into my head. "You must understand, Jacques," he said repeatedly. "It is your heart—not your circumstances—that will determine whether you become a man of honor or disgrace." I was fifteen and a prisoner in the Bastille when he first spoke those words to me. Of course, I did not believe him then. But I run ahead of myself. Let me begin my story by telling you of Paris and of my place in it on the eve of the Revolution.

THINKING ZONE

Up to this point in your text, you have been reading short selections such as stories and poems. Now you have begun an extended work of fictional prose, a novel. *In Search of Honor* is an example of **historical fiction**; that is, the **novel** is a fictional story that contains authentic historical characters or events that tell its story. When an author blends history with fiction in this manner, the story seems more real to the reader. Since by definition historical fiction takes place in the past, authors will sometimes write a prologue. A prologue is an introduction to a literary work. Prologues were a standard device in Greek drama. The **prologue** gave any background necessary to the listeners' understanding of the action that followed. The prologue to *In Search of Honor* acquaints the reader with the characters in the story and the time period of the French Revolution. The effect is to bring the reader "up to speed" before the author begins her story in earnest.

Narrator—*the person who tells a story*

Hero—*the protagonist or main character of a story*

1. *[critical]* What do you think is the purpose of Hess's **prologue** to this piece of **historical fiction**?

_____

_____

_____

_____

_____

_____

_____

_____

2. *[critical]* Based on the prologue, who do you think is the hero of the **novel**?

_____

_____

_____

3. *[literal]* In the prologue, what does the narrator reveal about himself?

_____

_____

_____

_____

_____

4. *[interpretive]* How does the narrator seem to feel about the story he is going to tell?

_____

_____

_____

5. *[interpretive/critical]* Within the prologue, the author includes many details that most likely foreshadow the main plot of her story. What are these details?

_____

_____

_____

_____

6. *[critical]* How do you think the opening verse of the prologue relates to the story?

_____

_____

_____

_____

7. *[critical]* Given that the novel is titled *In Search of Honor*, what about the prologue is ironic? How may this irony be instructive?

_____

_____

_____

_____

_____

PART ONE
THE ROAD TO THE BASTILLE
1787–1788

CHAPTER 1
SPRING, 1787

The revolution began for me the day my father was murdered. Though it was years ago, memories of that day have faded little. His death is still difficult to think upon and harder yet to write about, and I would not, were it not for the fact that the circumstances of his death reveal the temper of the times.

It was early one afternoon. My father and I were in our shop as usual. I was bent over the fire, stirring up a new batch of molding wax while he was busy carving on yet another marble bust of the great Rousseau. He had done many such busts that spring, for Rousseau, like Voltaire, had become an idol of the rich. Requests for his image seemed endless and were not limited to sculptured busts. The wealthy wanted the face of this dead philosopher on buttons, snuff boxes, shaving bowls, and inkwells. Indeed, for several months it seemed that everywhere I looked, a Rousseau was staring back at me.

There was one thing, however, that intrigued me about those myriad* faces that my father created: no two were alike. I have since come to realize that such diversity is the mark of a great artist. My father was a great artist, and I freely admit that any success I have achieved as a sculptor I owe to him. For it was he who first stood me on a stool before a block of stone, placed a chisel in my hand, and clasping his strong hand over mine, steadied the tool and laid the hammer to it. I was no more than three, but I still vividly remember the first time my hand felt iron meeting stone. From that day I was always at my father's side working with him in the shop.

myriad: a large number

I can still see him as he was that afternoon, poised on the edge of his stool, hovering over a low wooden worktable, the dust of chiseled stone clinging to his beard. I remember, too, how his face brightened the moment he laid his tools aside and bade me do the same.

"Jacques,* tomorrow is your mother's birthday," he reminded me. "What shall we get for her?"

Jacques (zhäk)

His look told me that he had no need of my suggestions. Still, he had asked. So, remembering her birthdays past, I suggested some colorful linen thread for her lace work.

"No, no, Jacques," he said, beckoning me to bring a stool and come to sit by him. "I want this year to be different. This year, I want to give your mother a memory—to wrap it up and place it on the table there before her."

I was just fourteen, but at that moment something in my father's voice made me understand that he spoke to me as man to man, and though uncertain of the full meaning in his words, I sensed enough to know that I wanted to be part of his plan. I paused only a moment before asking, "What kind of memory?"

He leaned forward, resting both hands upon his knees. "Well," he continued, his voice just above a whisper, "you know, we've never had much. Oh, my father and I had plenty of business, just as you and I do. But even good business does not provide artisans* like us with the delicacies of the rich. There was one time though—just once—when your mother and I enjoyed such a delicacy. It was on our wedding day. On that day my father somehow managed to get a pigeon and prepare it for our wedding supper. Ah, Jacques," he sighed, "you never tasted such a dinner."

---
artisans: skilled craftsmen

"However did grandfather get hold of a pigeon?" I asked.

"I've no idea," he confessed. "But this I do know: if he did it, so can I. Your mother has often reminisced to me about that bird. And when she speaks of it, it's enough to make your mouth water. She remembers it well."

"I think it's not just the bird that she's remembering," I said.

His smile grew so broad it threatened to eclipse his face. "You're right, Jacques! Every time she thinks about that bird, she remembers that she loves me. Indeed, I think it may have been that bird that won her heart. That's why you and I are going to close up shop and pay a visit to old Michel this afternoon. He's a good man, old Michel is, and I'll wager he'll let me hunt a bird out on his land."

"Hunt?" I said. "On his small plot of land? Not much for hunting I'd say."

"Michel farms more than that one small plot. He tends the fields all around him. It's a vast acreage."

"But he does not own all the land he farms," I reminded him. "The Comte de Guiche* owns most of it."

Comte de Guiche (kô[m]t de gēsh´)

A look of anger erased the smile from my father's face. "It is Michel who keeps the land thriving, and he does so with a worn-out plow and rusty sickle. What's more, he pays good money to that fat old Comte for the 'privilege' of doing so!" He then thrust his finger in my face for emphasis. "Michel nurses the land, makes it fruitful, and pays for it. Now you tell me, who 'owns' it?"

I could not better his argument, and yet I felt I had to try. "But the laws, Papa. They say the Comte owns most of the land and *all* of the game on it—even the game on Michel's plot."

"I have come to believe, Jacques, that only a fool would say that the birds which fly over a man's field are not his!"

"Well, then," I said cautiously, "France must be full of fools."

He gazed at me a moment and then burst into a hearty laugh. "There you have it!"

My father could see that fear made it hard for me to enjoy the laughter.

"Times are changing," he assured me. "Have you not listened to the talk of those who come into the shop? They have enshrined the ideas of Rousseau as surely as they have his face. Mark me, before long they will consider it fashionable to cast aside such laws."

"Still," I argued, "the laws aren't cast aside just yet. And we don't know if the Comte de Guiche is one who's heard of such ideas."

"Every beggar in the streets of Paris has heard of such ideas!" he chided. "Come, it is *one* bird to make your mother happy. My father succeeded in bagging one, and in his day the laws were even harsher. Besides, if you are right in saying that the Comte has managed to remain ignorant of Rousseau, then it should be easy to hide my hunt from him as well."

"We'd best be going then," I said, his confidence having won me over, "or the setting sun, not the Comte de Guiche, will keep us from that bird."

"Let's to it," he said, and we got up to go. It was then we heard my mother coming down the stairs that led up to our living quarters. "Jacques," she said, quickly entering the shop and handing me one of her neatly wrapped bundles, "I need for you to deliver this lace to—"

My father intercepted the bundle and gave it back to her. "Oh no," he said. "Jacques is coming with me."

My mother stared up at him in vague surprise. "And where in the world would you be going in the middle of the day?"

"None of your business," said my father merrily. And taking off his apron, he tossed it to her.

Caught up in my father's high spirits, I too whipped off my apron and tossed it to my mother. Then, fearing she might take this bravado somewhat amiss, I added, "We won't be long, and you'll be pleased with what we bring back for you."

As we headed toward the door my mother called out after us, "Go ahead you two, go off without a word. But I warn you, I'll not keep your dinner warm if you are late." I looked back just long enough to see that her scolding was all bluff.

* * *

My anxiety returned when we reached Michel's, for I could see my former apprehension mirrored in his weathered face. "I don't know—" he said. "The Comte, he's uncommon stingy with his birds."

"You know, Michel, I'd not ask you to answer for my actions," said my father carefully. "I don't want you to give me an official sanction.* I just want to know—friend to friend—if it were up to you, would you mind my bagging a bird on this property?"

"If it were up to me, you know I'd bag the bird for you myself," he said. Then he added hotly, "Why, I'd bag you a whole slew of 'em. Those flying thieves raid my seed at every harvest, then fly home to the safety of the Comte's dovecote!"* He paused and grew cautious once again. "What's mine I'd just as soon be yours. I can loan you a gun, but—"

---

sanction: official permission

dovecote: structure often raised on a pole for domesticated pigeons

---

My father stopped him. "That's all I ask, the loan of a gun and your word that whatever else you could give, you would give."

With that assurance, old Michel handed my father his gun, doffed* his ragged cap, and left us.

doffed: tipped or removed his hat

It was late afternoon by the time we finally set out, and another quarter of an hour passed before we came to an open stretch of land. "I'll wager," said my father, pointing out a brushy area in the distance, "I can flush a nice fat bird out of that brush over there."

"What can I do to help?" I asked.

"Wait here," he said, the excitement growing in his voice. "Two of us would make too much noise. You can keep a lookout for me."

I watched his lean, agile form set out across the field and thought proudly that he was yet a good man to have in any fight. The quiet beauty of the open land calmed my fears and restored my faith in him, and as I sat down under an old gnarled tree to

wait, I no longer doubted that he would bag that bird.

It was not long before a shot rang out. Jumping to my feet, I saw my father emerging from the brush, holding up his treasure for me to see. I was about to shout my congratulations, but before I could give voice to it, I spied a young man decked out in finery riding fast toward my father from the east. He too must have heard the shot. I tried to cry a warning, but the words stuck in my throat like some suffocating thing. Nor did I move. I simply watched the man as he came on, his fine muscular horse silhouetted against the burning brightness of the setting sun, its graceful form hardly touching hoof to ground.

He reached my father and reigned in but did not dismount. They spoke, and from where I stood, I saw neither fear nor shame upon my father's face during the course of this short exchange. Then I remember my father holding up that bird. I expected the young nobleman simply to reach down and take it. Instead he pulled a pistol from his riding boot, shot my father in the chest, and rode off as if he'd killed a rabbit.

I found my voice and took off at a run, crying out my father's name as I fled to him across the field. To this day I do not know if anyone heard my screaming. I know that I did not care. At that moment I cared for one thing only—the sound of my father's voice answering mine.

When I reached him, he lay sprawled on his back, his hand still clutching fast the lifeless bird. The blood was flowing freely from his heart, and I knew before I kneeled to touch him—he was dead. He looked so strange lying there amidst the new grown grass and wildflowers. How I wished that the same April sun that had but recently touched dry roots long sleeping, bringing them to life, could have touched my father also and awakened him again. The world changed for me that moment as I knelt beside my father, lifeless in the field.

*   *   *

My mother and I survived those days immediately following my father's death by keeping alive our hope that his murderer, whom we learned was the older of the Comte de Guiche's two sons, would be brought to justice. By summer's end, "justice" had been meted out. The Comte's wealth and influence insured that the court would be lenient;* the young nobleman was sentenced only "to pay a fee to the widow and orphan of the dead man."

---

lenient: permissive; tolerant

I well remember the rage on my mother's face when that young man, only a few years older than I, stepped forward and handed her his bulging bag of coins. I think he actually believed that she would take it, for he seemed genuinely astonished when she emptied its contents into her hand and threw it at his feet. He was doubly astonished when she spit in his face before turning on her heel and exiting the courtroom.

By the time we reached the shop, her rage had given way to grief. She wept almost unceasingly for several days. Then she stopped her weeping. Burying her hopes with my father, she gave way to complete despair.

THINKING ZONE

In your reading of this novel, you will study examples of various narrative devices as well as build upon literary concepts and terms that you have studied in the previous two units. The first of the new devices is **flashback**, a reference to events that occurred before the main story or the action that is occurring at the time the narrator is speaking. The short story "After Twenty Years" contains a kind of flashback when Bob tells the policeman about his dinner with Jimmy at "Big Joe" Brady's. In this story most of the action is presented as a flashback, with the prologue's having set up reader anticipation for finding out what has happened to Jacques.

Prologue—
introduction to a literary work

1. *[critical]* How might it be said that the last line of the prologue implies that Chapter 1 will begin as a **flashback**?

   _____

   _____

   _____

2. *[critical]* What purpose does the first sentence of Part One, Chapter 1, serve?

   _____

3. *[literal]* What occupation is Jacques learning from his father?

   _____

4. *[critical]* What do we know about Jacques's father, based on his words and actions?

   _____

   _____

   _____

5. *[literal/interpretive]* What does Jacques's father plan to give his wife? How does Jacques feel about his father's plan?

   _____

   _____

   _____

6. *[critical]* Biblically evaluate the decision of Jacques's father to take the bird.

_____

_____

_____

_____

7. *[critical]* What is sadly ironic about Jacques's father's words concerning the gift: "I want to give your mother a memory"?

_____

_____

_____

8. *[literal/critical]* What simile describes how the Comte de Guiche's son felt about his act toward Jacques's father? What does this simile mean?

_____

_____

_____

Simile— *comparisons of un-like objects using* like *or* as

9. *[critical]* What conflicts exist in Chapter 1? Do any of them foreshadow what happens in the chapter or what might possibly happen in future chapters?

_____

_____

_____

_____

_____

10. *[appreciative]* How would you respond to someone whose reaction to adversity is similar to Jacques's mother's reaction to her husband's death?

_____

_____

_____

CHAPTER 2
SPRING, 1788

Unlike my mother, I did not despair after my father's death. Nor did I vent my rage in public as she had done that day in the courtroom. Indeed, it would have been impossible for me to rid myself of such anger in a moment of passion. No, my rage went too deep, and deeply did I harbor it until it became so much a part of me that I ceased to see it for what it was. I believed my growing sullenness to be the outworking of genuine sorrow and my increasing peevishness* the legitimate reflection of a creative nature.

---
peevishness: irritation; anger

If there was any advantage to this melancholy brought on by anger, it was that it drove me to my work. I felt at peace only when I was busy in my shop. The sturdy feel of my hammer and chisel coupled with the measured sound of iron striking stone seemed somehow to quiet my feverish spirit. Such discipline hastened the establishment of my reputation. Within a year I was looked upon as a master artisan whose work could evoke a nod of approval from the most obstinate nobleman.

Still, the fact that I could satisfy wealthy customers did not insure that my mother and I would be well fed. There were several reasons for this, one of which affected all of us who labored in St. Antoine.* The year's harvest had been meager and the winter harsh. Food and firewood were scarce even for those who could afford them. Beggars in the streets of Paris had increased twofold, and I began to fear that my mother and I might soon be forced to join them. But during this unhappy time there was one bit of light I allowed into my otherwise dismal existence. It was Phillipe,* the eight-year-old son of the cabinetmaker Thomas Grammônd,* whose shop was also on our street.

St. Antoine (să[n]t ä[n]-twän´)

Phillipe (fē-lēp´)

Thomas Grammônd (tō-mä´ grä-mô[n]´)

Shortly after my father's death, Phillipe began his daily visits to my shop. He had wandered in one day and had become as intrigued with my work as I had been with my father's. I suppose that was what first endeared him to me—that and his boundless energy and unfailing good nature, both of which did much to lift my spirits as I worked. I remember one day in particular.

I had just completed a bust commissioned by a squire named Latude when Phillipe came bursting in and announced quite unnecessarily, "I'm here!" In a moment his cap and jacket were tossed into the corner, and he was dragging a stool over to my worktable. "It's Monsieur Latude,"* he said, as he climbed up on the stool.

Monsieur Latude (mœ-syœ´ lä-tüd´)

"And how do you know the 'good' monsieur?" I asked, gratified that I had apparently achieved a good likeness of the squire.

"He's been coming into Papa's shop for weeks," Phillipe informed me. "He has ordered a cabinet, but he's hard to please. Each time Papa thinks he's finished carving, Monsieur Latude demands another leaf or flower. You should hear Papa after he has gone. It's enough to scorch your ears!"

The news was not encouraging. "Perhaps he will like his face better than he likes his cabinet," I said.

It was then that I noticed Phillipe's expression. Something about the bust was bothering him. Though he was only eight, I had come to realize that Phillipe had a keen eye, and his appraisals, if nothing else, were always honest—sometimes brutally so. I braced myself. "What's the matter?" I asked. "Don't you like it?"

"Oh, it isn't that," he assured me.

"Well, what is it then?"

I can still see him as he leaned both elbows on the worktable and peered closely at the face. His unruly auburn hair fell down across his forehead and his blue-black eyes were fixed in concentration on my work.

"Well?" I prodded.

"His nose," said Phillipe. "It is the nose."

"What about the nose?"

"It's not big enough," he concluded. Then, with the confident air of a critic, he leaned back, folded his arms across his chest, and said yet more emphatically, "Monsieur Latude's nose is much bigger."

"But Monsieur Latude does not believe that," I explained.

Phillipe was yet too young—and honest—to enjoy the art of vain deceit. "How can he not believe it?" he demanded. "It is on *his* face."

"That is precisely why he does not," I said. Phillipe's trust in me began to erode his confidence, and I remember that he lifted his hand and rubbed his own nose as if to make certain that he knew its size.

"One day you'll understand," I assured him. "For now you must trust that I have made Monsieur Latude's nose exactly as he wants it." Of course, I did not admit to him the pleasure that it gave me to play upon the vanity of such men; it was a form of scorn.

"Speaking of what Monsieur Latude wants," I continued, "he has asked me to deliver this to Charpentier's café. Monsieur Charpentier* has promised me that he will deliver the bust *and* see that I am paid." For several months I'd been seeking out commissions at Charpentier's to supplement those that came directly to the shop.

Charpentier (shär-pä[n]-tyä´)

"Do you want me to stay and listen for the shop bell until your mother returns?" he asked.

"She's here—" I admitted; then I hesitated. "But she is upstairs—sleeping."

"She is always sleeping these days," he observed.

I ignored his comment and said instead, "If you will stay and listen for the bell, I will give you some molding wax to work with."

"And a story when you return?"

I nodded my consent.

"I will stay as long as you like," he promised.

"Good," I said, scooping some wax onto a pan and placing it in front of him. "I will be gone the remainder of the afternoon and perhaps on into early evening."

Carefully I wrapped a cloth about the bust of Latude. "Just get the name and address from any customers that come for me," I continued.

"If someone comes wanting to buy your mama's lace, do you want me to go upstairs and wake her?"

"No—" I said a bit too harshly.

Phillipe looked up. "Shall I tell them to come tomorrow then?"

"No," I said and tried to search for some excuse that would make him cease his questioning. "Just tell them that she is ill and that I—I'm not sure when she will be feeling better." As an afterthought I added, "Of course, they can leave their name if they would like."

Despite my efforts, Phillipe sensed my growing irritation, and although he had no idea why I had turned peevish, he tried in his childlike way to make things better, saying, "It's all right. I don't think that anyone will come. The bell does not ring much for her anymore."

I got up quickly, picked up the bust, and headed out. At the door I turned to see him staring after me. "You need not stay inside the whole time," I said, trying to sound more cheerful. "Go outside a little; you can easily see any customers approaching in this alley. Oh, and if you get hungry before I return, there's some fruit over on the table in the corner."

He smiled and waved before plunging both hands into the molding wax. I went out, closing the door behind me. As I did so, the soft tinkling of the shop bell reminded me of Phillipe's innocent observation, "The bell does not ring much for her anymore."

CHAPTER 3

I had hoped that the atmosphere at Charpentier's would lift my spirits. It often did, but this day when I entered, I sensed a subtle, unsettled feeling, as if something unusual or unpleasant were about to happen. Moving toward my usual corner, I studied the customers as I went. They seemed the usual clientele:* lawyers in court robes languidly* sipping cider and talking politics; town clerks and country squires* gaming* and grumbling at crowded tables. Everything seemed as always—the lawyers, the clerks, the low hum of conversation punctuated by the soft tapping of dominos and drinking mugs on marbled tabletops.

clientele: customers
languidly: listlessly
squires: landowners; gentlemen
gaming: gambling

Within moments Charpentier approached and diverted my attention with his usual friendly goading.* "So you are here again."

goading: prodding or urging

"Yes, I'm here again," I said, somewhat heartened by his greeting. "And I'll be here again tomorrow. Come, admit it, you would miss me if I stayed away."

"It's true," he said laughing. Then growing serious he added, "Still, Jacques, you might take an afternoon off now and then; you never seem to relax, to enjoy yourself."

"That's why I come here," I said. "The games and conversation are relaxing."

"And, of course, every *sou** is important."

---
sou (sōō): a coin of small value

"I do well enough," I said defensively; then catching myself, I softened my tone. "My mother's lace making is the pride of Paris. She does a good business. Along with what I make, we are doing better than most. But—you are right, I do enjoy earning a few extra *sous*—just for myself."

"As you should enjoy making an honest wage for honest work," he said, his jovial spirit restored. "I see you have brought Latude," he added.

I unwrapped the bust* and handed it to him. It was about twelve inches in height but when Charpentier took it in his massive hands, it seemed almost to disappear.

---
bust: sculpture representing a person's head, shoulders, and upper chest
---

"I will say this for you, Jacques," he said, a faint smile playing at the corners of his mouth. "Though you are sometimes gloomy, you are certainly gifted. I do not understand how you can make a block of marble look as supple and smooth as muscle and bone."

"My father would have told you that what you hold in your hand was never simply stone," I said, warming to the subject of my art. "He taught me that in every block of marble there is a living face or figure waiting to be freed; the sculptor's job is simply to release the captive from the unchiseled stone that binds him."

Charpentier knew well that the memory of my father might draw me deeper into melancholy, and he did his best to avert the possibility. "Well, I must say that you've let Latude escape. But I warn you, there may be some who will not thank you that he's freed."

"It's too late now," I said.

Setting the bust aside, he continued, "It won't be long before all of my customers will be begging for a bust of themselves. You have come to the right place, Jacques, for I tell you that wherever there are lawyers, a sculptor need not want for work. Such men love busts of themselves. They set them on their mantels next to their collection of Rousseaus and Voltaires. Ah yes," he sighed, "such men pride themselves on their image." Then leaning close, he added, "Though just between you and me, as I look at them I cannot see why."

I smiled, and seeing his success, he added, "Then again, next to the pinched and sallow* face of old Voltaire, would not even I look handsome?"

---
sallow: colorless; yellowish

"Indeed," I assured him, laughing outright.

"Poor old Voltaire. Had he lived another ten years, I am certain that he would have begged you to do a bust of him." Charpentier paused a moment to cast another glance at the face of Latude before adding, "I have noted that you rarely fail to make your subjects look a bit better than they really are. Eh?"

"Perhaps," I confessed.

"I knew it!" he said. "You are more than a good sculptor; you are a clever businessman. And I predict that both will pay you well one day."

"I hope that you are right."

"Charpentier is *always* right," he said. "Trust me, you will one day be the talk of Paris. You will not forget me?"

"Of course not," I said.

"Good. Now go settle yourself and I will bring you some cider."

Taking Charpentier's advice, I moved over to the staircase and leaned against one of the wooden beams to wait for the casual nod of a customer to summon me. As I waited, a vague sense of guilt came over me, for I knew that I had not been honest with Charpentier. I did need money—desperately—and not just because of a meager harvest and harsh winter. My mother and I together should have been able to survive better than most. Indeed, her lace making had been the pride of Paris, but not of late—not since the Comte de Guiche's son had murdered my father.

I had lied to Phillipe as well. My mother had been sleeping, but her sleep was more than that brought on by ill health; it was the sleep of drunkenness. The deft hands that once wove delicate patterns now did little more than clutch a flask of sour wine. For months I had made excuses to her customers, but I rarely had to do so anymore. Her commissions had dropped off drastically, and what little money she did make, she hoarded to buy more wine. She drank and slept only to awake and drink some more. The only people I lied to now were friends.

I closed my eyes, determined to push down unwanted thoughts and feelings. Then, as if in answer to the tension that had gripped me, a booming voice called out, "Citizens!" I snapped to attention, as did every other man in the café. It was not unusual for a customer to demand attention. But as this man emerged from a darkened corner of the room, I could see that he was no usual customer.

He was a giant of a man, and although he was fashionably dressed, fashion ill-suited him. The gray breeches and white stockings that he wore clung to his muscular legs and thighs as if every thread were strained; his red-striped waistcoat bulged at every button; and the lace-trimmed cravat* looked ludicrous* around his bull-like neck. As for his face—I had never seen such a profoundly ugly face. His skin was marred and pitted by the ravages of smallpox, and his large square jaw was rounded out by massive sagging jowls. There was a scar that split his upper lip, and the dark eyes receded beneath wild, bushy eyebrows.

cravat (krə-văt´): a scarf worn around the neck as a tie
ludicrous: silly; ridiculous

Not a sound could be heard as this stranger moved to the center of the room, and with cool impudence stated flatly, "I need money."

The customers were dumbfounded, unable to decide whether this powerful man were a great orator* or a mere mountebank.* He did not wait for their decision.

orator: a skilled speaker
mountebank: a fake or cheat

"I see you blush that I so boldly confess to you my plight. But why? Does not the King himself admit as much?" He pulled a tattered news sheet from his waistcoat and held it up. "We are told here that France is poor, that His Majesty is poor, and that we the people must be taxed to pay his debts. But I, Georges Danton,* cannot pay his debts. Can you? Or you? Are we not mere clerks and counselors? We know that the wealthy nobles will not pay. Then I ask you again, who shall pay? The peasants who strain to wrench the rye and buckwheat from the soil?"

Georges Danton (zhorzh dä[n]-tô[n]´)

As Danton began to move among the crowd, I noted what to my artist's eye was an amazing transformation. This strange man's eloquence* not only swayed his hearers but changed his face as well. The dark eyes sparkled brightly, and every facial muscle sprang to life. Such animation transformed this grotesque giant of a man into a mighty warrior.

eloquence: persuasiveness

"Where has the wealth of our great nation gone?" he bellowed. "We were not always poor. I tell you it has gone to support the profligate* living of that Austrian woman, Marie-Antoinette, whom His Majesty calls our queen. She is not *our* queen, and we will not pay her debts! We cannot! And though we love our King, we will not allow his wife to drive us into bankruptcy!"

profligate: extravagant; wasteful

A round of applause rang out. I could see that without doubt Danton had his audience now, and with the skill of a Roman orator he continued the harangue,* a harangue I felt sure would go on for hours. Such speakers were seldom brief once they succeeded in arresting the attention of Charpentier's clientele. My spirits sank. I realized that there would be no hope of new commissions this day. Nor could I expect Charpentier to interrupt this exchange between a café orator and his audience to wrench payment from Latude. What did such men know of poverty, men in velvet robes, silk waistcoats, and buckled shoes? To them all this was no more than rhetoric—not to me. Slowly I made my way along the wall, determined to slip out.

harangue: an impassioned speech

THINKING ZONE

Have you ever had the experience of a fellow student's bumping into you in the hall and knocking your books out of your hand? You may have responded by saying, "Thanks a lot!" or "That was really nice of you!" If you did, you responded with **sarcasm**, or mock praise. Sarcasm is a form of **verbal irony**, the use of language to convey meaning other than what is stated. In reality, you hardly thought of that person as being nice; in fact, you probably thought of him as exactly the opposite. Milne's *The Ugly Duckling* contains many examples of sarcasm as well as verbal irony. Near the beginning of the play, the Chancellor remarks that one of the King's quotations was "a profound and original thought, which may well go down to posterity." The audience presumably recognizes immediately the familiar quotation ("Uneasy lies the head that wears a crown") from Shakespeare's *Henry IV, Part 2*, and realizes that it is not original and is obviously already time-tested. This statement may be said to be verbal irony.

1. *[interpretive]* How does Jacques feel about his father's death?

   _____

   _____

   _____

2. *[interpretive/critical]* How can you tell that Jacques's statement to Phillipe about Monsieur Latude's being "the 'good' monsieur" is an example of **sarcasm**?

   _____

   _____

   _____

3. *[interpretive]* How is Jacques's statement about Phillipe's being "too young—and honest—to enjoy the art of vain deceit" ironic?

   _____

   _____

   _____

4. *[literal/interpretive]* What has brought about the decline of Jacques's mother's lace business? How has this change in her affected Jacques?

_____

_____

_____

_____

_____

5. *[interpretive]* What does Charpentier mean when he says, "Well, I must say that you've let Latude escape"?

_____

_____

_____

6. *[interpretive]* What does Charpentier mean by his statement that "wherever there are lawyers, a sculptor need not want for work"?

_____

_____

_____

7. *[critical]* How does Danton win the approval of the crowd at Charpentier's? As an artist, how does Jacques respond to Danton's speech?

_____

_____

_____

_____

_____

_____

8. *[interpretive]* How would you describe Jacques's mood at the end of Chapter 3?

_____

_____

_____

CHAPTER 4

As I stepped out into the street, the bells atop one of the cathedrals began to ring. The music of those bells was like laughter in that part of the city where the gaily dressed promenaded* along the Rue St. Honoré* and gossiped in shops lining the Palais-Royal.* But well I knew that when the soft winds on the river Seine* picked up this music and carried it away from the city's heart, its fading echoes would fall on the ear like weeping and, at length, die out as a sigh.

---

promenaded: walked

Rue St. Honoré (rü sănt´ ō-nōr-ā´)

Palais-Royal (pä-lā´ rwä-yäl´)

Seine (sĕn)

I looked across to the cobbled wharf that ran along the Seine. The amber hues of a dying sun made the gray stones seem warm, inviting. As I turned toward home, I crossed the street that I might walk along the water.

The cool, damp mist felt good upon my face, and as I walked, my thoughts were drawn more and more to the river, that river which for hundreds of years had pumped life into a thriving city. It seemed at that moment to be pumping life back into me as well, life that weeks and months of strain had sucked out of me. Undisturbed, the river flowed past palaces and prisons with the same ever-constant rhythm. An overwhelming desire rose in my heart, a desire to capture the secret of such constancy. Why, I wondered, can I not move through life like the river Seine, oblivious to pain—or even pleasure?

By the time I reached St. Antoine it was growing dark. I rounded the corner to my shop, still lost in thought, but was quickly jerked from my reverie* when through the dusk I saw the chalk-white face of Phillipe. He stood pressed against my shop door, clutching in his hands a bunch of grapes. A wild pig had cornered him and with a menacing look was eyeing the fruit that Phillipe grasped tightly in his hand.

---

reverie: daydream

Grabbing up a loosened stone, I flew down the alley, crying as I ran, "Throw the fruit, Phillipe! Throw it!" But Phillipe was too frightened to obey. Seeing that the animal was about to lunge, I skidded to a stop and hurled the rock. With a vicious squeal the lean, rangy thing turned. I had no time to find another stone. The animal was racing toward me. I threw my back against the alley wall and braced myself. When the beast attacked, I kicked at it with all my strength. A shooting pain went up my leg as its razor sharp teeth sliced across my ankle, but my kick had been sure enough to daze the animal. The pain that the animal inflicted unleashed in me all the pent-up rage of a long, frustrating day, and with renewed strength I jumped over the beast, sweeping up another stone as I landed on its other side. Screaming,

I lunged and threw again. It was enough; the animal took off squealing down the alley.

"Little wonder that there are no promenaders outside our shops!" I yelled at no one in particular. "It's not even safe for beggars where wild pigs run free!"

Then, remembering Phillipe, I turned to see him still standing, rooted to the spot. My blood was still up as I rushed to him. "How many times must I tell you, Phillipe?" I took him by the shoulders. "Never, never eat in the alley! You are sure to lose an arm—or worse."

He lifted a trembling hand and offered up his fruit. The slender fingers which held the grapes—quite crushed by now—reminded me of the talons of a tiny bird. My anger melted. "Go ahead and eat what's left of them," I said, slumping down to take a seat on the narrow steps. "It's safe now."

Phillipe sat down beside me. "Your leg—it's bleeding."

"It will stop in a moment," I said. "He didn't get his teeth into me. I was too fast for him."

"You *were* fast," he said, an admiring smile lighting up his face. As he shoved the dripping grapes into his mouth, he asked, "Do I still get a story?"

I marveled at how quickly he had shed his fear. "How about a story of a wild pig?" I said.

He gave me a look of scorn. "That wouldn't be a story," he said. "That's real."

"Real things *do* happen in stories," I reminded him.

He thought on that for a moment, then resolutely began, "That's not the kind of story I want. I want—" He stopped. "Who's that?"

I followed Phillipe's gaze down the alley to see a stranger moving slowly toward us, stopping long enough to briefly examine the shop signs as he passed. Despite the dusky shadows that clouded the features of his face, I soon recognized the man.

"I don't like the look of him," said Phillipe. "What do you think he wants?"

"We need not wait and see," I said, feeling no inclination to admit that I knew who he was. "Let's go inside."

As I reached for the shop door, I heard again that booming voice ring out. "There you are!"

Reluctantly I turned. Danton was fast approaching.

"I saw you slip out as I began my speech," he said, when at length he stood before us. "Oh, I don't blame you," he continued, ignoring the cool reception I was giving him. "I didn't care much for politics at your age either."

Danton reached down and placed one hand upon Phillipe. "I remember what I liked and did not like at your age too. Back then I was quite a scrapper. As a matter of fact, I was just about your age when I got this scar," he said, pointing proudly to his mouth. "I had a fight with a bull. It was his horn that split my lip. I didn't let him get away with it, though. Three days later, I was out in the pasture again with a stick and gave him as good a beating as he had given me. Of course, he also broke my nose that time. Still I felt I'd settled matters." He sighed contentedly before adding, "Yes, back then I was quite a scrapper."

"I'm not a scrapper," said Phillipe, pulling back.

It was obvious that he liked Danton no more than I did. Still, I'd had enough for one night, and wanting to make certain that there would be no confrontation, I said, "You'd better be getting home, Phillipe. I'll see you tomorrow."

Phillipe did not seem loath* to go. He lingered only a moment at his father's shop door. "Thanks, Jacques," he said, calling back to me. "You *were* fast."

loath: reluctant

Before Danton could inquire as to the cause of Phillipe's admiration, I turned to him and quickly asked, "What is it that you want?"

"Charpentier showed me the bust you brought to him and assured me that you are as skilled in sculpting wax as you are in chiseling stone." He paused only for a moment to see how I registered such praise. I did my best to keep my face impassive, and after a moment he continued. "He warned me, too, that you were a no-nonsense sort, so I will come quickly to my point. I have a commission for you."

I wanted to refuse outright, but my need of money forced me to hold my tongue.

"I'd like a portrait medallion of myself," he continued. Then leaning closer, he added with a smile, "It's for a lady."

The feeling of Danton's hot breath upon my face was loathsome, and instinctively I backed away. "It can be done," I said.

He did not seem to notice my aversion.* "Good! It need not be large. A miniature will do, one that she can carry in her hand. You understand?"

aversion: dislike

I nodded. "I have done such miniatures before."

"How long before it's done?" he asked.

I hesitated only a moment before saying, "I shall have it for you the day after tomorrow."

"Splendid!" he cried.

I knew that I would have to work day and night to meet such a deadline, but wanting to be done with this man soon as possible, I determined to do so.

"Shall I come in now and let you get a sketch of me then?" he asked.

"That's not necessary. I've a good memory for faces."

"Especially for ones like mine?" he asked, carefully gauging my expression. I said nothing, and just as the silence was becoming oppressive, he burst into a roar of laughter. "Day after tomorrow then!" he said. Turning on his heel, he headed down the alley, laughing as he went; the very walls shook with it, but somehow the sound was hollow, a laughter without merriment.

CHAPTER 5

I crushed the sculpted face beneath my fist, got up, and paced about the room. For the first time in my life, my artistry had utterly failed me. I had tried all day, through the night, and into the morning. But try as I would, the wax refused to yield to me. I cursed my own stupidity. This time I had expected too much of myself. Danton's was not a face for portraits. But how was I to explain that to him?

Wearily I returned to my worktable and gazed down upon the medallion once more. The pressure of my blow had twisted Danton's mouth into a macabre* grin. Oddly enough, the damage seemed almost unnoticeable beneath the strong forehead and penetrating eyes. Perhaps, I thought, I've gone about it wrongly. I've been trying to obscure* his ugliness, but there is no obscuring it.

macabre (mə-kä´brə): grotesque
obscure: hide

I thought back to the café and to the strange transformation that came over him as he warmed to his speech. I remembered that fine line between the ugliness of his features and their strength. That's it, I thought. I must see him as he was that evening. I set to work again, this time determined to fix my mind on that moment when one saw Danton not as hideous but as Herculean.*

Herculean: unusually powerful

I was well on my way to restoring the mouth when my concentration was broken by a stirring upstairs. My mother had awakened. Quickly I took the two wine bottles I had taken from her room the night before and put them out of sight with others I'd retrieved. I wanted desperately to stay at my work, but I knew that she needed to eat and would not unless I forced her to it. Reluctantly, I pulled myself away and went upstairs.

She gave me a halfhearted smile as she slowly shuffled across the room to sit down at the kitchen table. My heart sank as I watched her. She was terribly thin and sallow looking. Her long hair, which she—and my father—had been so proud of, now hung limp about her face, void* of any sheen. So too, her eyes that once reflected all the vibrant greens of summer were now dull, lifeless.

void: empty

As she sat down at the kitchen table, I saw her glance about, searching for the wine.

"Let me fix you some bread and cheese," I said quickly.

"I'm not hungry," she replied in a voice that was barely audible.

"You must eat. You're wasting away," I said, hurrying to prepare her meal. "You refused me all day yesterday, but I'm telling you that you *will* eat today."

She took no notice of either my firm-ness or my frantic preparations. Her con-centration remained fixed on searching out the room, even when I placed her meal before her.

"Where is it?" she said as she pushed the plate aside.

"I have put it away," I said resolutely, but I could not bring myself to look at her.

Gathering her strength, she raised her-self to face me. "Who are you to tell your mother when she must eat and when she must not drink?"

I forced myself to look her in the face. "I am your son and I refuse to let you starve!"

For a moment her green eyes flashed with their former beauty as she raised her hand to strike me. I caught her by the wrist be-fore the blow could fall. I felt her frailness, and she my strength. The fury in her seemed to melt. "Please, Jacques, you do not under-stand." Her pleading was more painful than any blow she could have given me.

I stood there fighting with myself, trying to steel my heart against the look in her eyes. But I could not. "I will give you more wine," I said, "after you have eaten."

She collapsed into the chair, pulled the food towards herself, and forced herself to eat.

I hated myself for giving in, but I could not fight her. But neither could I ease her pain. I could only keep her alive, and I *would* keep her alive. Yet as I looked at her sitting there, I felt that the mother I had known was already dead. This woman that sat before me was no more than her shadow. Still, I could not help but love even the shadow of her.

"I've eaten it all," she said looking up at me.

Reluctantly I went down into the shop, retrieved the wine, and brought it to her.

She took it from me and got up. Pausing a moment, she placed her hand on my shoul-der. "Thank you, son," she said. Then once again she disappeared behind the curtain where she slept.

I salved my conscience by telling myself that all she needed was a bit more time. I could give her that—time and patience. I determined more than ever to protect her (and myself) from those who would be quick to condemn. No one need know that my mother's heart, mind, and hands had all failed her.

I was still standing there, looking after her, when I heard the shop bell ring. I went downstairs to see Danton waiting for me.

"Good morning," he said cheerfully.

"Good morning," I returned without the cheer.

"Come," said Danton, "is working on my portrait that depressing?"

I drew my thoughts back to the business at hand. "I regret to say that I was unable to finish the medallion you requested."

"Was it the deadline or the subject that hindered you?"

I paused a moment. "To be honest, it was both. But I believe I could have mastered the subject if I had had the time."

"Take all the time you need," he said.

His response caught me off guard, for I fully expected him to turn on his heel and leave. Any of my other customers would have done so.

"I see you are unaccustomed to patience," he said wryly. "But I would wager that I am not like most of your other customers. They may not understand the value of hard labor, but I do. I have worked hard, and only re-cently has my work come to pay me well."

He stopped a moment and glanced about the shop. Then, reaching into his pocket, he pulled out some money—enough to pay for at least half of the commission—and held it out to me.

I forced myself to say, "You need not pay until I've finished."

"Take it," he urged. "I know you will finish as quickly as you can. And I have no doubt that I will be pleased with the work, for I know that you will not present it to me until you are well pleased with it yourself."

I took the money and casually laid it on my worktable, as if I were accustomed to having it about. "I will finish your commission as soon as possible," I promised.

"Take it to Charpentier's when you are done," he said. "I will see you there." He bowed politely and went out. I stood a moment, wondering if perhaps I had misjudged the man. At the time, I did not realize that for men like Danton, an act of kindness is merely a means of manipulation.

THINKING ZONE

Consider the following quotations from some of the Mother Goose nursery rhymes: "The little [ant] stops to suck his thumb." "The poor dog was laughing." "The cats went out to serenade / And on a banjo sweetly played." All of these quotations have something in common: animals are doing things that are very "un-animal-like." **Personification**, giving human characteristics to something that is nonhuman, helps you picture more precisely what the rhyme is trying to tell. Personification may also be applied to nonliving things. In Amy Carmichael's poem "Make Me Thy Fuel," the final stanza speaks of a love that leads, a faith that is capable of dismay, and a hope that can be tired. All of these are examples of personification of ideas. Writers use personification as a concrete way to visualize ideas and to help readers associate feelings and emotions with their topics. As you continue your reading of *In Search of Honor*, look for examples of personification.

1. [critical] How are **personification** and simile used at the beginning of Chapter 4 to describe the music of the bells? How is personification used to describe the city?

   _____

   _____

   _____

2. [literal/interpretive] What characteristic of the river Seine does Jacques desire to have within himself? Why do you think he feels this way?

   _____

   _____

   _____

   _____

3. [literal] Why does Danton visit Jacques?

   _____

   _____

   _____

4. *[critical]* What impression do you have of Danton, based on his actions, his words, his physical appearance, and the reaction of Jacques and Phillipe?

_____

_____

_____

5. *[critical]* What does the description of Danton's "laughter without merriment" suggest about him?

_____

_____

_____

6. *[interpretive]* How does the description of the wax at the beginning of Chapter 5 exhibit personification?

_____

_____

_____

7. *[appreciative]* What do you think of Jacques's response to his mother in Chapter 5?

_____

_____

_____

8. *[critical]* Why is Jacques taken by surprise by Danton's response to his request for more time?

_____

_____

_____

9. *[interpretive]* In spite of the fact that the sculpture is not done, what does Danton give Jacques? What line in the final paragraph foreshadows that things are not as they would seem?

_____

_____

_____

CHAPTER 6

Danton had scarcely left the shop before Phillipe came bursting in, his cap askew and his rumpled jacket obviously put on in haste. "Hurry, Jacques!" he shouted. "You must come quickly!"

"Come where? What are you talking about?" I asked, trying to get him to stand still long enough for me to make some sense of his errand.

"It's Papa. He's gone after Latude!" he said, growing even more frantic.

"What for?"

"The cabinet he's been working on for weeks—Latude sent word—he's changed his mind. He doesn't want it."

"He can't do that."

"Well, he has!" Phillipe assured me. "And now Papa's gone after him, saying he will get his due one way or another. Mama says that we must stop him!"

"All right, calm down. Just tell me which way he went. I've no idea where Latude lives."

"Just outside the city gate," Phillipe said, as he turned to race for the door. "I've got the address."

"Wait," I said catching hold of him. "Give it to me."

He obeyed. "All right, but I'm coming too," he added.

"No, you're not," I said as I threw aside my apron. "Go home and take care of your mother."

"I must come, Jacques," he pleaded.

"No," I said more sternly. "You'll only slow me down." The point hit home, and reluctantly he headed toward the door.

Grabbing up my jacket, I ran out behind him, locking the door behind me.

"I promise that I will bring your father home safely," I called back to him; then I flew down the alleyway, glancing at the address long enough to be certain which direction I should run.

I counted on the fact that Phillipe's father, Thomas, would take the most direct, albeit* crowded, route to the outskirts of the city. My instinct was correct, and within minutes I saw him up ahead of me. He was walking swiftly through the crowd, seemingly oblivious to the jostling he was giving several passers-by, and I could see that more than one of them turned on him angrily. He ignored them.

---

albeit: although

When I got closer, I shouted, "Thomas!" I was sure that he could hear my shouting; still, he didn't stop. So I kept on running, dodging people with greater care than he did.

"Thomas!" I called again when I was just about upon him.

He did not turn, but merely said, "I've got important business, Jacques. Go home."

"I know your business," I said, falling into step beside him, "and I'm not turning back. I've just left Phillipe with the promise that I would bring you home."

He stopped dead in the middle of the street, stared me in the face, and in a voice with an edge as hard as steel he said, "I, too, have made promises to Phillipe—promises to feed and clothe him. If you have found out where I'm going, then you know why I'm going. Don't try to stop me."

"I've no intention of trying to stop you," I told him flatly.

My answer was not what he expected. Indeed, it was not what I had planned to say, but it was out now. The look in his eye and the edge in his voice had awakened my own feelings of injustice. I saw myself as I had been more than a year before, standing in a courtroom expectantly waiting for some "justice" to be served upon the Comte de Guiche's son. The memory of it sickened me. "I—I will help you," I said.

He stood trying to reconcile my words with his first impressions of my mission.

"Do you have a plan?" I pressed him.

For the first time I saw him waver in his determination. "I will decide what to do when I get there," he said.

"Look, even if you can come up with a plan," I reasoned, "I doubt that you can accomplish it alone." He was listening intently to me now. "I think I know how you can get the money that is due you. Or is it revenge you're after?"

"I'd like revenge," he said honestly, "but I will settle for the money."

"Then I think we can succeed."

"You seem very sure of yourself," he said.

"Not of myself, but of Latude," I answered. "I know that he goes to Charpentier's every afternoon. If you can wait for a couple of hours, I think we can get into his chateau*—and out again—without being seen." I was growing more sure of the idea that was forming in my mind as I gave voice to it.

chateau (shă-tō´): a French manor house

"I'm willing to wait," he assured me. "But it will not hurt us to do our waiting just outside his gate."

"All right," I conceded. "But promise me that you—that we—will take no more than is our due."

"I am not a thief, Jacques. I am an honest artisan who has been robbed!"

His words salved* my guilty conscience for the moment, and we set out and arrived at Latude's with less than a quarter of an hour to wait.

salved: soothed

About half past three, from our hiding place we spotted Latude climbing into his carriage.

"Come on," Thomas urged.

"Not yet," I said, panicking. "His driver will see us."

"Not if we stay low and get into those bushes lining the gate. Come. If we don't get closer, we will never get inside. We have to get through the gate when it opens for the carriage."

I knew he had a point, for the iron gate that led into Latude's estate would not be easy to scale in daylight.

We moved forward slowly. "Get down! Get down! They're coming through," I said. But the sound of horses' hooves and carriage wheels on cobblestone had already convinced Thomas to press himself into the tangled foliage.

When the carriage reached the gate, a valet jumped down from the seat next to the driver. I thought that he had seen us, but I breathed a halting sigh when I realized that he'd alighted merely to swing open the gate. He opened first the side of the gate closest to us. He then moved to the opposite side of the carriage to open the other gate as well, and moving forward, he began to guide the horses through.

"Now!" I said.

Shielded by the carriage, we scrambled inside the gate and rolled into the shrubs which stood like sentinels along the bars of iron. The pawing of the horses—the only ones to sense our movement—obscured the noise we made.

"Whoa!" cried the surprised valet, and Thomas and I did not so much as breathe. It seemed hours rather than minutes before the horses calmed, allowing the valet to close the gate and mount his carriage seat again.

"We've done it!" Thomas cried when at last the sounds of the horses and their carriage had completely died away.

"We've not succeeded yet," I said, my apprehension growing. The stupidity of our plan was finally beginning to dawn on me, but I could see that Thomas was in no mood to turn back now.

"How long does he stay at Charpentier's?" he asked.

"Well into the evening," I assured him.

"Good." He sounded relieved. "We should be able to get what we want and hide back here until the sun goes down. We'll have to scale the fence once it is dark." I nodded my assent. His plan was as good as any I'd thus far conceived, for I had given no thought to the problem of getting out once we'd gotten in.

"What's next?" he asked me.

"I think the servants' entrance would be the best place to start."

"What if there are servants there?"

"Trust me," I said with a confidence I did not feel. "Now that Latude has departed for his nightly bout at the café, the servants will have vanished."

Cautiously we made our way across the grounds until we reached the back. "There it is," I said.

"How can you be sure?"

"They all look pretty much alike," I said. "I've delivered lace to many of my mother's wealthy customers. Believe me, they do not let the lace maker's son enter the front door."

"Well, I hope the inside is as familiar to you as the outside."

I was hoping the same thing as we crept along the wall, endeavoring to glimpse inside each window that we passed.

When we reached the door, we found it slightly ajar. I raised my hand to gently push it open but Thomas stopped me. "What will we do if someone's in there?"

"I—I'll just tell them that Latude has ordered some lace and that my mother misplaced his order. I've come for it again."

"Knock, then," he whispered.

"Knock?" I said, staring at him incredulously.

"Of course," he snapped. "That's the only way they would believe such a story."

I knocked gently. Thomas, seeing my timidity, stepped in front of me and rapped boldly on the door. No one stirred.

"I guess you were right," he said. "They must take off as soon as Latude heads out."

We entered cautiously and looked about. We were in the kitchen.

"Well, everything's in perfect order; they won't be coming back to tidy up," he said. "But what now? Should I look for the stairs?"

"No, over here," I said, moving across the room to stand before what looked like a large cupboard in the corner. I tried the door and it opened.

"What's that?" Thomas asked, peering over my shoulder to have a closer look.

"It's a sort of moving cupboard. They put dishes, drinks, all sorts of things into it and then pull on this rope to heave it all up to the next floor. I've seen it in other houses. A servant showed it to me once. Get in."

"Are you crazy?"

"I know it's a tight fit, but it's the safest way. I'll heave you up slowly. When you reach the top, crack open the cupboard and see if the coast is clear. If it is, get out and get your money's worth. If I'm not mistaken, you'll be in the dining room. A couple of pieces of silver should cover the cost of what he owes you. When you're back inside, tap twice and I'll haul you down."

Thomas ran his hands over every inch of the cupboard. "It's good sturdy wood," he finally said. "I guess it'll hold me."

Handing me his cap, he climbed up and wedged himself in sideways. The uncertain look upon his face as he crouched there made me think more of a frightened boy than of a thief. I imagine anyone looking on would have seen the same look on my face as well.

"Here we go," I said. "Remember, be careful but be quick. And it's two taps. I'll be waiting." I closed the cupboard door and pulled down on the rope; it took more strength than I'd imagined. My progress was slow but sure. I pulled and pulled until the rope would go no further; then I wound it round a hook on the wall to secure it, and I waited.

My nerves were as tightly wound as that cupboard rope. As I waited I heard every creak of the ancient mansion, and such sounds conjured up* all sorts of images. At one moment I believed there were footsteps behind me; the next instant I was certain that I'd heard the squeaking hinges of the kitchen door. Every sound—even my own breathing—became like a roaring in my ears until even the scampering of the kitchen mice across the floor seemed loud and menacing.*

conjured up: called to mind
menacing: threatening

At last I heard the long awaited tapping against wood. Quickly I unknotted the rope and slowly let him down—a much easier task than it had been to heave him up. As soon as the rope went slack, Thomas pushed open the door, but the smile on his face vanished. I had no time to discern the cause, for at that moment a calloused hand took me by the shoulder. I turned to see two men, each holding a kitchen knife.

"Need some help there, lad?" one servant said in a menacing tone. He turned to the other. "Go, raise the alarm." Then, turning back to us, he said, "I hope you two enjoy the smell of a musty stone cell as well as you've enjoyed the smell of a squire's kitchen, for that's what you'll be smelling next."

CHAPTER 7

To officials of state, the Bastille,* located at 232 Rue St. Antoine, was simply an obscure old fortress that served as a prison. But to those of us who lived near where it stood, the Bastille was much, much more. It was a castle of darkness and secrecy, a place into which one might disappear without warning, never to be heard from again. The fact that the Bastille's exterior courtyard was open to the public and that one might freely visit the gatekeeper did nothing to allay fears, for few availed themselves of such "privileges." Most of us had learned at our mothers' knees the Bastille's tales of horror—tales of slimy cells overrun with rats, of vicious criminals covered with vermin and desperate for food, of cruel guards who waited for prisoners to die, then sealed them up in the thick tower walls. To put it plainly, we believed that to enter such a place was to be buried alive. You can, therefore, imagine my thoughts when Thomas and I were informed that until our trial we would be held in the Bastille.

Bastille (bă-stē´yə)

Before the sun had set, we stood outside the fortress. The guard pushed us forward, and reluctantly we entered the prison's outer court. The gatekeeper hailed an officer, and at his command the massive drawbridge lowered and opened like a gaping wound, providing access to the inner court.

"Don't worry, Jacques," Thomas whispered in my ear as we were ushered in. "I'll think of something to get us out of here."

I said nothing.

The guard untied our hands. "Take them to the governor's quarters," he ordered one of his men who stood nearby.

I was surprised by the comfort and richness of the governor's rooms as well as by the governor himself. Bernard René de Launay* was not what I expected. He struck me as a tired man, somewhat dour to be sure, but hardly the vicious overseer I'd imagined.

Bernard René de Launay (bĕr-närˊ rə-näˊ də lōˊ-näˊ)

"Two more for you, sir," the guard said casually.

The governor did not look up from the work before him. "What's the charge?" he demanded.

"They tried to pinch a squire of his silver."

"I can explain," said Thomas, stepping forward.

But before he could speak, the guard interjected. "He had the goods in his thieving hands when they caught him. I'd like to see him explain that."

"I was after what he owed me!" shouted Thomas, turning on the man.

"Aye," countered the guard in a cynical tone.

Without thinking, Thomas made a move toward him, and the governor was on his feet in a moment. "Enough!" he shouted, startling Thomas and giving the guard time enough to get his prisoner in a strangle hold.

"Let him go," Launay ordered after a moment. Then, addressing Thomas, he warned, "I assure you that even if you were to succeed in knocking down one of my guards, I'd have another on you in a moment."

"I meant no harm," said Thomas. "I lost my head, but if you'd let me explain—"

"Save it," the governor said, the weariness returning to his voice. "I'm sure I've heard your story before. You'll get a chance to present your case, but not to me. Until then—"

"When?" Thomas demanded. "I've a family to care for—and Jacques here has his mother."

The governor looked from one of us to the other and then he said, "You should have thought of that before."

As we were led away, I noted that the conditions were much more commonplace than I'd been led to believe. Though dark and musty, the prisoners' quarters were far from the loathsome cells of horror I had pictured.

Our cells were oddly shaped, more octagonal than square, but there was room enough for comfort in them. There were also tables and chairs provided, along with a fireplace for warmth and mats for sleeping. But these newly discovered "comforts" did little to improve my spirit. In fact, the dissipation* of fear seemed only to make room for the anger I felt in being confined at all.

---

dissipation: dissolving

Of course, I told myself that my anger was directed at Latude and Thomas; it was they who had gotten me into such a mess. But even then I knew deep down, I was lying to myself. I believe it was this nagging awareness that kept me from lashing out at Thomas once we were settled in our cell.

Making my way to a corner, I sat down and propped myself against the wall—seething, sullen, and spoiling for a fight.

"Well," mused Thomas as he cautiously sat down beside me, "it's not as bad as I'd imagined."

"It's bad enough," I said.

"My wife and your mother are good, practical women," he said, perhaps trying to encourage me. "They shall see to things till we return."

I knew that his wife could manage, but my mother? She could have done so a few years before. But not now. I remembered the money Danton had given me, and I hoped that she would discover it and use it for food. I feared that she would not.

Although he did not understand why, Thomas could see that his words had only increased my misery. "Come, Jacques, they cannot keep us here long." A burst of laughter rang out and startled us. Until that moment neither Thomas nor I had noticed a third prisoner lying down in another corner of the cell.

"Are you wealthy?" the stranger asked nonchalantly.

"Oh, very!" I said, at last able to lash out at someone.

My tone had little effect upon the man, however. He sat up, stared at us for a moment, then lay back down. "No," he said with a good-naturedness that was maddening. "I can see now that you are not. And I'm sorry to say that since you are not, you may still be waiting for your trial this time next year."

I jumped to my feet and in two strides reached the man. Grabbing his collar, I hauled him up. "What do you mean!" I yelled.

Thomas quickly intervened. "Stop it, Jacques!" he said, freeing the man from my grip. "I know how you feel, but we've got to try to keep our tempers in check. It's the only way—"

"Testy, isn't he?" the man said as he relaxed again and leaned against the wall.

"He didn't mean it," Thomas said. "We're both a little testy."

"Oh, I don't mind," the stranger continued. "They're always testy when they're first brought in."

I returned to my seat feeling a bit better for having burned up some energy.

Thomas turned back to the man. "Tell me, were you serious—or just goading* us—about the time it would take to get a trial?"

---

goading: provoking to anger

"I was serious," the man said, dropping his nonchalance. "I have seen artisans like you—you are artisans, aren't you?"

Thomas nodded.

"I have seen men like you wait for years."

Thomas sat down wearily.

"It need not be that way, you know," the stranger continued cautiously.

I got up and moved toward him once again, this time without anger. "What other choice do we have?" I asked.

"A boy with your spirit has many choices." Both Thomas and I moved closer

to him. "I have a plan," he said, "but I cannot execute it alone."

"A plan?" said Thomas.

"I am going to escape," he said boldly.

"Can such a thing be done?" I asked.

"If you two are willing to help me," he said, "I am certain of it." He paused. "Can I count on you, or would you prefer to wait for the justice of the courts?"

The memories of my father's murder trial came flooding back to me. "You can count on me," I said.

Thomas hesitated a moment after my reply; then he added, "You can count on me as well."

THINKING ZONE

By now you have probably formed an opinion of some of the characters in the novel—Jacques, Phillipe, Danton, Thomas. These and other characters that you encounter in your reading can become almost lifelike to you. You laugh and cry with them; you like what they like and dislike what they dislike. How does an author create characters with whom you can identify? Sometimes an author uses **direct characterization**, the explicit authorial description of the traits and qualities of a character, to give the reader an image of the character. At other times, however, the author uses **indirect characterization**, characterization that presents the characters in action and leaves the reader to infer their traits. In "A Most Important Person," Margaret Weymouth Jackson uses indirect characterization when she describes a feisty little boy entirely with dialogue: "I know just how you feel. I saved a cat once. I was awf'ly fond of it afterwards. It wasn't much of a cat. . . . Its ears were chewed and it had fleas, but then—it liked me." And later, "It is better to get in an alley, or somewheres where the cops or teachers won't stop you." We learn from those two quotations that Chester is empathetic, sensitive, insightful, compassionate, lovable, intelligent, and spunky—all without Jackson's having to say so outright. Hess uses both types of characterization in her novel. Think about when you first met Danton in Chapter 3. Hess describes his size, clothing, lips, skin, and eyes (direct) and then includes a lengthy speech of Danton's (indirect). As you read and write, be aware of both kinds of characterization and the advantages and disadvantages of them.

1. *[literal]* What has Latude done to Thomas? What does Jacques suggest that they do to get even with Latude?

   _____

   _____

   _____

2. *[literal]* Why is Jacques able to identify so readily with Thomas's state of mind in Chapter 6?

   _____

   _____

   _____

3. *[critical]* Why is Thomas's response to Latude wrong? Support your answer with a specific Bible verse or passage.

_____

_____

_____

4. *[critical]* What does the author's **indirect characterization** of Latude tell you about him? Defend your answer with details from Chapter 6.

_____

_____

5. *[critical]* Does the author use **direct characterization** or indirect characterization to describe Thomas's character in Chapter 6? What character qualities do you detect from the chapter's description of Thomas?

_____

_____

_____

_____

_____

6. *[interpretive]* Are Thomas and Jacques penitent about their crime? Explain.

_____

_____

_____

_____

7. *[critical]* How does the stranger's question demonstrate verbal irony: "Can I count on you, or would you prefer to wait for the justice of the courts?"

_____

_____

_____

_____

Verbal irony—*the use of language to convey meaning other than what is stated*

CHAPTER 8

We learned that the stranger in our cell was Louis Alègre,* a soldier of fortune who had endeavored to win favor at court and failed. Despite his failures as a courtier,* however, he was nonetheless shrewd. As Thomas and I sat down with him the next day, we found that his plan for escape, though risky, was well thought through.

Louis Alègre (lōo-ē´ ä-lĕg´[r])

courtier: an attendant at court

He had been imprisoned for several months. In that time he had not only learned the intricate structure of the fortress but also devised a way to construct a ladder that would prove the key to our escape.

"I have the ladder well under way," he told us. "I've been making the rungs out of my firewood."

"The weather is growing warmer," Thomas noted. "They won't be giving us firewood much longer, will they?"

"They have already cut it back to just the evenings," Louis conceded. "That is why I need your help. I cannot finish it with my store only. Also, if each of us takes from the store that is given to us, it will be less noticeable. We must be quick—but careful."

"Where is this ladder?" I inquired.

"Behind a loosened brick in the prison chapel. I go there daily and add to it as I 'pray.'" He smiled. "The guards have come to think of me as a most holy man."

"How do you keep the rungs together?" I continued.

"A friend of mine is permitted to bring me clean shirts and bed linen every week. Just before her weekly visits, I tear the shirts and linen I've been wearing all that week into strips of cloth that I can knot and restitch into sturdy rope to put between the rungs."

"Are the guards not suspicious when she brings you clean shirts and never takes the soiled ones away?" I asked.

"Oh, I leave just enough for her to wrap up as dirty laundry. Needless to say, my wardrobe is growing rather thin. I must escape if for no other reason than to replenish it."

"Incredible," Thomas said, shaking his head in disbelief.

"So we have a ladder," I said, "but what are we to do with it?"

"You are so skeptical, Jacques," said Louis smiling.

"I am growing more so," I said and cast a glance at Thomas.

"That is wise," Louis conceded. "But you must also learn to trust those who can help you, and I am one of those who can." He paused a moment and then continued. "As to your question, it is legitimate, and one I've thought about. Over these months I have—because of good behavior—been permitted to take walks in the walled garden courtyards on the towers. During these little bouts of exercise, I've been able to observe firsthand how this fortress is constructed. As anyone on the outside can see, there are eight towers, and the shape of this cell proves that we are imprisoned in one of these towers. I've learned, too, that there are five to seven stories in each tower. Most of us are confined in the middle levels. There are those few, however, who are kept in the *calottes*.* Those are the levels immediately below the roof—"

---

calottes (kə-lôt′)

I interrupted him. "What kind of prisoners are kept there?"

He shrugged. "From what I can learn, only those who are excessively violent or insane. At any rate, one of us has to get up to the *calottes* before the ladder is finished."

"What for?" said Thomas, growing uneasy.

"To locate and examine the iron grates that I've observed on each tower roof," he said simply.

"How can one of us get up there if it's reserved for the violent and insane?" I asked flatly.

"Well, Jacques," Louis said, "I imagine it would be difficult for you to feign* insanity—but violence?"

---

feign: represent falsely

I was unsure at the moment if his appraisal was a compliment or insult, so I said, "Any man can fly off in a moment of passion, but to maintain such a state—"

"Oh, you don't have to maintain it," he assured me. "The guards have no notion as to your true temperament. They've seen you only a few times. I did observe, however, that one of the guards did see you collar me. We can build nicely on that first impression."

"I'm not sure I'm all that eager to be stuck up there indefinitely."

"It won't be indefinitely," he said. "The first time they put you there, it is as a warning. I've seen them do it often. They find one of the prisoners too hotheaded, and they send him to the top of the tower for a day or two, maybe a week—no more—believing that will cure him of his temper. For the most part, it works."

"What exactly do you want of me?" I asked, though I was growing more uncertain about really wanting to hear his answer.

"Tonight, when the guards bring in our firewood, I want you to slug one of them."

"Are you out of your mind?" asked Thomas, giving voice to the very words that were on the tip of my tongue.

"It's the only way," Louis said simply.

"And why don't you take the chance of slugging him?" I asked.

"Because they think of me as a holy man," he said. "Besides, you do not want me to be kept from my prayers, do you?"

My concern for my mother's welfare made me desperate to escape, and seeing no other alternative, I conceded. "All right," I said, "but this had better work."

"It will," Louis assured me. "I will make certain of it, for you must not forget that my success is tied up in yours."

CHAPTER 9

With some hope before me, I was finally able to relax, and I decided to lie down for a few hours' rest before the evening came and the guards arrived.

It seemed only moments before Louis was heaving me up from a dead sleep. "Hurry!" he hissed.

"What—what are you—"

"The guard's in the next cell. Come on—you've got to start a fight."

"About what?" I staggered to my feet.

The cell door next to ours slammed shut.

Louis said nothing, fearing he'd be overheard, but his look warned me that I'd better start yelling.

"Stay on your own side of the cell," I shouted, just as the guard approached our door.

"Sorry," Louis countered, feigning an appeasing tone.

"Sorry isn't good enough," I screamed. The guard's key turning in our lock had brought me fully to my senses. I lunged at Louis just as the guard entered.

"Break it up!" he ordered.

I ignored him and continued shaking Louis by the neck. "You fool, I'll teach you who's boss here!"

As we had hoped when planning our charade, the man dropped the firewood to the floor and came at me himself. As I turned on him, however, I saw that his age was

no match for my youthful strength, and I knew I had better push rather than hit him. Still, I put some muscle into it and knocked him up against the wall, then stepped back and maintained a menacing stance.

"Guards!" he bellowed, and two more guards appeared. "This young scoundrel needs a lesson."

For a moment I feared that they would all three set upon me, but to my relief one of them spoke up and said, "We'll give him some time in the *calottes*. That'll cool his temper."

They tied my hands behind my back and led me up three flights of stairs. The damp cold and darkness increased as we ascended, and I berated* myself for having left my jacket in the cell below.

---

berated: scolded

When we could go no higher, they freed my hands and unlocked one of the heavy doors. Then, shoving me inside, they slammed it shut.

Darkness and the pungent smell of mold and filth overwhelmed me. I stood a moment in the center of the cell, trying to get my bearings. It was then I heard soft, squeaking sounds, and, looking down, I saw that there were several rats about my feet. Instinctively I jumped back against the wall, which sent the rodents scampering, but the feel of that slimy, lichen*-covered stone against my back was even more revolting, and I quickly moved again toward the center of the room.

lichen (lī′kən): fungus

A low-burning torch, set in an iron ring, hung upon the wall. I took it down and slowly moved about to get a better picture of my "room." I saw at once that I had finally found the Bastille that had lived in my imagination.

An old trestle* table stood in one corner of the cell, and I started toward it, intending to sit down, for my heart was yet pounding in my chest. After a few steps forward, however, my heart ceased its pounding and threatened for a moment to stop altogether. Someone was already seated at the end of the table.

trestle: horizontal beam or bar held up by two pairs of legs used as support

Louis's words about those kept in the *calottes* came back to me: "only the exces-sively violent or insane." The man I saw before me was indeed a strange creature. He was old, very old—and still. He sat erect, one hand resting on his knee, the other stretched out upon the table. I had never seen the likes of the shirt and breeches that he wore and concluded that they must be as old as he. But despite the worn apparel, he had the bearing of an ancient king, a monarch who had ceased his reign and had at last been cast in stone.

Assuring myself that I was certainly a match for such an aged man—no matter what his state of mind—I moved slowly forward. The light from my torch fell upon him. The long, fleecy strands of his hair and beard were thin and fine like the delicate filaments of a spider's web, and his skin, mapped with a thousand wrinkles, appeared as fragile as a butterfly's wing. But his eyes—his eyes were riveting, milky pools with black, penetrating centers. It was his eyes that made me most uneasy, for it was evident that he saw me. Yet he said not a word. Nor did I,

and, unable to withstand his gaze for long, I turned and moved away.

I gave up the idea of sitting at the table and decided instead to get on with searching for a way out. I moved about the cell, scanning the ceiling for an opening which might lead to the tower roof. As far as I could see there was none. But there had to be, for Louis had insisted that he'd seen not one but several—eight to be exact—as many openings as towers.

I turned my attention to the walls themselves. The only thing I saw that held out any hope at all was the fireplace. There was no kindling, although I wished there had been, and upon inspection, I noticed that a puddle of rainwater had collected at the chimney's base. Using as much light from the torch as I could, I crouched down and looked up the chimney. Sure enough, there was the iron grille leading to the roof. It would be no easy task to climb up that narrow space, but it could be done.

My discovery cheered me somewhat, and since I could do little else, I determined that I would try to get some sleep. Before I did, however, I looked back to see what the old man was doing. He sat motionless, as before. I decided that he would not give me any trouble I could not handle, and I turned my attention to finding some bedding.

There were three mattresses in the cell. Two were by the table where the old man sat; the third lay in a heap by the torch ring. I replaced the torch and then picked up the bedding, purposely avoiding examining it under the light. I was afraid that if I did so I would find it was infested with worms or lice. I soon learned—even without the light—that my fears were justified.

THINKING ZONE

An important aspect of any story is the **setting**, or the time and place in which the action of the story occurs. The novel *In Search of Honor* is set in France during the time of the French Revolution, and that setting plays an important role in the story—from the unrest among the people to the attitude of the aristocracy to the imprisonment in the Bastille. The setting of a story often comments symbolically on what is going on within the story just as the unrest of the French Revolution is symbolic of the unrest in Jacques's soul.

Throughout your reading of *In Search of Honor,* your teacher has likely been filling you in on the background of some of the real people, places, and events in the story—Voltaire, Rousseau, Danton, the city of Paris, and the French Revolution. Sometimes as you read a work of literature, especially a work of historical fiction, it is useful to have additional information about the setting that will help you interpret what you are reading.

1. *[interpretive]* What character traits does Jacques attribute to Alègre?

   _____

   _____

2. *[critical]* How does the statement by Alègre that "the guards have come to think of me as a most holy man" exhibit verbal irony?

   _____

   _____

   _____

   _____

3. *[interpretive]* What does Louis mean when he tells Jacques, "My success is tied up in yours"?

   _____

   _____

   _____

   _____

4. *[literal]* List ways in which the *calottes* are different from the regular cells in the Bastille.

_____

_____

_____

_____

_____

5. *[critical]* What is ironic about the appearance of the old man that Jacques meets in the *calottes*?

_____

_____

_____

_____

_____

6. *[critical]* Identify factual details (about people, buildings, etc.) in Chapters 8 and 9 that the author would have needed to know to place the fictional story into its accurate historical **setting**.

_____

_____

_____

_____

_____

7. *[interpretive/critical]* Do you think that Louis seems like a trust- worthy person to this point in the story? Why or why not?

_____

_____

_____

_____

_____

_____

CHAPTER 10

I awoke abruptly to find myself clawing at my arms and legs. The lice had found me more to their taste than the filthy bedding. Jumping up, I kicked the mattress from me, but I still could not stop scratching.

"Don't scratch," a voice behind me said. Startled, I quickly turned and found myself face to face with the strange old man.

"I can't help it," I said irritably.

"You'd better," he said. "Or the sores you get will feel far worse than the itching. There is a bowl of water on the table," he continued, and he held out his gnarled hand. "Give me your clothes and go and wash yourself."

"What do you want with my clothes?" I said suspiciously.

He stared at me a moment, and I feared that he could read my thoughts of him. "Well, I certainly don't intend to wear them," he said. "You have lice."

"I imagine I'm not the only one," I replied, somewhat piqued* by the comment.

piqued: vexed by a perceived slight

"Yes, you are," he said. "I keep myself, my clothes, and my bedding clean. The man before you did not. You chose to sleep on his mattress."

"I didn't see another," I lied.

"Of course you did," he said plainly. "You saw that there were two by me. I would have gladly given you one."

"How was I to know that?"

"You might have asked," he said.

I searched his face for a hint of scorn but found there was none.

"You might have offered," I countered lamely.

He smiled. "Perhaps. But I have learned I must be cautious. I need to know what kind of man—or boy—they've sent to me before I speak to him. The company they provide is not always the best."

Without thinking, I gave vent to a derisive* laugh.

derisive: scornful

"Ah, I see that they have warned you I am mad," he said, and turning slowly, he began to move away.

The sadness in his voice shamed me, and I quickly added, "I believe they think us all mad."

He turned. "Yes," he said and began walking back to me. "My name is Pierre-Joseph Aumônt."* He bowed slightly. "What is yours?"

Pierre-Joseph Aumônt (pyâr-zhō-sĕf´ ō-mô[n])

"Jacques Chénier."*

Chénier (shān-yā´)

"Well, Jacques," he said, "it is my washday; will you allow me to wash your suit of clothes with mine? I've only one extra set, so I must keep up with laundry."

Deciding that there was no better way to rid myself of lice, I slipped out of my shirt and breeches and gave them to him.

He accepted the bundle with great care, holding them as far away as possible.

"You can slip on my old cloak until these things are dry—that is, *after* you have washed," he said. "You'll find it lying on the chair."

I watched him as he started off toward a corner of the room where I saw he had prepared a basin of water that he had set atop a small paving stone. A feeble coal fire glowed beneath the stone. I was surprised that I'd noticed neither the stone nor the basin the night before, but I suppose the rats, the madman, and chimney had so diverted my attention that I saw little else.

When he reached the basin, he left my belongings in a heap while he set about wringing out his own laundry, which had been soaking in the pot. When he finished, he took up my clothes and dropped them in.

He then pulled from his pocket several bits of bread crust and moved to the center of the room. Stooping down, he began to whistle softly. I was horrified to see the rats coming out from the corners in answer to his call.

"What are you doing?" I shouted.

He looked up at me. "Feeding the rats." Then, noting the panic on my face, he added, "I have found that if I feed them, they are not compelled to feed on me."

I stood gawking until I began to shiver. I then decided that it was time to begin washing. As I did, I wondered whether this frail old man was unusually clever or simply mad. I decided that in such a place as the Bastille they could well seem the same. Still, I wondered what circumstances could have brought him to this place, for though he was old, his bearing, his manner, and even his worn suit of clothes revealed that he had once been a gentleman.

The ice-cold water in the bowl numbed me, and by the time I threw Pierre-Joseph's cloak about my shoulders, the itching had somewhat subsided.

"How long have you been here?" I asked, sitting down at the table, for the cloak reminded me that I had never seen such clothes before.

He stopped his work and paused a moment as if he were trying hard to remember. "I've little way of knowing," he finally said. "All that I can say is that when I came here, I was much younger—" he looked down at his gnarled hands "—and stronger. I remember, too, that the Sorbonne Library had just opened and that an astonishing boy named Mozart had come to the city to play for the elite of Paris." A vague smile crossed his face. "Paris was a gay city then. Is it yet?"

"For some it is," I said. I'd never heard of Mozart, but the Sorbonne* Library had been open for as long as I could remember. I tried again. "This Mozart, did he play at court for the King and Queen?"

Sorbonne (sôr-bôn´)
_____

"For Louis XV? Not that I remember."

"Louis *XV*?"

He paused, and then asked, "He is dead then?"

"Yes," I said. "His grandson now sits on the throne, Louis XVI. Does no one speak to you?"

"You are the first person that I've had a real conversation with since—well, I can't remember. The men who are placed here with me are often drunk or violent. They do not care for conversation. I used to try to talk, but I learned that to do so was at best unwise. I suppose that is one reason they think me mad. Silence frightens people."

"Why did you decide to talk with me?" I asked.

"I watched you. You were neither drunk nor violent—which makes me wonder why you were put up here at all."

I could feel my face redden under his gaze. "I lost my temper," was all I said.

Noting my reticence,* he changed the subject. "How long ago did Louis die?"

---

reticence: restraint; reluctance

"The year after I was born," I said.

He nodded as he took the information in. "And how old are you?" he asked.

"Fifteen—almost sixteen."

He was silent. After a moment, he turned slowly and resumed his task.

As I continued watching him, the realization that this old man had been imprisoned for at least as long as I had been alive began sinking in. No wonder he was mad—or was he? I had certainly met greater fools—perhaps even greater madmen. I wanted to ask what horrid crime he had committed that kept him in this place, but he had been kind enough not to press me for information, and I knew I owed him the same.

Looking about for something to divert my attention, I spotted an object lying at the other end of the table. I reached over and picked it up. It seemed to be an iron bar with crude holes bored into it.

"Do you use this to protect yourself from the other prisoners?" I asked, holding up what I thought to be a weapon.

He turned, and seeing what was in my hand, he broke into a soft but merry laugh.

Somewhat chagrined* by his response, I said, "It certainly doesn't look good for much else."

---

chagrined: irritated; embarrassed

He ceased his laughter. "You don't think much of my handiwork."

"Tell me what it is," I demanded. "Perhaps then I'll change my mind."

"It is my flute," he said.

I looked at him, dumbfounded.

"I know it looks a bit primitive, but it plays well enough."

"However did you make it?" I asked.

"I did it many years ago when I first came to this place. Those first few days were terrible." He shook his head. "My hope revived the day after my arrival when I received a parcel from the guard. It was an extra suit of clothes. He would not tell me who had brought them, but I hoped that whoever it was would also return with books and possibly my flute. But as the days passed, I realized that all I would have to amuse myself would be what I brought with me: one Book—which I had about me when I was taken—and my ingenuity.* I decided I could use the latter to make myself a flute. I took a crossbar from that trestle table; I'm sure you've noticed it's unsteady."

---

ingenuity: creativity

He smiled at the thought before continuing. "I beat and fashioned it into a crude knife. Then I got one of the hollow bars from that iron grate at the chimney's base over there, and after much patience succeeded in boring holes in it. As I have said, I was stronger then."

"The guards did not try to stop you?"

He smiled. "I think they were afraid to try. I later learned that they thought my frantic pounding was simply madness."

"But surely when you'd finished they could see what you had done," I said.

"As you will recall," he reminded me, "you did not think much of my work when you first saw it."

"I'm sure you told them—as you did me—what it was you'd made."

"I did," he said. "I even played it for them, but you will find that first impressions die hard. They were less afraid to bring in

my supper but fearful enough to keep alive the idea that I was mad. Still," he sighed contentedly, "I had my flute."

By this time he had finished with the wash and joined me at the table.

"What kind of songs do you play?" I asked.

"My own," he said. "I was quite a good musician in my youth."

"They must be sad songs."

"What makes you think so?"

"What other kind of songs could you write in such a place as this?" I asked.

"Music reflects what's in the heart, not what is in one's surroundings."

"And what is that—what is in your heart, I mean?"

"I told you that I had one Book with me. I have spent these years hiding that Book in my heart, and I would like to think that my music in some measure reflects the peace that I have found there."

"Peace?" I said. "After the disgrace of imprisonment for all these years, how can you talk of peace when—" I hesitated, "when everyone believes you mad?"

"I have ceased to care what others think of me," he said. "Of course, there was a time when that was not the case, but I have since learned that it is my heart, not my

circumstances, that determines whether I am a man of honor or disgrace. The longer you live, Jacques, the more you will see that many of those held in honor are fools and that those counted as foolish are the wisest of men. The Book I speak of," he continued, "is more than just a book to me. You might say, it is part of my heritage. It has been in my family for over a hundred years."

"Your family," I said, taking an opportunity to learn more of him, "have they not been able in all these years to get your release?"

"As far as I know, they never knew that I was here," he said.

I waited for him to tell me more. When he did not, I asked, "May I see your book?"

He looked at me for what seemed a long time. "You may, if you promise that you will tell no one that I have it."

"The guards do not mind your flute; why would they mind your having a book?"

"I do not know if they would mind or not; but I will take no chance of losing it."

"All right," I said, "I promise."

He got up, went to the corner of the cell, and after rummaging under his bedding, pulled out a small but rather thick book. He brought it over, holding it in both hands, carefully but securely, as I would have held a new-made sculpture in which I took pride.

"Can you read?" he asked, as he returned and sat beside me.

"Of course," I said. "Artisans know how to read."

"Good," he said smiling. Then he began carefully thumbing through the delicate pages. "While I play for you, you can read the words that inspired my song. You shall see it is not sad." Handing me the book, he showed me the place. I looked down as he began to play:

"Ho! Everyone who thirsts,
Come to the waters;
And you who have no money,
Come, buy and eat. . . .
Why do you spend money for *what is* not
    bread,
And your wages for *what* does not satisfy?
Listen diligently to Me, and eat *what is* good,
And let your soul delight itself in abundance.
Incline your ear, and come to Me.
Hear, and your soul shall live. . . .
Seek the Lord while He may be found,
Call upon Him while He is near.
Let the wicked forsake his way,
And the unrighteous man his thoughts;
Let him return to the Lord,
And He will have mercy on him;
And to our God, For He will abundantly
    pardon."

"For thus says the High and Lofty One
Who inhabits eternity, whose name is Holy:
'I dwell in the high and holy *place*,
With him who has a contrite and humble
    spirit,
To revive the spirit of the humble,
And to revive the heart of the contrite ones.'"

The beauty of the words, the music, the scent of the Book's soft leather cover, and the feel of its delicate pages made me forget the musty, darkened cell until Pierre-Joseph broke off his music in haste. One of the guards was coming toward the cell. Quickly I closed the Book and gave it back to him. He had barely put it in its place before the guard came in with two bowls of gruel.

"You better watch out for him," the guard said, as he set down the bowls and started out. But when he reached the door, he turned, and, pointing to Pierre-Joseph, he added, "He's a sly one he is. He may be calm for now, but sometime when you're not looking—" He broke off his speech and made a mocking gesture as if to slit his throat.

I am ashamed to say that I said nothing in defense of this man who had been so kind to me. Instead, I simply watched the guard as he went out, shaking his head and laughing to himself.

CHAPTER 11

I am certain that the guards would have been disappointed had they known that my stay in the *calottes* was not the "horror" they intended. Indeed, as I was taken from the cell several days later, I found myself regretting my departure. I was, of course, glad to leave the rats and filth behind, but I was also saddened to leave the "mad" Pierre, for there was much about him—and his treasured Book—that yet intrigued me.

I was still thinking on Pierre-Joseph and on all of my unanswered questions when I entered my old cell. Thomas and Louis were seated at the table, but as soon as the guard closed and locked the door, they were both upon me.

"Well?" said Louis.

"Well what?" I asked.

"The opening—can we get out?" Thomas prodded.

"Oh!" I said, remembering my mission. "Well—we must go up through the chimney. It won't be easy—"

"But it's possible?" Louis interrupted.

"Yes," I said. "It's possible."

"Good! Come, sit down."

"The ladder's done," Thomas informed me, as we gathered round the table.

"No more need for praying now." Louis laughed.

"Unless it be for rain," said Thomas.

"Nature will take care of that," Louis assured him. "Spring is here, and with spring the rains will come."

"Why do we need rain?" I asked.

"To get rid of the night guards who walk atop the towers," Louis said. "The sentries do not make their rounds if it is raining."

"Where is the ladder? Still in the chapel?" I asked.

Louis shook his head and smiled. Then, motioning for Thomas to watch the door, he moved to the corner of the room and began rummaging amidst his bedding, which was piled up against the wall. Pulling out an unwieldy* bundle, he brought it to the table.

---

unwieldy: awkward

"I'm not sure you will be able to get that bulging thing up the chimney," I warned him.

"Oh, don't worry, I'll just unwind it a bit," he said. "Believe me, there's a way. I've not come this far only to allow such a trivial thing to deter me. Do you know what I call it?" he continued enthusiastically. "I call it Jacob's ladder; after all, it was kept in a chapel." He began to laugh as he fumbled with the bundle. "I've been six months in making this."

"How long is the thing?" I asked, astonished as he began unwinding it.

"About three hundred feet I'd guess."

He yanked and pulled on the ropes that bound the rungs together, smiling broadly at how well it held. Then, satisfied that he'd secured my admiration, he rewrapped his handiwork and placed it behind the heap of bedding by the wall.

"By the way," Louis said, as he and Thomas returned to their seats at the table. "What was it like up there?"

"The cell itself was as bad as it could get—all that we had feared," I said, pointing my remark to Thomas.

"Did you see anyone else up there?" asked Louis.

"Just an old man," I said.

"Must be an old lunatic—" said Thomas, moving closer. "Was he frightening too?"

"Hardly," I said. Then, turning to Louis, I inquired, "Do you know who he might be?"

"I have heard there is one old madman they keep up there. There's not much more to tell," he said, "except that he's been here more than twenty years. No one knows just why. I imagine they have all forgotten. There are tales, though, that he's violent when provoked."

"He hasn't enough strength for violence," I said scornfully. "Any young man could get the upper hand, at least in a battle of fists."

"But not in a battle of wits, huh?" Louis laughed.

"It's hard to say," I continued, ignoring his laughter. "He seems to have been well educated in his time and is quite the gentleman despite his horrid living conditions. That's what puzzles me. He looks as if he had his share of money once. Why didn't he buy his freedom?"

Louis shrugged. "Maybe his money ran out."

"Perhaps," I said. "Still, I've been thinking—" I hesitated.

"What?" coaxed Thomas.

"Well, since we must exit from the *calottes*, could we not take him with us?"

"An old lunatic! You *have* spent too much time with him," said Louis. "You've lost your mind as well!"

"I could see to him," I said, not at all sure that I really could.

"You didn't tell him of our plan, did you?" Louis queried.

"Of course not," I assured him.

"Besides, Jacques," Thomas interjected, "we've no assurance that we'll exit through his cell. Louis tells me that there are many cells up there."

"Come to think of it," I said, "how are we all three going to get up to the *calottes* at the same time?"

"That's easy enough," said Louis. "We'll get in such a row that they will be forced to throw us up there in order to get any peace."

"What if they put us into different cells?" questioned Thomas.

"They won't," Louis assured him. "I've conducted experiments with several other cellmates."

"Experiments?" I asked.

He nodded, a look of pride upon his face. "I'd pit one against another, subtly you understand, so that they had no notion I was doing so. Then I'd watch them break into a brawl. They were always taken up to the *calottes* and always to the same cell. The guards kept them together so that they could fight it out without disturbing anyone."

"Why did you not tell those other prisoners of your plans?" I asked.

"Because I was nowhere near finished with the ladder."

"So we got in on it by the luck of the draw, you might say," said Thomas.

"You might say that," said Louis. "Of course, I sized you up a bit as well," he added.

"And if we had not measured up?" I asked.

"Then I would have waited until they brought the next batch of prisoners in," he said. "Unlike you, Jacques, I'm a patient man. A month or two more would have meant little to me."

"What are we to do now?" I asked, feeling that there must be something that could occupy our time.

"Sit and wait for rain, as I have said."

"What you haven't said," I reminded him, making no effort to conceal my irritation at his flippant tone, "is how we are to know it is raining. We are in the center of a tower with three levels of stone overhead."

He got up, walked to the corner of the room, and sat down to lean against his mass of wadded bedding. "That friend of mine who does my laundry, she will not come again until a storm is raging."

I got up and began to pace about the room; life in a cell was once more pressing down on me. I wanted out—now. For whenever I stopped long enough to ponder, I remembered my mother and her desperate need of me.

"Relax, Jacques," Thomas said. "Your pacing will not make it rain."

"Perhaps not," I said, "but it will help me endure this place until it does."

THINKING ZONE

Great writers are very often great readers. Perhaps it is for this reason that so many authors make references to other works when they write. Sometimes the reference is quite obvious; other times the reference may go unnoticed except to the highly educated mind. Any reference to another work of literature within a piece is called an **allusion**. Allusions could be thought of as a type of "inside joke" between author and reader since they are not generally pointed out by the author. An allusion usually adds to the author's meaning either by illustrating a point or by highlighting the differences between the allusion and the topic. Author A. A. Milne accomplishes the latter when he alludes to Alfred, Lord Tennyson's *Idylls of the King* when the King in *The Ugly Duckling* mentions "a fierce light beating on a throne." He also alludes to Shakespeare's *King Henry IV, Part 2*, during the King and Chancellor's exchange about the uneasiness of the one who wears the crown. Milne hopes that his readers are familiar with those quotations and will associate them with the great and noble kings of literature. In this way he adds to the humor and irony of his allusion since Milne's King is a silly and shallow monarch. Now that you are aware of allusions, you will begin to see them often in your reading. When you do, try to figure out what "secret" message the author might be sending you and then smile to yourself and share a moment of connection with someone you don't even know.

1. *[interpretive]* What kind of character is Pierre-Joseph Aumônt? List some of his character traits.

   _____

   _____

   _____

   _____

   _____

2. *[interpretive]* What does Pierre-Joseph's flute playing suggest about his character?

   _____

   _____

   _____

   _____

   _____

3. *[interpretive/critical]* How is the Bible passage that Jacques reads relevant to Jacques's condition? What does he need at this point in the novel?

_____

_____

_____

_____

_____

_____

_____

4. *[literal/interpretive]* Why was Jacques reluctant to leave the *calottes*? How is this ironic?

_____

_____

_____

_____

5. *[interpretive]* What is the **allusion** Louis makes in reference to the ladder? Why is the name appropriate?

_____

_____

_____

_____

6. *[critical]* In Chapter 10 some of the novel's important ideas are directly expressed. Who states these themes, and what are they?

_____

_____

_____

_____

_____

_____

_____

CHAPTER 12

The spring rains were later than usual, and it was three miserable weeks before we finally heard the welcome words from Louis's friend: "The weather is frightful." As the guard ushered her in, she added, "I almost didn't come."

"I'm glad you did," said Louis, carefully framing his conversation, for the guard had remained just outside the door. "I'm in desperate need of clean shirts."

"Well, you need not have waited for me," she said. "You could have hung them outside for a thorough washing. Not only is the rain coming down in buckets, but the wind is whipping up something fierce."

"Perhaps it will stop by evening?" Louis asked pointedly.

"That's not likely," she reassured him. "The sky looks as if it will be rumbling all night. I'd say tomorrow's dawn will be the first sign of clearing."

"Well, the weather affects us little here," Louis said. He went to retrieve several old shirts for her—whole shirts this time.

"Well, I mustn't stay," she said, as she stuffed them into her basket. "I've yet to run my errands."

He bent to kiss her hand. "Until next week, then?"

"Or before," she replied with a knowing smile.

As soon as the guard was out of sight, Thomas asked the very question that was on my lips, "Tonight? It is tonight then?"

"Tonight it is," said Louis.

"How soon do we start up a brawl?" I asked impatiently.

"Let us first map out last-minute plans," he said, motioning us to the table. "Then we shall give them such a brawl that they'll be forced to shut us up in the calottes for weeks!"

* * *

The row that we invented went perfectly—as rows go. In moments, several guards came barging in. "Break it up! Break it up!" they shouted as they pulled us off one another.

"You never learn, do you?" said the one who collared me.

"Leave us to our fighting," shouted Louis. "It won't be settled until I knock both of them senseless!" he added for good effect.

"We'll see about that," Thomas chimed in. I decided not to join them; this being my second offense, I knew that I was already on my way upstairs. I feared to push my luck further.

"If you two don't keep quiet, I'll throw you both upstairs with this young rascal. Then you can all three rot together for a few days!"

"That suits me fine!" said Louis, with a sincerity that I feared was telling.

At this point, Thomas broke away from the guard that was holding him and lunged at Louis. That clinched it. "Round them all up," bellowed the guard at the door. "If we're lucky, they will kill each other, and we can save on gruel and kindling."

Louis feigned the cooling of his temper and convinced the guard to relax his grip long enough for him to scoop up his bundle of "belongings" to take with him. His reputation must have aided him, for neither Thomas nor I were afforded such a privilege, and for the second time I was hauled off without my jacket.

I was both relieved and disappointed that we were not put in Pierre-Joseph's cell. I had thought much of him over the past weeks. I had not, however, been able to come up with a realistic solution for including him in our plans, and I could not imagine facing him without asking him to come along.

By the time we reached the *calottes*, I was feeling the effects of our fray* in earnest. My lower lip had swelled to twice its size, and my nose had started spouting blood like one of the fountains in the Tuileries* gardens.

fray: scuffle or brawl
Tuileries (twē-lə-rē´)

"I think you two got a bit carried away down there," I said, when at last we'd been left alone again.

"Had to make it look like the real thing," said Louis, with that implacable* calm that over the weeks had begun to drive me to distraction.

implacable: unchanging

"From the looks of Thomas and the bleeding of my nose, it *was* the real thing," I said, as I forced my head back in an effort to stop my nosebleed.

"How'd you come out without a scratch?" Thomas inquired sullenly. He too had noticed that Louis barely looked rumpled, let alone battle scarred.

"Because I am as wily as I am patient," he said. "So this is our way out, huh, Jacques?" He began his examination of the chimney.

"That's it," I said. "Not very inviting but—"

He cut me off. "What's at the top will make it worth it."

"The top of the tower's just the start," interjected Thomas. "We've still got to get down the tower and across the moat," he reminded Louis. "Or have you forgotten those hurdles?"

"Small hurdles, Thomas," Louis said, "for we have Jacob's ladder." He patted the bundle that lay beside him.

"I'd feel better if they'd just let us out the front gate and across the drawbridge," Thomas sighed.

I agreed with Thomas.

"There would be no adventure in that," chided Louis.

My nosebleed had finally abated,* and Thomas and I joined him at the chimney's base.

abated: lessened

"Well, when do we begin this big adventure?" asked Thomas.

"No time like the present, for I'm sure the night has fallen," said Louis. Then he turned to me. "Now, Jacques, once you get to the top—"

"Once *I* get to the top?" I interrupted. "What makes you think I'm going to be the first one to stuff myself up that chimney? *You're* the mastermind behind this plan, remember. You can have the honor."

"You're going to be the first one," explained Louis in a most condescending tone, "because you are the lankiest. You are the only one of us that is lean enough to wedge himself in that space and climb up to the top. Once you're there, you should be able to loosen the grate with little difficulty. I've

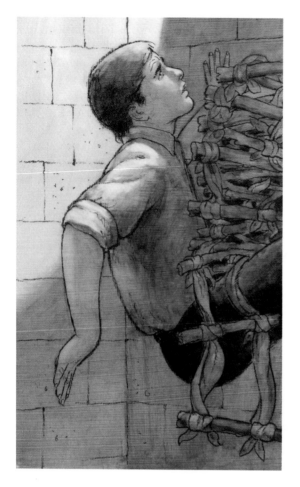

examined them as I've walked atop the towers; they're not secured by any means."

"Guess they never thought anyone would be dumb enough to try to crawl up the chimney," said Thomas.

"I wonder why?" I asked sarcastically.

I realized, however, that there was no way of arguing myself out of forging the way. So, anxious to get it over with as quickly as possible, I moved into position. "Don't forget the ladder," I said.

"Oh, you must take it with you," Louis informed me as he handed it over. "When you get onto the roof, you let it down a bit and use it to haul Thomas and me up. Don't worry," he added as he shoved me toward the opening; "I'll do my best to push you up as far as I can."

"Thanks," I said, snatching the bundle from him.

"Good luck, Jacques," I heard Thomas say as I stuck my head into the chimney.

The rain was leaking in, making an already dreadful task even worse. I placed my back against one side of the chimney wall, and with Louis's help I managed to draw my knees up to my chest and place my feet against the opposite wall. The ladder was cradled—or crammed—into my lap.

I felt the panic rising and I stopped a moment to breathe deeply. "What's wrong?" asked Louis.

"Nothing," I said. "Just give me a minute."

"Sure," he said. "Just tell me when you're ready for a push."

I leaned my head back and closed my eyes. The inch or two on either side of my shoulders helped to quell my fear. *You've got a bit of room*, I reasoned with myself. *Not much, but enough.*

My muscles began cramping up. Like it or not, I knew I had to get moving. "Push," I ordered, and Louis gave a heave—and then another—a large clot of loosened soot fell down upon me.

I can hardly relate the horror that I felt as that wet, suffocating mess covered my face. "Stop!" I managed to choke out. "Stop!"

"Jacques, Jacques," I could hear Thomas calling.

"He's all right," Louis reassured him. "Shake your head, Jacques. Get the soot out of your face."

His voice, though right below me, sounded as if it were coming from the end of a long tunnel. I imagine I was close to blacking out, but I heard enough to obey. Once I was able to brush the filthy substance from my face, I revived somewhat.

"Just breathe deeply for a few moments," Louis continued. "I'm sure the worst of it is loosened now. We'll take it slower. Just tell me when you're ready."

I desperately wanted to turn back, but I knew that I could not, and, steeling myself against my fear, I started slowly upward. Louis sensed my movement and did what he could to aid me.

It seemed hours before I reached the top. By the time I did, the muscles in my legs and back were nearly numb with aching, and my hands were cold and stiff. The thunder roared as I reached up and grabbed the grate, desperately hoping that it would give without much effort. It did. I managed to push it to one side, and, clinging to the edge of the opening, I pulled with all my strength to lift myself up a bit. After forcing my body into what seemed every conceivable contortion, I finally managed to roll out onto the roof. Flinging the bundle aside, I lay there for a moment with the rain beating down on me, my limbs stretched out to their full length.

A flash of lightning brought me to my senses and reminded me that if I were seen, my troubles would be multiplied tenfold.

Quickly I unwrapped the ladder, let it down, and waited until I felt a firm grip at the other end. I then began to pull. By the time I saw Thomas's smiling face, I had used my last ounce of strength.

"You'll have to get Louis up," I said, collapsing into a heap.

"Of course," said Thomas. "Save what breath you have left. You'll need it for the trip down the side of the tower."

Louis was out on the tower roof and ready to go on much sooner than I'd wished. "Keep low," he said as we moved to the parapet.

Cautiously he peered over the edge. "Well, it looks as if it's as quiet as it's going to get."

He threw the ladder over and anchored it around one of the jutting rows of bricks along the tower's ledge.

The panic in me began to rise again as I saw the long drop into the moat. The ladder looked ludicrously flimsy as it blew and twisted in the wind and rain. "Are you sure that thing will hold us?" I asked.

"So sure," said Louis, "that I will be the first one to descend it." And, throwing his leg over the wall, he started down.

Despite the height, I found that getting down the ladder was far easier than climbing out onto the roof. Louis, for all his faults, had made a flawless piece of work. So flawless in fact, that he was loath to leave it. "It is hard to leave behind such a rare and precious monument to human industry," he said as we pressed ourselves against the base of the tower wall, shivering in the moat.

"Come on," I said, kicking out from the wall, "this is no time for sentimentality."

"How can you be so callous to cast aside, without regret, the tools that helped us to our liberty?" Louis continued his lament as we swam to the other side. It was obvious he had worked less than I, for I had neither wind nor strength for conversation.

Thomas was losing patience as well. "Keep it down," he said. "We're not out of this yet."

"Look," I said, pointing up at the tower. We had been so intent upon getting through the moat that we failed to notice that the rain had stopped. The sentries had resumed their rounds, armed as usual with broad lanterns.

"What now?" hissed Thomas, for we had reached the other side.

"Get out," Louis said. We obeyed.

"Now, crawl—staying on your stomach—until you reach the gate. There are no sentries in the outer courtyard at night. They are too confident of their moat. If we make it that far, we'll be free."

"*If!*" I said it quietly, but with all the anger in my voice that I could muster. "It's a good two hundred yards over stones and who knows what else—on our stomachs?"

"Would you like to turn around?" Louis asked.

I put my face down to the dirt and started crawling.

CHAPTER 13

By the time we reached the outer courtyard, I was a matted mess of dirt, bruises, and bloodstains. But once outside that gate in the haven of a darkened street, I felt an exhilaration that I can scarcely put into words. Thomas and I were both eager to get home and paused only a moment before setting out in the direction of our shops.

Louis quickly followed after us. "Where do you two think you're going?"

"Home," said Thomas, without glancing back.

"Oh, that is brilliant," Louis said, and his derisive tone pulled us to a stop.

"What do you mean?" I said.

"You're going home? To do what? Wait until morning when the guards discover that you have escaped and come to fetch you back to prison?"

"Do you have a better idea?" asked Thomas.

"Of course, he does," I said. "He always has—"

Thomas cut me off. "Let's hear him out," he said.

"My friend," Louis began. "She lives in St. Germain.* Her father is a tailor; he will give us shelter for the night."

St. Germain (să[n] zhâr-mă[n]´)

"And tomorrow?" Thomas asked.

"Tomorrow he has promised to get me safely into the Low Countries.* I'm sure that he can do the same for you."

Low Countries: the Netherlands

"The Low Countries?" I said. "We can't leave Paris."

"Jacques is right," Thomas said. "I've a wife and son to care for."

"And how do you intend to care for them?" asked Louis. "Where else can a cabinetmaker and a sculptor find work in Paris but in St. Antoine, and I am telling you it is not safe for you to work there."

I could see Thomas wavering. "We'll manage," I said.

"How, Jacques?" questioned Thomas. "Louis is right. We're not thinking clearly."

"And he is?" I said sarcastically. "How can we support ourselves by fleeing Paris? Tell me that."

"I have connections," Louis said. "I already know that there will be work waiting for me. I will see that you find jobs as well."

"Why this sudden interest in our future? Inside the prison, you made it clear that we were chosen simply as a matter of convenience. Why exactly do you want us to go along now?" I said, trying to find something that would help me change Thomas's mind.

"You helped me escape. I like to pay my debts. Besides, if they find you, it will go very badly for you. And though I admit that I am prone to look to my own interests first, I am not averse to looking out for others when I can."

"How will we get the money that we make back to our families?" Thomas questioned, genuinely interested now.

"I have arrangements for that as well. I can also see that your families are notified of our plans, though I insist that they do not know our exact location."

I felt Thomas's gaze upon me, but I could not face him. I knew that I had no choice. I could not leave my mother, and though I knew it was unfair of me, I desperately wanted Thomas to return to St. Antoine as well. "Jacques?" he finally said.

I could hold out no longer. "I must stay here," I said. "But you go on. I'll tell your family that you'll be in touch."

"You're sure?" Thomas asked. "Your mother would understand."

"I'm sure," I said.

"Good-bye, Jacques," Louis said, offering his hand. "You have spirit. If anyone can survive as a fugitive in Paris, you can."

I took his hand then and said farewell to Thomas.

It was well into the night, but my shop was not far. When I reached it, I remembered that I'd left my key in my jacket pocket. Fortunately, I had long ago seen the necessity of preparing for emergencies and had done so by putting a clump of molding wax inside our shop bell and pressing an extra key into the wax. I reached up now and retrieved it, congratulating myself on my ingenuity.

The shop was dark, but despite the blackness, I could feel that I was home. I stood for a moment, taking in the smell of my leather aprons, molding clay, wax, and chiseled stone. Then, running my hand across the scarred surface of my wooden worktable, I found the cool, smooth form of my iron tools. I realized then just how much I'd missed the feel of them.

I found a candle and got it burning. As the light fell on the worktable, I saw that the money I'd left there so many weeks ago was gone. I took comfort in the fact, forcing myself to believe that my mother had spent it on food, not wine.

Heading up the stairs, I told myself that perhaps the fear brought on by my abrupt departure and the joy my mother would feel in knowing of my safe return might be enough to rekindle in her the desire to be the mother she once was.

Once upstairs, I made my way across the room as quietly as possible, for I did not want to startle her. Then, setting the candle on the table, I carefully pulled back the curtain and called softly, "Mother—"

She was gone.

I ran downstairs, out into the alley, and down to Thomas's shop. I banged upon the door and kept on banging until I saw the light of a lantern through the glass. I could see Phillipe and his mother cautiously approaching. "Open up, Madame Grammônd. It's me, Jacques," I called in to her.

Hearing my name, Phillipe ran ahead of his mother and opened up the door.

"Jacques!" he shouted.

His mother was quickly at his side. "Jacques, how—"

"My mother," I said. "I've just gone home. She isn't there."

I waited for an answer, but Phillipe and his mother just stood there staring.

"Surely, you saw her leave. Someone must have—"

"Jacques," Madame Grammônd interrupted; then she paused a moment. "I'm sorry," she finally said.

"Sorry?" I said, the truth beginning to weigh down on me.

Phillipe stood beside his mother, but he would no longer look up at me.

"I didn't know she needed help," his mother endeavored to explain. "Phillipe, he tried—two weeks or more had passed before I noticed that he'd been taking loaves of bread from the kitchen. I followed him one day to see that he was leaving them at your shop door—"

"The door was locked," he said, still refusing to look up. "I couldn't take the bread in to her. I rang the bell, but she never answered. I thought of telling Mama, but I—I didn't think you'd want me to."

His mother put out her hand to comfort him. "He did what he thought best, Jacques. He piled the bread up outside the door every day, hoping she would see it. She never did—the pigs would end up eating it. When I finally realized what he was doing, I went down to her myself. I banged and banged—and then began to worry. I got the locksmith to let me inside—but it was too late." Her voice dropped almost to a whisper. "She must have starved."

I stood there, stunned into silence, until I heard her voice once again. "Jacques, I

know this may not be the time, but—I must ask; have you news of Thomas?"

I told her all I knew, then, still numbed by what I'd learned, I turned and made my way back to my shop.

I walked through the open door and slowly went back up the stairs. The half-open curtains hung like a shroud about her bed, and on the table, I saw my candle's dying flame mirrored in one of the wine bottles she had cast aside. The sight of it awakened my dulled senses, and rushing to the table, I picked up the bottle and hurled it crashing to the wall. "I hate you!" I shouted. The years of seething anger at last erupted in fury, a fury that could not be quenched without revenge. "De Guiche—Latude—all of you. I'll kill you if I ever get the chance!"

I turned in search of something else to hurl but saw instead the small shadow of Phillipe standing on the stairs. I stopped. He came to me and gently took my hand in his. In that moment of stillness he looked up at me. "I will hate them too," he said.

THINKING ZONE

Style can be defined as a writer's personal signature. It is not *what* a writer says, but *how* he decides to say it. To give his signature "flair" and to draw his reader into the story, a writer will use many techniques. He might, for example, use descriptive details, concrete imagery, or figurative language to make the readers feel as though they are in the heart of the action. Additionally, some writers may use educated vocabulary in order to achieve a "high-toned" style, while others may express their thoughts using common speech to achieve the opposite effect. Sentence structure also affects a writer's style; some writers may compose long, complex sentences, while others use short, staccato-like sentences. A writer may vary sentence length and structure based on topic or audience. If a writer is composing a story for a newspaper, for instance, he may use short sentences. The writer may use longer sentences to write a scholarly essay.

Figurative language—*an artful deviation from the standard way of saying something*

1. *[literal/interpretive]* What are the "belongings" that Louis is able to scoop up and take with him to the *calottes*? Why does Jacques think the guards allowed Louis to do this?

_____

_____

_____

_____

_____

2. *[critical]* In the description of the escape from the Bastille, what elements of **style** does the writer demonstrate that help you to better imagine what it must have been like for Jacques and the others?

_____

_____

_____

_____

_____

3. *[critical]* What elements of the author's style serve to increase the tension that the reader feels as Jacques and the others make their getaway? Where else in these two chapters does the author demonstrate a similar tactic?

_____

_____

_____

_____

_____

_____

_____

4. *[interpretive]* What is ironic about the way Jacques felt once he reached the outer courtyard of the prison?

_____

_____

_____

5. *[interpretive]* After the men's escape, who has the best plan regarding where to go? Why is this plan the best?

_____

_____

_____

_____

6. *[interpretive/critical]* The author describes the curtains around Jacques's mother's bed as hanging "like a shroud." How is this simile appropriate? What other figurative language in that paragraph communicates a similar message?

_____

_____

_____

CHAPTER 14

That night as Phillipe and I sat in the shop together, I struggled to turn my thoughts to surviving as a fugitive in Paris. My only means of livelihood was my shop. I could not, would not, give it up. Despite the risk, I determined that I would continue as a sculptor in St. Antoine, and I set my mind to devising a plan that would enable me to do so.

"I need your help, Phillipe," I said to him. He nodded. "I'm going to make several busts and statues of the philosophers, princes—all the popular faces I've done before. When I'm finished, I want you to take them to Charpentier's café."

"You want me to sell them for you?"

"No," I said. "You will be my legs to deliver the work, but Charpentier shall be my eyes to seek out a clientele."

"But what am I to tell Monsieur Charpentier if he asks why you have not come to the café yourself?"

"If he does not already know, you can tell him what happened to your father and me. He'll understand why I must remain in hiding. Tell him that I will give him a portion of my commissions; enough to pay him for the time he takes on my behalf and for any inconvenience he may encounter in keeping my whereabouts a secret."

"When do you want me to go?"

"Tomorrow," I said. "You can explain our plans to him then. I will also try to have at least one thing finished for you to take along. I'm going to work the rest of the night—and every night while Paris sleeps. You can come each morning a little before sunrise and collect what I have finished."

"Will you work all day as well?" he asked.

"No. During the day I will have to lose myself among the hordes of beggars in the streets. No one must know that I have been in this shop. You understand?"

"Yes," he said, "but when will you sleep—and eat?"

"Whenever and wherever I can."

A worried frown creased his brow. "I will bring you bread when I come," he said.

"I will sleep—and eat—Phillipe. Don't worry."

"I'll bring you bread," he said dogmatically.

"Just tomorrow," I conceded. "Come an hour or so before dawn and we will eat together." The proposal cheered him. "Go home for now. You will have only a couple of hours sleep as it is."

I led him out and stood watching until he disappeared into his shop.

I stood alone in the alley, unwilling to go back inside my shop, reluctant to face all the bitter—and sweet—memories that were housed within. I was certain that our escape from the Bastille was as yet undetected. Perhaps I could still risk a walk through the city as a free man. I set out and soon found myself walking once again along the Seine.

The air was cool and the sound of the water's ebb and flow soothing—but not as soothing as it had been when I walked along the cobbled wharf so many weeks before. How much had happened since that night when I first saw Danton at Charpentier's! At that time, I believed that with my father's death the Comte de Guiche's murderous son had taken all there was to take from me. How wrong I was. Now I had lost my mother too, and in my mind, the young nobleman stood convicted of that crime as well. Had my father lived, my mother would have lived also. As I thought upon these things, any peace that still remained in my heart departed from me, and gazing down into the river, I felt as if the secret of the Seine's calm constancy was locked away from me forever. I turned toward home, determined to hold fast to the only solace left me—my work.

Entering the shop, I closed the door and locked it. Then, moving over to my worktable, I discovered the unfinished portrait of Danton lying just as I had left it. It startled me at first to see his face again. I picked up the medallion and examined it. As I did so, it occurred to me that Danton had been wise to demand the work in wax, for wax remained somewhat pliable.* Like Danton, with a bit of heat, it could be transformed in a moment. Only a fool would have chosen to cast such a man in stone.

---

pliable: moldable

I could see that the work I'd done was true—at least in part. I had captured Danton as an orator, a champion of the people. His speech came readily back to mind. It was true that the rich lived extravagantly and the poor paid for it in taxes. It had always been so. Perhaps Danton was a wiser man than I'd believed him to be. Even if he himself did not understand poverty, he understood its cause. I gazed at his image before me and knew that it would please him. I determined that I would finish the medallion that night, for I remembered that he had already paid me for half of the commission.

* * *

Phillipe arrived an hour or so before dawn, a loaf of bread under each arm. I took the bread from him and set it on the table. "You have told your mother of our plans?" I asked, as I handed the medallion to him.

"Yes," he said. "She is glad that I can help." He looked down at the medallion in his hand and asked, "Why did you make this?"

"It was an unfinished commission," I said. "This is what Danton wanted the night he came here. Charpentier knows of it. I only hope that Danton still visits the café, but even if he doesn't, perhaps Charpentier knows where to find him. You can at least ask if it can be delivered."

"All right," he said. Then, shaking his head, he added, "I can't see why he would ever want a picture of himself."

"He said it was for a lady." Phillipe looked doubtful. "I had my doubts as well," I confessed, "but that *is* what he told me. Come. We'd best get to eating what you brought. It will be light soon, and we must both be gone."

I spent that day wandering the back streets of St. Germain, for I felt no urge to sleep. I suppose what drew me to St. Germain was the faint hope that Thomas and Louis would still be there somewhere, but I saw no trace of them. I toyed with the idea of searching out the tailor whom Louis had claimed as friend, but thought better of it. There were almost as many tailors in St. Germain as brewers, and I could not risk asking questions of just anyone. Still, such thoughts gave a vague purpose to my wandering. I was glad when darkness finally fell and I could make my way back to St. Antoine.

Phillipe was faithful to come just at the time I'd told him.

"Were you able to deliver the medallion?" I asked when he had settled himself on a stool.

"Yes, and I've got the other half of the commission for you too," he said, digging into the ragged pocket of his breeches and pulling out the money.

"This is more than he owed me," I said. "Are you sure there is no mistake?"

Phillipe shrugged. "He said to give it to you. He said he was glad to pay for such work as yours even if he didn't really want the medallion anymore."

"He didn't want it?" I asked.

"That's what he said."

"What was wrong with it?"

"Nothing," Phillipe assured me. "He liked it well enough. But he said to tell you that he'd already won the lady's heart."

"Why ever did he take it then?" I asked.

"He wants to show it to a friend of his, a man he thinks can help you."

"Help me? How? You did not tell him I am working here."

A look of indignation came into his childish face. "Of course I didn't."

"I'm sorry," I said. "Go on. Help me how?"

"Danton said that he came here looking for you when you failed to show at Charpentier's. When he saw the shop deserted, he decided to get someone else to do the work. The man he found lives on the boulevard. He has a *cabinet** of waxworks there. Danton said that he is going to show the man your medallion and he thinks it will impress him. He can give you steady work."

----

cabinet (kä-bē-nä´): small private room or house set aside for a specific activity

----

"Does Charpentier know of this man?"

"Yes," Phillipe said. "I asked him what he thought of him."

"What did he say?"

"He said, 'Tell Jacques that he can trust Danton's advice.' I like Charpentier well enough," Phillipe continued unbidden, "but, Danton—I still don't like him much."

"Still, I need to make a living," I said. "If I decide to accept, how am I to meet this man?"

Phillipe looked down and assumed a look of strained concentration. "Tomorrow afternoon at three o'clock," he began slowly, as if he were struggling to remember the message just as it had been given, "you are to meet Danton on the boulevard next to the theater where the marionettes perform." He looked up again, a smile on his face. "That is just what he said."

I returned his smile but continued to weigh the content of his message. "I suppose if Charpentier says he's trustworthy, it is worth the risk," I said at length. "I only hope that Charpentier knows Danton as well as he thinks he does."

"He should," Phillipe remarked.

"Why? Does he go to the café often now?"

"Every day."

"Charpentier has taken to him then," I said, "or he would not encourage it."

"He has more than taken to him," Phillipe informed me.

"What do you mean?"

"Danton has married Charpentier's daughter."

"Danton!" I said astonished. "Married Gabrielle Charpentier?"

Phillipe nodded, then added thoughtfully, "I wouldn't want that face about my house."

I laughed at his predictable frankness, relieved to be reminded that some things were yet the same. "I agree," I said. Then I added, "But perhaps in time we shall grow used to him; after all, it seems that Charpentier and his daughter certainly did."

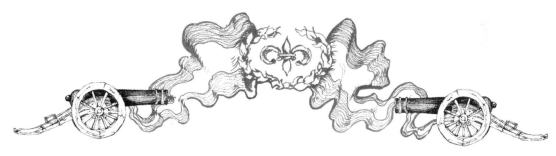

CHAPTER 15

The next day I returned to St. Germain, this time not to wander but to sleep in one of the many alleyways I'd found the day before. By two o'clock I was well rested and heading for the boulevard, that part of Paris where two kinds of people gathered: those hungering for an audience and those demanding to be entertained.

By the time that I arrived, the day's activities were well underway. Here and there clusters of men and women collected, elbow to elbow, talking and gesturing wildly. Painted mimes* and harlequins* jumped out to startle me, and the fruit vendors and flower girls tried to stop me in the street. Relentlessly I pushed past them all—the beggars, nobles, and *petite bourgeoisie*—until at last I stood before the theater.

---

mime: one who acts using gestures and no words

harlequins: clowns

petite bourgeoisie (pə-tēt′ boo[r]-zhwä-zē′): lower middle class

"I'm glad to see you have taken up my offer," called Danton as he approached me.

"I've not decided yet," I warned him. "I think you know my position. I can't trust just anyone. I want to know more about this man before I accept any proposals."

"Of course, of course," he said. "I'll tell you of him as we walk. His *cabinet* is just down the street."

"I want to know before I go," I said.

"Come, he is waiting. I've told him of you—but not your circumstances. He cares to know neither. He's interested only in your work, and I assure you, Jacques," he said, seeing I still hesitated, "that Dr. Curtius's cabinet is a safer place for you than here on the street."

"All right," I said. "I'll go along, but I'll not make any decisions until I meet the man myself."

"Shall we go?" he asked, pointing out the way.

Reluctantly I followed.

"As I've already mentioned," Danton continued, "his name is Dr. Curtius, and it may cheer you to know that you are not the first 'unsavory'* person to frequent his establishment. You need have little fear. But aside from that, all of Paris is in an uproar. Even if the authorities had the inclination, they wouldn't have the time to look for you."

unsavory: of bad reputation

"Uproar?" I said. "I've noticed nothing out of the ordinary."

"That's because you have not been to the cafés and clubs. I tell you plainly, Jacques, there is a revolution afoot." He said it with relish.

I stopped. "A revolution?"

Oh, you've nothing to fear," he said, "for it is the artisans and peasants—the working people—that stand the most to gain."

"And what are we to gain?" I asked, making no effort to conceal my scorn.

He stared at me a moment, then said, "You shall know soon enough." Resuming his jocund* air, he turned the conversation again to Dr. Curtius. "His waxworks have become the rage of Paris, for his figures are so lifelike that you almost expect them to speak to you while you gaze at them."

jocund: cheerful

"They are full figures—life-size?"

"Most of them are. He does some busts as well, but they are less popular," he said.

"I've never done life-size figures before," I said.

"I told him that. Still, he could see by your medallion that you have potential, and he is willing to teach you."

"I need a job, not a tutor," I said frankly, unwilling to think of any man aside from my father as my mentor.

"He will teach you as you work. Besides, even you must admit that there are things you've yet to learn. Ah, there it is."

I followed his gaze to where a tall, lean black man dressed in oriental robes sat before an ornamental gate. Majestic in his finery, the man took no notice of our approach but sat with a drum between his knees beating out a rhythm that kept pace with the rhythm of his speech. "Come, come see the Master's cabinet. Come, come see the famous brought to life. Come, come see villains brought to justice. Come, come see the waxworks that delight. Come . . ." His strange chant faded as we entered the inner courtyard.

The *cabinet* was a grand, two-storied apartment with a stone walk leading up to an enormous ornate door. The door was framed on either side by two large windows, each of which displayed numerous wax busts of popular Parisians—wealthy men, men like those that I had come to despise.

"I'm not impressed with those whom he chooses to display," I said.

"Nor is he," said Danton nonchalantly. "It is good business to keep them there for now, but I assure you the doctor shall cast them aside when they fall from grace."

"You speak as if you know when that will be," I said.

"Perhaps I do," he said as he opened the door and ushered me into a large, lavishly decorated room.

All about the room were tableaux* of life-size figures arranged on Indian-carpeted platforms. Some were posed as if sitting for a portrait. Others were arranged about tables—some eating, some flirting, and some engaged in lively arguments. All that I had seen on the boulevard paled in comparison to Curtius's cabinet.

---

tableaux (tă-blōz): costumed figures arranged in individual scenes

---

I was not permitted to gaze about undisturbed for long, however, for scarcely had my eyes come to rest on a grouping of well-dressed noblemen when one of them stepped forward. I jumped back, startled.

"I can fool anyone except Danton," said Dr. Curtius as he burst into a hearty laugh. Then, assuming a more businesslike air, he turned to Danton. "So this is Jacques," he said.

"It is," Danton replied, smiling upon me as if I were his prize.

Dr. Curtius then turned to me. "I've seen your work and it pleases me. What has Danton told you?"

"Only that you might have work for me."

"And that you are willing to teach him as he works," Danton added.

"That is so," said Dr. Curtius. "Have you ever worked with live models?" he asked.

"Yes," I said. "My father made me sketch from them for hours."

"How did a poor artisan get models?" he demanded.

I could feel my face redden at his question, but I tried hard to conceal the anger in my voice as I replied. "My father gave food to beggars and children who would sit for me."

"Then they were always living models?"

"Of course," I said. "What other kind are there?"

"The best kind—" he answered, "those that are dead. When you work only with the living you fail to see what lies beneath the flesh—the muscle, sinew, bone—all that gives life to what you see."

My expression must have revealed my distaste for his suggestion. "You are squeamish about working with cadavers?"

"I don't know," I said.

He stared at me for what seemed a long time. "You can put your mind at rest," he finally said. "I cannot get cadavers* for my study here. I assure you, however, that I have no need of them for I have studied so many that the models I will use to teach you will provide vivid enough instruction."

---

cadavers: dead bodies

"Dr. Curtius was trained as a surgeon," Danton explained.

"It was there that I began making my models of organs, limbs, whole skeletons," the doctor continued. "My professors were astonished at my accuracy and soon began using my work for teaching."

"It was then," Danton interjected, "that Dr. Curtius recognized his preference for molding rather than healing men." At this comment both men again broke into coarse, vulgar laughter.

"Come," said Curtius, recovering himself. "You have seen only what the casual observer sees. I will show you my most prized chamber, the chamber that my customers are willing to pay five extra *sous* to see."

He led us across the room until we stood before an enormous gothic door. "This was once a courtesan's drawing room—until now." He swung open the door. "Now it is my Den of Thieves."

He motioned me to enter, and as I did so, what I saw nearly took my breath away. Arrayed about the room were several gruesome scenes of torture.

"Here is where you see what lies beneath the flesh. Here is muscle, sinew, bone," said Dr. Curtius.

Danton stood by, a placid smile upon his face, as Dr. Curtius moved about the room, engrossed in what he considered his prize tour.

"This was Lescombert,"* he said, pointing up to a woman hanging from a gallows. "She murdered her husband, a most unwise thing to do." He moved past her. "And over here we have the madman Damiens.* You have heard of him? He tried to stab the King with a pocketknife." He stopped before the wax figure of a man bound to a table, an executioner leaning over him, tearing at the guilty hand with a horrible pincerlike* instrument.

Lescombert (lā-kôm-bär´)

Damiens (dä-myă´)

pincerlike: having a set of grasping parts

He made his way about the room describing each crime and punishment with relish.* "Of course," he sighed at the conclusion of his speech, "these executions were long ago, but there are still many in Paris who merit such rewards."

---

relish: enjoyment

"And there are yet many in Paris who would pay to see them get their just deserts," Danton added.

"Ah, that is true," Dr. Curtius agreed. "That is why they love coming here. In this chamber every man can imagine his enemy upon the rack and himself as tormentor."

The face of the Comte de Guiche's son rose up before me. I pushed him from my thoughts.

"Of course," Dr. Curtius continued, "not everyone who comes into this chamber does so for the horror of it."

"What other reason could there be?" I asked bluntly.

"Well, it could help you learn more of human anatomy. It's not as good as studying a cadaver but there are certain advantages, don't you think?"

I did not answer.

"I also have a friend, Dr. Guillotin, who comes here frequently to study the instruments of torture."

"And you do not see in that a curiosity for horror?" I asked.

"Quite the contrary," Curtius replied. "He believes that these instruments are far too brutal. He studies them merely to see how they work, for his dream is to invent a humane means of execution, one that will provide—in his words—'a clean, painless death for all.' And I think he may succeed. Still, I have warned him that Paris will not thank him for his efforts. As my coffers prove, the nature of man prefers not simple justice, but revenge." He smiled, then headed for the door. "Come, we must discuss your place and duties in my *cabinet*."

THINKING ZONE

You have already learned the importance of characterization in fiction. You have also discussed how an author reveals character by means of that character's behavior, physical description, words, thoughts, and feelings, and/or other characters' reactions to them. More than likely the writer will choose not to reveal all of these at the beginning of the novel or story. Rather, certain characters' traits will unfold as you read further. As a story develops, you will find yourself identifying with or having a favorable feeling toward certain characters. These characters are called **sympathetic characters**. Characters with whom you do not identify or for whom you have strong feelings of dislike are known as **unsympathetic characters**. Often, the extent to which we sympathize with a character will determine how deeply involved we become with the actual plot of the story. Most often, the hero of a story is a sympathetic character because the author wants the reader to learn important lessons from him.

Metaphor—*an expression of one thing in terms of another*

1. *[critical]* At the opening of Chapter 14, what metaphors does Jacques use when discussing Phillipe's helping him? What do the metaphors mean?

   _____

   _____

   _____

   _____

2. *[appreciative]* Consider how Jacques feels as he walks along the Seine River. Do you find him a **sympathetic** or **unsympathetic** **character**? Why?

   _____

   _____

   _____

   _____

3. *[interpretive]* What clues can you find that Jacques still does not fully trust Danton?

_____

_____

_____

_____

_____

_____

4. *[interpretive]* What does Danton tell Jacques on the way to Dr. Curtius's *cabinet* that foreshadows what we might expect in later chapters?

_____

_____

_____

_____

5. *[critical]* Do you find Danton to be a **sympathetic** or **unsympathetic character** at this point in the novel? Why?

_____

_____

_____

_____

6. *[critical]* According to Dr. Curtius, why do people enjoy coming to the Den of Thieves? What does this reveal about human nature?

_____

_____

_____

_____

PART TWO
THE REVOLUTION IN EARNEST
1789–1793

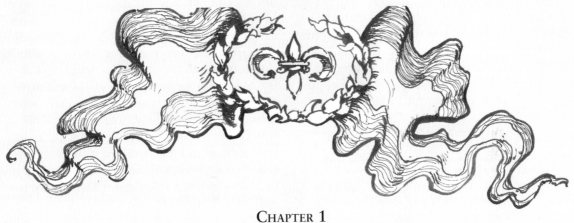

CHAPTER 1
SUMMER, 1789

For the next year, my "place" was, for the most part, in the basement, and my duties were so numerous that I scarcely had time to sleep or to reflect on the fact that I was a fugitive in hiding.

I began each morning by attending anatomy classes with two or three other apprentices. Aside from the evening meal, this was the only time I spent upstairs, for the classes were held on the second floor in Dr. Curtius's study, a room which could best be described as both a wonder and a horror. What initially caught your eye when you entered were the many shelves lined with skulls, most of which served as perches for powdered wigs. Your gaze would then be drawn to the tables upon which were strewn models of hands and arms, legs and bodies. There was also a large cupboard in the corner. Its door was always open, revealing drawers filled with glass eyes, cheap jewelry, and strands of hair and netting. I soon learned, however, that these "distractions" were essential to our lessons.

Curtius was a master craftsman whose fame as an anatomist* was known through all of Paris. But even without knowing of his fame, the lessons that he gave would have convinced me that he was unrivaled in this field. Although I cared little for the man and less for his art, I gleaned much from his medical knowledge. He was a hard taskmaster, and within weeks I had learned not only the purpose of every tendon, muscle, and joint but also the effects of movement, of aging, and even of disease upon the human form. My father had already bequeathed to me the greatest gift, the heart and eye of an artist, but my classes with Dr. Curtius made me better able to implement* what my heart and eye conceived.

---

anatomist: an expert in or student of anatomy

implement: put into concrete form

My afternoons were spent working in the basement, preparing figures for display. It was there that I met Anne Marie, Dr. Curtius's niece. She had but recently returned from Versailles,* where for several months she had served both as a sculptor for and companion to King Louis's sister, Princess Elizabeth. In appearance she was frail and pallid,* but the energy and intensity she put into her work were unequaled. She was exceedingly meticulous. If necessary, she would sit for hours repairing a minor flaw made by a less-skilled hand.

Versailles (vâr-sī)

pallid: pale

I remember clearly the night I recognized that she, not Dr. Curtius, was the one responsible for the "lifelikeness" of those who graced the cabinet. Those of us who were students not only worked but also slept in the basement. One night I awoke to see Anne Marie sitting at one of the tables, bent over the face of the *Dauphin*.* Having been dissatisfied with the way an apprentice had done the young prince's eyebrows, she had returned when she thought we were all sleeping. With only one candle to work by, she was plucking out each brow and reinserting the hairs—one by one.

Dauphin (dō-fä[n]´)

So intent was she upon her work that she did not notice that I'd awakened and was lying in the corner watching her. I continued to watch until at last she finished and slipped back up the stairs. I then got up and examined what she'd done. The Dauphin's brows had now the perfect arch and thickness. There would not be a beggar in Paris who would not know the prince.

Yet as I gazed upon that face, I recognized something else as well. Despite all of Anne Marie's noble efforts, the face that I

looked upon was no more than a shell; there was no soul to it. I had discovered that Anne Marie was the true artist of the family, but I could see as well that she could not fulfill her potential as an artist by working in her uncle's cabinet. I found myself wishing that I could take her back to my shop and show her how—with hammer, chisel, and stone—she could capture the strength of a man's character or that nuance* of weakness that lay hidden in his heart. Wax was too artificial, too insistent upon reflecting only what the naked eye could see. I saw clearly that it was the medium of a mimic, not an artist. I went back to bed, troubled by the realization that as long as I was forced to work in Curtius's cabinet I could not fully enjoy the only solace left to me—my art.

---

nuance: hint

---

* * *

I awoke the next morning in an ill humor and remained sullen throughout the day. I spoke to no one, and my mood and manner warned others that they had best not speak to me.

At six o'clock Dr. Curtius came down the stairs and to my disappointment announced, "All of you must be at dinner this evening. We are having guests."

I was in no mood to socialize. "I would like to be excused," I said.

"Not tonight, Jacques," Dr. Curtius said. "For Danton is among those who will dine with us, and he has asked specifically that you be there as well. He feels that the conversation may be of interest to you. Be cleaned up and in the dining room by seven o'clock." Before I could object further, he had disappeared back up the stairs.

I could think of nothing at the moment that Dr. Curtius, Danton, or anyone else might say that I would care to hear. Still, I knew I had no choice. Thus, I finished with my duties, cleaned up, and made my way upstairs.

The two other apprentices, Anne Marie, and Dr. Curtius were already there.

"Sit down," Dr. Curtius ordered as I entered. "I must greet our guests and bring them in."

I sat down next to Anne Marie. She seemed as loath* as I to be there. "What's so important that we must be here?" I whispered to her.

---

loath: unwilling or reluctant

"The men who are coming are the kind who insist upon an audience," she said.

"Who besides Danton?" I asked.

"Robespierre* is the only other one worth noting," she remarked without enthusiasm. "He seems at first to be simply tedious, but the more you are with him the more distasteful his company becomes."

Robespierre (rōbz´-pyâr´)

"Why?" I asked.

"You shall see." She had no time to say more, for Dr. Curtius had returned.

Six men came to dine with us that evening, but as Anne Marie had aptly observed, only two were worth noting. The others were but copies of either Danton or Robespierre. The two or three who kept close to Danton were like him, well dressed but coarse men who ate, drank, and talked more like peasants than like bourgeoisie. But those who hung upon Robespierre were clean-shaven, scented men, as impeccable* in manners as in appearance.

---

impeccable: flawless

"Have you heard that the King has dismissed Necker?" announced one of Robespierre's men as soon as we'd begun to eat.

I knew that Necker, the Minister of Finance, was popular with the people.

"Necker?" bellowed Curtius. "Jacques, did you not just finish a bust of him."

"Yes," I said.

"And already he is in disgrace!" moaned Dr. Curtius.

"Only with the King," Danton said.

"From what I have heard," Robespierre interjected, "it is not the King who is displeased with him. It is Marie Antoinette."

"What shall happen to us now!" Dr. Curtius shouted. "France, it seems, is run by a woman—a foreign one at that!"

"The King is weak," said Danton. "And a weak king is no king at all."

"He may be weak, but he is yet strong enough to be dangerous," said Robespierre.

"Louis—dangerous?" Danton laughed. "We shall have him eating out of our hand before the summer's end."

"Don't be so sure," said Robespierre. "A man who has enjoyed absolute power does not easily relinquish it."

"That's just it," countered Danton. "Louis has never ruled absolutely, and he will soon submit to the people's demands. I tell you, before the summer's end we shall have a constitutional monarchy* in France!"

---

constitutional monarchy: a form of government in which the monarchy's power is so limited by a constitution that the monarch is merely a figurehead

---

Danton raised his glass, and several at the table cheered him, but before the cheers could die away, Robespierre added in his dry, almost mechanical tone, "Then how do you explain the military guards who have been ordered by the King into the streets of Paris?"

"Those guards will do nothing to oppose us," said Danton, but with less conviction than he had used heretofore.

"They shall never have the chance," said one of Robespierre's followers, "for Parisians everywhere are out tonight in search of arms."

"In search of arms?" I said. "Whatever for?"

"To defend themselves," said Robespierre. He turned to Danton and spoke as if to warn him. "It is rumored that the King has sent out the troops for the express purpose of cutting down those who would oppose him."

Danton paused. Growing very serious, he said, "It may be wise then for the lovers of liberty to make certain that all Parisians have the means to protect themselves from such a king."

Robespierre smiled knowingly but said nothing. I began to understand Anne Marie's assessment of the man.

"This is ridiculous," said Anne Marie with a temper I had never seen. "The King would never order his soldiers to attack the people of Paris!"

"You are simply too young and innocent to understand such villainy," remarked Robespierre.

"I understand Versailles better than any of you," she said, "for I have lived there."

"I can't believe it," Danton said with a laugh. "Little Anne Marie at court? Curtius, you never told me."

"She was sent there simply to do some waxworks for the Princess Elizabeth," Dr. Curtius explained.

"But I knew the King as well," she continued, "and I tell you he would never do his subjects harm."

Robespierre glared at Curtius, at Danton, and even for a moment at me. Then the glare vanished and was replaced by a condescending smile. "Not all of those at court see the political side of things. The King may well be both an admirable host and a devil of a politician."

"I tell you—" started Anne Marie.

"Enough!" Dr. Curtius's voice was threatening, and his niece knew—as did we all—that any further comment would be perilous. There was a moment of tense silence before Robespierre broke in to change the mood.

"It is amazing, isn't it," said Robespierre, smiling, "that Anne Marie could have spent time at Versailles and returned home without even the slightest taint* of its corruption on her?"

---

taint: blemish

His comment had the desired effect upon the doctor's temper. "She is a Curtius," he said.

By supper's end, the conversation had returned to more mundane subjects. As the guests made their departure, however, Danton pulled me aside. "It won't be long until you may again be able to walk about the city freely."

"Why? What do you mean?"

"I cannot say just now, but in a day or two—watch for me," he said.

CHAPTER 2

Danton's cryptic* talk of freedom took away all hope of sleep. The following morning I was up long before dawn, bent over the fire, stirring up a fresh batch of molding wax that I would need for the day's casting. I could feel the beads of sweat forming on my forehead, for I'd been at the task for more than an hour. At last the wax was thinning. I reached for a bowl of turpentine and poured some in, then scooped up a handful of white and scarlet pigment.* Moving my stirrer round and round, I let the colors fall, watching as the lifeless wax took on the tone and texture of a child's skin.

---

cryptic: mysterious

pigment: coloring

As I pulled the mixture from the brazier* and set it on the stone hearth to cool, I heard someone coming down the stairs in haste. I looked up to see Dr. Curtius running toward me, his dressing gown, obviously thrown on in haste, flying out behind him as he ran.

---

brazier: metal pan for holding burning coals or charcoal

"Jacques, hurry! I've received word that a mob has gathered. We must be quick," he said. "Come. Follow me."

I ran up the stairs behind him. Through the windows I saw that a crowd of men, who looked as if they'd had more drink than sleep, were milling through the outer gate and coming up the walk.

"Whatever do they want?" I asked the doctor, who now stood smoothing down his hair and wrapping his robe securely about him in a futile effort to prepare himself to receive the "guests."

"Let's find out," he said.

Flinging open the cabinet doors, he called to them, "Good citizens, you have caught us unprepared. It is too early for tours of the cabinet or for selling you our wares."

"We do not come to buy," an unkempt* man said as he pushed himself to the front of the crowd. "Give us some heads!" he cried.

---

unkempt: untidy

The crowd roared out in unison.

"What's mine is yours," Dr. Curtius called above the tumult. "Which heads do you prefer?"

"We want our heroes," one man cried. "Necker, Lafayette—"

"The Prince d'Orléans," another said.

Another cheer went up. Curtius turned quickly to me, and his smile vanished. "I know we have Lafayette and Necker. But the duke—have you finished him?"

"I have," I said.

I saw a smile of relief replace the worried frown. "Well done, Jacques," he cried, fairly beaming now. "Keep them happy while I get those heads!"

I nearly panicked as I watched the doctor vanish, but as I turned around to face the mob, I saw Danton emerge. For the first time I was genuinely glad to see him.

"Citizens," he called out as he held up his hands. "I told you the good doctor was a patriot. We shall have what we have come for!"

As the crowd continued cheering, Danton stepped over the threshold and pulled me in. "A word with you," he said. "Your young friend—what is his name?"

"Phillipe, you mean?"

"Yes, Phillipe, that's it. Get him to come to me—at Charpentier's this afternoon.

"Why? What could you want with him?"

"I need someone to carry a message to the workers in St. Antoine."

"What kind of message?" I asked.

"It's nothing dangerous. I simply want him to spread the word that there is something planned for tomorrow. I want those in your neighborhood to have the knowledge—and to be prepared."

I hesitated. "I don't know," I said.

"Come, you must trust me," Danton hissed in a throaty whisper, "for I tell you plainly that after tomorrow you will never need to fear imprisonment again. Tomorrow we shall storm the Bastille."

"Storm the Bastille—"

"Lower your voice," he said. "No one must know until I've had time to prepare key men, men like those in St. Antoine. They await my word. You will tell Phillipe?"

"You are sure there is no danger for him?"

"I am sure," he said.

"All right," I said.

"Tell him to come to Charpentier's this afternoon. And you—you be at the café

early tomorrow morning—" He broke off as Dr. Curtius came puffing up the stairs holding the three heads he had obviously had to wrench from their wax bodies. I ran across the room to help him as Danton turned and once again addressed the crowd.

"Here are your prizes," Danton said as he took Lafayette and the duke from the doctor and tossed them into the crowd. Dr. Curtius, obviously relieved to see Danton and to hear the crowd's cheers of favor, stepped back inside and with a relieved sigh sat down on a velvet chair.

Danton took the head of Necker from me and tossed it into the crowd as well. Then, grabbing my arm, he pulled me back outside before the crowd. "And here, good citizens, is the worthy artist of your heroes!" Such cheering and applause rang out that I stood dumbfounded before them all. Danton leaned close and whispered in my ear, "See how easily honor comes to those who will but take it by the throat? Yesterday you were an unknown fugitive; today I have made you a hero of the Revolution."

He turned back to the crowd again. "Let us return to the cafés and drink to the Revolution!"

"To the Revolution!" they cried out, and as a single organ, laughing and jeering, they made their way again into the street.

I stood watching until they were out of sight. I was relieved to see them go. And yet—strange as it may seem—I, who had but recently scorned my work in wax, was now filled with pride as I watched those very heads paraded as trophies through the streets.

THINKING ZONE

What makes a novel or story interesting? Maybe you have identified closely with a character and are curious about what becomes of that character. Or maybe you have become so involved in the plot that you become intrigued about what will happen next. In either case the writer has been successful in creating **suspense**, reader uncertainty because of an author's withholding of plot details.

In a novel, the level of suspense that the author generates may determine the success of the **cliffhangers**. Cliffhangers are suspenseful situations strategically placed throughout different parts or chapters of a longer work. Often within novels, cliffhangers are found at the end of various chapters. The purpose of the cliffhanger is to make you want to keep reading until the end of the story. For instance, Chapter 12 of *In Search of Honor* ends with Jacques and his cellmates' having just escaped the Bastille. We are left hanging, wondering whether they will make it to safety. This curiosity compels the reader to continue to Chapter 13. Think about the ending of Part 1 of this novel. Did you find that to be a cliffhanger? Why or why not?

1. *[interpretive]* What did Jacques mean by his description of Dr. Curtius's study as both "a wonder and a horror"?

_____

_____

_____

_____

2. *[literal/interpretive]* What did Jacques recognize as the problem of using wax instead of stone for his sculpture? How might this be symbolic?

_____

_____

_____

_____

_____

3. *[critical]* After learning more about Dr. Curtius and meeting Anne Marie, for which character do you feel more sympathy? Why?

_____

_____

_____

_____

_____

_____

_____

_____

Sympathetic character—*a character with whom you identify or sympathize*

4. *[interpretive]* How has the revolution made Jacques a hero?

_____

_____

_____

5. *[critical]* Name two aspects of Part Two, Chapters 1 and 2 that generate **suspense** at this point in the story.

_____

_____

_____

_____

_____

_____

6. *[critical]* How is the ending to Chapter 1 a **cliffhanger**? What aspect of the cliffhanger provides suspense?

_____

_____

_____

_____

_____

_____

_____

CHAPTER 3

I arrived at Charpentier's by midmorning on July 14. The place was packed, for Danton was giving one of his orations. I scanned the room and saw Phillipe perched up on Charpentier's counter. I made my way over to him.

"I didn't expect to see you here today," I whispered.

"Danton said that you were coming, so I asked my mother if I could come as well. She said she'd let me if I made sure that you saw me home by evening. Of course, I told her that you would," he said smiling. Then he added seriously, "I don't see you half as often now that you live on the boulevard. When will you be coming back to St. Antoine?"

"If Danton can be trusted," I confided, "I should be able to return soon."

Danton brought his speech to a rousing conclusion and stepped aside to give the floor to a pale, pathetic-looking man, but the cheering for Danton continued and was so enthusiastic that the second man was virtually ignored.

At length he leaped up on the table. "You have listened to the wisdom of Danton," he cried from the height of his new-found perch. "He has told you of the treachery* of those in power; he has told you of their cruelties! But what will you do with such knowledge? Will it fall as a dead man in the street?"

_____
treachery: betrayal

The crowd as one voice gave answer. "No!"

"Let us right such wrongs! Let us cast aside all tyranny! And let us begin by setting the captives free! Who will lead us on our march to the Bastille?"

The noise in the café was deafening as the chants of "Danton! Danton! Danton!" rang out.

"I will lead you," Danton cried. "But by my side shall be the maker of your heroes, the artist at Curtius's *cabinet* and a youth who but a year ago was held captive in that prison. His name is Jacques Chénier!"

The crowd took up my name and sang it with Danton's.

Phillipe, ecstatic at the praise I was receiving, climbed from the counter onto my back. Holding me tightly with one hand, he took his cap in the other and waved it in the air, yelling as he did so, "Jacques Chénier!"

His action identified me clearly to those about the room and we were quickly swept to the head of the crowd, which now roared its approval.

"Let's waste no more time!" Danton shouted. "To the Bastille!"

"To the Bastille!" the crowd echoed, surging through the door.

The crowd continued swelling as we passed street after street, and those of nearly every rank and occupation fell in step beside us. As we marched, pikes,* clubs, and even guns were distributed through the crowd. I turned to inquire of Danton, whom I assumed would still be at my side. To my surprise, I found he'd vanished. It was I and the pale young man who now led the crowd. I began to feel uneasy.

---

pikes: long spear

Catching sight of the Bastille, I could see that others were already waiting for us at the gate. One of the men ran out to meet us. "The raid on the Invalides* this morning was successful," he said, addressing the pale young man. "We have two cannons waiting just beyond the outer gate."

Invalides (ă[n]-vä-lē´): veterans' hospital and retirement home

---

"Good!" the young man said.

By now we'd reached the entrance, and emotions were at a fever pitch. But the crowd fell back as soon as they passed through the gate and saw what awaited them there. Three of the Bastille's cannons stood facing the ones they had set up, and another ten or fifteen could be seen poised above us on the towers. A silence fell, and many hesitated, growing more uncertain. But, of course, the young man at my side did not. "We demand to see the governor," he cried.

No one emerged from the fortress and the crowd began once again to gather strength. At length a deputy called out. "The governor will allow only two delegates in to see him."

The young man motioned two men forward. "Go in and take three of our militia with you," he ordered them. "See if Governor de Launay is willing to release the prisoners without incident."

The men entered and remained for more than two hours while the crowd, growing restless under the heat of an unrelenting summer sun, became obstinate in their demands for action.

Another messenger was dispatched, instructing the governor that he must relinquish guns and powder—and that a unit of our militia must be admitted without delay.

This messenger entered—and returned within moments. "Impossible!" came the governor's reply. A cannon roared, a musket fired, and the fight began.

I was unprepared for the pandemonium* that erupted, and I fell to my knees as the surge of men and women stumbled over me. Fearing I'd be trampled, I thrashed about with all my strength and at last succeeded in getting to my feet, but I had lost Phillipe.

---

pandemonium: chaos

"Phillipe! Phillipe!" I called to him, but all that I could hear was the boom of the cannon, the crack of the muskets, and the cries of the dying.

Assuming that he had been swept with the crowd into the inner courtyard, I ran forward, dodging the swinging clubs and thrusting pikes as I did so. The shot of the muskets sprayed the ground around me, and the cannon kicked up so much dirt and debris that I was nearly blinded. Still, I stumbled on until I heard him calling, "Jacques! Jacques!"

I moved toward the sound of his voice and at last saw him through the veil of smoke, crouched against one of the courtyard walls. I got to him just as the drawbridge began to fall.

Grasping my hand as tightly as he could, he looked up and asked, "Are we going in?"

The crowds had blocked the gates. "We have no choice!" I said. It was then I thought of the *calottes*—and of Pierre. "Come on," I said. "I know a place where we may at least find space to breathe."

We moved with the crowd across the drawbridge, but once inside, we were able

to break away from the surge of humanity that headed toward the governor's quarters.

When the crowd had passed, I turned toward the towers, stopping only long enough to examine one of the guards who now lay dead.

"What are you doing?" shouted Phillipe as I reached out my hand to touch the corpse.

"Looking for his keys," I said, pulling the ring of cell keys from the dead man's pocket.

Taking Phillipe's hand again in mine, I made my way up the tower stairs.

"Jump up on my back and hold on tight," I ordered him, and he obeyed. Then, taking the stairs as fast as my legs could manage, I soon found myself outside Pierre-Joseph's cell.

"Climb down," I told Phillipe as I opened up the cell, "and wait here a moment."

I entered to see Pierre-Joseph at the table, sitting just as he had been that first night. He turned slowly to me. "Jacques?"

"Yes, it's me," I said, glad that he had recognized me. "I've come to take you out of here."

He remained seated as before. "What is the tumult? I have heard cannon and gunfire—"

"The Bastille has been taken."

"Taken?" he said, now standing upright. "By whom?"

"By those—" I stopped to search for words. "By those tired of tyranny," I said, remembering the rhetoric I had heard of late. "Now come. I think we may now be able to make our way outside the gates."

"Where will we be going then?" he asked.

I paused, for I had really given no thought to where I would be taking him. "You will come home with me," I said. "That is—if you would like to."

He stood a moment more, weighing my offer, then gathered up his few belongings and followed me out the door. Phillipe stood waiting where I had left him.

"And who is this?" asked Pierre-Joseph with a joy in his face that I had not seen before.

"A friend of mine," I answered. "His name's Phillipe."

"You are very old," said Phillipe, staring up at my aged friend.

"Yes, I suppose I am," said Pierre-Joseph as he reached out and touched Phillipe.

"And you are very young."

Phillipe smiled back at him. "Yes, I suppose I am."

"Come on, Phillipe, up on my back again. I'll not take the chance of losing you a second time," I said. I hoisted him up and the three of us made our way back down the stairs.

I tried to prepare Pierre-Joseph for the possible danger we might face when we reached the lower levels and the courtyard. But the danger had passed, leaving only the frightful corpses of dead guards and citizens strewn about here and there.

When we crossed the drawbridge, the frenzied sound of the crowd made mad by bloodshed told us that the mob was still gathered in the streets. I hesitated.

"Perhaps we should wait," Pierre-Joseph said.

"No. I don't want to spend another moment in this place," I said decisively and barged through the outer gate.

I will never forget the sickening sight that greeted me. Just outside, a man, laughing as if he were possessed, danced before the crowd. In his hand he held a pike atop of which bobbed the governor's severed head. I stumbled back into Pierre-Joseph, but before I could retreat, Danton pulled me forward.

"Here he is! Jacques, my boy, we thought we'd lost you!"

It was then that Pierre-Joseph stepped forward. I could see Danton's eyes light up as he gazed on this ancient man. "Was this a prisoner?" He did not wait for my answer but shoved me aside and pulled Pierre-Joseph to him. "Look, my friends!" he cried out to the crowd. "We may have released only seven prisoners this day, but one of them is the oldest captive in all of France!"

The crowd went wild, and before Pierre-Joseph could voice objection, Danton had lifted him up on the shoulders of two brawny men. "Let us celebrate!" he cried and swept my friend away. Phillipe and I could do no more than follow.

Pierre-Joseph was carried to Charpentier's café and celebrated as a hero. I could see, however, that the honor did not please him. Thus I made some excuse that would allow Phillipe and me to disentangle him from Danton and the admiring crowd.

"How disgraceful to be made—a—a relic!"* he said in disgust once we were outside the shop.

---
relic: an object of worship

"Come," I said, "they meant to do you honor."

He turned on me in anger for the first—and only—time. "Such men know nothing of honor! Do you call what we saw outside the Bastille tonight honorable? And they call me mad!"

"They have suffered wrongs," I said.

"Papa and Jacques suffered wrongs," Phillipe parroted in my defense.

"And so have I—for years," Pierre-Joseph said, "but I did not rejoice to see the Governor de Launay's head upon a pike."

"Nor did we," I said honestly.

"That is true," he said. "Come, bear with me. I am angered by such savagery. As for the honor those men meant to give me, you must see my point: they would have cheered a roasted pig as heartily as they cheered me if it had been lifted up before them by Danton."

I shrugged, unwilling to admit openly that he was right.

His voice grew calm and quiet once again. "Forgive me," he said. "I have not yet thanked you two for freeing me from prison—or from that horrid man Danton."

"He is rather horrid when you first get a look at him," said Phillipe, "but you get used to him. You'll see. Right, Jacques?"

I did not answer but said instead, "We'd best be getting home." The thought of St. Antoine at once lifted my spirits, and by the time we reached our street, I was in good humor.

"My shop is just two doors up from here," I told Pierre-Joseph when we had deposited Phillipe safely at his door.

"Are you sure that you do not mind my company?" he asked, as we made our way down the alley.

"Not if you don't mind mine," I said, reaching for the door.

"You're a good friend, Jacques," he told me, "and I will stay as long as I can do you good."

His words puzzled me, for I could think of no "good" that such an old man could do for me. Still, I knew now that he was far from mad, and I hoped that he might prove pleasant company as well.

CHAPTER 4
SUMMER, 1790

By the summer of the following year, I had learned what "good" an "old man" could do for me. Indeed, despite his age he did far more for me than I for him. He washed the clothes, made the meals, and in the winter rose and had the fires burning long before I ever stirred. He also cleaned my tools, swept the shop, and kept my aprons mended. Besides these daily acts of kindness, he also opened both his mind and heart to me, sharing with me the knowledge he had gleaned as a youth at the University of Paris and the wisdom he'd acquired as a prisoner in the Bastille.

When he was not waiting on or talking with me, he enjoyed taking walks or sitting in the shop, reading aloud his treasured Book and playing his flute.

"Do you remember, Jacques, the first day that I played for you?" he asked me one day. He settled himself into his favorite chair, flute and Book in hand.

"Of course," I said.

"You know, little has changed since then," he mused.

"Surely you don't mean that," I said, looking up from my work. "At least we are no longer prisoners."

"Oh, I do not mean that our circumstances have not changed. Of course they have, but—" he broke off. "You remember what I said: that it is the heart, not the circumstances, that determines whether we are men of honor or disgrace."

I nodded.

"Well, my heart is the same as it was that day. Is yours?"

"Mine is more content," I said. "As a matter of fact, I think all of Paris is more content."

"And to what do you attribute this newfound contentment?" he asked.

"For one thing we are better fed, and the King has accepted the proposal of a constitutional monarchy. The Revolution may have had a bloody start, but even you must admit that this past year has been relatively calm."

"I fear it is simply a calm before the storm," he said.

"Admit it," I chided him good-naturedly; "you just don't want to believe that Danton and those like him were right all along."

"Hmmm," was all he said.

"I felt the same as you did when I first met Danton," I told him. I resumed my work, delicately chiseling away the last vestiges* of unwanted stone. "But he has done much for me and—"

---

vestiges: visible traces

"And you have grown used to him," Pierre-Joseph said.

"Yes," I said, without looking up. "I have."

The soft tapping of my tools was the only sound for several minutes, and I was grateful for it. At length, however, Pierre-Joseph broke the silence with a warning: "Be careful, Jacques," he said. "A man like Danton is not to be trusted."

"He has done nothing to trouble me yet."

"That is because you have proved profitable to him. But I tell you—" He broke off, for he could see that I did not believe him. "You tell me that all of Paris is content now that they are better fed. How about you, is that what has made you more content?"

"That—and the fact that I am making more money in a week than I could have made in an entire year before the Revolution."

"And do you enjoy your work as much as you once did?" he asked.

"It is much the same," I said.

He laid his flute and Book aside and made his way over to one of my corner shelves. Taking down an old Rousseau my father had done, he turned it about in his hands. "This is marvelous workmanship—true art," he said.

"My father made that," I told him proudly.

"And this one?" he pointed to another on the shelf, a copy I made after studying my father's original.

"That one is mine," I said with equal pride.

"Then you have your father's hands, for they seem to me to be as one."

He saw the pleasure that his comment gave me. "Do you think that what you have there—" he said, pointing to the bit of stone before me, "is it as good?"

I looked down at my work. It was like many of the commissions I had done of late, a mere trinket carved from a stone that had been pried from the crumbling Bastille. "This is different. And besides," I added defensively, "this is what brings in all our profit."

"At what cost?" was all Pierre-Joseph said as he returned to his chair, picked up the Book, and opened it. "Shall I read to you?" he said.

I nodded, relieved to change the course of conversation.

Looking down he began to read:

And when a great multitude had gathered, and others had come to Him from every city, He spoke by a parable:

"A sower went out to sow his seed. And as he sowed, some fell by the wayside; and it was trampled down, and the birds of the air devoured it.

"Some fell on rock; and as soon as it sprang up, it withered away because it lacked moisture.

"And some fell among thorns, and the thorns sprang up with it and choked it.

"But others fell on good ground, sprang up, and yielded a crop a hundredfold. . . ."

Then His disciples asked Him saying, "What does this parable mean?"

And He said, . . . "The seed is the word of God.

"Those by the wayside are the ones who hear; then the devil comes and takes away the word out of their hearts, lest they should believe and be saved.

"But the ones on the rock are those who, when they hear, receive the word with joy; and these have no root, who believe for a while and in time of temptation fall away.

"And the ones that fell among thorns are those who, when they have heard, go out and are choked with the cares, riches, and pleasures of life, and bring no fruit to maturity.

"But the ones that fell on the good ground are those who, having heard the word with a noble and good heart, keep it and bear fruit with patience."

"You notice," he said, as he laid aside the Book and picked up his flute, "the difference was not in the word the sower sowed nor in the circumstances of those who heard, but in—"

"I know," I said. "The difference was in how their hearts received it. Come, play for me while I finish up this work, for we haven't much time before we must be going."

"Going?" he said.

"Have you forgotten? Today is the anniversary of the fall of the Bastille. All of Paris is celebrating."

"I am too old for celebrations," he said. "Phillipe can keep you company. But I will play for you until you go."

* * *

Phillipe and I reached the Champ-de-Mars* by the Seine early in the afternoon. It was to be a magnificent celebration. A vast amphitheater had been excavated for the ceremonies and a temporary triumphal arch and altar had been built. When we arrived, men and women from every walk of life were awaiting the festivities, and it was not long before the rolling drums of the military could be heard in the distance.

Champ-de-Mars (shä[m]-de-märs´)

"I can't see," Phillipe complained.

"Nor can I from here," I told him. "Let's move a bit farther down the river. It looks less crowded there."

We moved down to where the crowd thinned out, and though we had to wait a little longer, we at last caught sight of the parade as it came on.

"Let me up on your back for just a moment, Jacques!" Phillipe pleaded when he caught a glimpse of the military guards in blue, white, and red with guns and drums and banners waving.

"Only for a few moments," I said, letting him climb up. "You're growing like a weed and it's not easy anymore hauling you about," I teased him. "Soon you will be tall enough to see things for yourself."

Phillipe joined in the shouts of celebration which rose like waves washing over the marching guards as they came on. He was almost hoarse before all of them had passed to take their place in the hollow of the amphitheater.

After the parade, a mass was said in thanksgiving for the constitutional monarchy and the new era of freedom it had ushered in.

The mass was far less interesting than the parade had been, and many of the bystanders gathered in clusters to talk while the priest droned on.

"Look," said Phillipe, "over there's Latude."

I had not set eyes upon Latude since the day Thomas and I had seen him ride off in his carriage toward Charpentier's.

"He does not look pleased to be here," said Phillipe sullenly.

"I'm sure he's not," I said, my anger rising at the sight of him. "Men like him come merely out of duty. He shows his face here for fear that if he does not, he will be counted as a traitor."

"I would not call that a very good reason for coming, would you?" I turned to see Danton standing at my side. Although Pierre-Joseph refused to go near Danton, I had seen him often over the course of the year, for I still frequented Charpentier's café and Curtius's cabinet. I found both were good for business.

"Nonetheless he's here," I replied.

"And we shall keep our eye on him," Danton assured me. "By the way," he continued, "Dr. Curtius told me that he sent word to Pierre-Joseph several months ago, asking him to come and sit for him, but he received no answer to the request. Why?"

"You would have to ask him," I said. "He did not tell me anything about it."

"To be cast in wax and displayed in Curtius's *cabinet* is no mean honor."

"I doubt that Pierre-Joseph would agree," I said.

"You think not?" Danton said. "Well, I have heard some say he is mad."

"No, he's not," Phillipe interjected.

"To refuse to be made into wax is hardly a symptom of madness," I said.

"You're right," Danton said, laughing. "Still, Jacques, if he is your friend, you might encourage him to consent to a public appearance now and then. The people revere him now as much as they did a year ago, and it is unwise to scorn such admiration."

The priest had finally finished and the crowd broke out in song; afterwards they began milling about again in search of better entertainment. I was about to take Phillipe and go when Danton stopped me.

"It is too early to go home," he said. "And I have a good idea about how we can amuse ourselves."

"How's that?" I asked.

Danton looked down at Phillipe. "How would you like me to teach Latude a lesson? For I know that it was because of him that your father had to go away. And since he may soon be coming home, we want to be sure Latude gives him no trouble."

Phillipe looked up at me.

"Thomas need have no fear of Latude," I said. "It is the militia he must get past, for they are the ones who let no one who has been abroad back into Paris."

"It is for our safety," Danton said. "But even so, Phillipe's father would have been here now if Latude had not tried to cheat him."

"You're right there," I said.

"Come, let me show him a lesson," said Danton, encouraged by my agreement. "I promise you that he will be better for it."

I shrugged, and Danton at once took several strides through the crowd to collar the unsuspecting Latude.

"Citizens," Danton called out to anyone who would listen. "Here we have a squire turned patriot! Is that not so?" he said turning to Latude.

The captured Latude tried to maintain some semblance of respectability. He held himself upright and proclaimed, "It is true."

"Then you have seen the error of your ways?" Danton pressed him.

"I have," Latude confessed.

By this time quite a crowd had gathered.

"Well," Danton continued, as he moved Latude closer and closer to the river's edge, "I think it fitting that every convert should be baptized. What say you?" he shouted to the crowd, who cheered their affirmations back to him.

"Then Latude must at once be baptized!" he shouted and lifting up the squire, he dumped him into the river Seine.

Latude thrashed about wildly as the crowd looked on and jeered. He seemed to be desperately trying to make his way to the wharf but was having no success.

I had little sympathy for Latude but began to feel uneasy, for I did not want to think what Pierre-Joseph would say if this celebration ended as the Revolution had begun—with death. But to my relief Danton spoke up again. "What say you, good citizens? Should I go in to see our convert does not drown?"

There were yeas and nays of equal fervor, but at last Danton jumped in. His enormous girth* sent water splashing everywhere. Soon, however, he had Latude and was hauling him over to the wharf. As soon as the squire caught a few breaths, Danton again took hold of him. "Do you renounce your wealth?" he cried and dunked Latude, then brought him to the surface.

---

girth: size

"I do," Latude sputtered, with no thought of respectability now.

"And do you give up your manor and all the goods therein?" Danton shouted and dunked him once again.

"I do!" Latude confessed.

"And finally! Do you renounce your lands, your dovecotes, and your hunting rights?"

"Yes!" Latude screamed before he could be put under.

"Then you are indeed a convert!" Danton cried, and he heaved the squire, exhausted, up onto the wharf.

"I shall draw up the papers and bring them to your manor house tomorrow," Danton announced, as he too came climbing out. Then, lifting Latude to his feet, he said, "I would suggest that you go home now."

Latude, though staggering, went off as fast as his weak legs could carry him. The crowd was laughing wildly, Phillipe and I among the rest. After all, I told myself, he lost only his possessions, not his life, and such a loss might indeed prove good for him.

"Come. Let's go, for it will soon be dark," I told Phillipe, and we both turned toward home. As we did, my gaze fell on the troubled waters that still splashed violently against the wharf. The vague longing that had come upon me during my quiet walk along the Seine stirred in my heart again, and with it, all amusement faded.

THINKING ZONE

Authors reveal a character's traits through the character's actions, thoughts, and dialogue. Throughout the course of a story or novel, these aspects may change, thereby signifying changes within the various characters. Certain characters change very little as the story progresses, while others undergo many changes. A **static character** is one who remains essentially the same throughout a story. A **developing character** (also referred to as a dynamic character), on the other hand, will change as the story progresses. Developing characters in Scripture are some of the most encouraging to us. They remind us that God's grace can change people. Often in biblical narratives, people start out one way but then become very different because God has worked in their hearts. This change does not, however, totally alter the character's personality. If the change is to be believable, it must develop naturally out of the character's temperament. Consider Saul of Tarsus (who became Paul): he was still a strong personality after he met God on the Damascus road! Sometimes the changes can be for the better, and sometimes they can be for the worse. You have watched Jacques through some interesting developments in his story. Think about what kind of a character you think he is.

1. *[interpretive/critical]* Why do you think the words of Danton and the pale young man stir up the crowd gathered at Charpentier's? Explain your answer.

   _____

   _____

   _____

2. *[critical]* Name at least two factors that contribute to the suspense during the storming of the Bastille.

   _____

   _____

   _____

   _____

   _____

3. *[interpretive]* How does the mob respond when they see that Pierre-Joseph has been released from the Bastille? What does Pierre-Joseph believe to be the reason for the crowd's responding this way?

_____

_____

_____

_____

4. *[critical]* Is Jacques a **static** or **developing character**? Explain.

_____

_____

_____

_____

5. *[critical]* Is Pierre-Joseph a **static** or **developing character**? Explain.

_____

_____

_____

_____

6. *[appreciative]* How did you respond to Danton's treatment of Latude? Were his actions those of a hero?

_____

_____

_____

_____

7. *[critical]* What has Jacques realized at the end of Chapter 4? What major symbol from earlier in the novel is used to emphasize this realization?

_____

_____

_____

_____

CHAPTER 5

Seeing Latude rekindled my anger and robbed me of the contentment the year of profit had brought forth. I again became restless, sullen, and even peevish toward Pierre-Joseph. He said nothing and continued to behave toward me in the same calm, steady manner that he always had. I thought once or twice of unburdening my heart to him, but my pride would not allow it. Besides, I knew what he would say, and knowing made me all the angrier.

Events came to a climax about two weeks after the Bastille's anniversary celebration. Phillipe, whom I had sent on an errand to Charpentier's, returned with a message for me: "Danton wants you to convince Pierre-Joseph to sit for you at Dr. Curtius's."

"Sit for me?" I asked.

"Yes," said Phillipe. "And Dr. Curtius has promised that he will pay you well if you will come and work for him again—just long enough to get a figure of Pierre-Joseph done for his display."

"Pierre-Joseph will not consent to it," I told him.

"He might if you asked him," Phillipe said. "They know he would never do it for anyone else, but he might for you."

"I could try," I said, musing on the money that was promised and the undoubted prestige that such a commission would bring. "Yes. Go tell Danton that I will try. Why should he not consent to sit for me?" I concluded.

Phillipe was running out with his message just as Pierre-Joseph was returning from his walk. "And where are you off to in such a hurry?" he asked Phillipe, who glanced at me and saw that I did not wish him to disclose his errand.

"Oh, just off—" Phillipe said and hurried out.

"Look what I have," Pierre-Joseph said to me once Phillipe had disappeared.

I looked to see him holding a new, delicately carved flute.

"However did you get that?" I asked.

"It is a gift from a friend," he told me, smiling broadly.

"A friend?" I said, my tone betraying the slight I felt in not having been told of such a "friend."

"He is a very old friend. We went to the university together," Pierre-Joseph explained. "I went to the Sorbonne a month or two ago, and there he was, shuffling about among the books."

"He recognized you after all these years?" I asked.

"He has changed less than I," Pierre-Joseph admitted. "It was I who first recognized him. But it did not take him long to remember when I spoke to him. I've seen him many times since then; there is so much news to catch up on. You remember, Jacques," he continued, "my telling you about someone bringing me an extra suit of clothes when at first they had imprisoned me?"

I nodded.

"I have found out that it was he. I have learned, too, that he tried more than once to bring me other things, but the guards would not allow it." He shook his head and a momentary sadness clouded his face but passed again as quickly as it came. "Still, it is nice to know an old friend was remembering me, and it has been doubly good to renew his acquaintance once again. I imagine that those who see us at the Sorbonne must think it odd when they see two old, musty men laughing and remembering amidst the piles of old, musty manuscripts. Today when I arrived, he brought me this."

"It looks like an expensive gift," I said.

"It is valuable to be sure," he said, "for it cost him much in time. But not in money. He made it. He made one other for me, long ago when we were young. Of course, that one went the way of all my other goods the day I was imprisoned. I had showed him the one I'd so rudely carved, and today he offered to exchange it for this one."

"A good exchange I'd say."

"And so would I," he said, as he turned the new flute over in his hands, examining it proudly. Then, putting aside his memories, he brought his thoughts back to me. "And how is your work coming?"

"It could be better," I said.

"Is there anything that I can do to help?" he asked as he headed for his favorite corner.

"Yes," I said. "As a matter of fact there is."

He stopped. "And what is that?"

"I have just received a request from Dr. Curtius. He has asked me to come and do one more commission for him, one that will pay well in both money and future clientele."

"It sounds promising, but what can I do to help?"

"You can sit for me," I said.

I saw him stiffen in his chair. "Sit for you?"

"Yes. It seems that there is a demand for you as a display in Curtius's *cabinet*," I said, not letting on that I knew he'd turned down such a request before.

"No," he said firmly.

"Why not?" I asked.

"I think you know why," he said quietly.

"No, I don't," I said. "Oh, I know that you do not like to be thrust in front of a crowd—as you were that night at Charpentier's. But this is not the same."

"How is it different?"

"You shall sit for me in a quiet studio. There will be no thronging crowds. And I will do justice by you, you will see," I promised, imagining that I could easily win him over.

"I have never doubted your ability to do justice to any subject that you chose to do, but that has nothing to do with my reasons for refusing."

"Then what are your reasons?"

"Jacques, do you not see that to have people cheer and bow before me is something that is abhorrent to me? And for them to bow before a mere image of me is even worse. I have passed Curtius's *cabinet* on my walks, and I have seen how those poor, ignorant people gape and admire the images of those they call the heroes of their Revolution. They are not heroes, Jacques; nor am I. I am an old, sinful man, but a man who trusts implicitly in the goodness and mercy God has provided for me through His Son. If they desire to worship, I would have them worship Christ."

"This has nothing to do with God," I shouted. "You are just being selfish. What of me? You may not want such honors, but they are profitable to an artist like me. Why can you not think of my honor rather than your own?"

"That is precisely what I am thinking of," he said calmly. "I would wish for you all the honor that faith in Christ would bestow upon you. And the immutable* contentment that such faith would bring as well. But you refuse it."

---

immutable: unchanging

"I want an honor that I can see, hear, feel right now!" I cried. "That would content me!"

"No," he said. "It would not."

"How would you know?"

"I know better than you think, Jacques," he said. "I know that there is a high price for the praise of men, and I know that once you have it, you must then live in constant fear of losing it—as one day you will. And when it is gone, there is nothing left, nothing but a cold and black despair."

"And money," I said. "The honor that you spurn is what brings me clients, and clients are what bring in the money for our food, our wood, and every other thing. Or have you forgotten that?"

He said nothing.

I threw my tools aside and stomped toward the door. "Eat what you like," I said. "I will dine tonight at Charpentier's with friends."

"Good-bye, Jacques," I heard him say with a tenderness that might have made me weep had I the heart for it. Instead, I simply slammed the door.

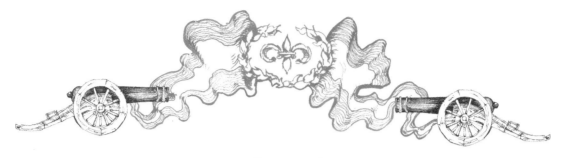

CHAPTER 6

I stayed away all that night and the next day as well. I did not care that my absence might cause Pierre-Joseph concern. I rather hoped it would, for I'd convinced myself that he had wronged me.

Before returning to the shop the next day, I forced myself to stop off at Curtius's *cabinet* and inform him of Pierre-Joseph's stubborn refusal. I feared that since this was the second offer, Dr. Curtius would not take such a rejection kindly.

The doctor's warm welcome only increased my apprehension. "I am sorry to have to tell you this," I began as soon as we were seated, "but Pierre-Joseph simply will not consent to a sitting. I have tried—"

"Forget the old man," the doctor interjected. "I've a better proposition for you."

"You have?"

"Oh, yes," he said, growing more and more excited. "Robespierre has consented to be part of my display. You know that he is fast becoming the rising star of the Revolution." He leaned closer. "He may yet surpass Danton, but don't tell Danton that I have said so. At any rate, I want you to do his figure! I tell you, Jacques, this Revolution is good for business, is it not?"

"It is," I said. "When would you like me to begin?"

"Two days from now. That should give you enough time to finish up any commissions you have now, for Danton and Charpentier have both told me that your popularity is growing."

"Things are going better than they ever have," I admitted. Then, taking my leave, I promised to be back in two days' time.

As I made my way toward home, I thought on my new commission. I had seen little of Robespierre since that night when he and Danton had come to dine at Curtius's *cabinet*, but I had heard much of him. He had amassed quite a following, though I wondered how he'd managed. He was a small, weak-looking man, with a lifestyle that was so rigid that Parisians referred to him as "The Incorruptible." In fact, he was the exact opposite of Danton. Perhaps that was why he had become popular; those repelled by the bombastic* Danton were drawn to the rigid Robespierre. In any case, I knew that I no longer needed Pierre-Joseph's help.

bombastic: showy

By the time I'd reached St. Antoine, I had determined to tell Pierre-Joseph about Robespierre. I would let him know that his stubbornness had not diminished my chances of success. But at the same time I told myself I would assure him that, even if I could not understand his obstinacy, I could excuse it, and I would still do all I could for him.

I entered the shop, admiring myself for the benevolent stance* I was taking toward my aged friend.

benevolent stance: kind attitude

Oddly, he was not about when I arrived. It was past the time for his daily walking, and I knew that he rarely went upstairs before the evening meal.

"Pierre-Joseph," I called out, not really expecting him to answer. With a slight twinge of guilt, I wondered if he might have gone out looking for me. Then I noticed that on my worktable lay his Bible with a letter folded neatly underneath it.

I picked it up and opened it, feeling a vague sense of dread.

Dear Jacques,

I told you that I would stay as long as I could do you good. Well, I feel that time has passed. Do not misunderstand, however. I am not leaving because I am in any way angry with you. Indeed, I love you as a son. But I know that every young man must find his own way, and I believe it is time for you to find yours.

You need not worry about my welfare. I am leaving early this morning for England. That friend of mine, the one who made my flute, also assured me that I yet have property across the Channel. It is property that my family acquired many years ago when they left France.

I'm sure you may be wondering why they left without me, just as you have probably wondered why I did not tell you how I became imprisoned in the Bastille. The two stories are closely linked, and I have not told you either of them, not because I do not trust you, but because it shames me yet to think about them. But I now feel the time has come when my experience may be of use to you. Besides, as you would expect, I cannot say good-bye without leaving behind a good sound lecture for you. It is the prerogative—or habit—of the old to insist upon such things. But I know you will bear with me.

As I have watched you these past two years, I have grown to understand just how much you are as I once was. My family circumstances were much different, but my youthful heart was so very much like yours.

My forefathers were not artisans, but titled, wealthy men. In my lineage were great soldiers, scholars, and noblemen, men whose deeds in times past called forth the praise of kings. But they were also Protestant Huguenots,* godly people who more than once were forced to choose between the honor of men and the praise of God. I know of only one who bears the name Aumônt—aside from myself—that chose men's praise over God's. Both of us have suffered for our folly. He was murdered in his bed on St. Bartholomew's Day in Paris in 1572. And I—as you know—was entombed in the Bastille.

But how came I to be there? During my years at the university, Protestants again began to suffer harassment from the Church of Rome. My father feared persecution—not for himself, but for my mother and my sisters, who were yet very young. He decided, therefore, to take them to England where they would be safe and where he could rear them as his conscience demanded. He begged me to go with them, but I was young and on the threshold of a promising career as a scholar and musician. I chose to stay behind. My father warned me that the day would come when the Protestants would again be forced either to renounce their faith or to suffer for it. I thought him foolish and I told him so. He did not rebuke me, but instead handed over his wealth and titles to me and assured me of his love and prayers. He also told me that as soon as they were settled, he would let me know their whereabouts and that if ever I had need of him, he would return without hesitation.

For more than a year, my life in Paris was all that I had hoped, but as you may guess, my father's predictions soon came true. At first, I was merely excluded from important social circles and denied prestigious posts. More than once my anger flared at such injustice, and I fought back, not just with words but also with my fists. It happened once too often. I was goaded into a fight with a young nobleman and beat him almost senseless. His father brought charges against me, but I was not especially fearful, for my wealth and rank were equal to his. I knew that in a court of law, I might be forced to pay some remuneration, but I thought I could afford it. What I did not know was that my adversary was also related to an influential bishop, a bishop who had the power to see that I—a Protestant—would never come to trial.

Two days before my scheduled hearing, I left the university and was on my way to send my father word of my predicament—just as a precaution. I was overtaken by the guards before I accomplished my mission. I was told that my wealth and titles would be confiscated and my family would never hear from me again. It grieves me even now to think of what they must have suffered, knowing only that I'd vanished and that the state now held their lands in France.

But God in His goodness saw to it that I had His Book about me when I was arrested. Under normal circumstances, I would not have had it with me, for I rarely read it much in those days. But a friend of mine had just returned it. He had wanted to examine how the French translation of the Scripture compared with his Latin Vulgate.

I remember the first night that I was left alone. The cell was a horror to one of my station. Trying to divert my thoughts, I opened God's Word and began to read at random. "Oh, that you had heeded My commandments!" the passage began. "Then your peace would have been like a river, And your righteousness as the waves of the sea." Those few words awakened in me the full extent of my folly. I had tried to cast aside my godly heritage, but God in His mercy had not allowed it. I prayed that night to be forgiven for my sins and to receive the contentment that I now knew could come only from Christ. My prayers were answered, and I can say that although my years of imprisonment were far from comfortable, they were filled with a peace that surpasses human understanding.

So you see, Jacques, I do know what it is to be young and to be ambitious. I know as well the anger one can feel when he is forced to suffer at the hands of unjust men. But I have learned that through Christ I can rise above any of life's circumstances. It is this lesson that I want to leave with you, this lesson and my family's greatest treasure. You have been like a son to me, and as my son, you shall inherit it. Take care; my love and prayers are with you. And remember, if you should ever need me—for any trifling* thing—my friend at the Sorbonne will know how to reach me. I shall return without the slightest hesitation.

Pierre-Joseph

Huguenots: followers of John Calvin

trifling: unimportant

My heart was yet unprepared to take in all the wisdom of his words, but I understood enough to know that I had been a fool to believe that he needed me. As I sat alone again in my shop, I knew that all along it had been I who needed him.

THINKING ZONE

In most stories and novels, an author creates one character to represent the author's worldview to the reader. That character is the one whom the author desires the reader to look to for the proper perspective of the situations and dilemmas in which characters find themselves. The character who provides this perspective is often referred to as the **normative character** (or sometimes the story's *moral norm*). That character is the mouthpiece for what the author believes to be good and right, and his is the attitude by which we measure other characters in the story. Very often a story's themes will be verbalized by or closely connected to the normative character. This character is usually a static one whose beliefs, ethics, and morals are unchanging throughout the story.

Christian readers must be especially aware of an author's perspective because an author will manipulate all of a reader's sympathies to be with the normative character. If a normative character is wicked or has a twisted worldview, the reader may be deceived into thinking that any wrong that this character does is unavoidable or excusable. For example, in Langston Hughes's "Thank You, M'am," the normative character is Mrs. Luella Bates Washington Jones since she is the one whom the reader admires, the one whose moral compass is unflinching from beginning to end. How would Hughes's story have been different had he presented Roger as a penniless, ragged, starving boy being attacked by a merciless giant of a woman who had an outstanding warrant for abusing children? The reader might have concluded that poor Roger had no choice! Society, after all, had driven him to this point. Searching for the normative character in a story will help you find out what is important to the author and what that author thinks should be important to you.

> **Internal conflict—** *conflict within a character's mind between opposing thoughts and emotions*
>
> **External conflict—** *conflict between a character and an outside force such as society or nature*

1. *[interpretive]* Give one example of each type of conflict (internal and external) that occurs in Chapter 5.

   _____

   _____

   _____

   _____

2. *[interpretive]* What is ironic about Jacques's accusation that Pierre-Joseph's refusal to pose for him is "selfish"?

_____

_____

_____

_____

3. *[critical]* What is the difference between the honor that Jacques seeks and the honor that Pierre-Joseph wishes him to achieve?

_____

_____

_____

_____

4. *[critical]* How do Pierre-Joseph's words to Jacques about the praise of men in Chapter 5 echo the novel's themes? (See page 263.)

_____

_____

_____

_____

5. *[critical]* Who is this novel's **normative character**? How can you tell?

_____

_____

_____

_____

6. *[appreciative]* Do you think this author presents a biblical perspective? Explain.

_____

_____

_____

_____

CHAPTER 7
SPRING, 1792

More than once I toyed with the idea of visiting Pierre-Joseph's friend at the Sorbonne, but I was too ashamed to do so. What message could I send to Pierre-Joseph that would make up for the way I'd scorned him? No, I could not go to him. Nor could I bear to read the Book he had left behind, for each time that I opened it I thought of him, and such thoughts only made me more miserable.

Phillipe again became the only bright spot in my dismal existence, but he came less often to the shop. Thomas had at last managed, through Danton's help, to slip back into Paris, and he now insisted that Phillipe begin to learn a cabinetmaker's trade. Thus, each day that passed seemed only to increase my gloom. I found that even my work brought me little satisfaction.

As I struggled, so did Paris. Pierre-Joseph had been right: the peace following the fall of the Bastille was a deceptive calm. Paris was on the brink of a violent, raging storm, a storm that broke in all its fury when the King tried to flee Paris with his family. He had hoped to obtain refuge in one of the royalist provinces and there gain support for his tottering throne. But His Majesty's hopes were never realized, for a postmaster recognized the royal family and stopped them at Varennes. They were brought back to the Tuileries in Paris as royal captives. Men and women now spurned the idea of a constitutional monarchy and demanded the overthrow of the King. Some, like Robespierre, even began to insinuate that it would be wise if the King and Queen were put to death. It is ironic that at the time the King's hopes were dashed, Dr. Guillotin's were realized.

"Have you heard?" cried Phillipe, dashing into the shop one afternoon. "There's to be no more gallows!"

I looked up at him.

"It's true," he said. "A man came into the shop today and said that the Paris deputies have at last listened to Dr. Guillotin. The poor as well as the rich can now simply have their heads cut off."

"That's good news, indeed," I said grimly.

"I say, Jacques," Phillipe chided. "Nothing cheers you anymore."

"I suppose I am bad company these days," I said.

"Not bad company," he said. "Just hard to cheer up."

"Try," I said. "Tell me what else you've learned. It seems that those who come to your shop are more talkative than those who come to mine."

"Well, according to gossip, Dr. Guillotin has a machine that can, as he puts it, 'separate the head from the body in less time than it takes to wink.'"

"That sounds like a bit of an exaggeration," I said.

"No, it's not," Phillipe assured me. "They say a surgeon has already tested it. He's cut off the heads of sheep, calves, and even corpses from the poorhouse. It works."

"Well, if it does, Dr. Curtius will be disappointed."

"Oh, I almost forgot," he said. "I had to run an errand for my father this morning, and while I was out, I stopped by Charpentier's. Danton was there, and he told me to tell you to stop by the *cabinet*. The doctor has another commission for you. He wants you to help him do a re-enactment of the first guillotine execution for his Den of Thieves."

"He likes to plan ahead, doesn't he?" I said.

Phillipe shrugged. "He did say that he will pay you better for this one than for any you have done before."

"Tell him when you see him next that I will think about it."

"I think you ought to," said Phillipe, growing very serious.

"Why?" I asked.

"I don't know," he said. "It's just—well, when Danton gave the message, it seemed more like a command than a suggestion."

"Are you afraid of Danton?" I asked.

"A bit," he said. "Papa is even a bit afraid of him, I think. I just don't think it's wise to cross him."

"You're not the first who has told me that," I said. "Perhaps you're right. Besides, I've done so many commissions for him, one more won't hurt. And although I never cared much for that Den of Thieves, I think I might be able to stand working on it for a while."

"Good," said Phillipe, relieved. "And who knows, maybe the guillotine will never be used."

"It will be used," I said.

And it was—within the week.

A forger named Pelletier was to be the guillotine's first victim. On the appointed

day I accompanied Dr. Curtius to the Place de Grève, the traditional site of executions. But scarcely had the crowd gathered round before the thing was done. The amazing efficiency of the execution did not please the masses. They began to jeer the executioner and eventually to chant and even cheer, "Give us back our gallows!"

"Did I not tell you that Paris would prove ungrateful?" said Dr. Curtius as we turned to go. "The nature of man does not crave justice, but revenge."

"This will prove a poor exhibit then," I said.

"Oh, no," he assured me. "We shall add a touch here and there. Before we are through, men will no longer look upon the guillotine as a humane instrument, but as an instrument of horror."

CHAPTER 8

Dr. Curtius was right. It took me several months to complete the guillotine exhibit, but when it was finally unveiled, people not only flocked to see it but revelled in its violent composition. Soon after my exhibit opened, the King and Queen were overthrown. Their demise unleashed in France a chaotic struggle for power. It was the Paris Commune, led by men like Danton and Robespierre, which emerged victorious from this political upheaval. To secure their power, these men instituted a special tribunal whose primary function was to round up, imprison, and eventually execute those suspected of once supporting the monarchy. Before summer's end, those same patrons who earlier frequented the *cabinet* were lining the streets to cheer as innocent men and women met their death by the guillotine.

In addition to the turmoil within the country, France was also embroiled in a war with Austria. By early September, news reached Paris that the enemy was closing in. In response, the Commune summoned "loyal patriots" to join the militia and defend the land. The call was answered by scores of men, but on the eve of their departure another crisis erupted. It was rumored that the imprisoned royalists were plotting to break free and restore Louis to his throne as soon as the militia had departed Paris. Prominent members of the Commune were quick to act. Organizing those of us who were not part of the mili-

tia into armed bands, they ordered us into the prisons to unmask the counteraries. We were instructed to try the prisoners. Of course, any who proved to be loyal citizens we could free. But those whom we found guilty were to be executed on the spot.

I set out with several others on the evening of September 2, assured that I was doing my civil duty and that I would be paid for the services I rendered. What followed was far from "civil," and I still shudder to think that I was offered pay for it.

We arrived at the first prison about nine o'clock that evening. I watched as prisoner after prisoner was hauled before our improvised court. It did not take long to see that these trials were a mere charade. Although a few prisoners were released, many more were executed, and as the night wore on, these armed bands of men—whipped up by rhetoric and fear—dispensed with the tribunals* altogether. Those of us who opposed such a travesty* of justice were afraid to protest for fear that we would be marked as royalist sympathizers. As we continued to break into cell after cell, I began hanging back, unwilling to partake in what was fast becoming wanton* slaughter, but one burly man soon noticed my apprehension. "You, there, come out from hiding and see to that next cell," he said.

---

tribunals: courts of justice

travesty: mockery

wanton: merciless and unjust

I felt I had no choice but to obey, and swinging open the cell door, I entered. Immediately my apprehension vanished, for there before me stood my father's murderer—the Comte de Guiche's older son. His father and his younger brother stood beside him.

"What do you want?" the indignant old Comte stepped forward and demanded.

I ignored him and turned my gaze upon his older son. I had grown much since he last saw me, so much in fact that I doubt he recognized me.

"What are you staring at?" he asked, and the tone of scorn in his voice sent me into abject* rage.

---

abject: contemptible

I ran at him, and with the handle of my pike pressed against his throat, I pinned him to the wall. "You murderer!" I cried.

Out of the corner of my eye I saw his father move forward, but immediately I heard a voice behind me saying, "No, you don't, old man." There was a moan and then a thud.

The young nobleman began struggling more violently, which only served to increase my blind fury. I held him fast and continued screaming—what, I don't remember. The next thing I knew, someone was pulling me back. "Let him go, now. I've finished him!"

I stepped back and released my grip. To my surprise the young nobleman sank to the floor.

"I thrust him through for you," the man beside me said.

I turned and saw that the Comte de Guiche also lay dead.

Just then the Comte's younger son, who had been stunned to silence, found his voice and ran toward the man who'd murdered both his father and his brother.

"You've killed them!" he screamed, beating his fists against the man's burly chest. The man thrust him away, and the boy, who was no more than thirteen, moved over to his dead father.

I saw him there—as I had been—so many years before. My fury melted, and I reached out to touch him.

In a flash of anger he thrust aside my hand. "Get away from me!"

But hardly had he spoken the words before the man who finished off the other two, stepped up behind me and thrust his pike into the boy. "That'll keep him quiet!" he said.

"You fool!" I yelled, turning on him. "You—" but he was gone, already heading for the next cell.

I took the boy up in my arms, intending to get help for him. But as I held him, I could feel the life blood flowing out of him. Help was useless now. I gently laid him down again, and as I did, I saw my bloodied hands.

"There's more down the way," another man called out to me as I staggered from the cell.

I stared at him a moment, then threw down my pike, turned, and walked away.

Once back home, I washed myself and put on a fresh suit of clothes, but the stench of death stayed with me. Though my hand had not actually performed the murders, I knew that the rage I felt against the Comte's son could well have killed him. As I sat alone that night in my darkened shop, I realized for the first time how much I'd become like those who cheered at executions.

THINKING ZONE

The chapters you have just read—Chapters 7 and 8—are pivotal in the development of the novel's protagonist. It is in these chapters that Jacques finally comes to realize several important things, both about himself and about the Revolution. These realizations lead to a crisis for the main character. In literature, **crisis** is the term used for the major turning point for the protagonist. It is the point at which something happens that affects the outcome of the story and determines the future of the protagonist. Many times, discerning the crisis requires close reading of the story.

As you read the chapters, were you able to detect elements of foreshadowing in the events that eventually brought Jacques to the crisis point in his development? The ability to examine evidence, draw conclusions, and formulate opinions regarding what will happen or why something did happen is an important one to develop, and it becomes increasingly important as you grow older since you will be bombarded with messages that are often meant to confuse and conflict. It is vital for a Christian to examine the details he is given and to evaluate conclusions in light of Scripture, using his God-given ability to reason.

1. *[interpretive/critical]* How is Jacques feeling emotionally at the beginning of Chapter 7? What passages from the text support your answer?

_____

_____

_____

_____

_____

_____

2. *[interpretive]* What words from Pierre-Joseph foreshadowing the revolution does Jacques remember?

_____

_____

_____

3. *[interpretive/critical]* What events from Chapter 7 lead Dr. Curtius to conclude that "the nature of man does not crave justice, but revenge"? Explain Dr. Curtius's statement.

_____

_____

_____

_____

_____

_____

4. *[critical]* By Chapter 8, do you see the revolutionaries as sympathetic or unsympathetic characters? Explain your answer.

_____

_____

_____

_____

_____

Sympathetic character—*a character that the reader identifies with or has a favorable feeling toward*

Unsympathetic character—*a character with whom the reader does not identify or for whom the reader has strong feelings of dislike*

5. *[critical]* What event finally causes Jacques to arrive at the **crisis** in his life? What statement in Chapter 8 reflects that this is a turning point for Jacques?

_____

_____

_____

_____

_____

6. *[critical]* Why do you think the author included the violent events of Chapter 8 in her novel?

_____

_____

_____

_____

_____

CHAPTER 9

I sat in the shop all through the night. I was afraid to sleep, and it was not until the first sign of sunrise that I got up and moved about. Crossing to the shop window, I wondered if perhaps the light of morning might dispel the darkness of my spirit as it dispelled the night. But my despair refused to leave me. Turning away, I wandered aimlessly about the shop.

At length my eye fell on the Bible Pierre-Joseph had bequeathed to me. It lay upon the same shelf where stood my father's prized Rousseau. I took it down and began leafing through it. Eventually I picked a random passage and began to read. It was a parable about a king who desired to settle accounts with his servants. I thought it appropriate for such a time in France, and thus continued reading:

"And when he had begun to settle accounts, one was brought to him who owed him ten thousand talents.

"But as he was not able to pay, his master commanded that he be sold, with his wife and children and all that he had, and that payment be made.

"The servant therefore fell down before him saying, 'Master, have patience with me, and I will pay you all.'

"Then the master of that servant was moved with compassion, released him, and forgave him the debt.

"But that servant went out and found one of his fellow servants who owed him a hundred denarii;* and he laid hands on him and took *him* by the throat, saying, 'Pay me what you owe!'

"So his fellow servant fell down at his feet and begged him, saying, 'Have patience with me, and I will pay you all.'

"And he would not, but went and threw him into prison till he should pay the debt.

"So when his fellow servants saw what he had done, they were very grieved, and came and told their master all that had been done.

"Then his master, after he had called him, said to him, 'You wicked servant! I forgave you all that debt because you begged me.

"'Should you not also have had compassion on your fellow servant, just as I had pity on you?'"

By this time I no longer thought of the parable as an analogy to France. It was I who mirrored the unjust servant, and Pierre-Joseph the noble king. All that he had done for me came flooding back to mind—the simple acts of kindness, the willing gift of his great heart and mind. And I—I who gave but a few worthless "denarii," had held it up to him as if it were a debt. Worse still—I had demanded even more than money from others who had wronged me: I had demanded that they pay me with their life.

The letter that he'd left for me fell from its place inside the Book. Carefully I unfolded it and smoothed it out upon the worktable. The feel of it was somehow comforting. How I missed my wise, old friend! I could write to him, I thought. Yes, I could write

denarii: ancient Roman silver coins

and ask him to forgive me. It was not much, but it was a start.

I began to scan the contents of the letter, but scarcely had I begun when I was startled by a banging at the door. I looked up and through the window saw Danton, Curtius, and Charpentier. I got up and opened the door to them.

"Have you heard?" said Danton, barging in. "Robespierre is trying to have the King put to death."

"From what I hear, the law forbids that," I said.

"Of course it does," Danton replied, pacing about in agitation.

"Robespierre's gaining influence, Jacques," Charpentier put in. "I fear that he will win."

"And we must be on the winning side with him," Danton said. "That is why we've come here. There's something Dr. Curtius and I want you to do."

"You see," Dr. Curtius endeavored to explain, "if we are to beat Robespierre at his own game, we must do something even more spectacular."

"I don't understand what you're driving at," I said.

"Robespierre is already pushing for the King's trial," Danton continued. "Of course, to him that is a formality. He needs the Commune behind him if he is to pull the whole thing off—which I have no doubt he will."

"Aye," added Charpentier, "he's a sly one all right."

"Not as sly as I am," Danton reminded him. "At any rate, once the King's condemned, Robespierre will look like a hero. I must have a means of diversion that will bring the attention back to me. Curtius here came up with the perfect plan."

"We shall do a wax of the beheaded King!"

"You shall do a wax of the King. I want no part of it."

Danton stepped forward and grabbed my arm. "What do you mean, you want no part of it? I have done enough for you. You owe me."

"What I owe you is a guilty conscience," I said, boldly. "Your Paris Commune not only authorized but ordered that charade last night."

"Charade?" Danton said.

"Yes," I replied. "You told us it was our civic duty to ferret out* a royalist plot, but those in the prisons were not plotting anything. They were waiting—waiting for trials, and for the chance to proclaim themselves as 'patriotic' as everyone else in France."

ferret out: uncover

"You young fool," he jeered. "They were deceiving you."

"I am no fool, Danton. I saw young boys mowed down!"

"Young boys?" said Charpentier.

"That's right," I said. Turning to face Danton again, I added, "Pierre-Joseph warned me not to trust you."

"Did he now?" Danton replied.

"Come, Jacques," Charpentier pleaded. "You're being too hotheaded. Danton here didn't order the murder of young boys."

"Besides being hotheaded, you're being stupid," added Curtius. "Think of the money the figure of the agonized King will bring. And what should the King care if we make a profit on him? He'll be dead."

"No," I said. "I tell you I have had enough."

"Fine," Danton said in a calm but icy tone. "We'd best be going, gentlemen."

I watched them as they headed for the door, but just before they reached it, Danton turned. "That reminds me, Jacques. The loan I gave you."

"Loan?" I said.

"Yes. You remember. I commissioned that medallion from you and paid for it ahead of time. But by the time you finally brought it to me, I had no need of it. You remember that I had already won Gabrielle's heart by then, don't you, Charpentier?" he asked.

Charpentier nodded, as if perplexed at what Danton was driving at.

"At any rate," Danton continued, turning back to me, "I pulled your little friend aside and told him that I would give you a loan until you were on your feet again. You are on your feet again, aren't you?"

It took only a moment before I knew what he was up to: he was making a point. In truth, I owed him nothing; the money he had given Phillipe was not a loan, but he knew I could not prove it, for he had given it in secret. His charade now was to impress me with the fact that he could withdraw his aid as easily as he gave it. I determined that I would "owe" such a man nothing. "Wait here," I said. "My money's upstairs."

When I came back down, I found Danton reading Pierre-Joseph's letter.

I walked over and snatched it from him. "Do you always read another's personal mail?" I snapped, and I thrust the money toward him.

"It rarely interests me," he said. "But that—" He pointed to the letter in my hand. "I didn't know that old Pierre-Joseph was once a nobleman. That would interest those peasants and artisans who once revered him."

"They would revere him still," I said.

"Perhaps," he said and turned to go. Dr. Curtius followed him out.

Charpentier lagged behind long enough to whisper, "Be careful, Jacques. Danton is not a man to trifle with. I know."

I spent the rest of the morning and the afternoon trying to decide what to do.

I knew that Charpentier was right, and though I had spoken boldly to Danton, I no longer trusted myself to remain firm under severe pressure. If I stayed in Paris, I felt sure that he would find a way to bend me to his will. I would not have it! But the only way I could be sure that I'd escape him was if I fled from France.

I looked down at the letter I still clutched in my hand and remembered, "If you need me—for any trifling thing. . . ." I sat down and wrote to Pierre-Joseph.

My letter was not simply a plea for aid. I poured out my heart to my friend, confessing not only the failures of the Revolution but my own as well. I told him of the King's overthrow and of Danton's and Robespierre's rise to power. I told him of my shame at having scorned him and of my murderous rage that night in the Comte de Guiche's cell. And, of course, I told him too of my discovery of Danton's self-serving cunning and of how he had discovered Pierre-Joseph's past. I told him everything, and it did me good to do so. Only then did I ask him if he could provide me safe passage across the Channel. I closed with the parable that I had read, and its effect upon me. I acknowledged that I had no right to ask anything of him. But I promised that if he could in good conscience aid me, I henceforth would do all I could to serve him, knowing that all the service I could render now would not repay my debt.

I delivered the letter to Pierre-Joseph's friend. Two weeks later, he summoned me to the Sorbonne and told me that Pierre-Joseph was on his way. I was to be ready and waiting outside the library at five o'clock the following afternoon.

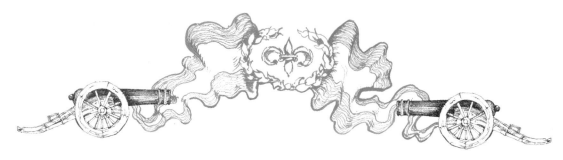

CHAPTER **10**

I packed up my tools, Pierre-Joseph's Bible, and a few belongings and was headed for the Sorbonne by four o'clock. When I arrived, Pierre-Joseph's friend was waiting.

"Where is he?" I asked.

"He is here," his old friend assured me, "but he wants you to go down to the wharf without delay. There is a seaman waiting. Here," he said, handing me a neatly wrapped cloth bundle. "I am to give this to you as well. Now go quickly."

"He will know where the boat is?"

The old man smiled. "He brought it here, did he not?"

"Of course," I said. "Thank you. Tell him I'll be waiting for him."

Within the hour I was at the wharf, looking for the seaman while keeping an eye out for Pierre-Joseph as well.

"You are Jacques?" a man behind me said.

I turned. "Yes—"

"Come. My boat is docked a bit further down."

As soon as we boarded, the seaman began untying the boat.

"You're not going just yet?" I asked him.

"We must," he said.

I grabbed the ropes from him. "But Pierre-Joseph—"

"Perhaps you'd better open that," he said, pointing to my bundle. Then he added, "Go down below. It is comfortable enough, and it's best if you stay there until we are out of port."

I released the ropes and went below.

Sitting down, I leaned myself against an old wooden barrel and opened the bundle. Out fell a packet of papers—and a letter. I took up the letter.

Dear Jacques,

As you must know by now, I am not coming with you. It is safer that way. You see, in the course of making arrangements for this trip, I learned that Danton knew of your plan to flee and that you had asked me for help. He made plans to insure that he could apprehend you as you fled, knowing that by catching you in "mid-flight" he could make fast his charge of treason against you.

I allowed his men to follow me yesterday as I completed my preparations for returning to England—preparations for myself, not for you. (The plans for your escape were all settled before I left home.) I believe that I convinced Danton's men that they were receiving the information about your escape that they sought. If events proceed as I hope, I will leave for England tomorrow. But just in case I am detained, you will find the deeds and titles to my property in England enclosed with this letter. Now that I've informed you of my plans, let me get on with more important matters.

I cannot tell you, Jacques, the joy your letter brought me! The grief you expressed assures me that God has answered my prayers and granted you one of His greatest gifts—the gift of godly sorrow, that sorrow which "worketh repentance to salvation." You now understand that the human heart is "deceitful above all things, and desperately wicked," and now that you comprehend the heart of man, you are ready to learn about the heart and nature of God.

Let me assure you first that "the Lord is nigh unto them that are of a broken heart; and saveth such as be of a contrite spirit." God is now calling to you as clearly as He called to Isaiah: "Come now, and let us reason together, . . . though your sins be as scarlet, they shall be as white as snow; though they be red like crimson, they shall be as wool."

There is no need to despair over your sins. Your only need is to come to Christ, to believe in Him and in the Father who sent Him to provide atonement for you. You will find God true to His Word. In place of your wicked heart, He shall give you a heart of honor, one that reflects the righteousness of Christ. With such a heart, no circumstance can defeat you or rob you of your peace.

I will see you again—one way or another—but until I do, know that you are in my thoughts and always in my prayers.

Pierre-Joseph

I closed my eyes; the secret of the Seine had at last become clear to me.

My time in England has proved to be rich and satisfying. The material wealth Pierre-Joseph bequeathed to me is more than I could have imagined. Still, such wealth is nothing compared to the spiritual legacy he provided. It is this legacy that has allowed me to drink the Water of Life freely, and in my months away from France I have found that whosoever drinks of the water Christ gives will never thirst. For I know now that the water He gives becomes a fountain of water springing up into everlasting life. Pierre-Joseph not only knew of this fountain but, through much patience, brought me to drink from it as well.

My only sadness is that I will never have the chance in this life to share with him my heartfelt gratitude for such a gift. You see, Pierre-Joseph was never able to return to England. Although the people of Paris refused to allow Danton to imprison the revered survivor of the Bastille, they had no quarrel with his forcing Pierre-Joseph to remain in France. Before long, however, Danton was robbed even of this petty revenge. Within a month after my departure, Pierre-Joseph died peacefully in his old friend's bed. "His last thoughts were of you," his friend wrote, and in his letter he included Pierre-Joseph's parting words to me: "Tell him that even though I cannot come to him, I know that he will one day come to me. And tell him that I won't mind waiting."

Why then am I returning now to France? Well, I am told that Danton is fast falling out of favor. (He may soon find himself a wax in Curtius's *cabinet*, but not as one of the heroes.) Unfortunately, those who have known and associated with Danton, including Phillipe, his parents, and Charpentier, may soon be forced to suffer as well. My gratitude for Phillipe's enduring friendship would be reason enough for my return, but you may recall that I once made a promise to Charpentier as well, the promise that I would not forget him. There is but little time to keep such promises and to provide those I love a way of escape. Thus I return, and I have peace that God will reward my journey. Indeed, it is He who sends me. If those I love must die, they shall die in Christ.

If, however, God sees fit to grant my friends and me a safe return to England, I will rejoice in my renewed fellowship with them. I especially look forward to those times that Phillipe and I will share. I hope one day to sit with him in the corner of my drawing room, with the bust I have made of Pierre-Joseph beside us on the mantel, and I will read to him as my old friend once read to me. The bust? Yes, I have made a bust of Pierre-Joseph. It is in stone, and I assure you that he would not object to this one, for I did not trust in only my artistry to reveal his noble soul. At the base of the sculpture is inscribed his attitude and mine concerning "images":

If you desire to worship, worship Christ.

Si tu désires adorer,
adore Jésus-Christ

ABOUT THE AUTHOR

Best known as the author of *A Father's Promise,* Donnalynn Hess (b. 1952) has also written historical dramas for stage and television productions in addition to several BJU Press publications. With degrees from Bob Jones University in both social studies education and dramatic production, Hess has chosen historical fiction as a vehicle to communicate her love of history and her conviction that the drama of the past can provide valuable lessons for the present. Hess teaches adolescent literature and is a favorite speaker at Christian school and homeschool conventions. She currently serves as the Director of Education at Bob Jones University Museum and Gallery in Greenville, SC.

THINKING ZONE

There are as many ways to end a story as there are to open a narrative. In every case, however, the ending should be both believable and satisfying. Sometimes in order to give the reader a greater sense of completeness, the author will provide an **epilogue**, or an addition to the story's ending that expounds on the fortunes of the main character or on the significance of the story's conclusion.

In Search of Honor contains both a prologue and an epilogue, making it a type of **frame story**: a story that contains another story or an introductory story from which another story springs. The term *frame* makes this device easy to remember: one story is "framed" by another, like a picture in a frame. Many frame stories contain multiple loosely related stories. One such frame story is *The Canterbury Tales* by Geoffrey Chaucer. In that work, a group of travelers makes its way toward Canterbury. Within that basic story (or frame), each of the travelers tells the others a tale. The book of Job is another frame story. There is a prose prologue (ch. 1–2) and a prose epilogue (ch. 42). The rest are poetic speeches between the characters. More recent literature, like the novel you have just finished reading, has tended toward a single tale within the frame of the other story. Whatever the type, you can be sure that when an author includes a frame story, she does so with purpose. Can you see Hess's purpose in the frame for this novel?

1. *[literal/interpretive]* How does Danton respond to Jacques's refusal to help with a gruesome new wax display? What does this action tell us about Danton?

_____

_____

_____

_____

_____

2. *[critical]* What actions of Jacques's are proof that the events of Chapter 8 were a genuine turning point in his life? List at least three.

_____

_____

_____

_____

3. *[interpretive]* Find at least two references for quotations from
   biblical passages in Pierre-Joseph's note to Jacques. (You may need
   to use a concordance.)

   _____

   _____

   _____

   _____

4. *[interpretive]* What does Jacques mean by his statement that the
   "secret of the Seine had at last become clear to [him]"?

   _____

   _____

   _____

   _____

5. *[critical]* What metaphor does Jacques use in the **epilogue** to describe what Christ has given him? How does this biblical allusion
   appropriately communicate what has happened to Jacques?

   _____

   _____

   _____   **Allusion**—*a reference*
                                                        within one work of
   _____   *literature to another*
                                                        work of literature
   _____

   _____

   _____

6. *[appreciative]* How do you think the **frame story** worked for this novel?
   What do you think the author's purpose was in using this device? Would
   you have ended the novel differently had you been the author?

   _____

   _____

   _____

   _____

WESLEY KO

TOM BROKAW

Heroes are not always on the battlefield. Heroes may be found in all walks of life and with many different backgrounds. This is the case of Wesley Ko, whose story is chronicled in Tom Brokaw's book *The Greatest Generation*, a collection of stories about the men and women who lived through World War II. In Ko, we discover a man who was heroic not only as a soldier but also as a civilian. This real-life hero never gave up—no matter what the challenge.

A sense of personal responsibility and a commitment to honesty is characteristic of this generation. Those were values bred into the young men and women coming of age at the time the war broke out. It's how they were raised. There are always exceptions to the common bonds of any generation, but in talking to the men and women whose stories make up this book I was struck by the connective cords of their lives, wherever they lived or in whatever circumstances.

One after another they volunteered how in their families and in their communities they were expected to be responsible for their behavior, how honesty was assumed to be the rule, not the exception. They also talked matter-of-factly about a sense of duty to their country, a sentiment not much in fashion anymore.

Moreover, in their communities there were always monitors outside their own families to remind them of the ethos* of their family and community. I've often said I was raised by the strict standards of my mother and father, and also of the parents of my friends, my teachers, my coaches, my ministers, and by the local businessmen who didn't hesitate to remind me "that's not how you were raised."

ethos: character or fundamental values

Those qualities didn't show up in a statistical survey of America's strengths as the country steeled* itself for what seemed an unavoidable war, but they were critical to the nation's preparations, for success depended as much on personal resolve as it did on tanks and planes and ships and guns.

steeled: made hard or strong; strengthened

The idea of personal responsibility is such a defining characteristic of the World War II generation that when the rules changed later, these men and women were appalled.

Wesley Ko is one of them. In 1988, at the age of seventy, his printing business failed, in part because of government regulations and in part because a relocation deal was seriously flawed. Ko was left with a debt of $1.3 million, a loan he'd personally guaranteed. It never occurred to him to declare personal bankruptcy. Ko had learned early in life the meaning of responsibility and self-sufficiency.

Ko grew up in the Philadelphia area, the son of a Chinese man brought to this country by an American missionary. His father was educated at Princeton and at Temple University and became pastor of a Methodist church for Chinese immigrants in Philadelphia. His mother was the daughter of a Chinese coolie* brought to America to work on the railroads, one of the laborers who in the late nineteenth and early twentieth centuries were subjected to the same vicious racial discrimination that African Americans suffered. They were treated like an alien and subhuman population, restricted to the backbreaking work on the railroad, or to hand laundries in their own well-defined ghettos.

coolie: Asian laborer; formerly in common use, the term is now considered derogatory

Ko's father hoped to escape that with his education, but the Great Depression was especially hard on preachers, who were dependent on their congregations for financial support. Wesley's father was just able to hold on to the family residence by opening a small laundry. Wesley, a bright young man, had hoped to go to college, but it was out of the question in those difficult times.

He went to work in a printing company, and when the war broke out his boss offered to get him a deferment,* but Wesley's buddies were all signing up and he wanted to volunteer as well. He was assigned to the officers' training school at Fort Benning, Georgia, and after ninety days he was a second lieutenant in the 82nd Airborne.

deferment: official delay of military service

I was apprehensive," he says, "being the only Oriental in the 82nd. I think the 82nd was apprehensive too; I wasn't assigned right away. I guess they thought Orientals couldn't be leaders. I didn't make an issue of it. I was born and raised in this country and I didn't think I was any different."

Asian complexions were real burdens for American citizens when their country was at war with Japan; too many of their fellow citizens made no distinction between the enemy and the Asian Americans in their midst. In the end, the Army did recognize Wesley Ko's qualities and installed him as a platoon leader in a new outfit: the 325th Glider Infantry Regiment.

It was the daredevil and dangerous new way to transport troops, including Dr. Van Gorder and his medical unit, when D-Day was launched. A pilot and a copilot steered the glider to what was a controlled crash landing in difficult terrain, ferrying thirteen troops and their equipment at a time.

In the spring of 1942 Ko and his outfit sailed for North Africa, for more training sessions in the demanding conditions of Morocco, Algeria, and Tunisia. "It was very, very hot," he recalls, "a hundred twenty degrees. We had to run for twenty minutes with our packs, then walk twenty minutes. At one point the whole regiment had dysentery.* We lost more men training in Africa than in our first combat."

dysentery: disease of the large intestine

It was the beginning of a three-year ordeal for Wesley Ko. After training in Africa he was almost constantly in combat—first in Sicily on Mount Saint Angelo de Cava, then during the occupation of Naples with steady shelling from Germany's big guns. After Italy, it was more hard-core training, this time in Ireland and England, for the Normandy invasion. Ko was promoted to first lieutenant and given command of a mortar platoon.

On June 7, D-Day* plus one, he was in a flight of 250 gliders headed for the north coast of France, where the fighting was very heavy. "When we arrived over Normandy," he says, "we started receiving machine-gunfire. We sat on our flak jackets* to give us a little more protection, we were flying so low."

D-Day: the day on which the World War II Allies invaded France; also, the day on which a military operation is to be launched

flak jackets: bulletproof vests or jackets

Ko was well trained. "I just didn't think of the danger," he says now. "I guess I was too young, too naive. But it turns out we lost twenty percent of our gliders—they never got into battle. They were either shot down or made a bad landing."

As soon as Ko scrambled from his glider, he was in the thick of the fighting. His regiment began fighting its way from village to village, losing many men along the way. Ko had some very close calls in hellish* days following D-Day. "I was standing next to one of the operations officers when he was shot and killed. I remember another time taking my binoculars from their case and shrapnel* had blown out a lens." Another time, "for the river crossing, the engineers had set up a bridge and we just ran across. We received tremendous fire but you had to keep pushing forward. Different fellows were hit and you had to keep jumping over their bodies."

hellish: indescribably abominable

shrapnel: fragments of ammunition

After thirty-three days straight of combat without replacements, Ko's battalion of 600 men had lost more than half, 323. And it was just the beginning of the drive for Berlin. Holland and the Battle of the Bulge lay ahead.

In the beginning of the Battle of the Bulge, that desperate but ultimately doomed attempt by Hitler to counterattack against the advancing Allied forces, Ko and his men were deployed in defensive positions, in heavy snow, to keep the enemy from overrunning Allied gains. "It was terrible weather, with snow up to your knees," he remembers, ". . . we had our olive-drab* uniforms, so we stuck out like sore thumbs."

olive-drab: olive brown or olive gray color used in military uniforms

During one withdrawal Ko and his sergeant were the last to leave. They looked to their left and saw a company of men in snowsuits. Ko relates: "The Germans! We were startled. There were only two of us, so we had to get out of there. We ran through a creek to keep out of sight. To this day I can't remember how I ever got dry"

Ko went on to more fierce fighting at close range, in the attack on the Siegfried line.* "The concrete pillboxes* were so thick that not even heavy artillery was effective, so the only option was for the men to get close enough to drop grenades. But in order to get close you had to suffer a lot of casualties. In my regiment alone, which had a couple of thousand men, we had close to two hundred killed, more than seven hundred fifty wounded, and forty-nine missing in action."

Siegfried line: German fortifications

pillboxes: low, concrete structures that held heavy artillery

Ko was promoted to captain and given command of a company as his outfit pushed east, participating in the battle for Cologne, Germany, and assisting in the capture of the 21st German army, which was trying to avoid the Russian troops advancing from the other direction. Ko and his men helped liberate the Wobbelin concentration camp at Ludwigslust. "We dug a mass grave and made every German citizen in the area who was aware of the situation help us and also attend the burial of the hundreds of dead inmates."

The war was at an end. Captain Wesley Ko had participated in six campaigns in two and a half years, under fire in some of the most important and ferocious battles of the war. He had accumulated enough points for a swift return home. As he put it, "Not many of us made it all the way."

On September 23, 1945, he arrived back in the United States aboard the *USS Constitution*.

When he returned from the war Ko decided to go back to his old printing-plant job, but after a year or so he teamed up with his brother and a friend to open their own business, Komak Printing. They specialized in silk-screening for advertising companies and then began doing custom work for electronics firms. It was hard work but Ko was thriving.

He married his wife, Ruth, in 1950 and they bought a home in the leafy Philadelphia suburb of Chalfont ("James Michener lived there," Ko is proud to point out). They raised a son and two daughters. It was anyone's American dream come true, but especially for the grandson of a Chinese coolie.

It didn't last.

By 1985, when he'd been in business for almost forty years, Ko faced some difficult decisions. The printing business involves a good many chemicals and waste, and the government was cracking down on disposal. His plant was outmoded.* Philadelphia was losing business to other metropolitan areas.

---

outmoded: obsolete, no longer usable

He accepted an offer to relocate to upstate New York, in Glens Falls, near Albany. It would be an expensive move—he'd have to personally guarantee the $1.3 million loan—but the Glens Falls chamber of commerce was offering lots of incentives and his son was interested in continuing the business there.

It all looked good on paper. The reality was a nightmare. Ko says the Glens Falls incentives took longer to get in place than promised. He was forced to shut down the Philadelphia plant before starting the other, so there was loss of income and, worse, a break in the continuity with his best customers. By the time he did get the new plant open it was too late. He went out of business after only a year.

"It was a big decision-making time. I couldn't retire. I hadn't taken out Social Security. So at the age of seventy I had to go get a job and start paying back that million-dollar loan." He adds, "I just didn't feel comfortable with declaring bankruptcy. I just didn't think it was the honorable thing to do, even though it would have been easier."

Lessons learned in training and during the war more than four decades earlier were critical during this trying time.

"In the war I learned to be self-sufficient. I matured. I learned to be a leader. When my business failed I was able to move on, whereas my wife was devastated by the loss."

Ko managed to preserve the plant's assets for his principal creditors, and his lawyers negotiated the settlement of other debts at reduced levels. Continuing to live in the small-town environment with local suppliers still carrying Komak debts on their books wasn't easy, but Wesley and Ruth persevered.

He managed to get a job as a quality-control manager at a local electronics company and applied the stock options he earned toward the debts he owed. Finally, at the age of seventy-six, Wesley retired, saying, "I have no regrets."

He and Ruth now live near their daughters, in Massachusetts. He's editor of *The Glider Towline*, the newsletter of the surviving members of the 325th Glider Infantry Association. It's filled with chatty reminders of coming re-unions and pictures of grandfatherly men in baseball caps bearing the regiment's insignia. One caption reads, "The youth of World War II are the senior citizens of today."

A column called "Taps" gets longer with every issue, as it marks the passing of the glider veterans or their wives.

Ko's only regret is that the lessons of his generation are lost on his grandchildren. He was disappointed when his grandson quit the private school he was attending. Now, however, the young man seems to have found a calling as a carpenter, and Wesley is feeling better about his direction.

However, Wesley Ko reflects the common lament of his generation when he says, "Everything comes too easy. Nowadays you just don't make the effort like you did in our day."

ABOUT THE AUTHOR

Tom (Thomas John) Brokaw (b. 1940) was born in Webster, South Dakota. Brokaw graduated from the University of South Dakota with a degree in political science. From 1960 to 1966 Brokaw worked for various television stations across the country. In 1966 Brokaw joined NBC in Los Angeles, California. Until his retirement from daily broadcasts in 2004, Brokaw hosted the *NBC Nightly News*, which became the most-watched cable or broadcast news program in the country. He continues to work for NBC periodically on special projects.

In his 1998 book, *The Greatest Generation*, Brokaw shares the stories, the struggles, and the triumphs of everyday people, both on the battlefield and at home. In 1999 Brokaw published *The Greatest Generation Speaks,* a collection of reminiscences from those who responded to the first book. In 2006 Brokaw was awarded the prestigious West Point Award for his raising public awareness and understanding of the sacrifices of men and women during World War II and for his war zone news coverage.

THINKING ZONE

A **biography** is a nonfiction work in which the author tells the true events that make up the life of a real person other than himself. Most works characterized as biographies are book-length works, and some are even several volumes. A **biographical sketch** is briefer than a full-length biography. Just as an artist's sketch has all the elements of the finished painting but with less attention to detail, so a written sketch has the elements of a biography but on a smaller scale. Tom Brokaw's book *The Greatest Generation*, from which "Wesley Ko" has been taken, is a compilation of many biographical sketches about people who contributed to the war effort during World War II, whether by joining the military or by serving at home in some way.

As you read, the theme of a work may reveal the **authorial purpose** (or intent), the reason the author composed the work. That purpose may be to correct what the author sees as an injustice or to defend the downtrodden or to present another side of an issue. Sometimes an author states his purpose at the outset; however, often a reader must infer the author's purpose through the specific details he includes (or omits) or the arguments he proposes.

1. *[critical]* What kind of opposition did Wesley Ko face in the military? How did Ko overcome that opposition?

_____

_____

_____

_____

2. *[interpretive]* What difficulty did Wesley Ko face after the war ended? How did he deal with that problem?

_____

_____

_____

_____

3. *[critical]* In what ways would you consider Wesley Ko a hero?

_____

_____

_____

_____

4. *[interpretive]* What do you think is the **authorial purpose** of this **biographical sketch**?

_____

_____

_____

_____

_____

_____

5. *[critical]* Brokaw says that the greatest generation was prepared to face the challenges of World War II by its shared "sense of personal responsibility and . . . commitment to honesty." What do you think had produced these values? What evidence do you find in this biographical sketch to support your answer?

_____

_____

_____

_____

_____

_____

_____

_____

Crown Him
with Many Crowns

Matthew Bridges

Crown Him with many crowns,
The Lamb upon His throne;
Hark! how the heavenly anthem drowns
All music but its own!
Awake, my soul and sing   5
Of Him who died for thee;
And hail Him as thy matchless King
Thro' all eternity.

Crown Him the Lord of love!
Behold His hands and side,—   10
Rich wounds, yet visible above,
In beauty glorified:
No angel in the sky
Can fully bear that sight,
But downward bends his wondering eye   15
At mysteries so bright.

Crown Him the Lord of life!
Who triumphed o'er the grave;
Who rose victorious to the strife
For those He came to save: 20
His glories now we sing,
Who died and rose on high;
Who died eternal life to bring,
And lives that death may die.

Crown Him the Lord of heaven!   25
One with the Father known,
One with the Spirit through Him given
From yonder glorious throne!
To Thee be endless praise,
For Thou for us hast died;   30
Be Thou, O Lord, through endless days
Adored and magnified.

The Ascension. Benjamin West, P.R.A.
From the Bob Jones University Collection

About the Author

Matthew Bridges (1800–1894), who is usually credited with authoring this hymn, was born in Malden, England. He served many years as a rector in the Church of England, during which time he wrote books of history and poetry and also compiled hymns for the church. "Crown Him with Many Crowns" first appeared in *Hymns of the Heart,* published in 1851. The text of the hymn is based on Revelation 19:12: "His eyes were as a flame of fire, and on his head were many crowns." Bridges first published the hymn with six stanzas. However, in 1874 Godrey Thring, a clergyman and hymnodist from Somerset, England, revised it. Because seven is the number of God, he felt there should be seven crowns mentioned in the song. As a result, he wrote the stanza that begins with "Crown Him the Lord of life." This stanza and three of the original stanzas by Bridges are those included in most hymnals.

DAVID AND GOLIATH

To this point in 1 Samuel, the Israelites have been suffering with the consequences of demanding a king at the wrong time. King Saul now rules over Israel. He has proved to be unstable, unwise, and sometimes cruel. The nation needs a leader with courage, integrity, and an unfailing love for God. The Israelites have known the pain and frustration of serving a king they have chosen. In this passage they will meet the king God has chosen.

Now the Philistines gathered together their armies to battle, and were gathered together at Shochoh, which belongeth to Judah, and pitched between Shochoh and Azekah, in Ephesdammim,

2 And Saul and the men of Israel were gathered together, and pitched by the valley of Elah, and set the battle in array against the Philistines.

3 And the Philistines stood on a mountain on the one side, and Israel stood on a mountain on the other side: and there was a valley between them.

4 And there went out a champion out of the camp of the Philistines, named Goliath, of Gath, whose height was six cubits and a span.

5 And he had an helmet of brass upon his head, and he was armed with a coat of mail; and the weight of the coat was five thousand shekels of brass.

6 And he had greaves of brass upon his legs, and a target of brass between his shoulders.

7 And the staff of his spear was like a weaver's beam; and his spear's head weighed six hundred shekels of iron: and one bearing a shield went before him.

8 And he stood and cried unto the armies of Israel, and said unto them, Why are ye come out to set your battle in array? am not I a Philistine, and ye servants to Saul? Choose you a man for you, and let him come down to me.

9 If he be able to fight with me, and to kill me, then will we be your servants: but if I prevail against him, and kill him, then shall ye be our servants, and serve us.

10 And the Philistine said, I defy the armies of Israel this day; give me a man, that we may fight together.

11 When Saul and all Israel heard those words of the Philistine, they were dismayed, and greatly afraid.

12 Now David was the son of the Ephrathite of Bethlehem-Judah, whose name was Jesse; and he had eight sons: and the man went among men for an old man in the days of Saul.

13 And the three eldest sons of Jesse went and followed Saul to the battle: and the names of his three sons that went to the battle were Eliab the firstborn, and next unto him Abinadab, and the third Shammah.

14 And David was the youngest: and the three eldest followed Saul.

15 But David went and returned from Saul to feed his father's sheep at Bethlehem.

16 And the Philistine drew near morning and evening, and presented himself forty days.

17 And Jesse said unto David his son, Take now for thy brethren an ephah of this parched corn, and these ten loaves, and run to the camp to thy brethren;

18 and carry these ten cheeses unto the captain of their thousand, and look how thy brethren fare, and take their pledge.

19 Now Saul, and they, and all the men of Israel, were in the valley of Elah, fighting with the Philistines.

20 And David rose up early in the morning, and left the sheep with a keeper, and took, and went, as Jesse had commanded him; and he came to the trench, as the host was going forth to fight, and shouted for the battle.

21 For Israel and the Philistines had put the battle in array, army against army.

22 And David left his carriage in the hand of the keeper of the carriage, and ran into the army, and came and saluted his brethren.

23 And as he talked with them, behold, there came up the champion, the Philistine of Gath, Goliath by name, out of the armies of the Philistines, and spake according to the same word: and David heard them.

24 And all the men of Israel, when they saw the man, fled from him, and were sore afraid.

25 And all the men of Israel said, Have ye seen this man that is come up? surely to defy Israel is he come up: and it shall be, that the man who killeth him, the king will enrich him with great riches, and will give him his daughter, and make his father's house free in Israel.

26 And David spake to the men that stood by him, saying, What shall be done to the man that killeth this Philistine, and taketh away the reproach from Israel? for who is this uncircumcised Philistine, that he should defy the armies of the living God?

27 And the people answered him after this manner, saying, So shall it be done to the man that killeth him.

28 And Eliab his eldest brother heard when he spake unto the men; and Eliab's anger was kindled against David, and he said, Why camest thou down hither? And with whom

has thou left those few sheep in the wilderness? I know thy pride, and the naughtiness of thine heart; for thou art come down that thou mightest see the battle.

29 And David said, What have I now done? Is there not a cause?

30 And he turned from him toward another, and spake after the same manner: and the people answered him again after the former manner.

31 And when the words were heard which David spake, they rehearsed them before Saul: and he sent for him.

32 And David said to Saul, Let no man's heart fail because of him; thy servant will go and fight with this Philistine.

33 And Saul said to David, Thou are not able to go against this Philistine to fight with him; for thou art but a youth, and he a man of war from his youth.

34 And David said unto Saul, Thy servant kept his father's sheep, and there came a lion, and a bear, and took a lamb out of the flock:

35 And I went out after him, and smote him, and delivered it out of his mouth: and when he arose against me, I caught him by his beard, and smote him, and slew him.

36 Thy servant slew both the lion and the bear: and this uncircumcised Philistine shall be as one of them, seeing he hath defiled the armies of the living God.

37 David said moreover, The Lord that delivered me out of the paw of the lion, and out of the paw of the bear, he will deliver me out of the hand of this Philistine. And Saul said unto David, Go, and the Lord be with thee.

38 And Saul armed David with his armour, and he put an helmet of brass upon his head; also he armed him with a coat of mail.

39 And David girded his sword upon his armour, and he assayed to go; for he had not proved it. And David said unto Saul, I

cannot go with these; for I have not proved them. And David put them off him.

40 And he took his staff in his hand, and chose him five smooth stones out of the brook, and put them in a shepherd's bag which he had, even in a scrip;* and his sling was in his hand: and he drew near to the Philistine.

scrip: bag or satchel

41 And the Philistine came on and drew near unto David; and the man that bare the shield went before him.

42 And when the Philistine looked about, and saw David, he disdained him: for he was but a youth, and ruddy, and of a fair countenance.

43 And the Philistine said unto David, Am I a dog, that thou comest to me with staves?* And the Philistine cursed David by his gods.

staves: plural of *staff*, sturdy cane or stick

44 And the Philistine said to David, Come to me, and I will give thy flesh unto the fowls of the air, and to the beasts of the field.

45 Then said David to the Philistine, Thou comest to me with a sword, and with a spear, and with a shield: but I come to thee in the name of the Lord of hosts, the God of the armies of Israel, whom thou hast defied.

46 This day will the Lord deliver thee into mine hand; and I will smite thee, and take thine head from thee; and I will give the car-

cases of the host of the Philistines this day unto the fowls of the air, and to the wild beasts of the earth; that all the earth may know that there is a God in Israel.

47 And all the assembly shall know that the Lord saveth not with sword and spear: for the battle is the Lord's, and he will give you into our hands.

48 And it came to pass, when the Philistine arose, and came and drew nigh to meet David, that David hasted, and ran toward the army to meet the Philistine.

49 And David put his hand in his bag, and took thence a stone, and slang it, and smote the Philistine in his forehead, that the stone sunk into his forehead; and he fell upon his face to the earth.

50 So David prevailed over the Philistine with a sling and with a stone, and smote the Philistine, and slew him; but there was no sword in the hand of David.

51 Therefore David ran, and stood upon the Philistine, and took his sword, and drew it out of the sheath thereof, and slew him, and cut off his head therewith. And when the Philistines saw their champion was dead, they fled.

52 And the men of Israel and of Judah arose, and shouted, and pursued the Philistines, until thou come to the valley, and the Philistines fell down by the way to Shaaraim, even unto Gath, and unto Ekron.

—1 Samuel 17:1–52

Unit 3 Review

Short Answer

Write the word, phrase, or sentence that best answers the question.

1. *In Search of Honor* has both a prologue and an epilogue, elements that make it a type of what kind of story?

   _____

2. Jacques's description of Latude as "the 'good' monsieur" is an example of what literary device?

   _____

3. The constancy of what gives Jacques the desire to discover its secret for being oblivious to pain and pleasure?

   _____

4. Why was Pierre-Joseph able to be content during his stay in the Bastille?

   _____

5. In Part 2 Robespierre's mysterious character and his reference to the king's placing guards on the street are examples of what type of literary device?

   _____

Multiple Choice

Choose the best answer from the choices given.

_____ 6. *In Search of Honor* is an example of what genre of literature?
   A. fiction
   B. historical fiction
   C. biography
   D. historical biography

7. Where does Jacques live at the writing of the "Prologue"?
   A. England
   B. France
   C. Phillipe's house
   D. Thomas's house

8. In Chapter 5 the reference to the wax as "refusing to yield" is an example of
   A. simile.
   B. metaphor.
   C. foreshadowing.
   D. personification.

9. Pierre-Joseph is able to play the flute from his prison cell because he
   A. hopes to relieve his depression over his circumstances.
   B. is in denial about his situation.
   C. believes that circumstances are irrelevant to his contentment.
   D. is senile from his long imprisonment.

10. The vivid description of Jacques's muscles cramping, his hands stiffening, and the rain beating down on him as he escaped the Bastille are examples of the author's use of
    A. style.
    B. conflict.
    C. foreshadowing.
    D. suspense.

11. Which of the following was *not* a difficulty that Wesley Ko faced?
    A. World War II
    B. starvation
    C. financial bankruptcy
    D. racial prejudice

TRUE/FALSE

If the statement is completely true, write *true*. If any part of the statement is false, write *false*.

_____ 12. The author's description of Latude's extravagant house to imply that Latude is probably wealthy is an example of indirect characterization.

_____ 13. Phillipe would probably consider Danton to be a sympathetic character.

_____ 14. The time and place in which the action of a story occurs do not contribute its setting.

_____ 15. Louis's reference to "Jacob's ladder" is an example of allusion.

_____ 16. Brokaw's authorial purpose in writing "Wesley Ko" is to emphasize personal responsibility and honesty.

MATCHING AND SHORT ANSWER

Match the following literary terms with their correct definitions. After each definition write an example of that type of character from *In Search of Honor*.

A. developing character

B. normative character

C. sympathetic character

D. static character

E. unsympathetic character

_____ 17. a character who presents the proper perspective for the situations of the story

_____

_____ 18. a character with whom you identify

_____

_____ 19. a character who changes as the story progresses

_____

_____ 20. a character with whom you do not identify

_____

_____ 21. a character who does not change as the story progresses

_____

ESSAY

In one paragraph completely answer each question below, using specific examples from the unit.

22. Discuss the proper viewpoint exhibited by Pierre-Joseph through-out the novel. In what ways is Jacques's viewpoint an improper one? What discovery (a truth shared by Pierre-Joseph when he first meets Jacques at the Bastille) finally brings about a change in Jacques's perspective?

_____

_____

_____

_____

_____

_____

_____

_____

_____

_____

23. Do you think Robespierre, who becomes a hero of the Revolution, possesses the qualities of true heroism? Explain your answer. How does Jacques develop into a true hero by the story's end?

_____

_____

_____

_____

_____

_____

_____

_____

_____

4

DISCOVERIES

In his painting Portrait of Louis Pasteur, *Albert Edelfelt (1854–1905), a well-known Finnish portraitist, takes the viewer inside Pasteur's laboratory as the famous scientist observes the contents of his jar.*

Do you think realism was a good style choice for this subject matter?

Besides the portrait's being a representation of what Pasteur looked like, what else does the portrait show about Edelfelt's subject?

Louis Pasteur discovered how to prevent the souring of milk, developed a rabies vaccine, and discovered a great deal about germs and bacteria. How does this painting emphasize his discoveries?

What do you think Pasteur has in the jar?

DISCOVERIES

ANTONY VAN LEEUWENHOEK STARED THROUGH A PRIMITIVE MICROSCOPE TO DISCOVER BACTERIA. SIR FREDERICK G. BANTING AND CHARLES H. BEST FOUND THAT BY ADMINISTERING CONTROLLED AMOUNTS OF INSULIN TO DIABETICS, THE EFFECTS OF THE DISEASE WERE CONTROLLED.

Circa AD 105 in China, Ts'ai Lun mixed and boiled bark and hemp to make paper. These and countless other discoveries—of electricity and DNA and plant respiration and plastics—changed our world. Not all discoveries, however, have the same impact. Some discoveries add to a single person's appreciation of nature; other discoveries evoke a strong emotional response for one individual.

In each of the selections in this unit, you will witness a discovery. The poems evidence a discovery on the part of the author; the story selections show the reader a discovery made by a character. In some stories a character discovers regret for present circumstances but does not alter his beliefs. In others a character confronts a new idea or problem, analyzes it, responds emotionally, and ultimately modifies his behavior in accordance with the discoveries he has made.

Still other characters experience the most important discovery—the comfort and strength afforded those who learn to view the world through eyes of a faith securely founded on an omniscient, omnipotent Savior. Such souls discover that the bleakest of circumstances can take on a radiant hue, and the most difficult of paths can lead to spiritual triumph.

Through studying the characters in the previous unit selections, you have been able to discover the importance of building good friendships, of making right choices, and of evidencing heroism. But what will you do with these discoveries? Will you simply add them to your store of knowledge? Or will you allow what you have learned to change your attitudes, beliefs, and behavior?

Characters' negative examples remind us of the value of learning not only from our personal experiences and discoveries but also from those of others. This truth captures for us one of the most significant reasons for studying good literature. In literature, we are given the opportunity to gain insight through the characters' discoveries, and we can do so without having to stumble over any obstacles or experience any unnecessary pain. Let us then allow the discoveries presented to us in our reading influence us for good.

WE LEARN WISDOM FROM FAILURE MUCH MORE THAN FROM SUCCESS. WE OFTEN DISCOVER WHAT WILL DO BY FINDING OUT WHAT WILL NOT DO; AND PROBABLY HE WHO HAS NEVER MADE A MISTAKE HAS NEVER MADE A DISCOVERY.

—SAMUEL SMILES
SELF-HELP

SHAGO

JAMES POOLER

Shago had a keen, sharp eye, an eye that not only allowed him to pitch a baseball with deadly accuracy but also enabled him to discern the subtle changes of a summer sun. Unfortunately, Shago's friends were not as quick to discover the subtle changes in their friend.

When the summer sun moves its heat a little low in the sky and there's a stir out of doors in the late afternoon's hush, I wonder if the Indian boys still gather under the bluff.

The bluff must be much the same. A gash of naked sand and stone upright for fifty feet and then the slope of green junipers and pines going to cover the top of the hill. And at the foot of the bluff the flat field where the marsh and quack grass grow, fed by the waves that in storms reach up to the very foot of the bluff. And, toward the lake, all those huge rocks, too big for man to move, and reasonless, stand in strange, silent rows for the waves to break on their outer sentinels.

That field was a fine one with the high wind singing in the pines of the bluff overhead and the colder wind outdistancing the waves to come across the rocks and freshen us at our play. Always around us the steady roar of the waves breaking and their hiss as they ran up the slope of sand to die.

The Indian lads must be there, and I know the island boys are. There, with the ebbing of the day and before cows must be sought in their roaming, the lads must join in their game.

We used a ball hard-woven of fisher twine with a rock of rubber for its heart. It was a grand hard ball and our bats were good—they came polished off the Michigan shore, but some of us fancied the island ones

cut and honed of our own woods. Shawn Laferty owned the gloves which the catcher and first baseman wore. And the bases were white driftwood.

Once we had a quarter ball, which one of the resort men bought us, but we played only a few innings before it got lopsided and sorry bits of wood and string flew from it, and we went back to our own wound ball.

It was Shago White, who had a curve that would break your back, who wound the balls. Shago lived in Indian Town, though his mother once was of the Irish. Shago would take twine from the fishing shanties and, with the old bits of hard rubber we carefully saved, wind a ball that was as round as any of the store kind.

When first I played I remember Shago's pitching well. He was not much older than I, but had been playing longer, and already he was a pitcher for at least a few innings of every game. He had feathers for feet, a strong arm, a sure eye. It always was Shago who was picked first if you won the choosing up.

The first time I came to bat, Shago was pitching. I was sick of heart, I was, and shaking and in great fear that I would make a fool of myself and the others would laugh. I still see Shago grinning there and whirling his arm like a windmill and the ball shooting at me and I making a helpless swing, a full ninny! And how I stood, decided to wait the next one out, and Shago blazing another one past me and the umpire calling it a strike.

And I spit on my hands as the older boys did and glared out at Shago. I'll never know if it was my luck or skill, or the kindness of Shago, that I hit the next ball and got on base. For I remember Shago rolled on the sand and laughed and laughed and so did I—except I stood still on the base. I felt a man.

It would have done you who love boys good to see Shago. He was lean and sharp like a knife blade, and there seemed to be the glint of steel in his eyes. But his mouth was merry and was quicker to laugh or shout than any other. There was a strange Indian madness on him, too.

I remember well the day that we had two men on the bases and Shago stopped his windup, pegged the ball to the catcher, and was away running fast to the foot of the bluff. He went up it like smoke up a chimney, only more quietly, and we saw him reach the summit, go swiftly along its edge, pounce, and hold up for us to see a young puppy, one of Pegh Mahone's brood, that might have tumbled down the bluff.

And again a day that the sun in strange complexion was dyeing all the sky and the hill and the rocks beside us, even our faces, with a grand blush, and Shago stopped the game. He would do it often when his side was way ahead by drawing back his arm and throwing the ball far over the catcher's head. It was what he did this evening and ran to a big rock right at the water's edge. We followed Shago up on the rock and sat beside him, perched like gulls. First he pointed out into the deep water where, just below the calm surface, you could see rocks big enough to farm and then he pointed to the sun.

"A blood sun," he said.

"A red sunset, a fine day tomorrow," John Gallagher answered.

"You lie there," said Shago. "A blood sun." And our eyes followed his over the bluff and the world that had grown a strange hue and still.

"A bad sun," said Shago. "Any tug not in by midnight will end on rocks like those. The sun says so."

We all grew still and looked out at the mountain rocks in the lake. Many of us had fathers who were fishermen, and we had some dread of the lake. And we listened to the little waves patting the big rocks. Color was over everything. It was Shago who spoke first.

"We'll have to hurry for the cows," he said. "They'll be restless, and it will be no night to be out late looking for them."

We went together up over the bluff, and toward the cows in the fields and the woods to hurry them home with clods and sticks. There was little shouting that night, for a mood was on us, and when we'd eaten we went to the docks and in the early night counted the tugs. They all were home.

That night the winds quarreled and slammed water on the island from all sides. You could hear the boom of water and the scream of wind when you first awoke the next morning. There were no ball games, for the waves poured through the rocks, up to the foot of the bluff. Beyond, out in deep water where Shago had pointed, you could see between the rolling waves the heads of rocks four times the size of a tug. Big rocks which should not have been lifting their heads up into our world.

It was in my third year of playing there afternoons below the bluff that I saw something strange in Shago. He would squint long from the box before he threw the ball. It always came fast and with a sweep, but

we were learning that if we waited, often we got a walk. As the summer went, they came oftener. Shago, too, was losing his skill at the plate and not hitting as well.

With the next spring we knew. Shago's eyes were red, and his pitching was hard, fast, and with great curves that did not seem to find the plate. Once in a while Shago would steady and pitch and his side never would lose, but by September he was a bad pitcher, a poor hitter, and had taken to playing with the fielders.

That winter, I remember, his mother bought him glasses from a man in Charlevoix, but because we laughed at him with the glint of glass on his dark face he only wore them going home.

The summer that came after found Shago early at the bench, but he no longer pitched. He pretended that he had no liking for that, and a custom grew up that whatever side took Shago always asked him if he would pitch. He would say "No," and would turn to go out into left field close to the bluff where the ball, if hit, never went far. His sight was such that he could not field well, and even when they would pitch easy to him he could not hit.

As fall came on, Shago, who had a pride to him, would come out late after the game had started, pretending he had been busy for his mother. He would sit with the little boys, who hoped to get into the game if we ran short.

School came to an end for him, too. The nuns, soon learning that sight was going from Shago, told his mother that she need not make him study any more, but to send him to school to listen. Shago went for a while, but after they asked him questions a couple of times to see if he were following the work, and he knew none of the answers, he would come no more. We saw him less and less. We found he had gone to work for one of the fishermen, cleaning hooks, which took nimble fingers and which one might do with only a sense of touch.

It was early spring, and a few plucky* crickets already had started their fiddling when Shago came slowly down the single street of St. James to stop in front of us. We stood in the light of the store where candy was sold and where we often met.

---

plucky: spirited

In Shago's hands there were five baseballs. They were wondrously tight in their winding and each as round as ever a baseball was. There never had been the like of such balls on the island.

"You'll be starting the game soon," said Shago. "So I got these ready."

We took them in our hands. We all told Shago how fine they were and thanked him. He stood curling his fingers around one wound so tightly you could feel where strand lay next to strand.

"But aren't you going to bat one?" Shago asked. "I think they have a fine fly to them."

We stood helpless and looked from one to the other. Why were we so thick of head we could not have said we would go for a bat and so changed his thoughts to other things? But we stood there as helpless as once we were at bat when Shago was in fine form. It was Laferty who blurted it out:

"We can't, Shago," he said.

It was night.

ABOUT THE AUTHOR

Not much is known about James S. Pooler (b. 1903), who was born in Sheboygan, Wisconsin. During his childhood Pooler traveled the Great Lakes area with his father, a commercial fisherman. He used his experiences from these times as a background for "Shago." In his early twenties he began writing a column for the *Detroit Free Press*. In 1932 Pooler won a Pulitzer Prize for Reporting for his coverage of the American Legion convention in Detroit. In addition to reporting, Pooler wrote newspaper stories that were sometimes adapted for radio and television.

THINKING ZONE

The way an author creates the story's characters, describes the setting, and builds the atmosphere can give the reader clues as to the author's **tone**, that is, his attitude toward his subject or toward the reader. The tone that an author adopts affects his style as well, making it formal or informal, academic or conversational. The tone of a story can either contribute to an author's message or detract from it. For instance, if an author's tone is overly sarcastic or snide, the reader may not identify with him. You may have read editorials in your local newspaper that struck you as being mean-spirited or antagonistic; you probably assumed that the author of the piece was angry either about the topic or at the person to whom the editorial was directed. You may even have dismissed the person as a crank. If, on the other hand, the author uses a gentler or more sympathetic tone, the reader is more likely to be convinced of the author's message.

1. *[interpretive]* From what point of view is "Shago" told?

   _____

2. *[interpretive]* Why does Shago stop pitching and become a fielder?

   _____

   _____

3. *[interpretive]* How does the author reveal the extent of Shago's visual impairment at the end of the story?

   _____

   _____

4. *[interpretive/critical]* Given the author's **tone** throughout the story, how do you think he feels about his boyhood days?

   _____

   _____

   _____

   _____

5. *[interpretive/critical]* What is the author's tone toward Shago at the beginning of the story? By the end of the story, how does the author feel?

_____

_____

_____

_____

6. *[critical]* What details or events in the story might be said to be symbolic?

_____

_____

_____

_____

_____

_____

7. *[critical]* Though the boys eventually recognize Shago's condition, why do they react the way they do at the end of the story? What is wrong about their reactions?

_____

_____

_____

_____

_____

8. *[appreciative]* Are you aware of the needs of those around you— at school, at home, at church? What could you do for those you think of?

_____

_____

_____

_____

THE LAST LESSON

ALPHONSE DAUDET

Translated anonymously from the French

As in "Shago," the boys in this selection make similar discoveries. As you read, think about what Franz's last lesson really is.

I started for school very late that morning and was in great dread of a scolding, especially because M.* Hamel had said that he would question us on participles, and I did not know the first word about them. For a moment I thought of running away and spending the day out-of-doors. It was so warm, so bright! The birds were chirping at the edge of the woods; and in the open field back of the sawmill the Prussian* soldiers were drilling. It was all much more tempting than the rule for participles, but I had the strength to resist, and hurried off to school.

M.: Monsieur (mə-sœ): French word for "mister"

Prussian: from Prussia, a large, powerful Germanic kingdom that united with other regions as Germany in 1871

When I passed the town hall there was a crowd in front of the bulletin board. For the last two years all our bad news had come from there—the lost battles, the draft, the orders of the commanding officer—and I thought to myself, without stopping:

"What can be the matter now?"

Then, as I hurried by as fast as I could go, the blacksmith, Wachter, who was there with his apprentice reading the bulletin, called after me:

"Don't go so fast, boy; you'll get to your school in plenty of time!"

I thought he was making fun of me and reached M. Hamel's little garden all out of breath.

Usually, when school began, there was a bustle which could be heard out in the street, the opening and closing of desks, lessons repeated in unison, very loud, with our hands over our ears to understand better, and the teacher's great ruler rapping on the table. But now it was all so still! I had counted on the commotion to get to my desk without being seen; but, of course, that day everything had to be as quiet as Sunday morning. Through the window I saw my classmates, already in their places, and M. Hamel walking up and down with his terrible iron ruler under his arm. I had to open the door and go in before everybody. You can imagine how I blushed and how frightened I was.

But nothing happened. M. Hamel saw me and said very kindly:

"Go to your place quickly, little Franz. We were beginning without you."

I jumped over the bench and sat down at my desk. Not till then, when I had got a little over my fright, did I see that our teacher had on his beautiful green coat, his frilled shirt, and the little black silk cap, all embroidered, that he never wore except on inspection and prize days. Besides, the whole school seemed so strange and solemn. But the thing that surprised me most was to see, on the back benches that were always empty, the village people sitting quietly like ourselves; old Hauser, with his three-cornered hat, the former mayor, the former postmaster, and

several others besides. Everybody looked sad; and Hauser had brought an old primer, thumbed at the edges, and he held it open on his knees with his great spectacles lying across the pages.

While I was wondering about it all, M. Hamel mounted his chair, and, in the same grave and gentle tone which he had used to me, said:

"My children, this is the last lesson I shall give you. The order has come from Berlin to teach only German in the schools of Alsace and Lorraine.* The new master comes to-morrow. This is your last French lesson. I want you to be very attentive."

Alsace and Lorraine: eastern French provinces annexed by
  Germany in 1871

What a thunderclap these words were to me!

Oh, the wretches; that was what they had put up at the town hall!

My last French lesson! Why, I hardly knew how to write! I should never learn any more! I must stop there, then! Oh, how sorry I was for not learning my lessons, for seeking birds' eggs, or going sliding on the Saar!* My books that had seemed such a nuisance a while ago, so heavy to carry, my grammar, and my history of the saints were old friends now that I couldn't give up. And M. Hamel, too; the idea that he was going away, that I should never see him again, made me forget all about his ruler and how cranky he was.

Saar: northeastern French river

Poor man! It was in honor of this last lesson that he had put on his fine Sunday clothes, and now I understood why the old men of the village were sitting there in the back of the room. It was because they were sorry, too, that they had not gone to school more. It was their way of thanking our master for his forty years of faithful service and of showing their respect for the country that was theirs no more.

While I was thinking of all this, I heard my name called. It was my turn to recite.

What would I not have given to be able to say that dreadful rule for the participle all through, very loud and clear, and without one mistake? But I got mixed up on the first words and stood there, holding on to my desk, my heart beating, and not daring to look up. I heard M. Hamel say to me:

"I won't scold you, little Franz; you must feel bad enough. See how it is! Every day we have said to ourselves: 'Bah! I've plenty of time. I'll learn it tomorrow.' And now you see where we've come out. Ah, that's the great trouble with Alsace; she puts off learning till tomorrow. Now those fellows out there will have the right to say to you: 'How is it; you pretend to be Frenchmen, and yet you can neither speak nor write your own language?' But you are not the worst, poor little Franz. We've all a great deal to reproach ourselves with.

"Your parents were not anxious enough to have you learn. They preferred to put you to work on a farm or at the mills, so as to have a little more money. And I? I've been to blame also. Have I not often sent you to water my flowers instead of learning your lessons? And when I wanted to go fishing, did I not just give you a holiday?"

Then, from one thing to another, M. Hamel went on to talk of the French language, saying that it was the most beautiful language in the world—the clearest, the most logical; that we must guard it among us and never forget it, because when a people are enslaved, as long as they hold fast to their language it is as if they had the key to their prison. Then he opened a grammar and read us our lesson. I was amazed to see how well I understood it. All he said seemed so easy, so easy! I think, too, that I had never listened so carefully, and that he had never explained everything with so much patience. It seemed almost as if the poor man wanted to give us all he knew before going away and to put it all into our heads at one stroke.

After the grammar, we had a lesson in writing. That day M. Hamel had new copies for us, written in a beautiful round hand; France, Alsace, France, Alsace. They looked like little flags floating everywhere in the schoolroom, hung from the rod at the top of our desks. You ought to have seen how everyone set to work, and how quiet it was! The only sound was the scratching of the pens over the paper. Once some beetles flew in; but nobody paid any attention to them, not even the littlest ones, who worked right on tracing their fishhooks,* as if that was French, too. On the roof the pigeons cooed very low, and I thought to myself:

"Will they make them sing in German, even the pigeons?"

---

tracing their fishhooks: making fishhooklike shapes as practice in forming the letters of the alphabet

---

Whenever I looked up from my writing I saw M. Hamel sitting motionless in his chair and gazing first at one thing, then at another, as if he wanted to fix in his mind just how everything looked in that little schoolroom. Fancy! For forty years he had been there in the same place, with his garden outside the window and his class in front of him, just like that. Only the desks and benches had been worn smooth; the walnut trees in the garden were taller, and the hop vine that he had planted himself twined about the windows to the roof. How it must have broken his heart to leave it all, poor man; to hear his sister moving about in the room above, packing their trunks! For they must leave the country next day.

But he had the courage to hear every lesson to the very last. After the writing, we had a lesson in history, and then the babies chanted their ba, be, bi, bo, bu.* Down there at the back of the room old Hauser had put

on his spectacles and, holding his primer in both hands, spelled the letters with them. You could see that he, too, was crying; his voice trembled with emotion, and it was so funny to hear him that we all wanted to laugh and cry. Ah, how well I remember it, that last lesson!

ba, be, bi, bo, bu (bä, bā, bē, bō, bü): sounds used for practicing French vowels

All at once the church clock struck twelve. Then the Angelus.* At the same moment the trumpets of the Prussians, returning from drill, sounded under our windows. M. Hamel stood up, very pale, in his chair. I never saw him look so tall.

Angelus (an'je-les): church bell rung at noon as a call to prayer

"My friends," said he, "I—I—" but something choked him. He could not go on.

Then he turned to the blackboard, took a piece of chalk, and, bearing down with all his might, he wrote as large as he could:
"*Vive la France!*"*

Vive la France (vēv' lä fräns): Long live France!

Then he stopped and leaned his head against the wall, and, without a word, he made a gesture to us with his hand:
"School is dismissed—you may go."

ABOUT THE AUTHOR

Alphonse Daudet (1840–97), an outstanding French author, certainly did not begin life in prosperous circumstances. Daudet was one of seventeen children, most of whom died when they were young. His family's silk-weaving business failed, plunging the Daudets into financial hardship. To help relieve the financial burden, Daudet left his own studies at the age of sixteen to become a teacher's assistant. This experience was apparently a humiliating one that Daudet later wove into one of his best-known works, *The Little Good-for-Nothing*. His days as an assistant teacher were few, ending as abruptly as they began when he moved to Paris to live with his brother and to focus his efforts on writing. Once he had settled into life in Paris, Daudet began to write; novels, short stories, and dramas established his name as a legend among French writers.

THINKING ZONE

The details that the author uses to describe the setting contribute to **atmosphere,** or the mood of a piece. It is the atmosphere that helps to determine what emotion the reader is supposed to share with the characters. In "Shago" the atmosphere was somber as you read about the baseballs Shago presented to the boys in the darkness. What was the atmosphere as you read "The Last Lesson"? How was it the same or different from the atmosphere of other stories you have read thus far?

1. *[interpretive]* What details from the story give the reader clues about the setting?

   _____

   _____

   _____

   _____

   _____

   _____

   Setting—*The time and place where the action of the story occurs*

2. *[interpretive]* How would you describe the **atmosphere** before Franz arrives at school? Give details from the story to explain your answer.

   _____

   _____

   _____

   _____

   _____

   _____

3. *[literal/interpretive]* How does the knowledge that this is his last French lesson alter Franz's outlook on school and on M. Hamel?

_____

_____

_____

_____

4. *[literal/interpretive]* What sound occurs at the same time that the bell indicates the noon hour? What is significant about this sound?

_____

_____

_____

_____

5. *[interpretive/critical]* What is the atmosphere at the end of the story? How does the author achieve this emotion?

_____

_____

_____

_____

_____

_____

6. *[appreciative]* How would you feel if your country's language were changed suddenly? How might the change affect daily life?

_____

_____

_____

_____

_____

_____

THE WILD DUCK'S NEST

MICHAEL MCLAVERTY

In both the Old and New Testaments, nature is used as a teaching tool. Solomon, for example, used the ant in Proverbs to illustrate industry and to warn against sloth. Our Lord, during His earthly ministry, used the vine, the mustard seed, and the fig tree to illuminate profound spiritual truths. The author of this story carries on this tradition, using nature to help us discover more about the world and about ourselves.

The sun was setting, spilling gold light on the low western hills of Rathlin Island. A small boy walked jauntily along a hoof-printed path that wriggled between the folds of these hills and opened out into a crater-like valley on the cliff-top. Presently he stopped as if remembering something, then suddenly he left the path, and began running up one of the hills. When he reached the top he was out of breath and stood watching streaks of light radiating from golden-edged clouds, the scene reminding him of a picture he had seen of the Transfiguration.* A short distance below him was the cow standing at the edge of a reedy lake. Colm ran down to meet her waving his stick in the air, and the wind rumbling in his ears made him give an exultant whoop which splashed upon the hills in a shower of echoed sound. A flock of gulls lying on the short grass near the lake rose up languidly,* drifting like blown snow-flakes over the rim of the cliff.

Transfiguration: of Christ (Luke 9:28–36)

languidly: slowly, lazily

The lake faced west and was fed by a stream, the drainings of the semi-circling hills. One side was open to the winds from the sea and in winter a little outlet trickled over the cliffs making a black vein in their gray sides. The boy lifted stones and began throwing them into the lake, weaving web after web on its calm surface. Then he skimmed the water with flat stones, some of them jumping the surface and coming to rest on the other side. He was delighted with himself and after listening to his echoing shouts of delight he ran to fetch his cow. Gently he tapped her on the side and reluctantly she went towards the brown-mudded path that led out of the valley. The boy was about to throw a final stone into the lake when a bird flew low over his head, its neck a-strain, and its orange-colored legs clear in the soft light. It was a wild duck. It circled the lake twice, thrice, coming lower each time and then with a nervous flapping of wings it skidded along the surface, its legs breaking the water into a series of silvery arcs. Its wings closed, it lit silently, gave a slight shiver, and began pecking indifferently at the water.

Colm, with dilated eyes, eagerly watched it making for the farther end of the lake. It meandered between tall bulrushes, its body, black and solid as stone against the graying water. Then as if it had sunk it was gone. The boy ran stealthily along the bank looking away from the lake, pretending indifference. When he came opposite to where he had last seen the bird he stopped and peered through the sighing reeds whose shadows streaked the water in a maze of black strokes. In front of him was a soddy islet guarded by the spears of sedge* and separated from the bank by a

narrow channel of water. The water wasn't
too deep—he could wade across with care.

---

sedge: grasslike plants

Rolling up his short trousers he began
to wade, his arms outstretched, and his legs
brown and stunted in the mountain water.
As he drew near the islet, his feet sank in
the cold mud and bubbles winked up at him.
He went more carefully and nervously. Then
one trouser fell and dipped into the water;
the boy dropped his hands to roll it up, he
unbalanced, made a splashing sound, and
the bird arose with a squawk and whirred
away over the cliffs. For a moment the boy
stood frightened. Then he clambered on
to the wet-soaked sod of land, which was
spattered with sea gulls' feathers and bits of
wind-blown rushes.

Into each hummock* he looked, pulling back the long grass. At last he came on the nest, facing seawards. Two flat rocks dimpled the face of the water and between them was a neck of land matted with coarse grass containing the nest. It was untidily built of dried rushes, straw and feathers, and in it lay one solitary egg. Colm was delighted. He looked around and saw no one. The nest was his. He lifted the egg, smooth and green as the sky, with a faint tinge of yellow like the reflected light from a buttercup; and then he felt he had done wrong. He put it back. He knew he shouldn't have touched it and he wondered would the bird forsake the nest. A vague sadness stole over him and he felt in his heart he had sinned. Carefully smoothing out his footprints he hurriedly left the islet and ran after his cow. The sun had now set and the cold shiver of evening enveloped him, chilling his body and saddening his mind.

hummock: a low mound or ridge

In the morning he was up and away to school. He took the grass rut that edged the road for it was softer on the bare feet. His house was the last on the western headland and after a mile or so he was joined by Paddy McFall; both boys, dressed in similar hand-knitted blue jerseys and gray trousers, carried home-made school bags. Colm was full of the nest and as soon as he joined his companion he said eagerly: "Paddy, I've a nest—a wild duck's with one egg."

"And how do you know it's a wild duck's?" asked Paddy slightly jealous.

"Sure I saw her with my own two eyes, her brown speckled back with a crow's patch on it, and her yellow legs—"

"Where is it?" interrupted Paddy in a challenging tone.

"I'm not going to tell you, for you'd rob it!"

"Aach! I suppose it's a tame duck's you have or maybe an old gull's."

Colm put out his tongue at him. "A lot you know!" he said, "for a gull's egg has spots and this one is greenish-white, for I had it in my hand."

And then the words he didn't want to hear rushed from Paddy in a mocking chant, "You had it in your hand! . . . She'll forsake it! She'll forsake it! She'll forsake it!" he said, skipping along the road before him.

Colm felt as if he would choke or cry with vexation.

His mind told him that Paddy was right, but somehow he couldn't give in to it and he replied: "She'll not forsake it! She'll not! I know she'll not!"

But in school his faith wavered. Through the windows he could see moving sheets of rain—rain that dribbled down the panes filling his mind with thoughts of the lake creased and chilled by wind; the nest sodden and black with wetness; and the egg cold as a cave stone. He shivered from the thoughts and fidgeted with the inkwell cover, sliding it backwards and forwards mechanically. The mischievous look had gone from his eyes and the school day dragged on interminably.* But at last they were out in the rain, Colm rushing home as fast as he could.

interminably: unendingly

He was no time at all at his dinner of potatoes and salted fish until he was out in the valley now smoky with drifts of slanting rain. Opposite the islet he entered the water. The wind was blowing into his face, rustling noisily the rushes heavy with the dust of rain. A moss-cheeper, swaying on a reed like a mouse, filled the air with light cries of loneliness.

The boy reached the islet, his heart thumping with excitement, wondering did the bird forsake. He went slowly, quietly, on to the strip of land that led to the nest. He rose on his toes, looking over the ledge to see if he could see her. And then every muscle tautened. She was on, her shoulders hunched up, and her bill lying on her breast as if she were asleep. Colm's heart hammered wildly in his ears. She hadn't forsaken. He was about to turn stealthily away. Something happened. The bird moved, her neck straightened, twitching nervously from side to side. The boy's head swam with lightness. He stood transfixed. The wild duck with a panicky flapping, rose heavily, and flew off towards the sea. . . . A guilty silence enveloped the boy. . . . He turned to go away, hesitated, and glanced back at the bare nest; it'd be no harm to have a look. Timidly he approached it, standing straight, and gazing over the edge. There in the nest lay two eggs. He drew in his breath with delight, splashed quickly from the island, and ran off whistling in the rain.

┌─ ABOUT THE AUTHOR ─────────────────────────

   Michael McLaverty (1907–92), who was born in Monaghan, Ireland, graduated from The Queen's University of Belfast, Northern Ireland, in 1933 and was married that same year. McLaverty's ability to understand young people stems not only from his being a father of four children but also from his experiences as headmaster of St. Thomas's Secondary School in Belfast. He is a well-received author who has had three of his novels translated into other languages.

THINKING ZONE

In Unit 1 you learned about the story plot. All plots share common elements and tend to follow a basic sequence. Over the course of the next three lessons, you will learn the elements that contribute to plot structure.

When telling a story, a storyteller tends to give some background so that his readers can acclimate themselves to the story. Most of the time, the **exposition** is the first element to occur. The exposition introduces the reader to the setting, characters, and situation within a story. Think of the fairytale formula: "Once upon a time, in a land far, far away (setting), there lived a beautiful princess (character) who was very sad (situation). . . ." Often occurring after the exposition, the **inciting incident** sets the rest of the plot in motion. Sometimes the order of these two elements is reversed. An example of this reversal of exposition and inciting incident is seen in O. Henry's "After Twenty Years," in which the inciting incident (the man meeting the policeman) occurs before the exposition (the man explains the bargain with Jimmy Wells).

Identifying plot elements requires careful reading and critical thinking. You can make the process easier by thinking about the literary elements you have studied and how they correspond to the various points of each story's plot.

Plot—*a series of events arranged to tell a story*

1. *[interpretive]* Where in the story does the **exposition** occur?

   _____

   _____

   _____

   _____

2. *[interpretive]* What is the **inciting incident**?

   _____

   _____

   _____

   _____

   _____

3. *[literal]* What is the setting of "The Wild Duck's Nest"?

_____

_____

4. *[critical]* What is the tone of the author toward nature? How do
you know?

_____

_____

Tone—*an author's attitude toward his subject or toward the reader*

5. *[critical]* What is the tone of the author toward Colm? Is he
sympathetic or critical?

_____

_____

_____

_____

6. *[critical]* Why does Colm feel regret about picking up the egg?

_____

_____

_____

7. *[interpretive]* What is the significance of what Colm sees when he
returns to the nest?

_____

_____

8. *[appreciative]* Have you ever made a bad decision in haste like
Colm did? How did you try to make things right?

_____

_____

_____

_____

HASTRMAN

JAN NERUDA

Translated from the Czech by Edith Pargeter

In this story the eccentric Mr. Rybář makes a startling discovery about his financial worth. It is this discovery that leads him to a new realization about himself and those around him.

He always walked with hat in hand, let the season threaten frost-stroke or heat-stroke; the greatest concession he ever made was to hold his low-crowned, rounded hat with the wide brim over his head like a parasol. His gray hair was smoothly combed to his skull, and drawn together behind in a queue* so firmly compressed and bound that it did not even wag—this must have been one of the last queues in Prague, for there were then no more than two or three of them left.

---
queue (kyo͞o): a pigtail at the back of the neck

His thin, slight little body was enveloped in a green frock-coat, which had only short fronts, but descended behind in tails so long that they slapped Mr. Rybář* on his emaciated* calves. A white waistcoat covered his stooped breast, black trousers reached only to just below his knees, where two silver buckles gleamed, and below these were snow-white stockings down to the second pair of silver buckles on his large, shambling* shoes. Whether these shoes were sometimes replaced by new ones I don't know, but they always looked as though the leather from them had been taken from the roof of a very old cab.

Rybář (rē′barzh)

emaciated: skinny

shambling: awkward or unsteady

The withered, pointed face of Mr. Rybář was illuminated by an eternal smile. Walking through the streets, he presented an odd spectacle. At every twenty paces he would stop and look round to right and left. It was as though his thoughts were not within him, but walked respectfully a pace behind, and were always entertaining him with some flash of wit, so that Mr. Rybář had to smile and look round from time to time at the jokers. When he greeted anyone, he lifted only the forefinger of his right hand into the air, and gave a thin whistle. The same soft whistling was heard also whenever he began to speak, and he regularly began with "Zhaw!" which had an affirmative* significance.

---
affirmative: positive

Mr. Rybář lived in Deep Street, just on the left beneath the prospect-tower on Petřín.* Even if he had almost reached his own home, if he caught sight of any strangers just turning to the right towards Hradčany,* he always went after them. When they stood on the prospect-tower and admired the beauty of our Prague, he stood beside them, lifted his finger, and whistled: "Zhaw, the sea!—Why don't we live by the sea!" Then he would follow them into the castle, and when the strangers admired the walls of St. Václav's* chapel, studded with semi-precious stones, he whistled again, and said: "You know what I think? Here in Bohemia a shepherd throws a stone after his herd, and the stone is often worth more than the whole herd!" He never made any other observations to them.

Petřín (pet´ərzh-in)
Hradčany (hräd´chä-nē)
St. Václav's (vät´slävz)

Because of his name, and his green coat,* and because of this cry of "The sea!" we called him "Hastrman." But, old and young, we all respected him. Mr. Rybář was a justiciary* from somewhere by Turnov, now retired on a pension. Here in Prague he lived with a young kinswoman of his, who was married to an official in a modest position and had already two or three children. It was rumored that Mr. Rybář was immensely rich, not so much in money, however, as in jewels. In his room he had, it was said, a tall black cupboard standing, and this cupboard was full of shallow, square black boxes, big ones, and the interior of every box was divided into squares with white pasteboard, and in each square, on a bed of cotton-wool, a jewel lay gleaming. There were people who had seen them. They said he had found and collected them all himself on Mount Kozák. We children used to tell one another, too, that when they washed the floor at the Šajvls'* house—these young relatives of Mr. Rybář were called Šajvl—they scattered over it, in place of sand, fine-ground sugar. On Saturday, which was cleaning day, we always desperately envied the Šajvl children. Once I sat above the moat,* to the left beyond the Bruska Gate, quite near to Mr. Rybář. He used to go there for an hour on every fine day, sit down comfortably in the grass, and smoke a short pipe. On that occasion two older students happened to come by. One of them spluttered, and said: "That one's smoking Mum's wadded jacket!" From

that time forth I considered the smoking of Mum's wadded jacket as a luxury which only the wealthiest of people could allow themselves.

his name, and his green coat: His name means "fisherman," and his green coat and braid were like those of the legendary hastrman, a water goblin.
justiciary (jŭ-stish´ē-er´ē): judge
Šajvls' (shä´yə-velz)
moat: a protective ditch surrounding a fortification

He walked, then, our Hastrman—but no, we won't call him that, since we're no longer children!—Mr. Rybář walked always along the Bruska ramparts.* If he met any of the canons,* who were also in the habit of taking their constitutionals there, he would stop and exchange a few friendly words with them. Once—I loved to listen to what grown-up people said to one another—I heard him talking with two canons who were sitting on a bench there. He was standing. They talked about "France" and something called "liberty," strange words in themselves. Suddenly Mr. Rybář lifted his finger and whistled: "Zhaw, I hold with Rosenau! Rosenau says: 'Liberty is like those rich foods and potent wine on which strong natures that are used to them thrive and grow stronger, but which only debauch,* intoxicate and ruin feeble constitutions.'"

---

ramparts: protective earth embankments

canons: the Roman Catholic clergy

debauch: corrupt

And then he waved his hat and went away.

The bigger canon, a fat man, asked then: "Who is this Rosenau he's always talking about?"

The smaller, but equally fat, canon replied: "A writer—most probably a writer."

But I remember this sentence as the sum of the entire higher wisdom. Of Rosenau and of Mr. Rybář I entertained the same exalted impression. When as a growing boy I took up a variety of books into my own hands, I found that Mr. Rybář had indeed quoted very faithfully on this occasion. But with this variation: that the judgment he had quoted was written not by Rosenau, but by someone called Rousseau.* Evidently unkind chance had misled Mr. Rybář by throwing in his way some frivolous printer's error.

Rousseau (rōō-sō´): French philosopher and writer

But he did not forfeit my respect on that account. A good, a very good man!

It was on a sunny August day, about three o'clock in the afternoon. The people who were walking along Spur Street suddenly stood at gaze; those who were merely standing outside their houses called in haste to those inside; customers hurried out of the shops. All of them were gazing after Mr. Rybář as he marched away down the hill.

"He's going somewhere to show off his riches," said Mr. Herzl, the innkeeper at the Two Suns.

"I declare!" cried Mr. Vitouš,* the shopkeeper on the corner. "Things must be bad, he's taking them off to sell them!" I'm sorry to have to report that Mr. Vitouš did not enjoy a very good reputation among the neighbors. It was said of him that once already he'd been near to bankruptcy, and even today your good Little Quarter citizen looks upon a bankrupt as totally different from the rest of humanity.

Vitouš (vi´touch)

But Mr. Rybář marched calmly on, a shade more quickly than on other days. Under his left arm he carried one of those square black boxes about which there existed so many legends. He clutched it firmly against his body, so that the hat he carried in the same hand was clamped against his thigh. In his right hand he carried a Spanish cane with a flat knob of ivory, which indicated that Mr. Rybář was going somewhere on a visit, for never at any other time did he carry a stick. When anyone greeted him he waved his stick, and whistled much more loudly than on other days.

He walked down Spur Street, crossed St. Nicholas's Square, and turned into the Žamberecký* house. There, on the second floor, lived a grammar school professor, Mr. Mühlwenzel, a mathematician and student of natural science, a man of unusually thorough education for those days. The visit did not last long.

Žamberecký (zhäm´bər-et´skē)

The professor was in a good humor. His powerful, compact body had just enjoyed the refreshment of an afternoon nap. His long gray hair, encircling a bald crown, stood on end in all directions, in comfortable disorder. His blue, intelligent and always kindly eyes were gleaming. His cheeks, invariably ruddy, now glowed. Those broad, benevolent cheeks were rather strongly marked by small-pox, and provided the professor with a pretext for constant jokes. "That's the way of the world," he would say. "If a girl smiles, and she has one dimple in her cheek, they say 'How charming!' When I smile I have a hundred dimples, but all they say is what a fright I am!"

He waved Mr. Rybář to the sofa, and asked: "What can I do for you?"

Mr. Rybář laid his box on the table and lifted the lid. A sparkle of variegated stones caught the light.

"I should—I only—These things—about what would their value be?" he stammered.

Then he sat down and leaned his chin on the knob of his cane.

The professor regarded the stones. Then he took out one dark one, weighed it in his hand, and examined it against the light. "That's moldavite,"* he said.

---

moldavite (mol´de-vīt): glass of meteoric origin

"What?"

"Moldavite."

"Zhaw, moldavite," whistled Mr. Rybář. In his face it could plainly be read that he now heard this word for the first time in his life.

"That would be a good item for our school collection, they're rather scarce now. You could sell it to us."

"Well, we'll see about that. About how much—"

"We could give you three zlatkas* for it, in twenties. What do you say?"

---

three zlatkas (zlät´kəs): small sum of money

"Three zlatkas!" Mr. Rybář whistled thinly. His chin jerked upward, then fell back again onto the knob of his stick. "And the rest?" he whispered after a pause, from a throat suddenly constricted.

"Chalcedony, jasper, amethyst, smoke-quartz*—there's nothing of value here."

---

chalcedony (kal-sed´ən-ē) . . . smoke-quartz: gems with less value than precious stones

---

After some minutes Mr. Rybář was again seen at the corner of Spur Street. He marched slowly up the hill. For the first time his neighbors saw him with his hat upon his head. The broad brim was pulled low upon his forehead, the Spanish cane dragged its tip along the ground and rattled over the pavement. He took no notice of anyone, he didn't whistle even once. On this journey he did not even look round. Plainly today not one of his thoughts was frolicking about outside him, they were all within him, deep within.

He did not go out of the house again that day, neither to the ramparts nor towards Bruska. And it was such a beautiful day!

It was almost midnight. The heaven was blue as at morning, the moon shone with its proudest, most magical radiance, the stars scintillated* like white sparks. Petřín was covered with a resplendent* silver mist, a flood of silver lay over the whole of Prague.

---

scintillated: twinkled

resplendent: brilliant

The smiling light flowed into Mr. Rybář's little room by both wide-open windows. At one of these stood Mr. Rybář, motionless as a statue. From below murmured the weirs* of the Vltava,* in a long, steady thunder. Did the old man hear them?

---

weirs (wērz): river dams

Vltava (vul´tä-vä): a Czech river

Suddenly he shook himself. "The sea!—Why have we no sea?" he whispered, and his lips were trembling.

Perhaps his own grief surged in him like the waves of the sea.

"Well!—" He jerked himself away from the window and turned towards the room. On the floor lay the open boxes, and his gaze lit upon them. Slowly he took up the nearest of them and plucked out of it a handful of stones. "Pebbles—just pebbles!" and he flung them through the open window.

Down below there was a crash and a splintering of glass. Today Mr. Rybář hadn't even remembered that there was a greenhouse down there in the garden.

"Uncle, whatever are you doing?" cried a pleasant young voice outside, evidently from the next window.

Mr. Rybář took an involuntary pace backwards.

The door creaked, and in came Mr. Šajvl. Perhaps it was the beauty of the night that had kept him so late at the window. Perhaps he had noticed in his old uncle signs of an unwonted disquiet,* and heard from his little room the sounds of an activity which had lasted for some time. Perhaps, even, the old man's heavy sighs had flown in to him through the open window.

---

unwonted disquiet: unusual lack of peace

"Uncle, you surely don't want to throw out all those beautiful stones?"

The old man's body twitched. He whispered, staring intently towards Petřín: "They're of no value—mere pebbles!"

"I know they have no great value in money, I recognized that myself. But they have a value, all the same, for us and for you. You collected them all yourself, at the expense of a great deal of effort—Uncle, please leave them all for my children. They'll learn from them, you'll explain all about them, how you gathered them—"

"But perhaps you've been thinking," whispered the old man again, in a labored monotone, "that I was rich—and indeed, I thought—"

"Uncle," said Mr. Šajvl in a firm but very soft voice, and clasping the old man's hand, "do you think we're not rich in you? My children would have no grandfather, my wife would be fatherless, if we hadn't got you. Surely you see how happy we are around you, you are our blessing in the house—"

Suddenly the old man drew away and walked back to the same window at which he had been standing before. His mouth was shaking, he felt in his eyes an indescribable pressure. He gazed out, seeing nothing distinctly, for everything glittered like a distillation* of diamonds, everything was surging into waves—up to his window—up to his eyes—the sea!—the sea!

---

distillation: a liquid condensed from vapor; a purified form of a substance

---

I won't tell any more; I can't.

┌─ ABOUT THE AUTHOR ──────────────────

Jan Neruda (1834–91) was born in Prague, where he also studied and became a schoolmaster. There he wrote for the newspaper and became influential in the realms of literary and theatrical criticism. However, it is for his accomplishments in writing prose tales and poetry that he is considered to be one of the greatest Czech writers of all time. But, in spite of his success as a writer, Neruda's personal life was a failure. He experienced a shattered romance, several unsuccessful career attempts, frequent illnesses, and a lonely life—circumstances that undoubtedly contributed to his choice of unhappiness as a frequent theme of his writing.

THINKING ZONE

In "The Wild Duck's Nest," you studied the exposition and inciting incident within a plot's structure. A good author arranges the plot elements of a story to lead the reader to a particular conclusion or idea, and he includes or omits facts to that same end. One way in which an author does this is by the inclusion of certain events in the rising and falling actions of a story or drama. **Rising action** involves the events following the inciting incident and leading up to the crisis, while **falling action** includes events after the crisis and continues to the end of the story. In "The Wild Duck's Nest," for example, the rising action takes place after Colm sees the wild duck (the inciting incident). He follows its flight path, treks after it on foot through muck and mire, and searches carefully amid the tall grass. The crisis is probably when Colm touches the egg and immediately realizes his mistake. The falling action is then the boy's fretting over whether the duck will forsake the nest. McLaverty's rising action about how the boy searched for the duck is evidence that the author wants the reader to be sympathetic to the boy; the events in the falling action are similar in that they lead the reader to believe that the boy meant no harm to the duck or the egg. How would your sympathies have been different had McLaverty related that Colm had been warned repeatedly not to touch a duck's egg or that he and Paddy had once tampered with a nest and seen the mother duck forsake the nest, killing all of the young? Always keep in mind that a story's author controls everything about the tale—including what you think about it.

> **Crisis**—*the major turning point for the protagonist*
>
> **Inciting incident**—*incident that sets the rest of the plot in motion*

1. *[literal]* What rumor exists about Mr. Rybář?

   _____

   _____

2. *[interpretive]* What does Mr. Rybář do that supports or refutes the rumors?

   _____

   _____

   _____

   _____

   _____

3. *[interpretive]* What is the crisis of the story?

_____

_____

_____

_____

4. *[critical]* Much of the story is exposition, introducing Mr. Rybář and filling the reader in on his characteristics. The inciting incident occurs when Mr. Rybář decides to go to Professor Mühlwenzel's home. What events are included in the **rising action** of the story? What events make up the **falling action**?

_____

_____

_____

_____

_____

5. *[interpretive/critical]* What is the theme of this story? What other story (from another unit) has a similar theme?

_____

_____

_____

_____

6. *[appreciative]* Do you find Mr. Rybář an admirable character? Explain your answer.

_____

_____

_____

_____

You've Got to Learn

Robert Murphy

Like Colm in "The Wild Duck's Nest," the hero of this story learns something through the natural world. His struggle, however, is more intense; his discovery, more personal; and his response, ultimately life changing.

It was a little after dawn when the big dog otter's broad, whiskered muzzle broke the calm and flawless mirror of the lake. A widening circle of ripples slid away from him, and he reared half length from the water to look about. The near shore was dim and quiet; on the far shore, the spruce and hemlock made a dark band against the paling sky. The otter whistled, cocked his head to the rolling echoes, and dropped back into the water again. He was an animal of great and happy vitality;* he began diving and rolling, with movements as effortless and fluid as a dance, hardly disturbing the calmness of the water.

vitality: energy

Presently, he vanished as silently as he had appeared. A swift line of bubbles followed him toward the banks; he dived deeper for the submerged entrance of the burrow, followed it above water line, and in the dark den bounded by roots found his mate with the one pup beside her, and waked them both. There was a short, good-natured scuffle among the three, and then they pushed the pup before them down the tunnel. When they all appeared on the lake's surface, the pup tried to climb upon his mother's back and ride. She shook him off and ducked him when he whimpered, and they began to hunt the bank. They hunted with great thoroughness, from surface to bottom, exploring every hole and cranny, every root hollow and crack among the stones, finding a few crawfish and an occasional frog. These were some easy kills and they let the pup make most of them. His little belly began to bulge, and his mother, growing hungry, left them to catch a pickerel in deeper water and bring it in. They climbed out on the bank and shared it; then, gleaming and sleek from the water, they rolled and galloped about, hissing at one another with mock ferocity.

Day stole in upon them. Out on the lake, the trailing mists of night thinned and vanished; the serrated* line of spruces on the distant shore took on depth and shape in the strengthening light. As the long rays of the sun fell on the otters, they gave over their play, cleaned their fur, and went into the water again. They continued up the lake toward one of the streams which fed it. When they reached the stream mouth, the mother and the pup swung away along the shore line. The otter remembered the great brown trout which lived above the bend of the stream, and left them. The trout was old and wise, and the otter had missed it so many times that the contest between them had become a fascinating game.

serrated: uneven

It was characteristic of the otter that he didn't go directly, his mind fixed on the trout. He zigzagged to and fro across the stream, playing as he went. When he came out of the water to cross the rocks at the first shallows, he heard the distant barking of a dog, up the lake in the direction his mate

and the pup had gone. He hesitated for a moment and went on.

He rounded the bend carefully, and began his stalk of the trout. He knew it would be lying like a shadow a little above the sandy bottom in the rushing green gloom of the pocket under a great gray rock. It would be facing upstream, and he would gain an advantage by coming up from the rear. He stretched out full length and, paddling gently and slowly with his forepaws, slid through the water like a stealthy shadow, close to the bank and halfway to the bottom. He came to the corner of the rock and paused, sank until his belly softly scraped the sand, and became one with the bottom's shadows; then sinuous* as a snake, he began to flow around the rock. He saw the trout several yards away, hanging motionless, and tensed for the spring.

sinuous: winding

The trout caught a slight movement of the otter's shadowy form in the tail of its eye. It drifted a little farther out and swung quartering to him; the otter arched his back swiftly, thrust against the water and darted in. An explosive burst of power sent the trout to the surface; the otter's teeth scored a thin bloody line on its side and the power of its tail stroke rolled him over and over. The trout reached the surface and shattered it by a leap, and the otter righted himself and breached* for air. Although a wild chase upstream and through the rapids was as much a part of the game as the stalk, this time the otter didn't follow. He lay for a moment resting, his sleek head dappled by the sunlight falling through the leaves, and then remembered the barking of the dog.

breached: broke the surface

His game with the trout was over. He started swiftly downstream and came to its mouth. Good fishing water was there, but he didn't hesitate; he turned up the lake. As he rounded the bend, he saw, fifty yards away, the head of his mate break water a good distance from the shore. The pup was just sliding down the bank; and, as the otter watched, the brown-and-white shape of the dog ran out of the hemlocks toward the pup and snapped at it. The pup was startled and confused; it scrambled between the dog's legs, turned again, and leaped from the bank. The dog leaped after it with a great splash; and, because the pup had lost time and couldn't get out of the shallows, the dog's long jaw closed on it and it was tossed into the air.

The otter was moving before the dog left the bank, swimming with desperate speed. As the pup curved into the air, a boy ran out on the bank, yelling, and although the otter avoided man above any other creature, he paid no attention to the boy now. He reached the dog a little before his mate, as it leaped for the falling pup, and, rising beneath it, fastened upon its throat. The female swirled away from them, getting behind the pup and driving it before her out into the lake.

The dog reared to free its throat, but the otter overbalanced it, fighting with deadly coolness to get it into deeper water. He was all about it, attacking and slipping away with disconcerting swiftness always maneuvering it a little farther out. The boy on the bank realized this; he grabbed a branch to use as a club, and, jumping from the bank, began to splash toward them. The otter saw the boy coming and pulled the dog into deeper water. The dog tried wildly to free itself, but the otter fastened implacably* on its haunches, pulled it down and entangled it in a pile of brush on the bottom. The dog struggled desperately in a world alien to it, but in which the otter was at home. But it was trapped; the air in its lungs fled in silver bubbles to the surface, and the otter struck again.

implacably: relentlessly; unyieldingly

Standing up to his chest in the water, Andy Gates stared in helpless anguish at the spot where the dog had gone down. He saw the bubbles burst to the surface, and, a short time later, a swirl far out where the otter breached for air as it followed its mate and the pup. At first he couldn't believe that the dog wouldn't come up again. But time drew out and realization finally came upon him; he dropped the branch he was holding, his fists clenched at his sides and his blue eyes filled with tears. The world about him was suddenly a new and terrible place. He forgot that the dog had been brash and foolishly quarrelsome, that no one had ever been able to teach it anything, and that it had usually been a nuisance. All that he remembered was his brother, standing by the gate before he left for the South Pacific, saying, "Take care of the pup, Andy. We'll make a bird dog of him when I get back."

He didn't realize that Joe, who knew the dog would never amount to anything, had said that to make them feel closer to each other for a moment and hold off the threatening tears, to make the parting easier for them both. The dog was a trust Joe had placed upon him, his most immediate link with his brother, and he had let it be killed. He turned and stumbled out of the water, tears blurring his sight. When his feet found the hard-packed surface of the path, he started along it toward home, stumbling a little now and then. There was an aching emptiness within him, an emptiness which seemed to have swallowed up all his strength; halfway up the long hill, he had to stop, and stood panting, unconscious of the dry fragrance of sun-warmed hemlock on the morning air.

He stopped crying after a while, and the world slowly came back to him. He grew aware of the birds that moved about him, the leaf shadows on the path, and the

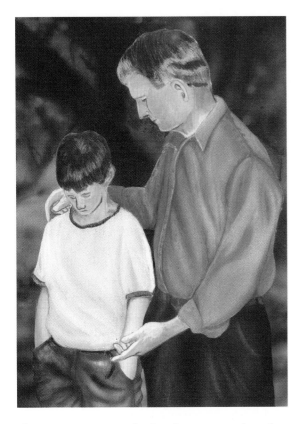

"Trouble, Andy?" he asked.

The boy's chin trembled. "Nicky," he said. "There was an otter—" He couldn't go on. He began to cry again, and suddenly went to his father as he hadn't done for years, and leaned against him, crying. "He went after the little one," he said, shaking with sobs, "and the big one drowned him. And Joe—" He couldn't talk about Joe.

"Joe would understand it, boy," his father said, sliding an arm around him. "Joe would know you couldn't help it."

"I was keeping him for Joe," Andy said. "Joe left him with me. He was Joe's and mine." He began to cry violently again.

"Joe's and mine," he repeated, remembering Joe at the gate, going away. "I'll kill him!" he burst out, thumping his father's broad chest.

"I'll find him and kill him!"

The man started to speak and checked himself, realizing the futility of words. The boy was extraordinarily moved; it was useless to talk against an emotion so deep that he could only guess at it. Time would have to smooth it out—time and what patient understanding he could give. The man was silent for a long time, holding the boy in the crook of his arm.

"Supper, Andy," he said finally. "Get ready for supper, boy."

"I don't want any supper, dad," Andy said. "I—I couldn't eat any supper."

"All right," Gates said. "Go along up to your room, then. Go up the front stairs. I'll tell mother you won't be down."

The boy went into the house; after waiting for a few minutes, Gates went around to the back door and into the warm kitchen. Mrs. Gates was taking a pie from the oven. She looked around, smiled, and straightened up to put the pie on top of the stove. She was small and very neat; her movements

slow movement of clouds across the sky. But he didn't go on. He sat down beside the path, dry-eyed now, but the emptiness hadn't gone, and he saw his surroundings as though from a great distance. Time stopped as his mind tried to rationalize the dog's death and soften the shock of it. The afternoon was growing late when he crossed the top of the hill and saw the farm in the little valley below, the big barn and the sprawling house among the willows, the file of ducks moving up from the stream shining white in the lowering sun, the cows coming in, and his father walking slowly between the house and the barn.

His father saw him and waited with his hands tucked into the top of his Levis. Gates was a kindly and unhurried man; he looked at the boy's face and didn't mention the chores that he'd done himself.

were deft and quick, and her eyes were blue like the boy's.

"Andy won't be down, Helen," Gates said. "We'd better eat without him."

"Why?" she asked. "What's the matter?"

"Well," Gates said. He took off his hat, hung it behind the door and thought a moment. "That fool dog," he said finally, "got himself killed by an otter. There was a young one, I think, and he went for it. Andy is—I've never seen him so worked up. Joe must have said something about taking care of the dog, and Andy thinks he's let Joe down. He's going to kill the otter, he says."

"But it's not like him," she said. "He doesn't just kill things, Harry."

"No," Gates said. "He's not a cruel boy."

"You'll have to talk to him," she said. "I don't want him to be that way. Vengeful like, I mean."

"It's not revenge," Gates said. "It's—he's—" He shook his head, irritated by his inarticulateness.* "This is a deep thing, Helen. He'll have to work it out himself. Maybe he'll kill that otter, but I hope not. If he kills it, then I'll have to talk to him."

---

inarticulateness: inability to speak

She looked at him, puzzled. "What do you mean, Harry?"

"That's the trouble," he said, exasperated. "I don't know what I mean. I can't say, I just feel it. Let's eat, shall we?"

"All right," she said, and began to fill their plates. Upstairs, the boy lay on his bed. The picture of Joe in his uniform smiled at him from the bureau, but he had stopped looking at it. He felt that he couldn't look at it again until he'd found the otter. As his father had said, he wasn't a cruel boy, but all his emotions confirmed the decision, made so suddenly, that the otter must pay with

its life for the life of the dog. The justice of the matter, the fact that the otter had been defending the pup, never occurred to him. Many plans went through his mind, but there was no pleasure, no anticipation of exciting sport, connected with any of them.

He went about his hunting with a singleness of purpose unusual in a boy, with a definite and unvarying schedule. First he'd do the chores, carefully and thoroughly, then get his old single-shot .22 rifle and go out. At first, he spent a lot of time at the lake, hiding near the place where the dog had been drowned. He knew, from remembered bits of Gates's talk, that otters didn't stay in one place, but made a wide, periodic circle about the ponds and streams of the countryside. Sooner or later, he thought, they'd come past him again. He spent days hidden among the hemlocks, and, although he learned a great deal about other animals and birds, he never saw the otters.

The thought came to him finally that they might have passed near dawn, before he got there, or after dusk, when he couldn't see them or had left for home. For several days, disappointment took all the energy out of him; he stayed at home, and his mother thought, with relief, that he'd given up.

"I'm glad it's over, Harry," she said to Gates. "It wasn't like a boy to act like that, going wherever he went, so regular all the time. It was more like a funny little old man."

But Gates had been quietly watching the boy, and he shook his head. "No," he said. "He's not through yet. He's just trying to get away from the place."

Gates was right; the boy was deciding that he would have to move about, to find the otters' route and intercept them somewhere. The place where the dog had died

had held him through a wistful, boyish hope that somehow it might come back again. But the bond weakened; reality came closer to him than it had ever come before, and, as hope died, some of his boyishness died with it. He finally broke away from the place and made his first circuit of the lake.

He went too fast at first and found nothing. The otters left very little indication of their passing along the shore line—a few fish scales and bones in widely separated places, a single rare pad mark in damp ground not covered by leaves or vines. On his first trip up the shore he found nothing. Slowing down and going very carefully, he found faint sign at last, and knew how painstakingly he would have to search from then on. He found the place where they left the lake, the stream they used, and how far they followed before leaving it.

In time he knew, between the actual points where they touched and guesses at the routes which connected these points, the otters' entire twenty-five-mile circuit of the country. It was an achievement in woodcraft which few men could have accomplished, because few men would have had the patience or the time. He had covered a tremendous amount of country; he was well scratched by briers, but he was brown and strong, and had filled out surprisingly.

He changed, little by little, during those weeks. The boyish heedlessness with which he had formerly moved through the woods was gone. He grew somewhat like an Indian, a part of the woods rather than an alien presence, drifting quietly about with a mind empty of thought, but blank and clean for the impressions which flowed into it. Time ceased to exist for him. He took no more account of hours than a squirrel, and learned the causes of sounds and the little chains of circumstance which stem from them—the techniques of the hunters and the defenses of the hunted. He saw young grouse freeze and blend with the leaves when the shadow of a hawk swung over them; he watched the steps by which a litter of young foxes learned to catch mice. The play of life about him increased with his skill in seeing it, but his understanding of it and his growing sympathy with it were both completely subconscious until his adventure with the lynx.*

lynx: a type of wildcat

He had found its tracks several times. They seemed to be near the places where he had walked or hidden, and he grew curious. He gave over the otters for a time and hunted it, and found that it was stalking him. He spent a good deal of time in the thick hemlock it liked best; finally, he went through this woods noisily, backtracked with great care, and hid in a very thick place.

A long time went by before he saw a movement, an indistinct blur as the pale fawn-colored fur slipped across a patch of sunlight. It came closer, silently, never distinct in the thicket; and then it was standing in a little opening not thirty feet away, the yellow eyes staring at him, the big, soft paws tense, and the tufted ears cocked. There was a good deal of wild power in it, but he never thought of being afraid. It stood regarding him, poised, unblinking and feral,* framed against the wild tangle of the thicket, but without menace. He smiled, and there suddenly seemed to come upon it a look, an expression, of shame that it had been outmaneuvered and taken in. It made a little sound, turned, and, with great care for its dignity, moved off and vanished.

feral: untamed

For the first time, he realized how much a part of his life the otters had become and how much he liked them. He realized, too, how clear and simple their reasons for action were, even when they killed.

His thought naturally came to the otters, and swung quickly away, but the fact that he had almost looked upon them sympathetically confused him. He got up, puzzled and a little ashamed, and went home. The disturbing questions which came to him refused to be dismissed. His father was alone in the kitchen; he looked up and saw that the boy was troubled.

"Yes, son?" he asked.

"Dad," he began, knowing that his father would help him, "the otters—"

Just then, his mother came in. "There's a letter from Joe for you, Andrew," she said. "I put it in your room."

His father watched the swift change of his expression, the closing of his mind against the question, with regret. "I wish you hadn't mentioned that letter, mother," he said after the boy left. "I wish you'd hidden it. I think he's seen something he liked about those otters, and it was about to change his mind."

"Oh, I'm so sorry," she said. "I'm so sorry, Harry. Do you think—"

"I think it's too late," Gates said. "He's right back now where he was before."

The uneasiness which at first had been like a formless shadow in the old dog otter's brain was sharper now, for he encountered the man-smell which evoked* it more frequently. To be followed was a new experience to him, and he didn't know what to make of it. It had not been difficult to avoid the infrequent and casual encounters all animals have with man sooner or later; his senses were superior to theirs, and vigilance and care were all that was necessary. He saw or heard or scented them and got out of the way; they passed and were gone, and places which held evidence of their presence were better left alone. But this was different; the smell waited in many places for him clinging to the underbrush or the banks. His temper grew short with constant watchfulness, and he began to avoid the daylight hours.

evoked: drew out

The female didn't take well to the curtailed* activity either. She was of a more casual temperament than her mate; she had never, as he had long ago, been caught in a trap and nearly drowned. She had not felt the blind terror of it nor lost two toes; her brain wasn't marked by an experience impossible to forget. She chafed* at being quiet in the dank* blackness of a bankside den when she knew that the world was filled with sunshine and freedom and sport a few feet away. She remembered so many happy places—gloomy thickets they went through between streams where a complexity of fine scents lingered and birds flashed in and out of shadow; deep pools below falls where trout hid among the sunken rocks; long, easy stretches of lazily sparkling water, and precipitous* banks where the three of them made slides and plunged down them until they were too weary for anything but lying happily in the sun.

curtailed: decreased

chafed: became annoyed

dank: damp

precipitous: steep

She grew morose* as they all did. Their rollicking vitality, with its urge toward ceaseless activity and play, was frustrated and turned against them. They bickered and snarled at one another.

morose: gloomy

But this retreat, which would eventually have discouraged the ordinary hunter, was doomed to failure with the boy. All his determination and effort were concentrated solely upon them, and because they could not exist by moving about altogether in the dark, it was inevitable that he find them. The impulse to change his range came to the old otter many times, but he resisted it. The old range was home, familiar and somehow comforting; the memories of his life along its banks and streams were deeply etched into his brain, and they held him there.

Clouds were beginning to cover the late-afternoon sun when the boy found the pad mark on the little sandy margin of the stream. It was very fresh; water was still oozing slowly into it, and he began to tremble. The facts that he had always got home before dark, to avoid worrying his mother, and that he wouldn't be able to do it this time if he didn't start at once were forgotten. A strange sort of surety came upon him, and, after a moment, the trembling stopped and he grew calm. He knew that the stream didn't go much farther; that within a quarter of a mile the otters would leave it and go across country, through a hemlock swamp and over a low ridge, to reach the stream on the other side which flowed finally into the lake.

He knew the thicket so well that he could predict where they would pass through it—a marshy little path which had once been a lumber road, cut through a high and tangled bank. He knew he could intercept them there by going through the woods; he knew he had them.

He had so often imagined the feeling of triumph that would be his when he found them that he was confused by the lack of it, by a sort of unwillingness that had suddenly come into his heart. This emotion was inexplicable* to him, and seemed like a betrayal of his brother. He thought of his father, who did not approve of the thing he was doing, but who had been patient and kind and

had said nothing against it, and suddenly he felt lost and alone. He stood indecisively for a moment in the darkening woods; the thoughts of his father changed to thoughts of Joe, and his back stiffened.

---

inexplicable: not able to be understood

He started to walk. A deeper gloom fell upon him as he went into the hemlock, and a deeper silence; he moved like a ghost, for his feet made no sound in the fallen needles. When he came to the place, the bank above the lumber road, the setting sun came out more brightly, and the thicket was filled with a banded, coppery light. The low branches were so thick that he had to crawl to the top on his hands and knees. He reached the top and lay down, stretching out with the rifle cocked in his hands. It was very quiet. The swampy little path lay before him for a few yards, meandering and crooked, masked here and there by low hemlock branches and brown old stumps rotting and green with moss.

The coppery light faded again, and after a long time the brooding silence was suddenly broken by a spitting snarl. The boy raised himself on his elbows quickly; there was a rapid, slurred pattering of feet, and the three otters were bunched below him. The old male's back was claw-raked and bleeding; he snarled at his mate and moved toward her as though to drive her along the path, then turned and galloped the other way. A lynx materialized in front of him, crouched and spitting, its ears laid flat and its teeth gleaming. He went at it hissing, and it gave ground; another bounded off the bank to-ward the pup, but he whirled and drove it off. Short-legged and awkward on land, he was at a great disadvantage before the pair of lynxes, but somehow he managed to be everywhere at once.

The snarling lynxes, trying to draw both otters away from the pup, were very quick, but the old otter moved like a dark flame. He closed with one of them, took his raking and punished it, and broke away in time to fasten on the throat of the other, which was batting with a hooked claw at his mate. He shook its big body, threw it aside and whirled again toward the first. Quiet suddenly fell; the lynxes drew off a little, and they all stood panting, glaring at one another.

The path had been so quiet and empty one moment and so full of violent action the next that the boy was held immobile and staring. The sudden quiet freed him. He got up on his knees, his eyes on the otter; he was so filled with a sudden overwhelming admiration for its courage that he nearly shouted encouragement as it stood, black and bloody, and so obviously ready to carry the fight on. One of the lynxes moved; it drew off a little farther, as though deciding to abandon the fight. The boy didn't think; he raised the rifle and fired a quick shot at it. The shot missed, but the lynx turned tail with a snarl and bounded off through the hemlocks. The other went after it, and the old otter turned its head and looked at him for a moment with curiosity, but no fear. Then it shook itself and drove the female and the pup before it down the path and out of sight.

It was well dark when the boy heard his father shouting in the distance and answered him; presently, he saw the lantern moving far off among the dark trees, and hurried toward it.

"Are you all right, Andy?" Gates called. "Are you all right, boy?"

"Yes, dad," he said. He came to the circle of yellow light and stopped.

"Your ma was a little worried," Gates said gently.

"I'm sorry," he said; and then, "I found them, dad."

Gates didn't say anything. He just stood there holding the lantern, and the boy could see a star or two among the scattering clouds and branches high above his head. "I found them," he said again. "There were two lynxes after them, and he—the old one, the otter—fought them off. He was wonderful, dad; he licked them both."

"Rabbits must be scarce," Gates said, "to make them tackle him."

"It was the little one," Andy said. "They were after him. But the old one—I—I shot at the lynxes, dad."

There was silence for a long moment, then Gates said, "You're not sorry?"

"No," the boy said. "No. He's not mean, dad. It was the little one all the time. He was watching out for it—even the day he took Nicky; but I didn't know it then. Do you think Joe will understand that, dad?"

"Sure," Gates said. "He'll understand it. He'll be glad you understand it too." His long arm went around the boy's shoulders. "Come on," he said. "Let's get on home."

ABOUT THE AUTHOR

Excellent writers usually write about subjects with which they are well acquainted. This principle holds true for Robert Murphy (1902–71), an avid sportsman who especially enjoyed hunting, fishing, and falconry. Many of his forty-four short stories, which were published in the *Saturday Evening Post* and other magazines, are set in the wild outdoors. His numerous fiction books include *Wild Geese Calling*, which was made into a movie for television, and *The Pond*, which won the Dutton Animal Book Award in 1964.

THINKING ZONE

The climax is often confused with the crisis or turning point of a plot. The **climax** is the moment at which the plot reaches the point of the protagonist's highest emotional intensity. In the last story that you read, "Hastrman," the climax occurs when Mr. Rybář's grief overwhelms him and he throws the stones through the open window. In "The Wild Duck's Nest," the story's climax occurs when Colm revisits the nest, "his heart thumping with excitement."

The **resolution** (sometimes called the denouement) is the final outcome of the plot. In most cases, the resolution ties up the story's "loose ends" and tells or suggests to the reader what has happened to the protagonist as a direct or sometimes indirect result of the crisis. In "Hastrman," the resolution is merely suggested by the symbolism of Mr. Rybář's looking out the window and considering his nephew's words. In "The Wild Duck's Nest," the resolution occurs when Colm realizes that the duck has not forsaken the egg.

Now that you have studied the basic elements of plot, think back over some of the stories you have read, either in this text or elsewhere, and see whether you can identify exposition, inciting incident, rising action, crisis, falling action, climax, and resolution in each.

1. *[interpretive]* Who is the protagonist of this story?

_____

2. *[interpretive]* What is the inciting incident in the plot?

_____

_____

_____

3. *[interpretive]* List at least one example of each type of conflict (internal and external) occurring in the story.

_____

_____

_____

_____

4. *[critical]* The rising action occurs when Andy decides to hunt the otter that killed his brother's dog and he begins studying the otters' movements. What is the story's crisis?

_____

_____

_____

_____

_____

_____

5. *[critical]* During what part of the story does the **climax** occur?

_____

_____

_____

_____

_____

6. *[critical]* What is the story's **resolution?**

_____

_____

_____

_____

_____

7. *[critical]* What do you think is meant by the story's title?

_____

_____

_____

_____

_____

_____

FROM

EVIDENCE NOT SEEN

DARLENE DEIBLER ROSE

In 1937 on her first wedding anniversary, Darlene Deibler arrived with her husband Russell on a small island in the Pacific. But the young missionary couple had barely settled into their work when war broke out in Europe. Japan soon joined the Axis powers and swept through the Pacific. One by one the islands fell, and on March 5, 1942, the Deiblers and their fellow missionaries found themselves at the mercy of Japanese invaders. The author vividly remembers being herded into a room by one of the commanding officers who announced that the men were being taken away as prisoners of war.

She recalls filling a pillowcase with a Bible, some clothing, and a few other things that her husband might need and then dashing outside to find him, only to see that he and the other men had been herded into a large truck. She states in her book *Evidence Not Seen* that she "handed [him] the pillowcase and looked into the face that had become so dear to me. A cry of protest, of fear, strangled itself in my throat. . . . The driver started the engine. Russell leaned over the tailgate and very quietly said, 'Remember one thing, dear: God said that He would never leave us nor forsake us.'" That was the last time she was to see her husband, but his words would come back to comfort her again and again during the months that lay ahead.

Those who had been left behind at the mission station were immediately forced into slave labor for the Japanese. For two years the prisoners endured indescribable hardship. But the suffering grew even worse in May 1944, when Deibler, accused of being an American spy, was taken from the Kampili prison camp by the dreaded Kempeitai, the secret police. Although the charges against her were groundless, she was forced to endure weeks of interrogation. In the following excerpt from her book, Darlene Deibler Rose shares one of her many discoveries of God's faithfulness during this time of trial.

Finally, around the sixth week, I was informed that the Kempeitai had positively established the fact of my involvement in espionage.* They refused to believe anything I had said.

espionage: spying

The Interrogator* looked at me and asked, "You know the penalty, don't you, for espionage work in war time?"

Interrogator: name given by Deibler to one of her torturers

I knew: I was condemned, without formal trial, to be beheaded as an American spy.

Missionary Darlene Deibler before her captivity

That afternoon the tears flowed more copiously than ever before. I felt the pressure of His hand upon the hurt; the anguish receded before the calm, reassuring quietness of knowing that His grace would sustain.

After this session, I was never again taken to the interrogation room. I lifted my heart in praise and thanksgiving to the God Who enabled me to endure. He had given me the strength to be a good soldier for Jesus Christ. What was to be in the future I left completely in His hands. Even my cell took on the beauty of a place of refuge—I didn't have to go back to the hearing room again.

About a week later, at the time of day when the guard herded the women from the front cell block into the courtyard, I decided to check on Margaret Kemp. There she was in my housecoat. I was so pleased that she had it and wished I dared call to her. With her in the graveled courtyard were several native women prisoners. They had been jailed for minor misdemeanors and were allowed to take air and exercise afternoons in the courtyard, whenever it pleased the officer in charge.

The actions of one woman in particular fascinated me. Every time the sentry on duty turned his back to her and marched to the other end of the courtyard, she inched over toward a fence covered with Honolulu Creeper. When the guard clicked his heels, turned about, and began to stroll in her direction, she stopped. There he went, and there she went. "Aha, intrigue. She's going to make contact with someone who's hidden in those vines. Isn't this exciting! Oh, do be careful. With no books to read, I'll watch the drama taking place here before my very eyes!" I empathized* with her. I wanted her to succeed, and not to be caught. Finally, reaching the vine-covered fence, the woman stood very still. The guard clicked his heels and went off again. At that moment, I saw a hand shoot through the tangle of vine. It held a big bunch of bananas. Quickly she grabbed the bananas, slipped them into the folds of her sarong,* and strolled nonchalantly* back to join the other women. Nobody knew she had those bananas. But I did—bananas!

empathized: identified with

sarong: skirt with colorful cloth wrapped around the waist

nonchalantly: calmly

I dropped to the floor of my cell. Exhausted from my efforts, I shook all over. Worse still, I began to crave bananas. Everything in me wanted one. I could see them; I could smell them; I could taste them. I got down on my knees and said, "Lord, I'm not asking You for a whole bunch like that woman has. I just want one banana." I looked up and pleaded, "Lord, just one banana."

Then I began to rationalize*—how could God possibly get a banana to me through these prison walls? I would never ask the guard. If he helped me and was discovered, it would mean reprisals.* I would certainly never ask a favor of the Interrogator or the Brain.* There was more chance of the moon falling out of the sky than of one of them bringing me a banana. Then I ran out of people. These three were the only ones. Of course, there was the old Indonesian night watchman. "Don't let it even enter his thinking to bring me a banana. He'd be shot if caught."

---

rationalize: reason

reprisals: retaliations

Brain: man who questioned Deibler and gave the orders to torture her during interrogation

---

I bowed my head again and prayed, "Lord, there's no one here who could get a banana to me. There's no way for You to do it. Please don't think I'm not thankful for the rice porridge. It's just that—well, those bananas looked so delicious!"

What I needed to do was link my impotence* to God's omnipotence,* but I couldn't see how God could get a banana to me through those prison walls, even after the knife episode* and my healing.

---

impotence: helplessness

omnipotence: limitless power

knife episode: Deibler recounts that earlier, a knife had mysteriously appeared and then disappeared after her prayers for its removal because she feared punishment if it were found.

When the Japanese officers from the ships docked in Macassar Harbor visited the prison, great hardships were inflicted upon the prisoners. We were laughed at, scorned, and insulted. When our cells were opened, we were expected to bow low at a perfect ninety-degree angle. If we didn't perform to their satisfaction, we were struck across the back with a cane. These were humiliating and desperate experiences.

The morning after the banana drama, I heard the click of officers' leather heels on the concrete walkway. The thought of getting to my feet and having to execute a bow was onerous,* to say the least. My weight had dropped during those months in the converted insane asylum, until now I was skin drawn over bones. One nice thing about my streamlined proportions was that the thinner I got, the longer my dress became, so I had more covering at night. I stretched out my hands often and laughed at my bird's claws. The meager daily meals were not designed for putting on weight. I had been healed, but I needed food for strength. I wondered if I could manage to get to my feet and remain upright, but I was determined that when that door opened, they would find me on my feet.

---

onerous: burdensome

The officers were almost at the door. I reached up, grabbed the window ledge, and pulled myself upright. "Now, Lord," I prayed, "officers are coming. Give me strength to make a proper bow." I heard the guard slip a key into the door, but he had the wrong one and ran back to the office to get the right key. I dropped to the floor to rest, then came to my feet again when I heard his tennis shoe–shod feet moving quickly down the walkway. My legs were trembling, and I clutched the bars of the window to steady myself. "Lord, please help me to bow correctly."

Finally the door opened, and I looked into the smiling face of Mr. Yamaji, the Kampili camp commander. This was early July, and it had been so long since I had seen a smiling or a familiar face. I clapped my hands and exclaimed, *Tuan Yamaji, seperti lihat sobat jang lama*, "Mr. Yamaji, it's just like seeing an old friend!"

Tears filled his eyes. He didn't say a word but turned and walked out into the courtyard and began to talk with the two officers who had conducted my interrogations. At roll call in Kampili, I had had to give certain commands in Japanese, but I had made a deliberate effort to learn as little of the Japanese language as possible. It was better not to know it. I couldn't understand what Yamaji was saying—but he spoke with them for a long time. What had happened to the hauteur* and belligerence* with which those two always conducted themselves toward me? I could see their heads hanging lower and lower. Perhaps he spoke to them of my work as a missionary, or maybe he shared with them concerning that afternoon in his office after I had learned of Russell's death, when I spoke of Christ, my Savior, Who gives us love for others—even for our enemies, those who use us badly.

hauteur (hō-tûr´): arrogance
belligerence: hostility

Finally Mr. Yamaji came back to my cell. "You're very ill, aren't you?" he asked sympathetically.

"Yes, sir, Mr. Yamaji, I am."

"I'm going back to the camp now. Have you any word for the women?"

The Lord gave me confidence to answer, "Yes, sir, when you go back, please tell them for me that I'm all right. I'm still trusting the Lord. They'll understand what I mean, and I believe you do."

"All right," he replied; then, turning on his heels, he left.

When Mr. Yamaji and the Kempeitai officers had gone and the guard had closed the door, it hit me—*I didn't bow to those men!* "Oh Lord," I cried, "why didn't You help me remember? They'll come back and beat me. Lord, please, not back to the hearing room again. Not now, Lord. I can't; I just can't."

I heard the guard coming back and knew he was coming for me. Struggling to my feet, I stood ready to go. He opened the door, walked in, and with a sweeping gesture laid at my feet—*bananas!* "They're yours," he said, "and they're all from Mr. Yamaji." I sat down in stunned silence and counted them. *There were ninety-two bananas!*

In all my spiritual experience, I've never known such shame before my Lord. I pushed the bananas into a corner and wept before Him. "Lord, forgive me; I'm so ashamed. I couldn't trust You enough to get even one banana for me. Just look at them—there are almost a hundred."

In the quiet of the shadowed cell, He answered back within my heart: *"That's what I delight to do, the exceeding abundant above anything you ask or think."* I knew in those moments that nothing is impossible to my God.

ABOUT THE AUTHOR

From the time she was a young girl, Darlene Deibler Rose (1917–2004) wanted to be a missionary. In 1938 she became the first American woman to enter the primitive Baliem Valley of New Guinea, where she served with her husband Russell for four years before being taken captive by the Japanese during World War II. Three years later, physically and emotionally devastated by the prison camp experience and the loss of her beloved husband, Deibler returned to the United States, certain that she would someday return to the island people. She spent the next two years sharing her experiences with others while recovering from the ordeals suffered during her imprisonment.

Shortly thereafter, in God's providence, a young missionary appointee to New Guinea, Gerald Rose, was given a copy of a film about Russell Deibler's ministry to use in his deputation ministry. Through the effort of mutual friends, he and Darlene Deibler became acquainted, and in 1948 they were married. A year later they headed back to the mission field she had left earlier, and there the Roses ministered to the primitive tribes while rearing two sons. After serving in New Guinea for many years, the Roses left in 1979 to begin a ministry in Australia. Rose has been an inspiration to many through her book *Evidence Not Seen*, published in 1988.

THINKING ZONE

Most of the prose selections that you have read so far in this text have been examples of fiction, or stories invented by the author. However, some of the best stories are real-life ones. **Nonfiction** relates the stories of real people and events. There are many different types of nonfiction. An **autobiography** is a nonfictional account of the author's own life. A more specific type of autobiography in which an author writes about a recollection from his or her life is called a **memoir**. Often, memoirs are shorter than autobiographies and do not seek to tell the reader about the author's whole life; rather, they center on one episode or one aspect of the person's life. The book of Nehemiah and parts of the book of Ezra (chapters 7–10) are memoirs.

Biography—a nonfiction work in which the author writes about the life of a person other than himself

1. *[interpretive]* Identify at least two instances from the excerpt from *Evidence Not Seen* in which the author was able to see God's hand and to sense His tender care despite her difficult circumstances.

   _____

   _____

   _____

2. *[interpretive]* Does this **autobiography** also qualify as a **memoir**? Explain your answer.

   _____

   _____

   _____

3. *[interpretive]* In this **nonfiction** work, how would you describe Darlene Deibler Rose's view of life?

   _____

   _____

   _____

   _____

4. *[critical]* What is the title *Evidence Not Seen* an allusion to? How is it an appropriate allusion?

_____

_____

_____

_____

_____

_____

5. *[critical]* Explain the irony in the title *Evidence Not Seen*.

_____

_____

_____

6. *[critical]* What portion or portions of the story demonstrate situational irony? Explain your answer.

_____

_____

_____

_____

_____

_____

Situational irony— *Irony in which the events of the story violate normal expectations*

7. *[appreciative]* Have you ever seen God at work in your life? Explain.

_____

_____

_____

_____

_____

SYMBOLS

CHRISTINA ROSSETTI

God's creation affords many opportunities for discovery. Can you find what the speaker in this poem learns about herself and about God?

I watched a rosebud very long
   Brought on by dew and sun and shower,
   Waiting to see the perfect flower:
Then, when I thought it should be strong,
   It opened at the matin* hour
And fell at evensong.*

I watched a nest from day to day,
   A green nest full of pleasant shade,
   Wherein three speckled eggs were laid:
But when they should have hatched in May,
   The two old birds had grown afraid
Or tired, and flew away.

Then in my wrath I broke the bough
   That I had tended so with care,
   Hoping its scent should fill the air:
I crushed the eggs, not heeding how
   Their ancient promise had been fair:
I would have vengeance now.

But the dead branch spoke from the sod,
   And the eggs answered me again:
   Because we failed dost thou complain?
Is thy wrath just? And what if God,
   Who waiteth for thy fruits in vain,
Should also take the rod?

matin: early morning
evensong: a daily evening prayer or worship service

— ABOUT THE AUTHOR —

Christina Rossetti (1830–94) was a remarkable poet. She had the ability to write exquisite devotional poetry that teaches God's truth through God's creation. Rossetti was a blend of her father's artistic nature and her mother's religious devotion. Her central religious theme is the love of God and the demands that that love places on the Christian. She evaluates all things by heavenly standards and sees nature as a textbook concerned with her personal relationship to God. Rossetti placed her relationship to God above all else: above her personal desires for a home and family, for she broke two engagements because of her religious convictions and never did marry; above her personal comfort, for she spent much of her time and limited energy caring for ailing family members and doing charity work among the lower-class women of Victorian England; above her personal ambition, for her work is almost all strongly religious in an age when Darwin's influence was quickly eroding the religious foundation. Rossetti has much to offer the reader through her work as well as her life. She desired God's will above all else and challenged those of her time and ours to do the same.

THINKING ZONE

You probably remember that a metaphor is an expression of one thing in terms of another. An **allegory** is a type of extended metaphor that forms a story with two levels of meaning: the literal and the figurative. The most famous allegory in English literature is *The Pilgrim's Progress* by John Bunyan. The tale of Christian and his journeys is understood on the literal level to be a story about a pilgrim carrying a heavy load. However, on the figurative level, the story of the pilgrim and his burden mirrors that of a person carrying a weight of sin and seeking to rid himself of it at the cross. Many of Christ's biblical parables can rightly be called allegories, such as the parable of the sower (a person witnessing) in Matthew 13. Aesop's fables also seek to communicate life lessons through allegory. Take time to reread "Symbols" and to think about how the episodes that the poet describes could be called allegorical.

1. *[literal]* What does the speaker in the poem expect of the rosebud in stanza 1 and the speckled eggs in stanza 2? How are her expectations disappointed?

   _____

   _____

   _____

   _____

2. *[critical]* What reason(s) does the reader have to expect the rosebud to grow and the eggs to hatch?

   _____

   _____

   _____

   _____

3. *[literal]* What is the speaker's response to this disappointment?

_____

_____

_____

_____

_____

4. *[interpretive]* How are the episodes in stanzas 1–3 an **allegory** for the way humans often respond to disappointment? How does it contrast with God's response when we disappoint Him?

_____

_____

_____

_____

_____

5. *[critical]* How do the dead branch and the eggs "speak" to the poet in stanza 4?

_____

_____

_____

_____

_____

6. *[critical]* What is the rhyme scheme of the first stanza? Does the entire poem follow this same general pattern?

_____

_____

_____

_____

_____

Rhyme scheme—
the pattern of rhyme sounds in a poem or in a stanza of poetry

THE SKY IS LOW, THE CLOUDS ARE MEAN

EMILY DICKINSON

Like Rossetti, Dickinson makes an important discovery by observing nature in action.

The Sky is low—the Clouds are mean.
A Travelling Flake of Snow
Across a Barn or through a Rut
Debates if it will go—

A Narrow Wind complains all Day
How some one treated him;
Nature, like Us is sometimes caught
Without her Diadem.*

diadem: **crown worn as a sign of royalty**

ABOUT THE AUTHOR

Born in Amherst, Massachusetts, Emily Dickinson (1830–86) is considered one of America's greatest poets. Following an education at Amherst Academy and Mount Holyoke Female Seminary, Dickinson became reclusive. By age twenty-three she spent most of her time in her room and ventured from the family property only occasionally. Dickinson occupied herself with baking, tending the garden, and writing voluminous amounts of poetry. She dressed almost entirely in white and communicated mostly by letter. Despite a number of regular visitors to the Dickinson home, the visitors she agreed to see were few. Dickinson often included poetry in the letters that she wrote, but her poetry did not receive public acclaim until after her death. In fact, her more than 1700 poems, the pages stitched together by hand in multiple volumes, were made public by her sister Lavinia. The last volume of Dickinson's poems was published in 1945. Dickinson's use of unusual punctuation and capitalization as well as unconventional rhyme and meter earned her recognition as an innovator in nineteenth-century poetry. She is also well-known for her atypical yet astonishingly apt metaphors.

SUNSET

OSWALD MBUYISENI MTSHALI

Have you ever witnessed a beautiful sunset? What did the sun remind you of? Perhaps it was like a ball of fire or a circle of light. In his poem, Mtshali uses an extended simile to create a picture for you.

The sun spun like
a tossed coin.
It whirled on the azure* sky,   azure: light purplish blue
it clattered into the horizon,
it clicked in the slot,
and neon-lights popped
and blinked "Time expired,"
as on a parking meter.

ABOUT THE AUTHOR

Oswald Mbuyiseni Mtshali [m bōō´və sān´ē m tə shäl´ē] (b. 1940) was born in the rural South African province of KwaZulu-Natal. At the age of eighteen he desired to enroll in the University of Witwatersrand in Johannesburg. He traveled to Johannesburg but was denied enrollment in the university because of South Africa's apartheid legislation. Mtshali worked numerous jobs before he published his first book of poetry, *Sounds of a Cowhide Drum*. He then moved to the United States to enroll in Columbia College, where he studied creative writing and education. Mtshali has served as an educator in both the United States and Africa and has been a vice-principal of Pace College in Soweto. Among his awards are the Olive Schreiner Poetry Prize and the Poetry International Award.

THINKING ZONE

When reading a poem containing rhyme, you will notice that some of the syllables are pronounced more strongly than others, contributing to the poem's even **rhythm**, or beat. Those syllables are referred to as **stressed syllables** because they receive greater emphasis when they are read. The regular arrangement of stressed and unstressed syllables within a poem is known as **meter**. Meter in poetry becomes more obvious when a poem is read aloud, though poetry should not normally be read in a way that overstates the meter or rhythm. Poetry with no distinguishable rhyme, meter, or line length is known as **free verse**. The translations of poems of Li Bai and José Martí from Unit 1 are examples of free verse, as is one of the poems you just read.

Writers often use analogies to help their readers picture a subject. An **analogy** is a detailed comparison of one thing to another dissimilar thing. Similes and metaphors are types of brief analogy. When Christ compared the kingdom of heaven to several things in Matthew 13 and proceeded after each one to further explain the comparison, he was using analogy. Emily Dickinson uses an analogy in her poem "The Sky Is Low, the Clouds Are Mean." Can you find it?

> **Rhyme**—the repetition of the last stressed vowel and all of the sounds following that vowel in two or more words

1. *[literal/interpretive]* Which of the poems contains rhyme, **meter**, and **rhythm**? What are the **stressed syllables** in line 1 of that poem?

_____

_____

2. *[literal]* Which of the poems is an example of **free verse**?

_____

3. *[interpretive/critical]* What do you think Dickinson means in line 5 when she mentions how the wind "complains"?

_____

_____

_____

_____

4. *[interpretive]* What **analogy** about human behavior is Dickinson making in lines 7 and 8?

_____

_____

_____

_____

_____

5. *[literal/interpretive]* In "Sunset" what specific type of analogy does the poet use in lines 1 and 2 and in lines 7 and 8 to describe the sunset? List both of the analogies.

_____

_____

_____

6. *[interpretive]* Explain the last four lines of "Sunset." What is happening in these lines?

_____

_____

_____

_____

_____

7. *[appreciative]* Which of the poems—"The Sky Is Low, the Clouds Are Mean" or "Sunset"—did you enjoy more? Why?

_____

_____

_____

_____

_____

_____

COLOSS. 3.3
OUR LIFE IS HID WITH CHRIST IN GOD

GEORGE HERBERT

As did several other authors studied in this unit, the poet George Herbert discovered that the Christian's focus must be toward heaven.

My words and thoughts do both express this notion,

That **Life** hath with the sun a double motion.

The first **Is** straight, and our diurnall* friend,

The other **Hid**, and doth obliquely bend.*

> diurnall: of or related to daytime hours; referring to the course the sun travels in one day
>
> obliquely bend: oblique = at an angle; referring to the course the sun travels in one year

One life is wrapt **In** flesh, and tends to earth.

The other winds towards **Him** whose happie birth

Taught me to live here so, **That** still one eye

Should aim and shoot at that which **Is** on high—

Quitting* with daily labour all **My** pleasure,

> quitting: conducting one's self in a certain way

To gain at harvest an eternall **Treasure**.

ABOUT THE AUTHOR

George Herbert (1593–1633) was the fifth of seven sons born to Richard and Magdalen Herbert of Wales. After having achieved a degree of prestige, he gave up his plans for a life of politics to become a minister at the age of thirty-seven. Three years later he died of tuberculosis, but he left behind a rich heritage of religious poetry in which he speaks to God as someone who knows God intimately. Herbert's poems are touchingly realistic portrayals of both the struggles and the triumphs of the Christian life.

THINKING ZONE

Many different patterns of rhymed lines exist within rhymed poetry, and the way a poet combines the lines makes up the poem's rhyme scheme. Some poets choose to include couplets in their poems. **Couplets** are rhymed pairs of poetic lines. As you read Herbert's poem, you will notice that it is made up entirely of couplets.

Herbert's poem also contains examples of a type of wordplay—known as a **pun**—in which the author combines different word meanings within a single word or phrase or uses homonyms (words that sound alike) in a sentence. Here is an example: A girl from Finland sits across the table from a boy from Russia. Self-conscious because he is the only diner still eating, the boy looks anxiously at the girl, who says kindly,

"Don't be Russian just because I'm Finnish." Of course, the puns are the plays on the words *Russian* (rushin') and *Finnish* (finished). The simplest forms of puns occur in riddles and jokes, but puns can be used in serious literature as well. One of the best-known Shakespearean puns occurs in *Romeo and Juliet* when Mercutio, fatally wounded, states that if one should try to find him the following day, he would be a "grave" man. The pun lies in the fact that *grave* may mean either "serious" or "a place in which dead bodies lie." Puns occur often in literature, yet they are difficult to do well. If they are too obvious or contrast too much in tone with the literary work, they take away from the work's literary merit.

1. *[literal/interpretive]* How many **couplets** make up this poem?

   _____

   _____

2. *[literal/interpretive]* What is the poem's rhyme scheme?

   _____

   _____

3. *[interpretive]* To what does Herbert compare life in line 2?

   _____

   _____

4. *[interpretive]* What specific similarities between the two does he notice within the poem?

_____

_____

_____

_____

_____

_____

5. *[critical]* Who is the "Him" referred to in line 6?

_____

_____

6. *[critical]* What is the significance of the emphasized words in this poem?

_____

_____

_____

_____

_____

_____

7. *[critical]* Look back at line 2. The word *sun* refers to the literal sun but could also be read as a **pun** that makes use of a homonym, the word *son*. Reading line 2 this way, and taking into account the emphasized portion, what deeper level of meaning does this add to the poem?

_____

_____

_____

CHRIST RETURNETH

H. L. TURNER

The greatest discoveries for a Christian must be the Resurrection and the second coming of the Savior—the receiving of Christ's "own."

It may be at morn, when the day is awaking,
When sunlight thro' darkness and shadow is
    breaking,
That Jesus will come in the fullness of glory,
To receive from the world "His own."

Chorus:
O Lord Jesus, how long, how long
Ere we shout the glad song,
Christ returneth!
Hallelujah! hallelujah! Amen.

It may be at midday, it may be at twilight,
It may be, perchance, that the blackness of
    midnight
Will burst into light in the blaze of His glory,
When Jesus receives "His own."

While its hosts cry Hosanna, from heaven
    descending,
With glorified saints and the angels attending,
With grace on His brow, like a halo
    of glory,
Will Jesus receive "His own."

Oh, joy! oh, delight! should we go without
    dying,
No sickness, no sadness, no dread and no
    crying,
Caught up thro' the clouds with our Lord into
    glory,
When Jesus receives "His own."

The Ascension. Gustave Doré.
From the Bob Jones University Collection

Not much is known about the hymnwriter H. L. Turner, but his hymn "Christ Returneth" was published in *Gospel Hymns and Sacred Songs,* a hymnal compiled by Ira Sankey, George Stebbins, and the hymn's composer, James McGranahan (1840–1907). Born in Pennsylvania, McGranahan became an accomplished singer early in his life and was teaching in singing schools by age nineteen. After the early death of P. P. Bliss in a train wreck in December 1876, McGranahan was chosen to replace Bliss as song leader for evangelist Major Dan Whittle. His first duty was to write the tune for "I Will Sing of My Redeemer," the hymn text found in Bliss's train trunk after the wreck. He went on to compose tunes for such well-known hymns as "I Know Whom I Have Believed" and "There Shall Be Showers of Blessing." After Bliss's death, Stebbins and McGranahan became co-compilers with Sankey of *Gospel Hymns and Sacred Songs* (vol. 3–6). The hymnal became the primary force in determining a song's popularity and influence. Though little is known of the text writer, thanks to James McGranahan, Turner's "Christ Returneth" is among today's well-known hymns.

ABRAHAM AND ISAAC

God called Abraham out of the land of Ur and promised that He would use him to change the world (Gen. 12:1–3). Specifically, God promised to give him many descendents. After waiting several decades, Abraham and Sarah had a son. Isaac was God's special instrument for fulfilling His promises and was used to bring Abraham to an important discovery.

And it came to pass after these things, that God did tempt Abraham, and said unto him, Abraham: and he said, Behold, here I am.

2 And he said, Take now thy son, thine only son Isaac, whom thou lovest, and get thee into the land of Moriah; and offer him there for a burnt offering upon one of the mountains which I will tell thee of.

3 And Abraham rose up early in the morning, and saddled his ass, and took two of his young men with him, and Isaac his son, and clave* the wood for the burnt offering, and rose up, and went unto the place of which God had told him.

---

clave: split

---

4 Then on the third day Abraham lifted up his eyes, and saw the place afar off.

5 And Abraham said unto his young men, Abide ye here with the ass; and I and the lad will go yonder and worship, and come again to you.

6 And Abraham took the wood of the burnt offering, and laid it upon Isaac his son; and he took the fire in his hand, and a knife; and they went both of them together.

7 And Isaac spake unto Abraham his father, and said, My father: and he said, Here am I, my son. And he said, Behold the fire and the wood: but where is the lamb for a burnt offering?

8 And Abraham said, My son, God will provide himself a lamb for a burnt offering: so they went both of them together.

9 And they came to the place which God had told him of; and Abraham built an altar there, and laid the wood in order, and bound Isaac his son, and laid him on the altar upon the wood.

10 And Abraham stretched forth his hand, and took the knife to slay his son.

11 And the angel of the Lord called unto him out of heaven, and said, Abraham, Abraham: and he said, Here am I.

12 And he said, Lay not thine hand upon the lad, neither do thou any thing unto him: for now I know that thou fearest God, seeing thou hast not withheld thy son, thine only son from me.

13 And Abraham lifted up his eyes, and looked, and behold behind him a ram caught in a thicket by his horns: and Abraham went and took the ram, and offered him up for a burnt offering in the stead of his son.

14 And Abraham called the name of that place Jehovah-jireh: as it is said to this day, In the mount of the Lord it shall be seen.

15 And the angel of the Lord called unto Abraham out of heaven the second time,

16 And said, By myself have I sworn, saith the Lord, for because thou hast done this thing, and hast not withheld thy son, thine only son:

17 That in blessing I will bless thee, and in multiplying I will multiply thy seed as the stars of the heaven, and as the sand which is upon the sea shore; and thy seed shall possess the gate of his enemies;

18 And in thy seed shall all the nations of the earth be blessed; because thou hast obeyed my voice.

19 So Abraham returned unto his young men, and they rose up and went together to Beer-sheba; and Abraham dwelt at Beer-sheba.

—Genesis 22:1–19

UNIT 4 REVIEW

SHORT ANSWER

Write the word, phrase, or sentence that best answers the question.

1. "Shago" is told from what point of view?

   _____

2. In "The Last Lesson" what is the significance of the soldiers' trumpets' sounding at noon?

   _____

   _____

3. What is the main lesson that "Hastrman" teaches?

   _____

   _____

4. Give an example of internal conflict found in "You've Got to Learn."

   _____

   _____

5. The climax of the story occurs at what point?

   _____

   _____

6. The title *Evidence Not Seen* is an allusion to what?

   _____

   _____

7. Rossetti's poem "Symbols" is a type of extended metaphor with two levels of meaning. What is the term for this type of metaphor?

   _____

   _____

8. Herbert's poem "Coloss. 3.3" contains pairs of lines called what?

   _____

   _____

MULTIPLE CHOICE

Choose the best answer from the choices given.

_____ 9. Shago predicts that
    A. a great storm is coming.
    B. he will go blind.
    C. his team will always win.
    D. he will lose his skill at pitching.

_____ 10. "The Last Lesson" is set in what country?
    A. Germany
    B. France
    C. Russia
    D. Italy

_____ 11. In "The Wild Duck's Nest," Colm observes all of the following upon returning to the nest _except_ that
    A. the bird is sitting on the nest, almost asleep.
    B. a snake is coiled in the nest.
    C. the bird has not forsaken the nest.
    D. there are two eggs in the nest.

_____ 12. The setting of "The Wild Duck's Nest" is
    A. an island.
    B. a mountain.
    C. a city.
    D. a park.

_____ 13. Darlene Deibler Rose's view of life in the excerpt from _Evidence Not Seen_ includes all of the following ideas _except_ that
    A. with God all things are possible.
    B. her faith was sometimes lacking.
    C. we always know what will happen to us.
    D. without God we can do nothing.

_____ 14. All of the following are true of the eggs in "Symbols" _except_ that
    A. they are crushed.
    B. they are abandoned.
    C. they are mistreated.
    D. they are hatched.

_____ 15. In "The Sky Is Low, the Clouds Are Mean," what does Dickinson mean when she says that "Nature, like Us is sometimes caught / Without her Diadem"?

A. Nature wants recognition just as people do.

B. Nature sometimes behaves badly just as people do.

C. Nature, like a person, wants to be thought of as royalty.

D. Nature, like a person, wishes to be treated better than anything else.

MATCHING

Match the following literary terms with their correct definitions.

_____ 16. Author's attitude toward his subjects or toward the reader

_____ 17. Detailed comparison of one thing to another dissimilar thing

_____ 18. Final outcome of the plot

_____ 19. Poetry with no distinguishable rhyme, meter, or line length

_____ 20. Event that sets the rest of the plot in motion

_____ 21. Mood of a written piece

A. resolution

B. free verse

C. tone

D. inciting incident

E. atmosphere

F. analogy

TRUE/FALSE

If the statement is completely true, write _true_. If any part of the statement is false, write _false_.

_____ 22. In "Shago" the story's ending with night (darkness) is symbolic of Shago's blindness.

_____ 23. In "The Last Lesson" the atmosphere in the story is one of a confident and relaxed spirit.

_____ 24. Exposition introduces a reader to the setting, characters, and situation in a story.

_____ 25. The rising action of "Hastrman" occurs after Mr. Rybář discovers that his jewels are useless and returns home and throws his jewels away.

_____ 26. A biography is a nonfictional account of the author's own life.

_____ 27. Mtshali's poem "Sunset" is an example of free verse.

ESSAY

Write a complete answer for each question below, using specific examples from the unit.

28. How does Darlene Deibler Rose's view of life reflect the truth taught in George Herbert's poem "Coloss. 3.3"?

_____

_____

_____

_____

_____

_____

_____

_____

_____

29. Explain the significance of the title of either "The Last Lesson" or "You've Got to Learn."

_____

_____

_____

_____

_____

_____

_____

_____

5

ADVENTURERS

Lepo Mikko (1911–78) was born to a farming family in Estonia. He belonged to a group of classical modernist painters who had roots in the classical painting style but who attempted to depict a subject in a fresh way—new angles, new materials, new purposes—much like some of the cubist painters.

What elements of cubism do you recognize in the painting?

What story is told by Lepo's painting?

This detail of his painting *Man and Space* was completed in 1971 just after the U.S. astronauts landed on the moon, ending the space race. Knowing that, what elements of Lepo's painting could you interpret as a commentary on his time?

Besides the astronauts, what other elements are recognizable in the picture?

ADVENTURERS

THE EXCITEMENT OF SEIZING AN OPPORTUNITY FILLED WITH RISK; THE THRILL OF DARING A FEAT THAT FEW OTHERS HAVE ACCOMPLISHED; THE WONDER OF DISCOVERING THAT YOU ARE THE FIRST, THE FASTEST, THE BEST—THESE EMOTIONS DRIVE THE ADVENTURER.

Adventurers deal with circumstances that are often extreme, even brutal. They do what others before them have either not wanted to do or not been able to do. They go for varying reasons—personal glory, fame, wealth—but they go.

Men and women have scaled mountains, dived to ocean depths, rocketed into space; they have reached both poles and landed on the surface of the moon. Like these adventurers, some of the adventurers you will read about in this unit confront unusual challenges head on. But not all adventures are of the extreme sort. Sometimes adventure creeps up unawares in everyday life—on a family road trip, along the way to school, in the grocery store. Adventure may involve confronting the unusual or unfamiliar, or it may mean looking at ordinary circumstances in an extraordinary way.

The Bible includes many accounts of adventurers: Abraham, Noah, and Paul are among them. Numbers 13 tells the exploits of twelve spies sent to search out the land of Canaan. What an adventure! Espionage, reconnaissance, danger, intrigue! Ten of the men returned to base camp with the report "We be not able to go up against the people" (Num. 13:31). But two of the spies, Joshua and Caleb, said instead, "Let us go up at once, and possess it" (13:30). They believed God's promises to His people and knew Him powerful enough to aid in their quest. They were two Bible adventurers whose ordinary faith led them to perform extraordinary feats for God.

Adventures demanding courage, wisdom, and determination are not limited to great Bible heroes of the past. Nor are they found only in the storybooks. God challenges each Christian to be a noble adventurer, and He promises success to those who accept that challenge.

GREAT ADVENTURE IS FACING RESPONSIBILITY DAY AFTER DAY.

—WILLIAM GORDON
TIME NOVEMBER 19, 1965

THE BANKS OF THE SACRAMENTO

JACK LONDON

The low groaning of the heavy ore-cables and the husky voices of working men had been silenced. The Yellow Dream mine was now like a peaceful hideaway cradled among the great pines high on a cliff overlooking the Sacramento River. The cable cars hung motionless above the river, and the only voices to be heard were those in quiet conversation. It is little wonder that young Jerry never suspected the perilous adventure that was soon to break the serenity of the morning.

"And it's blow, ye winds, heigh-ho,
For Cal-i-for-ni-o;
For there's plenty of gold so I've been told,
On the banks of the Sacramento!"

It was only a boy singing in a shrill treble the sea chantey,* which seamen sing the wide world over when they man the capstan bars* and break the anchors out for "Frisco" port. It was only a boy who had never seen the sea, but two hundred feet beneath him rolled the Sacramento. Young Jerry he was called, after Old Jerry, his father, from whom he had learned the song, as well as received his shock of bright-red hair, his blue, dancing eyes, and his fair and inevitably freckled skin.

---
chantey: sailor's song

capstan bars: levers used for hoisting a ship's anchor

For Old Jerry had been a sailor, and had followed the sea till middle life, haunted always by the words of the ringing chantey. Then one day he had sung the song in earnest in an Asiatic port, swinging and thrilling round the capstan-circle* with twenty others. And at San Francisco he turned his back upon his ship and upon the sea, and went to behold with his own eyes the banks of the Sacramento.

---
capstan-circle: apparatus used for hoisting weights

He beheld the gold, too, for he found employment at the Yellow Dream mine, and proved of utmost usefulness in rigging the great ore-cables across the river and two hundred feet above its surface.

After that he took charge of the cables and kept them in repair, and ran them and loved them, and became himself an indispensable fixture of the Yellow Dream mine. Then he loved pretty Margaret Kelly; but she had left him and Young Jerry, the latter barely toddling, to take up her last long sleep in the little graveyard among the great sober pines.

Old Jerry never went back to the sea. He remained by his cables, and lavished upon them and Young Jerry all the love of his nature. When evil days came to the Yellow Dream, he still remained in the employ of the company as watchman over the all but abandoned property.

But this morning he was not visible. Young Jerry only was to be seen, sitting on the cabin step and singing the ancient chantey. He had cooked and eaten his breakfast all by himself, and had just come out to take a look at the world. Twenty feet before him stood the steel drum round which the endless cable worked. By the drum, snug and fast, was the ore-car. Following with his eyes the dizzy flight of the cables to the

Young Jerry broke off his song at the sound of approaching footsteps. A tall, blue-shirted man, a rifle across the hollow of his arm, came out from the gloom of the pine trees. It was Hall, watchman of the Yellow Dragon mine, the cables of which spanned the Sacramento a mile farther up.

"Hello, younker,"* was his greeting. "What you doin' here by your lonesome?"

younker: youngster

"Oh, bachin,"* Jerry tried to answer unconcernedly, as if it were a very ordinary sort of thing. "Dad's away, you see."

bachin: living alone like a bachelor

"Where's he gone?" the man asked.

"San Francisco. Went last night. His brother's dead in the old country, and he's gone down to see the lawyers. Won't be back till tomorrow night."

So spoke Jerry, and with pride, because of the responsibility which had fallen to him of keeping an eye on the property of the Yellow Dream, and the glorious adventure of living alone on the cliff above the river and of cooking his own meals.

"Well, take care of yourself," Hall said, "and don't monkey with the cables. I'm goin' to see if I can't pick up a deer in the Cripple Cow Canyon."

"It's goin' to rain, I think," Jerry said, with mature deliberation.

"And it's little I mind a wettin'," Hall laughed, as he strode away among the trees.

Jerry's prediction concerning rain was more than fulfilled. By ten o'clock the pines were swaying and moaning, the cabin windows rattling, and the rain driving by in fierce squalls.* At half past eleven he kindled a fire, and promptly at the stroke of twelve sat down to his dinner.

squalls: short, intense periods of wind and rain

farther bank, he could see the other drum and the other car.

The contrivance* was worked by gravity, the loaded car crossing the river by virtue of its own weight, and at the same time dragging the empty car back. The loaded car being emptied, and the empty car being loaded with more ore, the performance could be repeated—a performance which had been repeated tens of thousands of times since the day Old Jerry became the keeper of the cables.

contrivance: mechanical device

No out-of-doors for him that day, he decided, when he had washed the few dishes and put them neatly away; and he wondered how wet Hall was and whether he had succeeded in picking up a deer.

At one o'clock there came a knock at the door, and when he opened it, a man and a woman staggered in on the breast of a great gust of wind. They were Mr. and Mrs. Spillane, ranchers, who lived in a lonely valley a dozen miles back from the river.

"Where's Hall?" was Spillane's opening speech, and he spoke sharply and quickly.

Jerry noted that he was nervous and abrupt in his movements, and that Mrs. Spillane seemed laboring under some strong anxiety. She was a thin, washed-out, worked-out woman, whose life of dreary and unending toil had stamped itself harshly upon her face. It was the same life that had bowed her husband's shoulders and gnarled his hands and turned his hair to a dry and dusty gray.

"He's gone hunting up Cripple Cow," Jerry answered. "Did you want to cross?"

The woman began to weep quietly, while Spillane dropped a troubled exclamation and strode to the window. Jerry joined him in gazing out to where the cables lost themselves in the thick downpour.

It was the custom of the backwoods people in that section of country to cross the Sacramento on the Yellow Dragon cable. For this service a small toll was charged, which tolls the Yellow Dragon Company applied to the payment of Hall's wages.

"We've got to get across, Jerry," Spillane said, at the same time jerking his thumb over his shoulder in the direction of his wife. "Her father's hurt at the Clover Leaf. Powder explosion. Not expected to live. We just got word."

Jerry felt himself fluttering inwardly. He knew that Spillane wanted to cross on the Yellow Dream cable, and in the absence of his father he felt that he dared not assume such a responsibility, for the cable had never been used for passengers; in fact, had not been used at all for a long time.

"Maybe Hall will be back soon," he said.

Spillane shook his head, and demanded, "Where's your father?"

"San Francisco," Jerry answered briefly.

Spillane groaned, and fiercely drove his clenched fist into the palm of the other hand. His wife was crying more audibly and Jerry could hear her murmuring, "And Daddy's dyin', dyin'!"

The tears welled up in his own eyes, and he stood irresolute* not knowing what he should do. But the man decided for him.

---
irresolute: indecisive

"Look here, kid," he said, with determination, "the wife and me are goin' over on this here cable of yours! Will you run it for us?"

Jerry backed slightly away. He did it unconsciously, as if recoiling* instinctively from something unwelcome.

---
recoiling: shrinking back in fear

"Better see if Hall's back," he suggested.
"And if he ain't?"
Again Jerry hesitated.

"I'll stand for the risk," Spillane added. "Don't you see, kid, we've simply got to cross!"

Jerry nodded his head reluctantly.

"And there ain't no use waitin' for Hall," Spillane went on. "You know as well as me he ain't back from Cripple Cow this time of day! So come along and let's get started."

No wonder that Mrs. Spillane seemed terrified as they helped her into the ore-car—so Jerry thought, as he gazed into the apparently fathomless* gulf beneath her. For it was so filled with rain and cloud, hurtling and curling in the fierce blast, that the other shore, seven hundred feet away, was invisible, while the cliff at their feet dropped sheer down and lost itself in the swirling vapor. By all appearances it might be a mile to bottom instead of two hundred feet.

---
fathomless: too deep to measure

"All ready?" he asked.

"Let her go!" Spillane shouted to make himself heard above the roar of the wind.

He had clambered in beside his wife, and was holding one of her hands in his.

Jerry looked upon this with disapproval. "You'll need all your hands for holdin' on, the way the wind's yowlin'."

The man and the woman shifted their hands accordingly, tightly gripping the sides of the car, and Jerry slowly and carefully released the brake. The drum began to revolve as the endless cable passed around it, and the car slid slowly out into the chasm,* its trolley wheels rolling on the stationary cable overhead, to which it was suspended.

---
chasm (kăz´əm): canyon

It was not the first time Jerry had worked the cable, but it was the first time he had done so away from the supervising eye of his father. By means of the brake he regulated the speed of the car. It needed regulating, for at times, caught by the stronger gusts of wind, it swayed violently back and forth; and once, just before it was swallowed up in a rain squall, it seemed about to spill out its human contents.

After that Jerry had no way of knowing where the car was except by means of the cable. This he watched keenly as it glided around the drum. "Three hundred feet," he breathed to himself, as the cable markings went by, "three hundred and fifty, four hundred, four hundred and—"

The cable had stopped. Jerry threw off the brake, but it did not move. He caught the cable with his hands and tried to start it by tugging smartly. Something had gone wrong. What? He could not guess; he could not see. Looking up, he could vaguely make out the empty car, which had been crossing from the opposite cliff at a speed equal to that of the loaded car. It was about two hundred and fifty feet away. That meant, he knew, that somewhere in the gray obscurity, two hundred feet above the river and two hundred and fifty feet from the other bank, Spillane and his wife were suspended and stationary.

Three times Jerry shouted with all the shrill force of his lungs, but no answering cry came out of the storm. It was impossible for him to hear them or to make himself heard. As he stood for a moment, thinking rapidly, the flying clouds seemed to thin and lift. He caught a brief glimpse of the swollen Sacramento beneath, and a briefer glimpse of the car and the man and woman. Then the clouds descended thicker than ever.

The boy examined the drum closely, and found nothing the matter with it. Evidently it was the drum on the other side that had gone wrong. He was appalled at thought of the man and woman out there in the midst of the storm, hanging over the abyss,* rocking back and forth in the frail car and igno-

rant of what was taking place on the shore. And he did not like to think of their hanging there while he went round by the Yellow Dragon cable to the other drum.

abyss: deep gulf

But he remembered a block and tackle in the toolhouse, and ran and brought it. They were double blocks, and he murmured aloud, "A purchase of four," as he made the tackle fast to the endless cable. Then he heaved upon it, heaved until it seemed that his arms were being drawn out from their sockets and that his shoulder muscles would be ripped asunder. Yet the cable did not budge. Nothing remained but to cross over to the other side.

He was already soaking wet, so he did not mind the rain as he ran over the trail to the Yellow Dragon. The storm was with him, and it was easy going, although there was no Hall at the other end of it to man the brake for him and regulate the speed of the car. This he did for himself, however, by means of a stout rope, which he passed, with a turn, round the stationary cable.

As the full force of the wind struck him in mid-air, swaying the cable and whistling and roaring past it, and rocking and careening the car, he appreciated more fully what must be the condition of mind of Spillane and his wife. And this appreciation gave strength to him, as, safely across, he fought his way up the other bank, in the teeth of the gale, to the Yellow Dream cable.

To his consternation,* he found the drum in thorough working order. Everything was running smoothly at both ends. Where was the hitch? In the middle, without a doubt.

consternation: bewilderment

From this side, the car containing Spillane was only two hundred and fifty feet away. He could make out the man and woman through the whirling vapor, crouching in the bottom of the car and exposed to the pelting rain and the full fury of the wind. In a lull between the squalls he shouted to Spillane to examine the trolley* of the car.

---
trolley: basket

Spillane heard, for he saw him rise up cautiously on his knees, and with his hands go over both trolley wheels. Then he turned his face toward the bank.

"She's all right, kid!"

Jerry heard the words, faint and far, as from a remote distance. Then what was the matter? Nothing remained but the other and empty car, which he could not see, but which he knew to be there, somewhere in that terrible gulf two hundred feet beyond Spillane's car.

His mind was made up on the instant. He was only fourteen years old, slightly and wirily* built; but his life had been lived among the mountains, his father had taught him no small measure of "sailoring," and he was not particularly afraid of heights.

---
wirily: leanly and strongly

In the toolbox by the drum he found an old monkey wrench and a short bar of iron, also a coil of fairly new Manila rope. He looked in vain for a piece of board with which to rig a boatswain's chair.* There was nothing at hand but large planks, so he was compelled to do without the more comfortable form of saddle.

---
boatswain's (bō´sənz) chair: makeshift chair used by sailors when working outside the boat
---

The saddle he rigged was very simple. With the rope he made merely a large loop round the stationary cable, to which hung the empty car. When he sat in the loop his hands could just reach the cable conveniently, and where the rope was likely to

fray against the cable he lashed his coat, in lieu of* the old sack he would have used had he been able to find one.

---
in lieu of: instead of

These preparations swiftly completed, he swung out over the chasm, sitting in the rope saddle and pulling himself along the cable by his hands. With him he carried the monkey wrench and short iron bar and a few spare feet of rope. It was a slightly uphill pull, but this he did not so much mind as the wind. When the furious gusts hurled him back and forth, sometimes half twisting him about, and he gazed down into the gray depths, he was aware that he was afraid. It was an old cable. What if it should break under his weight and the pressure of the wind?

It was fear he was experiencing, honest fear, and he knew that there was a "gone" feeling in the pit of his stomach, and a trembling of the knees which he could not quell.*

---
quell: suppress

But he held himself bravely to the task. The cable was old and worn, sharp pieces of wire projected from it, and his hands were cut and bleeding by the time he took his first rest, and held a shouted conversation with Spillane. The car was directly beneath him and only a few feet away, so he was able to explain the condition of affairs and his errand.

"Wish I could help you," Spillane shouted at him as he started on, "but the wife's gone all to pieces! Anyway, kid, take care of yourself! I got myself in this fix, but it's up to you to get me out!"

"Oh, I'll do it!" Jerry shouted back. "Tell Mrs. Spillane that she'll be ashore now in a jiffy!"

In the midst of pelting rain, which half-blinded him, swinging from side to side like a rapid and erratic* pendulum, his torn hands paining him severely and his lungs panting from his exertions and panting from the very air which the wind sometimes blew into his mouth with strangling force, he finally arrived at the empty car.

erratic: irregular

A single glance showed him that he had not made the dangerous journey in vain. The front trolley wheel, loose from long wear, had jumped the cable, and the cable was now jammed tightly between the wheel and the sheave block.

One thing was clear—the wheel must be removed from the block. A second thing was equally clear—while the wheel was being removed, the car would have to be fastened to the cable by the rope he had brought.

At the end of a quarter of an hour, beyond making the car secure, he had accomplished nothing. The key* which bound the wheel on its axle was rusted and jammed. He hammered at it with one hand and held on the best he could with the other, swinging and twisting his body, and made his blows miss more often than not. Nine-tenths of the strength he expended was in trying to hold himself steady. For fear that he might drop the monkey wrench, he made it fast to his wrist with his handkerchief.

key: bolt or pin

At the end of half an hour Jerry had hammered the key clear, but he could not draw it out. A dozen times it seemed that he must give up in despair, that all the danger and toil he had gone through were for nothing. Then an idea came to him, and he went through his pockets with feverish haste, and found what he sought for—a tenpenny nail.

But for that nail, put in his pocket he knew not when or why, he would have had to make another trip over the cable and back. Thrusting the nail through the looped

head of the key, he at last had a grip, and in no time the key was out.

Then came punching and prying with the iron bar to get the wheel itself free from where it was jammed by the cable against the side of the block. After that Jerry replaced the wheel, and by means of a rope, heaved up on the car till the trolley once more rested properly on the cable.

All this took time. More than an hour and a half had elapsed since his arrival at the empty car. He removed the detaining ropes, and the trolley wheels began slowly to revolve. The car was moving, and he knew that somewhere beyond, although he could not see, the car of Spillane was likewise moving, and in the opposite direction.

There was no need for a brake, for his weight sufficiently counterbalanced the weight in the other car; and soon he saw the cliff rising out of the cloud depths and the old familiar drum going round and round.

Jerry climbed out and made the car securely fast. He did it deliberately and carefully, and then, quite unheroiclike, he sank down by the drum, regardless of the pelting storm, and burst out sobbing.

There were many reasons why he sobbed—partly from the pain in his hands, which was excruciating; partly from exhaustion; partly from relief and release from the nerve-tension he had been under for so long; and in a large measure from thankfulness that the man and woman were saved.

They were not there to thank him; but somewhere beyond that howling, storm-driven gulf he knew they were hurrying over the trail toward the Clover Leaf.

Jerry staggered to the cabin, and his hand left the white knob red with blood as he opened the door, but he took no notice of it.

He was too proudly contented with himself, for he was certain that he had done well, and he was honest enough to admit to himself that he had done well. But a small regret arose and persisted in his thoughts—if his father had only been there to see!

ABOUT THE AUTHOR

John Griffith (Jack) London (1876–1916) was born into an extremely poor family in San Francisco. From a young age he worked long hours at a variety of jobs while also attending school. When he was ten years old, he delivered papers both before and after school, rising at 3 a.m. in order to accomplish the job. He also worked in a cannery, occasionally for as long as thirty-six hours straight, earning only ten cents an hour. Subsequent experiences as a hobo, an oyster pirate, a seaman, and a gold prospector provided experiences that served as background for many of his stories.

London experienced great public success as the author of such works as *The Call of the Wild* and *White Fang*. His private life, however, was very disappointing. For years he spent most of his money paying off debts incurred by his parents, and his first marriage failed after three years. When London was thirty-six, he began building his dream castle, which he named Wolf House, and this endeavor forced him to write almost nonstop to pay his expenses. Just before he was to move in, the house burned to the ground. Following this devastating blow, he wrote his daughter Joan a letter berating her for neglecting him and severing his ties with her. Three years later he wrote her another letter, making a desperate attempt to reconcile their differences. Unfortunately he died before she could even receive the letter. In spite of the enduring popularity that Jack London achieved as a writer, his life is an example of the miserable failure of a godless man seeking to attain happiness and success within himself.

THINKING ZONE

You may remember having discussed the two main types of point of view in Unit 1. The first-person point of view employs a narrator who is a part of the story and who tells the story using the pronoun *I*, while the third-person point of view uses the pronouns *he*, *she*, and *it* to tell the story. Within the third-person point of view, there are two further divisions: the omniscient point of view and the limited point of view.

With the **omniscient point of view**, the reader gains insight into the thoughts and feelings of all of the story's characters. The reader sees things from multiple perspectives, rather than from just one person's viewpoint, and can more easily understand the characters in the story. In the **limited point of view**, the reader's scope is limited, and he can comprehend the thoughts and feelings of only one (or, in some cases, a small number) of the characters. In "You've Got to Learn," we know what most of the characters are thinking—the otters, Andy, Mr. and Mrs. Gates—so the story is written from the omniscient point of view. "The Brothers" is written from the limited point of view because we hear only what Baard thinks and feels about the situation. Can you figure out what this story's point of view is?

1. *[interpretive]* Who is the protagonist in this story?

   _____

   _____

2. *[critical]* Would you say that this story was written predominantly from the **omniscient** or the **limited point of view**? Explain.

   _____

   _____

   _____

   _____

   _____

   _____

3. *[critical]* Is there any foreshadowing early in the story that hints at the crisis to come?

_____

_____

_____

_____

4. *[interpretive/critical]* Following the Spillanes' demand for Jerry to let them cross, we are told that "Jerry backed slightly away. He did it unconsciously, as if recoiling instinctively from something unwelcome." How does this description foreshadow the events to come?

_____

_____

_____

_____

_____

5. *[interpretive]* What positive character traits does Jerry show in the face of danger?

_____

_____

_____

_____

6. *[critical]* What does the phrase "if his father had only been there to see," expressed by Jerry, tell us about him?

_____

_____

_____

_____

YOU NEED TO GO UPSTAIRS

RUMER GODDEN

In "You Need to Go Upstairs," Godden dispenses with the narrator and allows the heroine to address the reader directly, telling her own story and describing her personal perceptions. This technique broadens our view and helps us see that for people like Ally, the most ordinary activity may be an extraordinary adventure.

And just when everything is comfortably settled you need to go upstairs.

You are sitting in the garden for the first time this year, sitting on a cushion on the grass by Mother. The feel of the grass is good; when you press it down and lift your hand the blades spring up again at once as strong as ever; they will not be kept lying down.

You sit with your legs straight in front of you; they have come out from their winter stockings and are very thin and knobbly, but the sun is beginning to warm them gently as if it were glad to see them again.

Your back is against Mother's chair and occasionally she puts her finger between your collar and your skin, to feel if you are warm; you are warm and you pick up your knitting because you can knit; with your fingers you follow the wool along the big wooden pins and you say, "Knit one—knit another"; with the slow puffs of wind. The wind brings the garden scents and the sounds to you; sounds of birds and neighbors and the street.

"I like it, Mother."

"So do I."

Then Doreen, who comes in the afternoons to help, brings out a visitor; voices and footsteps; Mother has to get up but you hang your head and go on knitting. Voices creaking and rustling and a sign. The visitor has sat down. Presently she whispers to Mother, "What is her name?"

"Her name is Alice," says Mother loudly and clearly to blot out the whisper. "We call her Ally. Ally, stand up and say how do you do."

"Ah, don't!" says the visitor and you do not stand up; you press the grass down flat with your hand. It is then that you know you need to go upstairs. The cloakroom is out of order; you have to go upstairs.

The visitor's voice falls from high up, almost into your lap, cutting off the wind and the birds, cutting off Mother, so that you have to stand up.

"Yes, Ally?"

"Mother, I need to go upstairs," and you hurry to say, "I can go by myself, Mother."

Mother is looking at your face—you cannot look yourself, yet you can always feel Mother's look; now she is doubtful, but she is proud, and after a moment she says, "Very well, dear." You understand what she does not say, *Be careful! Be careful!*

"Alone?" breathes the visitor, and prickles seem to rise all over you. You have said you will do it alone, and you will. You turn your back on the visitor.

From the chairs to the poplars is easy; you can hear them straining and moving their branches just enough to tell you where they are. There are two, and when you are up to them, you separate your hands the distance apart you think they will be and you do not hit them, you find them; their trunks

are under your hands and you stay to feel those trunks; they are rough and smooth together; they are like people, they are alive.

On the other side of the trees is a smell of cinders where, last winter, ashes were thrown down on the snow. The smell warns you. Move your feet along the grass, don't lift them, because the path is there and it has a little brick-edge hidden in the grass. You fell over it last summer; suddenly you were down on the grass and you have a fright about falling. You won't fall, the cinder smell has warned you. You find the path. Lift your feet—one—two. The cinders are crunching, now you can go along the path to where the flowers are.

"It's wonderful," says the visitor and her voice sounds like tears. "Her . . . little blue . . . jacket."

"It's a nice jacket, isn't it?" says Mother. "We got it at Pollard's bargain counter. Ally feels it's warm and gay."

That visitor there would be surprised if you picked the flowers, one by one, and took them to her and told her what they were. "I see no reason why you should not know your flowers," Mother has often told you. "Flowers have shapes and smells as well as colors." This is the hyacinth bed: hyacinths are easy, strong in scent and shaped like little pagodas*—"Remember, I told you about pagodas"—and these are crocuses and these are aconites—but Mother is not close and you remember that Schiff may be out on the path.

---

pagodas: Far Eastern religious structures

Schiff! You stop. Schiff is so small that you might easily step on him, but Schiff is large enough for you to fall over. Mother . . . but you must not call, you must go on. You think of falling, you can't help thinking of falling—down—into nothing until you get hit. Mother! Schiff! Mother! But you have not called and Mother is saying in what seems an ordinary voice to the visitor, but is her special loud voice for you. "How strange! With all this sun, our tortoise has not come out on the path today."

At the end of the path are two orange bushes with bitter-smelling leaves; they are bad little bushes, with twigs that catch on your coat; you don't like them and you think you will hurry past. There are two bushes in two tubs, and there are four steps; you can remember that, twice two are four. One—two—three—four, and your foot is on the last step, but you catch at the air, catch at the door with a sharp pain ringing in your shin, catch your breath and catch the door and save yourself.

Someone, somebody, has left the scraper* on the step. It has been pulled right out. You stand there shaking, boiling with anger, the pain hurting in your leg, but there is no sound from the garden; the visitor has not seen.

---

scraper: metal plate used for cleaning mud off footwear

Now you are in the house. At first it is always curiously still; and then always out of the stillness you find it. This is the hall and in it are the smells and sounds of all the rooms: furniture cream and hot pipes, carpet and dried roses from the drawing-room, tobacco and a little of pickles from the dining-room, mint and hot cake from the kitchen, and down the stairs comes soap from the bathroom. The loo* is up, next door to the bathroom—it has a piece of pine-smelling brick in a wire holder on the wall.

---

loo: a British term for bathroom, or specifically for the commode

With the smells come the house sounds, all so familiar: Doreen's footsteps in the kitchen, a whirring like insects from the refrigerator and the clocks, a curtain flapping in the wind and a tapping, a tiny rustle from the canary. You know all these things better than anyone else.

Now you let go of the door—like this— and you go across the hall. Of course you could have gone round by the wall to the stairs, feeling around the hat rack and chest, but you would not do that any more than you would go up the stairs on your hands and knees. No, you go across—like this—like this—and the big round knob at the bottom of the stair is in your hands. Dear knob. You put your cheek against the wood; it is smooth and firm. Now you can go upstairs.

You are not at all afraid of the stairs. Why? Because Mother has put signals there for you, under the rail where no one can find them, and they guide you all the way up; now your legs go up the stairs as quickly as notes up a piano—almost. At the top is a small wooden heart for you to feel with your fingers; when you reach it, it is like a message and your own heart gets steady. It was not quite steady up the stairs.

"Ally, always, always be careful of the landing." Mother has said that so many times. The landing feels the same to you as the hall but it isn't. Once you dropped

stairs behind you with your foot and they are still there but now you are afraid to let go in case you can't step away. It is steep—steep behind you. Suppose you don't move away? Suppose you hit something—like the chair—and pitch down backwards? Little stickers come out along your back and neck; the back of your neck is cold, your fingers are sticky too, holding the heart signal. Suddenly you can't move away from the stairs. Mother, Mother, but you bite your lips. You must not call out.

Through the window you hear voices—voices from the path.

Drops of water burst out on your neck and under your hair, and you leave the rail and step out on to the carpet and walk very boldly towards the verbena* and warm toweling and the hot-metal-from-the-bath-taps smell.

---

verbena: pleasant-smelling garden plant

---

a ball over, and the sound came from far away down; if you tripped on the landing you might drop like the ball.

Now? Or not now? Are you facing the right way? That is an old fright. Did you turn round without noticing? You feel the

"Is she all right? Is she?"

"Ally, are you managing?" calls Mother.

"Perfectly," you answer, and you shut the loo door.

ABOUT THE AUTHOR

Rumer Godden (1907–98), born Margaret Rumer Godden in Sussex, England, is best known for her fiction, which is an outgrowth of her own life experiences. From the age of nine months until age thirteen, Godden lived in India with her parents and three sisters. At age seven she wrote her first book. Her interest in writing continued but remained dormant until a vice principal with a special interest in the fine arts took her under her wing and helped her learn French, literature, and music. This training laid the groundwork for Godden's writing career. When she was about fifteen years old, Godden financed the publication of a book of poems under a pseudonym. Not one copy sold. However, persistence paid off when, in 1939, her novel *Black Narcissus* became a runaway bestseller in the United States. Several of Rumer Godden's novels and stories have been adapted for motion pictures or television. She is also renowned for her children's stories and books.

THINKING ZONE

Have you ever talked to yourself? "You better not be late again!" "Remember to take the garbage out." As you read "You Need to Go Upstairs," you probably noticed the main character's talking to herself throughout the story. For her story about a young blind girl's venturing to the house alone, author Rumer Godden uses stream-of-consciousness narration. **Stream of consciousness** is a type of writing in which the author attempts to reproduce the flow of thoughts in a character's mind with little attention to grammar or logic. The idea is that the reader is inside the character's head, listening to her unedited thoughts. Most of the story is a running commentary by Ally of her fears as she makes her way into the empty house. Since she is coaching herself around the various obstacles she encounters, she uses the second-person pronoun *you* throughout, even though it is a first-person account: "You need to go upstairs" actually means "I need to" and is worded so in the written dialogue of the story.

1. *[interpretive]* When did you realize Ally is blind? What details let you know?

_____

_____

_____

_____

_____

_____

2. *[literal]* What are the dangers that Ally faces on her excursion?

_____

_____

_____

_____

_____

_____

3. *[interpretive]* List at least two examples of concrete sensory imagery for each of these senses: (a) touch, (b) smell, and (c) sound.

_____

_____

_____

_____

_____

_____

_____

_____

4. *[critical]* What do you think the authorial purpose for writing this story was? What kind of response do you think Godden wanted from her readers?

_____

_____

_____

_____

_____

Authorial purpose—*the intent an author has in writing a story*

5. *[critical]* What are the implications of the last sentence of the story?

_____

_____

_____

6. *[appreciative]* Did you like the **stream-of-consciousness** method employed in this selection? Did it add to or detract from your enjoyment of the story?

_____

_____

_____

_____

_____

INCIDENT OF THE FRENCH CAMP

ROBERT BROWNING

War is often the time when adventuresome spirits answer the call to heroic actions.

You know we French stormed Ratisbon:*
    A mile or so away,
On a little mount, Napoleon
    Stood on our storming-day;
With neck out-thrust, you fancy how,   5
    Legs wide, arms locked behind,
As if to balance the prone* brow,
    Oppressive with its mind.

Just as perhaps he mused, "My plans
    That soar, to earth may fall,   10
Let once my army-leader Lannes
    Waver at yonder wall,"—
Out 'twixt the battery-smokes there flew
    A rider, bound on bound
Full galloping; nor bridle drew   15
    Until he reached the mound.

Then off there flung in smiling joy,
    And held himself erect
By just his horse's mane, a boy;
    You hardly could suspect   20
(So tight he kept his lips compressed,
    Scarce any blood came through),
You looked twice ere you saw his breast
    Was all but shot in two.

"Well," cried he, "Emperor, by God's grace   25
    We've got you Ratisbon!
The marshal's in the market-place,
    And you'll be there anon*
To see your flag-bird flap his vans*
    Where I, to heart's desire,   30
Perched him!" The chief's eye flashed; his plans
    Soared up again like fire.

Ratisbon: German city stormed by
    Napoleon in 1809

prone: forward and downward

anon: soon
vans: wings

The chief's eye flashed, but presently
Softened itself, as sheathes
   A film the mother eagle's eye   35
When her bruised eaglet breathes:
   "You're wounded!" "Nay;" his soldier's pride
Touched to the quick, he said,
   "I'm killed, sire!" And, his chief beside,
Smiling, the boy fell dead.   40

ABOUT THE AUTHOR

From early childhood Robert Browning (1812–89) showed signs of great creativity. By age twelve he had produced a book of poems that he later destroyed, and at age seventeen, he set out to be a poet after securing his father's financial support and encouragement. Perhaps one reason his father was willing to back Browning financially was an experience in which he had angered his own father, who then sent him a bill for all the expenses of rearing him, including those for his birth. Regardless of the reason, the allowance Browning received from his father for several decades allowed him to concentrate his efforts on his writing.

Browning wrote for years before achieving any degree of fame. However, his wife Elizabeth was already well-known as a writer when he met and fell in love with her. Robert and Elizabeth were happily married for sixteen years before Elizabeth died. Devastated by her death, Browning left their home in Italy and for two years withdrew from society and from writing. After re-entering society, he became a well-known figure at social gatherings. In 1889 Browning died at his son's home in Venice, and following his public funeral, his remains were buried in Poets' Corner of Westminster Abbey, London.

EMILY GEIGER

AUTHOR UNKNOWN

The story of Emily Geiger has become legend in the South. Her adventure
during the American Revolution is one of intrigue and bravery.

'Twas in the days of the Revolution,—
    Dark days were they and drear,—
And by Carolina firesides
    The women sat in fear;
For the men were away at the fighting,   5
    And sad was the news that came,
That the battle was lost; and the death-list
    Held many a loved one's name.

When as heart-sore they sat round the camp-fires,
    "What, ho! Who'll volunteer   10
To carry a message to Sumter?"
    A voice rang loud and clear.
There was a sudden silence,
    But not a man replied;
They knew too well of the peril   15
    Of one who dared that ride.

Outspoke then Emily Geiger
    With a rich flush on her cheek,—
"Give me the message to be sent;
    I am the one you seek.   20
For I am a Southern woman;
    And I'd rather do and dare
Than sit by a lonely fireside,
    My heart gnawed through with care."

They gave her the precious missive;*   25
    And on her own good steed
She rode away, 'mid the cheers of the men,
    Upon her daring deed.
And away through the lonely forests,
    Steadily galloping on,   30
She saw the sun sink low in the sky,
    And in the west go down.

missive: written message

"Halt!—or I fire!" On a sudden
    A rifle clicked close by.
"Let you pass? Not we, till we know you are   35
    No messenger or spy."
"She's a Whig,*—from her face,—and I will wager,"
    Swore the officer of the day.
"To the guard-house, and send for a woman
    To search her without delay."   40

No time did she lose in bewailing;
    As the bolt creaked in the lock,
She quickly drew the precious note
    That was hidden in her frock.
And she read it through with hurried care,   45
    Then ate it piece by piece,
And calmly sat her down to wait
    Till time should bring release.

They brought her out in a little,
    And set her on her steed,   50
With many a rude apology,
    For his discourteous deed.
On, on, once more through the forest black,
    The good horse panting strains,
Till the sentry's challenge: "Who comes there?"   55
    Tells that the end she gains.

Ere an hour, in the camp of Sumter
    There was hurrying to and fro.
"Saddle and mount, saddle and mount,"
    The bugles shrilly blow.   60
"Forward trot!" and the long ranks wheel,
    And into the darkness glides:
Long shall the British rue* that march
    And Emily Geiger's ride.

Whig: supporter of the colonies during the American Revolution

rue: regret

THINKING ZONE

In some instances, writers of poetry seek to tell a story within the poem they compose. Poems that tell a story are known as **narrative poems.** Some famous examples of narrative poetry are Henry Wadsworth Longfellow's "Song of Hiawatha" and Alfred, Lord Tennyson's "Enoch Arden." Long narrative poems about a great hero that are expressed in a formal, dignified style are called **epics.** Early Greek epics were told orally and were often sung in praise of the hero they described. Well-known examples of epics include *The Iliad* and *The Odyssey* by Homer and *Paradise Lost* by John Milton.

1. *[literal/interpretive]* What is the rhyme scheme of stanza 1 of "Incident of the French Camp"?

   _____

   _____

2. *[critical]* What is the irony in the fifth stanza of "Incident of the French Camp"?

   _____

   _____

   _____

   _____

   _____

   _____

   _____

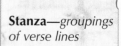

Stanza—*groupings of verse lines*

3. *[critical]* What makes the boy's actions in "Incident of the French Camp" heroic?

   _____

   _____

   _____

4. *[interpretive]* Is either (or both) of the two poems a **narrative poem?** Would you classify either as an **epic?**

_____

_____

_____

_____

5. *[literal]* What is the setting of "Emily Geiger"?

_____

_____

> **Setting**—*the time and place where the action of the story occurs*

6. *[interpretive]* After having been captured, what does Emily do with the note that she has been given to carry?

_____

_____

7. *[interpretive]* What character traits do the boy in "Incident of the French Camp" and Emily Geiger share? How do they differ?

_____

_____

_____

_____

_____

_____

8. *[appreciative]* Which of the two heroes did you admire the most— the boy or Emily Geiger? Why?

_____

_____

_____

_____

_____

THE FIRST ROBIN

HEYWOOD BROUN

What is success? People have different ideas of what success is. Being the best in one's field may be success for one person while another may consider success to be a life-long dedication to a calling that brings him little of this world's goods. After you read this selection, decide whether or not the robin was successful.

"York, Pa.—With the temperature at 10 degrees below zero the first robin of the year was seen in York today. It was found dead on Penn Common."

Penn Common: an area of open land that served as a popular gathering place

Call me an old sentimentalist if you will, but this seems to me the most tragic news note of the cold wave. I like people better than robins, and there has been widespread and agonizing suffering. But, you see, this was the first robin. He was by all odds the pioneer of his clan. He flew up from the South days, weeks and months before any reasonable robin weather was to be expected.

Without doubt the rest tried to discourage him. They spoke of the best recorded experience of bird kind. "Rome wasn't built in a day," some other robin told him. And no doubt he was advised that if he insisted on such precipitate* action he would split the group and no good would come of it.

precipitate: rapid and heedless

Somehow I seem to hear him saying: "If ten will follow me I'd call that an army. Are there two who'll join up? Or maybe one?"

But the robins all recoiled and clung to their little patches of sun under the Southern skies. "Later, maybe," they told him. "Not now. First there must be a campaign of education."

"Well," replied the robin who was all for going to York, Pa., without waiting for feathery reinforcements, "I know one who'll try it. I'm done with arguments, and here I go."

He was so full of high hopes and dedication that he rose almost with the roar of a partridge. For a few seconds he was a fast moving speck up above the palm trees, and then you couldn't spot him even with field glasses. He was lost in the blue and flying for dear life.

"Impetuous, I call it," said one of the elder statesmen while someone took him a worm.

"He always did want to show off," announced another, and everybody agreed that no good would come of it.

As it turned out, maybe they were right. It's pretty hard to prove that anything has been gained when a robin freezes to death on Penn Common. However, I imagine that he died with a certain sense of elation. None of the rest thought he could get there. And he did. The break in weather turned out to be against him. He just guessed wrong in that one respect, and so I wouldn't think of calling him a complete failure.

When the news gets back home to the robins who didn't go I rather expect that they'll make him a hero. The elder statesmen will figure that since he is dead his ideas can't longer be dangerous, and they cannot deny the lift and the swing of his venture.

After all, he was the first robin. He looked for the Spring, and it failed him. Now he belongs to that noble army of first robins.

Many great names are included. The honors of office and public acclaim, of ribbons and medals, the keys of the city—these are seldom the perquisite* of men or birds in the first flight. These go to fifth, sixth and even twentieth robins.

perquisite: a right reserved as an exclusive benefit

It is almost a rule that the first robin must die alone on some bleak common before mankind will agree that he was a hero. And sometimes it takes fifty years and often a hundred.

John Brown,* Galileo,* and those who sought goals before the world was quite ready are all in good standing.

John Brown: an American reformer who opposed slavery
Galileo: Italian scientist who held to the sun's being at the center of the universe

The man who says, "That would be swell, but, of course, you can't do it," is generally as right as rain; but who wants to get up and cheer for frustration? In the long haul the first robin is more right than any. It was his idea. He softened the way for the others. And with him even failure is its own kind of triumph.

He is not the victim of dry rot or caution or doomed eyestrain from too close an attention to ledgers.

"Here I go!" he cries, and I wouldn't be surprised to be told that the first minute of flight is reward enough, no matter what follows.

And so in a metaphorical way of speaking I bare my head and bow low in the general direction of the ice-covered plain which is known as Penn Common. And I think that the brief address should carry the statement: "You were the first, and after you will

come others. They will inherit the grubs and the nests and the comfort. But yours is the glory. You are the first robin."

ABOUT THE AUTHOR

Heywood Campbell Broun (1888–1939), the son of an English immigrant, was born in Brooklyn, New York. He began his professional writing career as a sports writer for the *New York Morning Telegraph*. He later worked at the *New York Tribune* as a drama critic and later covered World War I as a foreign correspondent in France. He then moved to the *New York World*, where he began writing his syndicated column "It Seems to Me," a column he continued to write until his death.

In his column Broun often wrote about social injustices and the plight of the "underdog" in American society. He became so disillusioned with American democracy that he ran as a socialist for Congress in 1930. In 1933 Broun founded the American Newspaper Guild, now known as The Newspaper Guild. Each year since Broun's death, the Guild has presented the Heywood Broun Award to a journalist whose work addresses some injustice.

THINKING ZONE

The literary genre you have just read is one that may well have changed the course of history! In December of 1776, George Washington read an important piece to his men at Valley Forge. The piece was written by Thomas Paine: "These are the times that try men's souls," the famous essay began. The men rallied, the war was won, and the rest is, as they say, history. An **essay** is a work that seeks to state a point of view, discuss a subject, or persuade a reader to accept an argument. Depending upon what the author seeks to communicate to the reader, essays can be formal, with rigid structure and strict adherence to the rules of grammar; or they can be in-formal, adopting a more conversational and candid tone.

The father of the modern essay is probably Michel de Montaigne, whose personal musings about a variety of sub-jects—from reason and repentance to cats and kidneys—are still considered among the best ever written. Other noted modern essayists were Francis Bacon, Joseph Addison, Richard Steele, and Samuel Johnson. More contemporary essayists include George Orwell and E. B. White. As you study the essay form further—both as an academic study and as a form of creative expression—you will no doubt discover the joy of expressing yourself through the essay.

1. *[interpretive]* Is the **essay** "The First Robin" a formal or informal one?

   _____

   _____

   _____

2. *[literal/critical]* What reason does the author give for his admira-tion of the dead robin? Are we supposed to read his explanation literally?

   _____

   _____

   _____

   _____

   _____

3. *[critical]* Look closely at the end of the essay. What is the author really trying to communicate through his story about the robin?

_____

_____

_____

_____

_____

4. *[critical]* What is the author's tone? Does the author keep a consistent tone throughout his essay?

_____

_____

_____

Tone—*the attitude of the author toward his subject*

_____

_____

_____

_____

_____

5. *[appreciative]* Besides Galileo and John Brown, can you think of another person from history who fits the characteristics of those that the author describes near the end of the essay? Explain your answer.

_____

_____

_____

_____

_____

The Way of the Water-Hyacinth

Zawgee

Translated from the Burmese by Lyn Aye

A flower seems an unlikely explorer. Notice, however, how the author speaks of the water-hyacinth as if it shares the characteristics of a determined adventurer.

Bobbing on the breeze blown waves
Bowing to the tide
Hyacinth rises and falls

Falling but not felled
By flotsam,* twigs, leaves   5
She ducks, bobs and weaves.

Ducks, ducks by the score*
Jolting, quacking and more
She spins through—

Spinning, swamped, slimed, sunk   10
She rises, resolute*
Still crowned by petals.

flotsam: floating trash

score: literally, twenty items; figuratively, many

resolute: determined

About the Author

    Zawgee, sometimes referred to as Zorjee, was a Burmese poet and librarian. Not much is known about him except through the person who translated his poem into English. Translator Lyn Aye was born in Burma (renamed Myanmar in 1989) but now lives in California, where he is an anesthesiologist. Aye remembers that poetry and reading were important parts of the lives of the people of Burma because they did not have access to television. A quiet, gentle man, Zawgee and his wife came often to the Aye home, and Aye remembers hearing recitations of "The Way of the Water-Hyacinth" as a child. Probably because water-hyacinths are so common in Burma along the lakes and rivers, Zawgee chose it as a symbol of the common people. Aye recalls that the poem was well-known in Burma. When Aye thinks of the poem, he remembers his childhood.

THINKING ZONE

In earlier units you learned that parallelism is one of the defining features of poetry. Because they highlight similarities of thought or sound, the literary devices of repetition, anaphora, and rhyme may be considered types of parallelism. Poets use these devices in order to better communicate their themes and to delight the reader through clever wordplay. Another literary device that can be a type of parallelism is alliteration. **Alliteration** is the repetition of initial consonant sounds (or sometimes the beginning sound of a stressed syllable in a word) in a group of words, and it can be used in poetry as well as in prose. Line two of "Emily Geiger" contains an example of alliteration: "*D*ark *d*ays were they, and *dr*ear." This repetition of sounds tends to add to the beauty of the spoken text as well as to support the meaning of the words. Consider the following lines from John Milton's *Paradise Lost*: "Of man's *f*irst disobedience, and the *fr*uit / Of that *f*orbidden tree." Milton alliterates the words *first*, *fruit*, and *forbidden* and in those three words alone gives the main thought of the opening of his poem. Pay attention to alliteration in the poetry you read, and you may be able to find extra meaning.

1. *[literal]* What are the obstacles that the water-hyacinth must face?

   _____

   _____

2. *[interpretive]* How does the poet use repetition and rhyme in this translation of the poem?

   _____

   _____

   _____

   _____

   _____

   _____

   _____

3. *[interpretive]* List examples of **alliteration** in this translation of the poem.

_____

_____

_____

_____

4. *[critical]* What does the author's tone toward the water-hyacinth seem to be?

_____

_____

_____

_____

5. *[appreciative]* How might one use this poem about the water-hyacinth to serve as an analogy of how humans should approach obstacles in their lives?

_____

_____

_____

_____

_____

Analogy—*a comparison of one thing to another*

6. *[critical]* What is ironic about the last stanza? How is this irony talked about in the Bible?

_____

_____

_____

_____

_____

_____

ALL THAT IS GOLD DOES NOT GLITTER

J. R. R. TOLKIEN

Sometimes an adventurer may be mistaken for a wanderer, or one who roams aimlessly. Do you think a true adventurer ever wanders? Why or why not? What does Tolkien's poem say about "those who wander"?

All that is gold does not glitter,

Not all those who wander are lost;

The old that is strong does not wither,

Deep roots are not reached by the frost.

From the ashes a fire shall be woken,

A light from the shadows shall spring;

Renewed shall be blade that was broken,

The crownless again shall be king.

ABOUT THE AUTHOR

J. R. R. (John Ronald Reuel) Tolkien (1892–1973) was born in South Africa to English parents. In 1896 Tolkien left South Africa with his mother and brother to return to England. His father was to follow soon after; however, his father contracted rheumatic fever and died while still in South Africa.

Tolkien was an avid reader and a good student. At Oxford he studied philology, the study of words and language. From his interest in Icelandic, Norse, and Gothic mythology, he developed the characters and names for which he is famous.

Tolkien married his childhood sweetheart, Edith Bratt, in 1916, shortly before he joined the World War I effort. Tolkien served for only a short time before he contracted trench fever and was sent back to England. During his recuperation he created a mythology that would later be a part of his celebrated books. Tolkien later became a professor at Oxford University and developed a longtime friendship with fellow author C. S. Lewis.

In 1936 Tolkien began *The Hobbit*. After the initial failure of his work *Silmarillion*, Tolkien began writing his trilogy *The Lord of the Rings*. The publication of Tolkien's books brought him unsought-for fame. He was pleased at his success but did not enjoy the intrusion into his family life. Tolkien died of pneumonia in 1973, two years after his wife died. In 2006 Tolkien's son Christopher completed a thirty-year editing project of one of his father's works, *The Children of Hurin*.

THINKING ZONE

Have you ever heard the expression "He couldn't see the forest for the trees"? This expression is sometimes used to convey the idea that though someone may have an understanding of the details of an issue and feel strongly in favor of or against it, he may not have as clear a picture of the entire issue as he believes he does. The expression is an example of a **paradox**, a statement that seems on its surface to be self-contradictory but when used at the right time makes good sense.

When interpreting a paradoxical statement within a work—or any portion of a larger work—one may need to examine that statement's **context**. Generally, the term *context* refers to any outside factors surrounding a work that may provide additional insight into its meaning. The term is usually used, however, to describe how surrounding passages affect the meaning of a specific portion (such as a quotation). This type of context is especially important in interpretation of the Bible. Often, people will misinterpret individual verses from the Bible because they ignore the larger context of those verses. Other types of context, such as historical context and authorial context, also contribute to the reader's understanding of the author's message. Historical context refers to the time period and events during which the work was written (or sometimes the time period of its setting), while authorial context refers to the background and ideas of the author.

1. *[critical]* The poem that you have read was taken from J. R. R. Tolkien's novel *The Fellowship of the Ring* and is known as "The Riddle of Strider." The poem talks about a character named Strider, whose real name is Aragorn. He knows that he is of noble descent but is living as a ranger roaming the countryside. When read in this context, what possible meaning might the **paradox** in lines 1 and 2 have?

_____

_____

_____

_____

2. *[critical]* Given the **context** above in question 1, how may one interpret lines 7 and 8?

_____

_____

3. *[interpretive]* Are there any other examples of paradox in the poem (besides lines 1 and 2)? What is the theme that is echoed throughout lines 3–8?

_____

_____

_____

_____

_____

4. *[critical]* The first line of the poem is a twist on the popular expression "All that glisters (or glitters) is not gold," from Shakespeare. Think about the meanings of both statements. How are they different? Do they contradict one another, or are the statements complementary?

_____

_____

_____

_____

_____

5. *[critical]* Tolkien himself disliked allegories, but one can see similarities between Tolkien's stories and the story of Scripture. In particular, consider how this poem and Philippians 2:5–11 are similar. How are they different?

_____

_____

_____

_____

_____

_____

_____

ELUSIVE REST AREA—JULY 11, 1976

ERMA BOMBECK

Perhaps you know someone who has had the following experience, or perhaps you have had the experience yourself. Feeling trapped in your vehicle can be quite frustrating. Was your experience (or one you know of) as humorous as this one?

Last summer when our family took to the highways, we noted that every 15 miles or so there was an exit on the freeway marked REST AREA. As we whizzed by, we saw happy families at play. Daddy was making yummies over a grill, the kids were tossing a Frisbee, Mother was moving a picnic table that was chained to the ground to the shade, and the dog was holding his stomach with laughter.

"We could do that," I said enviously. "It wouldn't take much to toss a cooler, a bag of charcoal and a few folding chairs in the backseat. We could stretch our legs, use the facilities, get a cold drink of water, and Daddy could read one of those big maps framed in glass to find out where we are."

This year, everyone forgot but me. When we packed the car, I announced, "No more driving for days to find a restaurant where grease is the beverage. This year, it's rest areas for the Bombecks."

We were on the road only 15 minutes when we saw our first rest area. "Want to stop?" asked my husband.

"No need." I smiled confidently. "There'll be another one in thirty miles."

I was right; 30 miles later was another rest area. Another 30 miles, we saw a third. Then lunchtime came and we never saw another one.

At two o'clock, the children became restless. One started to kick the back of the seat in protest. "Sit back and put your seat belt on," I commanded.

"I ate it," came the reply.

At 2:30, one child with his nose pressed against the window shouted, "Rest area spotted at nine o'clock!" We swiveled around and said numbly, "Rest area acknowledged . . . negative . . . on wrong side of turnpike."

At three o'clock, our stomachs were singing as a group. We were irritable, listless and one of the kids had raw hamburger breath, but I couldn't prove it.

"Check the road map," said my husband. "Isn't that a rest area marked with a little tepee? Don't you see it?"

"No. It's my saliva," I said.

By four o'clock we could stand it no longer. My husband pulled over to a soft shoulder under a sign that read NO PARKING ANYTIME. Here, we ripped through plastic with our teeth, ate cold wieners, and watched tomatoes drip off our elbows while we were blown off our feet by passing traffic.

We weren't on our way 15 minutes when we saw a sign: REST AREA.

I knew without looking that there would be one every 30 miles from here on in.

About the Author

Erma Bombeck (1927–96) was born in Dayton, Ohio. In 1949 she graduated from the University of Dayton with a degree in English. She began her career as a newspaper reporter, but after she married, she left her job and devoted her time to her family. Later, when her children were older, she began to write again. Bombeck distinguished herself as an American humorist in her daily newspaper column "At Wit's End." She received three dollars per column for her early submissions to the *Kettering-Oakwood Times*. By 1965 her column appeared nationally in more than five hundred newspapers. Bombeck spent the next thirty years writing and speaking about her life as a homemaker, wife, and mother. In 1973 she won the Mark Twain Award for humor, and in 1978 she was appointed to the President's National Advisory Committee for Women and was named one of the twenty-five most influential women in America by *World Almanac*. A television situational comedy in the 1980s was based on her life. In 1984 Bombeck appeared on the cover of *Time* magazine with the headline: "How Erma Copes: Working the House for Laughs."

In her lifetime Bombeck received sixteen honorary doctorates and numerous other awards for humor. She is best remembered for her humorous way of discussing everyday events. Collections of her columns have also appeared in book form.

THINKING ZONE

Ask any avid newspaper reader what he reads first in the morning paper, and he may respond with the name of a favorite columnist. Some enjoy the humor of a Dave Barry, some the etiquette advice of a Judith Martin, and some the political commentary of a Russell Baker. These and other essayists are noted for specializing in a kind of informal, often humorous, writing. The **informal** or **personal essay** is a type of essay in which the author adopts a friendly or conversational tone with the reader.

One device commonly used especially among writers of humor is **overstatement**, the exaggeration of details surrounding the events of a story. A form of obvious and extravagant overstatement used to make a point is **hyperbole**. The statement "I've made a *huge* mistake wearing these red shoes" would be overstatement. "Wearing these red shoes is the end of the world!" would qualify as hyperbole. In Shakespeare's *Macbeth*, Macbeth wishes that "all great Neptune's ocean wash this blood / Clean from my hand" (act 2, scene 2) after he murders the king of Scotland. Of course, that would not be physically possible, but the mental image reveals the depth of Macbeth's guilt. Hyperbole can have a humorous effect on a piece; other times the effect is serious or even ironic.

1. *[interpretive]* In paragraph 3, Bombeck announces to her family, "No more driving for days to find a restaurant where grease is the beverage." How is this statement an example of **hyperbole** or **overstatement**?

   _____

   _____

   _____

2. *[critical]* How might it be said that the entire incident described by Bombeck uses situational irony?

   _____

   _____

   _____

   _____

Situational irony— *a type of irony in which the story's events violate normal expectations*

3. *[interpretive]* Identify three more instances in which Bombeck uses hyperbole in her descriptions.

_____

_____

_____

_____

_____

_____

_____

_____

_____

4. *[appreciative]* Besides hyperbole, what other aspects did you find humorous in Bombeck's **informal essay?**

_____

_____

_____

_____

_____

_____

_____

_____

_____

_____

_____

_____

_____

_____

Che Fece . . . Il Gran Rifiuto

C. P. Cavafy

Translated from the Greek by Rae Dalven

What lies beyond a simple answer? You may think that an answer of yes or no may be simple and not important. This, however, is not necessarily true.

To certain people there comes a day
when they must say the great Yes or the great No.
He who has the Yes ready within him
reveals himself at once, and saying it he crosses over

to the path of honor and his own conviction.
He who refuses does not repent. Should he be asked
   again,
he would say No again. And yet that No—
the right No—crushes him for the rest of his life.

About the Author

Considered to be the finest modern Greek poet, C. (Constantine) P. Cavafy [kä-vä′fē] (1863–1933) was born in Alexandria, Egypt, to Greek parents. His father was involved in the import/export business in Alexandria. After the death of his father, Cavafy's family faced economic problems. For a while the family lived in England; they later lived in Alexandria and then Constantinople. Eventually Cavafy settled again in Alexandria, where he began writing poetry particularly for his Greek friends there. For a number of years he received no acclaim for his poetry; however, since his death, his work has been recognized and is taught in mainland Greek schools.

DRIVING TO TOWN LATE TO MAIL A LETTER

ROBERT BLY

The commonplace task of mailing a letter may become an adventure when done on a snowy evening. Notice the serendipity of Bly's late-night adventurer.

It is a cold and snowy night. The main street
   is deserted.
The only things moving are swirls of snow.
As I lift the mailbox door, I feel its cold iron.
There is a privacy I love in this snowy night.
Driving around, I will waste more time.

ABOUT THE AUTHOR

Robert Bly (b. 1926) was born in Minnesota to parents of Norwegian descent. After a two-year enlistment in the navy, he studied at Harvard, graduating in 1950. After his graduation he spent some struggling years in New York. In 1956 Bly traveled to Norway on a Fulbright grant to translate Norwegian poetry into English. Through his work he realized that many Norwegian authors were unknown in the United States. On his return to the United States, he began a literary magazine for poetry translation and introduced Americans to such poets as Gunnar Ekelöf and Cesar Vallejo.

Bly's writing has spanned the tumult of several decades, and the political, social, and racial unrest of the sixties, seventies, eighties, and nineties is reflected in much of his writing. Some of Bly's recent poems reveal his warm feelings for the Minnesota farm country of his boyhood. In his collection *Morning Poems*, Bly experimented with writing a poem every morning before he got out of bed. He described the experience as starting with the end of a piece of thread and just following it wherever it led him.

THINKING ZONE

Poets sometimes employ devices that help a reader determine how to interpret a poem. These devices are especially important to consider if the poem is to be read aloud. Sometimes a poet wants a reader to pause in the middle of a line of poetry before continuing with the line. That pause is called **caesura.** Caesura is usually indicated by a mark of punctuation, such as a dash, a comma, or a period. There are many reasons that a poet might use caesura, such as to make a transition or to emphasize a certain detail within the poem.

Another poetic device that indicates how a line should be read aloud is enjambment. **Enjambment** occurs when a poetic line flows past the end of one verse line into the next with no punctuation at the end of the first verse line. A poet may use enjambment to alert the reader that his thought has not been completed within the first verse line. When a rhymed poem is read aloud, enjambment also helps to lessen the impact of the rhythm so that the reader is better able to communicate the poet's intended message.

1. *[interpretive]* In "*Che Fece. . . Il Gran Rifiuto*," what happens when someone has "the Yes ready within him"? What does that phrase mean?

_____

_____

_____

2. *[critical]* In what lines does **caesura** occur in "*Che Fece . . . Il Gran Rifiuto*"? In what lines does **enjambment** occur?

_____

_____

3. *[interpretive/critical]* What irony can you detect in the last stanza of "*Che Fece . . . Il Gran Rifiuto*"? Explain.

_____

_____

_____

4. *[critical]* Though it is unlikely that Cavafy meant for his poem to have a Christian interpretation, how could a Christian apply the main idea of this poem? What further claim would a Christian make that Cavafy does not?

_____

_____

_____

_____

_____

_____

5. *[interpretive]* What kind of atmosphere does the author convey in "Driving to Town Late to Mail a Letter"?

_____

_____

_____

_____

Atmosphere—*the mood or emotion that the reader is supposed to share with the characters*

6. *[critical]* In what lines does caesura occur in "Driving to Town Late to Mail a Letter"? In what lines does enjambment occur?

_____

_____

7. *[appreciative]* What kinds of weather or types of situations make you feel the way Bly did in his poem?

_____

_____

_____

_____

_____

_____

BEN-HUR
AN ADAPTATION

LEW WALLACE

Before 600 B.C. Rome was a small, insignificant Latin settlement. By 509 B.C., however, this small settlement had grown into a powerful city-state. This city-state was to become the center of one of the world's greatest empires, an empire that dominated the Mediterranean world for more than four hundred years.

This story takes place at the peak of Rome's power at the time of Christ. Judea had been a Roman province for more than eighty years. A Roman guard kept the gates of the palace, a Roman judge dispensed justice both civil and criminal, and a Roman system of taxation crushed both city and country. Daily, hourly, and in a thousand ways, the Jews were taught the difference between a life of independence and a life of subjection.

Look now into one of the palace gardens on Mount Zion. The time is noonday in the middle of July when the heat of the summer is at its highest. Unmindful of the sun shining full upon them, two friends, one nineteen and the other seventeen, sit engaged in earnest conversation. Both boys are handsome and, at first glance, might be pronounced brothers, for both have dark hair and eyes, and their faces are deeply browned. The elder, Messala, wears a tunic that identifies him as a Roman. Messala's friend, Judah Ben-Hur, is slighter in form, and his distinctive features as well as his white linen garments confirm that he is of Jewish descent.

PART I
THE BETRAYAL OF BEN-HUR

"You say the new procurator* of Judea is to arrive tomorrow?" inquired Ben-Hur.

---
procurator (prŏk´yə-rā-ter): Roman administrator

"Yes, tomorrow," Messala answered. "Who told you?"

"I heard Ishmael, the new governor, tell my father so last night." Messala dismissed the subject as insignificant and turned his mind to other thoughts. "Our farewell took place in this garden. Your last words to me were, 'The peace of the Lord go with you.' 'The gods keep you,' I replied. Do you remember?"

"Yes. I watched you start for Rome, and wept. Five years are gone, and you have come back educated and princely—and yet—I wish you were the same Messala who went away."

"Tell me, friend, in what way have I changed?"

Ben-Hur reddened under Messala's scornful gaze, but he replied firmly, "You talk with the ease of a master, but your speech carries a sting. The old Messala had no poison in his nature. Not for the world would he have hurt the feelings of a friend."

Messala smiled as if complimented. "Be plain, Judah. Wherein have I hurt you?"

Ben-Hur drew a long breath and said, "In these five years, I too have learned, though my masters at the temple are not as those you heard in Rome. Their learning goes not out into forbidden paths. Those who sit at their feet arise enriched simply with the knowledge of God, the law, and Israel; and the effect is love and reverence for everything that pertains to them."

Messala raised his head a toss higher. "All things, even heaven and earth, change; but a Jew never! To him there is no backward, no forward; he is what his ancestors were in the beginning. Watch, Judah. In this sand I draw you a circle—there! Now tell me what more a Jew's life is? Round and round, Abraham here, Isaac and Jacob yonder, God in the middle!"

Ben-Hur arose, his face flushed.

"No, no; keep your place, Judah, keep your place," Messala cried, extending his hand.

"You mock me!"

"Listen a little further," urged Messala. "I am mindful of your goodness in walking from your father's house to welcome me back and to renew the love of our childhood. But if we are to remain friends you must see the world as it truly is. Judah, my teacher, in his last lecture said to us, 'Go, and to make your lives great, remember Mars* reigns and Eros* has found his eyes.' He meant that love is nothing, war everything. It is so in Rome, and Rome is now the world. Remember our childhood dreams? We were to be great warriors together."

Mars: Roman god of war

Eros: Roman god of love

Ben-Hur turned and moved closer to the garden pool. Messala's drawl deepened and a

flush of pride kindled on his haughty Roman face. "The world is not all conquered. Look to the glories that await us."

Ben-Hur looked hard at Messala, hesitated, then turned to go.

"Do not leave," said Messala.

"We had better part," Judah answered. "I wish I had not come. I sought a friend and find a—"

"Roman?" said Messala quickly. "Judah, renounce the follies of Moses and the traditions of Israel. They are past. Give yourself and your father's wealth to Rome. Together we will rule the future."

Ben-Hur's hands clenched tightly, and he started for the gate. Messala followed. When he reached Ben-Hur's side, he put his hand on his young friend's shoulder. "This is the way—my hand thus—we used to walk when we were children. Let us keep it as far as the gate." Judah permitted the familiarity, but when they reached the garden's entrance he stopped.

"I understand you because you are a Roman," he said taking Messala's hand gently from his shoulder. "But you cannot understand me, for I am an Israelite and will remain so. You have given me great suffering today by convincing me that we can never be the friends we once were—never. As we said our first farewell in this garden, so we shall say our last. The peace of the God of my fathers abide with you."

Messala offered him his hand, but Ben-Hur walked on through the gateway. When he was gone, Messala was silent a moment, then he too passed through the gate, saying to himself with a toss of the head, "Be it so. Eros is dead, Mars reigns!"

* * *

Ben-Hur was soon before the western gate of his house. He entered hastily, passed to the stairway, and ascended to the terrace.

Making his way to a doorway on the north side, he entered his apartment.

About nightfall a woman servant came to the door. Ben-Hur was lying motionless on his divan.* "Supper is long over. Are you not hungry?" she asked.

---

divan: a large sofa

"No," he replied.

"Are you sick?"

"I am indifferent, Amrah. Life does not seem as pleasant now as it did this morning."

"Your mother has asked for you."

"Where is she?"

"In the summer-house on the roof."

He stirred himself and sat up. "Very well. Bring me something to eat; then I shall go to her."

"What do you want?"

"What you please, Amrah."

After a while she returned, bearing on a wooden platter a bowl of milk, some thin cakes, a delicate paste of brayed wheat, a broiled bird, and honey and salt. Amrah was an Egyptian slave to whom not even the sacred fiftieth year could have brought freedom; she would not have accepted it, for the boy she was attending was her life.

"You remember, Amrah," he said as she placed the meal before him, "Messala who used to visit me here for days at a time?"

"I remember him."

"He went to Rome some years ago and is now back. I called upon him today." Ben-Hur shuddered in disgust.

"I knew something had happened," said Amrah, deeply interested. "I never liked Messala. Tell me all."

But Ben-Hur fell into musing and to her repeated inquiries only said, "He is much changed, and I shall have nothing more to do with him."

When Amrah took the platter away, Ben-Hur went out from his apartment and up to the roof. Through one of the openings, he saw his mother reclining against a cushion on the divan. At the sound of his steps upon the floor, the fan in her hand stopped, and he saw it glisten where the starlight struck the jewels with which it was sprinkled. She sat up and called his name.

"Judah, my son?"

"Yes, Mother," he answered, quickening his approach. His mother resumed her easy position against the cushion while Ben-Hur took his place on the divan. The city was still. Only the winds stirred.

"Amrah tells me something has happened," she said. Ben-Hur remained silent. "When you were a child, I allowed small things to trouble you, but now you are a man and you must face your doubts and find a way to banish them."

The words appeared to set him thinking anew. "Today, Mother, I have been made to think of many things that never had place in my mind before. Tell me, what am I to be?"

Her voice became very soft. "One day you are to be my hero."

"I will be your hero," he continued, "but you must put me in the way. You know the law—every son of Israel must have some occupation. Today I visited Messala." A certain change in his voice attracted his mother's attention. "He is very much changed."

"You mean he has come back a Roman?"

"Yes. I suppose all great people are proud," he went on, "but the pride of this people is unlike all others."

The young Israelite then rehearsed his conversation with Messala, dwelling on the Roman's speeches in contempt of the Jews and their customs.

His mother listened, discerning the matter plainly. Her voice became firm. "Your friend—or former friend—charged, if I understand you rightly, that we have had no great men. A just consideration of this charge requires a definition. A great man, my son, is one whose life proves him to be recognized, if not called, by God. In light of this definition, set our great men before you. You find patriarchs, legislators, warriors, singers, and prophets. Compare them to the best of Rome. Place Caesar against King David; Rome's consuls* against our judges; Augustus against Solomon. But do not stop here. Go on to the prophets—greatest of the great. Think of Elijah sitting on the hilltop outside Samaria amid the smoking bodies of captains and their fifties warning the son of Ahab of the wrath of our God. Finally, Judah, if such speech be reverent, place Jehovah against Jupiter.* Comparison ends here. You may judge our God by what His servants have done in His name. Rome and her gods are but the passing folly of vain men's imaginings.

consuls: highest officials of the Roman Republic

Jupiter: the chief Roman god

"And as for what you shall do—" She spoke these last words slowly, "You, my son, shall serve the Lord, the Lord God of Israel, not Rome. For a child of Abraham there is no glory except in the Lord's ways, and in them there is much glory."

"But can I be both a soldier and a servant of God?" inquired Judah.

There was a long silence in the summer chamber. "Your father, Judah, was a great merchant. But though all Rome recognized him as a wealthy man, they knew him first as a prince of Israel. You have my permission to pursue whatever occupation you desire if you will be as your father in this one point: remember that you serve the Lord, not Caesar."

* * *

When Judah awoke, the sun was up over the mountains, and the pigeons were abroad in flocks, filling the air with the gleams of their white wings. On the edge of the divan sat Tirzah his sister, scarcely fifteen. She was singing.

"Very pretty, Tirzah, very pretty!" he said with animation.

"The song?" she asked.

"Yes—and the singer, too. I am proud of you. Have you another song as good as the first?"

"Many. But let them go now. Amrah sent me to tell you that she will bring your breakfast and that you need not come down. She should be here by this time. She thinks you are sick and that a dreadful accident happened yesterday. What is it? Tell me and I will help Amrah doctor you.

"Tirzah," he continued cautiously, "I am going away."

"Going away? When? Where? For what?"

He laughed. "Three questions all in one breath!" But the next instant he became serious. "I am going to Rome."

"I will go with you."

"You must stay with Mother. If both of us leave her, she will die."

The brightness faded from her face. "But—must you go? Here in Jerusalem you can learn all that is needed to be a merchant as Father was."

"The law does not require a son to be what his father was."

"What else can you be?"

"A soldier," he replied, with a certain pride in his voice.

Tears came into her eyes. "You will be killed."

"If God wills, be it so. But, Tirzah, the soldiers are not all killed. War is a trade," he continued soberly. "To learn it thoroughly, one must go to school, and there is no school like a Roman Camp."

"You would fight for Rome?" she asked.

"Yes, I will fight for her, if, in return, she will teach me how one day to fight against her."

"When will you go?"

Amrah's steps were then heard.

"Hush!" he said. "Do not let her know what I am thinking."

The faithful slave came in with breakfast and placed it on the stool before them. Then she remained to serve them. They dipped their fingers into a bowl of water and were rinsing them when a noise arrested their attention.

"Soldiers from the Praetorium!* I must see them," Judah cried, springing from the divan and running out.

Praetorium: members of the royal bodyguard

In a moment he was leaning over the parapet* of tiles which guarded the roof, so absorbed that he did not immediately notice Tirzah, who was now at his side resting one hand on his shoulder.

---

parapet: protective railing

Ben-Hur knew of the custom by which chief commanders, to indicate their rank, appeared in public with a laurel vine upon their heads. By that sign he knew the officer—Valerius Gratus, the new procurator of Judea!

Judah leaned yet farther over the parapet to see him go by and in the act rested his hand on a tile which had long been cracked. The pressure was strong enough to displace the outer piece which started to fall. A thrill of horror shot through him. He reached out to catch the tile, and when he did so, it looked exactly as if he were pitching something from him. His effort failed. He shouted with all his might. The soldiers of the guard looked up; so did Valerius Gratus, and at that moment the tile struck him. He fell from his seat as dead. The cohort*

halted; the guards leaped from their horses and hastened to cover their chief with their shields.

cohort: a division of the Roman legion

Judah arose from the parapet, his face pale.

"Judah, what has happened?" Tirzah asked in sudden alarm.

"I have killed the Roman governor. The tile fell upon him. I did not do it purposely, Tirzah—it was an accident!"

"What will they do?" she asked.

To evade an answer, he peered over the parapet again and saw that the guards were assisting the Roman to remount his horse. "He lives, he lives, Tirzah! Blessed be the Lord God of our fathers! Do not be afraid. I will explain how it happened, and they will remember our father and his services and not hurt us."

He was leading her to the summer-house when the roof jarred under their feet. A cry of surprise and agony arose from the courtyard below. He stopped. The cry was repeated and followed by a rush of many feet and voices lifted in rage blending with voices lifted in fear. Then came the screams of women in mortal terror. He began to realize that the servants were being butchered.

The terrace at the foot of the steps was crowded with soldiers. Many other officers with drawn swords were running in and out of the chambers. At one place several women on their knees clung to each other and prayed for mercy. Apart from them, his mother, with torn garments, was struggling to tear loose from a man. Her cries were shrillest of all. Cutting through the clamor, they had arisen distinguishably to the roof. Judah sprang to her; his steps were long and swift, almost a winged flight. "Mother! Mother!" he shouted. She stretched her hand towards him; but when almost touching her, he was seized and forced aside. Then he heard someone cry aloud, "That is he!" Judah looked and saw—Messala. "That is his mother; yonder his sister. You now have the whole family."

Judah's love for his family made him forget his earlier quarrel with the young Roman. "Help them, Messala! Remember our childhood and help them. I—Judah—pray you!"

Messala pretended not to hear, and turning to the officer said, "I cannot be of further use to you. There is richer entertainment in the street. Down Eros, up Mars!" With these words he disappeared.

Judah understood; and in the bitterness of his soul, he prayed to heaven, "In the hour of Thy vengeance, O Lord, be mine the hand to put it upon Messala!"

THINKING ZONE

An **adaptation** seeks to take an author's original work and rework it for purposes of length, readability, or some other reason. In the case of *Ben-Hur*, the author of this adaptation took the full-length work and condensed it while retaining the basic plot of the story. Some adaptations alter the plot or defy the author's intent; others do justice to both. One well-known and widely accepted adaptation is Charles and Mary Lamb's *Tales from Shakespeare*, which tells the stories of Shakespeare's plays in language that is more understandable for younger readers.

You have already learned about the protagonist of a story. Most stories also contain a character in conflict with the protagonist, who is known as the **antagonist**. If the antagonist is an evil character, he is commonly known as a **villain**, though not all antagonists qualify as villains. In the biblical account of David and Goliath, David is the protagonist and Goliath is the antagonist and also a villain.

1. *[interpretive]* Although the story in your book is an **adaptation**, the characters remain the same as those in the novel. Who is the protagonist of *Ben-Hur*?

   _____

   _____

2. *[interpretive]* What character qualifies as the story's **antagonist**? How do you know? Is this character also a **villain**?

   _____

   _____

   _____

   _____

   _____

3. *[interpretive]* Think carefully about the conversation that Judah and his mother have on the roof of their house. Where might one detect an example of foreshadowing?

_____

_____

_____

_____

_____

_____

4. *[interpretive]* What conflicts are present in the first part of the story? Name at least two.

_____

_____

_____

_____

_____

_____

5. *[critical]* What would you say is Messala's chief character flaw? Give evidence from the chapter for your answer.

_____

_____

_____

_____

Character flaw—_an incidental weakness or serious moral fault that is revealed about a character through the story_

_____

_____

_____

_____

PART II
THE CAPTIVITY OF BEN-HUR

The next day a detachment of legionaries* went to the desolated place of the Hurs and, closing the gates permanently, nailed at each entrance the following notice:

"This is the property of the Emperor."

---
legionaries: soldiers of the Roman army

Several days later, a decurion* with his command of ten horsemen approached Nazareth from Jerusalem. His prisoner, Ben-Hur, was forced to make the long journey on foot. Upon reaching the well of Nazareth, the young Jew was in the last stage of exhaustion. The villagers would have helped him, but the hard look of the decurion as he dismounted stopped them. Ben-Hur sank down in the dust of the road unattended.

---
decurion: Roman cavalry officer

While the pitchers of water were passed among the soldiers, a man came down the road. At the sight of him one of the village women whispered, "Look! Yonder comes the carpenter. Now we will hear something." The man stopped close to the well to survey the crowd. "Good Rabbi Joseph," said the woman approaching him, "there is a Jewish prisoner here. Come ask the Roman soldiers about him that we may know who he is, what he has done, and what they are going to do with him."

The rabbi glanced at Ben-Hur, then went to the officer. "The peace of the Lord be with you," he said.

"And the gods with you," the decurion replied.

"Are you from Jerusalem?"

"Yes."

"Your prisoner is young."

"In years, yes."

"May I ask what he has done?"

"He is an assassin."

"Is he a son of Israel?"

"He is a Jew," said the Roman dryly. "I know nothing of your tribes, but I can speak of his family. You may have heard of the prince of Jerusalem named Hur—Ben-Hur they called him. He lived in Herod's day."

"I have seen him," Joseph said.

"Well, this is his son."

Exclamations became general, and the decurion hastened to stop them. "In the streets of Jerusalem, day before yesterday, he nearly killed the noble Gratus by flinging a tile upon his head."

There was a pause in the conversation, and the Nazarenes gazed at young Ben-Hur as at a wild beast.

"Did he kill him?" asked the rabbi at length.

"No."

"Is he under sentence?"

"Yes—the galleys for life."

"The Lord help him!" said Joseph.

At this time, a youth who had come up with Joseph laid down the axe he had been carrying. Going to the great stone standing by the well, he took a pitcher and filled it with water. The action was so quiet that before the guards could interfere he was stooping over Ben-Hur and offering him a drink. He laid his hand gently on Ben-Hur's shoulder. Judah revived; and, looking up, he saw a face he never forgot—the face of a boy about his own age. Ben-Hur's spirit, hardened though it was by suffering, melted under the stranger's look and became as a child's. He put his lips to the pitcher and drank long and deep. Not a word was said.

When the draught* was finished, the hand that had been resting on Judah's shoulder was placed on his head to say a blessing.

Having been appointed the new master of the ship, the tribune, Quintus Arrius, came to examine his slaves. His sharp eyes moved from seat to seat and came at last to number sixty. There they rested. Arrius observed Ben-Hur's youth. He also observed that he seemed of good height and that his limbs were a mass of muscle, which swelled and knotted like kinking cords as he rowed. Altogether there was in Ben-Hur's action a certain harmony which provoked Arrius's curiosity, and soon the tribune found himself waiting to catch a glimpse of Ben-Hur's face in full. Directly he caught the view he wished, for the young rower turned and looked at him.

"A Jew! and a boy!" he said to himself. "What could have brought a young Jew to this place reserved for barbarian convicts? I will know more of him." Arrius moved to the hortator.* "Do you know the man at number sixty?" he asked.

hortator (hôr´tä-tôr): man in charge of rowers

Then the stranger returned the pitcher to its place on the stone and taking his axe again went back to Rabbi Joseph. All eyes went with him, the decurion's as well as those of the villagers. And so, for the first time, Judah and the son of Mary met and parted.

draught: drink

* * *

For three years Ben-Hur had labored as a galley slave. No one knew his story nor even his name. There was no need of keeping the proper names of slaves brought to the galleys as to their graves. They were identified by the numerals painted on the benches to which they were assigned. Thus, Ben-Hur was known only as number sixty on the ship *Astroea.**

The chief looked sharply at the rower then going forward. "No," he replied.

"He is a Jew," Arrius remarked thoughtfully.

"The noble Quintus is shrewd," said the other.

"He is very young," Arrius continued.

"But our best rower."

"What is his disposition?"

"He is obedient. Otherwise I know nothing of him."

"Nothing of his history?"

"Not a word."

The tribune reflected awhile then turned to go. "If I should be on deck when his rowing time is up," he paused to say, "send him to me. Let him come alone."

About two hours later Arrius saw Ben-Hur approaching. "The chief said it was

your will that I should seek you here. I am come."

Arrius spoke as an older man to a younger, not as a master to a slave. "The hortator tells me you are his best rower."

"The hortator is very kind," Ben-Hur answered.

"Have you seen much service?"

"About three years."

"At the oars?"

"I cannot recall a day of rest from them."

"From your speech you are a Jew," said Arrius pointedly.

"My ancestors, further back than the first Roman, were Hebrews," answered Ben-Hur.

"The stubborn pride of your race is not lost in you," said Arrius, observing a flush on Ben-Hur's face.

"Pride is never so loud as when in chains."

"But what cause have you for pride?"

"That I am a Jew."

Arrius smiled. "I have not been to Jerusalem," he said. "But I have heard of its princes. I knew one of them. He was a merchant and sailed the seas. He was fit to have been a king. Of what degree* are you?"

---

degree: station in life

"My father was a prince of Jerusalem; and as a merchant, he sailed the seas. He was known and honored in the guest chamber of the great Augustus."

"His name?"

"Ithamar, of the house of Hur."

The tribune raised his hand in astonishment. "A son of Hur—you? What brought you here?" he said more sternly.

Judah lowered his head, and when his feelings were sufficiently mastered, he looked again at the tribune and answered, "I was accused of attempting to assassinate Valerius Gratus, the procurator."

"You?" cried Arrius, yet more amazed. "All Rome rang with the story!" His manner became more severe. "Do you admit your guilt?"

The change that came over Ben-Hur was wonderful to see; it was so instant and extreme. His voice sharpened, every fiber thrilled, and his eyes flamed. "You have heard of the God of my fathers," he said, "of the infinite Jehovah. By His truth and almightiness, I am innocent!"

The tribune was moved. "Did you have no trial?" he asked.

"No!"

The Roman raised his head surprised. "No trial—no witnesses? Who passed judgment on you?"

"They bound me with cords and dragged me to a vault in the tower of Antonia. I saw no one, and no one spoke to me. After what seemed several days of this torturous solitude, soldiers came, took me to the seaside, and placed me aboard this ship. I have been at the galleys ever since."

"Who was with you when the blow was struck?"

"Tirzah, my sister, was with me. Together we leaned over the parapet to see the legion pass. A tile gave way under my hand and fell upon Gratus. I thought I had killed him. Ah, what horror I felt!"

"Where was your mother?"

"In the chamber below."

"What became of her?"

Ben-Hur drew a breath like a gasp. "I do not know. I saw them drag her away—that is all. I, too, ask for her. Oh, for one word. She at least was innocent!"

Arrius listened intently. A whole family blotted out to atone an accident! The thought shocked him. For once Arrius was uncertain. His power was ample, and Ben-Hur had won his faith. Yet, he said to himself, there is no haste. The best rower cannot

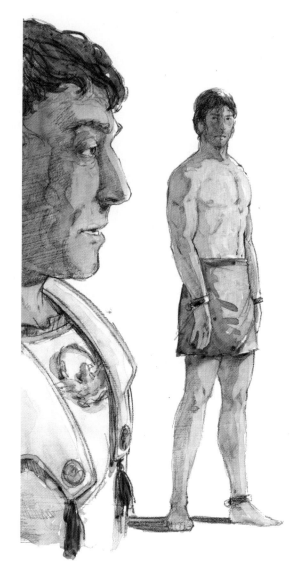

be spared. I will wait and learn more. I will at least be sure that this is the Prince Ben-Hur and that he is of the right disposition. Ordinarily slaves are liars. "It is enough," he said aloud. "Go back to your place."

Ben-Hur bowed, looked once more into his master's face, but saw nothing for hope. As he turned away, he said, "If you think of me again, tribune, let it not be lost in your mind that I prayed you only for a word of my people—Mother and sister." Ben-Hur moved on.

"Stay," said Arrius. Ben-Hur stopped; the tribune went to him. "If you were free, what would you do?"

"The noble Arrius mocks me," said Judah bitterly.

"No. No."

"Then I will answer. I would know no rest until my mother and Tirzah were restored to home. I would give every day and hour to their happiness. I would wait on them, never a slave more faithful. They have lost much; but, by the God of my fathers, I would find them more!"

The answer was unexpected by the Roman, and he momentarily lost his purpose. "I spoke of your ambition," he said, recovering. "If your mother and sister were dead, or not to be found, what would you do?"

"Tribune, I will tell you truthfully. Only the night before the dreadful day of which I have spoken, I obtained permission to be a soldier. I am of the same mind yet."

A short while after, Ben-Hur was at his bench again. That he had been called by a great man and asked his story was the bread on which he fed his hungry spirit. Surely something good would come of it. The light about his bench was clear and bright with promises, and he prayed, "Oh God, I am a true son of Israel whom Thou hast loved! Help me, I pray Thee!"

When the sun, going down, withdrew its last ray from the cabin, the galley still held northward. About nightfall, the smell of incense floated down the gangways from the deck. Ben-Hur noted this. The tribune is at the altar, he thought to himself. Could it be that we are going into battle? He became more observant.

Since becoming a galley slave, Ben-Hur had been in many battles though he had never seen one. He only heard them above

and about him, and he was familiar with all the notes, almost as a singer with a song. He waited anxiously, and it was not long before he heard Arrius addressing the commander of the marines. "The pirates are close by. Up and ready!"

Everyone aboard, even the ship, awoke now. Officers went to their quarters. The marines took arms and were led out. Sheaves of arrows and armfuls of javelins were carried on deck. The rowers assembled under guard in front of the chief while overhead could be heard the muffled noises of final preparations.

Presently, quiet settled about the galley again—quiet full of vague dread and expectation. No sound from without, none from within, yet each man in the cabin instinctively poised himself for a shock. The very ship seemed to catch the sense, hold its breath, and go crouched, tigerlike.

At last there was the sound of trumpets—full, clear, long blown. The chief beat the sounding board until it rang. The rowers reached forward, full length and deepening the dip of their oars, pulled suddenly with all their united force. The galley, quivering in every timber, answered with a leap. Forward rushed the *Astroea*; and as it went, sailors ran down into the cabin and plunging large cotton swabs into oil tanks, tossed them dripping to comrades at the head of the stairs. From this action Ben-Hur concluded that fire was to be added to the horrors of the combat. But he did not dwell long on this thought, for suddenly the *Astroea* stopped. The oars were dashed from the hands of the rowers, and the rowers from their benches. In the midst of this panic a body was plunged headlong down the hatchway falling at the feet of Ben-Hur. He beheld the face—a barbarian from the white-skinned nations of the North. Had an iron hand snatched him from the pirate's deck? Then the thought struck him—the *Astroea* had been boarded! The Romans were now fighting on their own deck!

A chill of horror smote the young Jew. Arrius was hard pressed. All Ben-Hur's hope of freedom rested in the noble tribune. What if Arrius were killed in battle? The tumult thundered above him; he looked around; in the cabin all was confusion. Only the chief kept his chair, unchanged, calm as ever—weaponless. A short space lay between Ben-Hur and the hatchway aft. He gave the chief a last look, then broke away—not in flight but to seek the tribune. With a single leap he was halfway up the steps—up far enough to catch a glimpse of the sky, blood-red with fire. The floor when he reached it seemed to be lifting itself and breaking into pieces; then, the whole after-part of the hull broke asunder. The sea, hissing and foaming, leaped in, and all became darkness and surging water to Ben-Hur.

The time he was under water seemed an age longer than it really was; at last he gained the top. With a great gasp he filled his lungs afresh and tossing the water from his hair and eyes, climbed higher on a plank he'd managed to grasp. He looked about him. Death had pursued him closely under the waves, and he found it waiting for him still when he reached the surface. The battle was yet on, nor could he say who was victor. But he had nothing to do with their struggles. They were all his enemies. There was not one of them who would not kill him for the plank on which he floated. He made haste to get away.

He struck out, pushing the plank, which was broad and unmanageable. Seconds were precious; half a second might save or lose him. He struggled with all his might, and in the crisis of this effort, up from the sea, within an arm's reach, a helmet shot like a gleam of gold. Then appeared two hands with fingers extended; they were large, strong hands. Ben-Hur swerved from them appalled. Then up came two arms which began to beat the water violently. The head turned back and gave the face to the light. Ben-Hur had never seen a more ghastly sight. The mouth was gaping wide, the eyes were open but sightless, and the face had a bloodless pallor. As the drowning man was going under again, Ben-Hur caught the chain of the man's helmet and drew him to the plank. The man was Arrius, the tribune.

The water beat violently about them, taxing all Ben-Hur's strength to hold to the plank and at the same time keep the Roman's head above the surface. A short distance from them were several others adrift. He turned toward them just as several galleys were heading toward them. The ships drove right through the floating men. In wild alarm Ben-Hur swerved, and he and the tribune barely escaped the stroke of the oars.

The battle moved on. Resistance had turned to flight. But who were the victors? Ben-Hur pushed the plank more securely under Arrius, then took care to keep him there.

* * *

The dawn came slowly, and Ben-Hur watched it coming with hope and fear, for he realized that both his freedom and the life of the tribune were dependent on the previous day's battle. At last the morning broke in full, the air without a breath. Ben-Hur looked about him. The sea was blackened by charred and sometimes smoking fragments, and in the distance could be seen a battered galley floating motionless, the oars all idle. Further on he noticed some moving specks, but he could not discern if they were ships or white birds a wing.

As the hours passed, his anxiety increased. If relief came not speedily, Arrius would die. Sometimes he seemed already dead, he lay so still. Ben-Hur took the Roman's helmet off, and then, with greater difficulty, the cuirass;* he found the heart fluttering. He took hope at the sign and held on. There was nothing to do but wait, and, after the manner of his people, pray.

---

cuirass (kwĭ-răs´): Roman soldier's armor

* * *

The throes of recovering from drowning are more painful than the drowning. These Arrius passed through and at length, to Ben-Hur's delight, reached the point of speech. "Our rescue, I see, depends on the result of that fight. I see also what you have done for me. To speak fairly, you have saved my life at the risk of your own. I make the acknowledgment broadly; and whatever comes you have my thanks. More than that, if fortune serves me kindly and we escape this peril, I will do you such a favor as becomes a Roman who has power and opportunity to prove his gratitude." Arrius rested again. "Are you indeed a son of Hur, the Jew?" he next asked.

"It is as I have said," Ben-Hur replied.

"I knew your father—" Judah drew himself nearer and listened eagerly; at last he thought to hear of home. "I knew him and loved him," Arrius continued. There was another pause, during which something diverted the speaker's thought. "Before I speak of my acquaintance with your father, let us discuss a more urgent matter. It is the custom of gentlemen in Rome to wear a ring. There is one on my hand. Take it now and put it on your own." Judah did as he was told. "This trinket has its uses. I have property and money, and am accounted rich even in Rome. I have no family, however, no heir to pass these fortunes on to. If you are rescued, show that ring to my freedman; he has control in my absence. You will find him in a villa near Misenum. Tell him how it came

to you and ask anything or all he may have. He will refuse you nothing. If we both are rescued by the Romans, I will do better by you." The tribune drew a deep breath to regain strength, then said, "Now, I desire a pledge from you."

"Tell me first your wish."

"Will you promise then?"

"That were to give the pledge, and—blessed be the God of my fathers! Yonder comes a ship!"

"In what direction?" asked Arrius.

"From the north."

"Can you tell her nationality by outward signs?"

"No. My service has been at the oars," said Ben-Hur.

"Has she a flag?"

"I cannot see one."

Arrius remained quiet some time, apparently in deep reflection. "Does the ship hold this way?" he said at length.

"Still this way," said Ben-Hur.

"Look for the flag now."

"She has none."

"Nor any other sign?"

"She has a sail set, is of three banks, and comes swiftly—that is all I can say of her."

"A Roman in triumph would have out many flags. She must be an enemy. Hear now," said Arrius, becoming grave again, "hear, while I may yet speak. If the galley be a pirate, your life is safe. They may not give you freedom. They may put you to the oar again, but they will not kill you. On the other hand, I—" The tribune faltered, "I am too old to submit to dishonor. In Rome let them tell how Quintus Arrius, as became a Roman tribune, went down with his ship in the midst of the foe. I want you to pledge me that if the galley prove a pirate, you will push me from the plank and drown me. Swear you will do it."

"I will not swear," said Ben-Hur firmly. "I will not do the deed. The Jewish law, which is to me most binding, tribune, would make me answerable for your life. Take back your ring." Ben-Hur took the seal from his finger. "Take it back, and all your promises of favor in the event of delivery from this peril. The judgment which sent me to the oar for life made me a slave, yet I am not a slave; and no more am I your freedman. I am a son of Israel and this moment, at least, my own master. Take back the ring." Arrius remained passive. "You will not?" Judah continued. "Not in anger then, nor in any despite, but to free myself from a hateful obligation, I will give your gift to the sea." He tossed the ring away. Arrius heard the splash where it struck and sank, though he did not look. "In the three years of my servitude, you are the first to treat me kindly—no, there was one other." His voice dropped, and he saw plainly, as if it were then before him, the face of the boy who helped him by the well in Nazareth. He pushed the thought aside and continued. "Tribune, I pray you to believe me. I would rather die with you than be your slayer. My mind is as firmly set as yours. Though you were to offer me all Rome, I would not kill you."

For a time they waited silently, Ben-Hur often looking at the coming ship and Arrius resting with his eyes closed, indifferent. "Are you sure she is an enemy?" Ben-Hur asked at length.

"I think so," was the reply.

"She is stopping to put a boat over the side."

Arrius became alert. "Do you see her flag?"

"Is there no other sign by which we may know if she is Roman?"

"If Roman, she will have a helmet over the mast's top."

"Then be of cheer. I see the helmet."

Arrius threw off his calm. "Thank your God," he said to Ben-Hur after straining to see the galley. "Thank your God, as I do my many gods." Judah raised himself on the plank, waved his hand, called with all his might, and at last drew the attention of the sailors.

* * *

Upon his return to Rome, Arrius had a warm welcome, and the young man attending him attracted the attention of his friends. To their questions about who he was, Arrius proceeded in a most affectionate manner to tell the story of his rescue and introduce Ben-Hur. He carefully omitted, however, any information that pertained to the young Jew's previous history. At the end of the narrative, the tribune called Ben-Hur to his side. "Good friends," he said, "this is now my son and heir, who, as he is to take my property, shall be known to you by my name. I pray you all to love him as you love me." As speedily as the opportunity permitted, the adoption was formally perfected, and Ben-Hur became the son of Arrius.

THINKING ZONE

You have already learned that overstatement refers to the exaggeration of details surrounding a story. By contrast, **understatement** is the representation of something as less important than it truly is. Instead of emphasizing the magnitude of an event, a writer will sometimes describe it as though it were an everyday occurrence. Shakespeare uses understatement when he has Macbeth say in reference to people's dying, "Blood hath been shed ere [before] now." Ironically, the use of understatement often serves to make a description even more memorable to the reader.

> **Overstatement—**
> *the exaggeration of details surrounding the events of a story*

1. *[literal]* Why is Ben-Hur taken to Nazareth by the decurion and his soldiers?

   _____

   _____

2. *[interpretive]* Whom does Ben-Hur meet at the well in Nazareth? How does the author use understatement to tell about the meeting?

   _____

   _____

   _____

   _____

   _____

3. *[interpretive]* What does Ben-Hur mean by his statement that "Pride is never so loud as when in chains"? What term have you learned that describes a statement like this that seems self-contradictory but actually makes sense?

   _____

   _____

   _____

4. *[critical]* Why do you think Ben-Hur attempts to save Arrius?

_____

_____

_____

_____

5. *[interpretive]* Given what Arrius tells Ben-Hur after the battle is over, can you think of a reason for Arrius's being sympathetic to Ben-Hur?

_____

_____

_____

_____

6. *[critical/appreciative]* Name two instances in which suspense is used effectively in this chapter.

_____

_____

_____

Suspense—*reader anxiety resulting from the author's withholding plot details*

_____

_____

_____

7. *[critical]* Examine Ben-Hur's dialogue in this chapter. What does it say about him as a character? Has he developed?

_____

_____

_____

_____

_____

_____

Arrius died soon after adopting Ben-Hur, but not before he had given the young Jew introduction into the Imperial world. Five years had passed since Ben-Hur had been taken from Jerusalem, and in that time he had learned to be cautious. For safety he desired to be known only as the son of Arrius, and he moved and carried out his business under that protective title. He had completed his training as a soldier in Rome and set out to travel the world and to enjoy the privileges reserved for wealthy Roman citizens. Presently, he was on board a ship bound for Antioch. For an hour or more he had occupied a seat in the shade of the sail. In that time several passengers of his own nationality had tried to engage him in conversation but without avail. His replies to their questions were brief, though gravely courteous, and in the Latin tongue.

It happened, however, that the galley stopped at a port in Cyprus and picked up a Hebrew of most respectable appearance: quiet, reserved, paternal. Ben-Hur could not refrain from speaking to the man. He ventured to ask him some questions, and the man's replies so won Ben-Hur's confidence that an extended conversation resulted.

During this conversation, the galley entered the receiving bay of the Orontes and two other vessels, which had been sighted out in sea, passed the river at the same time. As they did so, each threw out a flag of brightest yellow. There was much speculation as to the meaning of this signal, and at length one passenger interrupted Ben-Hur and addressed himself to the respectable Hebrew. "Do you know the meaning of those flags?" he inquired.

"Yes," replied the Hebrew. "They are simply marks of ownership."

"Do you know the owner?" asked another passenger.

"I have dealt with him," the Hebrew said.

All of the passengers, including Ben-Hur, looked at the speaker as if requesting him to go on.

"He lives in Antioch," the speaker continued in his quiet way. "He is vastly rich, and the talk about him is not always kind. You see, there used to be in Jerusalem a prince of an ancient family named Hur." Judah's heart beat quicker, but he managed to remain composed. "The prince was a merchant with a genius for business. He set on foot many enterprises, some reaching far east, others west. In the great cities he had branch houses. The one in Antioch was in the charge of a Greek in name, yet an Israelite. The master drowned at sea. His business, however, went on and was scarcely less prosperous. After a while misfortune overtook the family. The prince's only son, nearly grown, tried to kill the procurator Gratus in one of Jerusalem's streets. He failed by a narrow chance and has not been heard of since. In fact, Gratus's rage took in the whole house—not one of the name was left alive. Their palace was sealed up and is now a rookery for pigeons. The estate was confiscated as was everything that could be traced to the Hurs.

"To go on, Simonides,* once the Prince Hur's agent, now opened his own trade and in an incredibly brief time became the master merchant of the city. They say nothing goes amiss with him. His camels do not die, except of old age; his ships never founder; if he throws a chip into the river, it will come back to him gold."

Simonides (Sĭ-mŏ′nĭ-dāz′)

Judah gripped the rope he was holding with crushing force. "It is said," the narrator continued, "that there is not a sound bone in the man's body. The last time I saw him he sat in a chair, a shapeless cripple, propped against cushions."

"So tortured?" exclaimed several listeners in one breath.

"Disease could not have produced such deformity. Still, the suffering made no impression on him. All he had was his lawfully, and he was making lawful use of it—that was the most they wrung from him. Now, however, he is past persecution. He has a license to trade signed by Tiberius himself!"

"He paid roundly for it, I warrant,"* said a sympathetic listener.

warrant: guarantee

"How long has he been going on thus?"

"Not ten years."

"He must have had a good start."

"Yes, they say the procurator took only the prince's property ready at hand—his horses, cattle, houses, land, vessels, and goods. The money could not be found, though there must have been vast sums of it. What became of it has been an unsolved mystery—a mystery that haunts the procurator still."

"It is no mystery to me," said a passenger with a scorn.

"I understand you," the Hebrew answered. "Others have had your idea—that it furnished old Simonides his start is a common belief. The procurator is of that opinion, or has been, for twice in five years he has caught the merchant and put him to torture."

The story ended just as the city of Antioch came into full view. All the passengers now crowded on deck, eager that nothing of the scene might escape them, for the shores of this city were unsurpassed in beauty. But Judah scarcely noticed, and as the ship turned and made her way slowly to the wharf, he turned once again to the Hebrew. "Before saying farewell, let me trouble you for one moment more. Your story of the merchant has made me curious to see him. You called him Simonides."

"Yes, he is a Jew with a Greek name."

"Where is he to be found?"

The man considered an instant. Then approving of Ben-Hur, he gave the information requested. "One would think," he replied, "that the richest merchant in Antioch would have a house for business corresponding to his wealth. But if you would find him, you must follow the river to the bridge, then to a building that looks like the buttress* of a wall. Before the door there is an immense landing always covered with cargoes. The fleet that lies moored* there is his. You will find him in that building."

buttress: a supporting structure
moored: anchored

"I give you thanks," said Ben-Hur.

"The peace of our fathers go with you," said the Hebrew.

"And with you," replied Ben-Hur courteously.

Early the next day, Ben-Hur sought out Simonides. Now, at last, he thought to hear of his mother and sister. But if indeed Simonides had been his father's slave, would the man acknowledge the relation? To do so meant that he must give up his riches. This thought caused Ben-Hur to hesitate a moment, but he derived strength for the interview from faith in his rights and the hope in his heart. If the story which the Hebrew told of Simonides was true, then by right Simonides, as well as his riches, belonged to Ben-Hur. For the wealth he cared nothing. He only wished to hear of his family. When he started to the door, it was with this promise to himself: "Let him tell me of Mother and Tirzah, and I will give him his freedom without account."

As he entered, a man approached and spoke to him. "What would you have?"

"I would see Simonides, the merchant." He was led to the end of a darkened passage.

"A stranger to see the master," the man called out through a half parted curtain.

"Let him enter," a clear voice replied. Ben-Hur entered. In the middle of the room were two people. One was sitting in an ornate divan. This Ben-Hur assumed was Simonides. At the merchant's left, leaning against the back of the divan, was a girl well forward into womanhood.

"If you are Simonides, the merchant, and a Jew, then the peace of the God of our father Abraham on you and yours," said Ben-Hur.

"I am Simonides," the man answered in a voice singularly clear, "and a Jew. I return your salutation, with a prayer to know who calls on me."

"I am Judah, son of Ithamar, the late head of the House of Hur and a prince of Jerusalem."

Simonides' right hand lay outside the robe—a long, thin hand. It closed tightly. Otherwise, there was not the slightest expression of feeling on the merchant's part; nothing to warrant surprise or interest; nothing but his calm answer. "The princes of Jerusalem, of the pure blood, are always welcome in my house. You are welcome. Give the young man a seat, Esther." The girl took an ottoman and carried it to Ben-Hur.

He courteously refused the offered seat; his business was too urgent.

"I pray good master Simonides," began Ben-Hur cautiously, "that you will not hold me an intruder. But coming up the river yesterday, I heard you knew my father."

"I knew the Prince Hur. We were associated in some business enterprises."

Ben-Hur threw off his cautious manner. "Simonides, my father, at his death, had a trusted servant and I am told that you are that man!"

There was a sudden start of the wrenched limbs under the robe, but Simonides quickly regained himself and answered coldly, "Show me proofs of who you are."

Ben-Hur was stunned by the demand. He stammered, then turned away at a loss. Simonides pressed him. "The proofs, the proofs, I say! Set them before me! Lay them in my hands!"

Ben-Hur had not anticipated such a requirement. Now that it had been made, the awful fact came to him that the three years in the galley had carried away all proofs

of his identity. With his mother and sister gone, he did not live in the knowledge of any human being. Many were acquainted with him as the son of Arrius, but that was all. "Master Simonides," he said at length, "all my Roman connection with the noble Quintus Arrius I can prove. I have only to call the consul, at present the guest of the governor of this city, but I cannot prove your demand on me. I cannot prove I am my father's son. Those who would serve me in that, alas, are dead or lost! Since I have no proof, I will go and trouble you no further. Only let me say I did not seek your return to servitude nor account of your fortune. I have no need of any part thereof. When the good Quintus, my adopted father, died, he left me as his heir princely rich. If, therefore, you think of me again, let it be remembered that the chief purpose of my coming here was to know what you could tell me of my mother and sister. Can you tell me anything of them—even one word?"

Though Ben-Hur's earnestness brought Esther to tears, Simonides remained willful. In a clear voice he replied, "I have said I knew the Prince Ben-Hur. I also remember hearing of the misfortune which overtook his family, and I received the news with bitterness. Gratus and his officers, who wrought such misery on the widow of my friend, are the same who have since mercilessly tortured me. I will go further and say to you that I have made diligent search concerning the family, but—I have nothing to tell you of them. They are lost."

"Then the last hope is broken," he said, struggling with his feelings. "I am used to disappointments. I pray you to pardon my intrusion. If I have annoyed you, forgive it because of my sorrow. Farewell. I have nothing now to live for but vengeance on all that is Roman." With these words he departed.

Scarcely had Ben-Hur gone when Simonides seemed to wake as from sleep. His countenance flushed. The sullen light of his eyes changed to brightness, and he said with animation, "Esther, ring—quickly!" She rang a bell and behind them a door swung open and a man entered, passed round to the front of the merchant's divan and saluted him.

"Malluch, here—closer, closer to the divan," the master said excitedly. "I have a mission which shall not fail though the sun should. Listen! A young man is now descending to the storeroom—tall, comely, and in the garb of Israel. Follow him, his shadow not more faithful, and every night send me report of where he is, what he does, and the company he keeps. Do you understand? If he leaves the city, go after him—and mark my words, Malluch, be a friend to him." The man bowed and was gone.

When Ben-Hur exited the great warehouse, depression curtained him about with a sense of utter loneliness. He passed out of the city gate wandering aimlessly and eventually found himself one of a large procession. He had not enough interest to ask where they were going, yet he had a vague impression that they were in movement to the temples, the central attraction of Antioch's famous Grove of Daphne.

As the procession neared the grove, a breeze brought a wave of sweet smells toward them. Ben-Hur stopped as did the others and looked to see where the fragrance came from. "It is coming from a garden over there," Ben-Hur said to a man at his elbow.

"It looks like some priestly ceremony in performance—something to Diana* or Pan* or a deity of the woods," said the man. His answer was in Ben-Hur's mother tongue.

Diana: Roman goddess associated with the moon, hunting, and childbirth

Pan: Roman god associated with shepherds, fields, wild animals, and forests

---

"A Hebrew?" questioned Ben-Hur, turning toward the speaker.

The man replied with a smile, "I was born within a stone's throw of the market place in Jerusalem."

"Are you going my way?" asked Judah.

"I am going to the stadium, if that is your way."

"The stadium! Good friend," said Ben-Hur frankly, "I admit my ignorance of the grove. I did not know such a place had a stadium. If you will let me be your follower, I would be grateful."

"I would be delighted. Listen! I hear the wheels of the chariots now. They are taking the track."

Ben-Hur listened a moment, then completed the introduction by laying his hand on the man's arm and saying, "I am the son of Arrius, and you?"

"I am Malluch, a merchant of Antioch."

With the introductions completed, they moved on.

They came to a field with a track laid out on it. The course was of soft earth, rolled and sprinkled. There were also several stands shaded by awnings which provided seats for the scattered spectators. In one of these stands the two newcomers found places.

The chariots were already moving along the track. Ben-Hur counted them as they passed—nine in all. Eight of the fours* passed in front of them, some walking, others trotting, and all unexceptionally handled. Then the ninth one came on at a gallop. Ben-Hur burst into exclamation. "I have been in the stables of the emperor, Malluch; but by our father Abraham, I have never seen horses like these!" But before Ben-Hur stopped speaking, the horses fell into confusion. Someone in the stand uttered a sharp cry. Ben-Hur turned as he saw an old man half risen from an upper seat, his hands clenched, his eyes fiercely bright, and his long beard quivering in anger. The driver was exerting himself without avail to quiet the four. "Accursed Roman!" shouted the old man shaking his fist at the driver. "Did he not swear he could drive them—swear by all his Latin gods?" His servants tried to calm him. "Nay, hands off me—off, I say! Oh, fool, fool, that I was to put trust in a Roman!" Ben-Hur sympathized with him, while the others in the stand began to laugh.

fours: teams of four horses

"They should at least respect his age," said Ben-Hur. "Who is he?"

"Sheik Ilderim, a mighty man from the desert, somewhere beyond Moab," replied Malluch. "He owns those horses. They say that they are racers descended from the time of the first Pharaoh."

Suddenly a new contestant came into view. His progress was signalized by clapping and cheering. All eyes turned from the sheik and his driver to this new spectacle. The new driver's beautiful horses and resplendent chariot drew Ben-Hur's attention as well. While looking at the driver, Ben-Hur was struck with a vague sense of familiarity. "Who is that man?" Ben-Hur asked himself. He could not see the man's face or even his full figure yet. But the air and manner of the man pricked him keenly with a reminder of a period long gone.

From the shouting and the turnout, it was thought he might be some official favorite or a famous prince. Ben-Hur arose and forced a passage down nearly to the railing. His face was earnest, his manner eager. Directly the whole person of the driver was in view. Ben-Hur stood transfixed. His instinct and memory had served him faithfully—the driver was Messala!

Ben-Hur was yet staring at Messala, when an Arab arose and cried out, "Men of the east and west—listen! The good Sheik Ilderim needs a mighty man to drive his magnificent horses. Whoever will take them to his satisfaction, to him is promised enrichment forever. So says my master, Sheik Ilderim the Generous."

The proclamation awakened a great buzz among the people. Ben-Hur quickly turned his attention from Messala to the sheik. He then addressed Malluch who was by now at his side. "Good Malluch, may a man forget his mother?" The question was abrupt and without direction.

Malluch looked into Ben-Hur's face for some hint of meaning, but saw none. Thus, he answered mechanically, "No, never," he said. Then recovering himself he added with fervor, "If he is an Israelite, never!"

"Your words bring back my childhood," said Ben-Hur, "and, Malluch, they prove you a genuine Jew. I believe I can trust you.

My father bore a good name and was not without honor in Jerusalem, where he dwelt. My mother at his death was in the prime of womanhood; and it is not enough to say of her she was good and beautiful. In her tongue was the law of kindness, and her words were the praise of all in the gates. I also had a little sister; she and I were the family, and we were a happy family. But one day an accident happened to a Roman authority as he was riding past our palace. The legionaries burst the gate and rushed in to seize us. I have not seen my mother or sister since. I cannot say if they are dead or living. But, Malluch, the man in the chariot yonder was present at that separation. He gave us over to the captors, and despite my mother's prayer for her children, he laughed as they dragged her away. It is hard for me to say which lives deepest in my memory of that day, love or hate." Ben-Hur caught the listener's arm. "Malluch, that man knows and takes with him now the secret I would give my life for. He knows if my mother and sister live, where they are, and their condition. If they are dead, he could at least tell me where they died and where their bones await my finding."

"And he will not?"

"No."

"Why?"

"Because I am a Jew and he a Roman."

"But Romans have tongues; and Jews, though despised by Romans, have methods to beguile* them."

---
beguile: deceive

"Not for such as he," said Ben-Hur bitterly. "Besides, the secret is one of state."

Malluch nodded his head slowly, admitting the argument. Then he asked, "Would he recognize you?"

"He could not. I was sent to the galleys to die and have long been accounted as dead."

"I am amazed you did not rush at him and strike him," said Malluch yielding to a touch of passion.

"That would have been to put him past serving me forever. I would have had to kill him, and death keeps secrets even better than a guilty Roman." After a brief pause Ben-Hur resumed speaking. "I would not take his life, good Malluch, against that extreme the knowledge he possesses of my family's whereabouts is his safeguard. Yet I may punish him; and if you will help me, I will try."

"He is a Roman," said Malluch without hesitation, "and I am of the tribe of Judah. I will help you. If you choose, put me under oath—under the most solemn oath."

"Give me your hand; that will suffice." As their hands fell apart Ben-Hur said with lightened feeling, "What I would charge you with is not difficult, good friend; neither is

it dreadful to the conscience. Do you know Ilderim the sheik?"

"Yes. His Orchard of Palms lies beyond the village two hours by horse and one by swift camel."

"These games in which the chariots will race, have they been widely published?"

"Oh, yes."

"When will the games be?"

"They are scheduled for the sixth day from this."

"Then time is short, Malluch, but it is enough." The last words were spoken decisively. "One thing more now, Malluch. Can I be assured that Messala will drive?"

"He is committed to the race in many ways," said Malluch. "He has published it in the streets, in the palace, and in the soldiers barracks. Moreover, his name is on the tablets of every spendthrift in Antioch. He could not withdraw from the race now even if he desired to do so."

"Then I am satisfied. Now guide me to the Orchard of Palms and give me introduction to Sheik Ilderim the Generous."

"Now?"

"Now. I want to engage his horses, and by tomorrow someone else may have received the commission."

"You like them then?"

"They are of the blood which is the glory of the deserts. If all that is said of them be true and I can bring their spirit under control of mine, then I can—"

"Win the sestertii!"* said Malluch with enthusiasm.

---

sestertii (sə-stər′tə-ē′): silver coins

"No," said Ben-Hur quickly. "I will do much better than that, my friend. I will humble my enemy in a most public place, and as you and I know, a Roman can bear anything but humiliation!"

THINKING ZONE

As you read a short story or novel and analyze the characters, you will notice that each character tends to act a certain way. When you study **character motivation**, you are studying the reasons that a character behaves the way he does. Sometimes, character motivation is implied and requires careful attention to the details of the story, while other times, the author will state explicitly why a character does something. When you read "You Need to Go Upstairs," attention to the details surrounding Ally's trip into the house—the fear, the smells and sounds, the worry of the mother and guest—made you realize that the girl is blind. The author never tells the reader outright that Ally cannot see. On the other hand, when you read "The Last Lesson," you knew much of what motivates M. Hamel and Franz and the townspeople to take special care with their final French lessons. Reading for character motivation will enhance your understanding of and sympathy for the characters in the stories you read.

1. *[literal]* What is Ben-Hur's **motivation** for wanting to be known as the son of Arrius rather than the son of Hur?

   _____

   _____

2. *[critical]* Why is the Hebrew's story about the merchant Simonides of such interest to Ben-Hur?

   _____

   _____

   _____

   _____

3. *[critical]* How would you describe Ben-Hur's attitude after deciding to visit Simonides? Give evidence from the story to support your description.

   _____

   _____

   _____

   _____

4. *[critical]* What does Simonides do after Ben-Hur leaves him? What do you think his motivation for doing this is?

_____

_____

_____

_____

5. *[critical]* When Ben-Hur states that his father "was not without honor in Jerusalem," what does he really mean to emphasize? Is this an example of overstatement or understatement?

_____

_____

_____

_____

_____

Understatement—
the representation of something as less important than it truly is

6. *[critical]* What is Ben-Hur's motivation for wanting to drive Sheik Ilderim's horses?

_____

_____

_____

_____

7. *[critical]* Is it wrong for Ben-Hur to seek revenge? Cite Scripture to back up your answer.

_____

_____

_____

_____

8. *[critical]* What do you think will happen to Ben-Hur? What reason do you have for your prediction?

_____

_____

_____

_____

PART IV
THE BETRAYER IS BETRAYED

Simonides sat on the terrace looking down over the river. "Malluch is a laggard* tonight," he said, showing where his thoughts were.

---
laggard: a straggler

"Do you believe he will come?" Esther asked.

"Unless he has taken to the sea or the desert and is yet following the young man, he will come," Simonides said with quiet confidence. Just then a footstep was heard on the terrace—"Ha! Did I not tell you he would come, Esther? We will now have tidings."

Malluch approached. "Peace be to you, good master," he said, "and to you, Esther, most excellent of daughters."

Simonides, as was his habit in business, after answering the salutation went straight to the subject. "What of the young man, Malluch?"

Malluch recounted the events of the day in the simplest words; and until he was through, there was no interruption.

"You have done well—no one could have done better," said Simonides heartily. "Now, what say you of the young man's nationality?"

"He is an Israelite, good master, and of the tribe of Judah."

"You are positive?"

"Very positive."

"He appears to have told you only bits and pieces of his life."

"He has learned to be prudent.* I might call him distrustful, but I can answer with much assurance nonetheless. He is devoted to finding his mother and sister—that first.

Then he has a grievance against Rome. Messala whom I mentioned has something to do with that wrong, and the present object of the young Jew is to humiliate this Roman."

---

prudent: **wise**

"Messala is influential," said Simonides thoughtfully.

"Yes, but the meeting will be at the games."

"Well—what then?"

"The son of Arrius will win."

"How do you know?"

Malluch smiled. "I am judging by what he says."

"Is that all?"

"No, there is a much better sign—his spirit."

"Enough, Malluch. Go eat and make ready to return to the Orchard of Palms. You must help the young man in his coming trial. I will send a letter to Ilderim and tell him our secret. But make certain Ben-Hur remains ignorant of our acquaintance. He must not know I have sent you—at least not yet." Then in an undertone, as if to himself, he added, "I may attend the games myself this year."

* * *

Ben-Hur, having immediately answered Sheik Ilderim's publication, received the commission. The young Jew's skill with horses proved astounding, and Ilderim's enthusiasm knew no bounds. There was only one week for training, but when the time for the race arrived Ilderim, Malluch, and Ben-Hur were all confident—the fours and their driver were ready.

The afternoon before the games Ilderim's racing property was transported to the city and put in quarters adjoining the circus. As the sheik and Ben-Hur made their way into the city, Malluch approached them. He exchanged salutations, as usual, then produced a paper for the sheik saying, "I have here the notice of the editor of the games. It was just issued. In it you will find your horses published for the race. You will also find in it the order of the other exercises. And may I say even now, good sheik, that I congratulate you on your victory." He gave the paper to Ilderim and turned to Ben-Hur. "To you also, son of Arrius, my congratulations. There is nothing now to prevent your meeting Messala. Every condition preliminary to the race is complied with. I have assurance from the creditor himself, and may I add that I am certain you shall win."

"Thank you, Malluch," said Ben-Hur.

"Your color is white," Malluch continued, "and Messala's mixed scarlet and gold. The good effects are visible already. Boys are now hawking* white ribbons along the streets. Tomorrow I assure you every Arab and Jew in the city will wear them. In the circus you will see the white fairly divide the galleries with the red."

---

hawking: **peddling**

"Malluch, would you serve me perfectly?" said Ben-Hur.

"I would," replied Malluch.

"Then help me fix all the public eye on our race—Messala's and mine. Draw their attention away from all other contestants. Can that be done?"

"It can!"

"Then do it," said Ben-Hur.

At that moment the conversation was interrupted by a cry from Ilderim. "Ha! What is this!" He drew near Ben-Hur with a finger pointing on the face of the notice. "Read here!"

Ben-Hur took the paper. The names of the competitors were given, with their several nationalities and schools of training, the trials in which they had been engaged, the prizes they had won, and the prizes now offered. Over these parts of the program, Ben-Hur sped with rapid glance. At last he came to the announcement of the chariot race. He read it slowly. One thousand sestertii and a crown of laurel were the prizes. Then followed the particulars.

"I. A four of Lysippus the Corinthian—two grays, a bay, and a black; entered at Alexandria last year, and again at Corinth, where they were winners. Lysippus, driver. Color, yellow.

"II. A four of Messala of Rome—two white, two black; victors of the Circensian as exhibited in the Circus Maximus last year. Messala, driver. Colors, scarlet and gold.

"III. A four of Cleanthes the Athenian—three gray, one bay; winners at the Isthmian last year. Cleanthes, driver. Color, green.

"IV. A four of Dicaeus the Byzantine—two black, one gray, one bay; winners, this year at Byzantium. Dicaeus, driver. Color, black.

"V. A four of Admetus the Sidonian—all grays. Thrice entered at Caesarea, and thrice victors. Admetus, driver. Color, blue.

"VI. A four of Ilderim, sheik of the Desert. All bays; first race. Ben-Hur, a Jew, driver. Color, white."

Ben-Hur, a Jew, driver!
Why that name instead of Arrius?
Ben-Hur raised his eyes to Ilderim. He had found the cause of the Arab's outcry. Both rushed to the same conclusion.
The hand was the hand of Messala! He knew Ben-Hur!

* * *

In the purest sense the games were a gift to the public; consequently, everyone was free to attend. At midnight the day before the games were to start, the entrances were thrown open, and the rabble* came surging into every quarter. Nothing less than an earthquake or an army with spears could have dislodged them from their benches. They dozed the night away and breakfasted there, and in the morning they were found waiting, patient and sight-hungry.

---

rabble: common people

As the charioteers moved into the circus, the excitement increased. The people in the galleries filled the air with screams.
"Messala! Messala!"
"Ben-Hur! Ben-Hur!"
On hearing the crowd Ben-Hur knew his prayers had been answered. Malluch had done his work well. The eyes of the East were on his contest with Messala. In the midst of this excitement, four stout servants entered carrying the merchant Simonides up the aisle. Curiosity was much excited. Presently someone called out, "Simonides, that's Simonides; he's come to the games!" Those about caught it and passed it along the benches. There was a hurried climbing on seats to get sight of the man about whom common report had coined a romance so mixed of good and bad fortune that everyone was interested. Ilderim, who entered with Simonides and Esther, also brought attention. The merchant and his party were only just seated when the trumpet sounded short and sharp. The starters, one for each chariot, leaped down from behind the pillars of the goal, ready to give assistance if any of the four proved unmanageable. Again the trumpet sounded and simultaneously the gatekeepers threw open the stalls. The race was on and the souls of the racers were in it.

Ben-Hur was on the extreme left of the six racers. For a moment, like the others, he was half-blinded by the lights in the arena; yet he managed to catch sight of his antagonists* and divine* their purpose. At Messala, he gave one searching look. As he did so, he saw the soul of the man—cruel, cunning, desperate—not so much excited as determined, a soul in a tension of watchfulness and fierce resolve. In a time no longer than was required to turn his eyes back to his horses, Ben-Hur felt his own resolution harden to like temper. At whatever cost, at all hazards, he determined to humble this enemy!

---

antagonists: competitors
divine: guess

At the outset of the race, Ben-Hur swept around and took the course neck and neck with Messala, though on the outside. The marvelous skill shown in making the change from the extreme left across to the right without losing ground did not fail the sharp eyes of the spectators. The circus rocked with prolonged applause.

Now, racing together side by side, the two opponents neared the goal. Making this first turn was in all respects considered the telling test of a charioteer. A hush fell over all the circus so that, for the first time in the race, the rattle and clang of the cars plunging after the tugging steeds was distinctly heard.

Messala observed Ben-Hur. As they rounded the perilous curve, he turned to Ben-Hur and cried out, "Down Eros, Up Mars!" and with this shout he whirled his whip to lash Ben-Hur's steeds. The whip caught the horses a cut the like of which they had never known. The four Arabs sprang forward affrighted! The blow was seen in every quarter of the galleries, and the spectators' amazement was universal. The silence deepened until up on the benches behind the consul the boldest held his breath, waiting for the outcome. The strength obtained from years of rowing helped Ben-Hur now. He called to the four in a soothing voice, and with both might and skill he gripped the reins to guide the horses safely around the dangerous turn. The people cheered Ben-Hur then turned

their attention to Messala. Down from the balcony, as thunder falls, burst their indignant cry. Their feeling was so vigorous in its manifestation that Messala felt it unsafe to trifle* further. Before the people's fever abated,* Ben-Hur had totally regained the mastery of his horses, and on approaching the first goal, he was again side by side with Messala, bearing with him the sympathy and admiration of all in the crowd who were not Roman.

trifle: to act inconsiderately
abated: lessen

As the cars whirled around the goal, Esther caught sight of Ben-Hur's face. He was pale, but otherwise calm. There were yet five rounds to go. After three rounds Messala still held the inside position, but Ben-Hur moved closely at his side.

Messala had now attained his utmost speed, and slowly but certainly he was beginning to forge ahead. His horses were running with their heads low; from the balcony their bodies appeared to skim the earth; their nostrils showed blood-red in expansion; their eyes seemed straining in their sockets.

When the last round began, Ben-Hur turned in behind the Roman's car, and the joy of the Messala faction reached its bound. They screamed and howled and tossed the red and yellow colors. Malluch in the lower gallery found it hard to keep his cheer. Ben-Hur was barely holding a place at the tail of his enemy's car. Over in the east end, Simonides' party was silent. The merchant's head was bent low. Ilderim tugged at his beard and dropped his eyebrows till there was nothing to be seen of his eyes but an occasional sparkle of light. Esther scarcely breathed.

Messala, fearful of losing his place, hugged the stony wall with a perilous clasp.

As they whirled by Esther saw Ben-Hur's face again; it was whiter than before. Simonides, shrewder than Esther, said to Ilderim, "I am no judge, good sheik, if Ben-Hur be not about to execute some design. His face has that look."

All factions except the Romans joined hope in Ben-Hur and openly indulged their feeling.

"Ben-Hur! Ben-Hur!" they shouted.

From the benches above him as he passed, he heard the favor descend in fierce injunctions,* "Speed thee, Jew!" some cried. "Take the wall now! On! loose the Arabs! Give them rein and scourge!* Do not let the Roman have the turn on you again!" others cried.

injunctions: commands
scourge: a whip

Either Ben-Hur refused to listen or could not do better, for halfway round the course in the last round, he was still following. Now, to make the last turn, Messala began to draw in his left-hand steeds, an act which necessarily slackened their speed. His spirit was high, and confident, for they were only six-hundred feet from the finish.

At that moment Malluch saw Ben-Hur lean forward over his Arabs and give them the reins. Out flew the many-folded lash in his hand. Over the backs of the startled steeds it writhed and hissed and writhed again and again. Though it did not fall, there was both sting and menace in its quick report. Instantly, not one, but the four as one, answered with a leap that landed them alongside the Roman's car. Messala heard, but dared not look. At that moment the iron shod point of Ben-Hur's axle caught Messala's wheel and crushed it. A crash loud enough to send a thrill throughout the circus was heard. Quicker than thought, out over the course a spray of shining red and yel-

low fragments flew. Down on its right side toppled the bed of Messala's chariot! There was a rebound as the axle hit the hard earth; then another. The car dashed against the wall and went to pieces. Messala, entangled in the reigns, pitched forward headlong! To increase the horror of the sight, the Sidonian, who was behind Ben-Hur, could not stop or turn out. He drove into the wreck full speed, over Messala and into his horses all mad with fear. Presently, out of the turmoil, the fighting horses, the resound of blows, and the murky clouds of dust, crawled Messala. The race had been delayed only an instant.

The people arose, leaped on the benches, shouted and screamed. Their enthusiasm was beyond all restraint. Those who looked toward the wreckage caught glimpses of Messala, now under the trampling fours, now under the abandoned car. He was still; they thought him dead. But a far greater number never even

looked that way. Instead they followed Ben-Hur. When the Byzantine and Corinthian were halfway down the course, Ben-Hur made the last turn. The race was won.

* * *

The chariot race proved only the beginning of Messala's humiliation. He had escaped death, but his legs were crushed and forever useless. This proud Roman, who had encouraged Gratus to torture Simonides in an effort to find the Hurs' fortune, was now compelled to suffer the same affliction. His misery, however, was far greater than the noble merchant's. For all Messala's wealth was lost with the race, and the friends that had doted on him in prosperous times now deserted him. Only his pride remained as a bitter companion to mock him and daily remind him of lost dreams and the tragic life he was destined to endure.

THINKING ZONE

Galatians 6:7 states, "Be not deceived; God is not mocked: for whatsoever a man soweth, that shall he also reap." The biblical principle of sowing and reaping sums up the idea behind the literary concept of **poetic justice**, a term coined by a seventeenth-century literary critic to describe the occurrence within a story of earthly rewards or punishments being given to a character based on that character's previous actions. Poetic justice often satisfies the reader because readers want to see good characters achieve a happy ending and evil characters accorded their proper punishment. We are glad when the youngest brother in "The Magic Brocade" wins the beautiful maiden and feel gratified when the two older brothers are forced to slink away in poverty. As you read the rest of *Ben-Hur*, note which characters seem to receive poetic justice.

1. *[interpretive]* What is the main conflict in this chapter?

   _____

   _____

2. *[interpretive]* Why does Ben-Hur ask Malluch to help to "fix the public eye" on the race between him and Messala?

   _____

   _____

   _____

   _____

3. *[literal]* Why does Sheik Ilderim cry out when he reads the program for the games? Whose "hand" is behind the program's revelation?

   _____

   _____

   _____

   _____

4. *[critical]* How are Ben-Hur's horses different from the rest of those entered in the race?

_____

_____

_____

_____

_____

5. *[critical]* List some specific actions during the race that reveal Messala's villainous character.

_____

_____

Villain—*an evil character*

_____

_____

_____

_____

_____

_____

_____

6. *[critical]* Does poetic justice occur at the conflict's resolution? How?

_____

_____

_____

_____

_____

_____

_____

_____

Ben-Hur moved toward the house of Simonides with the excitement of the race still in his mind. After the race, Simonides had revealed his acquaintance with Ilderim, and now the whole party waited for Ben-Hur at the merchant's house. Malluch greeted him at the door and showed him into the main room. It was exactly as it had been at Ben-Hur's first interview.

"Son of Hur," said Simonides, repeating the address slowly, "son of Hur, take thou the peace of the Lord God of our fathers— take it from me and mine." The salutation could not be misunderstood. Simonides' address confirmed that he now recognized Ben-Hur as master.

Unable to find the appropriate words to convey his emotion, Ben-Hur remained silent while Simonides continued, "I have here a statement covering your property first, and then our relation. Will it please you to read it now?"

"Later, Simonides," he managed to say. "Later I will read the papers carefully. For the present I would prefer you to summarize their contents."

From the separate sheets, Simonides read the following:

CREDIT

By ships	60 talents
By goods in store	110 talents
By cargoes in transit.	75 talents
By camels, horses, etc.	20 talents
By warehouses	10 talents
By bills due	54 talents
By money on hand and subject to draft.	224 talents
TOTAL	553 talents

"To these five hundred and fifty-three talents gained, add the original capital I had from your father and you have six hundred and seventy-three talents! You are now, son of Hur, the richest Roman subject in the world!" Ben-Hur gazed at the speaker. Despite the broken limbs and the bloodless face, Simonides had a masterful air and a royal manner. His black eyes looked out under the white brows steadily, but not sternly. The pride perceptible in the faithful servant's manner was not offensive, for it was from a sense of duty well done. Simonides rolled the papyri* and offered them to Ben-Hur, who took them gently from the old man's hand. "Now, concerning our relation," said Simonides, dropping his voice but not his eyes, "What is your desire?"

---

papyri (pə-pī′rī′): ancient writing papers made from the papyrus plant

---

The moment was one of absorbing interest to all present, for a man is never so on trial as in the moment of excessive good fortune. Simonides folded his hands and waited. Esther scarcely breathed, and Ilderim fingered his beard anxiously.

Ben-Hur arose. He was yet struggling with emotion, but he mastered himself and began. "All this is to me as a light from heaven sent to drive away a night which has been so long I feared it would not end, so dark I had lost hope of seeing. I give thanks to the Lord, Who has not abandoned me, and next, to you, good Simonides. Your faithfulness outweighs the cruelty of others, and my father would have richly rewarded you. I desire to be like him. You have said there is nothing I cannot do; be it so. The goods recorded here—the ships, houses,

ministrative command, Pilate ordered an inspection of all the prisons in Judea and a return of the names of persons in custody with a statement of the crimes they had committed.

This order was received and promptly executed at the Tower of Antonia in Jerusalem. The next morning an officer from the tower appeared at Pilate's palace.

"Ah, Gesius! Come in," Pilate said.

The newcomer entered. Everyone present looked at him, and observing a certain expression of alarm on his face, became silent that they might hear what he had to say. "Tribune," he began, bending low, "I fear to tell you the news I bring."

"Another mistake—ah, Gesius?"

"If I could persuade myself it was but a mistake, I would not be afraid."

"A crime then, or worse, a breach of duty. You may laugh at Caesar and live; but if you have offended the eagles*—ah, Gesius you know your fate. Go on."

---

eagles: emblem of Rome

---

camels, horses, money, and of course your freedom, I give back to you. It is all yours with one exception and on one condition. That exception is that the hundred and twenty talents which were my father's be returned to me; and that condition is that you shall join me in the search for my mother and sister, holding all your wealth, as I shall mine, subject to the expense of their discovery." It was heartily agreed on, and before nightfall Ben-Hur was on his way to Jerusalem, with the promise that Simonides and Esther would soon follow.

* * *

A great change had come to pass in Jerusalem. Valerius Gratus had been succeeded by Pontius Pilate. As his first ad-

"It has been about eight years now since Valerius Gratus selected me to be keeper of the Tower of Antonia," said the man deliberately. "I remember the morning I entered upon the duties of my office. There had been a riot the day before. We slew many Jews and suffered on our side as well. The affair came, it was said, from an attempt to assassinate Gratus. I found him sitting where you now sit, his head wrapped in bandages. He told me of my selection and gave me these keys. They are numbered to correspond with the number of each cell in the Tower. He told me they were the badges of my office and not to be parted with. He also laid a roll of parchment on the table, and calling me over to him, he opened the roll. 'Here are the maps of the cells,' he said. There were three maps. He pointed to one. 'This one,' he said, 'shows the arrangement of the lower floor.' He then took care to spread the map out on the table. 'Notice this cell—cell number V.' He laid his finger on the picture of the cell. 'There are three men confined in that cell,' he continued, 'desperate characters, who by some means got hold of a state secret and suffer for their curiosity. They are blind and tongueless and are placed in this cell for life. They are to have nothing but food and drink, and that is to be given them through a hole which you will find in the wall. Do you understand, Gesius?' I nodded assent. 'It is well that you do.' He looked at me threateningly. 'One thing more, the door of their cell—cell number V—shall never be opened for any purpose, neither to let anyone in or out, not even yourself.'

"But if they die," I asked.

"'If they die,' he said, 'the cell shall be their tomb. They were put there to die. The cell is leprous. They cannot last long.' With that he gave me the parchments and let me go."

Gesius stopped and from the breast of his tunic drew three parchments, all much yellowed by time and use. Selecting one of them, he laid it before the tribune. "This is the lower floor as the map Gratus gave me shows." The whole company looked at the map. "But," Gesius continued, "this is not a true map," said the keeper. "It shows but five cells on that floor and there are six."

"Six, you say?"

"I will show you the floor as it is, or as I believe it to be." On the page of his tablet, Gesius drew another diagram and gave it to the tribune.

"You have done well," said Pilate, examining the drawing and thinking the narrative at an end. "I will have the map corrected; or, better, I will have a new one made and given to you. Come for it in the morning." Pilate then rose to go.

"But hear me further, tribune. The prisoners of state—those blind and without tongues—that was not a true story either."

"No?" said the tribune with returning interest.

"Hear and judge for yourself. As required, I visited all cells. Gratus's order that cell number V should not be opened had been respected all these years. Food and drink only had been passed through the wall for the three men; that was all. I went to the door yesterday, curious to see the wretches who, against all expectation, had lived so long. The locks refused the key. We pulled a little and the door fell down, rusted from its hinges. Going in, I found but one man—old, blind, and tongue-less. His hair dropped in stiffened mats below his waist. His skin was like the parchment there, and as he held out his hands, his fingernails curled and twisted like the claws of a bird. I asked him where his companions were. He shook his head in denial. Thinking to find the others, we searched the cell. The floor was dry; so were the walls. If three men had been shut up in the cell and two of them had died, at least their bones would have endured."

"What are you saying?"

"I believe that there has been but one prisoner there in the eight years."

The tribune regarded the keeper sharply and said, "Are you saying that Gratus lied?"

Gesius bowed, "I am saying he might have been mistaken."

"No, he must have been correct," the tribune said. "By your own admission he was right. For did you not say that for eight years food and drink were furnished for three men?"

"There is an explanation," Gesius continued. "Today the prisoner came back. He was brought to me. By signs and tears he at last made me understand that he wished to return to his cell, and I so ordered. As they were leading him off, he broke away and kissed my feet and by piteous dumb imploration* insisted that I should go also. I went. When we were in the cell again, the prisoner caught my hand eagerly and led me to the back wall of his cell. There I found a hole exactly like the one through which we passed the prisoner's food and drink. He pushed me aside and put his face to the hole and gave a beastlike cry. A sound came faintly back. I was astonished and drew him away. I called out, 'Ho, here!' At first there was no answer. I called again and received a reply. 'Be Thou praised, O Lord,' a faint voiced cried. What was more astonishing was that the voice was a woman's voice. 'Who are you?' I called. The reply came, 'A woman of Israel, entombed with her daughter. Help us quickly, or we die.' I told them to be of cheer and hurried here to know your will in the matter."

---

imploration: pleading

The tribune arose hastily. "You were right, Gesius," he said. "I see now. The map was a lie, and so was the tale of the three men. There have been better Romans than Valerius Gratus."

"I gleaned from the prisoner that he had regularly given the women of the food and drink that he received," continued Gesius excitedly.

"It is accounted for," replied the tribune. "Come let us rescue the women."

"We will have to pierce the wall," the keeper warned. "I found where a door had been, but it was filled solidly with stones and mortar."

"Send workman after me with tools," the tribune said to a clerk.

In a short time Ben-Hur's mother and his sister were released from their living tomb. As they emerged from their long confinement, however, the light revealed for them a fate worse than death—they were leprous.

* * *

About the same hour that Gesius was visiting the tribune, Ben-Hur was climbing the eastern face of Mount Olivet. He had left Simonides' house thirty days before and was now just arriving in Judea. The road was rough and dusty, for it was the dry season. He proceeded slowly, approaching his home town as one approaches an old acquaintance after a long separation, as if he were saying, "I'm glad to be with you again; let me see how you have changed."

His search for his mother and sister as yet had no definite plan. From Simonides he learned that Amrah, the Egyptian servant, was still living. On the morning the calamity overtook the Hurs, the faithful creature broke from the guard and ran back into the palace.

She was sealed up there. Simonides, while searching for the family, had discovered Amrah and secretly began supplying her with enough money to live comfortably. The Roman authorities assumed she had starved to death.

Gratus had tried diligently to sell the palace but could not. Its reputation was that of a haunted house. This idea was probably derived from the infrequent glimpses of poor old Amrah by passersby. Sometimes she would be seen on the roof, other times through a latticed window. Never was a palace so shunned or fitted for ghostly habitation after that tragic day.

Ben-Hur decided first to go to the old house and find Amrah. He would make further plans then. As he stopped at the gate on the north side, he saw plainly that the wax used in sealing the corners was still intact. No one had gone in or out of the gate since that fateful day. Should he knock as in old

times? It was useless, he knew. Still, he could not resist the temptation. Amrah might hear and look out one of the windows on that side. He mounted the broad stone step and tapped three times. A dull echo replied. He tried again, louder than before, pausing each time to listen. The silence was mocking, and he finally gave up and passed from the north side to the west.

There were four windows on this side and he watched them long and anxiously, hoping Amrah would appear. But when she made no sign, he stole round to the south. There, too, the gate was sealed and inscribed with the hated words: *This is the property of the*

Emperor. The mellow splendor of the August moon brought the lettering boldly out. As he read the inscription, Ben-Hur was filled with rage. He wrenched the board from its nailing and hurled it into the ditch. Then he sat down on the step and prayed until his blood cooled. After sitting a while, however, he began to feel the weariness caused by his long journey in the summer heat. He sank down lower and at last slept.

About this time two women approached the palace from the direction of the Tower of Antonia. They advanced with timid steps, pausing to make certain no one was about. They neared the house. "This is it, Tirzah," the widow said. Tirzah, after a look, caught her mother's hand and leaned heavily on her, quietly weeping.

"We must go on now, my child," the mother said. She hesitated and then added, "If they find us within the city in the morning, they will stone us. We must be out of the gates and to the lepers' tombs by then." At these words Tirzah sank almost to the stones. Her mother, however, supported her and encouraged her to move on. As she did so, she gave one last glance back toward the house and stopped. "Wait," she said. "I think I see someone lying on the steps—a man."

Looking carefully about her, the mother stepped cautiously into the street leading Tirzah closer to the house. As they emerged from the darkness, the bright moonlight revealed the extent of their affliction. Their faces and hands were dry and cracked. Their eyes were bleary. Their hair was long, stiff, loathsome, and ghastly white. Nor was it possible to tell the daughter from the mother, for they both seemed witch-like old. They crossed to the opposite side of the street quickly and moved on till they were before the gate. They were careful to keep close to the wall in the shadows.

"He is asleep, Tirzah! Stay here and I will get a closer look." She moved close to the gate. Looking down, she gasped, looked again, then ran back to Tirzah. "As the Lord lives, the man is my son—your brother!" she said in a frenzied whisper.

"Judah?" said Tirzah, unbelieving.

Her mother caught her hand eagerly. "Come!" she said, in the same enforced whisper. "Let us look at him together—once more—only once!" They moved close hand in hand ghostly-quickly, ghostly-still. When their shadows fell upon him, they stopped. One of his hands was draped across a step. Tirzah fell on her knees and would have kissed it, but her mother drew her back. "No! We are unclean!" Tirzah shrank from him, as if he were the leper. He stirred at that moment. They moved back. He muttered in his restless dreaming, "Mother! Amrah, where is—" He moved fitfully and then fell off into a deep sleep once again.

Tirzah stared wistfully. Her mother covered her face, struggling to suppress a sob so deep and strong it seemed her heart would burst. Almost she wished he would awaken. But he had asked for her, and she knew she was not forgotten. This had to be enough. She beckoned Tirzah and they arose, taking one more look, as if to imprint his image on their minds. They then turned and crossed the street again. When safely on the other side, they hovered in the shadows waiting—waiting for some revelation, they knew not what.

By and by another woman appeared at the corner of the palace. Tirzah and her mother saw her plainly in the light, a small figure, much bent, dark-skinned, gray-haired, and dressed neatly in servant's garb. She was carrying a basket full of vegetables. At the sight of Ben-Hur on the steps, the newcomer stopped. Then, as if deciding to walk on, very lightly she drew the wicket gate latch easily to one side and put her hand in the opening. One of the boards swung ajar without noise. She put her basket through and was about to follow, when, yielding to her curiosity, she lingered to have one look at the stranger. The spectators across the street heard her low exclamation and saw the woman rub her eyes as if to renew their power. She then leaned closer, gazed wildly about, and awoke the sleeper.

"Amrah! Oh, Amrah!" exclaimed Ben-Hur when he had regained his sense. "Is it really you?"

Amrah made no answer in words; she simply fell upon his neck, crying for joy. He gently kissed her. His tears of joy were only a little less than hers. Tirzah and her mother straining to listen from their hiding place heard him say, "Mother and Tirzah, tell me of them, Amrah. Speak, speak I pray you." Amrah only cried the more. "Have you seen them, Amrah? Tell me, are they at home?"

Tirzah moved forward as if to run to her brother, but her mother caught her firmly by the arm and whispered urgently, "You cannot go—not for life!" Her mother's love was in a tyrannical mood. Even though both of them desired more than anything to see him, the greater fear of making him leprous overruled.

In another moment Amrah and Ben-Hur disappeared into the house, leaving the two outsiders staring blankly at the gate—the gate which they might never enter more. Nestling together in the dust, they gave way to their despair.

The next morning they were found and driven from the city with stones, the sentence of their doom ringing in their ears as they went forth. "Begone! You are of the dead! Go to the dead."

* * *

Amrah had been accustomed to going to the market after nightfall. Stealing out unobserved, she would quickly make her purchases of meat and vegetables and return to shut herself within the palace. She had been on this errand the night she found Ben-Hur.

The pleasure she derived from his return was even more than she imagined it would be. Her only regret was that she could tell him nothing of his mother and sister. She desired that he move into the palace and take his own room again, but the danger of discovery would be too great and he refused. He came to see her as often as possible, however. She was satisfied and at once set about contriving ways of making him happy.

Several nights after his arrival she stole out with her basket to the Fish Gate market. Ben-Hur was coming to visit and she was in search of the best honey. Wandering about, she chanced to hear a man telling a story, and immediately her attention went to the storyteller. She could scarcely believe her ears, for he was relating the particulars of the rescue of the widow and Tirzah. Quickly she made her purchases and returned home as if in a dream, thinking only of the joy she would have in telling Ben-Hur the news.

As she entered the gate, however, another thought struck her. They were lepers. She had heard the man say so, and yet she had not let that idea sink into her mind until now, and it struck with crushing force. Such knowledge she knew would kill Ben-Hur. He would relentlessly wander through the tombs where the lepers lived until he found them, and eventually their fate would be his. Wringing her hands in despair, she sat down to think what she should do.

Like many others before her, she derived wisdom from her affliction and came to a profitable conclusion. The lepers, she knew, were accustomed to come down from their gravelike abodes every morning to get water from the well. Bringing their jars, they would set them on the ground and move far from the well, waiting for some merciful soul to take up the jars and fill them. The mistress and Tirzah must surely come to the well with the others, for a rich leper was no better than a poor one. Thus, Amrah decided not to speak to Ben-Hur of her discovery until she had gone to the well in the morning.

Shortly after sunrise the lepers began to appear, moving slowly from their tombs. Amrah kept watch on the ghostly group moving slowly. At first, distance softened the misery of the outcasts, but as they neared, their true condition became clear. Some leaned on the shoulders of others. A few—the utterly helpless—lay, like heaps of rags, on litters.* She had never seen such a ghastly spectacle. But she was determined. Those she sought must come down and she would wait.

---

litters: stretchers

At length Amrah beheld two women. They remained at the back of the crowd awhile. Then slowly, painfully they moved forward toward the well. They were fearful and obviously unaware that they could not come themselves to fill the jars. Several voices were raised to stop them from approaching. Someone even picked up some pebbles and made ready to drive them back. The company of lepers behind them shouted shrilly, "Unclean! Unclean!"

"Surely," thought Amrah, "surely they are strangers to the usage of lepers and have only recently come to the tombs." She arose and went to meet them, taking a jar of water. The alarm at the well immediately subsided and was replaced by mocking and laughter.

"What a fool," said one observer, "what a fool to serve water to the dead."

"And to think of her going so far," said another as she watched Amrah proceed without hesitation.

The further Amrah went, however, the more she doubted. What if she should be mistaken? Her heart rose to her throat. Four or five yards from where they stood she stopped. That woman could not be the mistress she loved, not the woman of matronly loveliness that Amrah treasured faithfully in her memory. Nor could the other leper be Tirzah whom she had nursed through babyhood, whose pains she had soothed and whose sports she had shared. Amrah's soul sickened at the sight of them. "These women are old," she said to herself. "I never saw them before. I will go back." She turned away.

"Amrah," one of the lepers called to her. The Egyptian nurse dropped the jar she was holding, spilling the water it contained. She looked back trembling.

"Who called me?" she asked.

"Amrah."

The servant's wondering eyes settled on the speaker's face. "Who are you?" she cried.

"We are those you are seeking," said the woman softly. Amrah fell on her knees. "Oh, my mistress, my mistress! As I have made your God my God, be He praised that He has led me to you!" The poor, overwhelmed creature moved forward to embrace them.

"Stay, Amrah! Don't come near." The words sufficed to stop her approach, but she was so overcome with her helplessness that she fell on her face and began to sob loudly. The people at the well heard her and wondered.

"Please, Amrah, rise, and bring us water."

The habit of the servant renewed itself. Immediately Amrah rose and taking up the jar she went to the well and refilled it. The people under whose eyes all this had passed made way for her and even helped her, for her countenance was so grief stricken, they could not help showing mercy.

"Who are they?" one woman asked.

Amrah answered meekly, "They used to be good to me." Raising the jar on her shoulder, she hurried back. She would have served them both, but the mistress restrained her, "No, Amrah. They may stone you and refuse us drink. Leave the jar, and we will carry it to the tomb with us. You have rendered us all the service that is lawful."

Amrah obeyed, and placing the jar on the ground, she stepped back a little way. "Is there nothing else I can do for you?" she asked.

"Yes," she said firmly. "I know that Judah has come home. I saw him at the gate asleep the same night you found him. I watched you awaken him."

"Mistress, you saw it and did not come?"

"That would have been to kill him. I can never take him in my arms again, never kiss him more." She paused to gain strength. "Oh, Amrah, I know you love him."

"I would die for him," said the servant earnestly.

"Then prove what you say."

"What do you want me to do?"

"Do not tell him where we are or that you have seen us—only that, Amrah."

"But he has come so far to find you."

"He must not! You shall tell us of him, but never, never, say anything of us. Do you hear?"

"It will be hard to hear him speak of you and see him constantly searching for you and say nothing—not so much as that you are alive."

"Can you tell him we are well, Amrah?"

"No," said the servant, grieved.

"Then be silent altogether. Go now and come again when you have news. Until then, farewell."

THINKING ZONE

Sometimes, within a longer work of literature, the author will introduce a second plot that may be equal in importance to the main plot yet will not be given the same amount of detail or story length. Any plot introduced in addition to the main plot is called a **subplot**. The subplot may sometimes reflect further (symbolically or otherwise) on the main plot.

Depending on how the subplot is handled within the story, the subplot may contain a degree of dramatic irony. **Dramatic irony** occurs when the reader of a story is aware of certain story details of which the characters within the story are unaware. If the subplot of a story is in any way related to the main plot, there is a good chance that there will be dramatic irony present within the story because the reader will be aware of details from both plots but the characters will probably not be. Shakespeare often uses dramatic irony when he has a female character dress up as a male character. The audience knows that the boy Ganymede in *As You Like It* is really the girl Rosalind, but since most of the other characters do not, a great deal of humor results.

1. *[interpretive]* How does the statement that "a man is never so on trial as in the moment of excessive good fortune" relate to Ben-Hur and his situation at the beginning of Part V?

_____

_____

_____

_____

_____

_____

2. *[literal]* How does Ben-Hur choose to deal with the faithful Simonides?

_____

_____

_____

3. *[interpretive]* Compare the characters of Simonides and Amrah. How are they alike?

_____

_____

_____

_____

_____

_____

4. *[critical]* What is the **subplot** that begins in this part of the novel?

_____

_____

_____

5. *[critical]* Look closely at the portion describing Tirzah and her mother's arrival at the family home and their secret reunion with Ben-Hur. What descriptive elements help to heighten the suspense of this portion?

_____

_____

_____

_____

_____

_____

6. *[critical]* Where does **dramatic irony** occur in this chapter?

_____

_____

_____

_____

_____

PART VI
THE BELOVED ARE RESTORED

Throughout the passing months, Amrah remained obedient to her mistress's command. Though daily she carried news of Ben-Hur to the leper's tomb, she returned to the palace bearing only the guarded silence of her hidden sorrow. She gave Ben-Hur no cause to hope, and eventually his hope died and was replaced by bitterness against all that was Rome.

Jerusalem's political situation was ripe for harvesting a bitterness like Ben-Hur's. The Nazarene had recently gained many followers, and rumors flourished that He would soon overthrow Rome and set up a kingdom of His own. By the time Simonides and Esther arrived in Jerusalem, Ben-Hur had formed a faithful band of Galileans who followed the son of Mary expectantly. Simonides joined their ranks, and though he could not join them in roaming the Judean countryside, he gave of his wealth to further their cause.

One evening as Ben-Hur was recounting the day's events to Simonides, Amrah chanced to overhear the conversation. As she listened to him, she became increasingly excited, for Judah spoke of the Nazarene's cleansing of ten lepers. By the time Simonides and Ben-Hur departed Amrah had determined to bear the news to the widow and Tirzah.

As the first traces of dawn colored the sky, she hurried out of the city, hastened to the eastern valley, and made her way past the well of En-rogel to the lepers' refuge. Early as it was, her unhappy mistress was up sitting outside with Tirzah.

"Mistress, mistress," called Amrah excitedly. "I have news!"

"Of Judah?" asked the widow.

"There is a wonderful man," Amrah continued, "who has the power to cure you. He speaks a word and the sick are made well. Even the dead come to life! Come, we must go to Him."

"Poor Amrah," said Tirzah thinking the servant had gone mad.

"No!" cried Amrah, detecting Tirzah's thoughts. "As the Lord lives, I speak the truth. Come with me; let us lose no time. This morning He will pass this way on His way to the city. Come. Come," she urged.

The mother listened eagerly. She had heard of this man but not heard of this wonderful story. "Who told you about this?" she asked.

"Judah."

The widow was silent awhile, then asked, "Did my son send you to tell us this?"

"No, I have kept my word. He still believes you dead."

"How does he know this man?"

"He has been traveling with Him these past months. He believes as many others that the Nazarene will use His powers to conquer Rome. Judah has formed a band of soldiers, Galileans, who travel with the Master and await the time when He shall need them."

"Does the Nazarene know of his band of soldiers?"

"No—they say nothing; they only follow and wait. That is how Judah saw the miracle of healing."

The widow sat musing awhile, then at length said, "There was a time when Jerusalem was filled with the story that the Messiah had been born. This must be He." She did not speak coldly like one reasoning away doubt, but rather as a woman of Israel familiar with God's promises to her race. "We will go with you," she said turning to Amrah.

The journey, though short, was difficult. The good servant toiled faithfully to lighten the way as they descended the hillside, but Tirzah moaned at every step. When they reached the roadside, she fell down exhausted. "Go on with Amrah, Mother. Leave me. I cannot go further."

"No, Tirzah. What would be the gain to me if I were healed and you were not? And when Judah asks for you, as he will, what would I say to him?"

"Tell him simply that I love him."

At that moment the widow noticed a stranger approaching. "Courage, Tirzah," she said. "Here comes one who may tell us of the Nazarene."

Amrah helped the girl sit up and supported her. "In your goodness, Mother, you forget what we are. The stranger will go round us. His best gift to us will be a curse, if not a stone."

"We will see," said the widow, though she knew that her daughter's fears were well-founded. The road was little more than a path or trail, and if the stranger kept his direction he must meet them face to face. He did so. When he was near enough to hear the cry, the widow called out shrilly, "Unclean, unclean!"

To her surprise the man came steadily on, and stopping not four yards off, he asked, "What can I do for you?"

"You see our condition; be cautious."

"Woman," the man said, "I am the messenger of Him who speaks but once to people as you are and they are healed. I am not afraid."

"Do you speak of the Nazarene?"

"I speak of the Messiah."

"Is it true that He is coming to the city today?"

"He is now at Bethphage."

"On what road, master?"

"This one, but for whom do you take Him?"

"The Son of God," she replied firmly.

"Then stay here but remain by the rock yonder, for there is a multitude with Him. When He goes by, do not fail to call to Him. Call and fear not." With these words the stranger moved on.

"Did you hear, Tirzah? Did you hear? Let us go to the rock. It is but a step."

The road became gradually more and more frequented until by the fourth hour a great crowd appeared. Many carried freshly cut palm branches. "He is coming," said the widow to Tirzah. Then turning to Amrah she asked, "When Judah spoke of the healing of the ten, what words did he say the lepers used to call to the Nazarene?"

"Some said, 'Lord, have mercy on us,' and others simply said, 'Master, have mercy.'"

"Only that?"

"No more that I heard."

By now the foremost of the crowd was in sight, but the gaze of the lepers fixed on the man riding in the midst of the company, the wonderful Nazarene.

"Come, my child," the widow urged moving to the front of the rock. Directly her daughter and servant were by her side. As the procession drew near, she arose, staggered forward, and called out. The people turned, saw her hideous face, and stopped awestruck. Tirzah drew back frightened.

"Lepers!" someone cried.

"Stone them!"

"The accursed of God! Kill them!"

Despite these cries the widow continued to move forward. Those familiar with the nature of the One to whom she appealed remained silent. Jesus rode up and stopped

in front of her. "Master, you see our need. Have mercy on us—make us clean."

"Believest thou that I am able to do this?"

"Thou art He of whom the prophets spake—thou art Messiah!"

His eyes grew radiant, His manner confident. "Woman," He said, "great is thy faith; be it unto thee even as thou wilt." He lingered an instant after, unconscious of the throng—an instant—then He rode away.

Ben-Hur was in the midst of the multitude and glancing past the lepers he saw Amrah. He hurried to her, passing his mother and sister without recognizing them. "Amrah, what are you doing here?"

"Oh, master, master," she cried weeping for joy, "thy God and mine, how good He is!" Amrah knew the transformation the lepers were undergoing, knew it and shared all their feeling to the full. Her expression, her words, her whole manner betrayed her thoughts. With swift perception, Ben-Hur knew that her mission was in some way connected with the women he had just passed. He turned quickly, just as the widow and Tirzah were rising to their feet.

His heart stood still. He would have run to them, but he was rooted in his tracks. Could he be mistaken? "Amrah, Amrah—my mother! Tirzah! Tell me if I see rightly!"

"Go. Speak to them, master!"

He waited no longer but ran with outstretched arms and embraced them.

The first ecstasy over, his mother said, "In this happiness, my children, let us not be ungrateful. Let us begin life anew by acknowledging Him to whom we are all so indebted." They knelt together and the mother's prayer was outspoken in a psalm. Tirzah repeated it word for word; so did Ben-Hur, but not with the same clear mind and unquestionable faith. He was waiting, waiting until the Nazarene proved Himself by setting up His kingdom—until He had overcome Rome.

* * *

Tirzah and her mother had to remain outside the city nine days. They could then enter the temple, be purified, and once again be accepted into the community. Ben-Hur went to the palace to await their return. Five of these days had passed when two of the Galileans rode full speed to the palace and, dismounting, urged Amrah to summon Ben-Hur.

"Peace be to you," he said as he entered the chamber where the men were waiting for him. "Be seated."

"No," said the older of the two Galileans, "to be at ease would be to let the Nazarene die! Rise, Judah, and go with us. Judgment has been given and the tree of the cross is already at Golgotha."

Ben-Hur stared at them in disbelief. How could this king whom the people had praised with hosannas be condemned to the cross? He quickly made preparations to depart. He sent the men ahead to give Simonides instructions to meet them at Golgotha.

When the party—Ben-Hur, Simonides, Esther, and the two Galileans—reached the place of crucifixion, Ben-Hur was leading them. When he caught sight of Jesus he stopped spellbound. Gazing at the figure on the hill, he became conscious of a change. The force of his bitterness began to fade. He heard again the saying of the Nazarene, *I am the Resurrection and the Life.* The words repeated themselves over and over in his mind. He tried to grasp the meaning. Who is the resurrection? He pondered. Who is the life? *I AM* the figure seemed to say—and say it for him. Judah was sensible of a peace such as he had never known, a peace which is the end of all doubt and mystery and the beginning of faith, love, and clear understanding.

From this dreamy state Ben-Hur was aroused by the sound of hammering. On the summit of the hill he observed then what had escaped him before, the soldiers and workmen preparing the crosses.

"The crosses are ready," said the centurion to the pontiff.

The high priest received the report and with the wave of his hand said, "Let the blasphemer go first. We shall see if the Son of God is able to save Himself."

The people, who to this time had assailed* the hill with continual cries of impatience, permitted a lull which directly became a universal hush, for the part of the infliction, the most shocking part, was at hand. As the soldiers laid their hands on Jesus, a shudder passed through the crowd.

assailed: verbally attacked

"How very still it is!" Esther said, as she put her arm about her father's neck.

Remembering the torture he himself had suffered in times past, he drew her face down on his breast and said trembling, "Avoid it, Esther, avoid it. I do not know but that all who stand and see this, the innocent as well as the guilty, may be cursed from this hour." Growing increasingly anxious, Simonides added, "Son of Hur, if Jehovah does not stretch forth His hand and quickly, Israel is lost. We are lost."

Ben-Hur answered calmly, "I have been as in a dream, Simonides, and heard in it why all this should be, and why it should go on. It is the will of the Nazarene; it is God's will. It is not for us to try to rescue Him. Let us hold our peace and pray."

The Nazarene's back was yet bloody from the morning's scourging when He was laid down on the wooden cross. The careless soldiers stretched His arms across the transverse* beams and roughly drove the first sharp spike through His tender palms. Then drawing His knees up until the soles of His feet rested flat against the wood, they placed one foot on the other and thrust in the final spike. Yet the spectators heard only the dull sound of hammering; there was no cry, nor word of rebuke from the sufferer.

transverse: crosswise

The workmen carried the cross to its place of planting and dropped it into the hole prepared. The body of the Nazarene hung heavily by bleeding hands. A cry was then heard—not of pain but of pity. "Father, forgive them, for they know not what they do." To this selfless proclamation the people answered with curses and jeers. Again and again their mocking salutation, "Hail, King of the Jews!" echoed across the darkening hillside. The dimness that filled the sky and covered the earth at first appeared only as the fading of day. But the blackness deepened. Only then did the noise of laughter and shouting subside, for men, doubting their senses, paused to gaze at one another curiously.

"It is only a mist or a passing cloud," said Simonides to comfort Esther. "It will brighten presently."

"It is not a mist or cloud," Ben-Hur said. "The spirits who live in the air—the prophets and the saints—are at work in mercy to themselves and nature. I say to you, Simonides, truly as God lives, He who hangs on that cross is the Son of God."

But even the darkness did not long silence the reckless jeering. "If you are the king of the Jews, save yourself," one soldier shouted.

"Yes," said a priest, "if He will come down to us now, we will believe Him."

"He called himself the Son of God; let us see if God will save Him," others called.

"Let's go home," Esther pleaded. "This darkness is the frown of God, Father. What other dreadful things may happen we cannot tell?"

But Simonides would not be moved. Though he said little, it was plain that he was under great agitation.

The second hour passed like the first one. For the Nazarene they were hours of insult, provocation, and slow dying. He spoke but once in that time. Some women came and knelt at the foot of His cross. Among them He recognized His mother with the beloved disciple. "Woman," He said raising His voice, "behold thy son!" And to the disciple, "Behold thy mother!"

The third hour came, and still people surged round the hill, held to it by some strange attraction. When the hour was about half gone, some men of the rudest class came and stopped in front of the center cross. "This is He, King of the Jews," said one of them.

The others cried out with laughter, "Hail, all hail, King!" Receiving no reply, they went closer.

"If you are the Son of God, come down," said one man boldly.

At this, one of the thieves quit groaning and called to the Nazarene, "Yes, if you are the Christ, save yourself and us!"

The people laughed and applauded; then, while they were listening for a reply, the other felon spoke, "Do you have no fear of God? We received due reward for our deeds, but this man has done nothing wrong." The bystanders were astonished. In the midst of the hush, the second felon spoke again, "Lord," he said, "remember me when you come into your kingdom."

Simonides gave a start. "When you come into your kingdom!" This was the very point of doubt in his mind.

"Did you hear?" said Ben-Hur. "The kingdom cannot be of this world. The felon declares that He is but going to His kingdom."

"Hush!" said Simonides to Judah. "Hush, the Nazarene may answer."

And as he spoke the Nazarene did answer, in a clear voice, full of confidence: "Verily, I say unto thee, today shalt thou be with me in paradise!"

Simonides folded his hands and said, "The darkness is gone, Lord. I see with the eyes of perfect faith." At last he understood. New life was now shown him, a life beyond this one, and its name was paradise. There he would find the kingdom which he and Ben-Hur had longed for. There his broken body would be restored and all the memories of undeserved suffering blotted out.

The breathing of the Nazarene grew harder, and His sighs became great gasps. Then there went out through the gloom, over the heads of those gathered on the hill, a cry of despair, "My God! My God! Why hast Thou forsaken me?" The voice startled all who heard it. But it touched Ben-Hur more than any; for there came to his memory a time long ago when he had despaired by the well of Nazareth. Quickly he moved toward the soldiers. They had brought with them a vessel of wine and water. Catching up a sponge on the end of a stick, he dipped it into the vessel and pushed his way through the crowd toward the cross.

"Let Him be!" the people in the way shouted angrily. But Ben-Hur pressed on, remembering the drink he had received at the well so long ago.

Reaching the Nazarene, Judah gazed up at the loving face now bruised and black with blood and dust, and at that moment the eyes opened wide and fixed on someone in the far heavens. In relief, even triumph, He gave a shout, "It is finished! It is finished!"

Ben-Hur quickly put the sponge to the Nazarene's lips, but the light in the eyes had dimmed and the head was slowly sinking on the laboring breast. "I am too late," he thought. But the fainting soul recollected itself and in a low voice said, "Father, into thy hands I commend my spirit." A tremor shook the tortured body. There was a scream of fiercest anguish, and the mission and earthly life were over. The heart, with all its love, broke and He died.

There was a murmur, at first a little more than a whisper, which spread from the hill in every direction. "He is dead! He is dead!" The people had their wish. Yet on hearing the news they drew back, as if for the first time they realized that His blood was upon them! While they stood staring, the ground began to tremble, and each man took hold of his neighbor to support himself. The crosses were reeling drunkenlike on the hill, and Ben-Hur could scarcely make his way back to his company.

Every man among them who had jeered at the Nazarene, everyone who had struck Him, everyone who had voted to crucify Him, everyone whose heart had wished Him dead, felt at that moment that he was being individually singled out for judgment. They started to run and ran with all their might to get away. Some mounted horses, others camels, and others tried escaping on foot. But the earthquake pursued them, tossed them about, flung them down, and terrified them yet more by the horrible noise of the great rocks grinding and rending beneath them. They shrieked in fear. If they called on the Lord, the outraged earth answered

for Him in fury and dealt with them all alike. The high priest was no better than his guilty brethren. Overtaking him, the rumbling earth tripped him, smirched the fringing of his robe, and filled his mouth with dust. They were all to blame. The blood of the Nazarene was on them all!

* * *

When the sunlight finally broke upon the crucifixion, the hill had nearly cleared. Only the mother of Jesus, the beloved disciple, the faithful women of Galilee, the centurion and his soldiers, and Ben-Hur's party remained. They had not observed the flight of the multitude, for they were too engaged in caring for their own safety. Realizing they need no longer fear, Ben-Hur turned to Esther and said, "Cover your eyes, and do not look up. Simply trust in God and the spirit of that just man so foully slain."

"No," said Simonides reverently, "call Him not a man. Let us henceforth speak of Him only as the Christ."

"Be it so," said Ben-Hur as he lifted Simonides in his strong arms to bear him home.

From that day forward, all who entered the palace of Ben-Hur were to hear not only of the crucifixion and resurrection but also of the coming kingdom of **GOD THE FATHER AND CHRIST THE SON.**

About the Author

By age thirteen Lew Wallace (1827–1905) had been branded as wicked. He cared little for formal education and often slipped away from school to scout the surrounding countryside. Because of his truancy, those observing his early life predicted inevitable failure. When he was sixteen, his father frankly denounced his lethargy and insisted that he support himself. Financial demands soon cured Wallace of sloth. He even became interested in studying, spending hours in his father's library. As a result of his study, Wallace was inspired to become both a soldier and a writer. And reach his goals he did. At age thirty-four he became the youngest man to attain the rank of major general, the highest army rank then possible. Twelve years later his first novel was published, establishing him as a romantic novelist. Wallace decided to focus his second novel, which was intended to bring him wealth and fame, on the conflict between a young Jew and a Roman. His interest in Christianity at the time was strictly professional and remained so until he met Robert Ingersoll, who was known as The Great Agnostic. As a result of their friendly debate, Wallace decided to search the Scriptures to find answers to the questions Ingersoll had raised. He then reworked his novel into a reply to Ingersoll's clever arguments. Again Wallace met his goals: *Ben-Hur* won for him both national acclaim and literary immortality. But more important, Wallace stated that its writing brought him to belief in Christ as the Son of God, winning for him a far greater immortality than his literary fame could ever give him.

THINKING ZONE

Because it blends actual people and settings from history with details that the author invented, *Ben-Hur* qualifies as historical fiction. It is important when reading a piece of historical fiction to keep in mind that while the settings and people may have actually existed, things may not have happened in exactly the way that the author presents them. Just as the author of *In Search of Honor* did, the author of this piece of historical fiction has tried to imagine a real historical incident and the effects that it may have had on those involved. The author will often add details that, while believable, are not verifiable. Be careful to discern the historical fact from the fiction.

1. *[critical]* What reason does Amrah have to change her attitude from hopeless to hopeful at the beginning of Part VI?

_____

_____

_____

_____

2. *[critical]* How does Ben-Hur's attitude differ from his mother's and sister's after they meet Christ?

_____

_____

_____

_____

3. *[critical]* What finally causes Ben-Hur to lose his bitterness?

_____

_____

_____

_____

4. *[literal]* What memory from Ben-Hur's past comes to his mind as he sees Christ on the cross?

_____

_____

_____

_____

5. *[critical]* How does the mob feel after Christ has died? Is this description a reasonable inference from Scripture (cf. Matt. 27:24–26, 50–54)?

_____

_____

_____

_____

_____

_____

_____

6. *[critical]* Read Isaiah 53:4–6, Acts 2:22–24, and Acts 4:24–28. Based on these verses, who was responsible for Christ's death?

_____

_____

_____

_____

_____

_____

_____

7. *[appreciative]* Did you enjoy this adaptation of the novel *Ben-Hur*?

_____

_____

_____

Rise Up, O Men of God

William P. Merrill

Notice the imperatives (nine in all, including three to "rise up") that the author includes in this triumphant hymn. The hymn is a command and an encouragement to Christian adventurers to follow in the steps of the King.

Rise up, O men of God!
Have done with lesser things;
Give heart and soul and mind and strength
To serve the King of kings.

Rise up, O men of God!
His kingdom tarries long:
Bring in the day of Christ our Lord
And end the night of wrong.

Lift high the cross of Christ!
Tread where His feet have trod:
As brothers of the Son of Man
Rise up, O men of God!

The Triumph of David. Jacopo Vignali.
From the Bob Jones University Collection

About the Author

In 1911 "Rise Up, O Men of God" flowed from the pen of William Pierson Merrill (1867–1954). A well-known Presbyterian pastor as well as composer, poet, and authority on hymnody, Merrill was well suited to author this call for action. Merrill was prompted to write the hymn after reading an article on the need for strong men to take a stand in the church.

To maintain consistency with the theme of the hymn, Merrill used a plain style that emphasizes by its lack of poetic devices the need for members of the body of Christ to stand firm in their convictions. Thus a hymn that crossed cultural, national, and denominational boundaries in its day reaches through the years to urge today's "men of God" to stand strong in their pursuit of Christlikeness, the goal of Christians everywhere in every time.

DAVID'S SONG OF PRAISE

The books of Samuel record David's many adventures—his battle with Goliath, his flight from the murderous king Saul, and his many wars against the enemies of God. At the end of these books, David sings a song praising the Lord for delivering him from all evil.

The Lord is my rock, and my fortress, and
    my deliverer;
The God of my rock; in him will I trust;
He is my shield, and the horn of my
    salvation,
My high tower, and my refuge, my saviour;
Thou savest me from violence.
I will call on the Lord, who is worthy to be
    praised:
So shall I be saved from mine enemies.

When the waves of death compassed me,
The floods of ungodly men made me afraid;
The sorrows of hell compassed me about;
The snares of death prevented me;
In my distress I called upon the Lord, and
    cried to my God:
And he did hear my voice out of his temple,
And my cry did enter into his ears.

Then the earth shook and trembled;
The foundations of heaven moved and
    shook, because he was wroth.
There went up a smoke out of his nostrils,
And fire out of his mouth devoured: coals
    were kindled by it.
He bowed the heavens also, and came
    down;
And darkness was under his feet.
And he rode upon a cherub, and did fly:
And he was seen upon the wings of the wind.
And he made darkness pavilions round
    about him,
Dark waters, and thick clouds of the skies.
Through the brightness before him were
    coals of fire kindled.

The Lord thundered from heaven,
And the most High uttered his voice.
And he sent out arrows, and scattered them;
Lightning, and discomfited them.
And the channels of the sea appeared,
The foundations of the world were
    discovered,
At the rebuking of the Lord,
At the blast of the breath of his nostrils.

He sent from above, he took me;
He drew me out of many waters;
He delivered me from my strong enemy,
And from them that hated me: for they
    were too strong for me.
They prevented me in the day of my
    calamity:
But the Lord was my stay.
He brought me forth also into a large place:
He delivered me, because he delighted in me.

The Lord rewarded me according to my
    righteousness:
According to the cleanness of my hands
    hath he recompensed me.
For I have kept the ways of the Lord,
And have not wickedly departed from my
    God.
For all his judgments were before me:
And as for his statues, I did not depart
    from them.
I was also upright before him,
And have kept myself from mine iniquity.
Therefore the Lord hath recompensed me
    according to my righteousness;
According to my cleanness in his eye sight.

With the merciful thou wilt shew thyself
    merciful,
And with the upright man thou wilt shew
    thyself upright.
With the pure thou wilt shew thyself pure;
And with the froward thou wilt shew thy-
    self unsavoury.
And the afflicted people thou wilt save:
But thine eyes are upon the haughty, that
    thou mayest bring them down.
For thou art my lamp, O Lord;
And the Lord will lighten my darkness.
For by thee I have run through a troop:
By my God have I leaped over a wall.

As for God, his way is perfect;
The word of the Lord is tried:
He is a buckler* to all them that trust in him.
For who is God, save the Lord?
And who is a rock, save our God?
God is my strength and power:
And he maketh my way perfect.
He maketh my feet like hinds' feet:
And setteth me upon my high places.
He teachest my hands to war;
So that a bow of steel is broken by mine
    arms.
Thou hast also given me the shield of thy
    salvation:
And thy gentleness hath made me great.
Thou hast enlarged my steps under me;
So that my feet did not slip.

I have pursued mine enemies, and destroyed
    them;
And turned not again until I had consumed
    them.
And I have consumed them, and wounded
    them, that they could not arise:
Yea, they are fallen under my feet.
For thou hast girded me with strength to
    battle:
Them that rose up against me hast thou
    subdued under me.

Thou hast also given me the necks of mine
    enemies,
That I might destroy them that hate me.
They looked, but there was none to save;
Even unto the Lord, but he answered them
    not.
Then did I beat them as small as the dust of
    the earth,
I did stamp them as the mire of the street,
    and did spread them abroad.

Thou also hast delivered me from the
    strivings of my people,
Thou hast kept me to be head of the heathen:
A people which I knew not shall serve me.
Strangers shall submit themselves unto me:
As soon as they hear, they shall be obedient
    unto me.
Strangers shall fade away,
And they shall be afraid out of their close
    places.*

The Lord liveth; and blessed be my rock;
And exalted be the God of the rock of my
    salvation.
It is God that avengeth me,
And that bringest down the people under
    me.
And that bringeth me forth from mine
    enemies:
Thou also hast lifted me up on high above
    them that rose up against me:
Thou hast delivered me from the violent
    man.
Therefore I will give thanks unto thee,
    O Lord, among the heathen,
And I will sing praises unto thy name.
He is the tower of salvation for his king:
And sheweth mercy to his anointed,
Unto David, and to his seed for evermore.

                 —2 Samuel 22:2–51

buckler: shield
close places: fortresses

UNIT 5 REVIEW

SHORT ANSWER

Write the word, phrase, or sentence that best answers the question.

1. How does the author foreshadow what will happen to Jerry in "The Banks of the Sacramento"?

   _____

   _____

   _____

2. From what point of view is "The Banks of the Sacramento" written?

   _____

   _____

3. Give two examples of concrete sensory imagery from "You Need to Go Upstairs."

   _____

   _____

   _____

   _____

   _____

   _____

4. Why is Ally's mother uneasy about sending her into the house alone?

   _____

   _____

5. Godden's use of *you* when Ally is really referring to herself ("you can remember that"; "you catch at the air") allows the reader to be inside Ally's mind and thoughts. What type of writing attempts to reproduce the flow of thoughts in a character's mind?

   _____

   _____

6. In "Emily Geiger" what does Emily do with the note she is carrying?

_____

_____

7. What is the setting of "Emily Geiger"?

_____

_____

8. In "The Way of the Water-Hyacinth," "Bobbing . . . breeze blown / Bowing" and "Spinning, swamped, slimed, sunk" are examples of what literary device?

_____

_____

9. Who is the chief antagonist in *Ben-Hur*?

_____

_____

10. What sort of poetic justice happens to Messala?

_____

_____

_____

MATCHING

Match each of the following literary terms with the best example of that term.

_____ 11. "To certain people there comes a day / when they must say the great Yes or the great No."

_____ 12. "All that is gold does not glitter, / Not all those who wander are lost."

_____ 13. "It is a cold and snowy night. The main street is deserted. / The only things moving are swirls of snow."

_____ 14. "My father . . . was not without honor in Jerusalem."

_____ 15. "We were blown off our feet by passing traffic."

A. caesura

B. understatement

C. paradox

D. hyperbole

E. enjambment

TRUE/FALSE

If the statement is completely true, write *true*. **If the underlined part of the statement is false, write** *false* **and change the underlined portion of the statement to make the statement true.**

> **Example: In "Incident of the French Camp," the boy delivers a message to <u>George Washington</u>.**
>
> *false—Napoleon*

16. An author's use of <u>omniscient point of view</u> gives the reader insight into only one of the story's characters.

17. In the story "You Need to Go Upstairs," the author uses <u>stream of consciousness</u> to relate Ally's story.

18. "Incident of the French Camp" is an example of the <u>informal essay</u>.

19. An irony of the <u>"Incident of the French Camp"</u> is that the boy smiles as he dies.

20. The real message of "The First Robin" is that <u>true adventurers attempt difficult tasks despite fear of failure</u>.

21. The author of "The First Robin" maintains a <u>consistent</u> tone throughout the piece.

22. In "The Way of the Water-Hyacinth," the water-hyacinth is symbolic of an <u>artist</u>.

23. In "All That Is Gold Does Not Glitter," the theme of life springing from that which is dead is an example of <u>understatement</u>.

24. Bombeck uses <u>hyperbole</u> to achieve humor in her essay "Elusive Rest Area."

25. An irony of "*Che Fece . . . Il Gran Rifiuto*" is that the individual who <u>says no</u> would do the same again although the consequences be grievous.

_____

26. The villain of *Ben-Hur* is <u>Malluch</u>.

_____

27. Ben-Hur passes through Nazareth because he is <u>on his way to be a slave on a ship</u>.

_____

28. Once Ben-Hur escapes, he desires to be known as the <u>son of Hur</u> because of fears for his own safety.

_____

29. Revealing his evil character in the midst of the chariot race, Messala <u>whips Ben-Hur's horses</u>.

_____

30. In the story of *Ben-Hur*, the subplot that develops focuses on <u>Simonides</u>.

_____

MULTIPLE CHOICE

Choose the best answer from the choices given.

_____ 31. In "The Banks of the Sacramento," Jerry displayed all of the following character traits *except*
  A. ingenuity.
  B. perseverance.
  C. rebellion.
  D. self-sacrifice.

_____ 32. An example of situational irony in "Elusive Rest Area" is that
  A. when the family wants to eat lunch, there are no rest areas on their side of the highway.
  B. everyone wants to eat at a restaurant except the mother.
  C. when they finally stop, the family discovers that their cooler has leaked.
  D. when they stop at a rest area, their lunch is stolen by other travelers.

33. Which statement about the similarities of the two poems "Incident of the French Camp" and "Emily Geiger" is *not* true?
   A. Both cover approximately the same period of time.
   B. Both have wartime settings.
   C. Both are narrative poems.
   D. Both tell of heroic acts.

34. At the beginning of the excerpt from *Ben-Hur*, Ben-Hur argues with
   A. Amrah.
   B. Messala.
   C. the Emperor.
   D. Joseph.

35. The effects of the chariot race in *Ben-Hur* include all of the following *except*
   A. the destruction of Messala's chariot.
   B. the death of Messala.
   C. the crushing of Messala's legs.
   D. the loss of Messala's wealth.

36. Why do Tirzah and her mother not awaken Ben-Hur when they find him at their house?
   A. Tirzah and her mother are convicted criminals.
   B. Tirzah and her mother do not recognize Ben-Hur.
   C. Tirzah and her mother do not want Ben-Hur to know that they are lepers.
   D. Tirzah and her mother have disowned Ben-Hur.

37. Jesus commends the Widow Hur for her
   A. bravery.
   B. virtue.
   C. humility.
   D. faith.

38. *Ben-Hur* is an example of
   A. fiction.
   B. historical autobiography.
   C. nonfiction biography.
   D. historical fiction.

ESSAY

In one paragraph completely answer the question below, using specific examples from the story.

39. What makes Ally in "You Need to Go Upstairs" an adventurer? Describe her "adventures" and tell what makes her admirable.

_____

_____

_____

_____

_____

_____

_____

_____

_____

_____

_____

_____

_____

_____

_____

_____

_____

_____

VIEWPOINTS

The role of photography as art is one that is widely debated. Should photography be strictly objective—what you see is what you get—or should photography be open to the same artistic freedoms that an artist takes with his artwork? With the computer age and the ability to manipulate images to appear to be what they are not, photography's place is perhaps changing. The unnamed photographer of this winding staircase in the Palazzo del Quirinale, Rome, Italy, chose an interesting viewpoint from which to take this photograph.

What do you notice first when you see this photograph?

How do light and shadow play a role in this photograph?

How many floors do you see? What do you think might be close by but unseen in the photograph?

In your viewpoint, is the photographer going up the stairs or coming back down?

VIEWPOINTS

POOR PETER THE DISCIPLE. HE WAS PROBABLY TIRED AND HUNGRY, AND HERE WERE THESE YOUNG SERVANT GIRLS BADGERING HIM. HE JUST WANTED TO BE LEFT ALONE TO WATCH WHAT HAPPENED TO JESUS. HE DIDN'T WANT TO BE IDENTIFIED WITH HIM. FROM HIS VIEWPOINT, IT WOULD BE BETTER TO DENY THAT HE EVEN KNEW THE MAN JESUS.

What had happened? Only a few short hours before, Peter had been with the Lord at the Passover feast, boldly and sincerely declaring, "Though all men shall be offended because of thee, yet will I never be offended" (Matt. 26:33). Why then did Peter, the first disciple to proclaim "Thou art the Christ," deny the Savior? Peter's statement at the Passover gives us a clue that his viewpoint was not what it should have been. Peter was focusing on self rather than on Christ.

Unfortunately Peter's sad experience is not unique. An improper viewpoint has caused many of Christ's followers to wander from the right path to tread upon forbidden ground. And as Peter did, they have always found the consequences of such wanderings painful.

Yet this painful experience proved to be a milestone in Peter's life; for following this denial, he confessed his sin and became the courageous, immovable servant he imagined himself to be before his fall. The book of Acts is a testimony to Peter's change in viewpoint. Failure had taught him his total dependence on Jesus Christ, not just for salvation, but also for the grace needed to walk the right path.

It is imperative, therefore, that each of us examine himself to determine whether his focus is as it should be. But how can we determine whether we are viewing things correctly? One way is to examine our behavior. If our viewpoint is flawed, what we do will betray an overemphasis on self, others, or things. Many of us are reluctant to change our viewpoints or relinquish our ideals of self, others, and things. As you observe the characters in the following stories and poems, remember the lesson each of them learned: a proper viewpoint is the surest road to contentment. ☩

WHAT YOU SEE AND HEAR DEPENDS A GOOD DEAL ON WHERE YOU ARE STANDING.
IT ALSO DEPENDS ON WHAT SORT OF PERSON YOU ARE.

—C. S. LEWIS
THE MAGICIAN'S NEPHEW

WOLVES OF FEAR

RICHARD SAVAGE

Consider the problem that plagues the main character in this story. How does he eventually experience a change in his viewpoint?

It was late at night in early December, and the veteran trapper's eighteen-year-old companion stirred sleeplessly in the rough, hand-hewn bunk, rustling the hay and marsh grass beneath him. The iron stove in the center of the cabin still threw off some heat, although he and the trapper, who snored softly on the other side of the room, had gone to bed several hours earlier. Why he had awakened suddenly, Paul didn't know at first—he had been tired enough after a day of sawing logs and making practice runs out from the cabin on snowshoes. He turned his head so he could gaze at one of the two small windows high off the floor. The thick, wavy glass was so frosted he could not see through, but the moon was out and the window pane shone a luminous* white against dark logs.

---
luminous: shining

Then suddenly the youth shivered, and he knew what must have awakened him. A long, quavering howl rose from the far shore of the lake, then another and another. Breaking the profound* quiet of the snow-covered wilderness, the sound seemed to fill the woods around them and the cabin itself. He tried to fight back his fear, keenly aware of how disappointed and scornful his father would be if he gave in to it and proved a failure on his trapping expedition.

---
profound: deep

When his father had arranged for him to spend these six months in the wilderness with an old trapper friend with whom he had gone through high school in Duluth years ago, he had talked of what a wonderful experience it would be for Paul before he started college. But Paul knew all too well why his father had urged him to go on this trip. He could almost remember when it all started.

When Paul was ten years old, his father had bought him a small tent one summer and helped him to pitch it at the edge of the wooded lot behind their home on the outskirts of Minneapolis. Then he had suggested that Paul try sleeping in it alone. Paul had been frightened at the idea to begin with, but he had been game to try, and even joined his father in overcoming his mother's protests.

Lying wide-eyed and sleepless in the tent, Paul had listened to the rustling noises in the little patch of woods behind the tent and had shivered when an owl hooted. Then the howling of a dog nearby had jerked him upright into a sitting position, stiff with fear. As he stared out the opening of the tent, he began to see fearful shapes of animals prowling about the edge of the wooded lot. It was all he could do to keep from crying out in terror. But he was too frightened even to move, and he sat there clutching with icy hands at the ground cloth beneath his father's sleeping bag.

At last from several blocks away, he heard a car door slam and voices calling good night. This comforting sound had given him just enough momentary reassurance. He scrambled out of the sleeping bag, grabbed his flashlight, and raced barefoot in his pajamas across the lawn to the back door. He opened it quickly but silently and tiptoed up to his room, praying that no one would hear him. He could tell his father that he came into the house to go to the bathroom in the early morning and then decided to stay in his room till breakfast.

But as he slipped his feet under the covers, the bedroom door opened, and there was his father, outlined by the hall light, standing large and forbidding in the doorway. "So you couldn't stick it out?" asked his father, trying to control the scorn in his voice.

The boy swallowed and turned his head away, unable to meet his father's gaze. "No," he whispered. "There were—I saw . . ." His voice trailed off in fear and humiliation.

There was a moment of silence, while his father shook his head and gazed at his son. "I hoped you wouldn't give in so easily," he said at last. "There was nothing out there that could harm you. Why were you afraid?"

"I—I don't know. I couldn't help it."

"Look, Paul," said his father, walking over to his bed, "maybe a person can't help being afraid, but they can keep from running away. Every time you run away you lose a little bit of yourself. You lose some respect for yourself. Remember the story I used to read to you about the gingerbread boy who ran away? And in the version we read he gets smaller and smaller as he runs? That's what happens when we let our fears make us run away. We get smaller."

As Paul lay there remembering all this, he suddenly realized the howling of the wolves had stopped. A deep silence settled again on the white solitude, broken only by the occasional sharp cracking of the frost in the trees. Struggling to push back the slow, dark waves of uneasiness, of fear, he tried to relax and drift back to sleep.

All at once the quavering chorus of wolves began again, moving along the shore of the lake, and so close now that the youth sat upright in bed, a cold tingling at the nape of his neck and a coldness at his heart. This time the trapper heard it too, and Paul could see him in the dim light sitting up and shaking his head, running a muscular hand through the thick iron-gray hair. Then Mac was out of bed and pulling on his heavy pants and boots.

"Come on, boy! Let's see what those wolves are up to. They'll not do the trapping any good. Come on, maybe we can bag a couple!"

Paul jumped out of bed and dressed hurriedly. He grabbed his old Remington rolling block rifle just as the trapper started out the door. With his long legs the youth made better time through the deep snow and caught up with the stocky trapper. They headed for the lake about a hundred yards beyond the cabin. The howling had stopped now, and in its place they heard a muted frenzy of vicious snarls. A three-quarter moon lighted the white world around them, and when they reached the lake, they could see what was happening on the ice a little way up the shore toward the outlet of the river.

Four wolves were attacking a moose they had driven into the open, their ghostly gray and brown forms whipping in and out like pursuing demons. The great moose was fighting a courageous but losing battle. Already the huge creature was down, almost in a sitting position, tossing its great antlers in a dying frenzy.

Mac stepped back from the shore into a thicket of balsam and spruce. "Come on," he said. "Keep to the trees. They might be too hungry to frighten away, but we won't take chances." Crouching low, he began to move

through the trees up the shore, and Paul followed, clutching his rifle so tightly his hands grew numb. About fifty yards away from the scene, the trapper stopped and then crept to the edge of the trees. The moose was completely down now, and the timber wolves were tearing at the flesh.

"Now!" whispered Mac, taking aim from a kneeling position. Several shots rang out. One wolf dropped instantly to the side and lay still. Another wolf, apparently wounded, gave a little leap into the air then, in snarling confusion headed almost directly toward the two men. The animal had covered nearly half the distance before Mac brought it down with one shot. The two remaining wolves sniffed the air for just an instant and then started toward the heavy timber, moving like gray ghosts in the dim light of the moon. Then they disappeared amidst several more shots.

"So!" exclaimed Mac, standing up. "There's two wolves that won't rob traps or scare game. But what happened to you, boy? Didn't you—" He stopped suddenly as he realized his young companion was no longer with him. "Hey, boy!" He gazed around, perplexed and a little annoyed. Then he spotted tracks that led back to the cabin.

When the trapper stepped inside, stamping snow from his boots, he saw the youth sitting on the edge of the bunk, his head in his hands and staring at the floor. Paul didn't look up. Mac hung up his rifle and lighted one of the deer-tallow* candles they had made. Then he put several logs into the stove and began stripping down to his woolen underwear. It wasn't until he had taken off his boots that the trapper spoke. "What's the matter, boy? You get sick or something?"

---

tallow: fat obtained from a deer

Slowly Paul raised his head, his large, soft-gray eyes gazing almost blankly into the semidarkness. "No," he said, his voice nearly a whisper.

"No, I—I—"

The trapper's jaw tightened underneath his beard, and the dark, piercing eyes smoldered with angry impatience. "Look here, boy," he began, and his voice had a threatening rumble to it. Then he stopped. Perhaps it was something that he had glimpsed in the boy's open and sensitive face, or a sudden remembrance that he was the son of a friend.

He shrugged at last, and his voice softened a little. "Guess a pack of wolves can be frightening the first time. But they're not ever likely to attack a man. That wounded critter didn't know where he was headed— just wanted to hit the timber."

Paul shifted on the edge of the bunk and shook his head. "I'm sorry, Mac." Drawing a deep breath, Paul tried to speak more forcefully. "I'll snap out of it, Mac. I'm not going to be a handicap to you."

After a few minutes he lay down on his bunk. "Mac," he said at last, trying to keep his voice casual, "if—if something did happen, like—like the cabin burning down and we had to go back before the ice broke, where would we head for?"

"Why, I suppose we'd head for that settlement that's about two days due south of here. If my old Indian-trapper friend is up here this winter, maybe we could head for his cabin if we needed. That's only a day's haul from here. Now, let's get some sleep, boy!"

Then all was still, except for the occasional loud snapping of the frost in the trees. A silence so deep that the earth itself seemed to have dropped away, leaving them in a cold, white void. Paul closed his eyes and eventually slipped off into a fitful sleep. But the wolves of fear ran through his dreams.

At breakfast the next morning nothing was said about the incident of the night before. Paul, however, could not bring himself to look the old trapper in the face—he was ashamed and afraid of what he might see there. While Paul cleaned up the breakfast utensils, Mac went out to see what could be salvaged from the moose. It appeared that no wolves had returned, wary perhaps of the two dead ones lying nearby, but the flesh was badly torn in places from the initial attack. He quickly set about to dress the animal. Paul came out as he was finishing, and they lugged the hindquarters back to the meat shelter.

The sky had become overcast, and the temperature had risen, becoming unexpectedly mild, though far from the point of melting. The trapper got together his equipment for a day's run and then knelt outside the cabin door to bind on his snowshoes. Paul stood by, gazing out over the lake toward the south.

"In a few more days, boy," said Mac. "I'll be able to take you along on some of the shorter runs. Right now I want to move around fairly fast and get the trap lines out in good shape. Maybe you can spend some time making that extra shelf we thought we could use—and taking an excursion* on your snowshoes. By this time you ought to be getting good enough so you won't slow me down. And see what you can think up for supper, eh?"

---
excursion: short journey

The youth nodded, mumbled good-bye, and watched the trapper set out on a line northeast of the cabin. He had really been looking forward to accompanying Mac as he made the rounds of the trap lines, but now he could only gaze miserably after the departing trapper.

All at once, his face strangely set, Paul hurried inside. He began to make up a bedroll and gather together food supplies and a few clothes. When his packsack was filled and ready to shoulder, he paused for a moment. Then he quickly began to search on his shelf for a pencil and a piece of paper. Having found them, he sat down at the table and scrawled a note.

Mac: Please don't try to follow me. I've headed for the settlement, and I'll make it O.K. It's better that I leave. Thanks for all you've done. Dad will understand. Paul

He shouldered his packsack, picked up his rifle, and went outside. He bound on his snowshoes and then, without looking back, headed directly across the lake, past the mouth of the river up which they had traveled in canoes during the beautiful days of mid-October. How long ago that seemed now! Driven by shame and by his haunting fear of the violent primitive forces of this wilderness, Paul felt there was nothing else to do but try to escape. Once at the settlement he could find a way to reach a train— but not to his home. He couldn't go back now to face his father. He would have to get a job somewhere and give up college, at least for a while.

As he plunged into the tamarack* swamp on the other side of the lake, he saw out of the corner of his eye the tracks of the wolves in the snow. He shuddered and hurried on. He traveled through dense stands of pines, across open meadows, over wooded hills, and across small lakes. He looked frequently at his compass and was satisfied that he was heading due south. Around noon he stopped. But so desperately did he want to continue on that he didn't bother to light a fire. Instead he cleared a place for himself in the protected hollow of a great hemlock* and collapsed wearily onto the ground, where he munched on some pemmican* and cold biscuits from the morning's breakfast. The sky was still partly overcast, and the mild temperature continued.

---

tamarack: a tree having short needles that grow off spur shoots

hemlock: a coniferous evergreen

pemmican: dried beef product

When Paul started on again, he was suddenly aware of a pain in both ankles—a pain that seemed to increase with almost every step. He was suffering from snowshoe lameness, which had actually been coming on for some time; but he had been concentrating so fiercely on covering as much ground as possible that he hadn't noticed it at first. Nonetheless, he kept on, even though the pain finally became so intense that his teeth were clenched and the tears came constantly to his eyes.

At last, when the pain in his ankles became so intense that he realized he could not go much farther, he began searching for a place to spend the night. It was while he was looking about him that one of his snowshoes caught under a fallen bough which arched a fraction above the snow. Because of the pain and weariness, he had become careless, and now he was flung onto the snow in a crumpled heap. The breath went out of him, and he gave a groan as he felt his right leg twist beneath him. When he tried to get to his feet, he cried out in pain, realizing with a sickening shock that he had wrenched the leg so badly he could not stand on it.

He struggled out of the packsack and then lay there in the snow, so exhausted, so stricken with pain from the twisted leg and the lameness in his ankles that he sank into a daze. Lying there with his eyes closed, listening to the deep soughing* of the wind in the tops of the pines and hemlocks, he felt the exhaustion and the pain recede at last. In their place a wave of drowsy contentment crept over him, drugging him. No longer was there any thought of moving, even to try to build a fire. He wanted only to lie there and rest, forgetting everything—forgetting his plight and all the torment and humiliation his fears had brought him.

---

soughing (sŭf´ĭng): rustling sound

Yet as he drifted closer toward complete unconsciousness and snuggled with drowsy comfort in his snow cocoon, he was still aware of a warning signal far back in his mind—a persistent, urgent nudging to move, to move, to move. . . . Then it seemed as if the warning took strangely the form of the barking of a dog—a barking that became as irritating and disturbing as the buzzing of a mosquito which won't let one make the final descent into sleep.

The barking continued and even seemed to become louder. Was he awake or dreaming? Finally with a grimace Paul half raised himself on one elbow. Gradually he became once more aware of his surroundings and at last realized bewilderedly, that he was not dreaming, that it was the barking of a dog.

Groaning slightly with the pain and the effort, he struggled onto his knees and crawled through the snow to where his rifle had landed. Then raising his head to determine where the barking was coming from, he began to crawl with painful slowness to the top of a little ridge a few yards ahead of him. There was still enough light to see the outlines of things, but the darkness was coming fast. Paul reached the top of the ridge and stared in disbelief into the hollow just a little below him.

No more than fifty yards away were a large bear, a gray dog, and an Indian boy. With the dog barking and snapping at its rear quarters, the bear, looming frighteningly large in the dim light, was lumbering in a dazed and awkward manner toward the boy, who was armed with only a bow and arrow. Legs apart, with the arrow notched and the bow bent, the boy courageously stood his ground. For a moment the bear paused to swat clumsily at the dog. The Indian released the arrow and then retreated a few paces and notched another. There was a low, hoarse growl from the bear, and it swung forward again and continued to advance, two arrows sticking from its shoulder and chest like banderillas* in a bull.

banderillas: darts stuck in a bull during a bullfight

In a moment Paul had shaken himself free of his dazed condition. He grasped at least partially what had happened. The boy had been hunting rabbits or other small game, and the dog had routed the bear out of its winter den. This accounted for the slow, stupefied* approach of the animal as it weaved toward the young hunter.

stupefied: stunned

Lying on his stomach, Paul took off his mittens and raised the rifle. He hesitated. If I miss, he thought. If I only wound the bear and draw his attention toward me? Then in his fear and indecision he heard himself gasping to the boy, "Run, you little fool! Run quick before it's too late." He had meant to shout, but it came out no more than a whisper.

Even as Paul wavered indecisively, the undaunted Indian boy drew back the arrow for another shot—and there was in that movement, in that stance, a timeless element which seemed to have in it all that men knew of resolution and courage. Sensing this, Paul clenched the rifle. Something within him clicked with the clean, sharp finality of a released trigger. In that instant he saw himself standing again before the oncoming wolf, as the boy stood before the bear, only this time he did not run—and knew now that he could not run again.

Taking a deep breath, Paul squeezed the trigger. At the sharp report the feisty* dog gave a loud yelp and ran to its master. The bear stopped suddenly and sat down in the snow, snarling and tossing its head. With numbed fingers Paul reloaded and fired again, and the great creature crumpled onto the snow. The gray dog raced over to the body, sniffing and growling.

feisty: spirited

The boy dropped his bow, gazed at the bear for a moment, and then began jumping up and down, clapping his hands. "Good! Good!" he cried with boyish delight, as if he'd been in no danger at all. "Fine shot!" Then he stopped and peered about him.

At last he spied Paul in the near darkness and without any hesitation walked directly up the ridge toward him. He stood in front of Paul, grinning down at him in the friendliest kind of manner. "You shot just in time, mister. A little while, maybe, and there would not be much of me." He continued to smile as if the thought did not disturb him.

Paul saw that he was no more than fourteen or fifteen and noted with surprise that although he was dressed in Indian fashion, almost entirely in buckskin, his skin was very light and his features only slightly resembled the characteristic Indian face. Paul couldn't help smiling too. "And if you hadn't come along with your dog, a little while, maybe, and I'd have been a frozen corpse."

The boy looked puzzled.

"My leg is twisted," said Paul. "I can't walk on it."

The Indian lad gave him a quizzical glance and then said, "Oh. You wait here. I'll bring back hunting sled."

In what seemed a relatively short time the Indian boy returned, dragging after him what looked like a narrow toboggan—two hand-hewn boards about six feet long and held in place by cross pieces with rawhide lashings and curved slightly in front. Paul got on with difficulty. He was numb with cold from lying so long in the snow.

Then the boy lugged the packsack to the sled. Paul motioned with his hand. "Leave it. You'll have a hard enough time as it is. We can get it later."

The boy hesitated a moment and then nodded. "Yes. I'll get it later. I'll come back to skin the bear." He hesitated again. "You'll let me have some bear meat?" he added, a look of real concern on his face. "My mother and I—"

"It's yours," said Paul with a smile, wondering curiously what the circumstances were of the boy and his mother living here in the midst of this wilderness. Why were they here? What had driven the boy to—

Suddenly the sled began to move with such vigor that Paul was nearly jerked into the snow. It was totally dark now, but the boy seemed to know exactly where he was going. After about a half mile they came to a clearing, and Paul, lying on his stomach with his rifle at his side, could see the dim

outline of a small cabin and beyond that a broad expanse of frozen lake.

With great difficulty he rolled himself off the sled and crawled through the doorway that the boy held open for him. Inside it was lighted dimly by a single deer-tallow candle. In the center of the single room stood a Chippewa squaw. She motioned him toward a deerskin rug that had been placed near the stove.

"There," she said. "Lie down."

Paul took off his fur-lined jacket, the bearskin cap that had been his father's, his mittens, and his boots. But instead of lying down, he sat holding his hands and feet toward the warmth of the stove.

The boy squatted beside him. "My name is John—John Burton. This is my mother."

The woman nodded, smiled a little, and then set about preparing something to eat.

Paul introduced himself and then said, "Your son came along just in time, Mrs. Burton. He saved me from freezing to death in the snow."

Again the squaw smiled a slow, hesitant smile. "He says you saved him," she said softly.

"Oh, I could not run," broke in the boy quickly. "Not while I had arrows to kill the bear. If I turn and run before then, I am nothing."

Paul stared at him in wonderment, remembering suddenly his father's whimsical words years ago about the gingerbread boy who ran away.

Then John held up a forefinger in front of Paul. "But you could not have run if the bear had come after you when you shot," he said softly. There was a pause. "We saved each other!" laughed John suddenly, clapping his hands in that childlike gesture so incongruous* with the amazingly calm and courageous manner he had faced the bear.

---

incongruous: inconsistent

Paul nodded and smiled, noticing then how strongly built the boy was, with his black hair and attractive, though somewhat dirty, features. He noticed also that he was too thin; so too was his mother, who was a strikingly attractive squaw—probably in her middle thirties, Paul decided, though it was hard to tell.

In a short time they began eating their meal, which consisted of nothing more than rice, bread, and tea, and Paul wished then that he had his packsack with him. So well did he and John strike it off that before long he had their confidence and was hearing, bit by bit from the woman and her son, their story. The woman's English was limited and hesitant, and the boy did most of the talking.

His mother was a full-blooded Chippewa and had married a white man, who had worked in a trading post in the settlement to the south. When he died a year ago—they didn't say how—several persons began to try to have the boy taken away from her. She had fled with her son to this cabin her husband had built some years ago when he was trapping. They had planned late last October to travel back to the settlement by canoe for more supplies. They had Indian friends there whom they could stay with and who would get for them the things they needed without betraying their presence. But the mother had become very ill, and before she was well enough to travel, the lake and river had frozen. Then the journey was impossible. Paul could see that she was still weak and had probably been giving most of what little food they had to her son.

Now they were almost without supplies of any kind, and the old rifle they had been so dependent upon had broken down two months before. They were subsisting almost entirely on what small game John could shoot with his bow and arrow. The mother planned to travel farther south when summer came, where she would not be known, and there she and John would sell woven baskets and moccasins to the tourists. Paul could see in the corner some of the beaded moccasins and baskets she had been working on.

When their story was finished, there was a brief silence. Then Paul put down his tin cup of tea. "I'll help you," he said quietly. "Somehow."

At eleven o'clock the next morning Mac came barging into the cabin, having set out around six and traveling in five hours the distance it had taken Paul eight or nine hours to cover. He had known of the existence of the

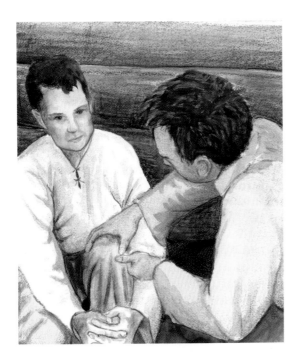

cabin, though he had not realized it was occupied now. Paul was not really surprised to see him. Deep in his subconscious he had known Mac would follow him. But in keeping with the inexplicable* folly of his whole attempted escape, he had pretended it was not so.

---

inexplicable: not able to be explained

Mac stood over the youth and began to roar angrily, ignoring the squaw who shrank into a corner of the cabin. "What kind of foolishness is this! Did you think I could let you go like that and ever face your dad again? If it weren't for your dad being my friend, I sure would have let you go—let you go so you could get lost and freeze to death or starve, or—"

Suddenly he was startled to feel small hands pushing and pounding against his shoulders and chest. "No, no!" cried the squaw. "He saved my son. He killed meat for us. It's not right to talk so!"

Mac stopped, backing away and staring at the woman, half in irritation, half

in amusement. He shrugged and fell silent; presently he heard the story, not from her or from Paul, but from John, who had been standing wide-eyed just inside the door, having just returned from dressing the bear.

"So you stuck it out this time, eh?" muttered Mac, and then was sorry for having said it. Paul looked away—and then with an effort went about the formality of introducing him to the woman and her son. Then he fell silent, not knowing what to say to the trapper.

Mac removed some of his outer clothing and knelt beside Paul to examine his leg. The woman withdrew to a corner to weave a basket, and John went outside to finish dressing the bear. "It will be all right in another day or two," said Mac, his voice quieter and showing some regret at his outburst. "Look, boy," he began after an awkward pause, "yesterday I met my Indian trapper friend while I was out on the trail. If you're really set on getting back to the city, he'll take care of my trap lines, and I'll take you out of here. Maybe that's what we'd better do, eh?"

Paul clenched his fists hard against his knees. "I want to stay, Mac," he said with quiet intensity. "I'm sure sorry for the trouble I've caused, and you have every right to be angry and want me to go. But, please— now I have to stay. I must stay! I must stay," he repeated in a fierce whisper.

The trapper seemed to understand the urgency in the voice and all that was left unspoken. He nodded and in a gruffly embarrassed gesture patted the youth's knee.

Then in a low voice Paul told him briefly the story of the Indian woman and her son. When he had finished, Mac nodded and said, "We'll give them some help. We'll see them through the winter." He glanced speculatively* toward the Chippewa squaw. "I'll do more than that. I'll give some help when she leaves here and see that she doesn't lose her son."

---

speculatively: with great thought

There was a long pause. Then the veteran trapper spoke again, looking directly at the youth. "I think things will go all right for us this winter, Paul. You'll make out in good shape. And it'll make your dad proud to hear it."

Paul lay back, stretching his slim body on the deerskin rug, his hands behind his head and a broad smile on his lips. He was pleased with Mac's words. Pleased mostly that the trapper had addressed him for the first time by his name. It was as if a hand of partnership had been extended to him.

When the trapper left his side a moment later, Paul closed his eyes, still smiling. "The gingerbread boy won't get any smaller," he murmured.

THINKING ZONE

As you read this story, you may have noticed that some of the author's vivid descriptions employ **onomatopoeia**, words that sound like what they mean. For instance, when we talk about a "bang on the door," the word *bang* is a suggestion of the sound that is being made. Using onomatopoeia is another way that a writer can *show* the reader what he means rather than just *tell* him.

Throughout this book, you have studied various literary devices and terms and have learned to identify them within a work of literature. With this selection, we will be reviewing many of the key terms and concepts that you have learned to this point. If you need to refresh your memory, you can use the glossary at the back of the book for help.

1. *[critical]* Briefly summarize what the exposition tells about Paul.

   _____

   _____

   _____

   _____

   _____

2. *[interpretive]* Where near the opening of the story is an example of flashback?

   _____

   _____

   _____

3. *[interpretive]* After the wolf attack, Paul asks the trapper what they would do "if something did happen . . . and they had to go back before the ice broke." How does this question foreshadow future events in the story?

   _____

   _____

   _____

4. *[critical]* Where is internal conflict present in the story? What about external conflict (or conflicts)?

_____

_____

_____

_____

External conflict—
conflict between a character and an outside force such as society or nature

Internal conflict—
conflict within a character's mind between opposing thoughts and emotions

5. *[interpretive]* What examples of **onomatopoeia** can you find in the author's description of the actions of animals within the story? Name at least three.

_____

_____

_____

_____

6. *[critical]* What would you identify as the crisis of the story? Why?

_____

_____

_____

7. *[interpretive]* What does Paul mean by his last statement: "The gingerbread boy won't get any smaller"? Has Paul's viewpoint changed in any way?

_____

_____

_____

_____

_____

_____

_____

_____

SOME LIKE POETRY

WISLAWA SZYMBORSKA

People are not all alike. Some like one thing and some another. Szymborska cleverly captures the idea that not everyone likes poetry.

Some—
thus not all. Not even the majority of all but the minority.
Not counting schools, where one has to,
and the poets themselves,
there might be two people per thousand.   5

Like—
but one also likes chicken soup with noodles,
one likes compliments and the color blue,
one likes an old scarf,
one likes having the upper hand,   10
one likes stroking a dog.

Poetry—
but what is poetry.
Many shaky answers
have been given to this question.   15
But I don't know and don't know and hold on to it
like to a sustaining railing.

— ABOUT THE AUTHOR —

Wislawa Szymborska (b. 1923) was born in Kornik, Poland. She studied Polish literature and sociology at Jagiellonian University and then from 1953 to 1981 was a columnist and poetry editor at a literary magazine in Krakow. She published her first poem, "Szukam slowa" ("I Am Looking for a Word"), in March 1945. Since then sixteen collections of her poetry have been published, and many of her poems have been translated into more than twelve languages. In addition, her poems have been published in for-eign anthologies of Polish poetry. Szymborska is both a Goethe and Herder Prize winner. She has received many additional honors, including an honorary doctorate from Poznan University in 1995 and the 1996 Polish PEN Club prize. She was awarded the Nobel Prize for literature in 1996. A 2002 work, *Nonrequired Reading: Prose Pieces*, was a break from her usual genre. An intensely private person, Szymborska avoids the public eye of literary society and continues to write from her home in Krakow.

HEIGHT

BILLY COLLINS

Perhaps you have stood on the observation deck of a tall skyscraper. As you looked out over the city, how did things appear to you? The cars and trucks probably looked like toys. But what of the people?

Viewed from the roof of a tall building,
people on the street
are said to take on the appearance of ants,

but I have been up here for so long,
gazing down over this parapet,*   5
that the ants below have begun to resemble people.

Look at that one lingering
near a breadcrumb on the curb,
does he not share the appearance of my brother-in-law?

And the beautiful young ant   10
in the light summer dress
with the smooth ovoid* head,

the one heading up the lamppost—
could she not double for my favorite cousin
with her glad eyes and her pulled-back hair?   15

Surely, one with the face
of my mother and another with the posture
of my father will soon go hobbling by.

parapet: a low protective wall or railing
    along the edge of a roof
ovoid: egg-shaped

"Height", from THE TROUBLE WITH POETRY by Billy Collins, copyright © 2005 by Billy Collins. Used by permission of Random House, Inc.

ABOUT THE AUTHOR

William J. "Billy" Collins (b. 1941) was born in New York City. He is often spoken of with the same fervor as American poetry legend Robert Frost because of his quality verse and broad appeal. Numerous anthologies, textbooks, and periodicals have included his poems, and he has published more than eight collections of poetry. Prizes awarded to Collins include the New York Public Library Literary Lion award, the Oscar Blumenthal Prize, the Frederick Bock Prize, the Bess Hokin Prize, and the Mark Twain Award.

Collins was named two-term United States Poet Laureate in 2001 and the New York Poet Laureate in 2004.

Collins is passionate about making his poetry accessible to the average reader. His book *Poetry 180: A Turning Back to Poetry* encourages students to read a poem a day. He is a frequent guest on National Public Radio. Collins has taught English for over thirty years at Lehman College at the City University of New York.

THINKING ZONE

You may remember that alliteration is the repetition of initial consonant sounds of words in a poem. **Assonance** is the repetition of similar vowel sounds in a series of words. Lyn Aye's translation of Zawgee's "The Way of the Water-Hyacinth" uses assonance in the second and third lines of the first stanza. In these lines the long *i* sound is repeated in "Bowing to the t*i*de / Hyacinth r*i*ses and falls." You will notice that it is not necessarily the spelling of a word that is important, but its sound.

Assonance also plays a part in rhyme. As you may remember, rhyme relies on the repetition of the last stressed *vowel* sound of a word and all the sounds following that vowel. One type of rhyme that appears throughout poetry is **internal rhyme**, or rhyme that occurs between words within a single line of poetry.

1. *[literal]* What things is poet Billy Collins comparing in his poem "Height"?

   _____

   _____

   _____

2. *[critical]* Where does **assonance** occur in the first stanza of Collins's poem?

   _____

   _____

3. *[interpretive]* What factor affects Collins's viewpoint the most? Is he speaking literally or figuratively throughout the poem?

   _____

   _____

   _____

4. *[critical]* Where does assonance occur in the last stanza of "Height"? Where does **internal rhyme** occur?

_____

_____

_____

_____

5. *[interpretive]* Based on "Some Like Poetry," what does Szymborska believe most people feel about poetry?

_____

_____

_____

_____

6. *[critical]* What poetic device involving repetition occurs in most of the lines in the second stanza of "Some Like Poetry"?

_____

_____

_____

_____

Anaphora—
repetition of words and phrases at the beginnings of lines of poetry

7. *[critical]* What is the irony of Szymborska's question in stanza 3 (especially when compared with what she says in stanza 1)?

_____

_____

_____

_____

_____

8. *[appreciative]* Which poem did you like better? Why?

_____

_____

_____

_____

_____

THE SHARK

E. J. Pratt

From poet E. J. Pratt's viewpoint, the shark is a mysterious and fascinating
creature. In this poem, he creates a clear visual picture of a shark. Notice
the closing line of the poem. Is it true?

He seemed to know the harbour,
So leisurely he swam;
His fin,
Like a piece of sheet-iron,
Three-cornered,   5
And with knife-edge,
Stirred not a bubble
As it moved
With its base-line on the water.

His body was tubular*   10   tubular: tube-like, cylindrical
And tapered
And smoke-blue,
And as he passed the wharf
He turned,
And snapped at a flat-fish   15
That was dead and floating.
And I saw the flash of a white throat,
And a double row of white teeth,
And eyes of metallic grey,
Hard and narrow and slit.   20

Then out of the harbour,
With that three-cornered fin
Shearing without a bubble the water
Lithely,*
Leisurely,   25
He swam—
That strange fish,
Tubular, tapered, smoke-blue,
Part vulture, part wolf,
Part neither—for his blood was cold.   30

lithely: gracefully, with flexibility

ABOUT THE AUTHOR

E. J. (Edwin John "Ned") Pratt (1882–1964) was born in Western Bay, Newfoundland, Canada. His father was a Methodist minister, and the family lived in many communities throughout the province. Although Pratt himself was an ordained minister, he pursued other avenues of work such as teaching and writing. He taught for thirty-five years at Victoria College at the University of Toronto, where a library is named after him.

Pratt's first collection of published poetry to gain popularity was *Newfoundland Verse*, published in 1923. Pratt was one of the founders of *Canadian Poetry Magazine* and was its first editor. Throughout his lifetime, Pratt received numerous literary honors. To this day the University of Toronto honors Canadian poets with the E. J. Pratt Medal for poetry. Previous winners of the medal include Margaret Atwood and Michael Ondaatje. E. J. Pratt is considered the foremost Canadian poet of the early twentieth century.

THE SLOTH

THEODORE ROETHKE

From just about anyone's viewpoint, the sloth is a slow-moving animal. Most sloths sleep between fifteen and eighteen hours a day. Can you separate fact from fiction in Theodore Roethke's poem?

In moving-slow he has no Peer.
You ask him something in his Ear,
He thinks about it for a Year;

And, then, before he says a Word
There, upside down (unlike a Bird),
He will assume that you have Heard—

A most Ex-as-per-at-ing* Lug.
But should you call his manner
   Smug,
He'll sigh and give his Branch a Hug;

Ex-as-per-at-ing: highly annoying

Then off again to Sleep he goes,
Still swaying gently by his Toes,
And you just know he knows he knows.

ABOUT THE AUTHOR

Theodore Roethke (1908–63), the son of German immigrant parents, was born in Saginaw, Michigan. During his years at the University of Michigan, Roethke worked a number of jobs, among which was a job in the Heinz pickle factory. Following his graduation, he pursued a master's degree in literature at Harvard. However, the Depression and accompanying financial problems forced him to withdraw.

Roethke's years as a young poet were difficult. He suffered several mental and emotional breakdowns and, probably as a result, moved from one teaching job to another. He taught at Lafayette, Penn State, Bennington, and the University of Washington. Roethke published his first book of poetry in 1941 and continued to publish somewhat erratically. In 1954 Roethke was awarded the Pulitzer Prize for *The Waking*, a collection of poetry. Roethke's poetry often uses natural imagery and ranges from poems with regular, metered stanzas to fluid free-verse pieces. In his later years Roethke taught at the University of Washington, where he had the opportunity to influence a number of poets from the American Northwest.

THINKING ZONE

The more familiar you become with poetry, the more you discover what goes into writing a poem. Poets use pauses and punctuation, rhyme, rhythm, meter, and a variety of other devices to guide the reader's impression and the thrust of the poem. One punctuation device you have studied already is caesura. Another punctuation device is **end-stopped lines**, poetic lines that end with a natural pause indicated by punctuation. Both caesura and end-stopping affect the reading of the poem when it is presented aloud.

Rhythm and meter also affect the way a poem is read. As you recall, meter refers to the arrangement of stressed and unstressed syllables in a poem. In a rhymed poem, there is often a pattern in the way the stressed and unstressed syllables appear. This repetitive pattern of stressed and unstressed syllables is what produces the rhythm of a poem. Each repetitive unit of the poetic line is called a **poetic foot**. The most common type of poetic foot is one unstressed syllable followed by a stressed syllable (as in "to-*day*"). This unstressed-stressed type of foot is called **iambic**, and the individual feet are known as **iambs**.

Students of poetry use a special type of marking to analyze the meter of the feet in a poem and to indicate the pauses in the lines. This marking is called **scansion**. Look at the first line of Emily Dickinson's poem "The Sky Is Low, the Clouds Are Mean." In order to **scan** or mark the poem, note the rhythm of the line and then draw a line between the poetic feet. Next draw an upward curved line (˘) over the syllables that are unstressed and an accent mark (/) over the stressed syllables. Below is an example of scansion.

The Sky | is low, | the Clouds | are mean.

1. *[interpretive]* What is Pratt's viewpoint or tone toward the shark in his poem? What details contribute to the tone?

_____

_____

_____

_____

2. *[interpretive]* What lines in stanza 1 of "The Shark" are **end-stopped**?

_____

3. *[interpretive]* Is Roethke's tone in "The Sloth" serious or playful? Explain.

_____

_____

4. *[critical]* **Scan** lines 1 and 2 of "The Sloth." Write your **scansion** below.

_____

_____

5. *[critical]* How many **poetic feet** does "The Sloth" have per line? Are they **iambic** feet (**iambs**)? How do you know?

_____

_____

6. *[critical]* How does the rhythm of "The Sloth" enhance the poem's meaning?

_____

_____

7. *[interpretive]* Which lines in "The Sloth" are end-stopped?

_____

8. *[critical]* What examples of hyperbole can you find in "The Sloth"?

_____

_____

_____

Hyperbole—*a form of obvious and extravagant overstatement used to make a point*

9. *[critical/appreciative]* Does a Christian have a reason to enjoy and even write poems like these? Why or why not?

_____

_____

_____

_____

_____

_____

THE TORN INVITATION

NORMAN KATKOV

Harry Wojick possesses a character flaw that threatens to harm someone he loves. Does Harry's viewpoint change before the end of the story? How does he compare to Paul from "Wolves of Fear"?

At fifteen, in the spring of his sophomore year at Hamilton High School, Harry Wojick was as big as a college senior, a long, thin, big-boned left-hander, who could anchor a leg in first base and stretch halfway to right field for a bad throw from his shortstop.

Now, in the waning* daylight, he turned into Glover Street toward his home, his arms swinging as he moved onto the un-paved road. For a few feet he ran easily, bringing his knees up high, until, without warning, he stopped short and bent low to field the imaginary ball cleanly, beating the runner by a mile. He straightened up, grinning in the half darkness, blushing a little from the applause at the brilliant play he had made.

---
waning: fading

Harry Wojick came off the street onto the opposite sidewalk. He passed the four-family flat* in the middle of the block. He passed the empty lot and beyond it the condemned building with all the windows long since broken, and then he turned into the cement walk which ran the length of his house.

---
flat: apartment on one floor of a building

The windows were raised in the kitchen and he smelled the roast. He smelled the asparagus for the roast and the fried potatoes with onions that nobody made like Ma, and he was suddenly terribly hungry after the three hours of baseball practice.

When he came into the kitchen, Theresa Wojick turned from the stove, smiling at her son, rubbing her hands on her apron as she walked to meet him. She held him at the elbows, examining him carefully, her face warm and her eyes gentle, welcoming him as though he had returned from a long and perilous journey. She was a tall woman with large, capable hands and black, unkempt hair shot through with gray. She held Harry and she said, "Hello, my little son. Will you eat supper?" joking with him as always.

He put his cheek to hers, noticing again the redness of her chapped hands. She could try to do something about it, he said to himself, as she released him, remembering the mothers of his teammates who lived above the flats on Livingston Drive and Harding Boulevard and scattered through Maple Heights. They were mothers with manicures and they were thin—and their hair was always set just right.

Harry went to the sink to wash and, turning, saw the table set for three. He thought for an instant that his father was home, that Peter Wojick had not gone to his night-watchman's job in the office building downtown. But he saw the hooks on the wall near the door empty of cap and coat.

"For Frankie Thomas," his mother whispered, looking at her son. "His mother is gone again till half the night, and leaves cold cuts. Boy like Frankie to eat cold cuts," she whispered. "You call him, Harry."

"Why can't she learn to speak English?" he asked himself savagely, turning away. "She's been here long enough!"

Harry walked through the short hall and stood under the arch which led into the living room. He saw the frail, black-haired boy with whom he had grown up, sitting in the chair under the lamp. "Hey, Frankie," Harry said. "Come on and eat." Harry whistled shrilly and came back into the kitchen.

He pulled the chair out and held it suspended off the clean, bare floor, his fingers tightening on the wood. There, next to his plate, was the white, square envelope, and atop it, covered by a transparent sheet of thin paper, was the embossed invitation.

Harry looked at his mother, who had her back to him, busy at the stove. He heard Frankie coming through the house and knew it was Frankie's work, *knew* it. He moved the chair at last and sat down and, without touching it, his hands holding his knees, he read the invitation from the faculty of Hamilton High School to an open house in honor of all the students' mothers.

It was for tomorrow.

Harry knew *that*, all right. Had known it for ten days and had kept it secret. He looked up as Frankie sat down across the table.

Harry's mother was sitting between them, and as she handed her son the roast she said, "I asked Frankie maybe he has this invitation, Harry. I heard by Celusik, the grocery man, about this open house. Must be open house for junior, senior mothers."

Frankie had skipped a grade.

Harry was busy with the roast. "It's for everyone," he said, watching the roast. "Didn't you get one, Ma?" He turned to his mother. "They mailed them out," Harry said, remembering now that morning when he had waited for the postman on the corner, taken the envelopes from him, searched for the square, white one, and had torn it, scattering the pieces in the empty lot before running home and dropping the rest of the mail in the black metal box beside the door.

"Maybe they make a mistake," his mother said.

She reached for a thick slice of the rye bread she baked herself and held it flat in her left hand. She buttered it completely and thickly and brought it to her mouth, taking a large bite, and Harry wanted to leave the table and this house. He remembered the homes on Maple Heights to which he had been invited, where they called it dinner and ate in a dining room with tablecloths; where

George Sidley's mother sat at one end of the table and broke her bread piece by piece, buttering it lightly and eating slowly.

"Frankie's ma got this invitation," Theresa Wojick said, nodding at their guest, who lived with his mother in one of the upstairs apartments of the four-family flat. "How long she got the open house, Frankie?"

"Mother had it," Frankie said. "She—we didn't talk about it."

She turned to Harry, smiling at her son. "You eat, Harry. Big ball-players must eat good," she said.

Harry ate. The three sat in silence.

Later, while Theresa Wojick set out the dessert plates, Frankie said, "How's practice going, Harry?"

"All right, I guess." He wanted this supper finished.

Theresa Wojick filled the dessert plates with pudding. As she sat down she said to Frankie, "Your ma goes to this open house?"

"I don't know," he answered. "She— well, you know, she's pretty busy. One of my aunts is sick and I think she's going to be with her for a few days. She packed her suitcase when she left today."

"Ma," Harry said.

She set her coffee cup down.

"I wanted to tell you, Ma," he said. "I meant to tell you about it and then I forgot, I guess."

"Easy to forget," she said.

"It wouldn't make any difference anyway, Ma," Harry lied. "We've got that game with Central next week and the coach is worried. He's been working us hard all week. He's got a game for tomorrow. You know, he picks two teams from the squad and we play each other."

"I've got to go," Frankie said. "Thanks very much for supper, Mrs. Wojick."

"You're welcome, Frankie. Here"—she reached across the table—"here is the invitation, Frankie," and she offered it to him.

He held it, shifting it from one hand to the other. "Thanks," he said, moving toward the kitchen door. "Thanks. Thanks." And he was gone.

"I won't be finished until about six o'clock, Ma," Harry said.

She nodded. Harry watched her walking to the sink. "Do you want me to miss practice, Ma?" he asked.

She had her back to him.

"We'll go next year, Ma. I'll be a regular on the team then. We can go next year," he said, but she didn't turn, nor move, nor did she answer him, and he left the kitchen quickly. He went into the living room and stood before the windows. He tried to blame Frankie and couldn't, and he tried to blame Theresa Wojick and couldn't. He was seldom a liar, but he just didn't want her there with George Sidley's mother and Eric Portland's mother.

Harry heard the water running in the sink and the clatter of dishes, and he went back into the kitchen. He opened the cabinet door, reaching for one of the dish towels his mother had cut from sugar sacks and washed white and soft. She took it from his hand.

"You rest, Harry," his mother said. "Big ball game tomorrow. You must rest up for the ball game." She turned from him to the sink.

"All right," he thought, and now he left the house, going out into the vestibule and then to the rear porch. "Let her wash her own dishes," he thought, and walked out to the sidewalk.

Frankie said, "Hi, Harry." He was leaning against the fence in front of Harry's house. He said, "I didn't want to jam you up, Harry."

"You didn't jam me up."

"That ought to be a pretty good game tomorrow, that intrasquad game," Frankie said. "Think I'll watch it."

"There isn't any intrasquad game," Harry muttered.

"You said—"

"I said. I say a lot of things." He felt the meanness in him. He started to walk away, but Frankie took his arm.

"I've got enough for a movie," Frankie said.

"I'm busy," Harry said, jerking his arm free. He left Frankie there, walking down Glover Street. He passed the corner and went on aimlessly.

When he came home he entered the house through the front door and moved through the living room in darkness, turning into his bedroom. He could see the cracks of light below the bathroom door and heard the water running; he wondered if there was ever a time in this house when the water *wasn't* running. He made it to his bedroom and undressed in the darkness, dropping his clothes on the floor and crawling into the turned-down bed.

"All right," he thought; "this time tomorrow it'll be over." He heard the bathroom door open and his mother moving around the house. He lay still, his eyes closed, his breath coming evenly as he simulated sleep, but the sound of her footsteps faded.

For a bad moment he thought of his ma, saw her again at the kitchen table, but he chased the scene from his mind and went, instead, to baseball, seeing himself leading infield practice, and thus, at last, fell asleep.

The first thing he noticed in the morning was his clothes, arranged neatly on the chair beside the bed, the shoes together on the floor and clean socks across them. He dressed quickly.

The kitchen was deserted. He saw his cornflakes and the orange juice and the milk before his chair, but he stood behind it, gulping the juice. As he set the empty glass on the table his mother came in from the rear porch.

"You didn't eat, Harry," she said.

"I'm late, Ma. I've got a test this morning. I've got to study for the test." He wanted to be out of here now as he turned from the table, saw that her hands were full.

She held the clean, freshly dried sweatshirt and the two pairs of wool socks, and he knew now why the water had been running in the bathroom last night. "For your game today, Harry," she said. "You bring me tonight your dirty stuff."

Harry watched her wrap the bundle and he wanted to kiss her, suddenly. He wanted to put his arms around her and hold her as she tied the bundle carefully with the string she always saved. But he only took the package from her and said thanks, and left.

All the way up to school he promised he'd make it up to her. He'd start tonight. He'd sit in the kitchen with Ma; she liked him there studying while she worked. He'd take her for a walk if she wanted. Saturday and Sunday he was staying home the whole time, that's all.

He came into school on the Livingston Drive side. His locker was on the first floor. He put the package inside, took his books, and slammed the locker shut. The bell sounded for first hour and Harry went to English.

Pete Overholt, the team's catcher, sat behind Harry. As they waited for the tardy bell, he nudged Harry. "Look at the women, man," he whispered. "Look at 'em, Harry!"

Harry looked. Not a girl in the class wore saddle shoes, or blue jeans, or boys' shirts with the sleeves rolled above the elbows.

They were in Sunday dresses and suits, and high heels.

"The open house," Pete whispered. "All of them showing off for their mothers."

The tardy bell sounded, and Harry saw Miss Liggett look up from the desk. He wasn't called on during the hour, and afterward, on his way to study hall, he waved to George Sidley, who played third base, and to Bernie Cremmens, the right-fielder. They were both wearing sports jackets and regular shirts, and they wore ties. Harry looked down at his sweater worn over the skivvy* shirt. His corduroys were clean, but they were corduroys, and around him, in the study hall, was a sea of gray flannels.

skivvy: underwear

There was only one lunch period today because they had to get the cafeteria ready for the open house. Harry bought a sandwich and a glass of milk. Then he saw that half the guys on the team, sitting at the table they shared every day, were dressed up, too. He sat down in a far corner with two guys he didn't know, ate quickly, and left by the side door so he wouldn't have to pass Sidley and Cremmens and the others.

He went to his locker for his afternoon books. He had only a French class left, because, for today, school was over after fifth hour. He sat half hearing Miss Formanek, gazing out the window until his name was called sharply.

Harry turned to the teacher, his face red, feeling the eyes of the whole class on him as Miss Formanek smiled. "Let's look alive there," said Miss Formanek. "Your mother will find her way, Harry," and she told him the place in the French book.

The bell sounded at last and Harry hurried to his locker. He saw the cafeteria cleared of tables, the floor bare and chairs lining the walls. He saw the huge coffeepots

steaming, and then he got his package out and threw his books into the locker and slammed it shut.

He was half running for the door when George Sidley stopped him: "Hey, where you headed for?"

Harry stared at him. "Headed for?" he asked. "Where do you think I'm headed for? Aren't you going to practice?"

"Not me," George grinned. "Coach said anybody who wanted to could be excused. Isn't your mother coming?"

"She had to go downtown," Harry said. "She had to see a doctor. She hasn't been feeling well."

"Hey, that's not good," George said, frowning. Then his face brightened. "Well, hang around anyway. Lots of fun."

Harry shook his head. He swung his left arm. "It feels like it's stiffening up," he said. "Guess I'll work out. See you."

He walked down Livingston Drive toward the baseball field. He crossed the playing area, moving toward the Quonset hut* that served as dressing room for the team. There was nobody inside but Art Hughes, the student manager.

Quonset hut: prefabricated, portable metal hut

"You alone, Harry?" Art asked.

"Yup."

Art turned and opened the doors of the uniform rack. "Anybody that's coming better come quick—that's all I got to say," he announced. "My mother is over at school waiting for me. I'm not keeping her waiting too long."

Harry sat down on the bench before the lockers and unwrapped the package. He pulled his sweater off and he was in his pants and skivvy shirt, standing in his socks on the cement floor when Oscar

Anderson walked in. In a few minutes they were joined by Chuck Kellerman, the shortstop, and Mr. Quint, who taught chemistry and was assistant baseball coach.

Mr. Quint came over to the bench. "Look, you fellows; my wife's outside in the car. It seems there are only three of you here. You won't mind if I go back to school, will you?"

"Go ahead, Mr. Quint," Chuck said.

"I don't want to run out on you," Mr. Quint said.

"It's just—well, with only three of you here, there doesn't seem to be much we could do."

"Can I get a ride back?" Art Hughes said. "You guys can check out your own uniforms today."

"Come ahead, Art," Mr. Quint said.

When they were gone, Chuck Kellerman slammed his baseball cap down on the cement floor. "All the way over here for nothing," he said.

He looked at Oscar Anderson. "How about you?" he asked. "Aren't you going to Mamma's Day and eat cookies?"

"Listen; I've got six brothers and sisters and I'm the baby," Oscar said. "My mother's tired of this stuff. I'm going home and get the grass cut, and then I got Saturday for myself."

"How about you, Harry?" Chuck asked.

"How about *you*, wise guy?" Harry said, beginning to tie his shoelaces.

Chuck got up from the bench and reached for a bat. "My mother is dead," he said, and he swung the bat desperately, as though he were hitting a line drive. Then he dropped the bat into the wicker basket. Harry watched him pick up his books and walk to the door and leave without turning to them.

"Will you lock up, Harry?" Oscar asked.

Harry saw his mother in the kitchen, and he reached for his sweater.

"Will you, Harry?"

He remembered the light under the bathroom door and the sound of water as she washed the sweatshirt and the socks.

"HARRY!"

"It isn't too late yet," Harry said. He had his sweater on.

"Are you nuts?" Oscar asked.

He'd call her. He'd use the phone in the principal's office. "See you tomorrow," he said, and he ran out of the Quonset hut. Far off, walking in left-center field, Harry saw Chuck Kellerman, and then he began to run.

He could call her, he thought as he ran, and she could even take a taxi. Just this once a taxi; Pa wouldn't care. Harry knew that. She could get dressed and be up there in half an hour, and he was suddenly breathless with anticipation. He'd wait out in front of the school, on Hamilton Avenue, and help her from the cab and hold her arm and lead her to the front door. He didn't care about the bread any more, or how she talked. She was his ma.

Harry was out of the alley now, running across Livingston Drive. There were cars all around the school, almost like it was graduation night. He cut across the grass, toward the long flight of steps that led up to the second floor. He was gasping for breath when he reached the door.

He stood there a moment, then pulled the heavy door open and stepped into the deserted corridor. There was nobody on the second floor, but from the cafeteria below he heard the muted murmur of a hundred voices.

The principal's door was open. There was a phone in the outer office, an ancient upright that Miss Tibbetts, the principal's secretary, used. Harry took the receiver off the hook, set it on the desk and, holding the upright with his left hand, dialed his home number.

He grinned with excitement thinking of her when she answered. Ma didn't like phones and couldn't hear good on them, but she'd hear this. He could see her listening and her face lighting up, and then, afterwards, ordering Pa around to help her, getting the gray dress ready and her coat. She never wore a hat, but let the wind command her hair, and Harry didn't care.

But she didn't answer.

Aloud he said, "Wrong number," but felt the first, tiny stabs of alarm in his chest. He dialed again, slowly now, holding the receiver to his ear, hearing the first ring, the second, the third, the eighth, the ninth, and finally, the operator's voice telling him there was no answer.

He felt the ache in his chest now, and his hands were wet. "Maybe Ma is sick or something," he thought, and he knew who had to take the blame. He dialed the 0 and asked the operator to check the number; maybe the phone was out of order. But all the time he knew it wasn't.

At last he thanked the operator and replaced the receiver and stood listlessly at the desk, wondering what to do. Now he remembered his ma helping him with fractions when he was at Crowley School. He remembered her at graduation, Ma and Pa sitting alone in the back row, and after he had his diploma, when the other guys were bringing their parents up to the front of the auditorium, he had led them out to the hall and home immediately. He remembered her walking over to the skating rink on Inverness Street, standing in a corner beside the fence to watch him skate under the floodlights, careful not to be seen, but he had seen her, all right. Seen her and kept away from that corner.

It seemed to him now, alone in the principal's office, that he had been hiding his ma all his life, and he was sick inside then, with a physical distaste in his mouth. He grimaced with self-hatred, wanting, somehow to feel a sharper pain, to hurt himself deliberately; and he left the office and almost ran into Mr. Quint and a woman.

"Hello, Harry," Mr. Quint said. "I thought you were practicing."

"I guess not, sir."

"This is my wife, Harry," Mr. Quint said. "Harry Wojick, Emma," he said. "Harry's our first baseman."

Mrs. Quint smiled and shook hands with him.

"Mrs. Quint wants to use the phone," the assistant coach said. "She's worried about our little girl. . . . I'll see you in the cafeteria, dear," he said to his wife.

She nodded, and Mr. Quint took Harry's arm. "Let's get some of those cookies, Harry."

"I can't sir. My mother isn't there," Harry said.

"Oh, yes. One of the boys told me. She's seeing a doctor. Hasn't been feeling well, eh?"

Harry pulled his arm away. "That's a lie," he said. "I didn't want her to come today."

Mr. Quint started laughing. He put his arm around Harry's shoulders and they walked toward the stairs. "You guys," he said, shaking his head. He looked at Harry. "Do I really look that old, Harry? An old fossil whose leg you all enjoy pulling?"

"What's the difference?" Harry thought. "What difference does it make now?" And his heart leaped as he thought of next year. There'd be an open house next year, but Ma wouldn't go. If she never went anywhere with him, he'd deserve it. If she never talked with him, he had that coming, too. "Just let me get away from Mr. Quint," he thought. Get out of here without trouble and without a fuss. But now they were in the cafeteria, in the midst of mothers and daughters and sons and teachers, and Mr. Quint was pulling him through the mob.

But they got separated and Harry was alone. He wanted to get out quickly now, away from all the laughter and gaiety. He saw Miss Formanek, the French teacher. He saw her wave at him, her finger curved beckoning him. He saw Frankie Thomas standing beside her and the woman between them. He was moving sideways, pushing through the people, and he looked up for Miss Formanek again, and then felt his heart stop. For a long time he remembered his heart stopping dead as he saw the woman in the gray dress.

He thought his legs would give away. His legs were shaking and he was shaking, and he couldn't move until someone pushed him clear and he was standing there before them. He couldn't get his hands free of sweat. He rubbed his hands up and down against the corduroys and looked at his ma.

"I was telling your mother how you were watching for her, Harry. You have a devoted son, Mrs. Wojick," the French teacher said.

Harry saw his ma smile and nod. She was beautiful.

Frankie was wearing a jacket and a tie. How come *he* was dressed up?

"And you're pinch-hitting for Frankie's mother, too," Miss Formanek said. "Frankie was my best student, Mrs. Wojick."

"Frankie's a good boy," Theresa Wojick said.

"They're all good boys," Miss Formanek said, and she excused herself and left them then.

"Ma," Harry said. He had to tell her.

She had her hand in Frankie's arm. She was smiling, and her hair was pulled back neat, and she was the loveliest woman he had ever seen. "Ma, I tore up the invitation," he said, and he looked right at her.

"I know," she said. "But Frankie has an invitation. We are two orphans: mother without a son, and son without a mother."

"I'm your son, Ma," Harry said, and saw Frankie slipping away, but his mother held the black-haired boy.

She was wearing white gloves and she looked right at him, and he was more afraid than he had ever been in his life.

"Ma." He held her elbows as she had held his and he didn't drop his eyes. He said, "Please, Ma, I'm your son. Please, Ma, let's get something to eat. There's my coach there. I want to introduce you to my coach."

"Yes," she said, and she smiled at him then, and for him. "Yes," she said, and put one hand through his arm and the other through Frankie's. "Introduce, please, to this coach, my little son."

┌─ ABOUT THE AUTHOR ─────────────────────────

"Go to school!" is a command that Norman Katkov (b. 1918) heard often as he was growing up. Born in a small Russian village, Katkov, at age three, moved with his family to America. Although the family-owned store provided a livelihood for the Katkovs, Norman's father wanted better things for his sons' futures and insisted on their getting the best education they could get. Katkov's father was rewarded for his persistence in running his sons out of the grocery store and sending them to school, as he saw his sons excel in the professional world. It was the grocery store, however, that helped to provide those "better things" for Norman as his stories, many of which are based on three brothers who work in a grocery store, gained popularity and began to earn him a degree of fame.

Katkov's writing career led him into various fields of work, including jobs as a police reporter and feature writer. For two years he wandered the streets of New York City all night and returned to the newspaper office before dawn to write a story about someone or something he had seen. In 1948 Katkov left the newspaper business to devote his time to writing fiction pieces, which include novels, television scripts, a motion picture script, and numerous short stories.

THINKING ZONE

Within a story, an antagonist often strives against the main character, or protagonist, thus motivating conflict. Other characters in the story may contrast sharply with the main character without being in direct conflict with him. A character who contrasts with the protagonist is called a **foil**. Though *foil* may suggest opposition, the foil character may even be a friend of the protagonist who possesses opposing character traits. These opposite traits purposefully emphasize the uniqueness of the protagonist's attitude or appearance. The two characters in Langston Hughes's "Thank You, M'am" illustrate a protagonist and a foil. The boy Roger is young—small enough to be picked up by his shirt—dirty, and selfish. In sharp contrast, Mrs. Luella Bates Washington Jones is "a large woman," excessively clean, and generous. As his foil, she is everything he is not; the kinder she is to him, the worse he feels about his own character flaws and the more the reader appreciates the change he must undergo. A good foil is instructive to the careful reader: What are the protagonist's strengths and weaknesses? Where might he need to change?

Antagonist—*a character in conflict with the protagonist*

1. *[interpretive]* How does Harry feel about his mother? Why does he feel this way?

_____

_____

_____

_____

_____

2. *[interpretive]* What does Mrs. Wojick's appearance suggest about her character?

_____

_____

_____

_____

_____

3. *[interpretive]* In addition to the invitation, what else is torn apart in the story?

_____

_____

_____

_____

4. *[critical]* Who is the protagonist and who is the chief **foil** in the story? Explain.

_____

_____

_____

_____

5. *[critical]* Is Harry a developing character in the story? Explain your answer.

_____

_____

_____

_____

_____

_____

_____

6. *[appreciative]* Harry was embarrassed by his mother; Peter denied even knowing Jesus (Matt. 27:69–75). Have you ever been embarrassed about someone or something when you ought not to have been? Explain what your feelings were and why they were wrong.

_____

_____

_____

_____

_____

_____

FRY, FRY AGAIN

RUSSELL BAKER

Do you get tired of the trite expressions that people use? How often do you hear someone say, "Last but not least" or "At the end of the day" or "Under the weather"? You will probably be able to identify, then, with Uncle Henry.

The present heat wave reminds me of my Uncle Henry who once fried chicken on the sidewalk. It was Uncle Henry's way of showing his contempt for newspapers.

At that time, as soon as a heat wave started going well the newspapers sent out photographers to take pictures of somebody frying an egg on the sidewalk. "Hot enough to fry an egg," was the invariable picture caption.

After fifty or sixty summers of looking at the same old egg-frying picture in his newspapers, Uncle Henry phoned his local papers one steamy* July day and said he was going to give them something new to photograph.

steamy: hot and humid

"I am going to fry a chicken on the sidewalk," he said.

"Are you crazy? You can't fry a chicken on the sidewalk," is more or less what all of the newspaper editors replied.

"But even if I fail," Uncle Henry said, "you'll have a new kind of picture for your heat-wave story. You can caption it, 'Not hot enough to fry a chicken.'"

Naturally the editors didn't send their photographers.

This pleased Uncle Henry, since it confirmed his suspicion that newspapers had no interest in anything that was new.

Aunt Jenny, who was practical, said he was acting like a fool.

"If you'd told those editors you were going to fry an egg on the sidewalk, you could have got your picture in the papers," she said.

"You don't understand," Uncle Henry told her. "I'm not interested in giving a fried food demonstration. I am dramatizing the press's enslavement to clichés."*

clichés: statements that are common or overly obvious

"If you told them you were going to fry both the chicken and an egg side by side out there on the cement, you could have got them interested in a nice heat-wave feature story. Think of the headline possibilities: 'Man answers age-old question—which fried first? The chicken or the egg?'"

Uncle Henry ignored her, as he usually did.

When he brought the chicken in from the sidewalk, of course, none of us wanted to eat it, but as Uncle Henry pointed out, "If I'd fried an egg out there in all those dog tracks, you wouldn't want to eat that either."

At this stage of his life Uncle Henry's distaste for newspaper clichés was drawing him toward eccentricity.*

eccentricity: strange or unusual behavior

Much as he hated heat waves because of the inevitability* of the fried-egg-on-the-sidewalk picture, he detested the autumnal* change of foliage* color even more.

inevitability: unavoidableness

autumnal: occurring in autumn

foliage: leafage

Uncle Henry had nothing against tree leaves changing their color, but he dreaded the same old annual newspaper stories about forests "ablaze in russet, gold and brilliant scarlet."

When he came into a sum of money from Great-Aunt Martha's will, he bought a wooded tract* and a considerable amount of spray painting equipment.

tract: a large area of land

His plan was to spray his trees with navy blue paint, thus challenging reporters coveting the annual fall foliage story to shed their clichés and write something fresh.

He knew, of course, that they wouldn't. "I'll bet when they see it, they'll write about "a forest ablaze in navy blue," he said.

Unfortunately, Uncle Henry was unable to carry out this ambitious* demonstration of the press's passion for the trite, for his paint and spraying equipment were destroyed in a four-alarm fire, which also destroyed his house.

ambitious: requiring a great deal of effort

Uncle Henry escaped uninjured, except by the newspaper report, which said that the fire had "roared through" his house.

After reading the account, he turned to Aunt Jenny with tears in his eyes.

"Roar for me, Jenny," he said. Aunt Jenny gave a passable imitation of a lion in a testy* mood.

testy: irritable

"Did you hear that?" he asked the editor, after he had Aunt Jenny roar a second time

into the telephone. "Does that sound to you, Mr. Editor, like the noise a fire makes?"

Though a mere adolescent in those days, I tried to comfort him. "Fires always roar in newspapers, Uncle Henry. They've roared since I began reading newspapers seven years ago at the age of six, and they'll probably still be roaring when I'm an old coot* of thirty-three."

coot: an odd or grouchy person

"That's not good enough, boy," he told me. "There's supposed to be progress in this old world of ours. It's time newspapers quit misleading people about fires roaring and started telling us something accurate about fires."

"I know what you're saying, Henry," said Aunt Jenny. "It would be so much more graphic* if, when a house burned down, the papers sent somebody around and you put an egg in a skillet and held it in the fire and they could write, 'It was hot enough to fry an egg.'"

graphic: vividly descriptive

If there hadn't been oppression of women in those days, Uncle Henry always said, Aunt Jenny would have made a great editor.

About the Author

Born in Morrisonville, Virginia, Russell Baker (b. 1925) began his writing career as a reporter for the *Baltimore Sun*. In 1954 he joined the staff of the *New York Times*, and in 1962 he began his "Observer" column. In the "Observer," Baker reveals his observations on politics and life in a humorous way. Baker received the Pulitzer Prize for commentary in 1979 and the Pulitzer Prize for his autobiography, entitled *Growing Up*, in 1983. He also hosted the PBS program *Masterpiece Theater* from 1992 to 2004. Baker is a contributor to such periodicals as *Sports Illustrated*, *McCall's*, and *Saturday Evening Post*.

THINKING ZONE

Have you ever run like the wind and afterward been so dog-tired that you felt deader than a doornail? **Clichés** are phrases, idioms, and expressions that have become so overused that they often detract from a work or a story rather than contribute to it. For instance, the well-known "It's raining cats and dogs" may be acceptable in conversation, but one should avoid using it in writing to describe the weather. It has become a stale and almost meaningless expression. The author of "Fry, Fry Again," however, takes part of a cliché ("If at first you don't succeed . . .") and creatively adapts it to title his entertaining essay.

Idioms—
expressions that cannot be defined by the meanings of the individual words

1. *[critical]* How does the author's opening draw you into the essay?

   _____

   _____

   _____

2. *[interpretive]* What is the first **cliché** to which Uncle Henry reacts? What reason does he give for reacting this way?

   _____

   _____

   _____

3. *[interpretive]* How is Aunt Jenny's first response to Uncle Henry a humorous spin on another old cliché?

   _____

   _____

   _____

4. *[critical]* What is ironic about the results of Uncle Henry's plan to paint the trees blue?

   _____

   _____

   _____

5. *[critical]* Aunt Jenny's final response to Uncle Henry's antics is another cliché. Why do you think Uncle Henry, who disliked this expression at the beginning of the essay, appreciated her response?

_____

_____

_____

_____

6. *[critical]* What is the authorial tone toward Uncle Henry and Aunt Jenny?

_____

_____

_____

7. *[appreciative]* Did you enjoy the personalities of Uncle Henry and Aunt Jenny?

_____

_____

_____

8. *[critical]* What message do you think Baker is trying to convey in this essay?

_____

_____

_____

9. *[appreciative]* Have you ever known a person like Uncle Henry? Describe that person.

_____

_____

_____

_____

_____

THE DIARY OF A YOUNG GIRL

ANNE FRANK

In central Europe during World War II, thousands of Jews were arrested by the secret police and sent to concentration camps or to immediate death. Through the diary of Anne Frank, we learn of the struggles, heartaches, and disappointments of a young Jewish girl in hiding.

SATURDAY, JUNE 20, 1942

Writing in a diary is a really strange experience for someone like me. Not only because I've never written anything before, but also because it seems to me that later on neither I nor anyone else will be interested in the musings* of a thirteen-year-old schoolgirl. Oh well, it doesn't matter. I feel like writing, and I have an even greater need to get all kinds of things off my chest.

"Paper has more patience than people." I thought of this saying on one of those days when I was feeling a little depressed and was sitting at home with my chin in my hands, bored and listless, wondering whether to stay in or go out. I finally stayed where I was, brooding.* Yes, paper *does* have more patience, and since I'm not planning to let anyone else read this stiff-backed notebook grandly referred to as a "diary," unless I

musings: meditations

From THE DIARY OF A YOUNG GIRL THE DEFINITIVE EDITION by Anne Frank. Otto H. Frank & Mirjam Pressler, Editors, translated by Susan Massotty, copyright © 1995 by Doubleday, a division of Random House, Inc. Used by permission of Doubleday, a division of Random House, Inc.

should ever find a real friend, it probably won't make a bit of difference.

brooding: in deep thought

Now I'm back to the point that prompted me to keep a diary in the first place: I don't have a friend.

Let me put it more clearly, since no one will believe that a thirteen-year-old girl is completely alone in the world. And I'm not. I have loving parents and a sixteen-year-old sister, and there are about thirty people I can call friends. I have a throng of admirers who can't keep their adoring eyes off me and who sometimes have to resort to using a broken pocket mirror to try and catch a glimpse of me in the classroom. I have a family, loving aunts and a good home. No, on the surface I seem to have everything, except my one true friend. All I think about when I'm with friends is having a good time.

I can't bring myself to talk about anything but ordinary everyday things. We don't seem to be able to get any closer, and that's the problem. Maybe it's my fault that we don't confide in each other. In any case, that's just how things are, and unfortunately they're not liable to change. This is why I've started the diary.

To enhance the image of this long-awaited friend in my imagination, I don't want to jot down the facts in this diary the way most people would do, but I want the diary to be my friend, and I'm going to call this friend *Kitty*.

Since no one would understand a word of my stories to Kitty if I were to plunge right in, I'd better provide a brief sketch of my life, much as I dislike doing so.

My father, the most adorable father I've ever seen, didn't marry my mother until he was thirty-six and she was twenty-five. My sister Margot was born in Frankfurt am Main in Germany in 1926. I was born on June 12, 1929. I lived in Frankfurt until I was four. Because we're Jewish, my father immigrated to Holland in 1933, when he became the Managing Director of the Dutch Opekta Company, which manufactures products used in making jam. My mother, Edith Holländer Frank, went with him to Holland in September, while Margot and I were sent to Aachen to stay with our grandmother. Margot went to Holland in December, and I followed in February, when I was plunked down on the table as a birthday present for Margot. . . .

After May 1940 the good times were few and far between: first there was the war, then the capitulation* and then the arrival of the Germans, which is when the trouble started for the Jews. Our freedom was severely restricted by a series of anti-Jewish decrees: Jews were required to wear a yellow star; Jews were required to turn in their bicycles; Jews were forbidden to use street-cars; Jews were forbidden to ride in cars, even their own; Jews were required to do their shopping between 3 and 5 P.M.; Jews were required to frequent only Jewish-owned barbershops and beauty parlors; Jews were forbidden to be out on the streets between 8 P.M. and 6 A.M.; Jews were forbidden to go to theaters, movies or any other forms of entertainment; Jews were forbidden to use swimming pools, tennis courts, hockey fields or any other athletic fields; Jews were forbidden to go rowing; Jews were forbidden to take part in any athletic activity in public; Jews were forbidden to sit in their gardens or those of their friends after 8 P.M.; Jews were forbidden to visit Christians in their homes; Jews were required to attend Jewish schools, etc. You couldn't do this and you couldn't do that, but life went on. Jacque always said to me, "I don't dare do anything anymore, 'cause I'm afraid it's not allowed." . . .

capitulation: act of surrender

WEDNESDAY, JULY 8, 1942

Dearest Kitty,

It seems like years since Sunday morning. So much has happened it's as if the whole world had suddenly turned upside down. But as you can see, Kitty, I'm still alive, and that's the main thing, Father says. I'm alive all right, but don't ask where or how. You probably don't understand a word I'm saying today, so I'll begin by telling you what happened Sunday afternoon.

At three o'clock (Hello* had left but was supposed to come back later), the doorbell rang. I didn't hear it, since I was out on the balcony, lazily reading in the sun. A little while later Margot appeared in the kitchen doorway looking very agitated. "Father has received a call-up notice from the SS,"* she whispered. "Mother has gone to see Mr. van Daan." (Mr. van Daan is Father's business partner and a good friend.)

Hello: Helmuth Silberberg, a boy whom Anne met shortly before going into hiding

Schutzstaffel: an elite group that served as Hitler's bodyguard and as special security forces

I was stunned. A call-up: everyone knows what that means. Visions of concentration camps and lonely cells raced through my head. How could we let Father go to such a fate? "Of course he's not going," declared Margot as we waited for Mother in the living room. "Mother's gone to Mr. van Daan to ask whether we can move to our hiding

Dutch Jewish Star

Statement provided by the United States Holocaust Memorial Museum: "The views or opinions expressed in this book, and the context in which the images are used, do not necessarily reflect the views or policy of, nor imply approval or endorsement by, the United States Holocaust Memorial Museum."

place tomorrow. The van Daans are going with us. There will be seven of us altogether." Silence. We couldn't speak. The thought of Father off visiting someone in the Jewish Hospital and completely unaware of what was happening, the long wait for Mother, the heat, the suspense—all this reduced us to silence. . . .

When she and I were sitting in our bedroom, Margot told me that the call-up was not for Father, but for her. At this second shock, I began to cry. Margot is sixteen—apparently they want to send girls her age away on their own. But thank goodness she won't be going; Mother had said so herself, which must be what Father had meant when he talked to me about our going into hiding. Hiding . . . where would we hide? In the city? In the country? In a house? In a shack?

When, where, how . . . ? These were questions I wasn't allowed to ask, but they still kept running through my mind.

Margot and I started packing our most important belongings into a schoolbag. The first thing I stuck in was this diary, and then curlers, handkerchiefs, schoolbooks, a comb and some old letters. Preoccupied by the thought of going into hiding, I stuck the craziest things in the bag, but I'm not sorry. Memories mean more to me than dresses.

Father finally came home around five o'clock, and we called Mr. Kleiman to ask if he could come by that evening. Mr. van Daan left and went to get Miep. Miep arrived and promised to return later that night, taking with her a bag full of shoes, dresses, jackets, underwear and stockings. After that it was quiet in our apartment; none of us felt like eating. It was still hot, and everything was very strange. . . .

Miep and Jan Gies came at eleven. Miep, who's worked for Father's company since 1933, has become a close friend, and so has her husband Jan. Once again, shoes, stockings, books and underwear disappeared into Miep's bag and Jan's deep pockets. At eleven-thirty they too disappeared.

I was exhausted, and even though I knew that it'd be my last night in my own bed, I fell asleep right away and didn't wake up until Mother called me at five-thirty the next morning. Fortunately, it wasn't as hot as Sunday; a warm rain fell throughout the day. The four of us were wrapped in so many layers of clothes it looked as if we were going off to spend the night in a refrigerator, and all that just so we could take more clothes with us. . . .

At seven-thirty we too closed the door behind us; Moortje, my cat, was the only living creature I said goodbye to. According to a note we left for Mr. Goldschmidt, she was to be taken to the neighbors, who would give her a good home. . . .

Yours, Anne

THURSDAY, JULY 9, 1942

Dearest Kitty,

So there we were, Father, Mother and I, walking in the pouring rain, each of us with a schoolbag and a shopping bag filled to the brim with the most varied assortment of items. The people on their way to work at that early hour gave us sympathetic looks; you could tell by their faces that they were sorry they couldn't offer us some kind of transportation; the conspicuous yellow star spoke for itself.

Only when we were walking down the street did Father and Mother reveal, little by little, what the plan was. For months we'd been moving as much of our furniture and apparel out of the apartment as we could. It was agreed that we'd go into hiding on July 16. Because of Margot's call-up notice, the plan had to be moved up ten days, which meant we'd have to make do with less orderly rooms.

The hiding place was located in Father's office building. That's a little hard for outsiders to understand, so I'll explain. Father didn't have a lot of people working in his office, just Mr. Kugler, Mr. Kleiman, Miep and a twenty-three-year-old typist named Bep Voskuijl, all of whom were informed of our coming. Mr. Voskuijl, Bep's father, works in the warehouse, along with two assistants, none of whom were told anything.

Here's a description of the building. The large warehouse on the ground floor is used as a workroom and storeroom and is divided into several different sections, such as the

The Annex (tallest building)

stockroom and the milling room, where cinnamon, cloves and a pepper substitute are ground. . . .

A wooden staircase leads from the downstairs hallway to the third floor. At the top of the stairs is a landing, with doors on either side. The door on the left takes you up to the spice storage area, attic and loft in the front part of the house. A typically Dutch, very steep, ankle-twisting flight of stairs also runs from the front part of the house to another door opening onto the street.

The door to the right of the landing leads to the "Secret Annex" at the back of the house. No one would ever suspect there were so many rooms behind that plain gray door. There's just one small step in front of the door, and then you're inside. Straight ahead of you is a steep flight of stairs. To the left is a narrow hallway opening onto a room that serves as the Frank family's living room and bedroom. Next door is a smaller room, the bedroom and study of the two young ladies of the family. To the right of the stairs is a windowless washroom with a sink. The door in the corner leads to the toilet and another one to Margot's and my room. If you go up the stairs and open the door at the top, you're surprised to see such a large, light and spacious room in an old canalside house like this. It contains a stove (thanks to the fact that it used to be Mr. Kugler's laboratory) and a sink. This will be the kitchen and bedroom of Mr. and Mrs. van Daan, as well as the general living room, dining room and study for us all. A tiny side room is to be Peter van Daan's bedroom. Then, just as in the front part of the building, there's an attic and a loft. So there you are. Now I've introduced you to the whole of our lovely Annex!

Yours, Anne

THINKING ZONE

As you read this selection, you probably noticed that Anne Frank writes in a very candid, informal style, expressing freely what she is feeling at different times during her and her family's confinement in the small Amsterdam annex. A **journal** or **diary** is intended as an informal (often daily) record of a person's life. Most of the time, those who keep diaries are not writing with the intention that anyone else will see their work; instead, they are writing for their own personal benefit. Diaries can be especially useful as records of historical events. For instance, some have cited Anne Frank's diary as part of the evidence that the Holocaust did happen. Another person whose diary has become important historically is Samuel Pepys (pronounced "peeps"), who kept a diary during the seventeenth century. His detailed record of his daily diet, exercise, and activities has proven a valuable resource for those researching culture and daily life of that time.

1. *[literal]* In the first excerpt, what does Anne give as the purpose for keeping her **diary**?

   _____

   _____

   _____

   _____

2. *[critical]* What is the irony in the first paragraph?

   _____

   _____

   _____

3. *[literal]* Who is Kitty?

   _____

   _____

4. *[interpretive]* What do you think is the meaning of Anne's quotation "Paper has more patience than people"?

_____

_____

_____

_____

5. *[interpretive]* According to her **journal** why are Anne and her family having to stay in the annex?

_____

_____

_____

_____

6. *[interpretive]* Anne says that she decided to keep a diary because she did not have a friend. What reason does she give for not having a friend? What advice would you give to a person like Anne?

_____

_____

_____

_____

_____

7. *[critical/appreciative]* What do you think makes the diary different from a biography or autobiography? What makes it seem better or worse than a formal work of nonfiction?

_____

_____

_____

_____

_____

_____

Dearest Kit,

I recently witnessed a fierce dogfight between German and English pilots. Unfortunately, a couple of Allied airmen had to jump out of their burning plane. . . .

Although it's undeniably hot, we have to light a fire every other day to burn our vegetable peelings and garbage. We can't throw anything into the trash cans, because the warehouse employees might see it. One small act of carelessness and we're done for!

All college students are being asked to sign an official statement to the effect that they "sympathize with the Germans and approve of the New Order." Eighty percent have decided to obey the dictates of their conscience, but the penalty will be severe. Any student refusing to sign will be sent to a German labor camp. What's to become of the youth of our country if they've all got to do hard labor in Germany? . . .

Yours, Anne

FRIDAY, JULY 23, 1943

. . . Since you've never been through a war, Kitty, and since you know very little about life in hiding, in spite of my letters, let me tell you, just for fun, what we each want to do first when we're able to go outside again.

Margot and Mr. van Daan wish, above all else, to have a hot bath, filled to the brim, which they can lie in for more than half an hour. Mrs. van Daan would like a cake, Dussel* can think of nothing but seeing his Charlotte, and Mother is dying for a cup of real coffee. Father would like to visit Mr. Voskuijl, Peter would go downtown, and as for me, I'd be so overjoyed I wouldn't know where to begin.

Dussel: another friend in hiding in the Annex

Most of all I long to have a home of our own, to be able to move around freely and have someone help me with my homework again, at last. In other words, to go back to school! . . .

MONDAY EVENING, NOVEMBER 8, 1943

Dearest Kitty,

. . . As you can see, I'm currently in the middle of a depression. I couldn't really tell you what set it off, but I think it stems from my cowardice, which confronts me at every turn. This evening, when Bep was still here, the doorbell rang long and loud. I instantly turned white, my stomach churned, and my heart beat wildly—and all because I was afraid.

At night in bed I see myself alone in a dungeon, without Father and Mother. Or I'm roaming the streets, or the Annex is on fire, or they come in the middle of the night to take us away and I crawl under my bed in desperation. I see everything as if it were actually taking place. And to think it might all happen soon! . . .

I simply can't imagine the world will ever be normal again for us. I do talk about "after the war," but it's as if I were talking about a castle in the air, something that can never come true. . . .

Yours, Anne

FRIDAY, DECEMBER 24, 1943

Dear Kitty,

. . . Whenever someone comes in from outside, with the wind in their clothes and the cold on their cheeks, I feel like burying my head under the blankets to keep from thinking, "When will we be allowed to breathe fresh air again?" I can't do that—on the contrary, I have to hold my head up high and put a bold face on things, but the thoughts keep coming anyway. Not just once, but over and over.

Believe me, if you've been shut up for a year and a half, it can get to be too much for you sometimes. But feelings can't be ignored, no matter how unjust or ungrateful they seem. I long to ride a bike, dance, whistle, look at the world, feel young and know that I'm free, and yet I can't let it show. Just imagine what would happen if all eight of us were to feel sorry for ourselves or walk around with the discontent clearly visible on our faces. Where would that get us? I sometimes wonder if anyone will ever understand what I mean, if anyone will ever overlook my ingratitude and not worry about whether or not I'm Jewish and merely see me as a teenager badly in need of some good plain fun. I don't know, and I wouldn't be able to talk about it with anyone, since I'm sure I'd start to cry. Crying can bring relief, as long as you don't cry alone. . . .

Yours, Anne

Dearest Kitty,

. . . As you can no doubt imagine, we often say in despair, "What's the point of the war? Why, oh, why can't people live together peacefully? Why all this destruction?" . . .

I don't believe the war is simply the work of politicians and capitalists. Oh no, the common man is every bit as guilty; otherwise, people and nations would have rebelled long ago! There's a destructive urge in people, the urge to rage, murder and kill. And until all of humanity, without exception, undergoes a metamorphosis, wars will continue to be waged, and everything that has been carefully built up, cultivated and grown will be cut down and destroyed, only to start all over again! . . .

I'm young and have many hidden qualities; I'm young and strong and living through a big adventure; I'm right in the middle of it and can't spend all day complaining because

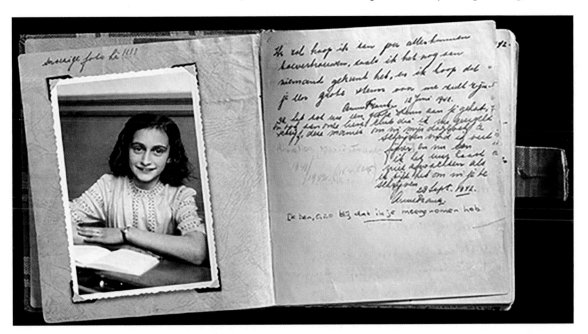

it's impossible to have any fun! I'm blessed with many things: happiness, a cheerful disposition and strength. Every day I feel myself maturing, I feel liberation drawing near. I feel the beauty of nature and goodness of the people around me. Every day I think what a fascinating and amusing adventure this is! With all that, why should I despair?

Yours, Anne M. Frank

ABOUT THE AUTHOR

Anne Frank (1929–45) was born in Frankfurt, Germany. In 1933 the family emigrated from Germany to Holland (the Netherlands) to escape the Nazis. By 1940, however, the Nazis had occupied Holland and required all Jews to wear the yellow Jewish star of David. Anne's life changed drastically in July of 1942 when her older sister, Margot, received an order to report for deportation. At this point, Anne's father knew that it was time to put into action the plan that he had prepared for such a time.

The family, along with four other people, spent the following three years in a secret place. In August 1944 the eight people were arrested and imprisoned in Amsterdam. From there they were taken to Auschwitz and then to Bergen-Belsen. Both Margot and Anne died of typhus at Bergen-Belsen in 1945. Anne became well-known after her death through the publication of her diary. Her writings give readers an insight into the struggles and hopes of a teenage girl who lived during the Nazi takeover of central Europe.

On the next page is a chart in which the inhabitants of the Annex are listed (along with the names Anne gave them in parentheses). On August 4, 1944, several members of the secret police arrived at the warehouse annex. They arrested the eight people in hiding and two others who had helped in hiding the eight. These people were sent to various prison camps without a trial.

Annex Chart

Margot Frank	Anne's sister	arrested at the Annex	taken to a prison camp; later transferred to Auschwitz and then to Bergen-Belsen	died in prison camp of typhus a few days before Anne in February or March of 1945
Otto Frank	Anne's father	arrested at the Annex	taken to a prison camp; later transferred to Auschwitz	survived Auschwitz; liberated and returned to Amsterdam; died 1980
Edith Frank	Anne's mother	arrested at the Annex	taken to prison camp in Auschwitz	died from hunger and exhaustion in 1945
Hermann van Pels (van Daan)	Otto Frank's business partner and friend	arrested at the Annex	taken to prison camp in Auschwitz	gassed to death in 1944 (according to testimony of Otto Frank)
Auguste van Pels (Petronells van Daan)	Hermann van Pels's wife	arrested at the Annex	taken to a prison camp and then transferred to many other prison camps	death date unknown, did not survive the war
Peter van Pels (van Daan)	son of Hermann and Auguste	arrested at the Annex	part of the death march from Auschwitz	died in 1945 just three days before the camp was liberated
Fritz Pfeffer (Albert Dussel)	friend of family in hiding in the Annex	arrested at the Annex	taken to Neuengamme concentration camp	died in camp in December 1944
Johannes Kleiman	friend who helped hide the Franks	arrested at the Annex	taken to prison camp without a trial	released because of poor health; died in 1959
Victor Kugler	worked in Otto Frank's office; helped hide the Franks	arrested at the Annex	taken to prison camp without a trial	escaped in 1945; settled in Canada where he died in 1989
Miep Gies	secretary at Otto Frank's office; helped hide the Franks; hid Anne's diary until her father's return	not arrested at the Annex		lives in Amsterdam
Jan Gies	husband of Miep	not arrested at the Annex		died in 1993
Elizabeth (Bep) Voskuijl	worker in Otto Frank's office; go-between with the outside world during their hiding	not arrested at the Annex		died in 1983
Mr. Voskuijl	Elizabeth's father; worked in the warehouse; built bookcase to conceal Annex door	not arrested at the Annex		

THINKING ZONE

The first set of diary entries that you read introduced you to Anne and made clear the reason that the Franks and others hid themselves in the Annex. Much of the content of the first set of entries deals with the concrete facts of Anne's life: when and where she was born, where she lived, what her father did for a living, and so on. But Anne's diary also discusses abstract feelings and emotions such as loneliness, love, and fear. An **abstract concept** is one that cannot be perceived by the five senses but must instead be discussed in general terms by describing its attributes or its effects on a concrete image. For example, since no one can see, smell, taste, touch, or hear happiness, a writer must describe how a person who is happy acts or looks or sounds. Writers attempt to assign concrete images to abstract concepts when they write. Think of the famous Burns line "My luve is like a red, red rose," in which he describes love (abstract) as both a June rose (concrete) and a sweet melody (concrete). As you look again at the diary excerpts, notice how Anne chooses to communicate the various abstract concepts she includes.

1. *[interpretive]* Besides their obvious danger, what other hardships and difficulties do Anne and her family face while hiding in the Annex? How does Anne cope with those difficulties?

   _____

   _____

   _____

   _____

   _____

   _____

2. *[interpretive/critical]* In her November 8, 1943, entry, Anne talks about her depressed moods. To what does she attribute her depression?

   _____

   _____

3. *[critical]* What are some of the concrete images Anne uses to describe her fear (an **abstract concept**)?

_____

_____

_____

_____

4. *[literal]* On July 23, 1943, Anne writes of the things that those in the Annex would want to do first upon going outside. What does Anne want most? What would you want to do first were you in her position?

_____

_____

_____

5. *[interpretive/critical]* What passages of the diary reflect that Anne wrote her diary "in a variety of moods" and often seemed to contradict herself in her feelings and opinions?

_____

_____

_____

_____

_____

6. *[critical]* What do you view as Anne's strengths as a person? What are her weaknesses?

_____

_____

_____

_____

_____

_____

_____

OPPORTUNITY

EDWARD ROWLAND SILL

As you read these poems, think about the lessons that they teach. How do their themes reflect on the stories that you have read in this unit? How might it be said that one poem cautions the reader while the other reassures?

This I beheld or dreamed it in a dream:—
There spread a cloud of dust along a plain;
And underneath the cloud, or in it, raged
A furious battle, and men yelled, and swords
Shocked upon swords and shields. A prince's banner   5
Wavered, then staggered backward, hemmed by foes.
A craven* hung along the battle's edge,
And thought, "Had I a sword of keener steel—
That blue blade that the king's son bears,—but this
Blunt thing!—" he snapt and flung it from his hand,   10
And lowering crept away and left the field.
Then came the king's son, wounded, sore bestead,
And weaponless, and saw the broken sword,
Hilt-buried in the dry and trodden sand,
And ran and snatched it, and with battle-shout   15
Lifted afresh he hewed his enemy down,
And saved a great cause that heroic day.

craven: coward

ABOUT THE AUTHOR

Edward Sill (1841–87), who was born in Connecticut, experienced a series of tragedies while he was still quite young. In 1847 his only brother drowned, and during the next six years, both his mother and father died. So, orphaned at the age of twelve, the young Sill moved to Ohio to live with his uncle and remained there until he was ready to attend college. After graduating from Yale and spending a few years in California, Sill went to Harvard to study theology. Sadly, this educational experience led only to his questioning whether one can know that God exists (agnosticism). Later Sill became both a teacher and a writer and spent his last years writing essays. His writing did not make him famous during his lifetime; however, several collections of poetry have been published since his death. Among the best known of his poems are "The Fool's Prayer" and "Opportunity."

THE MEANING OF THE LOOK

ELIZABETH BARRETT BROWNING

This poem is full of biblical allusion. Do you recognize the passages Browning is alluding to?

I think that look of Christ might seem to say—
"Thou Peter! art thou then a common stone
Which I at last must break my heart upon,
For all God's charge to his high angels may
Guard my foot better? Did I yesterday   5
Wash thy feet, my beloved, that they should run
Quick to deny me 'neath the morning sun?
And do thy kisses, like the rest, betray?
The cock crows coldly.—Go, and manifest
A late contrition*, but no bootless* fear!   10
For when thy final need is dreariest,
Thou shalt not be denied, as I am here;
My voice to God and angels shall attest*,
Because I KNOW this man, let him be clear."

contrition: repentance

bootless: unprofitable, useless

attest: affirm to be correct or true

The rooster and Saint Peter denying. Detail from *Saint Peter's Denial* (15-03-02/39). Mosaic (6th) S. Apollinare Nuovo, Ravenna, Italy
Erich Lessing/Art Resource, NY

ABOUT THE AUTHOR

After injuring her spine at the age of fifteen, Elizabeth Barrett Browning (1806–61) became a semi-invalid who struggled with health problems for the rest of her life. Much of her life was devoted to her writing, which earned her recognition among her peers as the foremost female poet. Although she was not known as a feminist, the famous Englishwoman fought for recognition as a writer without regard to gender in an era when many looked upon women with disregard, and some people even considered educated women to be dangerous.

Writing remained Elizabeth's main love in life until a favorable reference to Robert Browning's writing in one of her poems led to a correspondence that in turn sparked a romance. Four months after his first letter to her, Browning and Barrett met, and the next day Browning declared his love for her. For a year they wrote, sometimes as much as twice a day, and he called on her every few days. They eloped in 1846 and lived happily in Italy until Elizabeth's death in 1861.

Robert and Elizabeth's relationship provided the inspiration for her *Sonnets from the Portuguese*. She is also well-known for the conversational style of her letters, which have been published and widely read. Modern critics disagree about the quality of her writing, but perhaps the greatest proof of her place among the great writers is that she is still a topic of debate more than a century after her death.

THINKING ZONE

Occasionally within rhymed poetry, the poet may attempt to pair two lines whose ending words do not rhyme perfectly but instead have similar sounding endings. When this occurs, a poet is using **slant rhyme**. Emily Dickinson is well-known for employing slant rhyme in her poetry. For instance, in the last stanza of her poem "I Like to See It Lap the Miles," she ends two lines with the words *star* and *door*. Sometimes a poet repeats terminal consonant sounds in lines of poetry, as in "That the battle was lo*st*; and the death-li*st* / Held many a loved one's name" in "Emily Geiger." This device is known as **consonance**.

Between rhymed, metered poetry and free verse, there is a type of poetry that contains meter but does not rhyme. This type of poetry is known as **blank verse**. Blank verse contains five iambic feet per line. Generally, if a poem does not rhyme but appears to be uniform in line length throughout, there is a good chance that the poem may be blank verse. Occasionally, there may be a slight change from the iambic pattern in a poem written in blank verse, but overall the poem will contain five iambic feet per line. Much of William Shakespeare's playwriting is in blank verse.

1. *[critical]* Find three lines in which **consonance** occurs in "Opportunity." List the words that exhibit consonance in each of those lines.

   _____

   _____

   _____

   _____

2. *[interpretive]* What is the main difference in the viewpoints of the prince and the coward that allows the prince to accomplish great things with the sword that the coward cannot accomplish?

   _____

   _____

   _____

   _____

3. *[critical]* What does "Opportunity" teach the reader about how he should respond to challenging situations? What might a Christian response be to the poem?

_____

_____

_____

_____

_____

_____

_____

4. *[interpretive]* "The Meaning of the Look" is an allusion to what biblical event?

_____

_____

5. *[interpretive]* How is the ending of "The Meaning of the Look" ironic? Why is it at the same time reassuring?

_____

_____

_____

_____

6. *[interpretive]* Where does **slant rhyme** occur in "The Meaning of the Look"?

_____

_____

7. *[interpretive]* Which of the two poems exhibits **blank verse**? How can you tell?

_____

_____

_____

_____

A Christmas Carol

Charles Dickens

"Bah! . . . Humbug!" Scrooge's well-known response perfectly expresses his flawed viewpoint of Christmas, of mankind, and of life. It will take some very special visitors to change the detestable opinions of Dickens's "squeezing, . . . grasping, . . . clutching, covetous" protagonist.

Stave I
Marley's Ghost

Marley was dead: to begin with. There is no doubt whatever about that. Old Marley was as dead as a door-nail.

Scrooge knew he was dead? Of course he did. How could it be otherwise? Scrooge and he were partners for I don't know how many years.

Scrooge never painted out Old Marley's name. There it stood, years afterwards, above the warehouse door: Scrooge and Marley. Sometimes people new to the business called Scrooge Scrooge, and sometimes Marley, but he answered to both names: it was all the same to him.

Oh! But he was a tight-fisted hand at the grindstone, Scrooge! a squeezing, wrenching, grasping, scraping, clutching, covetous, old sinner. Hard and sharp as flint, from which no steel had ever struck out generous fire; secret, and self-contained, and solitary as an oyster. The cold within him froze his old features, nipped his pointed nose, shrivelled his cheek, stiffened his gait;* made his eyes red, his thin lips blue; and spoke out shrewdly in his grating voice.

gait: manner of walking

Nobody ever stopped him in the street to say, "My dear Scrooge, how are you? When will you come to see me?" No beggars implored him to bestow a trifle, no children asked him what it was o'clock, no man or woman ever once in all his life inquired the way to such and such a place, of Scrooge. Even the blind men's dogs appeared to know him; and when they saw him coming on, would tug their owners into doorways and up courts; and then would wag their tails as though they said, "No eye at all is better than an evil eye, dark master!"

But what did Scrooge care? It was the very thing he liked.

Once upon a time—of all the good days in the year, on Christmas Eve—old Scrooge sat busy in his counting-house. It was cold, bleak, biting weather, and he could hear the people in the court outside go wheezing up and down, beating their hands upon their breasts, and stamping their feet upon the pavement-stones to warm them. The City clocks had only just gone three, but it was quite dark already: it had not been light all day: and candles were flaring in the windows of the neighboring offices, like ruddy smears upon the palpable* brown air.

palpable: capable of being touched

The door of Scrooge's counting-house was open that he might keep his eye upon his clerk, who in a dismal little cell beyond was copying letters. Scrooge had a very small fire, but the clerk's fire was so very much

smaller that it looked like one coal. But he couldn't replenish it, for Scrooge kept the coal-box in his own room; and so surely as the clerk came in with the shovel, the master predicted it would be necessary for them to part. Wherefore the clerk put on his white comforter, and tried to warm himself at the candle.

"A merry Christmas, uncle! God save you!" cried a cheerful voice. It was the voice of Scrooge's nephew, who came upon him so quickly that this was the first intimation he had of his approach.

"Bah!" said Scrooge. "Humbug!"*

Humbug: a term meaning "all is deceit or fraud"

He had so heated himself with rapid walking in the fog and frost, this nephew of Scrooge's, that he was all in a glow; his face was ruddy and handsome; his eyes sparkled, and his breath smoked again.

"Christmas a humbug, uncle!" said Scrooge's nephew. "You don't mean that, I am sure."

"I do," said Scrooge. "Merry Christmas! What right have you to be merry? What reason have you to be merry? You're poor enough."

"Come, then," returned the nephew, gayly. "What right have you to be dismal?* What reason have you to be morose?* You're rich enough."

---

dismal: depressing

morose: gloomy

Scrooge having no better answer ready on the spur of the moment, said, "Bah!" again; and followed it up with "Humbug."

"Don't be cross, uncle," said the nephew.

"What else can I be," returned the uncle, "when I live in such a world of fools as this? Merry Christmas! Out upon merry Christmas! What's Christmas time to you but a time for paying bills without money; a time for finding yourself a year older, but not an hour richer? If I could work my will," said Scrooge, indignantly, "every idiot who goes about with 'Merry Christmas' on his lips should be boiled with his own pudding, and buried with a stake of holly through his heart. He should!"

"Uncle!" pleaded the nephew.

"Nephew!" returned the uncle, sternly, "keep Christmas in your own way, and let me keep it in mine."

"Keep it!" repeated Scrooge's nephew. "But you don't keep it."

"Let me leave it alone, then," said Scrooge. "Much good may it do you! Much good it has ever done you!"

"There are many things from which I might have derived good, but which I have not profited, I dare say," returned the nephew: "Christmas among the rest. But I am sure I have always thought of Christmas time, when it has come round—apart from the veneration* due to its sacred name and origin, if anything belonging to it can be apart from that—as a good time: a kind, forgiving, charitable, pleasant time: the only time I know of, in the long calendar of the year, when men and women seem by one consent to open their shut-up hearts freely, and to think of people below them as if they really were fellow-passengers to the grave, and not another race of creatures bound on other journeys. And therefore, uncle, though it has never put a scrap of gold or silver in my pocket, I believe it has done me good, and will do me good; and I say, God bless it!"

veneration: reverence

The clerk involuntarily applauded.

"Let me hear another sound from *you*," said Scrooge, "and you'll keep your Christmas by losing your situation.* You're quite a powerful speaker, Sir," he added, turning to his nephew. "I wonder you don't go into Parliament."

situation: job

"Don't be angry, uncle. Come! Dine with us tomorrow."

Scrooge said that he would not.

"But why?" cried Scrooge's nephew. "Why?"

"Why did you get married?" said Scrooge.

"Because I fell in love."

"Because you fell in love!" growled Scrooge, as if that were the only one thing in the world more ridiculous than a merry Christmas. "Good afternoon!"

"Nay, uncle, but you never came to see me before that happened. Why give it as a reason for not coming now?"

"Good afternoon," said Scrooge.

"I am sorry, with all my heart, to find you so resolute. We have never had any quarrel, to which I have been a party. But I have made the trial in a homage to Christmas, and I'll keep my Christmas humour to the last. So a merry Christmas, uncle!"

"Good afternoon!" said Scrooge.

"And a Happy New Year!"

His nephew left the room without an angry word, notwithstanding. He stopped at the outer door to bestow the greetings of the season on the clerk, who cold as he was, was warmer than Scrooge; for he returned them cordially.

"There's another fellow," muttered Scrooge, who overheard him: "my clerk, with fifteen shilling a-week, and a wife and family, talking about a merry Christmas."

Scrooge's nephew had let two other people in. They were portly* gentlemen, pleasant to behold, and now stood, with their hats off, in Scrooge's office. They had books and papers in their hands, and bowed to him.

portly: stout

"Scrooge and Marley's, I believe," said one of the gentlemen, referring to his list. "Have I the pleasure of addressing Mr. Scrooge, or Mr. Marley?"

"Mr. Marley has been dead seven years," Scrooge replied. "He died seven years ago, this very night."

"We have no doubt his liberality* is well represented by his surviving partner," said the gentleman, presenting his credentials.

liberality: generosity

It certainly was; for they had been two kindred spirits. At the ominous* word "liberality," Scrooge frowned, and shook his head, and handed the credentials back.

---
ominous: threatening

"At this festive season of the year, Mr. Scrooge," said the gentleman, taking up a pen, "it is more than usually desirable that we should make some slight provision for the poor and destitute, who suffer greatly at the present time. Many thousands are in want of common necessaries; hundreds of thousands are in want of common comforts, Sir."

"Are there no prisons?"* asked Scrooge.

---
prisons: debtors' prison; individuals or entire families were put
  here for not paying their debts

"Plenty of prisons," said the gentleman, laying down the pen again.

"And the Union workhouses?" demanded Scrooge. "Are they still in operation?"

"They are," returned the gentleman.

"Oh! I was afraid, from what you said at first, that something had occurred to stop them in their useful course," said Scrooge. "I'm very glad to hear it."

"Under the impression that they scarcely furnish Christian cheer of mind or body to the multitude," returned the gentleman, "a few of us are endeavouring to raise a fund to buy the Poor some meat and drink, and means of warmth. We choose this time, because it is a time, of all others, when Want is keenly felt, and Abundance rejoices. What shall I put you down for?"

"Nothing!" Scrooge replied.

"You wish to be anonymous?"

"I wish to be left alone," said Scrooge. "Since you ask me what I wish, gentlemen, that is my answer. I don't make merry myself at Christmas, and I can't afford to make idle people merry. I help to support the establishments I have mentioned: they cost enough: and those who are badly off must go there."

"Many can't go there; and many would rather die."

"If they would rather die," said Scrooge, "they had better do it, and decrease the surplus* population."

---
surplus: excess

Seeing clearly that it would be useless to pursue their point, the gentlemen withdrew.

Meanwhile a scant young singer gnawed by hungry cold as bones are gnawed by dogs, stooped down at Scrooge's keyhole to regale* him with a Christmas carol: but at the first sound of

"God bless you, merry gentlemen!
May nothing you dismay!"

Scrooge seized a ruler with such energy of action, that the singer fled in terror.

---
regale: entertain

At length the hour of shutting up the counting-house arrived. With an ill-will Scrooge dismounted from his stool, and tacitly* admitted the fact to the expectant clerk, who instantly snuffed his candle out, and put on his hat.

---
tacitly: without words

"You'll want all day tomorrow, I suppose?" said Scrooge.

"If quite convenient, Sir."

"It's not convenient," said Scrooge, "and it's not fair. If I was to stop half-a-crown for it, you'd think yourself ill-used, though you don't think *me* ill-used, when I pay a day's wages for no work. But I suppose you must have the whole day. Be here all the earlier next morning."

The clerk promised that he would; and Scrooge walked out with a growl.

Scrooge took his melancholy dinner in his usual melancholy tavern; and having read all the newspapers, and beguiled* the rest of the evening with his banker's-book, went home.

---
beguiled: pleasantly passed

He lived in chambers which had once belonged to his deceased partner.* Now, it is a fact, that there was nothing at all particular about the knocker on the door, except that it was very large. It is also a fact, that Scrooge had seen it, night and morning, during his whole residence in that place; also that Scrooge had as little of what is called fancy about him as any man in the City of London. Let it also be borne in mind that Scrooge had not bestowed one thought on Marley since his last mention of his seven-years' dead partner that afternoon. And then let any man explain to me, if he can, how it happened that Scrooge, having his key in the lock of the door, saw in the knocker, not a knocker, but Marley's face.

---
deceased partner: Marley

Marley's face. It was not in shadow as the other objects in the yard were, but had a dismal light about it like a bad lobster in a dark cellar. It was not angry or ferocious, but looked at Scrooge as Marley used to look: with ghostly spectacles turned up on its ghostly forehead. The hair was curiously stirred, as if by breath or hot air; and though the eyes were wide open, they were perfectly motionless. That, and its livid* color, made it horrible.

---
livid: pale

As Scrooge looked fixedly at this phenomenon, it was a knocker again.

To say that he was not startled, or that his blood was not conscious of a terrible sensation to which it had been a stranger from infancy, would be untrue. But he put his hand upon the key he had relinquished, turned it sturdily, walked in, and lighted his candle.

He *did* pause before he shut the door; and he *did* look cautiously behind it first, as if he half-expected to be terrified with the sight of Marley's pigtail sticking out into the hall. But there was nothing on the back of the door, except the screws and nuts that held the knocker on; so he said "Pooh, pooh!" and closed it with a bang. The sound resounded through the house like thunder. He fastened the door, and walked across the hall, and up the stairs: slowly too: trimming his candle as he went.

Half-a-dozen gas-lamps out of the street wouldn't have lighted the entry too well, so you may suppose that it was pretty dark.

Up Scrooge went, not caring a button for that: darkness is cheap, and Scrooge liked it. He walked through his rooms to see that all was right. He had just enough recollection of the face to desire to do that.

Sitting-room, bedroom. All as they should be. Quite satisfied, he closed his door, and locked himself in; double-locked himself in, which was not his custom. Thus secured against surprise, he took off his cravat;* put on his dressing-gown and slippers, and his nightcap; and sat down before the fire to take his gruel.

---

cravat: neck scarf

It was a very low fire indeed; nothing on such a bitter night. He was obliged to sit close to it, and brood over it, before he could extract the least sensation of warmth from such a handful of fuel.

His glance happened to rest upon a bell, a disused bell, that hung in the room, and communicated for some purpose now forgotten with a chamber in the highest story of the building. It was with great astonishment, and with a strange, inexplicable dread, that as he looked he saw this bell begin to swing. It swung so softly in the outset that it scarcely made a sound; but soon it rang out loudly, and so did every bell in the house.

This might have lasted half a minute, or a minute, but it seemed an hour. The bells ceased as they had begun, together. They were succeeded by a clanking noise, deep down below; as if some person were dragging a heavy chain over the casks in the wine-merchant's cellar. Scrooge then remembered to have heard that ghosts in haunted houses were described as dragging chains.

The cellar-door flew open with a booming sound, and then he heard the noise much louder, on the floors below; then coming up the stairs; then coming straight towards his door.

"It's humbug!" said Scrooge. "I won't believe it."

His color changed though, when, without a pause, it came on through the heavy door, and passed into the room before his eyes. Upon its coming in, the dying flame leaped up, as though it cried "I know him! Marley's Ghost!" and fell again.

The same face: the very same. Marley in his pigtail, usual waistcoat, tights and boots. The chain he drew was clasped about his middle. It was long, and wound about him like a tail; and it was made (for Scrooge observed it closely) of cashboxes, keys, padlocks, ledgers, deeds, and heavy purses wrought in steel. His body was transparent; so that Scrooge, observing him, and looking through his waistcoat, could see the two buttons on his coat behind.

He looked the phantom through and through, and saw it standing before him; though he felt the chilling influence of its death-cold eyes; and marked the very texture of the folded kerchief bound about its head and chin, which wrapper he had not observed before: he was still incredulous* and fought against his senses.

---

incredulous: unbelieving

"How now!" said Scrooge, caustic* and cold as ever. "What do you want with me?"

---

caustic: bitter

"Much!"—Marley's voice, no doubt about it.

"Who are you?"

"Ask me who I was."

"Who *were* you then?" said Scrooge, raising his voice.

"In life I was your partner, Jacob Marley."

"Can you—can you sit down?" asked Scrooge, looking doubtfully at him.

"I can."

"Do it then."

The Ghost sat down on the opposite side of the fireplace.

"You don't believe in me," observed the Ghost.

"I don't," said Scrooge.

"What evidence would you have of my reality beyond that of your senses?"

"I don't know," said Scrooge.

"Why do you doubt your senses?"

"Because," said Scrooge, "a little thing affects them. A slight disorder of the stomach makes them cheats. You may be an undigested bit of beef, a blot of mustard, a crumb of cheese, a fragment of an underdone potato. There's more of gravy than of grave about you, whatever you are!"

Scrooge was not much in the habit of cracking jokes, nor did he feel, in his heart, by any means waggish* then. The truth is, that he tried to be smart, as a means of distracting his own attention, and keeping down his terror; for the spectre's* voice disturbed the very marrow in his bones.

waggish: humorous

spectre: ghost

"You see this toothpick?" said Scrooge, wishing to divert the vision's stony gaze from himself.

"I do," replied the Ghost.

"You are not looking at it," said Scrooge.

"But I see it," said the Ghost, "notwithstanding."

"Well!" returned Scrooge. "I have but to swallow this, and be for the rest of my days persecuted by a legion of goblins, all of my own creation. Humbug, I tell you—humbug!"

At this the spirit raised a frightful cry, and shook its chain with such a dismal and appalling noise, that Scrooge held on tight to his chair, to save himself from falling in a swoon. But how much greater was his horror, when the phantom taking off the bandage round its head, as if it were too warm to wear indoors, its lower jaw dropped down upon its breast!

Scrooge fell upon his knees, and clasped his hands before his face.

"Mercy!" he said. "Dreadful apparition, why do you trouble me?"

"Man of the worldly mind!" replied the Ghost, "do you believe in me or not?"

"I do," said Scrooge. "I must. But why do spirits walk the earth, and why do they come to me?"

"It is required of every man," the Ghost returned, "that the spirit within him should walk abroad among his fellowmen, and travel far and wide; and if that spirit goes not forth in life, it is condemned to do so after death. It is doomed to wander through the world—oh, woe is me!—and witness what it cannot share, but might have shared on earth, and turned to happiness!" Again the spectre raised a cry, and shook its chain, and wrung its shadowy hands.

"You are fettered," said Scrooge, trembling. "Tell me why?"

"I wear the chain I forged in life," replied the Ghost.

"I made it link by link, and yard by yard; I girded it on of my own free will, and of my own free will I wore it. Is its pattern strange to *you*?"

Scrooge trembled more and more.

"Or would you know," pursued the Ghost, "the weight and length of the strong coil you bear yourself? It was full as heavy and as long as this, seven Christmas Eves ago. You have laboured on it since. It is a ponderous chain."

Scrooge glanced about him on the floor, in the expectation of finding himself surrounded by some fifty or sixty fathoms* of iron cable: but he could see nothing.

fathoms: one fathom equals six feet

"Jacob," he said imploringly. "Old Jacob Marley, tell me more. Speak comfort to me, Jacob."

"Seven years dead," mused Scrooge. "And travelling all the time!"

"The whole time," said the Ghost. "No rest, no peace. Incessant* torture of remorse."

"You travel fast?" said Scrooge.

"On the wings of the wind," replied the Ghost.

"You might have got over a great quantity of ground in seven years," said Scrooge.

The Ghost, on hearing this, set up another cry, and clanked its chain hideously in the dead silence of the night.

"Oh! captive, bound, and doubled-ironed," cried the phantom, "not to know, that ages of incessant labour, by immortal creatures, for this earth must pass into eternity before the good of which it is susceptible is all developed. Not to know that any Christian spirit working kindly in its little sphere, whatever it may be, will find its mortal life too short for its vast means of usefulness. Not to know that no space of regret can make amends for one life's opportunity misused! Yet such was I! Oh! such was I!"

"But you were always a good man of business, Jacob," faltered Scrooge, who began to apply this to himself.

"Business!" cried the Ghost, wringing its hands again. "Mankind was my business. The common welfare was my business; charity, mercy, forbearance, and benevolence were all my business. The dealings of my trade were but a drop of water in the comprehensive ocean of my business!"

It held up its chain at arm's length, as if that were the cause of all its unavailing grief, and flung it heavily upon the ground again.

Scrooge was very much dismayed to hear the spectre going on at this rate, and began to quake exceedingly.

"I have none to give," the Ghost replied. "It comes from other regions, Ebenezer Scrooge, and is conveyed by other ministers, to other kinds of men. Nor can I tell you what I would. A very little more is all permitted to me. I cannot rest, I cannot stay, I cannot linger anywhere. My spirit never walked beyond our counting-house—mark me!—in life my spirit never roved beyond the narrow limits of our money-changing hole; and weary journeys lie before me!"

It was a habit with Scrooge, whenever he became thoughtful, to put his hands in his breeches pockets. Pondering on what the Ghost had said, he did so now, but without lifting up his eyes, or getting off his knees.

"You must have been very slow about it, Jacob," Scrooge observed, in a business-like manner, though with humility and deference.

"Slow!" the Ghost repeated.

"Hear me!" cried the Ghost. "My time is nearly gone."

"I will," said Scrooge. "But don't be hard upon me! Don't be flowery, Jacob! Pray!"*

Pray: expression of pleading; "I beg of you"

"How it is that I appear before you in a shape that you can see, I may not tell. I have sat invisible beside you many and many a day."

It was not an agreeable idea. Scrooge shivered, and wiped the perspiration from his brow.

"That is no light part of my penance," pursued the Ghost. "I am here tonight to warn you, that you have yet a chance and hope of escaping my fate. You will be haunted by Three Spirits."

Scrooge's countenance fell almost as low as the Ghost's had done.

"I—I think I'd rather not," said Scrooge.

"Without their visits," said the Ghost, "you cannot hope to shun the path I tread. Expect the first tomorrow, when the bell tolls one."

"Couldn't I take 'em all at once, and have it over, Jacob?" hinted Scrooge.

"Expect the second one the next night at the same hour. The third upon the next night when the last stroke of twelve has ceased to vibrate. Look to see me no more; and look that, for your own sake, you remember what has passed between us!"

When it had said these words, the spectre took its wrapper* from the table, and bound it round its head, as before. Scrooge knew this, by the smart* sounds its teeth made, when the jaws were brought together by the bandage.

---

wrapper: loose dressing gown

smart: sharp

The apparition walked backward from him; and at every step it took, the window raised itself a little, so that when the spectre reached it, it was wide open. It beckoned Scrooge to approach, which he did. When they were within two paces of each other, Marley's Ghost held up its hand, warning him to come no nearer. Scrooge stopped.

Not so much in obedience, as in surprise and fear: for on the raising of the hand, he became sensible of confused noises in the air; incoherent sounds of lamentation and regret; wailings inexpressibly sorrowful and self-accusatory. The spectre, after listening for a moment, joined in the mournful dirge;* and floated out upon the bleak, dark night.

---

dirge: funeral hymn or lament

Whether these creatures faded into mist, or mist enshrouded* them, he could not tell. But they and their spirit voices faded together; and the night became as it had been when he walked home.

---

enshrouded: covered

Scrooge closed the window, and examined the door by which the Ghost had entered. It was double-locked, as he had locked it with his own hands, and the bolts were undisturbed. He tried to say "Humbug!" but stopped at the first syllable. And being much in need of repose, went straight to bed, without undressing, and fell asleep upon the instant.

THINKING ZONE

Now that you have learned about many of the various types of literary devices that authors use to communicate and have had experience analyzing the plot, characters, setting, and conflict of various literary works, you should be able to put those skills to good use when studying this famous story. Though you may have seen many film and television versions of *A Christmas Carol* or read a children's adaptation, a careful reading of Dickens's original language, combined with your knowledge of symbolism and other literary elements, will enhance your enjoyment of the story and help you to discover significant details you probably have not noticed before.

A Christmas Carol is one of the most famous novellas in all of English literature. A **novella** is a prose narrative that is longer than a short story but shorter than the typical novel, usually about two hundred pages. Novellas may have chapters or other kinds of subdivisions that make them similar to novels.

1. *[literal/interpretive]* To reveal Scrooge's character to the reader, much of paragraph four employs metaphor and simile. Identify at least one of each and explain what they reveal about Scrooge.

   _____

   _____

   _____

   _____

   _____

2. *[interpretive]* What is the authorial tone toward Scrooge?

   _____

   _____

3. *[interpretive]* How is the author's use of the cold at the beginning of the story symbolic? How do the setting and atmosphere reflect Scrooge's viewpoint?

_____

_____

_____

_____

4. *[interpretive]* How do Dickens's descriptions of Scrooge's nephew and clerk contrast symbolically with Scrooge?

_____

_____

_____

_____

_____

_____

5. *[interpretive]* What is ironic about the fact that Scrooge is rich but eats gruel and keeps a low fire?

_____

_____

_____

6. *[interpretive/critical]* Marley tells Scrooge that Scrooge has forged himself a "ponderous chain" much like the one Marley must wear. What might the chain symbolize?

_____

_____

_____

7. *[critical]* Has Scrooge developed as a character by the end of Stave I of the **novella**? Explain.

_____

_____

_____

STAVE II
THE FIRST OF THE THREE SPIRITS

When Scrooge awoke, it was so dark, that looking out of bed, he could scarcely distinguish the transparent window from the walls of his chamber. He was endeavouring to pierce the darkness with his ferret* eyes, when the chimes of a neighboring church struck the four quarters. So he listened for the hour.

---

ferret: weasel-like

To his great astonishment the heavy bell went on from six to seven, and from seven to eight, and regularly up to twelve; then stopped. Twelve! It was past two when he went to bed. The clock was wrong. An icicle must have got into the works. Twelve!

"Why, it isn't possible," said Scrooge, "that I can have slept through a whole day and far into another night. It isn't possible that anything has happened to the sun, and this is twelve at noon!"

The idea being an alarming one, he scrambled out of bed, and groped his way to the window. All he could make out was, that it was still very foggy and extremely cold, and that there was no noise of people running to and fro, and making a great stir, as there unquestionably would have been if night had beaten off bright day, and taken possession of the world. This was a great relief.

Scrooge went to bed again, and thought, and thought, and thought it over and over and over, and could make nothing of it. Marley's Ghost bothered him exceedingly. "Was it a dream or not?"

As Scrooge lay in this state he remembered, on a sudden, that the Ghost had warned him of a visitation when the bell tolled one. He resolved to lie awake until the hour was passed; and, considering that he could no more go to sleep than go to Heaven, this was perhaps the wisest resolution in his power.

The quarter was so long, that he was more than once convinced he must have sunk into a doze unconsciously, and missed the clock. At length it broke upon his listening ear.

"Ding, dong!"

"A quarter past," said Scrooge, counting.

"Ding, dong!"

"Half-past!" said Scrooge.

"Ding, dong!"

"A quarter to it," said Scrooge.

"Ding, dong!"

"The hour itself," said Scrooge, triumphantly, "and nothing else!"

He spoke before the hour bell sounded, which it now did with a deep, dull, hollow,

melancholy *One*. Light flashed up in the room upon the instant, and the curtains of his bed were drawn.

The curtains of his bed were drawn aside, I tell you, by a hand, and Scrooge, starting up into a half-recumbent* attitude, found himself face to face with the unearthly visitor who drew them.

recumbent: reclining

It was a strange figure—like a child: yet not so like a child as like an old man, viewed through some supernatural medium,* which gave him the appearance of having receded from the view, and being diminished to a child's proportions. Its hair, which hung about its neck and down its back, was white as if with age; and yet the face had not a wrinkle in it, and the tenderest bloom was on the skin. The arms were very long and muscular; the hands the same, as if its hold were of uncommon strength. Its legs and feet, most delicately formed, were, like those upper members, bare. It wore a tunic of the purest white; and round its waist was bound a lustrous* belt, the sheen of which was beautiful. It held a branch of fresh green holly in its hand; and, in singular contradiction of that wintry emblem, had its dress trimmed with summer flowers. But the strangest thing about it was, that from the crown of its head there sprang a bright clear jet of light, by which all this was visible; and which was doubtless the occasion of its using, in its duller moments, a great extinguisher* for a cap, which it now held under its arm.

medium: means

lustrous: radiant

extinguisher: a candle snuffer

Even this, though, when Scrooge looked at it with increasing steadiness, was not its strangest quality. For as its belt sparkled

and glittered now in one part and now in another, and what was light one instant, at another time was dark, so the figure itself fluctuated in its distinctness: being now a thing with one arm, now with one leg, now with twenty legs, now a pair of legs without a head, now a head without a body.

"Are you the Spirit, Sir, whose coming was foretold to me?" asked Scrooge.

"I am!"

The voice was soft and gentle.

"Who, and what are you?" Scrooge demanded.

"I am the Ghost of Christmas Past."

"Long past?" inquired Scrooge: observant of its dwarfish stature.

"No. Your past."

Perhaps, Scrooge could not have told anybody why, if anybody could have asked him: but he had a special desire to see the Spirit in his cap; and begged him to be covered.

"What!" exclaimed the Ghost, "would you so soon put out, with worldly hands, the light I give? Is it not enough that you are one of those whose passions make this cap, and force me through whole trains of years to wear it low upon my brow!"

Scrooge reverently disclaimed all intention to offend, or any knowledge of having wilfully "bonneted" the Spirit at any period of his life. He then made bold to inquire what business brought him there.

"Your welfare!" said the Ghost.

It put out its strong hand and clasped him gently by the arm.

"Rise! and walk with me!"

It would have been in vain for Scrooge to plead that the weather and the hour were not adapted to pedestrian purposes; that bed was warm, and the thermometer a long way below freezing; that he was clad but lightly in his slippers, dressing-gown, and nightcap; and that he had a cold upon him at that time. The grasp, though gentle as a woman's hand, was not to be resisted. He rose: but finding that the Spirit made towards the window, clasped its robe in supplication.

"I am a mortal," Scrooge remonstrated, "and liable to fall."

"Bear but a touch of my hand there," said the Spirit, laying it upon his heart, "and you shall be upheld in more than this!"

As the words were spoken, they passed through the wall and stood upon an open country road, with fields on either hand.

It was a clear, cold, winter day, with snow upon the ground.

"Good Heaven!" said Scrooge, clasping his hands together, as he looked about him. "I was bred in this place. I was a boy here!"

He was conscious of a thousand odours floating in the air, each one connected with a thousand thoughts, and hopes, and joys, and cares long, long forgotten!

"You recollect the way?" inquired the Spirit.

"Remember it!" cried Scrooge with fervour—"I could walk it blindfold."

"They walked along the road; Scrooge recognizing every gate, and post, and tree; until a little market-town appeared in the distance, with its bridge, its church, and winding river. Some shaggy ponies now were seen trotting towards them with boys upon their backs, who called to other boys in country gigs and carts, driven by farmers. All these boys were in great spirits, and shouted to each other, until the broad fields were so full of merry music, that the crisp air laughed to hear it.

"These are but shadows of the things that have been," said the Ghost. "They have no consciousness of us."

The jocund* travellers came on; and as they came, Scrooge knew and named them every one. Why was he rejoiced beyond all bounds to see them! Why did his cold eye glister, and his heart leap up as they went past! Why was he filled with gladness when he heard them give each other merry Christmas, as they parted at cross-roads and by-ways, for their several homes!

---

jocund: merry

What was merry Christmas to Scrooge? Out upon merry Christmas! What good had it ever done to him?

"The school is not quite deserted," said the Ghost. "A solitary child, neglected by his friends, is left there still."

Scrooge said he knew it. And he sobbed.

They left the high-road, by a well-remembered lane, and soon approached a mansion of dull red brick. It was a large house, but one of broken fortunes; for the spacious offices were little used, their walls were damp and mossy, their windows broken, and their gates decayed. Entering the dreary hall, and glancing through the open doors of many rooms, they found them poorly furnished, cold and vast.

They went, the Ghost and Scrooge, across the hall, to a door at the back of the house. It opened before them, and disclosed a long, bare, melancholy room, made barer still by lines of plain deal forms and desks. At one of these a lonely boy was reading near a feeble fire; and Scrooge sat down upon a form, and wept to see his poor forgotten self as he had used to be.

The Spirit touched him on the arm, and pointed to his younger self, intent upon his reading. Suddenly a man, in foreign garments: wonderfully real and distinct to look at: stood outside the window, with an axe stuck in his belt, and leading an ass laden with wood by the bridle.

"Why, it's Ali Baba!" Scrooge exclaimed in ecstasy. "It's dear old honest Ali Baba! One Christmas time, when yonder solitary child was left here all alone, he *did* come, for the first time, just like that. And Valentine," said Scrooge, "and his wild brother, Orson; there they go! And what's his name, who was put down in his drawers, asleep at the Gate of Damascus; don't you see him! And the Sultan's Groom turned upside down by the Genii; there he is upon his head! Serve him right. I'm glad of it. What business had *he* to be married to the Princess!"

To hear Scrooge expending all the earnestness of his nature on such subjects would have been a surprise to his business friends in the City, indeed.

Then, with a rapidity of transition very foreign to his usual character, he said, in pity for his former self, "Poor boy!" and cried.

"I wish," Scrooge muttered, putting his hand in his pocket, and looking about him, after drying his eyes with his cuff: "but it's too late now."

"What is the matter?" asked the Spirit.

"Nothing," said Scrooge. "Nothing. There was a boy singing a Christmas carol at my door last night. I should like to have given him something: that's all."

The Ghost smiled thoughtfully, and waved his hand: saying as it did so, "Let us see another Christmas!"

Scrooge's former self grew larger at the words, and the room became a little darker and more dirty. The panels shrank, the windows cracked; fragments of plaster fell out of the ceiling, and the naked laths* were shown instead; but how all this was brought about, Scrooge knew no more than you do. He only knew that it was quite correct; that everything had happened so; that there he was, alone again, when all the other boys had gone home for the jolly holidays. He was not reading now, but walking up and down despairingly. Scrooge looked at the Ghost, and with a mournful shaking of his head, glanced anxiously towards the door.

---

laths: substructure for plaster or shingles

It opened; and a little girl, much younger than the boy, came darting in, and putting her arms about his neck, and often kissing him, addressed him as her "Dear, dear brother."

"I have come to bring you home, dear brother!" said the child.

"Home, little Fan?" returned the boy.

"Yes!" said the child, brimful of glee. "Home, for good and all. Home, for ever and ever. Father is so much kinder than he used to be, that home's like Heaven! He spoke so gently to me one dear night when I was going to bed, that I was not afraid to ask him once more if you might come home; and he said Yes, you should; and sent me in a coach to bring you. And you're to be a man!" said the child, opening her eyes, "and are never to come back here; but first, we're to be together all the Christmas long, and have the merriest time in all the world."

She clapped her hands and laughed, and tried to touch his head; but being too little, laughed again, and stood on tiptoe to embrace him. Then she began to drag him, in her childish eagerness, towards the door; and he, nothing loath to go, accompanied her.

"Always a delicate creature, whom a breath might have withered," said the Ghost. "But she had a large heart!"

"So she had," cried Scrooge. "You're right. I'll not gainsay* it, Spirit. God forbid!"

gainsay: deny

"She died a woman," said the Ghost, "and had, as I think, children."

"One child," Scrooge returned.

"True," said the Ghost. "Your nephew!"

Scrooge seemed uneasy in his mind; and answered briefly, "Yes."

They had left the school behind them, and they were now in the busy thoroughfares of a city, where shadowy passengers passed and repassed; where shadowy carts and coaches battled for the way. It was made plain enough, by the dressing of the shops, that here too it was Christmas time again; but it was evening, and the streets were lighted up.

The Ghost stopped at a certain warehouse door, and asked Scrooge if he knew it.

"Know it!" said Scrooge. "I was apprenticed* here."

apprenticed: trained

They went in. At sight of an old gentleman in a Welsh wig, sitting behind a high desk, Scrooge cried in great excitement:—

"Why, it's old Fezziwig!"

Old Fezziwig laid down his pen, and looked up at the clock, which pointed to the hour of seven. He rubbed his hands; adjusted his capacious* waistcoat; laughed all over himself, and called out in a comfortable, oily, rich, fat, jovial voice:—

"Yo ho, there! Ebenezer! Dick!"

---

capacious: roomy

Scrooge's former self, now grown a young man, came briskly in, accompanied by his fellow-'prentice.

"Dick Wilkins, to be sure!" said Scrooge to the Ghost. "Bless me, yes. There he is. He was very much attached to me, was Dick. Poor Dick! Dear, dear!"

"Yo ho, my boys!" said Fezziwig. "No more work tonight. Christmas Eve, Dick. Christmas, Ebenezer! Let's have the shutters up," cried old Fezziwig, with a sharp clap of his hands.

You wouldn't believe how those two fellows went at it! They charged into the street with the shutters—one, two, three—had 'em up in their places—four, five, six—barred 'em and pinned 'em—seven, eight, nine—and came back before you could have got to twelve, panting like race-horses.

"Hilli-ho!" cried old Fezziwig, skipping down from the high desk, with wonderful agility. "Clear away, my lads, and let's have lots of room here!"

Clear away! There was nothing they wouldn't have cleared away, or couldn't have cleared away, with old Fezziwig looking on. It was done in a minute. Every movable was packed off, as if it were dismissed from public life for evermore; the floor was swept, the lamps were trimmed, fuel was heaped upon the fire; and the warehouse was as snug, and warm, and dry, and bright a ball-room, as you would desire to see upon a winter's night.

In came a fiddler with a music-book, and went up to the lofty desk, and made an orchestra of it, and tuned like fifty stomach-aches. In came Mrs. Fezziwig, one vast substantial smile. In came the three Miss Fezziwigs, beaming and lovable. In came the six young followers whose hearts they broke. In came all the young men and women employed in the business. In came the housemaid, with her cousin, the baker. In came the cook, with her brother's particular friend, the milkman. In they all came, one after another.

There were dances, and there were forfeits,* and more dances, and there was cake, and there was negus,* and there was a great piece of Cold Roast, and there was a great piece of Cold Boiled,* and there were mince-pies. But the great effect of the evening came after the Roast and Boiled, when the fiddler (an artful dog, mind! The sort of man who knew his business better than you or I could have told it him!) struck up "Sir Roger de Coverley." Then old Fezziwig stood out to dance with Mrs. Fezziwig. Top couple, too; with a good stiff piece of work cut out for them; three or four and twenty pair of partners; people who were not to be trifled with; people who *would* dance, and had no notion of walking.

---

forfeits: a parlor game

negus: sweet, spicy, hot beverage

Cold Boiled: possibly another cold meat or a dish made by boiling and then frying meat and vegetables

---

But if they had been twice as many: ah, four times: old Fezziwig would have been a match for them, and so would Mrs. Fezziwig.

When the clock struck eleven, this domestic ball broke up. Mr. and Mrs. Fezziwig took their stations, one on either side the door, and shaking hands with every person individually as he or she went out, wished him or her a merry Christmas. When everybody had retired but the two 'prentices, they did the same to them; and thus the cheerful voices died away, and the lads were left to their beds; which were under a counter in the back-shop.

During the whole of this time, Scrooge had acted like a man out of his wits. His heart and soul were in the scene, and with his former self. He enjoyed everything and underwent the strangest agitation.

"A small matter," said the Ghost, "to make these silly folks so full of gratitude."

The Spirit signed to him to listen to the two apprentices, who were pouring out their hearts in praise of Fezziwig: and when he had done so, said,

"Why! He has spent but a few pounds of your mortal money: three or four, perhaps. Is that so much that he deserves this praise?"

"It isn't that," said Scrooge, heated by the remark, and speaking unconsciously like his former, not his latter, self. "It isn't that, Spirit. He has the power to render us happy or unhappy; to make our service light or burdensome; a pleasure or a toil. Say that his power lies in words and looks; in things so slight and insignificant that it is impossible to add and count 'em up: what then? The happiness he gives is quite as great as if it cost a fortune." He felt the Spirit's glance, and stopped.

"What is the matter?" asked the Ghost.

"Nothing particular," said Scrooge.

"Something, I think?" the Ghost insisted.

"No," said Scrooge. "No. I should like to be able to say a word or two to my clerk just now! That's all."

His former self turned down the lamps as he gave utterance to the wish; and Scrooge and the Ghost again stood side by side in the open air.

"My time grows short," observed the Spirit. "Quick."

This was not addressed to Scrooge, or to anyone whom he could see, but it produced an immediate effect. For again Scrooge saw himself. He was older now; a man in the prime of life. His face had not the harsh and rigid lines of later years; but it had begun to wear the signs of care and avarice.*

---

avarice: greed

He was not alone, but sat by the side of a fair young girl in a mourning-dress:

"It matters little," she said, softly. "To you, very little. Another idol has displaced me; and if it can cheer and comfort you in time to come, as I would have tried to do, I have no just cause to grieve."

"What idol has displaced you?" he rejoined.

"A golden one."

"This is the even-handed dealing of the world!" he said. "There is nothing on which it is so hard as poverty; and there is nothing it professes to condemn with such severity as the pursuit of wealth!"

"You fear the world too much," she answered, gently. "All your other hopes have merged into the hope of being beyond the chance of its sordid* reproach. I have seen your nobler aspirations* fall off one by one, until the master-passion, Gain, engrosses you. Have I not?"

---

sordid: base
aspirations: ambitions

"What then?" he retorted. "Even if I have grown so much wiser, what then? I am not changed towards you."

"Our contract is an old one. It was made when we were both poor and content to be so, until, in good season, we could improve our worldly fortune by our patient industry.

You are changed. When it was made, you were another man."

"I was a boy," he said impatiently.

"Your own feeling tells you that you were not what you are," she returned. "I am. That which promised happiness when we were one in heart, is fraught with misery now that we are two. How often and how keenly I have thought of this, I will not say. It is enough that I have thought of it, and can release you."

"Have I ever sought release?"

"In words? No. Never."

"In what, then?"

"In a changed nature; in an altered spirit; in another atmosphere of life; another Hope as its great end. In everything that made my love of any worth or value in your sight. If this had never been between us," said the girl, looking mildly, but with steadiness, upon him; "tell me, would you seek me out and try to win me now? Ah, no!"

He seemed to yield to the justice of this supposition* in spite of himself. But he said with a struggle, "You think not."

supposition: assumption

"I would gladly think otherwise if I could," she answered, "Heaven knows! When I have learned a Truth like this, I know how strong and irresistible it must be. But if you were free today, tomorrow, yesterday, can even I believe that you would choose a dowerless* girl—you who, in your very confidence with her, weigh everything by Gain: or, choosing her, if for a moment you were false enough to your one guiding principle to do so, do I not know that your repentance and regret would surely follow? I do; and I release you. With a full heart, for the love of him you once were."

dowerless: without a dowry; poor

She left him, and they parted.

"Spirit!" said Scrooge, "show me no more! Conduct me home. Why do you delight to torture me?"

"One shadow more!" exclaimed the Ghost.

"No more!" cried Scrooge. "No more. I don't wish to see it. Show me no more!"

But the relentless Ghost pinioned* him in both his arms, and forced him to observe what happened next.

pinioned: held by force

They were in another scene and place; a room, not very large or handsome, but full of comfort. Near to the winter fire sat a beautiful young girl, so like the last that Scrooge believed it was the same, until he saw her, now a comely matron, sitting opposite her daughter. The noise in this room was perfectly tumultuous, for there were more children there, than Scrooge in his agitated state of mind could count.

Now the father came home attended by a man laden with Christmas toys and presents. The shouts of wonder and delight with which the development of every package was received!

The joy, and gratitude, and ecstasy! They are all indescribable alike. By degrees the children and their emotions got out of the parlour and by one stair at a time, up to the top of the house; where they went to bed, and so subsided.

And now Scrooge looked on more attentively than ever, when the master of the house, having his daughter leaning fondly on him, sat down with her and her mother at his own fireside.

"Belle," said the husband, turning to his wife with a smile, "I saw an old friend of yours this afternoon."

"Who was it?"

"Mr. Scrooge. I passed his office window; and as it was not shut up, and he had a candle inside, I could scarcely help seeing him. His partner lies upon the point of death, I hear; and there he sat alone. Quite alone in the world, I do believe."

"Spirit!" said Scrooge in a broken voice, "remove me from this place."

"I told you these were shadows of the things that have been," said the Ghost. "That they are what they are, do not blame me!"

"Remove me!" Scrooge exclaimed, "I cannot bear it!"

He turned upon the Ghost, and seeing that it looked upon him with a face, in which in some strange way there were fragments of all the faces it had shown him, wrestled with it.

"Leave me! Take me back. Haunt me no longer!"

In the struggle, if that can be called a struggle in which the Ghost with no visible resistance on its own part was undisturbed by any effort of its adversary, Scrooge observed that its light was burning high and bright; and dimly connected that with its influence over him, he seized the extinguisher-cap, and by a sudden action pressed it down upon his head.

The Spirit dropped beneath it, so that the extinguisher covered its whole form; but though Scrooge pressed it down with all his force, he could not hide the light, which streamed from under it, in an unbroken flood upon the ground.

He was conscious of being exhausted, and overcome by an irresistible drowsiness; and, further, of being in his own bedroom. He gave the cap a parting squeeze, in which his hand relaxed; and had barely time to reel* to bed, before he sank into a heavy slumber.

reel: stagger

THINKING ZONE

A good writer endeavors to show the reader much more than he tells outright. Hence, much of Dickens's novella relies heavily on the use of symbolism and understatement, leading the reader to draw conclusions based on the information given by the author. Read carefully the descriptions of the spirits and give careful attention to the symbolism conveyed by their appearances, which reflect various aspects of Christmases past, present, and future.

1. *[critical]* How does Dickens effectively create suspense at the beginning of Stave II (until the first ghost arrives)?

   _____

   _____

   _____

   _____

   _____

   _____

   _____

2. *[interpretive/critical]* What aspects of the appearance of the Ghost of Christmas Past exhibit paradox?

   _____

   _____

   _____

   _____

   _____

   _____

   _____

   _____

   _____

3. *[interpretive]* Why do you think Scrooge "seemed uneasy in his mind" after being reminded of Little Fan and her fondness for him?

_____

_____

_____

4. *[critical]* How has Scrooge's attitude changed from his time as Fezziwig's apprentice to the time when he ends his relationship with Belle?

_____

_____

_____

_____

5. *[critical]* Why is it appropriate that Belle is attired "in a mourning-dress"?

_____

_____

_____

6. *[interpretive]* What is symbolic about Scrooge's struggle with the ghost at the end of Stave II?

_____

_____

_____

_____

7. *[appreciative]* How might the gift of conscience be one of God's greatest gifts to humankind?

_____

_____

_____

_____

A waking in the middle of a prodigiously* tough snore, and sitting up in bed to get his thoughts together, Scrooge had no occasion to be told that the bell was again upon the stroke of One. He felt that he was restored to consciousness in the right nick of time, for the especial purpose of holding a conference with the second messenger despatched to him through Jacob Marley's intervention.

---

prodigiously: exceptionally

He was ready for a good broad field of strange appearance, and nothing between a baby and a rhinoceros would have astonished him very much.

Now, being prepared for almost anything, he was not by any means prepared for nothing; and, consequently, when the Bell struck One, and no shape appeared, he was taken with a violent fit of trembling. Five minutes, ten minutes, a quarter of an hour went by, yet nothing came. All this time, he lay upon his bed, the very core and centre of a blaze of ruddy* light, which streamed upon it when the clock proclaimed the hour; and which, being only light, was more alarming than a dozen ghosts, as he was powerless to make out what it meant. At last, however, he began to think—that the source and secret of this ghostly light might be in the adjoining room, from whence, on further tracing it, it seemed to shine. This idea taking full possession of his mind, he got up softly and shuffled in his slippers to the door.

---

ruddy: reddish

The moment Scrooge's hand was on the lock, a strange voice called him by his name, and bade him enter. He obeyed.

It was his own room. There was no doubt about that. But it had undergone a surprising transformation. The walls and ceiling were hung with living green. The crisp leaves of holly, mistletoe, and ivy reflected back the light, as if so many little mirrors had been scattered there; and a mighty blaze went roaring up the chimney. Heaped up on the floor, to form a kind of throne, were turkeys, geese, game, poultry, brawn, great joints of meat, sucking-pigs, long wreaths of sausages, mince-pies, plum-puddings, barrels of oysters, red-hot chestnuts, cherry-cheeked apples, juicy oranges, luscious pears, immense twelfth-cakes, and seething bowls of punch, that made the chamber dim with their delicious steam. In easy state upon this couch, there sat a jolly Giant, glorious to see; who bore a glowing torch, in shape not unlike Plenty's horn, and held it up, high up, to shed its light on Scrooge, as he came peeping round the door.

"Come in!" exclaimed the Ghost. "Come in! and know me better, man!"

Scrooge entered timidly, and hung his head before this Spirit. He was not the dogged* Scrooge he had been; and though the Spirit's eyes were clear and kind, he did not like to meet them.

---

dogged: unyielding

"I am the Ghost of Christmas Present," said the Spirit. "Look upon me!"

Scrooge reverently did so. It was clothed in one simple deep green robe, or mantle, bordered with white fur. This garment hung loosely on the figure. Its feet, observable beneath the ample folds of the garment, were bare; and on its head it wore no other covering than a holly wreath set here and there with shining icicles. Its dark brown curls

were long and free; free as its genial* face, its sparkling eyes, its open hand, its cheery voice, its unconstrained demeanour, and its joyful air. Girded round its middle was an antique scabbard; but no sword was in it, and the ancient sheath was eaten up with rust.

genial: friendly

"Spirit," said Scrooge, submissively, "conduct me where you will. I went forth last night on compulsion,* and I learnt a lesson which is working now. Tonight, if you have aught to teach me, let me profit by it."

on compulsion: under force

"Touch my robe!"

Scrooge did as he was told, and held it fast.

Holly, mistletoe, ivy, turkeys, geese, game, poultry, brawn, meat, pigs, sausages, oysters, pies, puddings, fruit, and punch, all vanished instantly. So did the room, the fire, the ruddy glow, the hour of night, and they stood in the city streets on Christmas morning, where (for the weather was severe) the people made a rough, but brisk and not unpleasant kind of music, in scraping the snow from the pavement in front of their dwellings.

The poulterers' shops were still half open, and the fruiterers' were radiant in their glory. There were great, round, pot-bellied baskets of chestnuts, shaped like the waistcoats of jolly old gentlemen, lolling* at the doors, and tumbling out into the street. There were pears and apples, clustered high in blooming pyramids; there were oranges and lemons, urgently entreating and be-seeching to be carried home in paper bags and eaten after dinner.

---

lolling: relaxing

Soon the steeples called good people all, to church and chapel, and away they came, flocking through the streets in their best clothes, and with their gayest faces. And at the same time there emerged from scores of by-streets, lanes, and nameless turnings, in-numerable people, carrying their dinners to the bakers' shops. The sight of these poor revellers appeared to interest the Spirit very much, for he stood with Scrooge beside him in a baker's doorway, and taking off the cov-ers as their bearers passed, sprinkled incense on their dinners from his torch. And it was a very uncommon kind of torch, for once or twice when there were angry words between some dinner-carriers who had jostled with each other, he shed a few drops of water on them from it, and their good humour was restored directly. For they said, it was a shame to quarrel upon Christmas Day. And so it was! God love it, so it was.

They went on, invisible, as they had been before, into the suburbs of the town—straight to Scrooge's clerk's; and on the threshold of the door the Spirit smiled, and stopped to bless Bob Cratchit's dwelling with the sprin-klings of his torch. Think of that! Bob had but fifteen "Bob"* a-week himself; and yet the Ghost of Christmas Present blessed his four-roomed house!

Bob: English shillings (coins)

Then up rose Mrs. Cratchit, dressed out but poorly in a twice-turned gown, but brave in ribbons, which are cheap and make a goodly show for sixpence; and she laid the cloth, assisted by Belinda Cratchit, sec-ond of her daughters, also brave in ribbons; while Master Peter Cratchit plunged a fork into the saucepan of potatoes. And now two smaller Cratchits, boy and girl, came tearing in, screaming that outside the baker's they had smelt the goose, and known it for their own; and basking in luxurious thoughts of sage and onion, these young Cratchits danced about the table.

"What has ever got your precious fa-ther?" said Mrs. Cratchit. "And your brother, Tiny Tim! And Martha warn't as late last Christmas Day by half-an-hour!"

"Here's Martha, mother!" said a girl, ap-pearing as she spoke.

"Why, bless your heart alive, my dear, how late you are!" said Mrs. Cratchit, kissing her a dozen times, and taking off her shawl and bonnet for her with officious* zeal.

---

officious: unnecessary

"We'd a deal of work to finish up last night," replied the girl, "and had to clear away this morning, mother!"

"Well! Never mind so long as you are come," said Mrs. Cratchit. "Sit ye down before the fire, my dear, and have a warm, Lord bless ye!"

"There's father coming," cried the two young Cratchits, who were everywhere at once.

In came Bob, the father, and Tiny Tim upon his shoulder. Alas for Tiny Tim, he bore a little crutch, and had his limbs supported by an iron frame!

The two young Cratchits hustled Tiny Tim, and bore him off into the wash-house, that he might hear the pudding singing in the copper.

"And how did little Tim behave?" asked Mrs. Cratchit.

"As good as gold," said Bob, "and better. Somehow he gets thoughtful, sitting by himself so much, and thinks the strangest things you ever heard. He told me, coming home, that he hoped the people saw him in the church, because he was a cripple, and it might be pleasant to them to remember upon Christmas Day, who made lame beggars walk and blind men see."

The active little crutch was heard upon the floor, and back came Tiny Tim before another word was spoken, escorted by his brother and sister to his stool before the fire; and while Bob compounded some hot mixture in a jug and stirred it round and round and put it on the hob* to simmer; Master Peter, and the two young Cratchits went to fetch the goose, with which they soon returned in high procession.

hob: a shelf at the back or side of a fireplace used for keeping food warm

Such a bustle ensued that you might have thought a goose the rarest of all birds; and in truth it was something very like it in that house. At last the dishes were set on, and grace was said. It was succeeded by a breathless pause, as Mrs. Cratchit, looking slowly all along the carving-knife, prepared to plunge it in the goose; but when she did, and when the long expected gush of stuffing issued forth, one murmur of delight arose all around the board, and even Tiny Tim, excited by the two young Cratchits, beat on the table with the handle of his knife, and feebly cried Hurrah!

There never was such a goose. Its tenderness and flavour, size and cheapness, were the themes of universal admiration. It was a sufficient dinner for the whole family; indeed, as Mrs. Cratchit said with great delight (surveying one small atom of a bone upon the dish), they hadn't eaten it all at last! Yet everyone had had enough. But now, the plates being changed by Miss Belinda, Mrs. Cratchit left the room alone—too nervous to bear witnesses—to take the pudding up and bring it in.

Suppose it should not be done enough! Suppose it should break in turning out! Suppose somebody should have got over the wall of the back-yard, and stolen it, while they were merry with the goose—a supposition at which the two young Cratchits became livid!* All sorts of horrors were supposed.

livid: pale

In half a minute Mrs. Cratchit entered— flushed, but smiling proudly—with the pudding, like a speckled cannon-ball, and bedight* with Christmas holly stuck into the top.

bedight: decorated

At last the dinner was all done, the cloth was cleared, the hearth swept, and the fire made up. The compound in the jug being tasted, and considered perfect, apples and oranges were put upon the table, and a shovelful of chesnuts on the fire. Then all the Cratchit family drew around the hearth, in what Bob Cratchit called a circle, meaning half a one; and at Bob Cratchit's elbow stood the family display of glass. Two tumblers and a custard-cup without a handle.

These held the hot stuff from the jug, however, as well as golden goblets would have done; and Bob served it out with beaming looks, while the chestnuts on the fire sputtered and cracked noisily. Then Bob proposed:—

"A merry Christmas to us all, my dears. God bless us!"

Which all the family re-echoed.

"God bless us every one!" said Tiny Tim, the last of all.

He sat very close to his father's side upon his little stool. Bob held his withered little hand in his, as if he loved the child, and wished to keep him by his side, and dreaded that he might be taken from him.

"Spirit," said Scrooge, with an interest he had never felt before, "tell me if Tiny Tim will live."

"I see a vacant seat," replied the Ghost, "in the poor chimney-corner, and a crutch without an owner, carefully preserved. If these shadows remain unaltered by the Future, the child will die."

"No, no," said Scrooge. "Oh, no, kind Spirit! say he will be spared."

"If these shadows remain unaltered by the Future, none other of my race," returned the Ghost, "will find him here. What then? If he be like to die, he had better do it, and decrease the surplus population."

Scrooge hung his head to hear his own words quoted by the Spirit and, trembling, cast his eyes upon the ground. But he raised them speedily, on hearing his own name.

"Mr. Scrooge!" said Bob, "I'll give you Mr. Scrooge, the Founder of the Feast!"

"The Founder of the Feast indeed!" cried Mrs. Cratchit, reddening. "I wish I had him here. I'd give him a piece of my mind to feast upon, and I hope he'd have a good appetite for it."

"My dear," said Bob, "the children! Christmas Day."

"It should be Christmas Day, I am sure, on which one drinks the health of such a stingy, hard, unfeeling man as Mr. Scrooge," said Mrs. Cratchit. "I'll drink his health for your sake and the Day's, not for his."

The children drank the toast after her. It was the first of their proceedings which had no heartiness in it. Tiny Tim drank it last of all, but he didn't care twopence for it. Scrooge was the Ogre* of the family. The mention of his name cast a dark shadow on the party, which was not dispelled* for full five minutes. But after it passed away, they were then merrier than before.

Ogre: cruel man

dispelled: driven away

They were not a handsome family; they were not well-dressed; their clothes were scanty. But, they were happy, grateful, pleased with one another, and contented with the time; and when they faded, and looked happier yet in the bright sprinklings of the Spirit's torch at parting, Scrooge had his eye upon them, and especially on Tiny Tim, until the last.

By this time it was getting dark, and snowing pretty heavily; and as Scrooge and the Spirit went along the streets, the brightness of the roaring fires in kitchens, parlours, and all sorts of rooms, was wonderful. But the Spirit did not tarry here, but bade Scrooge hold his robe, and sped on, above the black and heaving sea—on, on—until, being far away, as he told Scrooge, from any shore, they lighted on a ship. They stood beside the helmsman at the wheel, the look-out in the bow, the officers who had the watch; dark, ghostly figures in their several stations; but every man among them hummed a Christmas tune, or had a Christmas thought, or spoke below his breath to his companion of some by-gone Christmas Day, with homeward hopes belonging to it. And every man on board, walking or sleeping, good or bad, had had a kinder word for another on that day than on any day in the year; and had shared to some extent in its festivities; and had remembered those he cared for at a distance, and had known that they delighted to remember him.

It was a great surprise to Scrooge, while listening to the moaning of the wind, and thinking what a solemn thing it was to move on through the lonely darkness over an unknown abyss* whose depths were secrets as profound as Death: it was a great surprise to Scrooge, while thus engaged, to hear a hearty laugh. It was a much greater surprise to Scrooge to recognize it as his own nephew's and to find himself in a bright, dry, gleaming room, with the Spirit standing smiling by his side, and looking at that same nephew with approving affability.*

---

abyss: bottomless gulf

affability: kindliness

"Ha, ha!" laughed Scrooge's nephew. "Ha, ha, ha!"

Scrooge's nephew laughed: holding his sides, rolling his head, and twisting his face into the most extravagant contortions. Scrooge's niece, by marriage, laughed as heartily as he. And their assembled friends being not a bit behindhand, roared out, lustily.

"Ha, ha! Ha, ha, ha, ha!"

"He said that Christmas was a humbug, as I live!" cried Scrooge's nephew. "He believed it too!"

"More shame for him, Fred!" said Scrooge's niece, indignantly.

She was very pretty: exceedingly pretty. With a dimpled, surprised-looking, capital* face; a ripe little mouth, that seemed made to be kissed—as no doubt it was; all kinds of

good little dots about her chin, that melted into one another when she laughed; and the sunniest pair of eyes you ever saw in any little creature's head.

capital: excellent

"He's a comical old fellow," said Scrooge's nephew, "that's the truth; and not so pleasant as he might be. However, his offences carry their own punishment, and I have nothing to say against him."

"I'm sure he is very rich, Fred," hinted Scrooge's niece. "At least you always tell *me* so."

"What of that, my dear!" said Scrooge's nephew. "His wealth is of no use to him. He doesn't do any good with it. He don't make himself comfortable with it."

"I have no patience with him," observed Scrooge's niece. Scrooge's niece's sisters, and all the other ladies, expressed the same opinion.

"Oh, I have!" said Scrooge's nephew. "I am sorry for him; I couldn't be angry with him if I tried. Who suffers by his ill whims? Himself, always. Here, he takes it into his head to dislike us, and he won't come and dine with us. What's the consequence? He doesn't lose much of a dinner."

"Indeed, I think he loses a very good dinner," interrupted Scrooge's niece. Everybody else said the same, and they must be allowed to have been competent judges, because they had just had dinner; and, with the dessert upon the table, were clustered around the fire, by lamplight.

"Well! I'm very glad to hear it," said Scrooge's nephew, "because I haven't any great faith in these young housekeepers. What do *you* say, Topper?"

Topper had clearly got his eyes upon one of Scrooge's niece's sisters, for he answered that a bachelor was a wretched outcast, who had no right to express an opinion on the subject. Whereat Scrooge's niece's sister—the plump one with the lace tucker:* not the one with the roses—blushed.

---
tucker: lace or cloth worn around the neck and shoulders

"Do go on, Fred," said Scrooge's niece, clapping her hands. "He never finishes what he begins to say! He is such a ridiculous fellow!"

"I was only going to say," said Scrooge's nephew, "that the consequence of his taking a dislike to us, and not making merry with us, is, as I think, that he loses some pleasant moments, which could do him no harm. I am sure he loses pleasanter companions than he can find in his own thoughts, either in his mouldy old office, or his dusty chambers. I mean to give him the same chance every year, whether he likes it or not, for I pity him. He may rail at Christmas till he dies, but he can't help thinking better of it—I defy him—if he finds me going there, in good temper, year after year, and saying 'Uncle Scrooge, how are you?' If it only put him in the vein to leave his poor clerk fifty pounds,* that's something; and I think I shook him yesterday."

---
pounds: British money

After tea, they had some music. When the music sounded, all the things the Ghost had shown him, came upon his mind; he softened more and more; and thought that if he could have listened to it often, years ago, he might have cultivated the kindnesses of life.

The Ghost was greatly pleased to find him in this mood, and looked upon him with such favour, that he begged like a boy to be allowed to stay until the guests departed. But this the Spirit said could not be done.

And he and the Spirit were again upon their travels.

Much they saw, and far they went, and many homes they visited, but always with a happy end. The Spirit stood beside sick beds and they were cheerful; on foreign lands, and they were close at home; by struggling men, and they were patient in their greater hope; by poverty, and it was rich. In almshouse, hospital, and jail, in misery's every refuge, where vain man in his little brief authority had not made fast the door, and barred the Spirit out, he left his blessing, and taught Scrooge his precepts.

It was a long night, if it were only a night; but Scrooge had his doubts of this, because the Christmas Holidays appeared to be condensed into the space of time they passed together. It was strange, too, that while Scrooge remained unaltered in his outward form, the Ghost grew older, clearly older. Scrooge had observed this change, but never spoke of it, until they left a children's Twelfth Night party, when, looking at the Spirit as they stood together in an open place, he noticed that its hair was gray.

"Are spirits' lives so short?" asked Scrooge.

"My life upon this globe is very brief," replied the Ghost. "It ends tonight."

"Tonight!" cried Scrooge.

"Tonight! at midnight. Hark! The time is drawing near."

The chimes were ringing the three quarters past eleven at that moment.

"Forgive me if I am not justified in that I ask," said Scrooge, looking intently at the Spirit's robe, "but I see something strange, and not belonging to yourself, protruding from your skirts. Is it a foot or a claw?"

"It might be a claw, for the flesh there is upon it," was the Spirit's sorrowful reply. "Look here."

From the foldings of its robe, it brought two children; wretched, frightful, hideous, miserable. They knelt down at its feet, and clung upon the outside of its garment.

"Oh, Man! look here. Look, look, down here!" exclaimed the Ghost.

There were a boy and girl. Yellow, meagre, ragged, scowling, wolfish; but prostrate,* too, in their humility. Where graceful youth should have filled their features out, and touched them with its freshest tints, a stale and shrivelled hand, like that of age, had pinched, and twisted them, and pulled them into shreds. Where angels might have sat enthroned, devils lurked, and glared out menacing. No change, no degradation,* no perversion of humanity, in any grade, through all the mysteries of wonderful creation, has monsters half so horrible and dread.

prostrate: lying face-down
degradation: lowering in value; humiliation

Scrooge started back, appalled. Having them shown to him in this way, he tried to say they were fine children, but the words choked themselves, rather than be parties to a lie of such enormous magnitude.

"Spirit! are they yours?" Scrooge could say no more.

"They are Man's," said the Spirit, looking down upon them. "And they cling to me, appealing from their fathers. This boy is Ignorance. This girl is Want. Beware them both, and all their degree, but most of all beware this boy, for on his brow I see that written which is Doom, unless the writing be erased. Deny it!" cried the Spirit, stretching out his hand toward the city. "Slander those who tell it ye! Admit it for your factious* purposes, and make it worse! And bide the end!"

factious: divisive

"Have they no refuge or resource?" cried Scrooge.

"Are there no prisons?" said the Spirit, turning on him for the last time with his own words. "Are there no workhouses?"

The bell struck twelve.

Scrooge looked about him for the Ghost, and saw it not. As the last stroke ceased to vibrate, he remembered the prediction of old Jacob Marley, and lifting up his eyes, beheld a solemn Phantom, draped and hooded, coming, like a mist along the ground, towards him.

THINKING ZONE

You have learned about static and developing characters (pp. 259–60) and sympathetic and unsympathetic characters (pp. 239–40) in previous stories. Here is another distinction that writers make: flat and round characters. A **flat character** is a character with little individuality, whose mindset the reader knows little about. On the other hand, a **round character** is a character whose personality is well defined by the author. For example, in Donnalynn Hess's *In Search of Honor*, Jacques is an example of a round character. We find out much about Jacques's motivations and understand the reasons for his reactions. Jacques's young friend Phillipe is an example of a flat character. The novel reveals little about Phillipe's character traits or his personality. Typically, a story will have more flat characters than round ones.

Static character— *one who remains essentially the same throughout a story*

Developing character— *a character that changes as the story progresses*

1. *[interpretive]* Name one example of a **flat character** and one example of a **round character** from Stave III.

   _____

   _____

   _____

   _____

2. *[interpretive]* How does the appearance of the second spirit compare with that of the first?

   _____

   _____

   _____

   _____

   _____

   _____

   _____

   _____

3. *[interpretive]* How does the physical appearance of the second
spirit symbolize Christmas Present?

_____

_____

_____

_____

_____

4. *[critical]* Why do you think Scrooge was hesitant to look into
the spirit's "clear and kind" eyes? (Think specifically about how
Scrooge reacted to the previous spirit and its revelations.)

_____

_____

_____

_____

5. *[critical]* What is ironic about the responses of Bob Cratchit and
Fred to Scrooge?

_____

_____

_____

_____

_____

_____

6. *[interpretive]* What "children of man" does the spirit reveal? Why
does the spirit believe that the boy is more dangerous?

_____

_____

_____

_____

STAVE IV
THE LAST OF THE SPIRITS

The Phantom slowly, gravely, silently approached. When it came near him, Scrooge bent down upon his knees; for in the very air through which this Spirit moved it seemed to scatter gloom and mystery.

It was shrouded in a deep black garment, which concealed its head, its face, its form, and left nothing of it visible save one outstretched hand. But for this it would have been difficult to detach its figure from the night, and separate it from the darkness by which it was surrounded.

"I am in the presence of the Ghost of Christmas Yet To Come?" said Scrooge.

The Spirit answered not, but pointed downward with its hand.

Although well used to ghostly company by this time, Scrooge feared the silent shape so much that his legs trembled beneath him, and he found that he could hardly stand when he prepared to follow it. The Spirit paused a moment, as observing his condition, and giving him time to recover.

"Ghost of the Future!" he exclaimed, "I fear you more than any Spectre I have seen. But, as I know your purpose is to do me good, and as I hope to live to be another man from what I was, I am prepared to bear you company, and do it with a thankful heart. Will you not speak to me?"

It gave him no reply. The hand was pointed straight before them.

"Lead on!" said Scrooge. "Lead on! The night is waning fast, and it is precious time to me, I know. Lead on, Spirit!"

The Phantom moved away as it had come towards him. Scrooge followed in the shadow of its dress, which bore him up, he thought, and carried him along.

The Spirit stopped beside one little knot of business men. Observing that the hand

was pointed to them, Scrooge advanced to listen to their talk.

"No," said a great fat man with a monstrous chin, "I don't know much about it, either way. I only know he's dead."

"When did he die?" inquired another.

"Last night, I believe."

"Why, what was the matter with him?" asked a third, taking a vast quantity of snuff out of a very large snuff-box. "I thought he'd never die."

"God knows," said the first, with a yawn.

"What has he done with his money?" asked a red-faced gentleman.

"I haven't heard," said the man with the large chin, yawning again. "Left it to his Company, perhaps. He hasn't left it to *me*. That's all I know."

This pleasantry was received with a general laugh.

"It's likely to be a very cheap funeral," said the same speaker; "for upon my life I don't know of anybody to go to it. Suppose we make up a party and volunteer?"

"I don't mind going if a lunch is provided," observed the red-faced gentleman. "But I must be fed, if I make one."

Another laugh.

Speakers and listeners strolled away, and mixed with other groups.

Scrooge was at first inclined to be surprised that the Spirit should attach importance to conversations apparently so trivial; but feeling assured that they must have some hidden purpose, he set himself to consider what it was likely to be. For he had an expectation that the conduct of his future self would give him the clew he missed, and would render the solution of these riddles easy.

He looked about in that very place for his own image; but another man stood in his accustomed corner, and though the clock pointed to his usual time of day for being there, he saw no likeness of himself among the multitudes that poured in through the Porch. It gave him little surprise, however; for he had been revolving in his mind a change of life, and thought and hoped he saw his new-born resolutions carried out in this.

They left the busy scene, and went into an obscure part of the town, where Scrooge had never penetrated before, although he recognized its situation, and its bad repute.* The ways were foul and narrow; the shops and houses wretched; and people half-naked, drunken, slipshod, ugly. Alleys and archways, like so many cesspools, disgorged* their offences of smell, and dirt, and life, upon the straggling streets; and the whole quarter reeked with crime, with filth, and misery.

repute: reputation

disgorged: emptied

Far in this den of infamous resort, there was a low-browed, beetling* shop, below a pent-house roof, where iron, old rags, bottles, bones, and greasy offal* were brought. Upon the floor within, were piled up heaps of rusty keys, nails, chains, hinges, files, scales, weights, and refuse iron of all kinds. Secrets that few would like to scrutinize were bred and hidden in mountains of unseemly rags, masses of corrupt fat, and sepulchres of bones. Sitting in among the wares he dealt in, by a charcoal-stove, made of old bricks, was a gray-haired rascal, nearly seventy years of age; who had screened himself from the cold air without, by a frowzy* curtaining of miscellaneous tatters, hung upon the line, and smoked his pipe in all the luxury of calm retirement.

beetling: machine used for finishing cloth

offal: garbage

frowzy: dirty, untidy

Scrooge and the Phantom came into the presence of this man, just as a woman with a heavy bundle slunk into the shop. But she had scarcely entered, when another woman, similarly laden, came in too; and she was closely followed by a man in faded black, who was no less startled by the sight of them, than they had been upon the recognition of each other. After a short period of blank astonishment, in which the old man with the pipe had joined them, they all three burst into a laugh.

"Let the charwoman* alone to be the first!" cried she who had entered first. "Let the laundress alone to be the second, and let the undertaker's man alone to be the third. Look here, old Joe, here's a chance! If we haven't all three met here without meaning it!"

charwoman: woman hired to do cleaning in a building

"You couldn't have met in a better place," said old Joe, removing his pipe from his mouth. "Come into the parlour."

The parlour was the space behind the screen of rags. The old man raked the fire together with an old stair-rod, and having trimmed his smoky lamp (for it was night) with the stem of his pipe, put it in his mouth again.

While he did this, the woman who had already spoken threw her bundle on the floor, and sat down in a flaunting* manner on a stool; crossing her elbows on her knees, and looking with a bold defiance at the other two.

flaunting: arrogant

"What odds then! What odds, Mrs. Dilber?" said the woman. "Every person has a right to take care of themselves. *He* always did!"

"That's true, indeed!" said the laundress. "No man more so."

"Very well, then!" cried the woman. "That's enough. Who's the worse for the loss of a few things like these? Not a dead man, I suppose."

"No, indeed," said Mrs. Dilber, laughing.

"If he wanted to keep 'em after he was dead," pursued the woman, "why wasn't he natural in his lifetime? If he had been, he'd have had somebody to look after him when he was struck with Death, instead of lying gasping out his last there, alone by himself."

"It's the truest word that ever was spoke," said Mrs. Dilber. "It's a judgment on him."

"I wish it was a little heavier one," replied the woman; "and it would have been, you may depend upon it, if I could have laid my hands on anything else. Open that bundle, old Joe, and let me know the value of it. Speak out plain. I'm not afraid to be the first, nor afraid for them to see it. We knew pretty well that we were helping ourselves,

before we met here, I believe. It's no sin. Open the bundle, Joe."

But the gallantry of her friends would not allow of this; and the man in faded black, mounting the breach first, produced *his* plunder. It was not extensive. A seal or two, a pencil-case, a pair of sleeve-buttons, and a brooch of no great value, were all. They were severally examined and appraised by old Joe, who chalked the sums he was disposed to give for each, upon the wall, and added them up into a total when he found there was nothing more to come.

"That's your account," said Joe, "and I wouldn't give another sixpence, if I was to be boiled for not doing it. Who's next?"

Mrs. Dilber was next. Sheets and towels, a little wearing apparel, two old fashioned silver teaspoons, a pair of sugar-tongs, and a few boots. Her account was stated on the wall in the same manner.

"And now undo my bundle, Joe," said the first woman.

"What do you call this?" said Joe. "Bed-curtains!"

"Ah!" returned the woman, laughing and leaning forward on her crossed arms. "Bed-curtains!"

"You don't mean to say you took 'em down, rings and all, with him lying there?" said Joe.

"Yes I do," replied the woman. "Why not?"

"His blankets?" asked Joe.

"Whose else's do you think?" replied the woman. "He isn't likely to take cold without 'em, I dare say."

"I hope he didn't die of anything catching? Eh?" said old Joe, stopping in his work, and looking up.

"Don't you be afraid of that," returned the woman. "I ain't so fond of his company that I'd loiter about him for such things, if he did. Ah! you may look through that shirt till your eyes ache; but you won't find a hole in it, nor a threadbare place. It's the best he had, and a fine one too. They'd have wasted it, if it hadn't been for me."

"What do you call wasting of it?" asked old Joe.

"Putting it on him to be buried in, to be sure," replied the woman with a laugh. "Somebody was fool enough to do it, but I took it off again. If calico ain't good enough for such a purpose, it isn't good enough for anything. It's quite as becoming to the body. He can't look uglier than he did in that one."

Scrooge listened to this dialogue in horror. As they sat grouped about their spoil, in the scanty light afforded by the old man's lamp, he viewed them with a detestation and disgust, which could hardly have been greater, though they had been obscene demons, marketing the corpse itself.

"Ha, ha!" laughed the same woman, when old Joe, producing a flannel bag with money in it, told out their several gains upon the ground. "This is the end of it, you see! He frightened everyone away from him when he was alive, to profit us when he was dead! Ha, ha, ha!"

"Spirit!" said Scrooge, shuddering from head to foot, "I see, I see. The case of this unhappy man might be my own. My life tends that way, now. Merciful Heaven, what is this!"

He recoiled in terror, for the scene had changed, and now he almost touched a bed: a bare, uncurtained bed: on which, beneath a ragged sheet, there lay a something covered up, which, though it was dumb, announced itself in awful language.

Scrooge glanced towards the Phantom. Its steady hand was pointed to the head. The cover was so carelessly adjusted that the slightest raising of it, the motion of a finger upon Scrooge's part, would have disclosed the face. He thought of it, felt how easy it would be to do, and longed to do it; but had no more power to withdraw the veil than to dismiss the spectre at his side.

Oh cold, cold, rigid, dreadful Death, set up thine altar here, and dress it with such terrors as thou hast at thy command: for this is thy dominion! But of the loved, revered, and honoured head, thou canst not turn one hair to thy dread purposes, or make one feature odious.

No voice pronounced these words in Scrooge's ears, and yet he heard them when he looked upon the bed. He thought, if this man could be raised up now, what would be his foremost thoughts? Avarice,* hard dealing, griping cares? They have brought him to a rich end, truly!

Avarice: greed

He lay, in the dark empty house, with not a man, a woman, or a child, to say that he was kind to me in this or that, and for the memory of one kind word I will be kind to him. A cat was tearing at the door, and there was a sound of gnawing rats beneath the hearth-stone. What *they* wanted in the room of death, and why they were so restless and disturbed, Scrooge did not dare to think.

"Spirit!" he said, "this is a fearful place. In leaving it, I shall not leave its lesson, trust me. Let us go!"

Still the Ghost pointed with an unmoved finger to the head.

"I understand you," Scrooge returned, "and I would do it, if I could. But I have not the power, Spirit. I have not the power."

The Ghost conducted him through several streets familiar to his feet; and as they went along, Scrooge looked here and there to find himself, but nowhere was he to be seen. They entered poor Bob Cratchit's house; the dwelling he had visited before; and found the mother and the children seated round the fire.

Quiet. Very quiet. The noisy little Cratchits were as still as statues in one corner, and sat looking up at Peter, who had a book before him. The mother and her daughters were engaged in sewing. But surely they were very quiet!

"'And He took a child, and set him in the midst of them.'"

Where had Scrooge heard those words? He had not dreamed them. The boy must have read them out, as he and the Spirit crossed the threshold. Why did he not go on? The mother laid her work upon the table, and put her hand up to her face.

"The colour hurts my eyes," she said.

The colour? Ah, poor Tiny Tim!

"They're better now again," said Cratchit's wife. "It makes them weak by candlelight; and I wouldn't show weak eyes to your father when he comes home, for the world. It must be near his time."

"Past it rather," Peter answered, shutting up his book. "But I think he's walked a little slower than he used, these few last evenings, mother."

They were very quiet again. At last she said, and in a steady cheerful voice, that only faltered once:—

"I have known him walk with—I have known him walk with Tiny Tim upon his shoulder, very fast indeed."

"But he was very light to carry," she resumed, intent upon her work, "and his father loved him so, that it was no trouble—no trouble. And there is your father at the door!"

Bob was very cheerful with them, and spoke pleasantly to all the family. He looked at the work upon the table, and praised the industry and speed of Mrs. Cratchit and the girls. They would be done long before Sunday he said.

"Sunday! You went today, then, Robert?" said his wife.

"Yes, my dear," returned Bob. "I wish you could have gone. It would have done you good to see how green a place it is. But you'll see it often. I promised him that I would walk there on a Sunday. My little, little child!" cried Bob. "My little child!"

He broke down all at once. He couldn't help it. If he could have helped it, he and his child would have been farther apart perhaps than they were.

He left the room, and went upstairs into the room above, which was lighted cheerfully, and hung with Christmas. There was a chair set close beside the child, and there were signs of someone having been there, lately. Poor Bob sat down in it, and when he had thought a little and composed himself, he kissed the little face. He was reconciled to what had happened, and went down again quite happy.

"Spectre," said Scrooge, "something informs me that our parting moment is at hand.

I know it, but I know not how. Tell me what man that was whom we saw lying dead?"

The Ghost of Christmas Yet To Come conveyed him, as before—though at a different time, he thought: indeed, there seemed no order in these latter visions, save that they were in the Future—into the resorts of business men, but showed him not himself.

Indeed, the Spirit did not stay for anything, but went straight on, as to the end just now desired, until besought by Scrooge to tarry for a moment.

"This court," said Scrooge, "through which we hurry now, is where my place of occupation is, and has been for a length of time. I see the house. Let me behold what I shall be in days to come!"

The Spirit stopped; the hand was pointed elsewhere. "The house is yonder," Scrooge exclaimed. "Why do you point away?"

The inexorable* finger underwent no change.

---

inexorable: unrelenting

Scrooge hastened to the window of his office, and looked in. It was an office still, but not his. The furniture was not the same, and the figure in the chair was not himself. The Phantom pointed as before.

He joined it once again, and wondering why and whither he had gone, accompanied it until they reached an iron gate. He paused to look round before entering.

A churchyard. Here, then, the wretched man whose name he had now to learn, lay underneath the ground. It was a worthy place. Walled in by houses; overrun by grass and weeds, the growth of vegetation's death, not life; choked up with too much burying; fat with repleted appetite, A worthy place!

The Spirit stood among the graves, and pointed down to One. He advanced towards it trembling. The Phantom was exactly as it had been, but he dreaded that he saw new meaning in its solemn shape.

"Before I draw nearer to that stone to which you point," said Scrooge, "answer me one question. Are these the shadows of the things that Will be, or are they shadows of things that May be, only?"

Still the Ghost pointed downward to the grave by which it stood.

"Men's courses will foreshadow certain ends, to which, if persevered in, they must lead," said Scrooge. "But if the courses be departed from, the ends will change. Say it is thus with what you show me!"

The Spirit was immovable as ever.

Scrooge crept towards it, trembling as he went; and following the finger, read upon the stone of the neglected grave his own name, EBENEZER SCROOGE.

"Am I that man who lay upon the bed?" he cried, upon his knees.

The finger pointed from the grave to him, and back again.

"No, Spirit! Oh no, no!"

The finger still was there.

"Spirit!" he cried, tight clutching at its robe, "hear me! I am not the man I was. Why show me this, if I am past all hope!"

For the first time the hand appeared to shake.

"Good Spirit," he pursued, as down upon the ground he fell before it: "Your nature intercedes for me, and pities me. Assure me that I yet may change these shadows you have shown me, by an altered life!"

The kind hand trembled.

"I will honour Christmas in my heart, and try to keep it all the year. I will live in the Past, the Present, and the Future. The Spirits of all Three shall strive within me. I will not shut out the lessons that they teach. Oh, tell me I may sponge away the writing on this stone!"

In his agony, he caught the spectral hand. It sought to free itself, but he was strong in his entreaty, and detained it. The Spirit, stronger yet, repulsed him.

Holding up his hands in one last prayer to have his fate reversed, he saw an alteration in the Phantom's hood and dress. It shrank, collapsed, and dwindled down into a bedpost.

THINKING ZONE

You have already studied the difference between the literal and figurative uses of language. Often it is easy to detect the difference between expressions meant to be read literally and those meant to be interpreted figuratively. It can be more difficult, however, to distinguish the denotative and connotative meanings of words. The **denotative meaning** of a word is its exact meaning found in the dictionary. The **connotative meaning** is the dictionary meaning of the word plus all of its implications and emotional associations. For instance, the words *lean* and *skinny* have similar denotative meanings, yet when those words are used to describe people, they carry different connotative meanings. The connotation of *lean* suggests someone who is toned, healthy, and strong. The connotation of *skinny*, however, suggests a person who is probably unhealthy or lacking in muscular development. The connotative meanings of words are important because they can do more to establish an impression in a reader's mind. The more you read, the more sensitive you will become to the connotations of various words. Dickens and other masters of language choose their words very carefully, so pay attention to the words chosen by the authors you read. And be choosey yourself when you write!

1. *[interpretive/critical]* The words *spirit* and *ghost* are used to describe all of the entities that visit Scrooge, but the last figure is also called a "phantom." Though the **denotative meanings** are similar, how are the **connotative meanings** different? Why is *phantom* a particularly appropriate word to describe this third spirit?

_____

_____

_____

_____

2. *[interpretive]* How does the third spirit differ from the previous two in appearance? What does this difference symbolize?

_____

_____

_____

3. *[interpretive/critical]* What clues foreshadow the spirit's final revelation to Scrooge concerning his destiny? Name at least three.

_____

_____

_____

_____

_____

4. *[critical]* How do the two groups of people at the beginning of Stave IV compare to Scrooge?

_____

_____

_____

5. *[critical]* Read Mark 9:36 (the verse Peter Cratchit reads) in context. What is the significance of this verse for the Cratchits? What is its significance for Scrooge?

_____

_____

_____

_____

6. *[interpretive]* Where does the crisis of the novella occur?

_____

_____

_____

7. *[critical]* How does Dickens generate suspense throughout Stave IV?

_____

_____

_____

STAVE V
THE END OF IT

Yes! and the bedpost was his own. The bed was his own, the room was his own. Best and happiest of all, the Time before him was his own, to make amends in!

"I will live in the Past, the Present, and the Future!" Scrooge repeated, as he scrambled out of bed. "The Spirits of all Three shall strive within me. Oh Jacob Marley! Heaven, and the Christmas Time be praised for this! I say it on my knees, old Jacob, on my knees!"

He was so fluttered and so glowing with his good intentions, that his broken voice would scarcely answer to his call. He had been sobbing violently in his conflict with the Spirit, and his face was wet with tears.

"They are not torn down," cried Scrooge, folding one of his bed-curtains in his arms, "they are not torn down, rings and all. They are here: I am here: the shadows of the things that would have been, may be dispelled. They will be. I know they will!"

His hands were busy with his garments all this time: turning them inside out, putting them on upside down, tearing them, misleading them, making them parties to every kind of extravagance.

"I don't know what to do!" cried Scrooge, laughing and crying in the same breath; and making a perfect Laocoön* of himself with his stockings. "I am as light as a feather, I am as happy as an angel, I am as merry as a schoolboy. I am as giddy as a drunken man. A merry Christmas to everybody! A Happy New Year to all the world. Hallo here! Whoop! Hallo!"

Laocoön (lā-ŏk′ō-ŏn): a Trojan priest who was killed for having warned his people about the Trojan horse

---

He had frisked into the sitting-room, and was now standing there: perfectly winded.

"There's the saucepan that the gruel* was in!" cried Scrooge, starting off again, and frisking round the fireplace. "There's the door, by which the Ghost of Jacob Marley entered! There's the corner where the Ghost of Christmas Present sat! There's the window where I saw the wandering Spirits! It's all right, it's all true, it all happened. Ha, ha, ha!"

---

gruel: thin, watery porridge or soup

Really, for a man who had been out of practice for so many years, it was a splendid laugh, a most illustrious laugh. The father of a long, long line of brilliant laughs!

"I don't know what day of the month it is!" said Scrooge. "I don't know how long I've been among the Spirits. I don't know anything. I'm quite a baby. Never mind. I don't care. I'd rather be a baby. Hallo! Whoop! Hallo here!" He was checked in his transports by the churches ringing out the lustiest peals he had ever heard. Clash, clang, hammer, ding, dong, bell. Bell, dong, ding, hammer, clang, clash! Oh, glorious, glorious!

Running to the window, he opened it, and put out his head. No fog, no mist; clear, bright, jovial, stirring, cold; cold, piping for the blood to dance to; golden sunlight; heavenly sky; sweet fresh air; merry bells. Oh, glorious. Glorious!

"What's today?" cried Scrooge, calling downward to a boy in Sunday clothes, who perhaps had loitered in to look about him.

"EH?" returned the boy, with all his might of wonder.

"What's today, my fine fellow?" said Scrooge.

"Today!" replied the boy. "Why, CHRISTMAS DAY."

"It's Christmas Day!" said Scrooge to himself. "I haven't missed it. The Spirits have done it all in one night. They can do anything they like. Of course they can. Of course they can. Hallo, my fine fellow?"

"Hallo!" returned the boy.

"Do you know the Poulterer's, in the next street, the one at the corner?" Scrooge inquired.

"I should hope I did," replied the lad.

"An intelligent boy!" said Scrooge. "A remarkable boy! Do you know whether they've sold the prize Turkey that was hanging up there? Not the little prize Turkey: the big one?"

"What, the one as big as me?" returned the boy.

"What a delightful boy!" said Scrooge. "It's a pleasure to talk to him. Yes, my buck!"

"It's hanging there now," replied the boy.

"Is it?" said Scrooge. "Go and buy it."

"Walk-ER!" exclaimed the boy.

"No, no," said Scrooge, "I am in earnest. Go and buy it, and tell 'em to bring it here, that I may give them the direction where to take it. Come back with the man, and I'll give you a shilling. Come back with him in less than five minutes, and I'll give you half-a-crown!"

The boy was off like a shot. He must have had a steady hand at a trigger who could have got a shot off half so fast.

"I'll send it to Bob Cratchit's!" whispered Scrooge, rubbing his hands, and splitting with a laugh. "He shan't know who sends it. It's twice the size of Tiny Tim. Joe Miller never made such a joke as sending it to Bob's will be!"

The hand in which he wrote the address was not a steady one, but write it he did, somehow, and went down stairs to open the street door, ready for the coming of the poulterer's man. As he stood there, waiting his arrival, the knocker caught his eye.

"I shall love it, as long as I live!" cried Scrooge, patting it with his hand. "I scarcely ever looked at it before. What an honest expression it has in its face! It's a wonderful knocker!—Here's the Turkey. Hallo! Whoop! How are you! Merry Christmas!"

It *was* a Turkey! He could never have stood upon his legs, that bird. He would have snapped 'em short off in a minute, like sticks of sealing-wax.

"Why, it's impossible to carry that to Camden Town," said Scrooge. "You must have a cab."

The chuckle with which he said this, and the chuckle with which he paid for the turkey, and the chuckle with which he paid for the cab, and the chuckle with which he recompensed the boy, were only to be exceeded by the chuckle with which he sat down breathless in his chair again, and chuckled till he cried.

Shaving was not an easy task, for his hand continued to shake very much; and shaving requires attention, even when you don't dance while you are at it. But if he had cut the end of his nose off, he would have put a piece of sticking-plaster over it, and been quite satisfied.

He dressed himself "all in his best," and at last got out into the streets. The people were by this time pouring forth, as he had seen them with the Ghost of Christmas Present; and walking with his hands behind him, Scrooge regarded everyone with a delighted smile. He looked so irresistibly pleasant, in a word, that three or four good-humoured fellows said, "Good morning, Sir! A merry Christmas to you!" And Scrooge said often afterwards, that of all the blithe sounds he had ever heard, those were the blithest in his ears.

He had not gone far, when coming on towards him he beheld the portly gentleman, who had walked into his counting-house the day before and said, "Scrooge and Marley's, I believe?" It sent a pang across his heart to think how this old gentleman would look upon him when they met; but he knew what path lay straight before him, and he took it.

"My dear Sir," said Scrooge, quickening his pace, and taking the old gentleman by both his hands. "How do you do? I hope you succeeded yesterday. It was very kind of you. A merry Christmas to you, Sir!"

"Mr. Scrooge?"

"Yes," said Scrooge. "That is my name, and I fear it may not be pleasant to you. Allow me to ask your pardon. And will you have the goodness"—here Scrooge whispered in his ear.

"Lord bless me!" cried the gentleman, as if his breath were gone. "My dear Mr. Scrooge, are you serious?"

"If you please," said Scrooge. "Not a farthing less. A great many back-payments are included in it, I assure you. Will you do me that favour?"

"My dear Sir," said the other, shaking hands with him. "I don't know what to say to such munifi—"

"Don't say anything, please," retorted Scrooge. "Come and see me. Will you come and see me?"

"I will!" cried the old gentleman. And it was clear he meant to do it.

"Thank'ee," said Scrooge. "I am much obliged to you. I thank you fifty times. Bless you!"

He went to church, and walked about the streets, and watched the people hurrying to and fro, and patted children on the head, and questioned beggars, and looked down into the kitchens of houses, and up to the windows; and found that everything could yield him pleasure. He had never dreamed that any walk—that anything—could give him so much happiness. In the afternoon, he turned his steps towards his nephew's house.

He passed the door a dozen times, before he had the courage to go up and knock. But he made a dash, and did it:—

"Is your master at home, my dear?" said Scrooge to the girl.

"Yes, Sir."

"Where is he, my love?" said Scrooge.

"He's in the dining-room, Sir, along with mistress. I'll show you upstairs, if you please."

"Thank'ee. He knows me," said Scrooge, with his hand already on the dining-room lock. "I'll go in here, my dear."

He turned it gently, and sidled* his face in, round the door. They were looking at the table (which was spread out in great array*) for these young housekeepers are always nervous on such points, and like to see that everything is right.

---

sidled: slowly moved

array: display

"Fred!" said Scrooge.

Dear heart alive, how his niece by marriage started! Scrooge had forgotten, for the moment, about her sitting in the corner with the footstool, or he wouldn't have done it, on any account.

"Why, bless my soul!" cried Fred, "who's that?"

"It's I. Your uncle Scrooge. I have come to dinner. Will you let me in, Fred?"

Let him in! It is a mercy he didn't shake his arm off. He was at home in five minutes. Nothing could be done heartier. His niece looked just the same.

So did Topper when *he* came. So did the plump sister, when *she* came. So did everyone when *they* came. Wonderful party, wonderful games, wonderful unanimity,* wonderful happiness!

---

unanimity: complete agreement

But he was early at the office next morning. Oh, he was early there. If he could only be there first, and catch Bob Cratchit coming late! That was the thing he had set his heart upon.

And he did it; yes he did! The clock struck nine. No Bob. A quarter past. No Bob. He was full eighteen minutes and a half behind his time. Scrooge sat with his door wide open, that he might see him come in.

His hat was off, before he opened the door; his comforter too. He was on his stool in a jiffy; driving away with his pen, as if he were trying to overtake nine o'clock.

"Hallo!" growled Scrooge, in his accustomed voice as near as he could feign it. "What do you mean by coming here at this time of day?"

"I am very sorry, Sir," said Bob. "I *am* behind my time."

"You are?" repeated Scrooge. "Yes. I think you are. Step this way, Sir, if you please."

"It's only once a year, Sir," pleaded Bob. "It shall not be repeated. I was making rather merry yesterday, Sir."

"Now, I'll tell you what, my friend," said Scrooge, "I am not going to stand this sort of thing any longer. And therefore," he continued, leaping from his stool, and giving Bob such a dig in the waistcoat that he staggered back again: "and therefore I am about to raise your salary!"

Bob trembled, and got a little nearer to the ruler. He had a momentary idea of knocking Scrooge down with it; holding him; and calling to the people in the court for help and a strait waistcoat.

"A merry Christmas, Bob!" said Scrooge, with an earnestness that could not be mistaken, as he clapped him on the back. "A merrier Christmas, Bob, my good fellow, than I have given you for many a year! I'll raise your salary, and endeavour to assist your struggling family, and we will discuss your affairs this very afternoon, over a Christmas bowl of smoking bishop, Bob! Make up the fires, and buy another coal-scuttle before you dot another i, Bob Cratchit!"

Scrooge was better than his word. He did it all, and infinitely more; and to Tiny Tim, who did NOT die, he was a second father. He became as good a friend, as good a master, and as good a man, as the good old city knew, or any other good old city, town, or borough, in the good old world. Some people laughed to see the alteration in him, but he let them laugh, and little heeded them; for he was wise enough to know that nothing ever happened on this globe, for good, at which some people did not have their fill of laughter in the outset; and knowing that such as these would be blind anyway, he thought it quite as well that they should wrinkle up their eyes in grins, as have the malady* in less attractive forms. His own heart laughed: and that was quite enough for him.

malady: ailment

He had no further intercourse* with Spirits, but lived upon the Total Abstinence Principle, ever afterwards; and it was always said of him, that he knew how to keep Christmas well, if any man alive possessed the knowledge. May that be truly said of us, and all of us! And so, as Tiny Tim observed, God Bless Us, Every One!

intercourse: communication

About the Author

Charles Dickens (1812–70) was born into a very poor family in England, and although his father loved his wife and children, he was incapable of caring for them financially. Because they were unable to pay their debts, the family was consigned to debtors' prison while Charles, only ten years old, entered the working world and supported himself. For most of two years he saw his family only on Sundays. During the remainder of the week, he boarded with an elderly lady but otherwise cared entirely for himself, including providing his own food. Young Charles was usually hungry and was "miserably unhappy."

Dickens worked without complaint, however, and many years later the hardships paid him dividends as many of the people he had met and experiences he had had during that time made their way into his books and stories. His active imagination stayed busy. He loved to read when he could and often pretended for days or even weeks that he was a character from some favorite book. At other times he made up stories about the lives of people he saw around him. Dickens's childhood, though full of hardship, gave him an understanding of the common people and enhanced his ability to create captivating characters that made him the well-loved author that he was and is today.

THINKING ZONE

What do you think of when you hear the word *criticism*? Harsh words from someone who doesn't like you, or maybe a newspaper editorial that condemns a certain practice? In studies of literature, **criticism** is the analysis of literary works. Literary critics formulate general principles for interpreting and evaluating literature. They then study works of literature, explaining them and identifying their strengths and weaknesses. Ultimately, many literary critics evaluate whether the work is a true representation of reality. Like the parables of Christ, literature should represent people and events in a way that gives insight into reality.

Not all critics agree on which works are good. Everyone sees the world through his **worldview**: the viewpoint from which a person examines the world and draws conclusions. It includes beliefs about the origin of the world, the nature of good and evil, and the reason humans exist. Christians see the world from the perspective of biblical teaching expressed in the themes of the Creation (God made a world filled with life, righteousness, and love), the Fall (this world has become twisted because of sin), and Redemption (God is working to restore this world). For the Christian, the best works of literature are those that skillfully and truly represent these themes. It is ironic that some of the most compelling representations of a Christian worldview are not written by Christians. This irony is not surprising when one considers that the Christian worldview is God's view of reality communicated to humans. Skilled, sensitive authors often unintentionally produce works that reflect Creation, Fall, and Redemption. And since humans are made in God's image (Gen. 1:26), these themes are also woven into every author's being.

1. *[interpretive]* How do the imagery, setting, and atmosphere in the opening of Stave V contrast with those of Stave I? In other words, how has Scrooge's **worldview** changed?

_____

_____

_____

_____

_____

2. *[interpretive]* What symbolic act does Scrooge perform when Bob Cratchit enters the office? How does it contrast with Stave I?

_____

_____

_____

3. *[interpretive]* God's created world was originally good. What reflections of the theme of Creation can be found in *A Christmas Carol*?

_____

_____

_____

4. *[interpretive]* The theme of the Fall concerns how what was once good has become twisted because of sin. What representations of the Fall can be found in Dickens's story?

_____

_____

_____

5. *[interpretive]* Redemption concerns restoring what has become fallen, often in a way that involves loss or sacrifice. How is this theme represented in *A Christmas Carol*?

_____

_____

_____

_____

_____

6. *[appreciative]* What makes Dickens's story memorable? Why do you think people have found it appealing for so long?

_____

_____

_____

_____

_____

SPIRIT OF GOD, DESCEND UPON MY HEART

GEORGE CROLY

The author of this hymn implores God's Spirit to change his viewpoint from an earthly one to a heavenly one.

Spirit of God, descend upon my heart;
Wean* it from earth, through all its pulses move;
Stoop to my weakness, mighty as Thou art,
And make me love Thee as I ought to love.

Hast Thou not bid us love Thee, God and King?
All, all Thine own, soul, heart and strength and
   mind;
I see Thy cross—there teach my heart to cling:
O let me seek Thee, and O let me find.

Teach me to feel that Thou art always nigh;
Teach me the struggles of the soul to bear.
To check the rising doubt, the rebel sigh;
Teach me the patience of unanswered prayer.

Teach me to love Thee as Thine angels love.
One holy passion filling all my frame;
The baptism of the heav'n-descended Dove,
My heart an altar; and Thy love the flame.

Pentecost. Vincente Juan Macip, called Juan de Juanes
Spanish c. 1510–d. 1579
From the Bob Jones University Collection

wean: detach

ABOUT THE AUTHOR

George Croly (1780–1860) was born in Dublin, Ireland, and was educated there. He was a well-known and highly regarded preacher. He was also very interested in writing. About 1810 he decided to move to London in order to concentrate on his writing. Croly made many contributions to *Blackwood's Magazine*, a conservative publication that printed works of various writers. His writings include poems, dramas, novels, histories, and theological works. Croly also wrote *Scenes from Scripture and other Poems* and *Psalms and Hymns for Public Worship*, where the selection "Spirit of God, Descend upon My Heart" can be found.

THE WAY TO EMMAUS

Jesus' death deals a crushing blow to His followers. How could His teachings and His promises be true if He is dead? From their viewpoint, all hope is gone. But their outlook is soon to change because of a stranger they meet on the road to Emmaus.

And, behold, two of them went that same day to a village called Emmaus, which was from Jerusalem about three-score furlongs.

14 And they talked together of all these things which had happened.

15 And it came to pass, that, while they communed together and reasoned, Jesus himself drew near, and went with them.

16 But their eyes were holden that they should not know him.

---
furlong: 1/8 mile or 201 meters
---

17 And he said unto them, What manner of communications are these that ye have one to another, as ye walk, and are sad?

18 And the one of them, whose name was Cleopas, answering said unto him, Art thou only a stranger in Jerusalem, and hast not known the things which are come to pass there in these days?

19 And he said unto them, What things? And they said unto him, Concerning Jesus of Nazareth, which was a prophet mighty in deed and word before God and all the people:

20 And how the chief priests and our rulers delivered him to be condemned to death, and have crucified him.

21 But we trusted that it had been he which should have redeemed Israel: and beside all this, to day is the third day since these things were done.

22 Yea, and certain women also of our company made us astonished, which were early at the sepulchre;

23 And when they found not his body, they came, saying, that they had also seen a vision of angels, which said that he was alive.

24 And certain of them which were with us went to the sepulchre, and found it even so as the women had said: but him they saw not.

25 Then he said unto them, O fools, and slow of heart to believe all that the prophets have spoken:

26 Ought not Christ to have suffered these things, and to enter into his glory?

27 And beginning at Moses and all the prophets, he expounded unto them in all the scriptures the things concerning himself.

28 And they drew nigh unto the village, whither they went: and he made as though he would have gone further.

29 But they constrained him, saying, Abide with us: for it is toward evening, and the day is far spent. And he went in to tarry with them.

30 And it came to pass, as he sat at meat with them, he took bread, and blessed it, and brake, and gave to them.

31 And their eyes were opened, and they knew him; and he vanished out of their sight.

32 And they said one to another, Did not our heart burn within us, while he talked with us by the way, and while he opened to us the scriptures?

—Luke 24:13–32

UNIT 6 REVIEW

SHORT ANSWER

Write the word, phrase, or sentence that best answers the question.

1. In "Wolves of Fear," why does Paul's father encourage Paul to spend the winter in the wilderness?

   _____

2. What flashback does the author include in "Wolves of Fear"?

   _____

   _____

3. A poet who used *glitter* to rhyme with *wither* would be using what type of rhyme?

   _____

4. In "The Torn Invitation," who is Harry's foil?

   _____

5. In the selections from *The Diary of a Young Girl*, what does Anne give as the purpose for keeping her diary?

   _____

   _____

6. Anne writes about the things that those in the Annex would want to do first upon going outside. What does Anne want most?

   _____

   _____

7. "Opportunity," a poem with meter (five iambic feet per line) but no rhyme, is an example of _____ _____.

   _____

8. "The Meaning of the Look" is an allusion to what biblical event?

   _____

9. In *A Christmas Carol*, what does Marley's chain symbolize?

   _____

10. Name a round character from *A Christmas Carol*.

   _____

11. Where is the crisis of *A Christmas Carol*?

_____

12. In Stave V what symbolic act does Scrooge perform when Bob
    Cratchit enters the office?

_____

MULTIPLE CHOICE

Choose the best answer from the choices given.

_____ 13. In "Wolves of Fear," all of the following are examples of onomato-
        poeia *except*
        A. snarls of the wolves.
        B fear of the surroundings.
        C. buzzing of a mosquito.
        D. growl of the bear.

_____ 14. Katkov's story "The Torn Invitation" reveals the true worth of
        character over
        A. wealth.   C. fame.
        B. appearance.   D. happiness.

_____ 15. In Stave II of *A Christmas Carol*, why is it appropriate that Belle is
        wearing mourning clothes?
        A. because Scrooge has died
        B. because Fezziwig has died
        C. because her relationship with Scrooge is over
        D. because she is so poor that she has only one dress

_____ 16. In Stave III all of the following describe the Spirit of Christmas
        Present *except* that he
        A. is a giant.   C. wears a green robe.
        B. has a shiny belt.   D. wears a holly wreath on his head.

_____ 17. According to Stave V, which of the following statements is *not* true?
        A. Some people laugh at the change in Scrooge.
        B. Scrooge sees many ghosts throughout the rest of his life.
        C. People say that Scrooge knows how to keep Christmas
           well, if anyone does.
        D. Tiny Tim does not die.

Matching

Match the following literary terms with their correct definitions.

_____ 18. Words that sound like what they mean

_____ 19. Unstressed-stressed type of foot in poetry

_____ 20. Overused phrases, idioms, and expressions

_____ 21. Repetition of terminal consonant sounds in poetry

_____ 22. Marking to analyze meter of the feet in a poem and to indicate pauses in the lines

A. consonance

B. onomatopoeia

C. scansion

D. iambic

E. clichés

True/False

If the statement is completely true, write *true*. If any part of the statement is false, write *false*.

_____ 23. In "Height," Billy Collins speaks both figuratively and literally.

_____ 24. The line "With its base-line on the water" from E. J. Pratt's "The Shark" contains an example of internal rhyme.

_____ 25. Szymborska's poem "Some Like Poetry" asserts that most people like poetry.

_____ 26. In "The Sloth" the sloth's viewpoint on life is that "he knows."

_____ 27. In "Fry, Fry Again" Uncle Henry reacts violently to the cliché "It's raining cats and dogs."

_____ 28. A journal is a formal (often daily) writing form.

_____ 29. In *The Diary of a Young Girl*, Anne's expressions of her fear as "alone in a dungeon" and her hope as "a castle in the air" are examples of using concrete images to illustrate abstract concepts.

_____ 30. In Stave I of *A Christmas Carol*, the author's use of cold is symbolic of Scrooge's viewpoint.

_____ 31. In Stave II, Scrooge's visit to Fezziwig's makes Scrooge realize that he has become like Fezziwig—cold and heartless.

ESSAY

Write a complete answer for each question below, using specific examples from the unit.

32. What kinds of problems result from a worldview characterized by an overemphasis on material things? Give examples from *A Christmas Carol*.

_____

_____

_____

_____

_____

_____

_____

_____

_____

33. Show how an overemphasis on self leads to pride in "The Torn Invitation" or "Wolves of Fear."

_____

_____

_____

_____

_____

_____

_____

_____

_____

GLOSSARY OF LITERARY TERMS

abstract concept. A concept that cannot be perceived by the five senses but must instead be discussed in general terms by describing the image's attributes or its effects upon a concrete subject.

act. A major division in the action of a play.

adaptation. A rewritten version of an author's work that has been changed for reasons such as length or readability.

allegory. A type of **extended metaphor** that forms a story with two levels of meaning.

alliteration. The repetition of initial consonant sounds.

allusion. A reference within a work to something else, usually another artistic work.

analogy. A detailed comparison of one thing to another dissimilar thing.

anaphora. The repetition of words or phrases at the beginnings of lines of poetry.

antagonist. The **character** who struggles against the **protagonist**.

assonance. The repetition of similar vowel sounds in a series of words.

atmosphere. The mood or emotion that the reader is supposed to share with the characters.

authorial purpose. The reason that the author composed his or her work.

autobiography. A nonfictional account of the author's own life.

biographical sketch. A brief descriptive biographical essay. See also **sketch**.

biography. A **nonfiction** account in which the author tells the true events that make up the life of a real individual other than himself.

blank verse. Unrhymed poetry with consistent meter (most often pentameter, or five feet per line).

caesura. A pause in the middle of a line of poetry, usually indicated by a mark of punctuation.

character. A person or being who performs the action of the story.

character flaw. An incidental weakness or serious moral fault that a **character** reveals through the story.

character motivation. See **motivation**.

character trait. Features or attributes that distinguish one **character** from another.

chronological order. The order in which events actually occur in a story.

cliché. A phrase, **idiom**, or expression that has become so overused that it often detracts from rather than contributes to a story.

cliffhanger. **Suspenseful** situations strategically placed throughout different parts or chapters of a longer work.

climax. The point at which the **plot** reaches the moment of highest emotional intensity.

concrete language. Words that appeal to one or more of the five senses.

conflict. The struggle of the story's main **character** or characters against an opposing force.

connotative meaning. The meaning of a word plus all of its implications and emotional associations.

consonance. The repetition of terminal consonant sounds (as in "bi*t* . . . figh*t* . . . le*t*").

context. The influence of factors surrounding a work of literature that may provide additional insight into its meaning.

couplet. A pair of rhymed lines.

crisis. The major turning point for the main **character**; the point at which something happens that affects the outcome of the story and determines the future of the main **character**.

criticism. The analysis of a literary work.

denotative meaning. The exact definition of a word as found in a dictionary.

description. Writing that seeks to aid the reader in seeing or feeling whatever the author is trying to convey.

developing character. A **character** who changes as the story progresses.

dialogue. A conversation between **characters**.

diary. See **journal**.

direct characterization. Characterization in which the author describes the traits and qualities of a **character** explicitly.

drama. Literature written to be acted.

dramatic irony. A type of **irony** in which the reader is aware of a **plot** development of which the **characters** of the story are unaware.

end rhyme. **Rhyme** that occurs at the ends of corresponding lines of **poetry**.

end-stopped lines. Lines of **poetry** that end with a natural pause indicated by punctuation.

enjambment. A poetic device in which lines flow past the end of one verse line and into the next with no punctuation at the end of the first verse line.

epic. A long **narrative poem** about a great **hero**, expressed in a formal, dignified style.

epilogue. An addition to a story's ending that expounds on the fortunes of the main **character** or on the significance of the story's conclusion.

essay. A work that seeks to state a **point of view**, discuss a subject, or persuade a reader to accept an argument.

explicit theme. A **theme** stated outright within a work of literature.

exposition. The part of a story's **plot** that introduces the reader to the situation and **setting**.

extended metaphor. A **metaphor** that is developed beyond a single sentence or comparison.

external conflict. **Conflict** that occurs between a **character** and an outside force (such as society or nature).

fable. A brief fanciful story that seeks to expand on a **moral**.

falling action. The **plot** element that unfolds the results of the **crisis** and leads to the **resolution**.

fiction. A work that contains events invented by the author.

figurative language. An artful deviation from literal speech.

first-person point of view. The **point of view** in which the author, as one of the characters, refers to himself as *I* throughout the piece.

flashback. A reference to events that occurred before the action of the main story or to action that occurred before the time that the **narrator** is speaking.

flat character. A **character** with little individuality whose mindset the reader knows little about.

foil. A **character** used to emphasize another character's opposing traits within a work.

folklore. The collective term for the tales and myths passed along primarily by word of mouth within a society or culture.

folktale. A short tale passed along by word of mouth throughout a given culture.

foot. See **poetic foot**.

foreshadowing. Hinting at events that will occur later within a story.

frame story. A story that contains another story or an introductory story from which another story springs.

free verse. Poetry with no distinguishable **rhyme**, **meter**, or line length.

genre. A type or category of literature.

haiku. A seventeen-syllable poem about nature, composed of three lines of five, seven, and five syllables. Example: "Daffodils in spring / Lift their golden trumpets and / Breathe a melody."

hero/heroine. A male or female **protagonist** who behaves virtuously within a story.

historical fiction. A fictional story that employs authentic historical **characters** or **settings**.

humor. A **genre** that seeks to amuse the reader through wordplay, **irony,** or other means.

hyperbole. A type of obvious **overstatement** used by writers to make a point.

iamb. A type of **poetic foot** that contains one unstressed syllable followed by one **stressed syllable** (also known as an *iambic foot*).

idiom. An expression that is unique to itself and cannot be defined from the meanings of the individual words (e.g., *pass the buck*).

imagery. Descriptive words or phrases used to create an impression.

implicit theme. A **theme** that is not stated outright but must be discerned from the details that the author includes in the work.

inciting incident. The incident that sets the events of the **plot** in motion.

indirect characterization. Characterization in which the author presents the **characters** in action and leaves the reader to infer their traits.

informal essay. A type of **essay** in which the writer adopts a friendly or conversational **tone** with the reader (also known as a *personal essay*).

internal conflict. **Conflict** that occurs between a **character** and his own thoughts or emotions.

internal rhyme. A type of **rhyme** that occurs between words within a single line of **poetry**.

irony. The use of language to convey meaning other than what is stated or a contradiction in what is expected to happen and what actually happens.

journal. An informal daily record of a person's life.

limited point of view. The **point of view** that limits the reader's scope of knowledge about the thoughts and feelings of the story's **characters**.

literal meaning. A standard definition of a word or expression.

memoir. A type of **nonfiction** that recounts a personal recollection of the author.

metaphor. An expression of one thing in terms of another.

meter. The regular arrangement of stressed and unstressed syllables in a poem.

moral. A simple statement that sums up a truth about life.

motivation. The reason that a **character** behaves as he or she does.

myth. A **fictional** story that was at one time held to be true within a certain cultural group.

narrative poem. A poem that tells a story.

narrator. The individual telling the story to the reader.

nonfiction. **Prose** that tells of real people and events.

normative character. The **character** who is the mouthpiece for what the author believes to be good and right (also known as the moral norm).

novel. An extended work of fictional **prose**.

novella. A **prose** work of medium length, longer than a **short story** yet shorter than a **novel**.

omniscient point of view. The **point of view** in which the reader gains insight into the thoughts and feelings of all the **characters**.

onomatopoeia. The use of words that sound like what they mean (e.g., *hiss, buzz*).

oral tradition. The audible means by which much **folklore** and mythology was transferred from person to person before the prevalent use of written language.

overstatement. The exaggeration of details surrounding the events of a story.

parable. A brief story told to illustrate or clarify a truth, often biblical in nature.

paradox. A statement that seems to be self-contradictory yet actually makes sense when applied at the right moment.

parallelism. Similarity in the structure of two or more phrases, clauses, or sentences.

personification. Giving human characteristics to something that is not human.

playwright. The author of a **drama** or play.

plot. A series of events arranged to tell a story.

plot twist. A **plot** development that violates the reader's expectations.

poetic foot. The unit by which **meter** is measured within **poetry**.

poetic justice. The term given to the reward or punishment that a **character** receives for his virtue or vice within a story.

poetry. Artfully compressed thought in the form of elevated expression.

point of view. The perspective or angle from which a story is told.

prologue. An introduction to a literary work.

prose. Writing that resembles speech and differs from **poetry**, such as a **short story** or an **essay**.

protagonist. The main **character** of a story.

proverb. A brief but wise saying.

pun. A type of wordplay in which the author combines two word meanings within a sentence.

refrain. A phrase or line repeated throughout a poem.

resolution. The final outcome of a story and the last element of the **plot** (also known as the *denouement*).

rhyme. In two or more words, the quality of having identical sounds in the last stressed vowel and all of the sounds following that vowel.

rhyme scheme. The pattern of **rhyme** sounds in a poem or in a **stanza** of poetry.

rhythm. A regular pace or beat.

rising action. The events that follow the **inciting incident** and lead up to the **crisis** in a story.

round character. A **character** whose personality is well defined by the author.

sarcasm. A type of **irony** that takes the form of mock praise.

scansion. The analysis of the **meter** of a poetic line or **stanza** and the marking of the **stressed syllables** or pauses in the lines.

scene. In a **drama**, a subdivision of an **act** that does not contain a change of time or place.

setting. The time and place in which the action of the story occurs.

short story. A brief work of prose **fiction**.

simile. A comparison of two unlike objects using *like* or *as*.

situational irony. A type of **irony** in which a story's events violate normal expectations.

sketch. A brief descriptive **essay**.

slant rhyme. **Rhyme** between words that sound similar but do not display perfect rhyme.

stage directions. Instructions for lighting, movement, and action included within a **drama** script.

stanza. A grouping of verse lines within a poem.

static character. A **character** who remains essentially the same throughout the story.

stream of consciousness. A type of writing in which the author attempts to reproduce the flow of thoughts in a character's mind with little attention to grammar or logic.

stressed syllable. A syllable that receives greater emphasis when read.

style. An author's manner of expression in **prose** or verse, in written or oral discourse.

subplot. A secondary **plot** within a piece of literature that accompanies the main plot yet is lesser in importance or significance.

surprise ending. A violation of the reader's expectations that occurs at the end of a story. See also **plot twist**.

suspense. Reader anxiety resulting from the author's withholding of **plot** details.

symbol. A person, place, thing, or idea that means something in addition to itself.

symbolism. The use of **symbols**.

sympathetic character. A **character** with whom the reader identifies or for whom the reader has favorable feelings.

theme. A recurring or emerging idea in a work of literature.

third-person point of view. The **point of view** in which the author refers to the **characters** as *it*, *he*, or *she*.

tone. The attitude of an author toward his or her subject.

understatement. The representation of something as less important than it truly is.

unsympathetic character. A **character** with whom the reader cannot identify or for whom the reader has strong feelings of dislike.

verbal irony. **Irony** occurring when an author's or character's meaning differs from what he or she expresses in words.

villain. An evil or cruel **antagonist**.

worldview. The viewpoint from which a person examines the world and draws conclusions.

INDEX

Entries in SMALL CAPITALS refer to authors of works. Entries in *italics* refer to titles of selections. Entries in **bold** refer to literary terms.

ILLUSTRATORS

A Most Important Person John Roberts

Being Neighborly Mike McDermott, Kathy Pflug

The Doll's House Roger Bruckner, Paula Cheadle

Thank You, M'am Roger Bruckner

After Twenty Years Bryan Martin

Half a Gift John Roberts

Christian Beholds the Cross

Weep No More, My Lady Sam Laterza, Dave Schuppert

Mama and the Graduation Present Kathy Pflug

The Brothers Mary Ann Lumm

Pleasing All the World Courtney Godbey

The Magic Brocade Courtney Godbey

The Blacksmith's Dilemma Ethan Mongin

The Golden Touch Sandy Mehus

The Ugly Duckling Courtney Godbey

In Search of Honor Keith Neely, Vincent Barnhart

Shago Mike McDermott

The Last Lesson Johanna Berg

The Wild Duck's Nest Gabriela Dellosso

Hastrman Bryan Martin

You've Got to Learn Sam Laterza

From *Evidence Not Seen* John Nolan

The Banks of the Sacramento Keith Neely, Kathy Pflug

You Need to Go Upstairs Mary Ann Lumm

Emily Geiger Kathy Pflug

Ben-Hur Del Thompson, Roger Bruckner

Wolves of Fear Sam Laterza

The Torn Invitation Mike McDermott

A Christmas Carol Tim Davis, Del Thompson

PHOTOGRAPH CREDITS

The following agencies and individuals have furnished materials to meet the photographic needs of this textbook. We wish to express our gratitude to them for their important contribution.

Alamy

Anne Frank Fonds - Basel/Anne Frank House Amsterdam

Art Resource

Associated Press

Bob Jones University Collection

The Bridgeman Art Library

Dohnavur Fellowship

Getty Images

Dr. and Mrs. Bill Henry

istockphoto.com

JupiterImages/Photos.com

Wesley Ko

Library of Congress

Marie Austria Instituut/MAI Amsterdam

Matton Images

Museum & Gallery at Bob Jones University

National Archives

PhotoDisc/Getty Images

Stock.XCHNG

United States Department of Defense

United States Holocaust Memorial Museum

UNIT 1
Friends, 2001 (oil on board) by Bootman, Colin (Contemporary Artist) © Private Collection/ The Bridgeman Art Library xxiv (also ix); © Classic Image/Alamy 50; M Freeman/ PhotoLink/Getty Images 54; www.istockphoto .com/Pavel Losevsky 57; From the Bob Jones University Collection 60; www.istockphoto .com/Spauln 64

UNIT 2
Forseth, Einar (29th CD) © Copyright. *Prodigal Son*. Stained glass cartoon for Church in Oretoro, Sweden. 1952. Inv.: E356–1956. Victoria & Albert Museum, London / Art Resource, NY 70 (also x); www.istockphoto .com/Jeff Doane 115; www.istockphoto.com/ agency by 131; © Dohnavur Fellowship 132; From the Museum & Gallery at Bob Jones University Collection 157

UNIT 3
National Archives/DOD 164 (also xii); Courtesy of Wesley Ko 287, 289, 290; From the Bob Jones University Collection 293

UNIT 4
Edelfelt, Albert (1854–1905). Louis Pasteur in his laboratory. The great French chemist and microbiologist discovered and developed various vaccines, among them against rabies, 1885. Oil on canvas, 154 × 126 cm. Musee d'Orsay, Paris, France. Erich Lessing/ Art Resource, NY 302 (also xiii); Picture courtesy of Dr. and Mrs. Bill Henry, Faith Bible Church, Ooltewah, TN. 346; www .istockphoto.com/Loretta Hostettler 352; www .istockphoto.com/David Raboin 355; www .istockphoto.com/Robyn Mackenzie 356; www .istockphoto.com/Joe Ho 359; From the Bob Jones University Collection 362

UNIT 5
Man and Space, 1971 by Mikko, Lepo (1911–78) © Tartu Art Museum, Estonia / The Bridgeman Art Library 370 (also xiv); Library of Congress 390; www.istockphoto.com/Tony Campbell 397; © 2007 JupiterImages/Photos.com. All rights reserved. 400, 406; © 2007 JupiterImages/ Thinkstock.com. All rights reserved. 410; www .istockphoto.com/Michael Braun 411; From the Bob Jones University Collection 475

608